ABOUT THE AUTHOR

Bob Sehlinger is the creator of the *Unofficial Guide* travel series and author or coauthor of over 25 travel guides. He makes his home in Birmingham, Alabama, where the catfish are jumping and the cotton is high.

Published by:

WILEY PUBLISHING, INC.

111 River St.
Hoboken, NJ 07030-5774

ISBN 978-0-470-43208-2

Editor: Jamie Ehrlich
Production Editor: Heather Wilcox
Cartographer: Roberta Stockwell
Photo Editor: Richard Fox
Production by Wiley Indianapolis Composition Services

Front cover photo: The Strip: Overview at dusk

For information on our other products and services or to obtain technical support, please contact our Customer Care Department within the U.S. at 877/762-2974, outside the U.S. at 317/572-3993 or fax 317/572-4002.

Wiley also publishes its books in a variety of electronic formats. Some content that appears in print may not be available in electronic formats.

Manufactured in the United States of America

5 4 3 2 1

Frommer's®

Las Vegas with Kids

4th Edition

by Bob Sehlinger

Here's what the critics say about Frommer's:

"Amazingly easy to use. Very portable, very complete."
—BOOKLIST

"Detailed, accurate, and easy-to-read information for all price ranges."
—GLAMOUR MAGAZINE

"Hotel information is close to encyclopedic."
—DES MOINES SUNDAY REGISTER

"Frommer's Guides have a way of giving you a real feel for a place."
—KNIGHT RIDDER NEWSPAPERS

WILEY
Wiley Publishing, Inc.

CONTENTS

LIST OF MAPS vii

1 HOW TO FEEL LIKE A LAS VEGAS FAMILY 1

1 Frommer's Favorite Las Vegas Family Experiences . . . 4
2 Best Hotel Bets . . . 7
3 Best Dining Bets . . . 10
4 The Rest of the Best . . . 12

2 LAS VEGAS IN DEPTH 14

1 Las Vegas Today . . . 14
2 A Look at the Past . . . 15
Dateline . . . 16
Farewell to Frank . . . 23
3 Getting the Kids Interested in Las Vegas . . . 24
Tips for Having a Great Family Vacation . . . 25
4 Recommended Reading for Adults . . . 26

3 PLANNING A FAMILY TRIP TO LAS VEGAS 28

1 Visitor Information . . . 28
More Winning Websites . . . 29
2 Entry Requirements & Customs . . . 29
Destination: Las Vegas—Red Alert Checklist . . . 31
3 When to Go . . . 32
Major Convention Dates . . . 33
Las Vegas Calendar of Kid-Friendly Events . . . 34
New Year's Eve in Las Vegas . . . 36
4 What to Pack . . . 37
Taking a Cellphone on Your Trip . . . 38
5 Getting There . . . 39
Flying with Film & Video . . . 41
6 Money & Costs . . . 47
What Things Cost . . . 48
7 Health . . . 50
8 Safety . . . 51
Curfew, According to the Law: When & Where Children Shouldn't Be Without an Adult . . . 52
9 Specialized Travel Resources . . . 53
10 Packages for the Independent Traveler . . . 58
11 Tips on Flying with Your Children . . . 59

In-Flight Fun for Kids ... 64
12 Planning Your Trip Online ... 66
Frommers.com: The Complete Travel Resource ... 68
Online Traveler's Toolbox ... 69
13 Tips on Accommodations ... 70
14 Babysitters & Child-Care Centers ... 73
What Parents Can Do in Vegas If They Have a Sitter/Child Care ... 74

4 SUGGESTED LAS VEGAS ITINERARIES FOR FAMILIES 76

1 The Heart of the Strip: East Side ... 77
Quick Takes: Itineraries by Kids' Age Groups ... 78
2 From Monte Carlo to the Top: The West Strip ... 80
3 Bombs & Boulders ... 82

5 GETTING TO KNOW LAS VEGAS 84

1 City Layout ... 84
2 Getting Around ... 87
A Word on Parking ... 89

6 FAMILY-FRIENDLY ACCOMMODATIONS 93

1 Condominiums & Vacation Homes ... 98
2 South Strip Accommodations ... 101
Cleaning Up ... 104
So Your Trip Goes Swimmingly ... 106
Nice Places to Visit (but You Wouldn't Want to Stay There) ... 109
3 Center Strip Accommodations ... 110
4 North Strip Accommodations ... 117
5 Accommodations East of the Strip ... 121
6 Accommodations West of the Strip ... 130
7 Accommodations Outside of Las Vegas ... 133

7 FAMILY-FRIENDLY DINING 136

1 Tips for Dining in Las Vegas ... 137
Dining Out in Peace ... 138
2 Restaurants by Cuisine ... 139
3 South Strip ... 141
Tea for Two ... 148
Cheap Eats ... 149
Las Vegas's Chinatown ... 151
4 Center Strip ... 151
Sweets for the Sweet ... 154
The Kult of Krispy Kreme ... 156
5 North Strip ... 158
6 East of the Strip ... 160
7 West of the Strip ... 163
8 Downtown ... 164
9 Buffets ... 165
10 Just the Two of Us: Romantic Dining ... 169

8 WHAT KIDS LIKE TO SEE & DO IN LAS VEGAS 170

1 Attractions for Kids 171

Free Attractions 172

If I Could Talk to the Animals 174

Arcades Abound 178

Photo Ops 180

2 Thrill Rides 180

3 Art Galleries & History Museums 186

Hey, Sport! 188

4 Factories & Food 190

Trivia: Viva Las Vegas 192

5 Kid-Friendly Tours 193

For Your Little Race Car Enthusiast 194

9 LAS VEGAS FOR THE ACTIVE FAMILY 196

1 Places to Run & Walk 196

2 Family Fun Centers & Indoor Playgrounds 199

3 Sports 199

Not for the Faint of Heart 200

4 Classes & Workshops 202

For the Special-Needs Child 202

10 SHOPPING FOR THE WHOLE FAMILY 204

1 The Shopping Scene 205

2 Shopping A–Z 210

11 ENTERTAINMENT FOR THE WHOLE FAMILY 227

1 What's Playing Where 228

Buying Show Tickets 229

2 Major Production Shows 229

3 Headliner Showrooms 239

4 Comedy Clubs 241

5 Spectator Sports 241

6 Local Performing Arts 244

Look & Listen 245

7 What to Do If You've Gotten a Babysitter 245

12 SIDE TRIPS FROM LAS VEGAS 254

1 Hoover Dam & Lake Mead 254

Did You Know 257

2 Valley of Fire State Park 263

Take a Hike: Desert Hiking Advice 266

3 Red Rock Canyon 267

4 Bonnie Springs Ranch/Old Nevada 272

5 Spring Mountains National Recreation Area 275

6 Primm 276

7 The Grand Canyon: Grand Canyon West 277

8 Outdoor Activities & Tour Companies 281

APPENDIX: FAST FACTS, TOLL-FREE NUMBERS & WEBSITES 282

1 Fast Facts: Las Vegas. 282
2 Toll-Free Numbers & Websites. . . 290

INDEX 297

LIST OF MAPS

Las Vegas & Environs 5
Las Vegas at a Glance. 85
South Strip Accommodations 103
Center Strip Accommodations . . . 111
North Strip Accommodations 119
Accommodations East of the Strip 123
Accommodations, Dining & Entertainment West of the Strip 131
Accommodations, Dining & Attractions in Henderson. 135
South Strip Dining 143
Center Strip Dining. 153
North Strip Dining. 159
Dining East of the Strip 161
South Strip Attractions 175
Center Strip Attractions. 177
North Strip Attractions 179
Downtown Attractions & Dining. 181
Attractions & Entertainment East of the Strip. 183
Las Vegas for the Active Family. 197
Las Vegas's Shopping Scene 207
South Strip Shopping 211
Center Strip Shopping. 213
North Strip Shopping. 215
Shopping East of the Strip 217
Shopping West of the Strip 219
South Strip Entertainment. 231
Center Strip Entertainment 233
North Strip Entertainment. 235
Las Vegas's Sports Venues, Stadiums & Local Performing Arts Venues. 243
Side Trips from Las Vegas 255
Lake Mead & Vicinity 261
Valley of Fire State Park. 265
Red Rock Canyon. 269
Grand Canyon West & Environs . . . 279

AN INVITATION TO THE READER

In researching this book, we discovered many wonderful places—hotels, restaurants, shops, and more. We're sure you'll find others. Please tell us about them, so we can share the information with your fellow travelers in upcoming editions. If you were disappointed with a recommendation, we'd love to know that, too. Please write to:

Frommer's Las Vegas with Kids, 4th Edition
Wiley Publishing, Inc. • 111 River St. • Hoboken, NJ 07030-5774

AN ADDITIONAL NOTE

Please be advised that travel information is subject to change at any time—and this is especially true of prices. We therefore suggest that you write or call ahead for confirmation when making your travel plans. The authors, editors, and publisher cannot be held responsible for the experiences of readers while traveling. Your safety is important to us, however, so we encourage you to stay alert and be aware of your surroundings. Keep a close eye on cameras, purses, and wallets, all favorite targets of thieves and pickpockets.

FROMMER'S STAR RATINGS, ICONS & ABBREVIATIONS

Every hotel, restaurant, and attraction listing in this guide has been ranked for quality, value, service, amenities, and special features using a **star-rating system.** In country, state, and regional guides, we also rate towns and regions to help you narrow down your choices and budget your time accordingly. Hotels and restaurants are rated on a scale of zero (recommended) to three stars (exceptional). Attractions, shopping, nightlife, towns, and regions are rated according to the following scale: zero stars (recommended), one star (highly recommended), two stars (very highly recommended), and three stars (must-see).

In addition to the star-rating system, we also use **six feature icons** that point you to the great deals, in-the-know advice, and unique experiences that separate travelers from tourists. Throughout the book, look for:

Finds	Special finds—those places only insiders know about
Fun Facts	Fun facts—details that make travelers more informed and their trips more fun
Moments	Special moments—those experiences that memories are made of
Overrated	Places or experiences not worth your time or money
Tips	Insider tips—great ways to save time and money
Value	Great values—where to get the best deals

The following **abbreviations** are used for credit cards:

AE	American Express	DISC	Discover	V	Visa
DC	Diners Club	MC	MasterCard		

FROMMERS.COM

Now that you have this guidebook to help you plan a great trip, visit our website at **www.frommers.com** for additional travel information on more than 4,000 destinations. We update features regularly to give you instant access to the most current trip-planning information available. At Frommers.com, you'll find scoops on the best airfares, lodging rates, and car rental bargains. You can even book your travel online through our reliable travel booking partners. Other popular features include:

- Online updates of our most popular guidebooks
- Vacation sweepstakes and contest giveaways
- Newsletters highlighting the hottest travel trends
- Podcasts, interactive maps, and up-to-the-minute events listings
- Opinionated blog entries by Arthur Frommer himself
- Online travel message boards with featured travel discussions

1

How to Feel Like a Las Vegas Family

If you sprang for this guide, you no doubt have Las Vegas on the brain. Is it a good family destination? You're probably hoping the reply is "yes." As it happens, the question is a lot more straightforward than the answer.

Las Vegas offers everything a family could want: world-class resorts; eye-popping neon; ersatz replicas of Egypt, Venice, Paris, ancient Rome, King Arthur's castle, and New York City; one of the most dynamic dining scenes in America; top-notch entertainment for all ages; sports and outdoor recreational opportunities rivaled by few cities; and an assortment of attractions ranging from exploding volcanoes to the Hoover Dam. As icing on the cake, all of this is available for a fraction of what you'd pay at most other destinations. Without spending a nickel in the casinos, you'll discover more to see and do in Las Vegas than a family can cram into 6 weeks.

But there, you see, is the rub. For many parents (perhaps including you), Las Vegas is on the short list for family vacation destinations precisely because mom and dad want to enjoy a little gambling. Gambling, after all, is what subsidizes those bargain hotel rooms, free pirate battles, and gut-busting buffets. It would seem almost un-American not to spend some time in the casino. Once you've started down that path, however, you're well on the way to taking the "family" out of "family vacation."

Gambling and spending time as a family are mutually incompatible. Children are not allowed in casinos. Period. So if you want to play some blackjack, the children will have to be someplace else. Where would that be exactly? Well, the 12-and-up crowd will eke out a couple hours a day at the pool (some pools require a parent present for children 15 and under); spend as much on buffets, burgers, and snacks as your budget allows; and then go cruising. This last activity consists of roaming up and down the Strip or Fremont Street ducking into arcades, gift shops, and hotels; riding the monorail; and checking out the freebie sex brochures available on street corners. Though cruising is good exercise, quite educational (every imaginable form of humanity is on display), and definitely horizon expanding, you might not be altogether pleased with the discoveries your children make.

For children aged 11 years and younger, your options are even more constrained. One spouse can watch the kids while the other gambles, you can plop the kids in day care (generally not available on the Strip or Downtown), or you can hire an in-room sitter. If you pick up the tab and sign some waivers, a number of in-room sitters will even take your kids out for sightseeing or other activities. The problem with all of these alternatives, however, is that they turn your family vacation into an occasionally overlapping medley of solitary pursuits. You've become, in effect, just like all the other adults in town—a person who has come to Las Vegas to get away from children.

Can you have it both ways? Of course. After all, it's essentially a matter of degree. Even at Walt Disney World parents hire sitters in order to enjoy an occasional adult night out. Problem is, in Las Vegas it's very easy to let that adult evening expand into an adult vacation with your grown-up agenda supplanting the family one.

WHO LOVES YOU, BABY?

Possibly the most effective PR campaign ever launched on behalf of Las Vegas was the **Las Vegas Convention and Visitors Authority (LVCVA)** broadside of the early '90s that attempted to recast Las Vegas as a family destination. Today, more than a decade later, the misconceptions introduced by that nifty piece of marketing still run rampant.

LVCVA had a couple of objectives. First, it wanted bodies to fill all those hotel rooms that sat empty except on weekends. Second, it sought to make gambling seem more mainstream and wholesome, sort of like bowling. Because family vacations are generally a few days longer than the average Las Vegas stay, and because a high percentage of families travel during the hot summer (historically Las Vegas's slowest time of year), an ad campaign targeting families seemed like a perfect strategy for boosting occupancy rates and visitors' average length of stay.

LVCVA's logic seemed reasonable to most outsiders and was buttressed by the opening of the Excalibur, a resort that, like its older sister, Circus Circus, actually pursued the family trade. Arriving at about the same time was the new MGM Grand Hotel & Casino with its on-site Grand Adventures theme park. The message could not have been clearer: "Families! Las Vegas is the place for you!" Unfortunately, though the hype for the new theme park was world-class, the park itself was a total disaster. And while on the surface it appeared that the MGM Grand was targeting families, its actual position was one of confused ambivalence, an ambivalence that was resolved pretty quickly in the wake of the dud theme park. Of course, by the time these events had transpired, LVCVA had long since bought into its own press releases.

Though LVCVA's family campaign seemed cogent enough and was successful in stimulating a lot of families to consider Las Vegas, there was a very big pea under the proverbial mattress. It seems that LVCVA had failed to solicit the support of the casinos, and that likewise it had failed to take the views of the Las Vegas bread-and-butter adult visitor into account.

As for the resorts, the last thing they wanted was a bunch of kids tearing around the casinos and roaming up and down the Strip. The casinos *had* bothered to consult their regular customers. These folks responded resoundingly and unambiguously that they came to Las Vegas to have an adult experience. As one recreational gambler put it, "When we want to be around kids we'll go to Disneyland." Looking at it from another angle, LVCVA failed to notice that there was no hospitality infrastructure to support a large population of vacationing families. When it launched its campaign, there were only two resorts that solicited family business. That should have been a clue. Today, more than a dozen years later, only the same two resorts—Excalibur and Circus Circus—still greet families with a warm smile. As for LVCVA, it now works more cooperatively with casinos and pays more attention to the repeat adult visitor. To make amends for letting the "Families Welcome" monster out of the bag, LVCVA runs ads and commercials that depict Las Vegas as a lusty, 24-hour-a-day den of iniquity where adults can find just about any kind of action they're looking for.

THE BOTTOM LINE

For you, two questions are paramount: What are the practical implications of not being wanted by the casinos, and can you have a great family vacation in Las Vegas? We'll take them one at a time.

In practical terms, casino resorts are open to the public. They may not want you, but they won't turn you away either. And once you're there they'll treat you cordially, just like any other guest. The business logic is straightforward. Once you've arrived, they want you to have a good experience, to recommend the resort to others (preferably to adults), and hopefully to come back someday without the children. Security will be none too gentle if they catch your kids in the casino, and other guests will demonstrate their displeasure if your little ones are disruptive at the pool or in other public areas.

If, however, your children are generally well behaved and comfortable around adults, you can expect smooth sailing. Be aware that casinos aren't the only game in town. Dozens of nongaming hotels and motels exist in Las Vegas. These properties range from budget to luxury, and, unlike the casinos, will be happy to have your entire family's business. You won't be able to sneak down to the craps table in the middle of the night, but you'll enjoy certain other benefits, such as easy access to your car, that are absent from the product mix of the large casino resorts.

On to question two. You can most definitely enjoy a whale of a vacation in Las Vegas if your real objective is to have fun as a family. The way to accomplish this, however, is to commit to being together, or, expressed differently, to pretty much swear off gambling. Go to Las Vegas with the attitude that you'll let the grinds and high rollers subsidize your bargain four-star resort, your endless buffets, and your lush Disney-esque swimming pool. The casinos are full of people busily losing money. Ride their coattails. Let them pick up the tab for the pirate battles, exploding volcanoes, and dancing fountains. Allow their losses to turn your beer budget into a champagne vacation.

BRING IT ON

Las Vegas is designed to separate you from your money, whether by gambling—the preferred manner—or spending, which does not offer quite as high a profit margin for proprietors. The malls of the resorts and hotels, as discussed in chapter 10, "Shopping for the Whole Family," are, for the most part, over-the-top castles of commerce. Though the city's exotic hotels are low priced in comparison to rooms in other destination locations, such attractions (reviewed in chapters 8, 9, and 11) as roller coaster and gondola rides, aquariums, dolphin habitats, IMAX movies, arcades, Humvee tours of the desert, simulated weightless flights, and numerous other (kid and adult) magnets will nibble away at your vacation budget. That said, while some of Las Vegas's memorable experiences aren't exactly cheap, you can definitely have an amazing time whether you are on a budget-conscious vacation or a price-be-damned adventure.

Along with visiting the glitzy tourist attractions, consider discovering the city's past and present through its cultural offerings (also discussed in chapter 11), many of which are offered in settings that are a pleasant change from the man-made environments of the casino hotels. Hoover Dam, the Mormon Fort, and the Atomic Testing Museum obviously provide very different views of the area than what you can garner "just" from the Strip.

The history and culture of Las Vegas are explored not only in museums and monuments, but also with diverse outdoor happenings. Rodeos, recreations of posse shootouts, and festivals celebrating the different traditions of the area's settlers help families explore Las Vegas's past. During the summer, there are opportunities to see classic family films screened outdoors under the stars. Nearby Nellis Air Force Base provides a chance to watch fighter jets up close, while those inclined toward the terpsichorean arts can see the ballet and/or a luau. Athletically inclined families can race BMX bikes and sports cars, or participate in or simply watch any number of indoor and outdoor sports. We were reminded by several locals that "kids under 12 fish free," meaning that fishing licenses are not required for that age group to try their hand at the fishing holes around town as well as at giant Lake Mead, which features fishing along with a slew of other water-related recreation. See chapters 8, 9, and 12 for more information on the many available activities and experiences in and around Las Vegas.

All that activity can build up an appetite, and though Las Vegas can be a gourmet's paradise of foie gras with chocolate sauce—something we actually saw on one restaurant's menu—feeding the kids is no problem because every Strip hotel has a food court with a variety of quick meals and fast food. The inevitable buffets and round-the-clock coffee shops are around, too, where your kids should be able to find *something* they'll like. We've made it a point to consider your family when reviewing the restaurants in chapter 7. Theme restaurants are a big draw here, especially for boys who can be coddled, entertained, *and* fed by the likes of Harley-Davidson or ESPN. And while some fancy restaurants ban children 4 and under, others welcome children of all ages, going beyond offering booster chairs to actually making custom dishes for the little ones. Vegetarian or vegan family members will also find something for their dietary concerns on almost every menu.

Being a vegetarian in Vegas is easy, but being a teenager is always difficult, and in Vegas it can be especially hard. Unless you are 21 or over you are not allowed on the casino floor, and if you look underage, trust us, you will be carded. Less than a handful of all-age nightclubs exist, and none of those are located in the actual Las Vegas area. Teens and 'tweens are too old for day care at most hotels, yet too young to be allowed alone in the pool areas. They are not allowed on the Strip after 9pm or in arcades unescorted during the late night and early morning hours. But do not despair; teens who live in Vegas manage to have plenty of fun, and so can yours. In fact, even the grumbling Goth, rebellious rocker, and truculent teen should find something cool to do, see, eat, or buy in Las Vegas, which is saying a lot.

We are continually amazed at the number of fun activities for families in Las Vegas and even more impressed with the educational opportunities that can be cleverly disguised as fun. A trip to one museum lets you examine live, exotic desert creatures from just inches away; a visit to another lets you explore sound waves and soap bubbles. In one casino hotel, you can take a quick trip to an Egyptian tomb, and others transport you to other distant times and places: Renaissance Venice, ancient Rome, the New York of the 1930s, a perfect Paris, and exotic deserts. Here in Vegas, you get quite a bang from your vacation buck!

When in Vegas, you won't be able to help noticing the number of tourists (from around both the country and the world) who have traveled to Vegas, kids in tow, to take advantage of both the adult- and child-oriented attractions the city offers. They know what you're about to find out: You can't help but be overwhelmed by the sheer amount of stuff to do and see in Las Vegas—but then again, if all you like to do on vacation is relax and lounge around the pool, that, too, can be accomplished with minimum effort in this city. In reality, Las Vegas is a great family vacation spot, with something for everyone. Just don't let the casino hotels in on the secret!

1 FROMMER'S FAVORITE LAS VEGAS FAMILY EXPERIENCES

- **Hike to the Calico Tanks at Red Rock Canyon:** Less than 3 miles round-trip, this hike climbs up a narrow, rocky canyon to the Calico Tanks, a natural water repository situated high on a ridge overlooking the Las Vegas Valley.

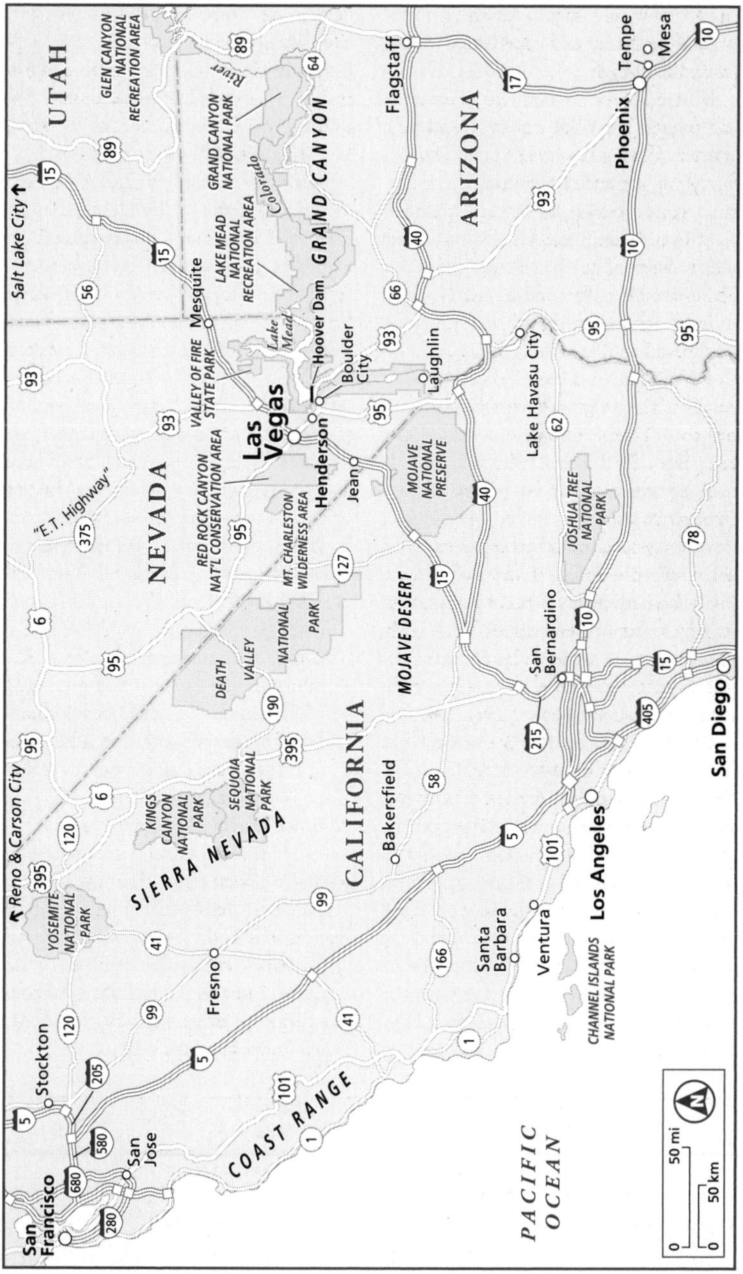

UTAH
GLEN CANYON NATIONAL RECREATION AREA
Salt Lake City
Mesquite
NEVADA
"E.T. Highway"
VALLEY OF FIRE STATE PARK
RED ROCK CANYON NAT'L CONSERVATION AREA
Las Vegas
Henderson
Jean
Hoover Dam
Boulder City
Lake Mead
Colorado River
LAKE MEAD NATIONAL RECREATION AREA
GRAND CANYON NATIONAL PARK
GRAND CANYON
Flagstaff
ARIZONA
Phoenix
Tempe
Mesa
Laughlin
Lake Havasu City
MT. CHARLESTON WILDERNESS AREA
DEATH VALLEY NATIONAL PARK
MOJAVE NATIONAL PRESERVE
MOJAVE DESERT
JOSHUA TREE NATIONAL PARK
San Bernardino
CALIFORNIA
Bakersfield
KINGS CANYON NATIONAL PARK
SEQUOIA NATIONAL PARK
SIERRA NEVADA
Reno & Carson City
YOSEMITE NATIONAL PARK
Fresno
Stockton
San Francisco
San Jose
COAST RANGE
Santa Barbara
Ventura
Los Angeles
San Diego
CHANNEL ISLANDS NATIONAL PARK
PACIFIC OCEAN
0 50 mi
0 50 km

Children love the adventure and easy boulder hopping. Adults and kids alike love the view from the top. See p. 267.

- **Witness a Simulated Atomic Bomb Explosion at the Atomic Testing Museum:** Located less than 5 minutes from the Strip, this new museum traces the history of the atomic bomb and the tests conducted at the atomic test facility northwest of Las Vegas. The museum's many exhibits, films, and simulations are in a re-creation of a bunker used to shield test witnesses from the heat and shock wave of bomb detonations. Boys in particular will find the museum way cool. See p. 186.
- **Why Must There Always Be Snakes?:** The answer to this question posed by Indiana Jones is that almost all of us are either fascinated or powerfully terrified by these primitive reptiles. Every species of venomous reptile native to southern Nevada can be found at the Southern Nevada Zoological-Botanical Park. Also on display are endangered cats, apes, and eagles, among others. See p. 174.
- **Kayak or Raft the Black Canyon of the Colorado River:** Starting below Hoover Dam, paddle 11 miles to Willow Beach, deep within the dramatic towering walls of the Black Canyon. Along the way are beaches for picnics and a multitude of side canyons to explore. There's a good current to speed you along but no rapids. A permit is required (easy to obtain) to run the river so don't wait until the last minute to make your plans. If you forget to acquire a permit you can opt for a more passive voyage through the canyon on a motorized pontoon raft. See p. 260.
- **Take an All-Day Excursion to Death Valley National Park:** The lowest point of elevation in the Western Hemisphere is in Death Valley. This is Desert 101 at its best—high desert, low desert, sand dunes, salt flats, coyotes, rattlesnakes, curious rock formations, ghost towns, cacti, and in the spring, glorious wildflowers. The drive to Death Valley National Park is about 2 hours from Las Vegas via the shortest route. If you get an early start, that leaves plenty of time to explore one of the park's 18 hiking trails. Finally, one of the coolest things (pun intended) about Death Valley is that January and February are ideal months to visit.
- **Watch Statues at Caesars Palace:** The "statues" come astoundingly alive at two locations in Caesars Palace in the Forum Shops, accompanied by music, lasers, and fog, enthralling everyone around them. The Fountain Festival, the original statue show, stars Bacchus, the god of wine, and might actually get your children interested in Greco-Roman mythology. The newer show, more loosely drawn from classical literature, is full of explosions, thunder, and lightning. Both are huge favorites with children of all ages. For more information, see p. 171.
- **Check Out the Night Lights at Fremont Street:** Fremont Street, the site of U2's video for "I Still Haven't Found What I'm Looking For," is now closed to cars, and a projection canopy of 12.5 million LEDs electrifies the evening sky with brilliant changing colors. A 540,000-watt sound system accompanies the light-and-laser show. Between shows, which run five times a night, live music and entertainers perform along this 5-block-long promenade lined with shops and cafes. The Neon Museum provides additional glow with the original lamp from the Aladdin and other classic Vegas signs. See p. 172.
- **Explore Lied Discovery Children's Museum:** Your entire family will have a blast piloting the space shuttle and composing tunes with their feet at this museum, where over 100 exhibits are designed to be played with and touched. See p. 176.

- **See the Pirate Battle at Treasure Island:** Five times nightly cannons boom as a ship of lusty sirens does battle with a ragtag troop of pirates. The sirens, scantily clad, were substituted for the British Navy in an effort to make the pirate battle more adult. Though still pretty adolescent, the presentation features hard-driving music, some good choreography, and an arsenal of special effects. Swords are drawn, swashbucklers swash and buckle, plus there's fire and a sinking ship. All in all, it's a very satisfying experience (watch it from the simulated docks outside Treasure Island), and, for fun after the crowds have cleared, you can watch the sunken ship rise from the watery depths to do battle again. See p. 173.
- **Ride the Monorail:** Take a ride from the MGM Grand to the Sahara on the Las Vegas Strip Monorail. The ride takes 14 minutes each way and affords behind-the-scenes glimpses of famous strip hotels before racing past the Wynn Las Vegas golf course and the Las Vegas Convention Center, to the end of the line at the Sahara. See p. 88.
- **Toss Balls with the Dolphins at the Dolphin Habitat:** Nothing is cooler than playing ball with a water mammal. These dolphins don't do tricks, per se, but they will bounce balls back to you and their trainers, stand up on their tails, and do flips, not because they're trained to, but because they want to. See p. 178.
- **Count the Moray Eels at Shark Reef, Mandalay Bay:** Supposedly, more than 20 of the slinky, spotted sea creatures live in the vast coral reef here, but we managed to count only 8. It's also fun to give them names, because each has a distinctive look. Ella Eel, Elvis Eel, Irwin . . . you get the idea. See p. 177.
- **Feel Brave After the Stratosphere Thrill Rides:** Your family will bond from the adrenaline rush before, during, and after a trip on the High Roller, the world's highest roller coaster; a drop on the Big Shot, a 160-foot free-fall ride on the Stratosphere's spire; and being dangled over the edge of the tower on X Scream. See p. 182.
- **Explore the International Marketplace:** This vast warehouse, a secret to most visitors, stocks thousands of different foods from around the world. Gooey Japanese fruit candies in neon wrappers share space with tarragon soda pop from the Middle East and purple yam ice cream from the Philippines. See p. 222.
- **See the Dinosaurs Dance at the Las Vegas Museum of Natural History:** Equipped with motion sensors, the re-creations of T. rex and his dino buddies come alive, roaring and moving when you enter their display room. Live sharks swim in a nearby tank, and there's a cool collection of stuffed animals in displays designed to replicate their natural environment. See p. 188.
- **Order in a Pizza:** Take a break from your sightseeing to relax in front of the TV and order up a pay-per-view movie. Then call out for a large pie from Metro Pizza, the city's best, which will actually deliver to your hotel room. Those ingredients should add up to decadent, silly fun that will help remind you of what being a family is all about. It will also hopefully revitalize you for your next adventure. See p. 163.

2 BEST HOTEL BETS

For the full descriptions of the hotels below, please see chapter 6, "Family-Friendly Accommodations."

- **Most Family Friendly on the Strip:** Both **Excalibur,** 3850 Las Vegas Blvd. S. (✆ **800/937-7777** or 702/597-7777), and its North Strip sibling, **Circus Circus,** 2880 Las Vegas Blvd. S. (© **800/634-3450** or 702/734-0410), were designed with families in mind and feature regularly scheduled free entertainment and large arcades. Circus Circus also has its own theme park (with rides for all ages) and miniature golf. See p. 107 and 119, respectively.

- **Most Family Friendly off the Strip:** The **Orleans,** 4500 W. Tropicana Ave. (© **800/ORLEANS** [675-3267] or 702/365-7111), has a bowling alley and movie theaters and offers child care. **Sam's Town,** 5111 Boulder Hwy. (© **800/897-8696** or 702/456-7777), also features a multiplex theater plus the free Sunset Stampede show and a large, beautiful indoor park with animatronic animals. See p. 132 and 128 respectively.
- **Best Suite Deals Close to the Strip:** The **Carriage House,** 105 E. Harmon Ave. (© **800/221-2301** or 702/798-1020), offers plenty of room for families in a nongaming environment 2 minutes from the Strip. A full kitchen in each suite also makes eat-in meals an option. And unlike hotels, there's full cable TV with over 40 channels, along with Nintendo at an hourly rate, plus free board games. See p. 122.
- **Best Suite Deals off the Strip:** A nongaming resort ideal for short- or long-term stays, **Desert Paradise,** 5165 S. Decatur Blvd. (© **800/424-1943** or 702/579-3600), offers complete apartments with their own washer/dryers, huge kitchens, full cable, and patio. With a barbecue area, lounge with large-screen TV, and a nice pool, this resort was designed with families in mind, and is a perfect getaway location. See p. 130.
- **Most Peace & Quiet on the Strip & the Most Child-Pampering Hotel:** You can't beat the nongaming **Four Seasons,** 3960 Las Vegas Blvd. S. (© **877/632-5000** or 702/632-5000), located at the southernmost tip of the Strip. The luxurious hotel pampers children as well as parents, providing small bathrobes and gift baskets for the kiddies. Rooms can be childproofed in advance of your arrival, ensuring your peace of mind. See p. 101.
- **Most Peace & Quiet off the Strip:** Staying in Henderson at the ultrarestful **Green Valley Ranch** resort, 2300 Paseo Verde Dr. (© **702/617-7777** or 866/782-9487), will give you plenty of peace and quiet in luxurious surroundings, plus many activities for the children. There's a casino, but you can avoid it completely and just go to the on-site multiplex, play golf, or sun by the pool. See p. 133.
- **Best View:** Unless you are on a low floor, at night, you should get a view of something sparkling no matter where you stay. But the view standing on the tower atop the **Stratosphere,** 2000 Las Vegas Blvd. S. (© **800/998-6937** or 702/380-7777), located at the northernmost end of the Strip, tops them all. See p. 118.
- **When Price Is No Object: Caesars Palace,** 3570 Las Vegas Blvd. S. (© **800/634-6661** or 702/731-7110), with its hilarious Greco-Roman theme, provides an over-the-top vacation experience for all ages. And the Fountain Show and Forum Shops just add to the fun. See p. 110.
- **Best Lobby:** A wall-sized relief map of the ancient city, ceiling frescoes in gilded frames, and an M.C. Escher–like marble floor greet you when you walk into **The Venetian,** 3355 Las Vegas Blvd. S. (© **888/2-VENICE** [283-6423] or 702/414-1000), making this a jaw-dropper for almost everyone. See p. 113.
- **Best Pool:** You can bob on a lazy river ride or bodysurf the gentle swells in the pools at both the (otherwise not quite kid-friendly) **Mandalay Bay,** 3950 Las Vegas Blvd. S. (© **877/632-7800** or

702/632-7777), or the **Monte Carlo Resort & Casino,** 3770 Las Vegas Blvd. S. (© **800/311-8999** or 702/730-7777), but the best pool scene is at **The Flamingo,** 3555 Las Vegas Blvd. S. (© **800/732-2111** or 702/733-3111), where five pools, two whirlpools, a kiddie pool, and water slides are set in a tropical environment complete with exotic birds and koi ponds. See p. 109, 104, and 114 respectively.

- **Best Hotel Arcade:** Even though it's not a 24-hour game room, the Coney Island arcade in **New York–New York,** 3790 Las Vegas Blvd. S. (© **800/NY-FOR-ME** [693-6763] or 702/740-6969), is the cleanest, best-lit arcade in the entire city, with gleaming hardwood floors instead of the usual dark carpet. See p. 105.
- **Best Fitness Center:** Though the **Four Seasons,** 3960 Las Vegas Blvd. S. (© **866/536-9403** or 702/632-5000), is a very expensive hotel, unlike at other casinos/resorts in the area, the use of its ultramodern, state-of-the-art health club is free. Other hotels, such as the **Fairfield Inn by Marriott,** 3850 Paradise Rd. (© **800/228-2800** or 702/791-0899), also offer free use of their exercise rooms, which, though small, can still make you break a sweat. For those who don't mind paying $35 a day for access to spa facilities, **The Venetian,** 3355 Las Vegas Blvd. S. (© **888/2-VENICE** [283-6423] or 702/414-1000), offers Canyon Ranch, a branch of what is considered one of the best spas in the United States. The fee gets you access to all the machines, saunas, and exercise classes Canyon Ranch offers, including yoga and Pilates. There's also a rock-climbing wall. See p. 101, 127, and 113, respectively.
- **Best Bathrooms:** Marvelous marble everywhere graces the very large bathrooms at **The Venetian,** 3355 Las Vegas Blvd. S. (© **888/2-VENICE** [283-6423] or 702/414-1000), but for sheer shower and bathroom opulence, we opt for **Mandalay Bay,** 3950 Las Vegas Blvd. S. (© **877/632-7800** or 702/632-7777), with glassed-in showers and sunken tubs, plus bathrobes available upon request. See p. 113 and 109, respectively.
- **Best Shopping Area:** Although grown-ups may love the luxuries on display at **Via Bellagio** in **Bellagio,** 3600 Las Vegas Blvd. S. (© **888/987-6667** or 702/693-7444), kids will have more fun at **Caesars Forum Shops** at **Caesars Palace,** 3570 Las Vegas Blvd. S. (© **800/634-6661** or 702/731-7110), **The Venetian's Grand Canal Shoppes,** 3355 Las Vegas Blvd. S. (© **888/2-VENICE** [283-6423] or 702/414-1000), or even the **Miracle Mile Shops** at **Planet Hollywood,** 3667 Las Vegas Blvd. S. (© **877/333-WISH** [333-9474] or 702/785-5555), for their mix of family entertainment and eye candy. **Las Vegas Premium Outlets,** 875 S. Grand Central Pkwy. (© **702/474-7500**), located near Downtown Las Vegas, offers 120 prestige-brand outlet stores. See p. 206, 208, 210, 209, and 206, respectively.
- **Best Hotel Coffee Shop:** Kids 11 and under will enjoy the carousel theme of the **Pink Pony** cafe inside **Circus Circus,** 2880 Las Vegas Blvd. S. (© **800/643-3450** or 702/734-0410), with its circus place mats and crayons. The hipster groove of **Mr. Lucky's 24/7** at the **Hard Rock Hotel & Casino,** 4455 Paradise Rd. (© **800/473-ROCK** [473-7625] or 702/693-5000), is more appealing to teens. But hands down, visitors go out of their way to visit **Calypsos** at the **Tropicana Resort & Casino,** 3801 Las Vegas Blvd. S. (© **800/634-4000** or 702/739-2222), an old-fashioned coffee shop that allows you to build your own burger and features classic coffee shop fare (try the slab of pound cake topped with fruit and frozen yogurt) in a tropical-themed environment. See p. 158, 163, and 148, respectively.

- **Best Hotel Restaurant for Kids:** The **Rainforest Cafe at MGM Grand,** 3799 Las Vegas Blvd. S. (✆ **800/929-1111** or 702/891-8580), features a kid's menu, crayons, good food, and, best of all, animatronic animals and thunderstorms. See p. 145.
- **Best Hotel Kids' Program: KidsQuest,** in the Sunset Station, 1301 W. Sunset Rd. (✆ **888/786-7389** or 702/547-7777), is a fun, safe place to tuck the kids for awhile. See p. 74.
- **Best Hotel Pet Programs: Desert Rose Resort,** 5051 Duke Ellington Way (✆ **800/527-1133** or 702/739-7000), welcomes any size, well-behaved Fido. See p. 57.
- **Best Hotel Buffet for Families: The Flamingo,** 3555 Las Vegas Blvd. S. (✆ **800/732-2111** or 702/733-3111), feeds kids 7 and under for a discount price at breakfast, brunch, and dinner, with a view of birds, habitat, and fishponds. See p. 167.
- **Tops for Toddlers:** For sensory stimulation, **Circus Circus,** 2880 Las Vegas Blvd. S. (✆ **800/634-3450** or 702/704-3986), offers a midway, clowns, jugglers, and lots of flashing lights. The **Excalibur,** 3850 Las Vegas Blvd. S. (✆ **800/937-7777** or 702/597-7777), also has jugglers and throws in puppet shows and story times as well. See p. 119 and 107, respectively.
- **Tops for Teens:** Staying at the **Hard Rock Hotel & Casino,** 4455 Paradise Rd. (✆ **800/473-ROCK** or 702/693-5000), can fill your teen with rock star dreams, plus *you'll* get points for being cool. Young sophisticates will enjoy the **Monte Carlo Resort & Casino,** 3770 Las Vegas Blvd. S. (✆ **800/311-8999** or 702/730-7777), and **The Venetian,** 3355 Las Vegas Blvd. S. (✆ **888/2-VENICE** [283-6423] or 702/414-1000), with their luxurious European style. See p. 122, 104, and 113, respectively.

3 BEST DINING BETS

For more information, please see chapter 7, "Family-Friendly Dining."

- **Best Burger:** Lots of folks love the 24-hour **Tiffany's Cafe** at **White Cross Drugs,** 1700 Las Vegas Blvd. S. (✆ **702/444-4459**), on the north end of the Strip, but we are actually partial to the juicy (and pricey) burger available at lunchtime only at **Delmonico Steakhouse** in The Venetian, 3355 Las Vegas Blvd. S. (✆ **702/414-3737**)—it's served with caramelized onions and Vermont cheddar, and made according to celebrity chef Emeril Lagasse's specifications. For drive-through, you can't beat **In-N-Out Burger,** 4888 Industrial Rd. at the Tropicana (✆ **800/786-1000**). Many locals consider this the best burger joint in town. See p. 158, 152, and 148, respectively.
- **Best Kids' Menu:** Buffets that offer price breaks for kids, such as those at **Luxor,** 3900 Las Vegas Blvd. S. (✆ **800/288-1000** or 702/262-4000), or **The Flamingo,** 3555 Las Vegas Blvd. S. (✆ **800/732-2111** or 702/733-3111), actually can give kids a feeling of empowerment as they choose their own meals. Children can eat for half price at the buffet in the **Las Vegas Hilton,** 3000 Paradise Rd. (✆ **888/732-7117** or 702/732-5111), but the best actual kids' menu is at the **Verandah** at the **Four Seasons,** 3960 Las Vegas Blvd. S. (✆ **702/632-5000** or 702/632-5000), which offers lots of kids' favorites, including pizza, hot dogs, and PB&J sandwiches. See p. 165, 167, 168, and 148, respectively.

- **Best Tacos: El Sombrero,** at 807 S. Main St. (© **702/382-9234**), serves by far the best tacos in Las Vegas, and they have been doing so for more than 50 years. Ask for any kind you like; Chef Jose will put them together for you. See p. 164.
- **Best Secret Meal:** It's not on the menu, and it's a real deal—steak and shrimp, a Vegas classic, for $8.95 at **Mr. Lucky's 24/7** in the Hard Rock Hotel & Casino, 4455 Paradise Rd. (© **800/473-ROCK** [473-7625] or 702/693-5592). Someone in your party should order it, just to prove that parents know cool stuff that isn't always written down. See p. 163.
- **Best Food Court:** Most of the hotels have the same offerings (McDonald's, Nathan's, Häagen-Dazs, Starbucks, and the like), so that it's nice to find some different options. The food court at the **MGM Grand,** 3799 Las Vegas Blvd. S. (© **800/929-1111** or 702/891-1111), has the usual suspects mentioned above, but also has Mama Ilardo's Pizza, which does a nice slice, and Studio Wok, which serves good Chinese food. See p. 102.
- **Best Alternative Breakfast:** Some kids, and grown-ups, just don't like breakfast food. And even if you're a fan of eggs and waffles, that fare can get pretty dull day after day. Along with the usual morning meals, **Chin Chin,** in **New York–New York,** 3790 Las Vegas Blvd. S. (© **800/NY-FOR-ME** [693-6763] or 702/740-6300), serves traditional Chinese breakfast foods such as *congee* (rice porridge) and dim sum (small individual dishes, such as steamed dumplings filled with meat, vegetables, or seafood, and many other dishes), including the Chinese version of a barbecue sandwich, *cha su bao,* comprising chunks of pork or chicken and sweet sauce tucked inside a white doughy bun. See p. 146.
- **Best Pizza:** Practically every hotel food court has a pizza stand, and such nouvelle-style places as **California Pizza Kitchen,** in **The Mirage,** 3400 Las Vegas Blvd. S. (© **702/791-7111**), and **Wolfgang Puck Bar & Grill,** in the **MGM Grand,** 3799 Las Vegas Blvd. S. (© **800/929-1111** or 702/891-3000), can be found throughout Vegas for fans of exotic toppings. However, **Metro Pizza,** 1395 E. Tropicana Ave. (© **702/736-1955**), located about 15 minutes away from the Strip, not only serves up the best slice in town, but also delivers to all major hotels. See p. 155, 145, and 163, respectively.
- **Best Ice Cream: Schrafft's** in **New York–New York,** 3790 Las Vegas Blvd. S. (© **800/NY-FOR-ME** [693-6763] or 702/740-6969), serves up frozen custard, along with its own brand of ice cream. See p. 105.
- **Best Educational Restaurant: America,** located in **New York–New York,** 3790 Las Vegas Blvd. S. (© **800/NY-FOR-ME** [693-6763] or 702/740-6451), features food from around the United States; each menu item is designated with its reputed place of origin. That alone makes for some interesting conversation, but the really neat (yet educational) feature is the 90×20-foot map of the United States, complete with geographic and topographic features. See p. 146.
- **Best Milkshake: Tiffany's Cafe at White Cross Drugs,** 1700 Las Vegas Blvd. S. (© **702/382-1733**) on the North Strip, serves them cold, thick, and creamy. If you'd rather sample the fountain goods in a hotel coffee shop, **Roxy's,** in the **Stratosphere,** 2000 Las Vegas Blvd. S. (© **800/998-6937** or 702/380-7777), pours a good one. See p. 158 and 118, respectively.
- **Best Thai: Lotus of Siam,** 953 E. Sahara Ave. (© **702/735-3033**), located about 10 minutes east of the Strip, serves the best Thai food in the entire United States, according to food critics, both amateur and professional

(*Gourmet* magazine's Jonathan Gold being one of the LoS's biggest fans). If you have a craving for satay, this is the place to sate it, because you won't find much Thai food at any of the casinos/resorts. See p. 162.

- **Best Hot Dog:** Ubiquitous **Nathan's** franks have perfect texture, savory taste, and low cost, making them a great snack or quick meal. You'll find a Nathan's at **Monte Carlo Resort & Casino,** 3770 Las Vegas Blvd. S. (✆ **800/311-8999** or 702/730-7777); **New York–New York,** 3790 Las Vegas Blvd. S. (✆ **800/NY-FOR-ME** [693-6763] or 702/740-6969); and **MGM Grand,** 3799 Las Vegas Blvd. S. (✆ **800/929-1111** or 702/891-1111). See p. 104, 105, and 102, respectively.
- **Best Selection:** The **Grand Lux Café** at **The Venetian,** 3355 Las Vegas Blvd. S. (✆ **888/2-VENICE** [283-6423] or 702/414-3888), gives you a choice of over 150 entrees, appetizers, salads, and desserts, all of which are big enough to split between two or three people. The cuisine jumps from Italian to Pan-Asian to American, with stops in Europe, providing a huge, mostly very tasty selection. Plus, there's a kids' menu, which your server will recite for you, because it's not printed in the book-size menu you are handed at the table. See p. 157.
- **Best Romantic Outdoor Restaurant:** The patio at **Mon Ami Gabi** at **Paris Las Vegas,** 3655 Las Vegas Blvd. S. (✆ **702/944-4224**), faces the Bellagio water show, making this French bistro the most romantic spot on the Strip as the fountains spray and dance in time to music. After a meal of oysters, grilled steak, or roasted chicken; wine; profiteroles; and espresso, stroll through the adjacent casino hotel. Then whisper in your beloved's ear, "We'll always have Paris . . . Las Vegas." See p. 152.
- **Best Romantic Restaurant View (for a Night When You Hired a Sitter):** The food at **Alizé** is as impressive as its view from three huge windows overlooking the Strip from atop the **Palms Hotel,** 4321 W. Flamingo Rd. (✆ **702/951-7000**). Chef Andre Rochat, from Andre's French Restaurant and Andre's at the Monte Carlo (two of the city's most acclaimed French restaurants) and Chef Jacques Van Staden continually create and execute meals of epicurean perfection. See p. 169.

4 THE REST OF THE BEST

- **Best Place to Run Around:** Providing a variety of outdoor diversions, from picnicking to skateboarding and in-line skating, plus a dog park, a radio-controlled miniboat area, and a horseshoe pitch, **Sunset Park,** 2601 E. Sunset Rd. (✆ **702/455-8200**), located south of the Strip near McCarran International Airport, is a welcome respite from much of the city's artificial atmosphere. See p. 198.
- **Best Bookstore:** Although **Borders Express** in the Fashion Show Mall, 3200 Las Vegas Blvd. S. (✆ **702/733-1049**), is easily accessed from the Strip, **Dead Poet Books,** 937 S. Rainbow Blvd. (✆ **702/227-4070**), has a huge selection of used books for adults and children, and is the perfect place to fill up on literature at a discount. See p. 212 for both.
- **Best Toy Store: FAO Schwarz,** located in the Forum Shops at **Caesars Palace,** 3500 Las Vegas Blvd. S. (✆ **702/796-6500**), is three stories of fabulous toys—including a room of Barbies for

girls, action figures for boys, and the store's trademark supersoft stuffed animals—stocked in a section that replicates Homer's Trojan Horse. Plus, they can hold a birthday party for your wee one, which could include a sleepover in the treehouse section of the store, if you want (and can afford it). See p. 225.

- **Best History Lesson:** Your child can join the posse and head out to hunt down the bad guy or watch the goofy Western melodramas that are staged every half-hour in **Old Nevada on the Bonnie Springs Ranch** (**✆ 702/875-4191**). Explore Boot Hill Cemetery—and other locations that re-create pioneer icons—with your family. Along with the Western town, cowhands, and petting zoo, there's a caged collection of rescued wildlife and the most reasonably priced horseback rides in the Las Vegas area. See p. 272.
- **Best Place to Beat the Heat:** Head for **Mount Charleston** in the Spring Mountains 40 minutes to the northwest of Las Vegas. While everyone else is sizzling in the desert heat, you'll be walking among tall conifers and drinking in the cool mountain air. Best of all, it's free! See p. 275.

2

Las Vegas in Depth

There has rarely been a time in Vegas's post-Bugsy history when the city wasn't booming, but it's been on a particular roll for the past two decades. A new megaresort seems to go up at least once a year, and each brings something new to the party: great works of art, five-star world-renowned chefs, rock clubs and arenas that attract significant and still-current acts—you get the idea. In other words, everything old is new again, and Vegas glamour is back, while the sightseeing, thrill rides, and animals continue as a draw for all ages.

1 LAS VEGAS TODAY

The Vegas-as-family-vacation experiment didn't quite meet corporate expectations, so much so that the city continues to repudiate the idea. Now, the powers that be are returning to the idea of Vegas-as-adult-fun with a vengeance—and, this time around, they're determined not only to recapture that long-ago Vegas elegance (if, indeed, it ever existed) but also to persuade potential visitors to view Vegas as a luxury resort destination. This means creating a place where lounging, recreation, food, and shopping are given greater emphasis than ever before—even, hotel owners say, over the sacred gaming tables.

But don't let any of this make you think that you shouldn't come to Vegas with your kids. Thankfully, there seems to be a tacit understanding in Sin City that many visitors do have children and they like to go on vacation as a family. With that in mind, though hotels are hardly wooing families as hard as they did in the 1990s, they are in no way overlooking children either (hence, the arcades, rides, animals, and more).

Keep in mind that Vegas is, has been, and will always be first and foremost a gambling destination. After all, if they really didn't want you to gamble, they would have left the casinos out of the new luxury resorts. But, as we stress, there is more to Las Vegas than the cling-clang bling-bling of the casinos: The city is surrounded by beautiful desert mountains; history comes alive at the city's many museums; and the income generated from the gaming resorts has helped build the city's arts and leisure activities—all of which are great for families.

Whether Las Vegas's current experiment in luxury will succeed remains to be seen, but its effects are already being felt. Vegas has 17 of the 20 largest hotels in the United States, with nearly 40 million tourists filling all those rooms. But so far, so good: The occupancy rate is running at an impressive 90%. And for every new glistening hotel that goes up, another old-timer comes down, or undergoes a face-lift because it looks so shabby next to its shining new neighbor.

The phenomenal growth in tourism is being paralleled by a population explosion. Las Vegas has had a 28% increase in its population over the last 5 years, and an average of 3,000 people are relocating into the area monthly, many of whom have families or are looking to start them. This is the only city in America where the phone book is published twice a year in order to keep up with all the changes and newcomers. Unfortunately, the highways

Hotel	Location	Rooms
1. MGM Grand	Las Vegas	5,690
2. Luxor	Las Vegas	4,408
3. Mandalay Bay	Las Vegas	4,341
4. The Venetian	Las Vegas	4,027
5. Excalibur	Las Vegas	4,008
6. Bellagio	Las Vegas	3,993
7. Circus Circus	Las Vegas	3,774
8. The Flamingo	Las Vegas	3,565
9. Hilton Hawaiian Village	Honolulu	3,386
10. Caesars Palace	Las Vegas	3,348
11. Palazzo	Las Vegas	3,066
12. The Mirage	Las Vegas	3,044
13. Monte Carlo	Las Vegas	3,002
14. Las Vegas Hilton	Las Vegas	2,956
15. Paris Las Vegas	Las Vegas	2,916
16. Treasure Island	Las Vegas	2,885
17. Gaylord Opryland Resort	Nashville	2,881
18. Disney's Pop Century Resort	Walt Disney World	2,880
19. Bally's	Las Vegas	2,814
20. Wynn Las Vegas	Las Vegas	2,716

can't expand as rapidly as the phone books, and school construction is lagging behind the population boom. For tourists, the town's all-too-rapid growth is most evident along the Strip, which is totally inadequate to accommodate such huge numbers of cars and people. While people movers, monorails, and overpasses have helped smooth pedestrian travel and other traffic solutions are slowly being integrated, Strip traffic remains frustratingly bumper-to-bumper at almost all times.

Snarled traffic notwithstanding, families visiting Las Vegas will be awestruck by the variety of eye candy and amusements offered to them, overwhelmed at times by the plethora of options for exploration, food, fun, attractions, and shopping. Each time something new opens up, you think, "They can't possibly top this." And yet they do. And one thing's for sure—somehow, they always will.

2 A LOOK AT THE PAST

For many centuries, the land that would become Nevada was inhabited only by several Native American tribes: the Paiute, Shoshone, and Washoe. It wasn't until 1826 that Europeans set foot in the future state, and not until 1829 that Rafael Rivera, a scout for Mexican traders, discovered a small spring in the middle of a huge desert valley and called it Las Vegas ("the Meadows"). From 1831 to 1848, these springs served as a watering place on the Old Spanish Trail for trading caravans plying the route between New Mexico and the California coast. Explorer, soldier, and pathfinder Col. John C. Frémont (for whom the main thoroughfare in Downtown is named) rehydrated at the spring at Las Vegas on an overland expedition in 1844. A decade later, Congress established a monthly mail route through Las Vegas Springs.

In 1855, Mormon leader Brigham Young sent 30 missionaries to Las Vegas to help expand Mormonism between Salt Lake City and Southern California. Just north of what is today Downtown (what would these missionaries think if they could see it today?), the Mormon colony built an adobe fort and dwellings. They raised crops, baptized Paiutes, and mined lead in the nearby mountains. However, none of these ventures proved successful, and the ill-fated settlement was abandoned after just 3 years.

The next influx into the area came as a result of mining fever in the early 1860s. Gold fever gave way to a fervor for land as pioneers moved ever westward. In 1865, gold prospector Octavius Decatur Gass homesteaded the 640-acre Las Vegas Ranch, using structures left by the Mormons as his base. Because Gass controlled the valley's water, he finally found "gold" offering services to travelers passing through. Gass planted crops and fruit orchards, started vineyards, raised cattle, established cordial relations with the Paiutes (he even learned their language), and served as a legislator. Thus was born the first significant settlement in the area. By 1900, the Las Vegas valley had a population of 30.

A TENT CITY IN THE WILDERNESS

The city of Las Vegas was officially founded in 1905, when the Union Pacific Railroad connecting Los Angeles and Salt Lake City decided to route its trains through this rugged frontier outpost, selected for its ready supply of water and the availability of timber in the surrounding mountains. On a sweltering day in May, 1,200 townsite lots were auctioned off to eager pioneers and real-estate speculators who had come from all over the country. The railroad depot was located at the head of Fremont Street (site of today's Plaza Hotel). Championing the spot was Montana senator William Clark, who had paid the astronomical sum (for that time) of $55,000 for the nearby Las Vegas Ranch and springs. The coming of a railroad more or less ensured the growth of the town. As construction began, tent settlements, saloons, ramshackle restaurants, boardinghouses, and shops gradually emerged. (The early tent hotels charged a

DATELINE

- **1831–48** Artesian spring waters of Las Vegas serve as an oasis on the Old Spanish Trail.
- **1855** Mormon colony of 30 missionaries establishes settlement just north of today's Downtown. Unsuccessful in its aims, the colony disbands in 1858.
- **1864** President Lincoln proclaims Nevada the 36th state of the Union. Las Vegas, however, is still part of Arizona Territory.
- **1865** Gold prospector Octavius D. Gass establishes Las Vegas Ranch, the first permanent settlement in Las Vegas, on the site of the old Mormon fort.
- **1895** San Francisco inventor Charles Fey creates a three-reel gambling device—the first slot machine.
- **1904** The San Pedro, Los Angeles and Salt Lake Railroad lays railroad track through Las Vegas Valley.
- **1905** The railroad company lays out a town site for Las Vegas and auctions lots.
- **1907** Fremont Street, the future "Glitter Gulch," gets electric lights.
- **1909** Gambling is made illegal in Nevada, but Las Vegas pays little heed.
- **1928** Congress authorizes construction of Boulder Dam 30 miles away, bringing

dollar to share a double bed with a stranger for 8 hr.!)

By present-day standards, the new town was not a pleasant place to live. Prospectors' burros roamed the streets braying loudly, generally creating havoc and attracting swarms of flies. There were no screens, no air conditioners, and no modern showers or bathrooms (the town's bathhouse had but one tub) to ameliorate the fierce summer heat. The streets were rutted with dust pockets up to a foot deep that rose in great gusts as stagecoaches, supply wagons, and 20-animal mule teams careened over them. It was a true pioneer town, complete with saloon brawls and shootouts. Discomforts notwithstanding, gaming establishments, hotels, and nightclubs—some of them seedy dives, others rather luxurious—sprang up and prospered in the new railroad town. A red-light district emerged on Second Street between Ogden and Stewart avenues. And gambling, which was legal until 1909, flourished.

THE EIGHTH WONDER OF THE WORLD

For many years after its creation, Las Vegas was a mere whistle-stop town. That all changed in 1928 when Congress authorized the building of nearby Boulder (later renamed Hoover) Dam, bringing thousands of workers to the area. In 1931, gambling once again became legal in Nevada, and Fremont Street's gaming emporiums and speak-easies attracted workers from the dam. Upon the dam's completion, the Las Vegas Chamber of Commerce worked hard to lure the hordes of tourists who came to see the engineering marvel (it was called "the Eighth Wonder of the World") to its casinos. Las Vegas was about to make the transition from sleepy desert town to desert town that never sleeps. But it wasn't until the early years of World War II that visionary entrepreneurs began to plan for its glittering future.

LAS VEGAS GOES SOUTH

Contrary to popular lore, Bugsy Siegel didn't actually stake a claim in the middle of nowhere—he just built a few blocks south of already existing properties. Development a few miles south of Downtown on Hwy. 91 (the future Strip) was already underway in the 1930s, with such establishments as the Pair-O-Dice Club and the Last Frontier.

And in 1941, El Rancho Vegas, ultra-luxurious for its time, was built on the same remote stretch of highway (across the street from where the Sahara now stands). According to legend, Los Angeles hotelier Thomas E. Hull had been driving by the site when his car broke down. Noticing the extent of passing traffic, he decided to build there. Hull invited scores of Hollywood stars to his grand opening and

thousands of workers to the area. Later, Las Vegas will capitalize on hundreds of thousands who come to see the engineering marvel.

- **1931** Gambling is legalized once again.
- **1932** The 100-room Apache Hotel opens Downtown.
- **1933** Prohibition is repealed. Las Vegas's numerous speak-easies become legit.
- **1934** The city's first neon sign lights up the Boulder Club Downtown.
- **1941** The luxurious El Rancho Vegas becomes the first hotel on the Strip. Downtown, the El Cortez opens.
- **1942** The Last Frontier opens 2 miles south of El Rancho Vegas.
- **1946** Benjamin "Bugsy" Siegel's Flamingo extends the boundaries of the Strip. Sammy Davis, Jr., debuts at the El Rancho Vegas. Downtown (dubbed "Glitter Gulch") gets two new hotels: the Golden Nugget and the Eldorado.
- **1947** United Airlines inaugurates service to Las Vegas.
- **1948** The Thunderbird becomes the fourth hotel on the Strip.
- **1950** The Desert Inn adds country club panache to the Strip.
- **1951** The first of many atomic bombs is tested in the desert just 65 miles from

continues

El Rancho Vegas soon became the hotel of choice for visiting film stars.

Beginning a trend that still continues today, each new property tried to outdo existing hotels in luxurious amenities and thematic splendor. In 1942, the Last Frontier (the Strip's second hotel) created an authentic Western setting by scouring the Southwest in search of authentic pioneer furnishings for its rooms, hiring Zuni craftsmen to create baskets and wall hangings, and picking up guests at the airport in a horse-drawn stagecoach. And with that, Las Vegas was on its way to becoming the entertainment capital of the world.

Las Vegas promoted itself in the 1940s as a town that combined Wild West frontier friendliness with glamour and excitement. As Chamber of Commerce president Maxwell Kelch aptly put it in a 1947 speech, "Las Vegas has the impact of a Wild West show, the friendliness of a country store, and the sophistication of Monte Carlo." Throughout the decade, the city was largely a regional resort—Hollywood's celebrity playground. Clara Bow and Rex Bell (a star of westerns) bought a ranch in Las Vegas, where they entertained the Barrymores, Norma Shearer, Clark Gable, and Errol Flynn. The Hollywood connection gave the town glamour in the public's mind. So did the mob connection (something Las Vegas subsequently spent decades trying to live down), which became clear early on when the notorious underworld gangster Benjamin "Bugsy" Siegel (with partners Charles "Lucky" Luciano and Meyer Lansky) built the fabulous Flamingo, a tropical paradise and "a real class joint." In 1947, the Club Bingo opened across the street from El Rancho Vegas, bringing yet another new game to town.

A steady stream of name entertainers began to make their way to Las Vegas. In 1947, Jimmy Durante opened the showroom at The Flamingo. Other headliners of the 1940s included Dean Martin and Jerry Lewis, tap-dancing legend Bill "Bojangles" Robinson, the Mills Brothers, skater Sonja Henie, and Frankie Laine. (Future Las Vegas legend Sammy Davis, Jr., debuted at El Rancho Vegas in 1945.)

While the Strip was expanding, Downtown kept pace with new hotels such as the El Cortez and the Golden Nugget. By the end of the decade, Fremont Street was known as "Glitter Gulch," its profusion of neon signs proclaiming round-the-clock gaming and entertainment.

THE 1950S: BUILDING BOOMS & A-BOMBS

Las Vegas entered the new decade as a city (no longer a frontier town) with a population of about 50,000. Photographs remind us that Las Vegas celebrated a more formal nightlife in the 1950s than it does today.

Las Vegas. An explosion of another sort takes place when Frank Sinatra debuts at the Desert Inn.

- **1952** The Club Bingo (opened in 1947) becomes the desert-themed Sahara. The Sands also opens; its Copa Room enhances the city's image as an entertainment center.
- **1954** The Showboat pioneers buffet meals and bowling alleys in a new area of Downtown.
- **1955** The Strip gets its first high-rise hotel, the nine-story Riviera, which pays Liberace the unprecedented sum of $50,000 to open its showroom. The Riviera is the ninth hotel on the Strip. A month later, the Dunes becomes the 10th.
- **1956** The Fremont opens Downtown, and the Hacienda becomes the southernmost hotel on the Strip.
- **1957** The Dunes introduces bare-breasted showgirls in its *Minsky Goes to Paris* revue. The most luxurious hotel to date, the Tropicana, opens on the Strip.
- **1958** The 1,065-room Stardust opens as the world's largest resort complex with a spectacular show from France, the *Lido de Paris.*
- **1959** The Las Vegas Convention Center opens, presaging the city's future as a major convention city. Another French production, the

Men donned suits and ties and women wore floor-length gowns to attend shows and try their luck in the casinos. The hotel growth of the time was phenomenal. The Desert Inn, which opened in 1950 with headliners Edgar Bergen and Charlie McCarthy, brought country club elegance (including an 18-hole golf course and tennis courts) to the Strip.

In 1951, the Eldorado Club Downtown became Benny Binion's Horseshoe Club, which would gain fame as the home of the annual World Series of Poker. In 1954, the Showboat sailed into a new area east of Downtown. Although people said it could never last in such a remote location, they were wrong. The Showboat not only innovated buffet meals and a bowling alley (at 106 lanes, the largest in Nevada for decades—until it closed in 2003), but offered round-the-clock bingo.

In 1955, the Côte d'Azur–themed Riviera became the ninth big hotel to open on the Strip. Breaking the ranch-style mode, it was, at nine stories, the Strip's first high-rise. And Liberace, one of the hottest names in show business, was paid the unprecedented sum of $50,000 a week to dazzle audiences in The Riviera's posh Clover Room.

The 15-story Fremont Hotel Downtown became the tallest building in Las Vegas, and the Hacienda extended the boundaries of the Strip by opening 2 miles south of the nearest resort.

Elvis appeared at the New Frontier in 1956 but wasn't a huge success; his fans were too young to fit the Las Vegas tourist mold. In 1957, the Tropicana joined the Hacienda at the far end of Las Vegas Boulevard. In 1958, the $10-million, 1,065-room Stardust upped the spectacular stakes by importing the famed *Lido de Paris* from the French capital. It became one of the longest-running shows ever to play Las Vegas.

Throughout the 1950s, most of the above-mentioned hotels competed for performers whose followers spent freely in the casinos. The advent of big-name Strip entertainment tolled a death knell for glamorous nightclubs in America; owners simply could not compete with the astronomical salaries paid to Las Vegas headliners. Major '50s stars of the Strip included Rosemary Clooney, Nat King Cole, Peggy Lee, Milton Berle, Judy Garland, Red Skelton, Ernie Kovacs, Abbott and Costello, Fred Astaire and Ginger Rogers, the Andrews Sisters, and Marlene Dietrich. Two performers whose names have been linked to Las Vegas ever since—Frank Sinatra and Wayne Newton—made their debuts there. Mae West not only performed in Las Vegas, but also cleverly bought up a half-mile of desolate Strip frontage between the Dunes and the Tropicana.

Competition for the tourist dollar also brought nationally televised sporting events such as the PGA's Tournament of Champions to the Desert Inn golf course

still-extant *Folies Bergere,* opens at the Tropicana.

- **1960** The Rat Pack, led by Chairman of the Board Frank Sinatra, holds a 3-week "Summit Meeting" at the Sands. A championship boxing match, the first of many, takes place at the Convention Center. El Rancho Vegas, the Strip's first property, burns to the ground.
- **1963** McCarran Airport opens. Casinos and showrooms are darkened for a day as Las Vegas mourns the death of President John F. Kennedy.
- **1965** The 26-story Mint alters the Fremont Street skyline. Muhammad Ali defeats Floyd Patterson at the Las Vegas Convention Center.
- **1966** The Aladdin, the first new hotel on the Strip in 9 years, is soon eclipsed by the unparalleled grandeur of Caesars Palace. The Four Queens opens Downtown. Howard Hughes takes up residence at the Desert Inn. He buys up big chunks of Las Vegas and helps erase the city's gangland stigma.
- **1967** Elvis Presley marries Priscilla Beaulieu at the Aladdin.
- **1968** Circus Circus opens, giving kids a reason to come to Las Vegas.

continues

(the winner got a wheelbarrow filled with silver dollars). Also in the 1950s, the wedding industry helped make Las Vegas one of the nation's most popular venues for "goin' to the chapel." (Nevada requires no blood test or waiting period.) Celebrity weddings of the 1950s that sparked the trend included singer Dick Haymes and Rita Hayworth, Joan Crawford and Pepsi chairman Alfred Steele, Carol Channing and TV exec Charles Lowe, and Paul Newman and Joanne Woodward.

On a grimmer note, the '50s also heralded the Atomic Age in Nevada, with nuclear testing taking place just 65 miles northwest of Las Vegas. A chilling 1951 photograph shows a mushroom-shaped cloud from an atomic-bomb test visible over the Fremont Street horizon. Throughout the decade, about one bomb a month was detonated in the nearby desert.

THE 1960S: THE RAT PACK & A PACK RAT

The very first month of the new decade made entertainment history when the Sands hosted a 3-week "Summit Meeting" in the Copa Room that was presided over by "Chairman of the Board" Frank Sinatra with Rat Pack cronies Dean Martin, Sammy Davis, Jr., Peter Lawford, and Joey Bishop (all of whom were in town filming *Ocean's Eleven*).

The building boom of the '50s took a brief respite. The Strip's first property, the El Rancho Vegas, burned down in 1960. And the first new hotel of the decade, the first to be built in 9 years, was the exotic Aladdin in 1966. A year after it opened, the Aladdin hosted the most celebrated Las Vegas wedding of all time when Elvis Presley married Priscilla Beaulieu. In 1966, Las Vegas also hailed Caesar—Caesars Palace, that is—a Lucullan pleasure palace whose grand opening was a million-dollar, 3-day Roman orgy with 1,800 guests.

During the '60s, negative attention focused on mob influence in Las Vegas. Of the 11 major casino hotels that had opened in the previous decade, 10 were believed to have been financed with mob money. Attorney General Robert Kennedy ordered the Department of Justice to begin serious scrutiny of Las Vegas gaming operations. Then, like a knight in shining armor, Howard Hughes rode into town. He was not, however, on a white horse. Ever eccentric, he arrived (for security rather than health reasons) in an ambulance. The reclusive billionaire moved into a Desert Inn penthouse on Thanksgiving Day 1966 and didn't set foot outside the hotel for the next 3 years. It became his headquarters for a $300-million hotel- and property-buying spree, which included the Desert Inn itself (in 1967). Hughes was as "bugsy" as Benjamin Siegel any day, but his pristine reputation helped

- **1969** The Landmark and the International (today the Hilton) open within a day of each other on Paradise Road. Elvis Presley makes a triumphant return headlining at the latter.
- **1973** The ultraglamorous 2,100-room MGM Grand assumes the mantle of "world's largest resort." Superstars of magic, Siegfried and Roy, debut at the Tropicana.
- **1976** Pioneer aviator Howard Hughes dies aboard a plane en route to a Houston hospital. Dean Martin and Jerry Lewis make up after a 20-year feud.
- **1978** Leon Spinks dethrones "The Greatest" (Muhammad Ali) at the Las Vegas Hilton. Crime-solver Dan Tanna (Robert Urich) makes the streets of *Vega$* safer, and better known.
- **1979** A new international arrivals building opens at McCarran Airport.
- **1980** McCarran International Airport embarks on a 20-year $785-million expansion program. Las Vegas celebrates its 75th birthday. A devastating fire destroys the MGM Grand, leaving 84 dead and 700 injured. Bally's takes over the property.
- **1981** Siegfried and Roy begin a record-breaking run

bring respectability to the desert city and lessen its gangland stigma. For a while, it worked.

Las Vegas became a budding family destination in 1968, when Circus Circus burst on the scene with the world's largest permanent circus and a "junior casino" comprising dozens of carnival midway games on its mezzanine level. In 1969, the Landmark and the dazzling International (today the Hilton) ventured into a new area of town: Paradise Road near the Convention Center. That same year, Elvis made a triumphant return to Las Vegas at the International's showroom and went on to become one of the city's all-time legendary performers. His fans had come of age.

Hoping to establish Las Vegas as "the Broadway of the West," the Thunderbird Hotel presented Rodgers and Hammerstein's *Flower Drum Song.* It was a smash hit. Soon The Riviera picked up *Bye Bye Birdie,* and, as the decade progressed, *Mame* and *The Odd Couple* played at Caesars Palace. While Broadway played the Strip, production shows such as the Dunes' *Casino de Paris* became ever more lavish, expensive, and technically innovative. Showroom stars of the 1960s included Barbra Streisand, Phyllis Diller, Carol Burnett, Little Richard (who billed himself as "the bronze Liberace"), Louis Armstrong, Bobby Darin, the Supremes, Johnny Carson, Bob Newhart, the Smothers Brothers, and Aretha Franklin. Liza Minnelli filled her mother's shoes, while Nancy Sinatra's boots were made for walking on stage, and Tom Jones wowed 'em at The Flamingo.

THE 1970S: MERV, MIKE, MGM & MAGIC

In 1971, the 500-room Union Plaza opened at the head of Fremont Street on the site of the old Union Pacific Station. It had what was, at the time, the world's largest casino, and its showroom specialized in Broadway productions. The same year, talk-show host Merv Griffin began taping at Caesars Palace, taking advantage of a ready supply of local headliner guests. He helped popularize Las Vegas even more by bringing it into America's living rooms every afternoon. Rival Mike Douglas soon followed suit at the Las Vegas Hilton.

The year 1973 was eventful: The Holiday Inn (today Harrah's) built a Mississippi riverboat complete with towering smokestacks and foghorn whistle, which was immediately dubbed "the Ship on the Strip." Dean Martin headlined in the celebrity room of the magnificent new MGM Grand, named for the movie *Grand Hotel.* And over at the Tropicana, illusionists extraordinaire Siegfried and Roy began turning women into tigers and themselves into legends in the *Folies Bergere.*

in their own show, *Beyond Belief,* at the Frontier.

- **1982** A Las Vegas street is named Wayne Newton Boulevard.
- **1989** Steve Wynn makes headlines with his spectacular Mirage, fronted by an erupting volcano. He signs Siegfried and Roy to an unprecedented $57-million showroom contract.
- **1990s** The family-friendly medieval Arthurian realm of Excalibur opens as the new "world's largest resort" titleholder with 4,032 rooms, a claim it relinquishes when the MGM Grand's new 5,005-room megaresort/theme park opens in 1993, with a *Wizard of Oz* theme. Other properties geared toward families open in the 1990s, most notably Luxor, with its pyramid and Egyptian motifs, and the pirate-themed Treasure Island. The rock-'n'-roll Hard Rock, Mandalay Bay, Bellagio, Venetian, and Paris Las Vegas carry concept gaming resorts to new heights, while New York–New York is built with a roller coaster running around it. Celebrity chefs come to town.
- **2000** The new Aladdin opens. MGM Grand buys out Mirage Resorts. Steve Wynn buys the Desert Inn and promptly

continues

However, two major disasters hit Las Vegas in the 1970s. First, a flash flood devastated the Strip, causing more than $1 million in damage and sweeping away hundreds of cars in the raging waters. Second, gambling was legalized in Atlantic City, which caused Las Vegas's hotel business to slump as fickle tourists decided to check out the new East Coast gambling mecca.

On a happier note, audiences were moved when Frank Sinatra helped to patch up a 20-year feud by introducing Dean Martin as a surprise guest on Jerry Lewis's 1976 Muscular Dystrophy Telethon at the Sahara, where Martin and Lewis hugged and made up.

As the decade drew to a close, Dan Tanna began investigating crime in glamorous *Vega$,* an international arrivals building opened at McCarran International Airport, and dollar slot machines caused a sensation in the casinos. Hot performers of the '70s included Ann-Margret, Tina Turner, Englebert Humperdinck, Bill Cosby, Sonny and Cher, Tony Bennett, Mel Tormé, Bobby Darin, Gregory Hines (with his brother and dad), Donny and Marie Osmond, the Jackson 5, Gladys Knight and the Pips, and that "wild and crazy guy," Steve Martin. Debbie Reynolds introduced daughter Carrie Fisher with a duet performance before a Desert Inn audience. Shirley MacLaine began an incarnation at The Riviera. And country was now cool: The names Johnny Cash, Bobbie Gentry, Charley Pride, and Roy Clark went up in marquee lights.

THE 1980S: THE CITY ERUPTS

Las Vegas was booming once again. McCarran Airport began a 20-year $785-million expansion program. On a tragic note, in 1980, a devastating fire swept through the MGM Grand, leaving 84 dead and 700 injured. Shortly thereafter, Bally acquired the property and reopened newly named Bally's Las Vegas.

Siegfried and Roy were no longer just the star segment of various stage spectaculars. Their own show, *Beyond Belief,* ran for 6 years at the Frontier, playing a record-breaking 3,538 performances to sellout audiences every night. It became the most successful attraction in the city's history.

In 1989, Steve Wynn made Las Vegas sit up and take notice. His gleaming white-and-gold Mirage was fronted by five-story waterfalls, lagoons, and lush tropical foliage—not to mention a 50-foot volcano that dramatically erupted, spewing great gusts of fire another 50 feet into the air every 15 minutes after dark! Wynn gave world-renowned illusionists Siegfried and Roy carte blanche (and more than $50 million) to create the most spellbinding show Las Vegas had ever seen.

---

implodes it to begin building Wynn Las Vegas.

- **2001** The events of 9/11 hit Las Vegas especially hard; it takes nearly a year for the steamroller to build up a new head of steam.
- **2004** The Las Vegas Strip Monorail debuts.
- **2005** Wynn Las Vegas, the first major new casino resort to open in 5 years, debuts on the Strip. Las Vegas celebrates its 100th birthday.
- **2006** The Boardwalk Hotel and Casino and the legendary Stardust close to make way for multi-billion-dollar resort, residential, and entertainment developments. The Red Rock Resort opens in Summerlin, ushering in a new vision for off-Strip hotels.
- **2007** Condo mania hits Las Vegas, with luxury high-rises rising on and around the Strip. The Aladdin turns into Planet Hollywood. The Stardust and New Frontier are imploded. Palazzo opens.
- **2008** Las Vegas is hit hard by the economic downturn, especially in the local housing market. Construction on Boyd's Echelon Place is suspended. The Cosmopolitan is taken over by its lending bank. But Wynn's Encore opens, and MGM MIRAGE's Project CityCenter and the Fontainebleau continue to rise on the Strip, with anticipated openings in 2009–10.

Farewell to Frank

Only a few times in its history have the lights of Vegas been turned off at night. Twice it happened in the '60s: for President Kennedy (when the casinos themselves actually closed) and for Martin Luther King, Jr. And it happened twice in the '90s; the Strip went completely dark for 10 minutes to honor the passing of Sammy Davis, Jr., and when Dean Martin died in 1996, the Strip dimmed again.

So when Frank Sinatra, the man who practically built this town, died in 1998, we were sure Vegas would do something big to honor the paramount Rat Packer. We were wrong. The Strip went dark, but for 1 lousy minute. (Did we mention Sammy got 10?) And some of the lesser casinos and buildings never shut off at all. Still, some of the hotels put up tributes to Frankie on their signs, while cars drove down the Strip honking their horns, and a few of the hundreds of tourists who lined the boulevard to watch this historic moment burst into applause for the Voice.

It was something. And it's unlikely we will ever see anything like it happen again. (Though in 2004, the reaction when the Strip went dark again in honor of President Reagan, who'd performed in several casinos during his acting days, came pretty close.)

Stars of the '80s included Eddie Murphy, Don Rickles, Roseanne Barr, Dionne Warwick, Paul Anka, the Captain and Tennille, Donna Summer, Rich Little, George Carlin, Barry Manilow, Bernadette Peters, and Diahann Carroll. Country continued to be cool, as evidenced by frequent headliners Willie Nelson, Kenny Rogers, Dolly Parton, Crystal Gayle, Merle Haggard, and Barbara Mandrell. Joan Rivers posed her famous question, "Can we talk?" and bug-eyed comic Rodney Dangerfield complained he got "no respect."

THE 1990S: KING ARTHUR MEETS KING TUT

The decade began with a blare of trumpets heralding the rise of a turreted medieval castle fronted by a moated drawbridge and staffed by jousting knights and fair damsels. Excalibur's interior had so many stone castle walls that a Strip comedian quipped, "It looks like a prison for Snow White." Excalibur also reflected the early '90s marketing trend to promote Las Vegas as a family-vacation destination.

More sensational megahotels followed on the Strip, including the *new* MGM Grand hotel, backed by a full amusement park (it ended Excalibur's brief reign as the world's largest resort), Luxor, and Steve Wynn's Treasure Island.

On October 27, 1993, a quarter of a million people crowded onto the Strip to witness the implosion of the 37-year-old Dunes Hotel. In true Vegas style, it went out with a bang. Later that year, a unique pink-domed 5-acre indoor amusement park, Grand Slam Canyon (now Adventuredome), became part of the Circus Circus hotel. In 1995, the Fremont Street Experience was completed, revitalizing Downtown Las Vegas. Closer to the Strip, rock restaurant magnate Peter Morton opened the Hard Rock Hotel & Casino, billed as "the world's first rock-'n'-roll hotel and casino." The year 1996 saw the advent of the French Riviera–themed Monte Carlo and the Stratosphere, its 1,149-foot tower the highest building west of the Mississippi. New York–New York arrived in 1997 and set a new Las Vegas standard for themed architecture.

Then, in 1998 and 1999, Vegas hastily repositioned itself (again), going from "family destination" to "luxury resort," as several new hotels, once again eclipsing anything that had come before, opened up. Bellagio, created by Vegas visionary Steve Wynn, was an attempt to bring grand European style to the desert, while at the far southern end of the Strip, Mandalay Bay also charmed, topped with floors entirely owned and run by the highly regarded Four Seasons (an *actual* luxury resort hotel in Vegas, which pampers children almost as well as it spoils adults). As if this weren't enough, The Venetian's ambitious detailed re-creation of everyone's favorite Italian city came along in May 1999, and was followed in short order by the opening of Paris Las Vegas in the fall of 1999.

And then everything got shaken up again when the MGM Grand purchased Steve Wynn's Mirage Corporation to become MGM MIRAGE, which led to a large number of the Strip's properties being placed under one corporate umbrella. Never one to rest, Wynn responded by purchasing the Desert Inn, and then designing and building the $2.7-billion Wynn Las Vegas that opened in April 2005.

But that was hardly the end of the city's corporate wheeling and dealing. In 2004, Planet Hollywood took over the bankrupt Aladdin, Colony Capital bought the Las Vegas Hilton, Harrah's acquired and reopened Downtown's famous Binion's Horseshoe, and two 30-something dot. com superstars purchased the Golden Nugget. But the two biggest merger blockbusters came in the summer of 2004, when Harrah's Entertainment moved to acquire Caesars Entertainment, and MGM MIRAGE reached an agreement to merge with Mandalay Resort Group. The two surviving companies now control 16 of the 25 major Strip properties. Clearly, no one can rest on their laurels in Vegas, for this is not only a city that never sleeps, but one in which progress never stops moving, even for a heartbeat.

3 GETTING THE KIDS INTERESTED IN LAS VEGAS

To help children get interested in their upcoming trip, have them write, e-mail, or call the **Las Vegas Convention and Visitors' Authority,** 3150 Paradise Rd., Las Vegas, NV 89109 (✆ **877/VISITLV** [847-4858] or 702/892-0711; www.visitlasvegas.com), or the **Las Vegas Chamber of Commerce,** 3720 Howard Hughes Pkwy., #100, Las Vegas, NV 89109 (✆ **702/735-1616;** www.lvchamber.com), and ask for its *Visitor's Guide,* which contains extensive information about accommodations, attractions, excursions, children's activities, and more.

For information on all of Nevada, including Las Vegas, they can contact the Nevada Commission on Tourism (✆ **800/638-2328;** www.travelnevada.com). It has a comprehensive information packet on Nevada. Your kids will get excited when they receive large envelopes and magazines addressed to them. Have them explore the kid-friendly Las Vegas websites listed above and make their own notes about what they want to see and do.

Very few books for children have been written about Las Vegas, but older children and teens may enjoy *Cult Vegas* by

Tips for Having a Great Family Vacation

- Family vacations are about spending time together and having fun. It's not a marathon to cover as much territory as possible. Pick and choose what you're going to see and do judiciously, and keep in mind that you aren't going to see and do everything.
- Tired people, no matter their age, are difficult to deal with, so keep the pace slow on your trip, and make sure you schedule time to rest.
- Hungry people are even worse than tired people, so carry snacks (protein bars are a wise choice) if you can't manage to feed everyone at regular intervals.
- You may have arrived together, but you don't have to travel in a pack. If it's possible to split up the kids among the adults to give everyone a break, do so, even if it's just for an hour.
- Be flexible and maintain a sense of humor. If the line for a particular buffet or ride is too long, perhaps that's just nature's way of telling you to try something else.
- Ask your children what they would like to do during this trip. Give them some options, make a calendar, and follow through on some of their suggestions. This doesn't mean they are in charge. It means they get to participate in a bit of decision making. And if they want to ride the coaster six times in a row, why not? That could just be what great vacation memories and family stories are made of.

Mike Weatherford, entertainment reporter for the *Las Vegas Review-Journal,* which lays out the history and legends of Las Vegas. Packed full of facts and photos, this is a fun book.

On the cinematic front, Las Vegas has mainly been shown from an adult perspective. Films such as *Casino, Leaving Las Vegas,* and *Indecent Proposal* are geared for mature audiences. *Honeymoon in Las Vegas* and the Brad Pitt/George Clooney version of *Ocean's Eleven,* along with the *Ocean's Twelve* and *Ocean's Thirteen* sequels, are good for those over 13; none shows too much sex and they all have plenty of humor and excitement. And you can't go wrong with *Viva Las Vegas,* which can introduce your kids to Elvis Presley, as well as providing a goofy glimpse of the city in the 1960s. Prehistoric Vegas appears in *The Flintstones Viva Rock Vegas,* suitable for preteens. More television shows are about or set in Las Vegas than your kids have time to watch. They range from the highly regarded *CSI* crime series to celebrity poker tournaments. A number of documentaries about Las Vegas, especially on the Discovery and Travel channels, seem more designed to titillate than to inform. Not so with the acclaimed PBS history series *The American Experience,* which aired an excellent 3-hour documentary titled *Las Vegas: An Unconventional History.* It doesn't shy away from the seamier side of Las Vegas's past, but presents it in a serious educational manner. If your kids watch it, it will be sort of like them learning about the birds and bees in a sex-ed class instead of from older brother's squirreled away *Playboy* magazine. We think it's the best Las Vegas introduction possible for children 11 years old and up. If you miss the documentary on TV, you can buy the

DVD for $25 on www.pbs.org. On the home page click "Shop PBS" on the black bar at the top of the screen. When the shopping page comes up, type "Las Vegas" into the search block at the top of the page. There's a beautifully illustrated book of the same name that you can purchase along with the DVD (or video) as a set for $60.

Considering the rich imitation of cultures on display in Las Vegas, you'll want to get your children excited about Egypt and the legends of the Middle East, Medieval Europe, Paris, Rome, and New York City.

For a stay at Luxor—along with history books about Egypt (*The Egyptians, The Cultural Atlas for Young People Series: Ancient Egypt,* and the very cool *Eyewitness: Ancient Egypt*)—consider fictional books: *Mara, Daughter of the Nile* by Eloise McGraw tells the story of Cleopatra's servant girl, and is good for reading levels 7 through 13. Award-winning children's author Zilpha Keatley Snyder has written about modern children incorporating Egyptian history into their daily lives in *The Egypt Game,* which will also entrance children in the 7 to 13 age range. Additionally, the Elizabeth Taylor/Richard Burton cinematic epic *Cleopatra* is a beautiful and compelling spectacle, but some kids might find parts boring.

Relating to Planet Hollywood, check out *The Mailroom: Hollywood History from the Bottom Up* by David Rensin.

In preparation for a stay at the Excalibur, consider movies about Robin Hood and his band of Merry Men. *Robin Hood, Prince of Thieves* with Kevin Costner, the comedy *Robin Hood: Men in Tights,* and Errol Flynn's *Adventures of Robin Hood* are all easy to find on video. The recent release *A Knight's Tale,* with the late Heath Ledger, also gives a rollicking portrayal of the Middle Ages. The classic books *The Story of Sir Lancelot and His Companions* and *King Arthur and the Knights of the Round Table,* both written by Howard Pyle, are available in editions designed for various reading levels.

Older children can experience Paris before visiting Paris Las Vegas via the big screen extravaganza *Moulin Rouge,* while younger children will enjoy the Madeline series of books and videos.

A Visitor's Guide to Ancient Rome and *Coloring Book of Ancient Rome* are good places to start interesting younger kids on the subject and prepare them for a visit to the wonders of Caesars Palace, while preteens and teens may want to watch movies. *A Funny Thing Happened on the Way to the Forum* (fine for all ages) and the violent, albeit Oscar-winning, movie *Gladiator* each deliver decidedly different visions of ancient Rome. The miniseries *I, Claudius* may prove popular with history buffs.

New York City has been captured in books and on film seemingly more than any other place on earth. *Eloise, Harriet the Spy,* and *A Cricket in Times Square* are excellent places to start with reading material for younger children, while older ones can discover the city by reading or watching *Breakfast at Tiffany's, On the Town, A Tree Grows in Brooklyn* (both book and film), and *One of a Kind Family,* which provide perspective on the lives of immigrants, visitors to the city, and first-generation Americans during the early part of the 20th century.

4 RECOMMENDED READING FOR ADULTS

If you believe in "reading more about it," here are a select few of our favorites you might turn to:

- Castleman, Deke, *Whale Hunt in the Desert: The Secret Las Vegas of Superhost Steve Cyr* (Huntington Press, 2009). If you've ever wondered how super-rich gamblers (whales) get treated in Las Vegas, this book contains all the answers. Interwoven is an interesting high-roller history of the city.

- Ferrari, Michelle and Ives, Stephen, *Las Vegas: An Unconventional History* (Bulfinch Press, 2005). This hardcover, full-color, coffee-table edition starts out at the inception of modern Las Vegas—with its hardscrabble origins and the impact of the Hoover Dam project—through the legalization of gaming and the advent of the city's burgeoning tourism market. Vintage photos and illustrations augment the well-written narrative. Chapters move through the years chronicling "Bugsy" Siegel and the gangster influence, wedding chapels and the marriage mills, ersatz architecture, and the Rat Pack, and wraps up with the authors' vision of Las Vegas's future. The PBS series *The American Experience* produced an excellent documentary to go along with the book. Both can be purchased online at www.pbs.org.
- Fleming, Charles, *The Ivory Coast* (St. Martin's, 2002). A fictionalized look at Las Vegas in the glamour and glory years of the mid-'50s, centered on segregation. The Ivory Coast represents, and is loosely modeled after, the Moulin Rouge, which opened in 1955 and was the only black-owned Las Vegas casino until Don Barden bought Fitzgeralds more than 45 years later.
- Ridley, John, *Everybody Smokes in Hell* (Ballantine, 1999). John Ridley has written some big-name screenplays (*Three Kings* comes to mind), and his books are mordant slices of tragic lives. In *Everybody,* a loser, possessing the only extant tape of a dead superstar rocker, runs into the underside of Vegas with bad guys on his trail.
- Swain, James, *Grift Sense* (Pocket Books, 2001). A senior/former cop gets hauled out of retirement in Florida to investigate some shady doings at a major Vegas casino. The book has good insider info in addition to laughs and action. It may be fiction, but the background material is all fact.
- Thompson, Hunter S., *Fear and Loathing in Las Vegas* (Random House, 1971). A gonzo journalist and his Samoan lawyer head to Sin City for the all-time binge.
- Wilkerson, W.R. III, *The Man Who Invented Las Vegas* (Circo Books, 2000). This book, written by the son of Billy Wilkerson II, a Hollywood restaurant and nightclub owner, presents compelling evidence that Wilkerson envisioned and launched construction of The Flamingo in 1945. Subsequently, Benjamin Siegel not only stole the hotel from Wilkerson, but actually hoodwinked history into crediting him with the idea.

3

Planning a Family Trip to Las Vegas

Before any trip, you need to do some advance planning. In the pages that follow, you'll find everything you need to know to handle the practical details of planning your trip in advance: airlines and area airports, a calendar of events, a list of major conventions you may want to avoid, resources for those of you with special needs, what you can do to get your kids interested in a trip to Las Vegas, and much more.

We also suggest that you check out chapter 11, "Entertainment for the Whole Family," before you leave home; if you want to see the most popular shows, it's a good idea to call ahead and order tickets well in advance to avoid disappointment. The same goes if you want to dine in one of the city's top restaurants; head to chapter 7, "Family-Friendly Dining," for full restaurant reviews and contact information.

1 VISITOR INFORMATION

For advance information, call or write the **Las Vegas Convention and Visitors Authority,** 3150 Paradise Rd., Las Vegas, NV 89109 (✆ **877/VISITLV** [847-4858] or 702/892-0711; www.visitlasvegas.com). They can send you a comprehensive packet containing brochures, a map, a show guide, an events calendar, and an attractions list; help you find a hotel that meets your specifications (and even make reservations); and tell you whether a major convention is scheduled during the time you would like to visit Las Vegas. Or, stop by when you're in town. They're open daily from 8am to 5pm.

Another excellent information source (more oriented toward local businesses rather than convention business) is the **Las Vegas Chamber of Commerce,** 3720 Howard Hughes Pkwy., Las Vegas, NV 89109 (✆ **702/735-1616;** www.lvchamber.com). Ask them to send you their *Visitor's Guide,* which contains extensive information about accommodations, attractions, excursions, children's activities, and more. They're open Monday to Friday 8am to 5pm.

For information on all of Nevada, including Las Vegas, contact the **Nevada Commission on Tourism** (✆ **800/638-2328;** www.travelnevada.com), which has a comprehensive information packet on Nevada.

There's also a lot of great information for visitors on the Internet, including specific Las Vegas websites dedicated to children. **Las Vegas Kids** (www.lasvegaskids.com) lists basic information, including information on local child care and accommodations, and has an e-mail list that features family-related discounts.

Check out the **Las Vegas Advisor** (www.lasvegasadvisor.com) for a comprehensive listing of casino restaurants, entertainment options, meal deals, freebies, reviews, and everything you'd want to know about gambling. Although it primarily covers all things Disney, **Mousesavers** (www.mousesavers.com) is the best site on the Internet for scoring great deals on rental cars. Similarly, **Travelaxe** (www.travelaxe.com) will make finding the best deals on lodging a breeze, especially in Las Vegas.

Tips More Winning Websites

When you consider the enormous popularity of Las Vegas, it should come as no surprise that hundreds of websites are devoted to the destination. There is a lot of good—and bad—information about everything from the casino hotels to dining suggestions.

If you want to pick the brains of the local populace—and whom better to ask about life in Las Vegas?—head over to **www.lasvegasweekly.com**. You'll find out where locals go for fun, and you can browse through reviews of nightclubs, restaurants, and amusement parks.

For the most comprehensive Vegas dining resource on the Web, go to **www.nightonthetown.com**. The site arranges its plethora of restaurants by cuisine and location so you can find what you want, where you want it.

If you like your information with a side order of humor, then head to **www.cheapovegas.com**. This fun site offers lots of sassy reviews and unbiased opinions, especially on the Las Vegas casino hotels. There's also a small section on getting freebies while you're in town.

Websites maintained by the local papers will give you and your family an overview of Las Vegas's current events, politics, and entertainment. Check out the ***Las Vegas Review-Journal*** (www.lvrj.com) and the alternative newspaper, the ***CityLife*** (www.lasvegascitylife.com), for lots of information.

Citysearch offers comprehensive city information for hundreds of locations across America. Click onto **www.lasvegas.citysearch.com** for both real-people and professional critics' reviews of restaurants, shows, and other attractions. **Openlist** (www.openlist.com) is a similar city guide site.

Designed for travelers, **Vegas4Visitors** (www.vegas4visitors.com) offers reviews, articles, and commentary, with a special "for families" section. **Vegas.com** (www.vegas.com) reviews hotels, restaurants, and shows; a sidebar to the shows comments on the age appropriateness and nudity factor.

Also see "Planning Your Trip Online" later in this chapter, which recommends more useful sites.

2 ENTRY REQUIREMENTS & CUSTOMS

ENTRY REQUIREMENTS

Passports

For information on how to get a passport, go to **"Passports"** in the **"Fast Facts: Las Vegas"** section of the Appendix, the websites listed provide downloadable passport applications as well as the current fees for processing passport applications. For an up-to-date, country-by-country listing of passport requirements around the world, go to the "Foreign Entry Requirement" Web page of the U.S. State Department at **http://travel.state.gov**. International visitors can obtain a visa application at the same website.

Visas

For information on how to get a Visa, go to **"Visas"** in the **"Fast Facts: Las Vegas"** section of the Appendix.

The U.S. State Department has a **Visa Waiver Program** allowing citizens of the following countries (at press time) to enter the United States without a visa for stays of up to 90 days: Andorra, Australia, Austria, Belgium, Brunei, Denmark, Finland, France, Germany, Iceland, Ireland, Italy, Japan, Liechtenstein, Luxembourg, Monaco, the Netherlands, New Zealand, Norway, Portugal, San Marino, Singapore, Slovenia, Spain, Sweden, Switzerland, and the United Kingdom. Citizens of these nations need only a valid passport and a round-trip air or cruise ticket upon arrival. If they first enter the United States, they may also visit Mexico, Canada, Bermuda, and/or the Caribbean islands and return to the United States without a visa. Further information is available from any U.S. embassy or consulate. Canadian citizens may enter the United States without visas; they need only proof of residence.

Citizens of all other countries must have (1) a valid passport that expires at least 6 months later than the scheduled end of their visit to the United States, and (2) a tourist visa, which may be obtained without charge from any U.S. consulate.

Medical Requirements

Unless you're arriving from an area known to be suffering from an epidemic (particularly cholera or yellow fever), inoculations or vaccinations are not required for entry into the United States. If you have a medical condition that requires **syringe-administered medications,** carry a valid signed prescription from your physician—the Federal Aviation Administration (FAA) no longer allows airline passengers to pack syringes in their carry-on baggage without documented proof of medical need. If you have a disease that requires treatment with **narcotics,** you should also carry documented proof with you—smuggling narcotics aboard a plane is a serious offense that carries severe penalties in the U.S.

For **HIV-positive visitors,** requirements for entering the United States are somewhat vague and change frequently. For up-to-the-minute information, contact **AIDSinfo** (✆ **800/448-0440** or 301/519-6616 outside the U.S.; www.aidsinfo.nih.gov) or the **Gay Men's Health Crisis** (✆ **212/367-1000;** www.gmhc.org).

CUSTOMS

International visitors arriving by air, no matter what the port of entry, should cultivate patience and resignation before setting foot on U.S. soil. Getting through immigration control can take as long as 2 hours on some days, especially on summer weekends, so be sure to carry this guidebook or something else to read. This is especially true in the aftermath of the September 11, 2001, terrorist attacks, when security clearances have been considerably beefed up at U.S. airports.

People traveling by air from Canada, Bermuda, and certain countries in the Caribbean can sometimes clear Customs and Immigration at the point of departure, which is much quicker.

WHAT YOU CAN BRING INTO LAS VEGAS

Every visitor 21 or over may bring in, free of duty, the following: (1) 1 liter of wine or hard liquor; (2) 200 cigarettes, 100 cigars (but not from Cuba), or 3 pounds of smoking tobacco; and (3) $100 worth of gifts. These exemptions are offered to travelers who spend at least 72 hours in the United States and who have not claimed them within the preceding 6 months. It is altogether forbidden to bring into the country foodstuffs (particularly fruit, cooked meats, and canned goods) and plants (vegetables, seeds, tropical plants, and the like). Foreign tourists may carry in or out up to $10,000 in U.S. or foreign currency with no formalities; larger sums must be declared to U.S. Customs on entering or leaving, which includes filing form CM 4790. For details regarding U.S. Customs and Border Protection, consult your nearest U.S. embassy or consulate, or **U.S. Customs** (✆ **202/927-1770;** www.customs.ustreas.gov).

Destination: Las Vegas—Red Alert Checklist

- Did you bring copies of vaccination records if you plan on leaving your children at any of the hotel child-care centers?
- Did you bring copies of insurance cards for you and your children?
- Did you pack sunblock, sunglasses, and wide-brimmed hats for the entire group?
- Did you pack lightweight, long-sleeved, button-down shirts to keep off both the hot sun and the chilly casino air?
- Did you pack collared shirts and khakis or slacks for the men and a dress or nice blouse and pants or skirt for women for dinner in a finer, more expensive restaurant?
- Do any theater, restaurant, or travel reservations need to be booked in advance? If at all possible, Cirque du Soleil's productions, the Blue Man Group, "Tournament of Kings," and other top attractions you may want to see should be booked well before you arrive in Las Vegas, as should some restaurants.
- Did you make sure that the attractions you want to see are open? Some attractions, such as the Hoover Dam observation decks, may be closed for security reasons. Also note that outdoor roller coasters and the Sirens of TI pirate battle close during windy and inclement weather. It's also possible that scheduled tours, festivals, and special events may be canceled or rescheduled. Additionally, you should double-check the opening and closing hours of places you really want to go.
- If you purchased traveler's checks, have you recorded the check numbers and stored the documentation separately from the checks?
- Did you pack your camera, an extra set of camera batteries, and purchase enough film? If you packed film in your checked baggage, did you invest in protective pouches to shield it from airport X-rays?
- Did you pack an extra battery and the charger for your cellphone?
- Do you have a safe, accessible place to store money?
- Did you bring your ID cards that could entitle you to discounts, such as AAA and AARP cards, student IDs, and so on?
- Do your children who are old enough to need photo ID have them?
- Did you bring emergency drug prescriptions and extra glasses and/or contact lenses?
- Do you have your credit card PINs?
- If you have an e-ticket, do you have documentation?
- Did you leave a copy of your itinerary with someone at home?

WHAT YOU CAN TAKE HOME FROM LAS VEGAS

Canadian Citizens

For a clear summary of Canadian rules, write for the booklet *I Declare,* issued by the **Canada Border Services Agency** (✆ **800/461-9999** in Canada, or 204/983-3500; www.cbsa-asfc.gc.ca).

U.K. Citizens

For information, contact **HM Customs & Excise** at ✆ **0845/010-9000** (020/8929-0152 outside the U.K.), or consult its website at **www.hmce.gov.uk**.

Australian Citizens

A helpful brochure available from Australian consulates or Customs offices is *Know Before You Go.* For more information, call the **Australian Customs Service** at ✆ **1300/363-263,** or log on to **www.customs.gov.au**.

New Zealand Citizens

Most questions are answered in a free pamphlet available at New Zealand consulates and Customs offices: *New Zealand Customs Guide for Travellers, Notice no. 4.* For more information, contact **New Zealand Customs,** The Customhouse, 17–21 Whitmore St., Box 2218, Wellington (✆ **04/473-6099** or 0800/428-786; **www.customs.govt.nz**).

3 WHEN TO GO

Because most of a Las Vegas vacation is usually spent indoors, you can have a good time here year-round. That said, the most pleasant seasons here are spring and fall, especially if you want to experience the great outdoors.

Weekdays are considerably less crowded than weekends. Holidays are always a mob scene and come accompanied by high hotel prices. Hotel prices also skyrocket when big conventions and special events are taking place. The slowest times of the year are July and August, the week before Christmas, and the week after New Year's.

If a major convention is to be held during your trip, you might want to change your date because rooms will be hard to get and will be more expensive during that time. Check the box later in this section for convention dates, and contact the **Las Vegas Convention and Visitors Authority** (✆ **877/VISITLV** [847-4858] or 702/892-0711; www.visitlasvegas.com), because convention schedules often change.

THE WEATHER

First of all, Vegas isn't always hot, but when it is, it's *really* hot. One thing you'll hear again and again is that even though Las Vegas gets very hot, the dry desert heat is not unbearable. This is true, except in most of the hotel pool areas, which are surrounded by massive hotels covered in mirrored glass, which acts like a giant magnifying glass on the antlike people below. Still, generally, the humidity in Vegas averages a low 22%, and even on very hot days, there's apt to be a breeze. Also, except on the hottest summer days, there's almost always at least a little relief at night when temperatures often drop by at least 20°F.

Las Vegas's Average Temperatures (°F & °C)

	Jan	Feb	Mar	Apr	May	June	July	Aug	Sept	Oct	Nov	Dec
Average Temp. (°F)	47	52	58	66	75	86	91	89	81	69	55	47
(°C)	8	11	14	19	24	30	33	32	27	21	13	8
High Temp. (°F)	57	63	69	78	88	99	104	102	94	81	66	57
(°C)	14	17	21	26	31	37	40	39	34	27	19	14
Low Temp. (°F)	37	41	47	54	63	72	78	77	69	57	44	37
(°C)	3	5	8	12	17	22	26	25	21	14	7	3
Precip. (in.)	.6	.7	.6	.2	.2	.1	.4	.5	.3	.2	.3	.4

Major Convention Dates

Listed below are Las Vegas's major annual conventions for 2009 (30,000 and up expected visitors), with projected attendance figures; believe us, unless you're actually coming to town to attend them, you probably want to avoid the biggies. Contact the **Las Vegas Convention and Visitors Authority** (✆ **877/VISITLV** [847-4858] or 702/892-0711; www.visitlasvegas.com) to double-check the latest info before you commit to your travel dates, because convention schedules frequently change.

Event	**Dates**	**Expected Attendance**
Consumer Electronics Show	Jan 8–11	148,000
Adult Entertainment Expo	Jan 8–11	37,000
World of Concrete Exposition	Feb 3–6	85,000
World Market Center	Feb 9–13	62,000
World Shoe Association	Feb 12–14	37,000
Nightclub/Bar Convention & Trade Show	Mar 3–6	38,000
Associated Surplus Dealers	Mar 15–18	64,000
National Association of Broadcasters	Apr 20–23	115,000
National Hardware Show	May 5–7	50,000
RECon	May 18–20	50,000
JCK Show	May 30–June 2	50,000
Truck Show-Western Addition	June 7–9	30,000
Int'l Esthetics, Cosmetics & Spa Conference	June 13–19	32,000
Assn. of Woodworking/Furniture Suppliers	July 15–18	45,000
World Shoe Association	July 27–29	37,000
Associated Surplus Dealers	Aug 12–16	62,000
Pack Expo	Oct 5–7	30,000
Specialty Equipment Market Association	Nov 2–5	120,000
Automotive Aftermarket Association	Nov 3–6	130,000

But this is the desert, and it's not hot all year-round. It can get quite cold, especially in the winter, when, at night, it can drop to 30°F (–1°C) and lower. Every few years it even snows in Las Vegas, and accumulations can reach a couple of inches. There's nothing quite like the sight of Luxor's Sphinx covered in snow. The breeze can also become a cold, biting, strong wind of up to 40 mph and more. And so, you won't be using that hotel swimming pool at all for entire portions of the year (even if you want to—be aware that many of the hotels close huge chunks of those fabulous swimming pool areas for "the season," which is usually mid-Oct to mid-Mar). Even in the height of summer, bring something for warmth; the casinos are air-conditioning with a vengeance, and savvy gamblers carry sweaters in July. Also, remember sunscreen and hats—even if it's not all that hot, you and your kids can burn very easily and very fast in these parts. You should see (and not be among!) all the lobster-red people glowing in the casinos at night.

LAS VEGAS CALENDAR OF KID-FRIENDLY EVENTS

You may be surprised to learn that Las Vegas actually does have annual community events. Granted, they don't have as many as most tourist cities, and the reason for that is Las Vegas's very raison d'être: the gaming industry. This town wants its visitors spending their money in the casinos, not at Renaissance fairs and parades. However, we know you'd like to spend your vacation doing fun things with your family, so we compiled a list of the best family-friendly events below.

When in town, check the local paper and call the **Las Vegas Convention and Visitors Authority** (✆ **877/VISITLV** [847-4858] or 702/892-0711; www.visitlasvegas.com) or the **Chamber of Commerce** (✆ **702/735-1616;** www.lvchamber.com) to find out about other events that may be scheduled during your visit.

The **Clark County Parks and Recreation Department** (✆ **702/455-8200;** www.accessclarkcounty.com/depts/parks/pages/homepage.aspx) also provides an excellent resource for children's activities and will, upon request, mail you a catalog of upcoming events.

Additionally, Las Vegas is rich in performing arts organizations and has teams for all major sports, so there's almost always a performance or sporting event to be seen, if that's your family's cup of tea.

January

Martin Luther King, Jr., Parade. This lively parade along Fremont Street, held on MLK's birthday, January 15, is the culmination of a weeklong celebration honoring the slain civil rights leader, which includes a gospel concert and poetry reading.

February

Chinese New Year. Las Vegas's Asian community comes out in full force for this lunar festival, with an all-day celebration that includes a parade, drummers, dancers, martial artists, and a large variety of Asian food. Held at Chinatown Plaza, 4255 Spring Mountain Rd., the New Year can fall between the last week of January and the third week of February. ✆ **702/221-8448;** www.lvchinatown.com.

March

Great Las Vegas Craft Festival. One-of-a-kind arts and crafts are on display indoors at Cashman Field, a huge athletic park, during this semiannual event (also held in Nov), including handmade toys like kaleidoscopes, puppets, and whirligigs. Musicians and magicians perform throughout the 3-day event, which usually takes place on the second-to-last weekend in March. ✆ **702/386-7184;** www.stevepowers.com.

April

Clark County Rodeo and Fair. Riding and roping are just part of the fun at this traditional Western fair. There's also a junior rodeo, livestock shows, carnival food, talent shows, and best of all, pig races. The rodeo and fair is held in mid-April in Logandale, roughly 60 miles from the city. ✆ **888/876-FAIR;** www.ccfair.com.

May

Cinco de Mayo Festival. This large fiesta, held in Lorenzi Park on one of the first weekends in the month, has a special children's area, plus crafts, music, and dancing, as well as food from almost two dozen vendors. ✆ **702/229-6792.**

Pride Festival. Gay, lesbian, bi, and transgender families have their own groups marching in the parade along Fourth Street in Downtown, and the festival at the parade's end has a children's play area with clowns, magicians, and face-painting. Naturally, open-minded straight families are welcome to this celebration of unity in diversity, held in mid-May. ✆ **702/615-9429;** www.lasvegaspride.org.

June

Friday Family Film Fest. As the sun sets, the stars come out on-screen. Pack a picnic meal or grab snacks from the vendors and enjoy adventure and family films, all PG- or G-rated. The locations vary between various county parks; call for details, location, and screening schedule toward the beginning of May for the most up-to-date information for the Fest, which usually begins the first weekend in June. ✆ **702/455-8200;** www.accessclarkcounty.com/depts/parks/Pages/events_calendar.aspx.

Jazz in the Park. This free outdoor evening series at the Clark County Amphitheatre runs through July, drawing all ages of jazz fans. Big names and local combos perform styles ranging from Chicago to New Orleans to West Coast jazz. The series is a good way to introduce your children to this truly all-American music genre. The series begins the second week in June. ✆ **702/455-8200.**

CineVegas International Film Festival. Ooh la la! Las Vegas shows its Cannes-do spirit with a variety of independent foreign and domestic films, both feature-length and shorts, including those shot by University of Nevada, Las Vegas students, all screened during the second week of June. If you have a budding Spielberg at home, call ahead for the schedule and make sure to order tickets as quickly as you can—this festival has caught a buzz. Keep in mind that sometimes "independent" can be synonymous with a hard R-rating, so read over the film descriptions carefully, and call festival organizers if you have any questions about age-appropriate content. ✆ **702/992-7979;** www.cinevegas.com.

September

Oktoberfest. Families will enjoy the folk dancers, singalongs around a roaring fire, special decorations, and Bavarian cookouts at the **Mount Charleston Resort** during this festival. On Sundays, the entertainment includes oompah bands, with accordions and brass, that play traditional Bavarian music. Visitors can also take advantage of the easy hiking trails on the resort's property, which provide a spectacular outdoors experience. This boisterous autumn holiday is celebrated on weekends from mid-September through the end of October. ✆ **800/955-1314** or 702/872-5408.

International Mariachi Festival. Mandalay Bay started hosting this worldwide mariachi music festival almost a decade ago, and it has become one of the city's most eagerly anticipated events, though it's now held at Planet Hollywood. The traditional, festive music of Mexico incorporates folk guitars and brass; the songs are sung in Spanish by colorfully costumed men and women. Often mariachi groups of children are around as well. It is usually held the second week in September. Call the Mariachi Festival Hotline at ✆ **800/637-1006.**

San Gennaro Feast. New York's Little Italy comes to Vegas at this traditional festival, known as the Feast of Feasts. Celebrate Italian culture with plenty of pasta and pastries, sausage sandwiches, local headliners, games, rides, and a petting zoo. It's loud, lively, and fun, and held in mid-September at Flamingo Road and Grand Canyon Drive. ✆ **702/286-4944;** www.sangennarofeast.com.

October

Nevada Shakespeare in the Park. The enduring works of the Bard, performed by local theater actors, are featured at Liberty Point Park. The sword fights in

Romeo and Juliet and the costumes and merry making in *A Midsummer Night's Dream* might keep kids interested. Even if you never go, it's nice to know it's there (for a weekend in mid-Oct). ✆ **702/384-8427;** www.cityofhenderson.com/relocation_guide/recreational.php.

Age of Chivalry Renaissance Festival. If visiting the Excalibur hasn't sated your child's passion for all things knightly, step back into the Middle Ages at this festival in Sunset Park, where crowds in T-shirts and jeans munch turkey legs and mingle with elaborately costumed lords and ladies. Jousting, battles, and pageants, plus artisans and others hawking their wares, can all be seen at this festival, which is held in mid-October. ✆ **702/455-8200;** www.lvrenfair.com.

November

Great Las Vegas Craft Festival. This event is also held in mid-November. See information for this listing under "March," above.

December

Tree & Menorah Lighting Ceremonies. Fremont Street goes ablaze with holiday spirit in these two separate ceremonies, held in early December, proving that not all the lights in Vegas are neon. ✆ **800/249-3559;** www.vegasexperience.com.

National Finals Rodeo. This is the Super Bowl of rodeos, attended by close to 170,000 people each year (usually during the first week of Dec). The top 15 male rodeo stars compete in six different events: calf roping, steer wrestling, bull riding, team roping, saddle bronco riding, and bareback riding. And the top 15 women compete in barrel racing. An all-around "Cowboy of the Year" is also chosen here. In connection with this event, hotels book country stars in their showrooms, and there's a cowboy shopping spree—the **NFR Cowboy Christmas Gift Show,** a trade show for Western gear—at Cashman Field. The NFR runs for 10 days during the first 2 weeks of December at the 17,000-seat Thomas and Mack Center of the University of Nevada, Las Vegas (UNLV). Order tickets as far in advance as possible. ✆ **888/NFR-RODEO** [637-7633]; http://nfr-rodeo.com.

Moments New Year's Eve in Las Vegas

More and more people have been choosing Las Vegas as their party destination for New Year's Eve. In fact, some estimates indicate that more people are ringing in the New Year in Nevada than in New York City's Times Square.

From experience, we can tell you that it's not a good bet with kids. A lot of people come here on December 31. We mean *a lot* of people. Figure on just about every room being sold out. Traffic is a nightmare, parking is next to impossible, and there is not a square inch of the place that isn't occupied by a human being.

A major portion of the Strip is closed down, sending the masses and their mass quantities of alcohol into the street. Each year's celebration is a little different but usually includes a streetside performance by a major celebrity, confetti, the obligatory countdown, fireworks, and, if you're lucky, maybe even a building implosion. This has become one of the city's biggest annual events.

4 WHAT TO PACK

IN GENERAL

One of the most important articles of clothing you can pack is a lightweight, long-sleeved, button-down shirt, preferably in white or another light color, for you and your kids. This will keep the sun off while outside and will help you adjust to the often-chilly hotels.

If you're going to Las Vegas in the summer, pack for hot weather and balmy nights. Shorts on men and women are seen everywhere, as are tank tops, though sometimes it's not a pretty sight. Bring bathing suits, naturally, as well as cover-ups to get you from room to pool and back again, along with sandals for the same purpose.

Desert winters can be cold, so make sure you bring some warmer clothes with you. A hooded sweat jacket can be especially handy. In winter, spring, and especially summer, sudden downpours can strike, but when that happens, umbrellas and inexpensive plastic ponchos appear in almost every hotel gift shop and convenience store, so hard-core rainwear shouldn't be an issue.

You'll be doing plenty of walking in Las Vegas, so comfortable shoes are a must, as are wide-brimmed hats and sunglasses, even during the cooler winter months. Hikers will want their boots, rock climbers theirs.

At one time, gentlemen couldn't get into any show or a restaurant after 5pm without a jacket and tie, but these days for the most part, Las Vegas has gone casual. At the highest-end restaurants, however, a jacket or collared shirt may still be required, along with long pants (khakis and chinos are fine; jeans are not), so if you're in doubt, call ahead. Women should pack one lightweight skirt or dress that can be worn to such a restaurant, if that's on your agenda, or a semidressy blouse to go with khakis. If you plan on taking your kids out for a "grown-up meal" at Mon Ami Gabi or a similar restaurant, they should have one nice, though not-too-dressy, outfit (sundress or khakis and a collared shirt).

You may want to leave your stroller at home and invest in a strap-on baby carrier if you don't already have one, because strollers are frowned on, if not banned, on the casino floors. Some hotels ban strollers except for registered guests. Also, negotiating a stroller in a crowded mall or on the sidewalk can be burdensome. All hotels are close to 24-hour drugstores that stock major brands of disposable diapers, infant formula, and over-the-counter medications; some of these items can even be found at gas station minimarts and in the convenience stores of the hotels/resorts, so you shouldn't worry about leaving the essentials behind—anything you forget can be easily found here.

FOR TRAVEL WITH YOUR KIDS

If you're flying with kids, don't forget a deck of cards, coloring books and crayons, toys, and magnetic board games; let each child pack his or her own backpack with favorite toys. Kindly ask your kids to keep their iPods and Game Boys turned to a

Tips Quick ID

Tie a colorful ribbon or piece of yarn around your luggage handle or slap a distinctive sticker on the side of your bag. This makes it less likely that someone will mistakenly appropriate it. And if your luggage gets lost, it will be easier to find.

Tips Taking a Cellphone on Your Trip

All wireless companies in North America provide roaming services, which means you'll be able to use your own cellphone on your trip. Check with your carrier and see whether it offers discounted or free long-distance calling plans, so that you can use the cellphone to make local calls while in Las Vegas (otherwise roaming charges might cost you up to $1 a minute to make a local call).

If you don't own a cellphone, consider renting one before you leave. The phone is delivered to you via Federal Express, UPS, or the like and activated immediately. When you get home, you simply return the phone in the prepaid package provided for you.

Taking your cellphone, or bringing a rental, has its advantages: You know the phone number in advance to give to family and friends at home who might need to reach you; you familiarize yourself with the phone before you leave home, instead of spending quality vacation time reading instructions; and your kids have more time to memorize the number.

Most wireless rental companies require a credit card deposit and bill the customer at the end of the trip. Although prices vary widely, in general, using a rented cellphone is more expensive than using a telephone calling card but cheaper than calling direct from your hotel room. Most companies charge a basic rental fee (which may include activation and shipping fees) of $40 to $75, plus a per-minute rate for both outgoing and incoming calls. In addition, airtime rates vary from network to network. Bottom line: Shop around for the best deal.

A highly recommended wireless rental company is **InTouch USA** (✆ **800/872-7626;** www.intouchusa.com).

So-called disposable cellphones, with a preprogrammed amount of minutes, can also be bought at some convenience stores. If you use a short-term phone, make sure your entire family has the number written down.

low volume out of courtesy to your fellow passengers. Chewing gum helps relieve ear pressure buildup during ascent and descent. If your child is still in diapers, be sure to pack plenty of extras, plus baby wipes and plastic bags for wrapping up the used diaper before tossing it in the airplane bathroom's trash. When altitude is reached, you might want to hand out additional books about Las Vegas and the various cultures and histories represented there.

When driving to Las Vegas, make sure to have a cooler of snacks and plenty of water and diluted juice. Take time out to stretch your legs or grab a snack at a local diner or even a fast-food joint. Again, baby wipes, paper towels, and plastic bags for trash are important, as well as plenty of extra diapers.

Playing road games such as license-plate bingo and counting out-of-state cars can keep kids occupied, and so can magnetic board games, Game Boys, coloring books, and MP3 players. We know one mom who bought a cheap, portable, DVD player to keep her young kids entertained on family road trips and swears that it makes driving a more pleasurable experience for both her and her kids.

5 GETTING THERE

BY PLANE

The following airlines have regularly scheduled flights into Las Vegas (some of these are regional carriers, so they may not all fly from your point of origin): **Air Canada** (© 888/247-2262; www.aircanada.ca) does not offer direct service but will book on partner airlines, usually with a change in San Francisco; **Alaska Airlines** (© 800/426-0333; www.alaskaair.com); **Allegiant Air** (© 877/202-6444; www.allegiantair.com); **American Airlines** (© 800/433-7300; www.aa.com); **Continental** (© 800/525-0280; www.continental.com); **Delta** (© 800/221-1212; www.delta.com); **Frontier Airlines** (© 800/432-1359; www.flyfrontier.com); **Hawaiian Airlines** (© 800/367-5320; www.hawaiianair.com); **Japan Airlines** (© 800/525-3663; www.jal.co.jp/en); **JetBlue** (© 800/538-2583; www.jetblue.com); **Midwest Airlines** (© 800/452-2022; www.midwestexpress.com); **Northwest** (© 800/225-2525; www.nwa.com); **Southwest** (© 800/435-9792; www.southwest.com); **Spirit Airlines** (© 800/772-7117; www.spiritair.com); **United** (© 800/241-6522; www.ual.com); **US Airways** (© 800/428-4322; www.usairways.com); and **Virgin Atlantic Airways** (© 800/862-8621; www.virgin-atlantic.com).

We've always enjoyed Southwest's relaxed attitude, and its service leaves few complaints. However, it mostly features first-come, first-served seating, so if you want to avoid that, try one of the other carriers.

In fact, now might be the time to talk about the spiffy leather seat/DirecTV wonder that is JetBlue. First-time passengers usually turn into longtime converts (including a number of Frommer's editors, who swear by this airline). Currently, they fly to Vegas from Long Beach and Burbank, California, and New York City, Boston, Washington, D.C., and Salt Lake City, often for very low prices.

FLIGHTS FOR INTERNATIONAL VISITORS

A number of U.S. airlines offer service from Europe to the United States, though a number of those same airlines are having financial troubles, and may perhaps be in different shape by the time you read this. If they do not have direct flights from Europe to Las Vegas, they can book you straight through on a connecting flight. You can make reservations by calling the following numbers in the U.K. or U.S.: **American** (© **0845/7789-79** in the U.K., 800/433-7300 in the U.S.; www.aa.com), **Continental** (© **0845/607-6760** in the U.K., 800/525-0280 in the U.S.; www.continental.com), **Delta** (© **0845/600-0950** in the U.K., 800/221-1212 in the U.S.; www.delta.com), and **United** (© **0845/8-444-777** in the U.K., 800/241-6522 in the U.S.; www.united.com).

And, of course, many international carriers serve Los Angeles and/or San Francisco International Airport. From LAX or San Francisco International Airport, you can take a domestic airline to Las Vegas. Helpful numbers to know include **Virgin Atlantic** (© **0870/380-2007** in the U.K., 800/862-8621 in the U.S.; www.virgin-atlantic.com), **British Airways** (© **0870/850-9850** in the U.K., 800/AIRWAYS [247-9297] in the U.S.; www.british-airways.com), and **Aer Lingus** (© **0818/365-000** in Dublin, 800/IRISH-AIR [474-7424] in the U.S.; www.aerlingus.com). **Qantas** (© **13-13-13** in Australia, 800/227-4500 in the U.S.; www.qantas.com.au) has flights from Sydney to Los Angeles and San Francisco; you can also take United from Australia to the West Coast. **Air New Zealand** (© **0800/737-000** in New Zealand, 800/262-1234 in the U.S.; www.airnewzealand.co.nz) also offers service to LAX. Canadian readers can book flights on **Air Canada** (✆ **888/249-2262;** www.aircanada.ca), which offers direct service from Toronto, Montréal, Calgary, and Vancouver to San Francisco and Los Angeles, and will book your final leg on a partner airline.

JetBlue (✆ **800/538-2583;** www.jetblue.com) is a highly rated low-cost carrier that operates out of a number of U.S. cities, and has daily direct service to Las Vegas out of New York City and Long Beach, California.

INTERNATIONAL AIRLINE DISCOUNTS Overseas visitors can take advantage of the APEX (Advance Purchase Excursion) reductions offered by all major U.S. and European carriers. For more money-saving airline advice, see "Flying for Less: Tips for Getting the Best Airfare" in this chapter. For the best rates, compare fares and be flexible with the dates and times of travel.

Operated by the European Travel Network, **www.discount-tickets.com** is a great online source for regular and discounted airfares to Las Vegas and other destinations around the world. You can also use this site to compare rates and book accommodations, car rentals, and tours. Click "Special Offers" for the latest package deals.

GETTING INTO TOWN FROM THE AIRPORT

McCarran International Airport is just a few minutes drive from the southern end of the Strip, and minibuses run daily between McCarran to all major Las Vegas hotels and motels. One of the major providers, **Bell Trans** (✆ **702/739-7990**) provides transportation almost round-the-clock (4:30am–2am). Several other companies offer the same service as well, along with taxis. Cabs cost $12 to $15 from the airport to South Strip hotels and $18 to $20 to Downtown, and carry up to five passengers; the minibuses charge $5 per person to the South Strip, $6.50 to Downtown, and carry up to 20 passengers, stopping at hotels along the way. When your vacation comes to an end, make reservations the night before with a bus company to pick your party up at least 2½ hours before your departure time. The hotel's concierge may be able to help you with this as well. Or take a cab from in front of the hotel.

All major car-rental companies are represented in Las Vegas, should you choose to rent one while in town. Grab one of the continuous shuttles from outside the terminal to the McCarran Rent-A-Car Center. From there, take a right onto Gilespie from the lot and another right on Warm Springs to reach Las Vegas Blvd. S. Take a third right on the Boulevard and you'll be headed north toward the Strip and downtown.

For complete information on renting a car in Las Vegas, see "Renting a Car" in chapter 5.

AIR TRAVEL SECURITY MEASURES

With the federalization of airport security, security procedures at U.S. airports are more stable and consistent than ever. Generally, you'll be fine if you arrive at the airport **90 minutes** before a domestic flight and **2½ hours** before an international flight; if you show up late, tell an airline employee and he or she will probably whisk you to the front of the line.

Try **not to drive your car** to the airport because terminal access can be restricted at a moment's notice. If you do drive, be sure to allow extra time to get from the long-term parking lots to the main terminal, because these aren't always close to each other.

Bring a **current, government-issued photo ID** such as a driver's license or passport, and if you've got an e-ticket, print out the **official confirmation page;** you'll need to show your confirmation and your ID at the ticket counter to get a boarding

Flying with Film & Video

Never pack unprotected, undeveloped film in checked bags, which may be scanned. The film you carry with you can be damaged by scanners, too. X-ray damage is cumulative; the slower the film, and the more times you put it through a scanner, the more likely the damage. Film under 800 ASA is usually safe for up to five scans. If you're taking your film through additional scans, request a hand inspection. In domestic airports, the Federal Aviation Administration guarantees hand inspections. Keep in mind that airports are not the only places where your camera may be scanned: Highly trafficked attractions are X-raying visitors' bags with increasing frequency.

Most photo supply stores sell protective pouches designed to block damaging X-rays. The pouches fit both film and loaded cameras. They should protect your film in checked baggage, but they also may raise alarms and result in a hand inspection.

You'll have little to worry about if you are traveling with **digital cameras.** Unlike film, which is sensitive to light, the digital camera and storage cards are not affected by airport X-rays, according to Nikon. Still, if you plan to travel extensively, you may want to play it safe and hand-carry your digital equipment or ask that it be inspected by hand. See "Digital Photography on the Road," p. 70.

Carry-on scanners will not damage **videotape** in video cameras, but the magnetic fields emitted by the walk-through security gateways and hand-held inspection wands will. Always place your loaded camcorder on the screening conveyor belt or have it hand-inspected. Be sure your batteries are charged, as you may be required to turn the device on to ensure that it's what it appears to be.

pass. (Children 17 and under do not need photo IDs for domestic flights, but the adults checking in with them need them.)

Security lines are getting shorter than they were a couple of years ago, but some doozies remain. We've heard reports of security checks and gridlocks causing delays of up to 4 and 5 hours, with plenty of missed flights as a result. If it's a busy convention or holiday weekend, you might want to plan accordingly. Better a long wait at the airport than a missed flight. If you have trouble standing for long periods of time, tell an airline employee; the airline will provide a wheelchair. Speed up security by **not wearing metal objects** such as big belt buckles or clanky earrings. If you've got metallic body parts, a note from your doctor can prevent a long chat with the security screeners. Keep in mind that only **ticketed passengers** are allowed past security, except for folks escorting passengers with disabilities, or children. If you're bringing a child who will be traveling solo to the airport, be sure to call in advance to confirm the proper procedure.

The Transportation Security Administration (TSA) regularly adjusts its list of **what you can carry on** and **what you can't,** which seems to get more and more idiosyncratic, so be sure to check its website (**www.tsa.gov/travelers/index.shtm**) for the latest details. As this book goes to print, for example, the TSA is enforcing strict rules for liquids, gels, and aerosols: They must be kept in containers that are

3 ounces or smaller (even a half-empty 4 oz. toothpaste tube is off limits); and these containers "must be placed in a single, quart-size, zip-top, clear plastic bag," ready for inspection. Nail clippers and safety/disposable razors (but not razor blades) are okay in a carry on, but almost all other sharp objects should be placed in checked bags.

The TSA is phasing out **gate check-in** at U.S. airports. Passengers with e-tickets and without checked bags can still beat the ticket-counter lines by using **electronic kiosks** or even **online check-in.** Ask your airline which alternatives are available, and if you're using a kiosk, bring the credit card you used to book the ticket. If you're checking bags, you will still be able to use most airlines' kiosks; again, call your airline for up-to-date information. **Curbside check-in** is also a good way to avoid lines.

Airport screeners may decide that your checked luggage needs to be searched by hand. You can now purchase luggage locks that allow screeners to open and relock a checked bag if hand-searching is necessary. Look for Travel Sentry certified locks at luggage or travel shops and Brookstone stores (you can buy them online at www.brookstone.com). These locks, approved by the TSA, can be opened by luggage inspectors with a special code or key. For more information on the locks, visit www.travelsentry.org. If you use something other than TSA-approved locks, your lock will be cut off your suitcase if a TSA agent needs to hand-search your luggage.

FLYING FOR LESS: TIPS FOR GETTING THE BEST AIRFARE

Passengers within the same airplane cabin are rarely paying the same fare. Business travelers who need to purchase tickets at the last minute, change their itinerary at a moment's notice, or get home for the weekend pay the premium rate.

Passengers who can book their ticket **long in advance,** who can **stay over Saturday night,** or who **fly midweek** or **at less-trafficked hours** will pay a fraction of the full fare. If your schedule is flexible, say so, and ask if you can secure a cheaper fare by changing your flight plans. ***Note:*** Southwest Airlines does not require you to stay over Saturday to obtain its lowest fares. It is thus often the best choice for business travelers and others whose schedules rule out a Saturday overnight.

Here are a few other easy ways to save:

- You can save on airfares by keeping an eye out in local newspapers for **promotional specials** or **fare wars,** when airlines lower prices on their most popular routes. You'll almost never see a sale during the Thanksgiving or Christmas seasons; but if you can travel in the off months, you may snag a bargain. If you

Travel in the Age of Bankruptcy

Airlines go bankrupt, so protect yourself by **buying your tickets with a credit card,** because the Fair Credit Billing Act guarantees that you can get your money back from the credit card company if a travel supplier goes under (and if you request the refund within 60 days of the bankruptcy). **Travel insurance** can also help, but make sure it covers against "carrier default" for your specific travel provider. And be aware that if a U.S. airline goes bust midtrip, a 2001 federal law requires other carriers to take you to your destination (albeit on a space-available basis) for a fee of no more than $25, provided you rebook within 60 days of the cancellation.

already hold a ticket when a sale breaks, it may pay to exchange your ticket, even though that usually incurs a $100 to $150 charge. ***Note:*** The lowest-priced fares are often nonrefundable, require advance purchase of 1 to 3 weeks and a certain length of stay, and carry penalties for changing dates of travel.

- **Consolidators,** also known as bucket shops, are great sources for international tickets, although they usually can't beat the Internet on fares within North America. Start by looking in Sunday newspaper travel sections; U.S. travelers should focus on the *New York Times, Los Angeles Times,* and *Miami Herald.* For less-developed destinations, small travel agencies that cater to immigrant communities in large cities often have the best deals. ***Beware:*** Bucket-shop tickets are usually nonrefundable or rigged with stiff cancellation penalties, often as high as 50% to 75% of the ticket price, and some put you on charter airlines with questionable safety records. **FlyCheap** (✆ **800/FLY-CHEAP** [359-2432]; www.flycheap.com) is owned by package-holiday megalith MyTravel and so has especially good access to fares for sunny destinations. **Air Tickets Direct** (✆ **800/778-3447;** www.airticketsdirect.com) is based in Montréal and leverages the currently weak Canadian dollar for low fares. And **TravelHub** (www.travelhub.com) represents nearly 1,000 travel agencies, many of whom offer consolidator and discount fares.
- Search **the Internet** for cheap fares. Great last-minute deals are available through free weekly e-mail services provided directly by the airlines. See "Planning Your Trip Online," later in this chapter, for more information.
- Book a seat on a **charter flight.** Discounted fares have pared the number available, but they can still be found. Most charter operators advertise and sell their seats through travel agents, thus making these local professionals your best source of information for available flights. Before deciding to take a charter flight, however, check the restrictions on the ticket: You may be asked to purchase a tour package, to pay in advance, to be amenable if the day of departure is changed, to pay a service charge, to fly on an airline you're not familiar with (this usually is not the case), and to pay harsh penalties if you cancel—but be understanding if the charter doesn't fill up and is canceled up to 10 days before departure. Summer charters fill up more quickly than others and are almost sure to fly, but if you decide on a charter flight, seriously consider buying cancellation and baggage insurance. Also be prepared for late departure hours and long airport delays, because charters usually do not have priority.
- Join a travel club such as **Moment's Notice** (✆ **718/234-6295;** www.moments-notice.com) or **Travelers Advantage** (✆ **800/433-9383,** or 877/259-2691 to join; www.travelersadvantage.com), which supply unsold tickets at discounted prices. You pay an annual membership fee to get the club's hot line number. Of course, you're limited to what's available, so you have to be flexible.
- Join **frequent-flier clubs.** Accrue enough miles and you'll be rewarded with free flights and elite status. It's free, and you'll get the best choice of seats, faster response to phone inquiries, and prompter service if your luggage is stolen, your flight is canceled or delayed, or if you want to change your seat. You don't need to fly to build frequent-flier miles—**frequent-flier credit cards** can provide thousands of miles for doing your everyday shopping.

Tips Canceled Plans

If your flight is canceled, don't book a new fare at the ticket counter. Instead, find the nearest phone and call the airline directly to reschedule. You'll be relaxing while other passengers are still standing in line.

HOW TO HAVE AN (ALMOST) FIRST-CLASS EXPERIENCE IN COACH

Anyone who has traveled in coach or economy class in recent years can attest to the frustrating reality of cramped seating. But with a little savvy and advance planning, you can make an otherwise unpleasant coach experience downright comfy.

Here are some tips for finding the right seat:

- Your choice of airline and airplane will definitely affect your legroom. Find more details at **www.seatguru.com**, which has extensive details about almost every seat on six major U.S. airlines. For more legroom, check in early and ask for an aisle seat in an emergency-exit row or bulkhead. The former is often restricted to able-bodied adults, so your kids may not be able to sit in that row. The latter, however, is where the airlines tend to stick passengers traveling with bassinets.
- You also may want to reserve a window seat so that your child can watch the scenery, rest his head, and avoid being bumped in the aisle.
- If you're traveling with a single child, try and book an aisle and a window seat. Middle seats are usually booked last, so chances are good you'll end up with three seats to yourselves. And in the event that a third passenger is assigned the middle seat, he or she will probably be more than happy to trade for a window or an aisle.
- To sleep, avoid the last row or the row in front of the emergency exit, as these seats are the least likely to recline.

Here are some tips for making yourself comfortable during your flight:

- Wear comfortable, low-heeled shoes and dress in loose-fitting layers that you can remove as cabin temperature fluctuates. Don't underdress: Airline cabins can be notoriously chilly and blankets may be unavailable. Wear breathable natural fabrics instead of synthetics. Bring light, long-sleeved shirts for the kids.
- Hydrate before, during, and after your flight to combat the lack of humidity in airplane cabins—which can be as dry as the Sahara. Bring a bottle of water on board. Sugary sodas and diet drinks don't count as water and can actually dehydrate you if they contain caffeine. Have the children drink club soda or diluted juice throughout the flight.
- Preorder special meals for some of your group if that option is available (most airlines no longer serve meals on short-haul flights except in first class). The airlines' vegetarian, high-protein, low-sodium, and kosher meals are healthier than standard plane fare, and you get served faster. By having a couple regular meals arrive as well, you'll be able to share desserts and other items that will vary from plate to plate. Or pack a lunch in each child's backpack, plus have some snacks in yours.
- Get up, walk around, and stretch every 60 to 90 minutes to keep your blood flowing. Escort your younger children to the bathroom so you get some exercise. This helps avoid **deep vein thrombosis,** or "economy-class syndrome," a potentially deadly condition that can be caused by sitting in cramped conditions for too long.

- Bring a toothbrush and moisturizer to stay fresh.
- When flying with kids, don't forget a deck of cards, toys, extra bottles, pacifiers, diapers, and chewing gum to help them relieve ear pressure buildup during ascent and descent. Let each child pack his or her own backpack with favorite toys.
- Ask about entertainment options. Many airlines offer seatback video systems where you get to choose your movies or play video games—but only on some of their planes.
- If you're flying with a cold or chronic sinus problems, use a decongestant 10 minutes before ascent and descent, to minimize pressure buildup in the inner ear.
- Try to acclimate yourself and your kids to the local time as quickly as possible. Stay up as long as you can the first day, and then try to wake up at a normal hour the next morning.

COPING WITH JET LAG

Jet lag is a pitfall of traveling across time zones. If you're flying north-south—say, from Canada to Chile—and you feel sluggish when you touch down, your symptoms will be the byproduct of dehydration and the general stress of air travel. When you travel east to west or vice versa, however, the bodily functions that operate cyclically—your hormone levels, blood pressure, body temperature, digestive enzymes, kidney, heart, and brain activity—fall into a sort of time warp. This is because they are, in part, someplace else, inclined to do the things they normally would have been doing back home. Traveling east, say, from Chicago to Paris, is more difficult on your internal clock than traveling west, say, from Atlanta to Hawaii. Traveling east, you lose time, whereas traveling west you gain time, and thus gain sleep, which will help your body recover more quickly. Children seem more affected by traveling long distances than adults, but maybe they are just excited about the trip.

Here are some tips for combating jet lag:

- **Drink lots of water** before, during, and after your flight.
- **Reset your watch** according to your destination time before you board the plane.
- **Avoid drinking alcohol** before and during your flight.
- **Exercise, sleep well, and eat especially healthy foods** during the few days before your trip.
- **Eat more lightly** than you would, both before and during your flight.
- When you reach your destination, **don't sleep longer than you normally would** to try to "catch up."
- **Daylight** is the key to resetting your body clock and your kids'. At the website for **Outside In** (www.bodyclock.com), you can get a customized plan of when to seek and avoid light.
- **Some doctors recommend melatonin for adults** 2 hours before bedtime. A natural, sleep-inducing hormone, it's thought that melatonin will trick your body into thinking night has fallen earlier and help you adjust to a new time zone. **Children usually sleep well on planes, and adjust to jet lag with Calms Forte,** an inexpensive homeopathic medication available over-the-counter at health food stores. Check,

Tips Under Pressure

According to folk wisdom, ear pressure can be relieved by placing a hot, damp, paper towel in a cup and holding it over the affected ear(s).

however, with your doctor before taking any over-the-counter medication.

- Remember that eating **carbohydrates** (such as pasta or whole-grain bread) **before bedtime** will allow you to sleep better. High-protein foods—such as meats, fish, eggs, and dairy products—eaten before bedtime will give you energy.

BY CAR

The main highway connecting Las Vegas with the rest of the country is I-15; it links Montana, Idaho, and Utah with Southern California. The drive from Los Angeles is quite popular, and thanks to the narrow two-lane highway, can get very crowded on Friday (heading east) and Sunday (heading west) afternoons with hopeful weekend gamblers making their way to and from Vegas. By the way, as soon as you cross the state line, three casinos are ready and able to handle your immediate gambling needs, as well as an outlet shopping mall, and most importantly for children, thrill rides and a video arcade.

From the east, take I-70 or I-80 W. to Kingman, Arizona, then U.S. 93 N. to Downtown Las Vegas (Fremont St.). From the south, take I-10 W. to Phoenix and then U.S. 93 N. to Las Vegas. From San Francisco, take I-80 E. to Reno, then U.S. 95 S. to Las Vegas. If you're driving to Las Vegas, be sure to read the driving precautions in "Getting Around," in chapter 5.

Vegas is 286 miles from Phoenix, 759 miles from Denver, 421 miles from Salt Lake City, 269 miles from Los Angeles, and 586 miles from San Francisco.

BY TRAIN

We don't really recommend this method if traveling with children because **Amtrak** (© **800/USA-RAIL** [872-7245]; www.amtrak.com) does not currently offer direct rail service to Las Vegas. If you take the train to Los Angeles or Barstow, Amtrak will get you to Vegas by bus. It's a long trip and not a lot of fun. Plans have been in the works to restore the rails between Los Angeles and Las Vegas for years now. At some point, Amtrak might restore service using the Talgo. This European-designed "casino train" completes the trip from Los Angeles in about 5½ hours, with a wholesale seat price of $99 round-trip. (There's some talk that the train's route may continue on to Salt Lake City.) But don't hold your breath; we believe this won't happen in our lifetime.

Much of the train will be presold to various hotels, so the final price to the traveler will depend on how you get the ticket. High rollers will probably end up with freebies, but the ticket will most likely be $99 if you purchase at the counter.

FURTHER TRAVEL FOR INTERNATIONAL VISITORS

BY PLANE Some large airlines (for example, Northwest and Delta) offer travelers on their transatlantic or transpacific flights special discount tickets under the name **Visit USA,** allowing mostly one-way travel from one U.S. destination to another at very low prices. These discount tickets are not on sale in the United States and must be purchased abroad in conjunction with your international ticket. This system is the best, easiest, and fastest way to see the United States at low cost. You should obtain information well in advance from your travel agent or the office of the airline concerned, since the conditions attached to these discount tickets can be changed without advance notice.

BY CAR Though you don't necessarily have to rent a car while in Las Vegas, the most cost-effective, convenient, and comfortable way to travel around the United States is by car. See "Renting a Car" in chapter 5 for more information on car rentals.

BY BUS Although bus travel is often the most economical form of public transit for short hops between U.S. cities, it can also be slow and uncomfortable—certainly not an option for everyone (particularly when Amtrak, which is far more luxurious, offers similar or slightly higher rates).

Greyhound/Trailways (✆ **800/231-2222;** www.greyhound.com), the sole nationwide bus line, offers an **International Ameripass** that must be purchased in a bus terminal. Passes are available for 7, 15, 30, or 60 days; prices vary seasonally. Note that the opening page on Greyhound's website makes no mention of the International Ameripass. Special ticket rates are available for seniors and students. Information is available at **www.greyhound.com/deals**.

Though bus stations are often located in undesirable neighborhoods, the one in Las Vegas is conveniently located in a safe part of Downtown.

6 MONEY & COSTS

ATMS

An automated teller machine (ATM) is within feet of you at almost all times in Las Vegas; no one in the city wants you to find yourself without cash that you could lose in a slot! Beware of withdrawal charges, though, which can often run as high as $2 or $3 per transaction; the highest charges are usually for commercial machines in convenience stores and hotel lobbies. (One way around ATM fees is to ask for cash back at grocery stores that accept ATM cards and don't charge usage fees. Of course, you'll have to purchase something first.) On top of this, the bank from which you withdraw cash may charge its own fee. Nevertheless, ATMs are a safe and convenient way of accessing cash while you're away from home.

Almost all of the ATMs in Las Vegas are linked to a national network that most likely includes your bank at home. **Cirrus** (✆ **800/424-7787;** www.mastercard.com) and **PLUS** (✆ **800/843-7587;** www.visa.com) are the two most popular networks; check the back of your ATM card to see which network your bank belongs to, and use the 800 numbers or Web addresses above to locate the ATMs closest to your Las Vegas destination.

Additionally, make sure you know your four-digit PIN and daily withdrawal limit before you depart. You can get cash advances on your credit card at an ATM, but keep in mind that credit card companies try to protect themselves from theft by limiting the funds someone can withdraw away from home. It's therefore best to call your credit card company before you leave and let them know where you're going and how much you plan to spend.

TRAVELER'S CHECKS

Traveler's checks are something of an anachronism from the days before the ATM made cash accessible at any time. Traveler's checks used to be the only sound alternative to traveling with dangerously

Tips Small Change

Always keep some small bills on hand when you're in Las Vegas. Petty cash will come in handy for tipping and public transportation. Consider keeping your small bills separate from your larger bills, so they are readily accessible. This system will also help you become less of a target for theft.

What Things Cost	US$	UK£	C$	Euro€
Hot dog at hotel snack bar	2.00	1.05	2.35	1.60
Medium soda at hotel snack bar	1.50	0.75	1.75	1.20
Apple juice at hotel shop	2.00	1.05	2.35	1.60
Bottled water at hotel shop	2.00	1.05	2.35	1.60
Slice of pizza at hotel food court	3.00	1.55	3.50	2.40
McDonald's Happy Meal	2.50	1.30	3.00	2.00
4-oz. jar baby food	0.80	0.50	0.95	0.65
Tube of sunblock	10.00	5.15	11.75	8.00
Package of diapers	7.70	3.60	8.25	5.60
Admission to movie:				
Child	6.50	2.80	6.50	4.40
Adult	9.75	4.85	10.30	8.00
Admission to Imperial Palace Auto Collection:				
Child	3.00	1.80	4.10	2.80
Student	3.00	1.55	3.50	2.40
Adult	6.95	3.55	8.15	5.55
Admission to *Tournament of Kings:*				
Children 3 and under	free			
Ages 4 and above	61.75	42.00	77.20	48.00
Cab fare: Strip to Downtown	18.00	7.70	17.65	12.00
One game of bowling	2.00	1.05	2.35	1.60
One video game	1.00–2.00	0.50–1.05	1.20–2.35	0.80–1.60

large amounts of cash. They were as reliable as currency, but, unlike cash, could be replaced if lost or stolen.

These days, however, traveler's checks seem less necessary because most cities have 24-hour ATMs that allow you to withdraw amounts of cash as needed. And, naturally, in Las Vegas, the casinos have ATMs at every turn. However, keep in mind that you will likely be charged an ATM withdrawal fee if the bank is not your own (and in Las Vegas's casinos and hotels, the bank is *never* your bank), so if you're withdrawing money every day, you might be better off with traveler's checks—provided that you don't mind showing identification every time you want to cash one.

You can get traveler's checks at almost any bank. **American Express** offers denominations of $20, $50, $100, $500, and (for cardholders only) $1,000. You'll pay a service charge ranging from 1% to 4%. You can also get American Express traveler's checks over the phone by calling ✆ **800/221-7282;** Amex gold and platinum cardholders who use this number are exempt from the 1% fee.

Visa offers traveler's checks at Citibank locations nationwide, as well as at several other banks. The service charge ranges between 1.5% and 2%; checks come in denominations of $20, $50, $100, $500, and $1,000. Call ✆ **800/732-1322** for information. AAA members can obtain Visa checks without a fee at most AAA offices. **MasterCard** also offers traveler's checks. Call ✆ **800/223-9920** for a location near you.

If you're traveling from abroad, make sure your checks are denominated in U.S. dollars, because foreign-currency checks are often difficult to exchange.

Tips **Dear Visa: I'm off to Vegas!**

Some credit card companies recommend that you notify them of any impending trip, so they don't become suspicious when the card is used numerous times away from home and block your charges. Even if you don't call your credit card company in advance, you can always call the card's toll-free emergency number (see below) if a charge is refused—a good reason to carry the phone number with you. But perhaps the most important lesson here is to carry more than one card with you on your trip; a card might not work for any number of reasons, so having a backup is the smart way to go.

CREDIT CARDS

Credit cards are invaluable when traveling. They are a safe way to carry money and provide a convenient record of all your expenses. You can also withdraw cash advances from your credit cards at any bank (though you'll start paying hefty interest on the advance the moment you receive the cash). At most banks, you don't even need to go to a teller; you can get a cash advance at the ATM. If you've forgotten your PIN number, call the number on the back of your credit card and ask the bank to send it to you. It usually takes 5 to 7 business days, though some banks will provide the number over the phone if you tell them your mother's maiden name or pass some other security clearance. All credit cards—American Express, Diners Club, Discover, MasterCard, and Visa, along with their foreign counterparts such as JCB and Barclays—are accepted in Las Vegas.

WHAT TO DO IF YOUR WALLET IS LOST OR STOLEN

Be sure to tell all of your credit card companies the minute you discover your wallet has been lost or stolen and file a report at the nearest police precinct. Your credit card company or insurer may require a police report number or record of the loss. Most credit card companies have an emergency toll-free number to call if your card is lost or stolen; they may be able to wire you a cash advance immediately or deliver an emergency credit card in a day or two. Visa's U.S. emergency number is ✆ **800/847-2911** or 410/581-9994. American Express cardholders and traveler's check holders should call ✆ **800/221-7282.** MasterCard holders should call ✆ **800/307-7309** or 636/722-7111. For other credit cards, call the toll-free number directory at ✆ **800/555-1212.** If you choose to carry traveler's checks, be sure to keep a record of their serial numbers separate from your checks. You'll get a refund faster if you know the numbers.

If you need emergency cash over the weekend when all banks and American Express offices are closed, you can have money wired to you via **Western Union** (✆ **800/325-6000;** www.westernunion.com).

Identity theft or fraud is a potential complication of losing your wallet, especially if you've lost your driver's license along with your cash and credit cards. Notify the major credit-reporting bureaus immediately; placing a fraud alert on your records may protect you against liability for criminal activity. The three major U.S. credit-reporting agencies are **Equifax** (✆ **888/567-8688;** www.equifax.com), **Experian** (✆ **888/397-3742;** www.experian.com), and **TransUnion** (✆ **800/680-7289;** www.transunion.com). Finally,

Tips **According to the Record**

Before you travel, take an inventory of the contents of your billfold. List the customer service and "lost card" numbers from the back of your credit cards, phone cards, and ATM cards, as well as the numbers of your frequent-flier accounts and important memberships such as AAA and AARP. Also record relevant info from your health insurance card and auto insurance card. Finally, make a copy of your driver's license and passport to have as a backup.

if you've lost all forms of photo ID call your airline and explain the situation; they might allow you to board the plane if you have a copy of your passport or birth certificate and a copy of the police report you've filed.

7 HEALTH

THE HEALTHY TRAVELER

Staying Healthy

It can be hard to find a doctor you can trust when you're in an unfamiliar place. Try to take proper precautions the week before you depart to avoid falling ill while you're away from home. Amid the last-minute frenzy that often precedes a vacation, make an extra effort to eat and sleep well—especially if you feel an illness coming on. It's a drag to be sick on vacation, and a head cold can make a plane flight intolerable.

Once in Vegas, limit your exposure to the sun, especially during the first few days of your trip, and, thereafter, from 11am to 2pm. Use a sunscreen with a high protection factor and apply it liberally. Remember that children need more protection than adults do.

What to Do If You Get Sick Away from Home

If you worry about getting sick away from home, you may want to consider **medical travel insurance** (see "Medical Insurance" in the appendix). In most cases, however, your existing health plan provides all the coverage you need. Be sure to carry your identification card in your wallet.

If you suffer from a chronic illness, consult your doctor before your departure. For conditions such as epilepsy, diabetes, or heart problems, wear a **MedicAlert Identification Tag** (✆ **888/633-4298;** www.medicalert.org), which will immediately alert doctors to your condition and give them access to your records through MedicAlert's 24-hour hot line.

Pack **prescription medications** in your carry-on luggage, and carry prescription medications in their original containers, with pharmacy labels—otherwise they won't make it through airport security. Also bring along copies of your prescriptions in case you lose your pills or run out. And don't forget an extra pair of contact lenses or prescription glasses.

If you do get sick, ask the concierge at your hotel to recommend a local doctor, even his or her own. You can also try the emergency room at a local hospital; many have walk-in clinics for emergency cases that are not life threatening. You may not get immediate attention, but you won't pay the high price of an emergency room visit (usually a minimum of $300 just for signing your name).

Also see the "Fast Facts" section in the Appendix. There, you'll find listings for hospitals, dental referrals, and even a clinic, right on the Strip.

The nearest poison control center is at **Humana Medical Center,** 3186 Maryland Pkwy. (✆ **702/732-4989**).

8 SAFETY

THE SAFE TRAVELER

Las Vegas has very strict laws regarding children. No one under 21 is allowed in casinos. Children may not watch you so much as drop a nickel in a slot machine. This law also covers infants and babies in strollers. Additionally, strollers are not allowed on the casino floors. However, because in most hotels you have to walk through the casino to get to your room, your child may walk *with you* to and from your room as long as you stay on "the path," usually designated by a different-colored strip of carpet.

The curfew in arcades for children under 18 unaccompanied by parents or a responsible adult 21 and over is 10pm to 5am of the succeeding day, Sunday through Thursday; and from midnight to 5am of the succeeding day, Friday through Saturday. From Memorial Day through Labor Day and on school holidays, the start of curfew is extended until midnight.

The majority of arcades in hotels are monitored by security guards, who, by law, must patrol the arcade four times an hour. Some hotel arcades have full-time security present in the arcade, rather than quarter-hourly patrols. Very few arcades comply with security ordinances by relying upon video surveillance. These arcades will have a prominently featured sign indicating that security cameras are in use.

SAFETY FOR INTERNATIONAL VISITORS

Although tourist areas are generally safe, crime is a national problem, and U.S. urban areas tend to be less safe than those in Europe or Japan. You should always stay alert. It's wise to ask your hotel front-desk staff if you're in doubt about which neighborhoods are safe.

Avoid carrying valuables with you on the street and don't display expensive cameras or electronic equipment. Hold on to your pocketbook and place your billfold in an inside pocket. In theaters, restaurants, and other public places, keep your possessions in sight.

Remember also that hotels are open to the public, and in a large hotel, security may not be able to screen everyone entering. Always lock your room door—don't assume that once inside your hotel you are automatically safe and no longer need to be aware of your surroundings. In Las Vegas, many hotels inspect room keys at the elevators at night, providing some extra security. Many Las Vegas hotels also have in-room safes; if yours doesn't and you're traveling with valuables, put them in a safe-deposit box at the front desk.

Pamphleteers who line the Strip passing out colorful ads for private exotic dancers and the like are not allowed to hand these to minors and, thankfully, will probably ignore you as well if you are with your children. That said, discarded pamphlets often end up on the Strip's sidewalks and may give your child an unintended eyeful.

You will see people walking the streets with alcoholic drinks in hand. Yes, this is legal, and is one of Las Vegas's many draws for those who like that sort of thing.

For more ordinances regarding minors and other public safety issues, see **http://municipalcodes.lexisnexis.com/codes/clarknv**.

Curfew, According to the Law: When & Where Children Shouldn't Be Without an Adult

This is not a town for teens to explore on their own after dark: The fine for violating curfew is $300, and the offending juvenile will most likely be cited and taken into custody and then placed with juvenile services until his or her parents or guardians can be located. Some of Clark County's Codes on Minors and Curfews are listed below. For a full list, head to **http://municipalcodes.lexisnexis.com/codes/clarknv**. (Click on "Title 12" and then "Chapter 12.12" for the information you see listed below.)

It is unlawful for any child under the age of 18 to be without adult supervision in or upon the following streets or sidewalks adjacent thereto and all parking lots, driveways, and walkways which are open to the public and located on properties that adjoin such designated streets between the hours of 9pm and 5am of the succeeding day on Friday, Saturday, and legal holidays, and between 6pm on December 31 and 5am of the succeeding day:

- Las Vegas Boulevard South between Sahara Avenue and Sunset Road
- Harmon Avenue between Las Vegas Boulevard South and Koval Lane
- Dunes Road/Flamingo Road between I-15 and Koval Lane
- Spring Mountain Road/Sands Drive between Vegas Plaza Drive and Koval Lane
- Stardust Road between Industrial Road and Las Vegas Boulevard South
- Convention Center Drive
- Riviera Boulevard
- Circus Circus Drive

It is unlawful for any child under the age of 18 to be in or upon the following streets or sidewalks adjacent thereto and all parking lots, driveways, and walkways which are open to the public and located on properties that adjoin such designated streets between the hours of 6pm on the last Wednesday, Thursday, Friday, and Saturday in the month of April and 5am of the succeeding days:

- Casino Drive, from block number 1500 through block number 3000

As in any location with vacationers, pickpockets try to work their skills. Keep your wallet in the front pocket of your pants, or firmly zipped inside your purse. Don't carry all your credit cards or cash with you. Also, see the "What to Do If Your Wallet Is Lost or Stolen" section above for more information.

The only part of Downtown Las Vegas we recommend visiting, except during parades, is Fremont Street, which has been turned into a pedestrian mall. Though streets parallel to and intersecting Fremont Street are safe, little to nothing of interest to families can be found there. Don't worry about your safety walking from nearby parking garages and public transportation centers.

The streets of Las Vegas are very wide and full of tourists walking and driving.

Tips Don't Wear It Out

Children should never wear clothing with their names displayed. Doing so can put them at risk—a stranger can call them by name, thus establishing a level of trust with the child.

Cross only on the "walk" signal, even if you see the foolhardy folks next to you jumping off the curb against the light. Use the crosswalks; do not jaywalk! And you should hold the hands of younger children while crossing the street.

Hats on parents can help children spot them in a crowd, and brightly colored shirts also help family members find each other. Always make sure each child carries the name of your hotel on a piece of paper, along with your cell phone number.

If separated in a casino/resort, your child should immediately approach a uniformed security guard or other employee, including staff in a shop or restaurant, explaining that they are lost, and ask that you be paged.

No casino wants a stray child roaming about. Security can find your child anywhere in the building; those "eye in the sky" surveillance cameras are good for more than just catching card sharks.

9 SPECIALIZED TRAVEL RESOURCES

Because Las Vegas was designed for tourists, the city accommodates the majority of visitors with ease. Most hotels were built in the last 20 years, so tens of thousands of rooms are compliant with the Americans with Disabilities Act (ADA). The city actively woos seniors, who love to travel here. A single parent will have no trouble keeping kids busy and amused in Las Vegas because so many attractions are kid-friendly. And nobody really notices or cares if you're gay, lesbian, bi, or transgender. This accommodating attitude makes Vegas a great place to visit, even though families sometimes face obstacles to their fun, such as crossing large smoky casinos to get to their rooms, no-stroller and no-children policies, and occasional hostile stares from those who don't think kids belong in Sin City. Don't let it get you down, however. As well as those who visit, plenty of families live in Las Vegas, and they all enjoy a myriad of fun activities at this neon oasis.

TRAVELERS WITH DISABILITIES

Most disabilities shouldn't stop anyone from traveling. More options and resources are out there than ever before.

On the one hand, the distance between Vegas hotels (particularly on the Strip) makes a vehicle of some sort virtually mandatory for most people with disabilities, and it may be extremely strenuous and time-consuming to get from place to place (even within a single hotel, because of the crowds). Additionally, the casinos can be quite difficult to maneuver in (particularly for a guest in a wheelchair); they're crowded and the machines and tables are often laid out close together, with chairs and such blocking easy access. You should also consider that it's often a long trek through larger hotels between the entrance and the room elevators (or, for that matter, anywhere in the hotel), and then add a crowded casino to the equation.

Tips Menus for the Blind

In 1999, activist Gordon DeWitty formed Abilities 2000, an organization that works with hotels, resorts, and restaurants to provide Braille and large-print menus for the blind in accordance with the Americans with Disabilities Act, which mandates accessibility to goods and services for all. Thanks to his efforts, the Monte Carlo Resort & Casino, Treasure Island, Excalibur, The Riviera, Bally's, and Harrah's Las Vegas now offer these menus in their coffee shops, food courts, and other high-traffic restaurants. DeWitty is also working with hotels and resorts to provide room service directories in Braille and large print.

On the other hand, Las Vegas is fairly well equipped for people with disabilities, with virtually every hotel having accessible rooms, ramps, and other requirements. (If mobility is a problem, we suggest basing yourself in a South or Center Strip location.)

The city provides for travelers with disabilities, not only with ADA rooms and TTY phones, but with ADA coordinators. You can get assistance in booking your room by voice or TTY from the Las Vegas Convention and Visitors Authority ADA Coordinator (✆ **800/884-2592** or 702/892-7406; www.visitlasvegas.com). Showrooms also have assisted listening devices and wheelchair seating.

All taxi vans have wheelchair access, casinos have roll-up tables and slot machines, and wheelchair seating is available at most restaurants.

The U.S. National Park Service offers a **Golden Access Passport** that gives free lifetime entrance to U.S. national parks and recreation areas (such as Lake Mead National Recreation Area; see chapter 12) for persons who are blind or with a permanent disability, regardless of age. You may pick up a Golden Access Passport at any NPS entrance fee area by showing proof of a medically determined disability and eligibility for receiving benefits under federal law. Besides free entry, the Golden Access Passport also offers a 50% discount on federal-use fees charged for such facilities as camping, swimming, parking, boat launching, and tours. For more information, click onto **www.nps.gov/fees_passes.htm** or call ✆ **888/GO-PARKS.**

Agencies/Operators

- **Flying Wheels Travel** (✆ **507/451-5005;** www.flyingwheelstravel.com) offers escorted tours and cruises that emphasize sports and private tours in minivans with lifts.
- **Accessible Journeys** (✆ **800/TINGLES** [846-4537] or 610/521-0339; www.accessiblejourneys.com) caters specifically to slow walkers and wheelchair travelers and their families and friends.

Organizations

- **The Southern Nevada Center for Independent Living Program,** 6039 Eldora St., Ste. H-8, Las Vegas, NV 89146 (✆ **702/889-4216;** www.sncil.org), can recommend hotels and restaurants that meet your needs, help you find a personal attendant, advise about transportation, and answer all sorts of other questions.
- The **Nevada Commission on Tourism** (✆ **800/638-2328;** www.travelnevada.com) offers a free accommodations guide to Las Vegas hotels that includes access information.
- **The MossRehab Hospital** (✆ **215/456-9603;** www.mossresourcenet.org) provides friendly, helpful phone assistance through its **Travel Information Service.**

- **The Society for Accessible Travel & Hospitality** (✆ **212/447-7284;** www.sath.org) offers a wealth of travel resources for all types of disabilities and informed recommendations on destinations, access guides, travel agents, tour operators, vehicle rentals, and companion services. Annual membership costs $45 for adults, $30 for seniors and students.
- **The American Foundation for the Blind** (✆ **800/232-5463;** www.afb.org) provides information on traveling with Seeing Eye dogs.

Publications & Websites

For more information specifically targeted to travelers with disabilities, the website www.makoa.org/travel.htm has destination guides and several details on accessible travel. Also check out the quarterly magazine ***Emerging Horizons*** ($16.95 per year, $21.95 outside the U.S.; www.emerginghorizons.com).

SINGLE PARENTS

Single parents face special, unique challenges when they travel with their children. **Parents Without Partners** (✆ **561/391-8833;** www.parentswithoutpartners.org) provides links for numerous single parents' resources.

Single mom Brenda Elwell's website (**www.singleparenttravel.net**) is full of advice garnered from traveling around the world with her two children.

Single parents also can find travel tips at **www.solosingles.com**.

GAY, LESBIAN, BI & TRANSGENDER (GLBT) FAMILIES

Many gay, lesbian, bi, and transgender families live in Las Vegas. And the city's nonjudgmental attitude toward tourists makes this a great place for GLBT families to visit.

We Are Family (**www.wearefamilylv.com**) provides activities such as movie groups, outings, and socials for the area's gay, lesbian, bi, and transgender families. The organization also works to promote accurate messages about GLBT families within the southern Nevada area. Its website lists events and resources for the community.

The Gay and Lesbian Community Center of Southern Nevada, 953 E. Sahara Ave., Ste. B-31 (✆ **702/733-9800;** www.thecenterlv.com), provides another important resource, with links to Parents, Families & Friends of Lesbians & Gays (PFLAG) and other GLBT family organizations, including spiritual groups.

The International Gay & Lesbian Travel Association (IGLTA; ✆ **800/448-8550** or 954/776-2626; www.iglta.org) links travelers up with gay-friendly hoteliers, tour operators, and airline and cruise-line representatives. It offers monthly newsletters, marketing mailings, and a membership directory that's updated once a year. Membership is $225 yearly, plus a $100 administration fee for new members.

Agencies/Operators

- **Above and Beyond Tours** (✆ **800/397-2681;** www.abovebeyondtours.com) offers gay and lesbian tours worldwide and is the exclusive gay and lesbian tour operator for United Airlines.
- **Now, Voyager** (✆ **800/255-6951;** www.nowvoyager.com) is a San Francisco–based gay-owned and -operated travel service.
- **BluWay** (**www.bluway.com**) dedicates its Internet-exclusive travel service to the GLBT community.

Publications

The following publications are directed more toward the single or childfree GLBT traveler, but some of the information will apply to families.

- ***QVegas,*** a monthly magazine serving the gay community, provides information about bars, workshops, local politics, support groups, shops, events, and more. A subscription costs $25 for 12 issues. You can find the magazine in bars, music stores, and most libraries and bookstores. For details, call ✆ **702/650-0636** or check its online edition at www.qvegas.com.

- ***Out and About*** (✆ **866/313-6373** or 415/834-6550; www.outandabout.com) offers guidebooks and a newsletter 10 times a year packed with solid information on the global gay and lesbian scene.
- ***Spartacus International Gay Guide*** and ***Odysseus*** are good, annual English-language guidebooks focused on gay men, with some information for lesbians. You can get them from most gay and lesbian bookstores, or order them from **Giovanni's Room** bookstore, 1145 Pine St., Philadelphia, PA 19107 (✆ **215/923-2960;** www.giovannisroom.com).
- ***Gay Travel A to Z: The World of Gay & Lesbian Travel Options at Your Fingertips,*** by Marianne Ferrari (Ferrari Publications; Box 35575, Phoenix, AZ 85069) is a very good gay and lesbian guidebook series.

SENIOR TRAVEL

One of the benefits of age is that travel often costs less. Mention the fact that you're a senior when you make travel reservations. Although all of the major U.S. airlines except America West have canceled their senior-discount and coupon-book programs, many hotels still offer discounts for seniors. In most cities, people over the age of 60 qualify for reduced admission to theaters, museums, and other attractions, as well as discounted fares on public transportation.

Members of **AARP** (formerly known as the American Association of Retired Persons), 601 E St. NW, Washington, DC 20049 (✆ **888/687-2277** or 202/434-2277; www.aarp.org), get discounts on hotels, airfares, and car rentals. AARP offers members a wide range of benefits, including *AARP The Magazine* and a monthly newsletter. Anyone 50 or over can join.

The Alliance for Retired Americans, 888 16th St. NW, Washington, DC 20006 (✆ **202/974-8222;** www.retiredamericans.org), offers a newsletter six times a year and discounts on hotel and auto rentals; annual dues are $10 per person or couple. ***Note:*** Members of the former National Council of Senior Citizens receive automatic membership in the Alliance.

The **U.S. National Park Service** offers a **Golden Age Passport** that gives seniors 62 years or older lifetime entrance to U.S. national parks for a one-time processing fee of $10, which must be purchased in person at any NPS facility (Lake Mead National Recreation Area, p. 259, sells them) that charges an entrance fee. Besides free entry, a Golden Age Passport also offers a 50% discount on federal-use fees charged for such facilities as camping, swimming, parking, boat launching, and tours. For more information, head online to **www.nps.gov/fees_passes.htm** or call ✆ **888/GO-PARKS.**

Agencies/Operators

Many reliable agencies and organizations target the 50-plus market. **Elderhostel** (✆ **800/454-5768;** www.elderhostel.org) arranges study programs for those aged 55 and over (and a spouse or companion of any age) in the United States and in more than 80 countries around the world. Most courses last 5 to 7 days in the United States (2–4 weeks abroad), and many include airfare, accommodations in university dormitories or modest inns, meals, and tuition. Its Las Vegas options include sessions on the city's entertainment, hotel, and gaming industries.

Publications

Recommended publications offering travel resources and discounts for seniors include the quarterly magazine ***Travel 50 & Beyond*** (www.travel50andbeyond.com);

Travel Unlimited: Uncommon Adventures for the Mature Traveler (Avalon); and ***101 Tips for Mature Travelers,*** available from Grand Circle Travel (✆ **800/959-0405** or 617/350-7500; www.gct.com).

ONLINE RESOURCES FOR FAMILY TRAVEL

- **Family Travel Network** (www.family travelnetwork.com) offers travel tips and reviews of family-friendly destinations, vacation deals, and thoughtful features such as "What to Do When Your Kids Are Afraid to Travel."
- **Travel with Your Kids** (www.travel withyourkids.com) is a comprehensive site offering sound advice for traveling with children.
- **Family Travel Files** (www.thefamily travelfiles.com) offers an online magazine and a directory of off-the-beaten-path tours and tour operators for families.

TRAVELING WITH PETS

Many of us wouldn't dream of going on vacation without our pets. Under the right circumstances, it can be a memorable experience. And these days, more and more lodgings and restaurants are going the pet-friendly route. Many hotel and motel chains, such as Best Western, Motel 6, Holiday Inn, and Four Seasons–Regent Hotels, welcome pets. Policies vary, however, so call ahead to find out the rules.

Frankly, bringing your pets to Las Vegas anytime from mid-May to early October is a bad idea: It's just too hot. The searing heat will cook their paws during walks on the endless hot concrete and forget about letting them run and frolic in the desert. In other words, there's nothing for them to do. But if you must, only one hotel in Vegas, the **Desert Rose Resort,** has no size limit on animals.

All city parks allow dogs on leashes, and **Sunset Park** has a special area set aside for off-leash dogs. There are also boarding kennels in the city. Make sure to bring copies of your pet's vaccination records with you, in case you encounter any problems.

An excellent resource is **www.pets welcome.com**, which dispenses medical tips, names of animal-friendly lodgings and campgrounds, and lists of kennels and veterinarians. Also check out *The Portable petswelcome.com: The Complete Guide to Traveling with Your Pet* (Howell Book House), which features the best selection of pet travel information anywhere.

If you plan to fly with your pet, the FAA has compiled a list of all requirements for transporting live animals at **http://air consumer.ost.dot.gov/publications/animals.htm**. You may be able to carry your pet on board a plane if it's small enough to put inside a carrier that can slip under the seat. Pets usually count as one piece of carry-on luggage. Note that summer may not be the best time to fly with your pet: Many airlines will not check pets as baggage in the hot summer months. The ASPCA discourages travelers from checking pets as luggage at any time; storage conditions on planes are loosely monitored, and fatal

Tips The Peripatetic Pet

Never leave your pet inside a parked car in hot climates with the windows rolled up. It's a good idea never to leave a pet inside a hot car even with the windows rolled down for any length of time.

Make sure your pet is wearing a name tag with the name and phone number of a contact person who can take the call if your pet gets lost while you're away from home.

accidents are not unprecedented. Your other option is to ship your pet with a professional carrier, which can be expensive. Ask your veterinarian whether you should sedate your pet on a plane ride or give it antinausea medication. Never give your pet sedatives used by humans.

Keep in mind that dogs are prohibited on hiking trails and must be leashed at all times on federal lands administered by the National Park Service national parks and monuments, including Red Rock Canyon and the Valley of Fire.

10 PACKAGES FOR THE INDEPENDENT TRAVELER

Before you start your search for the lowest airfare, you may want to consider booking your flight as part of a travel package. What you lose in adventure, you'll gain in time and money saved when you book accommodations, and maybe even food and entertainment, along with your flight.

Package tours are not the same thing as escorted tours. Package tours are simply a way to buy the airfare, accommodations, and other elements of your trip (such as car rentals, airport transfers, and sometimes even activities) at the same time and often at discounted prices—kind of like one-stop shopping. Packages are sold in bulk to tour operators—who resell them to the public at a cost that drastically undercuts standard rates.

RECOMMENDED PACKAGE TOUR OPERATORS

One good source of package deals is the airlines themselves. Most major airlines offer air/land packages, including **American Airlines Vacations** (✆ 800/321-2121; www.aavacations.com), **Continental Airlines Vacations** (✆ 800/301-3800; www.coolvacations.com), **Delta Vacations** (✆ 800/654-6559; www.deltavacations.com), **United Vacations** (✆ 888/854-3899; www.unitedvacations.com), and **US Airways Vacations** (✆ 800/455-0123 or 800/422-3861; www.usairwaysvacations.com).

Another good bet is **Southwest Airlines** (✆ **800/243-8372;** www.swavacations.com), which has dozens of flights in and out of Las Vegas every day. Sheer volume of flights allows them to offer some relatively inexpensive vacation deals with lots of options in terms of travel time and hotels.

Vacation Together (✆ **877/444-4547;** www.vacationtogether.com) allows you to search for and book packages offered by a number of tour operators and airlines.

The **United States Tour Operators Association**'s website (www.ustoa.com) has a search engine that allows you to look for operators that offer packages to a specific destination.

Travel packages are also listed in the travel section of your local Sunday newspaper. **Liberty Travel** (✆ **888/271-1584;** www.libertytravel.com), one of the biggest packagers in the Northeast, often runs full-page ads in Sunday papers. Or check ads in the national travel magazines such as *Arthur Frommer's Budget Travel Magazine, Travel + Leisure, National Geographic Traveler,* and *Condé Nast Traveler.*

If you're unsure about the pedigree of a smaller packager, check with the Better Business Bureau in the city where the company is based, or go online to **www.bbb.org**. If packagers won't tell you where they're based, don't fly with them.

The biggest hotel chains, casinos, and resorts also offer package deals. If you already know where you want to stay, call the resort itself and ask whether it offers land/air packages.

THE PROS & CONS OF PACKAGE TOURS

Packages can save you money because they are sold in bulk to tour operators, who sell them to the public. They offer group prices but allow for independent travel. The disadvantages are that you're usually required to make a large payment upfront; you may end up on a charter flight; and you have to deal with your own luggage and with transfers between your hotel and the airport, if transfers are not included in the package price. Packages often don't allow for a wide range of choices (the hotels may be unremarkable and are usually located more for the packager's convenience than for yours), or have a fixed itinerary that doesn't allow for an extra day of shopping. Some packages offer a better class of hotels than others. Some offer the same hotels for lower prices than their competitors. Some offer flights on scheduled airlines and others book charters. In some packages, your choices of travel days may be limited. Some packages let you choose between escorted vacations and independent vacations; others allow you to add on a few guided excursions or escorted day trips (also at prices lower than if you booked them yourself) without booking an entirely escorted tour. Your choice of travel days may be limited as well. Which package is right for your family depends entirely on what you want. Prices vary according to the season, seat availability, hotel choice, whether you travel midweek or on the weekend, and other factors.

QUESTIONS TO ASK IF YOU BOOK A PACKAGE TOUR

- What are the **accommodations choices** available and are there price differences? Once you find out, look them up in this guide and check their rates for your specific dates of travel online.
- What **type of room** will you be staying in? Don't take whatever is thrown your way. Request a nonsmoking room, a quiet room, a room with a view, or whatever you fancy.
- Look for **hidden expenses.** Ask whether airport departure fees and taxes are included in the total cost.

11 TIPS ON FLYING WITH YOUR CHILDREN

SAFE SEATS FOR KIDS

The practice of allowing children younger than 2 to ride for free on a parent's lap is still allowed. The FAA has yet to require all children under 40 pounds to have their own tickets and be secured in a child seat.

At press time, with jet fuel prices rising and airlines struggling, a number of them have dropped their discounted tickets for children 2 years of age or younger who occupy a separate adjacent seat in a restraining device. Be sure to check with your airline to find out the latest policy.

For now, if a seat adjacent to yours is available, your "lap child" can sit there free of charge. When you check in, ask if the flight is crowded. If it isn't, explain your situation to the agent and ask whether you can reserve two seats—or simply move to two empty adjacent seats once the plane is boarded. (You might want to shop around before you buy your ticket and deliberately book a flight that's not very busy for this reason—ask the reservationist which flights tend to be most full and avoid those.) Only one extra child is allowed in

Kids with Colds

It's difficult for kids to make their ears pop during takeoff and landing, because the eustachian tube is especially narrow in children. This passage becomes even tighter when kids are sick and their mucous membranes are swollen, which can make ascent and descent on planes especially painful—even dangerous—for a child with congested sinuses. If your little one is suffering from a cold or the flu, it's best to stay grounded to recuperate, if that's an option. (If you simply must travel with your child as scheduled, give him an oral child's decongestant an hour before ascent and descent or administer a spray decongestant before and during takeoff and landing.)

each row, however, due to the limited number of oxygen masks.

On international journeys, children can't ride free on parents' laps. On flights overseas, a lap fare usually costs 10% of the parent's ticket. Children who meet the airline's age limit (which ranges from 11–15 years old) can purchase international fares at 50% to 75% of the lowest coach fare in certain markets. Some of the foreign carriers make even greater allowances for children. Note, however, that children riding for free will usually not be granted any baggage allowance.

Some airlines offer child meals, if requested in advance, for ticketed babies. All major airlines except Alaska and Southwest will warm bottles on request.

Alaska Airlines lets babies fly as soon as they're born, but most airlines require that an infant be 2 weeks old to travel, though American and Continental require only that the child be 7 days old. (Bring a birth certificate if you're traveling with a very young baby to avoid any possible problems.)

CHILD SEATS: THEY'RE A MUST

The National Transportation Safety Board says that the deaths of several children and injury to a number of others could have been prevented had the children been sitting in restraint systems during their flights. Even in the event of moderate turbulence, children sitting on a parent's lap can be thrust forward and injured. When you consider that a commercial aircraft hits a significant amount of turbulence at least once a day on average, you'd do well to think about investing a few hundred dollars for a safety seat. In the event of an accident, unrestrained children often don't make it—even when the parent does. Experience has shown that it's impossible for a parent to hold onto a child in the event of a crash, and children often die of impact injuries. Sudden turbulence is a real danger to a child who is not buckled into his own seat belt or seat restraint. According to *Consumer Reports Travel Letter,* the most common flying injuries result when unanticipated turbulence strikes and hurtles passengers from their seats.

The FAA recommends that children under 20 pounds ride in a rear-facing child-restraint system and says children that weigh 20 to 40 pounds should sit in a forward-facing child restraint system. Children over 40 pounds should sit in a regular seat and wear a seat belt.

All child seats manufactured after 1985 are certified for airline use, but make sure your chair will fit in an airline seat—it must be less than 16 inches wide. You may not use booster seats or seatless vests or harness systems on airplanes. Safety seats must be placed in window seats—except in exit rows, where they are prohibited, so as not to block the passage of other travelers in the case of an emergency.

The airlines themselves should carry child safety seats on board. Unfortunately, most don't. To make matters worse, overzealous flight attendants have been known to try to keep safety seats off planes. One traveler recounts in the November 2001 issue of *Consumer Reports Travel Letter* how a Southwest attendant attempted to block use of a seat because the red label certifying it as safe for airline use had flaked off. That traveler won her case by bringing the owner's manual and appealing to the pilot—you should do the same.

Getting safety seats on an international flight may be even more difficult. Ask to make sure you can use your safety seat when you book a flight on a foreign airline.

If you can't afford the expense of a separate ticket, book a ticket toward the back of the plane at a time when air travel is likely to be slowest—and the seat next to you is most likely to be empty. The reservationist should also be able to recommend the best (meaning the least busy) time for you to fly.

CHILDREN TRAVELING SOLO

Although individual airline policies differ (check with the specific airline for details), for the most part, children aged 5 to 11 pay the regular adult fare and can travel alone as unaccompanied minors on domestic flights only with an escort from the airlines—a flight attendant who seats the child, usually near the galley, where the flight crew is stationed; watches over the child during the flight; and escorts the child to the appropriate connecting gate or to the adult who will be picking up the child. Unaccompanied minors typically board first and disembark last.

On domestic flights, the service costs between $30 and $75, depending on the airline and whether the child will have to change planes. On all the major airlines, several children traveling together from the same family will have to pay only one fee.

Unaccompanied children are never left alone; escorts stay with them until turning them over to an escort on the connecting flight or to a designated guardian.

In order to accompany your solo traveling child to the gate you will need to obtain a gate pass from the check-in counter of your airline. Present the gate pass along with photo ID at the security checkpoint and you will be allowed onto the concourse. For questions concerning airport security contact the **Transportation Security Administration** at © **866/289-9673** or check out **www.tsa.gov**.

Airlines require attending adults to furnish a name, address, and government-issued photo ID. The adult who drops the child off at the airport must designate then the name and address of the adult who is authorized to pick the child up. At the destination city, the airline will not release the child to anyone but the authorized adult, after receiving a signature and seeing a photo ID.

Children aged 5 to 7 generally may travel unaccompanied on direct and nonstop flights only; in other words, they're not allowed to change planes for connecting flights at that age (though Northwest and Delta do allow all children to travel on connecting flights). Children aged 8 to 14 may make connecting flights with an escort, with the exception of Southwest and America West, which do not allow any unaccompanied child under the age of 12 to take a connecting flight.

Children 15 and older are considered adults and may travel without an escort on every major airline. However, even if the children are over age 14, they still qualify for assistance from the airline for the extra fee. Southwest is the only airline that does not allow children to use the escort service once they are able to fly without one, at age 12.

Because airlines want to avoid the responsibility of having to shepherd children overnight, minors are usually not allowed to take the last connecting flight of the day, when the risk of missed connections is greatest. Minors are usually not allowed to travel on standby, and they must have confirmed reservations.

On connecting flights, ask when you book whether the child will be flying on more than one airline. (Due to airline code-sharing alliances, your child may end up on a Northwest aircraft, even though you booked the flight through Continental.) If so, make sure you know each airline's policy for unaccompanied minors. Once you receive the ticket, review it yourself to make sure the city of origin and the destination are accurate. Review the ticket carefully with your child and explain in simple terms how it works.

If you're booking a flight for your child, the airlines will request your name, telephone number, and address—along with the name, number, and address of the guardian who will meet your child at the destination city. An adult guardian must accompany the child to the gate or plane, furnish reasonable proof that another adult will meet the child at the final destination, and remain at the airport until the plane is in the air. The accompanying adult at the destination will have to sign a release form and furnish government-issued photo identification, such as a license or passport. If a child is unusually big or small, it's wise to bring a birth certificate to the airport as proof of age.

MINOR ORIENTATION

With stricter security measures at airports, parents must now get a gate pass from the ticket agent for permission to escort their children to the departure gate. (Adults picking up unaccompanied minors at arrival gates also need this pass.) If your child has never flown before, it makes sense to show up at the airport a little early to wander around, watch other planes take off and land, and prepare your child in advance for how flight is going to feel. Be sure to discuss the danger of talking to strangers—even if you have had the same discussion before. You will be allowed to escort your child to the gate, but not onto the plane.

Some airlines allow unaccompanied minors to board first, so the flight crew has more time to meet the child, orient the child to the location of bathrooms and emergency exits, store carry-ons, review safety procedures, and—kids love this part—introduce the child to the cockpit crew. Make sure minors understand that they should contact an attendant in case of any type of problem—from sickness, to a malfunctioning headset, to a bothersome neighbor. Be sure to introduce your child to the gate attendant and to ensure that he or she will receive help boarding if necessary.

Some airlines offer special meals for children, such as hamburgers, hot dogs, or peanut butter sandwiches, which must be ordered in advance when you make the reservation. It's still wise to send your child off with a bagged lunch, snack, and drinks. Also pack books and other entertainment in a carry-on and make sure your child knows how to get at them on board the plane.

Additionally, make sure your child has cash and knows how to make a collect phone call. In one place, record your child's name, your own name, address, and phone number, along with the names and phone number of your child's hosts at the final destination. Review the information with your child and place it in a safe purse, pocket, or neck pouch. Be sure, however, that your child knows not to share this information with strangers—not even a friendly seat neighbor in the cabin.

If your child is taking medication, it may be wise to postpone the trip unless you are certain your child is responsible for self-administering dosages properly—flight attendants are not allowed to administer drugs to minors.

EASING TRAVEL WITH THE TOTS IN TOW

Several books on the market offer tips to help you travel with kids. A reliable tome, with a worldwide focus, is ***Adventuring with Children*** (Avalon House; $15).

Family Travel Times (✆ **212/477-5524;** www.familytraveltimes.com) is an excellent online newsletter. Subscriptions are $39 a year, $49 for 2 years. Sample articles are available on the newsletter's website.

If you plan carefully, you can actually make it fun (or at least less stressful) to travel with kids.

- **Save yourself a good bit of aggravation by reserving a seat in the bulkhead row.** You'll have more legroom, and your children will be able to spread out and play on the floor underfoot. You're also more likely to find sympathetic company in the bulkhead area; families with children tend to be seated there.
- **Be sure to pack items for your children in your carry-on luggage.** In case you're forced to check one of your carry-ons, consolidate the children's things in one bag or in your purse. If you're forced to check a carry-on, be sure to keep the one that holds the kid's things. When you're deciding what to bring, ready yourself for the worst: long, unexpected delays without food, bathrooms without changing tables, airline meals that feature your children's least favorite dishes, and more.
- **Have a long talk with your children** before you depart for your trip. If they've never flown before, explain to them what to expect. If they're old enough, you may even want to describe how flight works and how air travel is even safer than riding in a car. Explain to your kids the importance of good behavior in the air—how their own safety can depend on being quiet and staying in their seats during the trip.
- **Pay extra careful attention to the safety instructions** before takeoff. Consult the safety chart behind the seat in front of you and show it to your children. Be sure you know how to operate the oxygen masks, because you will be expected to secure yours first and then help your children with theirs. Be especially mindful of the location of emergency exits. Before takeoff, plot out an evacuation strategy for you and your children in your mind's eye.
- **Ask the flight attendant whether the plane has any special safety equipment for children.** Make a member of the crew aware of any medical problems your children have that could manifest during flight.
- **Be sure you've slept sufficiently for your trip.** If you fall asleep in the air and your child manages to break away, all sorts of sharp objects could cause injury. Especially during mealtimes, it's dangerous for a child to be crawling or walking around the cabin unaccompanied by an adult.
- **Be sure your child's seatbelt remains fastened properly,** and try to reserve the seat closest to the aisle for yourself. This will make it harder for your children to wander off—in case, for instance, you're taking the red-eye or a long flight overseas and you do happen to nod off. You will also protect your child from jostling passersby and falling objects—in the rare but entirely possible instance that an overhead bin pops open.
- **Try to sit near the lavatory,** though not so close that your children are jostled by the crowds that tend to gather there. Consolidate trips there as much as possible.
- **Try to accompany children to the lavatory.** They can be easily bumped and possibly injured as they make their way down tight aisles. It's especially dangerous for children to wander while flight attendants are blocking passage

In-Flight Fun for Kids

With one of these children's game books on board, even the longest plane ride will go faster.

Gladstones Games to Go: Verbal Volleys, Coin Contests, Dot Duel, and Other Games for Boredom-Free Days
by Jim Gladstone
Retail price: $9.95
Ages 4 to 12
This book is full of entertaining educational games to help your kids while away the miles. Each game is highly engaging and entertaining and requires few materials and very little space.

Brain Quest for the Car: 1,100 Questions and Answers All About America
by Sharon Gold
Retail price: $11
Ages 7 to 12
This book features cards with questions about American geography, culture, and customs.

Vacation Fun Mad Libs: World's Greatest Party Game
by Roger Price
Retail price: $3.99
Ages 8 to 12
As suggested by the title, this book is chock-full of Mad Libs. Your kids will want to keep playing even after you've touched down.

with their service carts. On crowded flights, the flight crew may need as much as an hour to serve dinner, so it's wise to encourage your kids to use the restroom as you see the attendants preparing to serve.

- **Be sure to bring clean, self-contained, compact toys.** Leave electronic games at home. They can interfere with the aircraft navigational system, and their noisiness, however lulling to children's ears, will surely not win the favor of your adult neighbors (note, however that some airlines do offer personal video screens with in-flight games—check when you make your reservation). Magnetic checker sets, on the other hand, are a perfect distraction, and small coloring books and crayons also work well, as do card games like Go Fish.
- **Visit the library before you leave home and check out children's books about flying or airplane travel.** Geography-related books and coloring books that include their departure point and destination will also help engage them during air travel.
- **A portable CD or tape player with a few favorite recordings will also come in handy**—especially if you throw in some sleepy-time tunes. By all means, don't leave home without a favorite blanket or stuffed animal—especially if it's your kid's best friend at bedtime.
- **Some airlines serve children's meals first.** When you board, ask a flight

attendant if this is possible, especially if your children are very young or seated toward the back of the plane. After all, if your kids have a happy flight experience, everyone else in the cabin is more likely to as well.

- **You'll certainly be grateful to yourself for packing tidy snacks,** such as rolled dried fruit, which are much less sticky and wet and more compact and packable than actual fruit. Blueberry or raisin bagels also make for a neat, healthy sweet and yield fewer crumbs than cookies or cakes. Ginger snaps, crisp and not as crumbly as softer cookies, will also help curb mild cases of motion sickness. And don't forget to stash a few resealable plastic bags in your bag. They'll prove invaluable for storing everything from half-eaten crackers and fruit to checker pieces and matchbox cars.
- **Juice or cookies** will not only keep your kids distracted during ascent and descent—often the scariest parts of flight for a child—they will also help their little ears pop as cabin air pressure shifts rapidly. Juice (paper cartons travel best) will also keep them swallowing and help them to stay properly hydrated. Avoid giving young children gum or hard candies because sudden turbulence may cause them to choke.
- **If your children are very young, bring pacifiers.** The act of sucking will keep their ears clear. By the same logic, takeoff and landing are the perfect time for feedings. Your kids will be distracted from the deafening cabin noise, and their ears will pop more easily. If your schedule won't allow this, try placing drops of water on an infant's tongue, to facilitate swallowing. Don't forget to pack bottles and extra milk or formula as well, because these are unavailable on most aircraft. Many airlines prohibit flight attendants from preparing formula, so it's best to pack your baby's food premixed.

TASTELESS: DEALING WITH AIRLINE FOOD

Most airlines have cut back on food service recently—and even if you do get a "meal" on a domestic flight, it's likely to be a limp turkey sandwich. Your best bet is to brown-bag homemade sandwiches. Unlike fruit, for example, they have no leftover parts to throw away, and you won't have to tussle with airport security over silverware. But if you insist on eating economy-class cuisine, some tips follow:

- **Order a special meal.** Most airlines allow coach-class passengers to order from a range of special meals, including low-fat, low-cholesterol, vegetarian, and children's meals (usually a hamburger or hot dog). These meals aren't necessarily fresher than the standard ones, but at least you'll know what's in them. Call your airline 2 days before your flight to secure your meal. Then double-check that they're still available when you check in.
- **Become a vegetarian.** Dieticians and frequent flyers say vegetarian and vegan meals are often better than standard airline fare. Vegan meals skip cheese and sweets, leading to a healthier but more spartan platter.

In general, coach-class passengers now get meals only on flights crossing two thirds of the country or more; everyone else gets peanuts or other minibags of snacks.

Most low-fare airlines generally serve only snacks, even on cross-country flights, though some sell heartier fare onboard for somewhat inflated prices. At press time, a "kids' meal" on Song, for example, includes Nabisco Teddy Grahams, Nabisco Fruit Snacks, Goldfish Crackers, and Motts Strawberry Applesauce and costs $5.

THE ECONOMY-CLASS MEAL POLICIES OF MAJOR AIRLINES

- **Alaska:** Food served on flights of 3 hours or more. Meal times: breakfast 6 to 8:30am; lunch 10:30am to 1:30pm; dinner 4 to 7pm.
- **American:** Food served only on flights of 4 hours or more. In-flight meals can be purchased before the flight and taken on board. Breakfast 5 to 8:30am; lunch noon to 1pm; dinner 5:30 to 7pm.
- **Continental:** Food served on flights of 2 hours or more. Breakfast 7 to 9am; lunch 11am to 1pm; dinner 5 to 7pm.
- **Delta:** Food served only on flights of more than 5 hours or to Alaska or Hawaii. Times vary according to flight time.
- **Northwest:** Meals available for purchase on board during selected flights. Breakfast 6 to 9:45am; lunch 11am to 1:15pm; dinner 4:30 to 7:15pm.
- **United:** Food is available for purchase on flights of more than 3 hours. Breakfast 5 to 10am; lunch 11am to 1:30pm; dinner 4:50 to 7:30pm.
- **US Airways:** Food is available for purchase on flights of more than 3½ hours. Breakfast 6 to 10am; lunch 11am to 1pm; dinner 4 to 7:30pm.

12 PLANNING YOUR TRIP ONLINE

SURFING FOR AIRFARES

Tip: When searching for good airfares, remember that (with the exception of citywide conventions) Las Vegas is a weekend town. You'll save yourself a bundle if you can arrange to fly in and out on a weekday.

The "big three" online travel agencies, **Expedia, Travelocity,** and **Orbitz,** sell most of the air tickets bought on the Internet. (Canadian travelers should try Expedia.ca and Travelocity.ca; U.K. residents can go for Expedia.co.uk and Opodo.co.uk.) Each has different business deals with the airlines and may offer different fares on the same flights, so it's wise to shop around. Expedia and Travelocity will also send you **e-mail notification** when a cheap fare becomes available to your favorite destination. Of the smaller travel agency websites, **SideStep** (www.sidestep.com) has gotten the best reviews from Frommer's authors. It's a browser add-on that purports to "search 140 sites at once," but in reality beats competitors' fares only as often as other sites do.

Tip: Keep in mind that because several airlines are no longer willing to pay commissions on tickets sold by online travel agencies, the online agencies may either add a $10 surcharge to your bill if you book on that carrier—or neglect to offer those carriers' schedules.

Also remember to check **airline websites,** especially those for low-fare carriers such as Southwest, JetBlue, or AirTran, whose fares are often misreported or simply missing from travel agency websites. Even with major airlines, you can often shave a few bucks from a fare by booking directly through the airline and avoiding a travel agency's transaction fee. But you'll get these discounts only by **booking online:** Most airlines now offer online-only fares that even their phone agents know nothing about. For the websites of airlines that fly to and from your destination, go to "Getting There," earlier in this chapter.

Great **last-minute deals** are available through free weekly e-mail services provided directly by the airlines. Most of these are announced on Tuesday or

Wednesday and must be purchased online. Most are valid only for travel that weekend, but some (such as Southwest's) can be booked weeks or months in advance. Sign up for weekly e-mail alerts at airline websites or check megasites that compile comprehensive lists of last-minute specials, such as **Smarter Travel** (www.smartertravel.com). For last-minute trips, **site59.com** in the U.S. often has better deals than the major-label sites.

If you're willing to give up some control over your flight details, use an **opaque fare service** such as **Priceline** (www.priceline.com; www.priceline.co.uk for Europeans) or **Hotwire** (www.hotwire.com). Both offer rock-bottom prices in exchange for travel on a "mystery airline" at a mysterious time of day, often with a mysterious change of planes en route. The mystery airlines are all major, well-known carriers—and the possibility of being sent from Philadelphia to Las Vegas via Miami is remote; the airlines' routing computers have gotten a lot better than they used to be. But your chances of getting a 6am or 11pm flight are pretty high. Hotwire tells you flight prices before you buy; Priceline usually has better deals than Hotwire, but you have to play their "name our price" game. If you're new at this, the helpful folks at **BiddingForTravel.com** do a good job of demystifying Priceline's prices. Priceline and Hotwire are great for flights within North America and between the U.S. and Europe. But for flights to other parts of the world, consolidators will almost always beat their fares. ***Note:*** In 2004 Priceline added nonopaque service to its roster. You now have the option to pick exact flights, times, and airlines from a list of offers—or opt to bid on opaque fares as before.

SURFING FOR HOTELS

Shopping online for hotels is much easier in the U.S., Canada, and certain parts of Europe than it is in the rest of the world. Of the "big three" sites, **Expedia** may be the best choice, thanks to its long list of special deals. **Travelocity** runs a close second. Hotel specialist sites **hotels.com** and **hoteldiscounts.com** are also reliable. ***Tip:*** Always check the individual casino hotel websites, as they often feature deals you won't find anywhere else.

The best site for finding discounts on Las Vegas hotels is **Travelaxe.com.** Travelaxe allows you to download a free software program that compares room rates offered by more than a dozen of the top Internet discounters. You click on the price you like and the program will send you straight to

Tips Hey, Google, Did You Get My Text Message?

It's bound to happen: The day you leave this guidebook back at the hotel for an unencumbered stroll through [neighborhood in your destination], you'll forget the address of the lunch spot you had earmarked. If you're traveling with a mobile device, send a text message to ✆ **46645 (GOOGL)** for a lightning-fast response. For instance, type "carnegie deli new york," and within 10 seconds you'll receive a text message with the address and phone number. This nifty trick works in a range of search categories: Look up weather ("weather philadelphia"), language translations ("translate goodbye in spanish"), currency conversions ("10 usd in pounds"), movie times ("harry potter 60605"), and more. If your search results are off, be more specific ("the abbey gay bar west hollywood"). For more tips and search options, see www.google.com/intl/en_us/mobile/sms/. Regular text message charges apply.

the website offering it. And, unlike most websites, Travelaxe prices include hotel tax, so you actually see the total price of the room. Unfortunately the program works on PCs only.

Priceline and Hotwire are even better for hotels than for airfares; with both, you're allowed to pick the neighborhood and quality level of your hotel before offering up your money. Priceline's hotel product covers several of the major casino hotels, including The Venetian, The Mirage, and MGM Grand. Be sure to do your research before putting in a bid, however, because their prices aren't always the best available in Vegas.

BiddingForTravel.com has an excellent Las Vegas board in its hotel section. If you plan on bidding on Priceline, it's a must-stop. It also frequently posts hotel discount codes and available packages.

SURFING FOR RENTAL CARS

Although it primarily covers all things Disney, **Mousesavers.com** is the best site on the Internet for scoring great deals on rental cars.

Other good deals can also be found at rental-car company websites, although all the major online travel agencies also offer rental-car reservations services. Priceline and Hotwire work well for rental cars, too; the only "mystery" is which major rental company you get, and for most travelers the difference between Hertz, Avis, and Budget is negligible.

SMART E-SHOPPING

The savvy traveler is armed with insider information. Here are a few tips to help you navigate the Internet successfully and safely:

- **Know when sales start.** Last-minute deals may vanish in minutes. If you have a favorite booking site or airline, find out when last-minute deals are released to the public. (For example, Southwest's specials are posted every Tuesday at 12:01am CST.)
- **Go straight to the source.** After finding the best possible room rate on the Internet, check both the website and the reservations desk of the hotel in question. Ask whether a better rate is available by booking direct. Always call

Frommers.com: The Complete Travel Resource

For an excellent travel-planning resource, we highly recommend **Frommers.com** (www.frommers.com), voted Best Travel Site by *PC Magazine.* We're a little biased, of course, but we guarantee that you'll find the travel tips, reviews, monthly vacation giveaways, bookstore, and online-booking capabilities thoroughly indispensable. Among the special features are our popular **Destinations** section, where you'll get expert travel tips, hotel and dining recommendations, and advice on the sights to see for more than 3,500 destinations around the globe; the **Frommers.com Newsletter,** with the latest deals, travel trends, and money-saving secrets; our **Travel Talk** area featuring **Message Boards,** where Frommer's readers post queries and share advice (sometimes even our authors show up to answer questions); and our **Photo Center,** where you can post and share vacation tips. When your research is done, the **Online Reservations System** (www.frommers.com/book_a_trip) takes you to Frommer's preferred online partners for booking your vacation at affordable prices.

Online Traveler's Toolbox

Veteran travelers usually carry some essential items to make their trips easier. Following is a selection of handy online tools to bookmark and use.

- **Airplane Seating and Food.** Find out which seats to reserve and which to avoid (and more) on all major domestic airlines at **www.seatguru.com**. And check out the type of meal (with photos) you'll likely be served on airlines around the world at **www.airlinemeals.com**.
- **Intellicast** (www.intellicast.com) and **Weather.com** (www.weather.com). Both sites give weather forecasts for all 50 states and for cities around the world.
- **Mapquest** (www.mapquest.com). This best of the mapping sites lets you choose a specific address or destination, and in seconds, it will return a map and detailed directions.
- **Time and Date** (www.timeanddate.com). See what time (and day) it is anywhere in the world.
- **Universal Currency Converter** (www.xe.com/ucc). See what your dollar or pound is worth in more than 100 other countries.
- **Visa ATM Locator** (www.visa.com), for locations of PLUS ATMs worldwide, or **MasterCard ATM Locator** (www.mastercard.com), for locations of Cirrus ATMs worldwide.

the hotel's local number as opposed to a chain's central reservation number. When speaking to the hotel reservations desk on the phone, be sure to ask about specials. Because a given hotel manages its room inventory almost on a minute-by-minute basis, you'll often bump into deals that will never be offered on the Web.

- **Shop around.** If you're looking for bargains, compare prices on different sites and airlines—and against a travel agent's best fare. Try a range of times and alternative airports before you make a purchase.
- **Stay secure.** Book only through secure sites. Look for a key icon (Netscape) or a padlock (Internet Explorer) at the bottom of your Web browser before you enter credit card information or other personal data.
- **Avoid online auctions.** Sites that auction airline tickets and frequent-flier miles are the number-one perpetrators of Internet fraud, according to the National Consumers League.
- **Maintain a paper trail.** If you book an e-ticket, print out a confirmation, or write down your confirmation number, and keep it safe and accessible—or your trip could be a virtual one!

INTERNET ACCESS AWAY FROM HOME

Travelers have any number of ways to check their e-mail and access the Internet on the road (and your teens may be horrified at the thought of forgoing e-mail nowadays). Of course, using your own laptop—or even a PDA (personal digital assistant) or electronic organizer with a modem—gives you the most flexibility. But even if you don't have a computer, you can still access your e-mail from cybercafes (or even from your own hotel room).

Digital Photography on the Road

Many travelers are going digital these days when it comes to taking vacation photographs. Not only are digital cameras left relatively unscathed by airport X-rays, but with digital equipment you don't need to lug armloads of film with you as you travel. In fact, nowadays you don't even need to carry your laptop to download the day's images to make room for more. With a **media storage card,** sold by all major camera dealers, you can store hundreds of images in your camera. These memory cards come in different configurations—from memory sticks to flash cards to secure digital cards—and different storage capacities (the more megabytes of memory, the more images a card can hold) and range in price from $30 to over $200. (***Note:*** Each camera model works with a specific type of card, so you'll need to determine which storage card is compatible with your camera.) When you get home, you can print the images on your own color printer or take the storage card to a camera store, drugstore, or chain retailer. Or have the images developed online with a service like **Snapfish** (www.snapfish.com) for something like 25¢ a shot. See "Flying with Film & Video," p. 41.

WITHOUT YOUR OWN COMPUTER

It's hard nowadays to find a city that *doesn't* have a few cybercafes, and Las Vegas has its share. Although there's no definitive directory for cybercafes—these are independent businesses, after all—three places to start looking are at **www.cybercaptive.com**, **www.netcafeguide.com**, and **www.cybercafe.com**.

Competition, especially among hotels that offer meeting and convention facilities, has spurred the addition of computer terminals in most guest rooms. Those hotels, moreover, that do not provide direct connections now are scrambling to have them installed. Unless you opt for a small or budget hotel, you'll probably have Internet access from your hotel room.

Most major airports now have **Internet kiosks** scattered throughout their gates. These kiosks, which you'll also see in shopping malls, hotel lobbies, and tourist information offices around the world, give you basic Web access for a per-minute fee that's usually higher than cybercafe prices. The kiosks' clunkiness and high price means they should be avoided whenever possible.

To retrieve your e-mail, ask your **Internet Service Provider (ISP)** whether it has a Web-based interface tied to your existing e-mail account. If your ISP doesn't have such an interface, you can use the free **mail2web** service (www.mail2web.com) to access your home e-mail. For more flexibility, you may want to open a free, Web-based e-mail account with **Yahoo! Mail** (http://mail.yahoo.com) or **Microsoft's Hotmail** (www.hotmail.com). Your home ISP may be able to forward your e-mail to the Web-based account automatically.

13 TIPS ON ACCOMMODATIONS

For information on the various types of accommodations that you'll find in Las Vegas, see chapter 6, "Family-Friendly Accommodations."

TIPS FOR SAVING ON YOUR HOTEL ROOM

The rack rate is the maximum rate that a hotel charges for a room. It's the rate you'd get if you walked in off the street and asked for a room for the night. Hardly anybody pays these prices, however, especially in Vegas, where prices fluctuate wildly with demand, and there are many ways around them.

- **Don't be afraid to bargain.** Most rack rates include commissions of 10% to 25% for travel agents, which some hotels may be willing to reduce if you make your own reservations and haggle a bit. Get in the habit of asking for a lower price than the first one quoted. Always ask politely whether a less expensive room is available than the first one mentioned, or whether any special rates apply to you. You may qualify for corporate, student, military, senior, or other discounts. Be sure to mention membership in AAA, AARP, frequent-flier programs, or trade unions, which may entitle you to special deals as well. Find out the hotel policy on children—do kids stay free in the room or is there a special rate? If you belong to one of the slot clubs at a hotel casino, you may be able to secure a better deal on a hotel room. Of course, you will also be expected to spend a certain amount of time, and money, gambling there, which might not be practical with children. (See the "Sign Up to Save" box on p. 108 for more details on slot clubs.)
- **Rely on a qualified professional.** Certain hotels give travel agents discounts in exchange for steering business their way, so if you're shy about bargaining, an agent may be better equipped to negotiate discounts for you.
- **Dial direct.** When booking a room in a chain hotel, compare the rates offered by the hotel's local line with that of the toll-free number. Also check with an agent and online. A hotel makes nothing on a room that stays empty, so the local hotel reservation desk may be willing to offer a special rate unavailable elsewhere.
- **Remember the law of supply and demand.** Las Vegas hotels are most crowded and therefore most expensive on weekends. So the best deals are offered midweek, when prices can drop dramatically. If possible, go then. Business hotels in Downtown locations are busiest during the week, so you can expect discounts over the weekend. Avoid high-season stays whenever you can: Planning your vacation just a week before or after official peak season (or a large convention) can mean big savings. You can contact the **Las Vegas Convention and Visitors Authority** (**© 877/VISITLV** [847-4858] or 702/892-0711; www.visitlasvegas.com) to find out whether an important convention is scheduled at the time of your planned visit; if so, you might want to change the dates of your trip. Some of the largest and most popular conventions are listed in the "Major Convention Dates" box earlier in this chapter.
- **Look into group or long-stay discounts.** If you come as part of a large group, you should be able to negotiate a bargain rate, because the hotel can then guarantee occupancy in a number of rooms. Likewise, if you're planning a long stay (at least 5 days), you might qualify for a discount. As a general rule, expect 1 night free after a 7-night stay.
- **Avoid excess charges.** When you book a room, ask whether the hotel charges for parking. Many hotels charge a fee just for dialing out on the phone in your room. Find out whether your hotel imposes a surcharge on local and long-distance calls. A pay phone, however inconvenient, may save you money, although many calling cards charge a fee when you use them on pay phones. Finally, ask about local taxes and service charges, which could increase the cost of a room by 25% or more.
- **Watch for coupons and advertised discounts.** Scan ads in your local Sunday

newspaper travel section, an excellent source for up-to-the-minute hotel deals.

- **Consider a suite.** You can pack more people into a suite (which usually comes with a sofa bed), and thereby reduce your per-person rate. Remember that some places charge for extra guests.
- **Join hotel frequent-visitor clubs,** even if you don't use them much. You'll be more likely to get upgrades and other perks. A hotel-branded credit card usually gives its owner "silver" or "gold" status in frequent-guest programs for free.
- **Many hotels offer frequent-flier points.** Don't forget to ask for yours when you check in.
- **Investigate reservations services.** These outfits usually work as consolidators, buying up or reserving rooms in bulk, and then dealing them out to customers at a profit. You can get 10% to 50% off; but remember, these discounts apply to inflated rack rates that savvy travelers rarely end up paying. You may get a decent rate, but always call the hotel as well to see if you can do better.

Among the more reputable reservations services, offering both telephone and online bookings, are **Hotels.com** (© **800/2-HOTELS** [246-8357]; www.hotels.com); **Hotel Reservations Network** (© **800/364-0801;** www.hoteldiscounts.com); and **Quikbook** (© **800/789-9887,** includes fax-on-demand service; www.quikbook.com). Online, try booking your hotel through **Frommers.com** (www.frommers.com).

LANDING THE BEST ROOM

Somebody has to get the best room in the house. It might as well be you.

Always ask about a corner room. They're often larger and quieter, with more windows and light, and they often cost the same as standard rooms.

When you make your reservation, ask whether the hotel is renovating, pretty much a given in Las Vegas, where most of the hotels seem to have something old being torn out and something new going in its place. If this is the case, request a room away from the construction. Ask about nonsmoking rooms, rooms with views, and rooms with twin, queen-, or king-size beds. If you're a light sleeper, request a quiet room away from vending machines, elevators, restaurants, bars, and discos. Ask for one of the rooms that have been most recently renovated or redecorated, if that's possible. If you aren't happy with your room when you arrive, talk to the front desk. If they have another room, they may be willing to accommodate you. And, if you join the hotel's frequent-visitor club, you may qualify for upgrades.

Some other questions you may want to ask before you book a room include:

- What's the view like? Cost-conscious travelers may be willing to pay less for a back room facing the parking lot, especially if they don't plan to spend much time in their room.
- Do the windows open? Few hotels have windows that open more than just an inch, the notable exception being the Hard Rock Hotel & Casino.
- What is the noise level outside the room? Some hotels on the Strip can be noisy because of attractions on-site or close by. Rooms on lower floors, overlooking the Strip, can be loud, as can ones that open into the casino atrium.
- What's included in the price? Your room may be moderately priced, but if you're charged for sports equipment and other amenities, you could end up spending more than you bargained for.
- Is the hotel pool heated year-round? (Most pools in Las Vegas stop heating their pools in the fall and some close them down altogether in the winter.)
- Are airport transfers included in the price? Some Vegas hotels charge a small

fee, per person, for shuttles to and from the airport; others provide this service gratis.

- If it's off season, will any facilities be shut down while you're there?
- What programs are available for kids?
- How far is the room from the pool? From the elevator? We know one exercise fanatic who didn't mind skipping her workouts in Vegas because her room was almost a mile away (or felt like it), one-way, from the hotel's entrance. The distance issue will be magnified only when it comes to small kids (or parents who've been pushing strollers all day).
- What is the cancellation policy?

14 BABYSITTERS & CHILD-CARE CENTERS

BABYSITTERS

Major hotels can arrange a sitter for you from agencies with whom they frequently work; however, you may prefer to screen the sitter yourself. Keep in mind that babysitters, like all casino employees, must have a sheriff's card, which proves that they have undergone a 10-year background check. Sitters requested by a hotel must check in with the concierge, who will verify her ID and sheriff's card with their files.

When calling an agency yourself, ask for faxed proof that all employees have been cleared by the health department, the Clark County Sheriff, and the FBI, and that they know CPR.

Along with watching kids in your hotel room, sitters can—with your permission—take children to the pool and to see kid-appropriate shows, shopping, or on outings to arcades. You may want to consider having a sitter accompany you if you take a tour or simply as you stroll about as a family, especially if you have more children than adults in your party.

Sitters base their rates on the number of children and the number of families involved, meaning sets of parent(s). In other words, cousins don't count as the same family, but brothers, stepsisters, and half-siblings do. All services charge a 4-hour minimum.

Reputable sitters can be arranged by your hotel concierge: In order to work as a sitter in a casino hotel, like all casino employees, sitters must have a casino card, a form of ID that proves they have been cleared by law enforcement agencies to work in casinos and that they have a "clean record." If your hotel doesn't offer this service, you can try one of the following sitter services:

- In business since 1987, **Around the Clock Child Care** (**✆ 800/798-6768** or 702/365-1040) is a reputable company that clears its energetic, outgoing sitters with the health department, the sheriff, and the FBI, and carefully screens references. Charges for a sitter at most casino hotels are $65 for 4 hours for one or two children, $15 for each additional hour, with surcharges for additional children, children from different families, and on holidays. Sitters are on call 7 days a week, 24 hours a day, and they will come to your hotel. Call at least 3 hours in advance.
- At **Grandma Dottie's Babysitting** (**✆ 702/456-1175**), Grandma Dottie and her able crew of sitters—all with sheriff's cards and health cards—charge $55 for one or two children for the 4-hour minimum, and $12 for each additional hour, with surcharges for additional children, children from different families, and on holidays.

CHILD-CARE CENTERS

Four supervised activity centers (run by two different providers) for children serve casino hotel guests. Residents of Clark County must show current vaccination records; it's a good idea to have a copy of your child's with you. Your ID will be checked when you drop off and pick up your child. Under these facilities' licensing rules, at least one parent must stay on the gaming property while their child is at the center.

Rest assured that all staffs are trained and certified in CPR and first aid, and have undergone background checks. The maximum a child can stay at any supervised activity center is 5 hours. If you want your kids to munch on snacks (pizza, chips, sodas, juice, hot dogs), you can prepay for the food or trust your child with the cash.

KidsQuest is a chain of supervised play centers, and its six Las Vegas outposts are located at **Texas Station Gambling Hall & Hotel,** 2101 Texas Star Lane (✆ **800/654-8888** or 702/631-1000); **Boulder Station,** 4111 Boulder Hwy. (✆ **800/683-7777** or 702/432-7777); **Sunset Station,** 1301 W. Sunset Rd. (✆ **888/786-7389** or 702/547-7777); **Palms Resort & Casino,** 4321 W. Flamingo Rd. (✆ **866/942-7777** or 702/942-7770); **Red Rock Casino Resort Spa,** 11011 W. Charleston Blvd. (✆ **800/797-8777** or 702/797-7646); and **Santa Fe Station,** 4949 N. Rancho Dr. (✆ **800/658-4900** or 702/658-4966).

Other than the Palms, these casino hotels are way off the beaten path for most visitors, but locals visit them regularly to bowl, go to the movies, and gamble.

A fun, safe place to leave children for a few hours, KidsQuest has a giant soft slide/jungle gym, plus computers, games, and toys. For safety reasons, each child receives a sticker with his or her name and a SKU bar code, which is copied onto the parent's receipt. The hourly rate for children from 3 to 12 years old is $6.25 per

What Parents Can Do in Vegas If They Have a Sitter/Child Care

Being a family is great, but sometimes parents want to have fun on their own, and Las Vegas is certainly the place to do it. Gambling is one of the first things that comes to people's minds when they think of Vegas (see our brief discussion on p. 246), so go ahead, drop three bucks in a Megabucks machine and see whether you hit the jackpot. Chances are 1 in 50,000,000 that you will.

Or maybe you'd prefer to spend your time and money catching up on the spectacular adult-oriented shows for which Vegas is famous. If topless women in feather headdresses don't appeal to you, perhaps you'd rather see *Mystère, O,* Bette Midler, or other headliners (see chapter 11, "Entertainment for the Whole Family," and especially the section called "What to Do If You've Gotten a Babysitter," p. 245) as a couple, rather than in a group.

And then, of course, there's the food: Las Vegas has top-notch restaurants with plenty of romantic appeal (see chapter 7, "Family-Friendly Dining," and especially the section called "Just the Two of Us: Romantic Dining," p. 169), so take a night off and rediscover the fun of dating again. Enjoy!

hour from Monday to Thursday. Friday through Sunday, it costs $7.40 per hour, with a 2-hour minimum. Reservations must be made for children 6 weeks to 2½ years old, and their rate is $6.65 per hour with a 2-hour minimum from Monday through Thursday and $7.65 per hour with a 2-hour minimum from Friday though Sunday. KidsQuest is open Sunday through Thursday from 9am to 11pm and Friday through Saturday from 9am to 1am.

The **South Coast Hotel & Casino,** 9777 Las Vegas Blvd S. (✆ **702/796-7111**) has a Kid's Tyme Child Care Facility available to its guests. It offers an in-house babysitting service with a 3-hour maximum, though games and a climbing gym are available for the kids to use.

Accepting children ages 2½ to 12 years old, the Kid's Thyme child-care center at the **Orleans Hotel & Casino,** 4500 W. Tropicana Ave. (✆ **800/675-3267** or 702/365-7111), has the most reasonable rates, and allows you to leave your children for as little as 15 minutes. Their maximum is 5 hours. Children must be completely toilet trained: no pull-ups or diapers allowed. A record of up-to-date immunizations is required. Hourly rates are $6 per child, no minimum stay; you'll get a $1 per hour discount if you show an Orleans gaming card at checkout. Facilities include a movie room, supervised arts and crafts, a jungle gym, a playroom, and a small games arcade.

4

Suggested Las Vegas Itineraries for Families

Possible Las Vegas itineraries for families number in the thousands. The three main itineraries we present in this chapter blend free sights and attractions with those that charge admission. Because it's easy to wear yourself out touring Las Vegas, our itineraries are designed to last about 6 hours, including a lunch break. This should leave ample time for a nap or swim at your hotel before dinner.

The attractions and sights in the itineraries are, in our opinion, the best Las Vegas has to offer. Understand, however, that the itineraries are created to help you have a good time. They're not cast in stone. It's your day—if there's a sight or attraction on an itinerary that doesn't interest you, skip it or substitute something else. Conversely, if you bump into something that interests you, but it isn't on the itinerary, go ahead and check it out. In general, feel free to customize the itineraries to better suit your needs. Also, you don't have to complete an itinerary or do it all in 1 day. How much you see will depend on the size of your group, how fast you move, and how often you stop for breaks, meals, or to experience sights and attractions not included in the itineraries.

Understand too that in Las Vegas less is sometimes more. Don't pack so much into your touring agenda that you wear yourself out. If you stayed a month you still couldn't see and do everything. So relax and sample Las Vegas in small bites with plenty of rest in between.

TOP PICKS FOR KIDS 7 & UNDER All of our itineraries demand more walking than the average 7-and-under child can handle. In addition, Las Vegas is not a great place for strollers. Add to the above the fact that the best sights and attractions for the under-7 crowd are spread all over creation, and you'll understand how difficult it is to work up an itinerary for them. Even if you have a car, hitting the best 7-and-under sights involves more logistics than fun. Listed below are our recommendations for this age group. We suggest that you try two or three of those most convenient to your hotel:

- Bonnie Springs Ranch/Old Nevada, for ages 4 and up. See p. 272.
- Circus acts at Circus Circus, free, for all ages. See p. 171.
- Fountains of Bellagio at Bellagio, free, for all ages. See p. 172.
- Fremont Street Experience, free, for ages 4 and up. See p. 172.
- Kiddie rides at Adventuredome, at Circus Circus, for ages 3 and up. See p. 180.
- Lied Discovery Children's Museum, for ages 4 and up. See p. 176.
- Playing on the rocks at the Red Rock Canyon National Conservation Area, for ages 3 and up. See p. 268.
- Siegfried & Roy Secret Garden and Dolphin Habitat at The Mirage, for all ages. See p. 178.
- Southern Nevada Zoological-Botanical Park, for all ages. See p. 174.
- Stratosphere Tower Observation Deck, for ages 4 and up. See p. 118.
- Stuffed animals and fish at Bass Pro Shops Outdoor World in Silverton, free, for all ages. See p. 187.

- The Birdman of Las Vegas at the Hawaiian Marketplace near the MGM Grand, free, for ages 3 and up. See below.
- The Lion Habitat at the MGM Grand, free, for all ages. See p. 172.

1 THE HEART OF THE STRIP: EAST SIDE

This tour covers the opulent, extravagantly entertaining world of the Strip, traveling north on the east side of the boulevard. Be forewarned that Strip hotels are huge. It can take, for example, 10 minutes to walk from the sidewalk in front of Caesars Palace to the hotel's coffee shop. Also, while you can do a quick walk-through of a major Strip property in about 25 minutes, a thorough exploration, depending on the hotel, might require a couple hours. This tour is recommended for children ages 8 and up and covers approximately 3 miles, so wear shoes appropriate for hiking. ***Start:*** *New York–New York at 10:30am.*

❶ New York–New York

Start the itinerary at the corner of Tropicana and the Strip in front of **New York–New York** (p. 105). Check out the **Statue of Liberty, Brooklyn Bridge, Empire State Building,** and other New York icons that form the front and facade of the hotel.

Take the escalator from the sidewalk to the second-floor entrance, then descend to the casino floor and (keeping to the far right) proceed along the edge of the casino to the New York neighborhood street scenes, especially the (Greenwich) Village Eateries area, where you can grab a bite. Optional: If you're a roller coaster fan, consider trying the **Manhattan Express** (p. 181) before departing ($13 per person—certainly no bargain). Make a grand circuit by staying on the perimeter of the casino.

Exit New York–New York on the second level where you entered. Cross the pedestrian bridge to the:

❷ MGM Grand

Once inside the MGM Grand, descend to the ground level and enjoy the **Lion Habitat.** Take the Studio Walk to the back of the building, stopping off at the arcade along the way. Have lunch here at the food court, Rainforest Cafe, or one of the many restaurants; if it's a buffet you want, skip this one and head for Planet Hollywood. Be ready to continue the itinerary by 12:45pm.

Exit the MGM Grand via the ground-floor Strip entrance and turn right.

❸ Hawaiian Marketplace or Miracle Mile Shops (2 options)

If a Friday, Saturday, or Sunday, stop at the **Hawaiian Marketplace** for the 1pm free performance of the Birdman of Las Vegas. Rare, exotic, and endangered birds talk and fly in this educational and fast-paced show.

Continue north on the Strip to **Planet Hollywood** (p. 106) and the **Miracle Mile Shops** (p. 209). In 2007 the Arabian Nights theme was replaced in a total renovation with a hip, Hollywood theme. Take a stroll though the mall. If you haven't had lunch yet, try the Planet Hollywood Spice Market Buffet, one of the best buffets in Las Vegas.

Exiting Planet Hollywood, continue north on the Strip to:

❹ Paris Las Vegas

Take a quick tour of **Paris Las Vegas** (p. 112). Take the elevator up the **Eiffel Tower** replica for a super view of the Strip. Adults are charged $10; children ages 4 to 11 and seniors 65 and older pay $7 (before 7:30pm, $12/$10 after).

Quick Takes: Itineraries by Kids' Age Groups

FOR TODDLERS TO AGE 6

If you have 1 day: We've grouped the major Vegas sites and things to do by location. You know your toddlers better than we do; if you think they can handle the trek from one location to another, you may expand your day to include more than one location.

If you're staying on the South Strip, start off at Mandalay Bay to visit **Shark Reef.** Then take the elevated tram up to Excalibur and its midway of carnival games. Then stroll over to the MGM Grand to watch the big cats in the **Lion Habitat** and eat at the **Rainforest Cafe.**

If you're on the North Strip, the **circus acts** and the **Adventuredome** indoor park, which has rides suitable for small children (both at **Circus Circus,** listed on p. 119), should certainly keep your children thrilled.

Guests staying on the Center Strip can visit the **Dolphin Habitat and Secret Garden. Caesars Palace** has the **Forum Shops,** which is an excellent place to take children of all ages. Definitely plan on eating **dinner at a buffet** in the resort closest to where you wind up, because you can't beat the variety and because at most of them, children under 4 eat free.

If you have 2 days: Make a point to wander through the **Flamingo Wildlife Habitat** that surrounds The Flamingo's pool area, so your kids can spot flamingos, swans, and koi fish, or eat at the buffet seated by the window and watch the birds. Afterward: Those staying on the North Strip should head south to see some of the offerings on the South Strip, such as Excalibur's midway and MGM Grand's Lion Habitat, while South Strip guests should explore Circus Circus's free big-top circus and the Adventuredome.

If you have 3 days: Along with the above itineraries, toss in a visit to the **Lied Discovery Children's Museum,** located north of the Strip, where kids are encouraged to poke, touch, and yell. Consider a babysitter at night so the adults can enjoy a show or a romantic dinner (see "What to Do if You've Gotten a Babysitter," in chapter 11).

If you have 4 days: Located about a half-hour outside of Las Vegas is **Bonnie Springs Ranch/Old Nevada.** You may not think that the shootout and simulated hanging are appropriate entertainment for your little ones. The town, however, is a nice replica of a Wild West frontier village.

FOR AGES 7 TO 9

If you have 1 day: Start your day with breakfast at the MGM Grand's **Rainforest Cafe,** check out the **Lion Habitat,** and then stroll to the **New York–New York Coney Island arcade.** Taller children should take a trip on the **Manhattan Express** roller coaster at New York–New York, along with catching other South Strip sights, including the **Shark Reef** at Mandalay Bay and the wonder of **Luxor,** or the medieval midway at **Excalibur,** along with the SpongeBob Squarepants motion simulator. Head to the North Strip and spend awhile watching the circus acts at **Circus Circus,** and make a point to see the view from the top of the **Stratosphere** and brave the rides there. The **fountain**

shows at the **Forum Shops** in Caesars Palace are a must. Eat at the food court or try one of the many restaurants in the casino or mall. If your children want even more nightlife after all this, fit in a viewing of The **Mirage's volcano** and the **dancing fountains** at **Bellagio.**

If you have 2 days: Visit Paris and a real pyramid via **Paris Las Vegas** and **Luxor.** Explore the history of M&Ms and check out the Coca-Cola memorabilia at the **Showcase Mall.** Then visit the Dolphin Habitat at The **Mirage** or take a trip to the **Lied Discovery Children's Museum,** plus go for a nighttime stroll Downtown for the **Fremont Street Experience.** Consider the magic of **Mac King (Harrah's).** Substitute Fremont Street for the early show of **Blue Man Group, *O,* Lance Burton, *KÀ,* LOVE,** or ***Mystère*** if you've got money to burn (see chapter 11).

If you have 3 days: No question about it—head for **Adventuredome** on Day 3. After a day riding the roller coaster and flume and playing laser tag, order up a pay-per-view movie along with a pizza or room service, then have the kids rest with a sitter while you parents enjoy a grown-up few hours on the town.

If you have 4 days: Red Rock Canyon, located less than a half-hour from Las Vegas, offers stunning desert landscapes. Take the 13-mile loop when the park first opens, and follow up with a jaunt to **Old Nevada/Bonnie Springs Ranch,** where you can watch live-action melodramas and explore the zoo.

FOR AGES 10 TO 13

If you have 1 day: Follow the Day 1 itinerary for 7- to 10-year-olds and add in an evening trip to **GameWorks** or a show, if the kids (and you) have the stamina.

If you have 2 days: Follow Day 2's itinerary for 7- to 10-year-olds, but add in a ride on the roller coaster at **New York–New York.**

If you have 3 days: Adventuredome will keep your child busy for hours. Then head over to the Rio for the ***Masquerade in the Sky*** show, or just go back to your hotel, where the kids can watch TV and rest. Consider a sitter so you can explore adult Las Vegas (see "What to Do if You've Gotten a Babysitter," in chapter 11).

If you have 4 days: Hoover Dam is (oh no) educational and impressive. If your kids balk at the idea of an hour-long tour of the dam, just let them look at rushing water and read the information at the visitor center, then head off to explore **Lake Mead** or **Valley of Fire State Park.** See chapter 12.

FOR KIDS OVER 13

The same itineraries as for the 10- to 13-year-olds, but consider adding in or substituting **Madame Tussaud's Wax Museum** or the **Hard Rock Hotel & Casino exhibits, Flyaway Indoor Skydiving,** and one of the many **impersonator shows** as options for the star-struck. Of course, an unlimited game pass at **GameWorks** might be just as much fun for some.

Back on the Strip, continue north. Pass Bally's (nothing interesting to see) and cross Flamingo Road. Poke your head in:

❺ Bill's Gamblin' Hall and Saloon

This is Old Las Vegas. There are no volcanoes or pirates, only serious gamblers, at 3595 Las Vegas Blvd. (✆ **800/634-6755** or 702/737-7111).

Moving next door, check out the neon over the entrance to:

❻ The Flamingo

The **Flamingo** hotel (p. 114) is the most photographed marquee on the Strip, and it appears in almost every TV show or movie about Las Vegas. Enter the casino and make your way back to The Flamingo's elaborate gardens and wildlife exhibits flanking the swimming complex. Don't be surprised if your children want to switch hotels after seeing The Flamingo's pool.

Continue north on the Strip, passing O'Shea's, Harrah's Las Vegas, and Casino Royale. But car buffs should stop at:

❼ The Imperial Palace

This hotel boasts one of the best and largest vintage car collections in the world. If you or your kids are into cars, this is a must see. Admission is $7 for adults and $3 for children ages 5 to 12 and seniors ages 60 and older; look for hawkers handing out coupons for free admission. A quick walk-through will take about 30 to 40 minutes, but real car buffs could spend an afternoon.

And now, ta-da!

❽ The Venetian

Spend some time surveying **The Venetian**'s (p. 113) entrance plaza before entering via the hotel lobby entrance. Work your way from the lobby to the casino and then to the **Grand Canal Shoppes** and its winding canal and indoor replica of St. Mark's Square. Optional: **Gondola rides** at $15 per person. Also optional at The Venetian is **Madame Tussaud's Wax Museum** (p. 176). Covering two floors and 28,000 square feet, the attraction is home to approximately 100 wax figures ranging from Tupac Shakur to Frank Sinatra. The cool thing is that you can touch the figures (or hug them or hold their hands), which make for some dynamite photos. Wait until your jealous sister sees you locked in an embrace with George Clooney. Admission is $25 for adults, $15 for children 7 to 12, free 6 and under. Discount admission coupons can commonly be found in freebie visitor magazines.

Depart The Venetian and continue north crossing Sands Avenue to:

❾ Wynn Las Vegas

The **Wynn Las Vegas** (p. 250) is a very adult place with beautiful landscaping, water features, floral displays, and fine art. One thing that may crank a youngster's tractor is the Ferrari and Maserati dealership (you have to pay a $10 admission for ages 13 and up just to go in and look). Another is the spiral escalator from the Parasol Bar to the lake level. But that's about it. You can easily skip the Wynn and end this tour at The Venetian.

Getting back: To return to New York–New York where the itinerary began, it's a 1.8-mile walk. Another option is to take the Wynn Las Vegas Convention Center shuttle to the Convention Center and from there take the Las Vegas Monorail back to the MGM Grand. The most convenient option is to have Dad walk back to the car, then pick up the rest of the family. Failing all that, there's always a taxi cab.

2 FROM MONTE CARLO TO THE TOP: THE WEST STRIP

This itinerary offers more fun on the Strip, traveling south on the west side of the boulevard. See "The Heart of the Strip: East Side" above for general notes. Note that this itinerary concludes with a meal at Top of the World atop the Stratosphere tower (✆ **702/380-7711;** entree range $28–$45), so you'll need to make reservations ahead of time (shoot for a half-hour before sunset). If you need time to go to your hotel before dinner, begin the itinerary at 10:30am (and if you go this route, eat an early lunch at the excellent Mirage Cravings Buffet). Like the East Strip tour, this one's appropriate for children ages 8 and up and includes approximately 2 miles of walking. ***Start:*** *TI–Treasure Island Hotel & Casino at 1pm.*

❶ Treasure Island

Begin at **Treasure Island** (p. 116) at the bridge to the main entrance where the *Sirens of TI* perform in the evening. Take a quick look around inside, heading up the escalator toward the parking garage; to the left is the tram for the short ride to The Mirage.

Ride south to the:

❷ Mirage

Exit the tram and pause to view lush front grounds of The **Mirage** (p. 115). Enter through the main entrance. Take an immediate right once inside to the hotel registration lobby for a look at the world-famous shark tank behind the registration desk.

Backtrack to the entrance and turn left toward the casino, passing through the rainforest atrium. The atrium helped The Mirage break new ground by being the first hotel to allow natural light to penetrate the timeless depths of the casino.

Take a quick walk-through tour, keeping in mind that this casino revolutionized Las Vegas and led the way to the 1990s building boom of megaresorts that continues today. Optional: Visit the **Siegfried & Roy's Secret Garden and Dolphin Habitat** (p. 178), home to white lions, Royal White tigers, and Atlantic bottlenose dolphins, among others. Admission is $15 for adults and $10 for children ages 4 to 12, one of the better attraction deals on the Strip. FYI, the exploding volcano doesn't crank up until 6pm.

Depart The Mirage through the south entrance. When you exit the building, turn right on the Strip.

Approaching Caesars Palace, take the first available entrance into the:

❸ Forum Shops

The **Forum Shops** (p. 208) area is a tidy rendition of the Appian Way and the Roman marketplace. This place will knock you out, and, if you try to see everything, it'll gobble up the rest of your day. The Forum Shops are linear, extending back from the Strip. We recommend catching at least one of the **animatronic Roman statue shows,** held on the hour. The **Festival Fountain show** (the first big fountain you encounter) is excellent, but the **Atlantis show in the Great Hall** (toward the back of the complex) is really over the top, with a fire- and smoke-filled battle that takes place around a 50,000-gallon aquarium. Best of all: Both shows are free.

Between the two show fountains is a third fountain in a large rotunda with a wide street branching off to the south at a right angle. After you're done touring the shopping complex, take this street to the amazing:

❹ Caesars Palace

Once in **Caesars Palace** (p. 110), keep to the far left and you'll pass the **Colosseum theater** where Bette Midler and Cher perform (through mid-2009, at least) and continue to the hotel registration area, and from there head to a shopping concourse that points you southeast toward the Strip.

Exit Caesars Palace via this concourse. Back on the Strip, cross the pedestrian bridge to:

❺ Bellagio

The signature dancing-fountain show (free) at **Bellagio** (p. 109) runs every half-hour Monday through Friday from 3pm and from noon Saturday and Sunday, and every 15 minutes nightly after 8pm.

Architecturally, Bellagio's most creative and interesting spaces are found in its signature conservatory, botanical gardens, and restaurants. As you walk in the main entrance, the primary garden is straight ahead. Although the opulent and oversize displays do change seasonably, there may be a new permanent resident. Rescued from a Florida development, a once-failing 100-year-old-plus banyan tree (the same kind of tree Buddha sat under when he gained enlightenment) is a powerful and poised backdrop for the theatrical floral whimsies of the supremely accomplished botanical staff.

Optional: The **Bellagio Gallery of Fine Art** (p. 187) is touted as Las Vegas's premier art gallery. Each year the gallery presents world-class exhibitions of artworks and objects drawn from internationally acclaimed museums and private collections, such as an impressive body of Impressionist works and the photographs of Ansel Adams. Adult admission is $15 while children older than 12, students, and seniors ages 60 and over pay $12; children 12 and under are free. Because the gallery is so popular, call ✆ **702/693-7871** for reservations before leaving home.

Depending on how fast you toured, the number of optional attractions you've experienced, and the time of year, it should be almost time for your Top of the World restaurant reservation. To commute to the Stratosphere, we recommend a cab. Give yourself extra time—traffic will be very heavy this time of day.

❻ Stratosphere

At the **Stratosphere** (p. 118), proceed up the escalator to one level above the main casino, then through the shopping area to the base of the tower and the double-decker high-speed elevators. With a reservation at **Top of the World** (see below), there is no admission charge to access the tower. Think of this benefit as a $10-per-person saving on the cost of dinner. There are three thrill rides at the top the tower. If before or after dinner you decide you want to ride, you can buy tickets on the floor below the rides' loading area. **Insanity** and the **Big Shot** are great rides and well worth the cost of the ticket. **X Scream** might look tame, but waiting an extra turn to get the front seats is well worthwhile. There's a 48-inch minimum height for **Big Shot** and a 52-inch minimum for the other two rides. Also, before or after dinner, you can enjoy the observation platform and lounge at no additional charge.

7 TOP OF THE WORLD ★★

The restaurant is pricey, but the food is dependably good. The real draw here, however, is the view. The restaurant revolves as you dine, providing truly spectacular vistas of the city and surrounding mountains. Reservations are a must. The best time to reserve is for about 30 minutes before sunset; you might have to wait a few minutes if you want a window seat. Note that if you have a restaurant reservation, you don't have to pay the normal fee to access the tower. Further, there's a separate elevator for restaurant guests. In Stratosphere, 2000 Las Vegas Blvd. S. ✆ **702/380-7711.**

3 BOMBS & BOULDERS

This tour is designed to get you away from the Strip and expose you to some of the area's natural and educational attractions. Needless to say, **a car is required.** Wear shoes appropriate for hiking and bring at least 1 liter of bottled drinking water per person. Tear a roadmap from one of the freebie visitor magazines; *What's On* has a particularly good one. This tour is recommended for children ages 8 and up and it covers 50 miles of driving and 3 miles of walking. ***Start:*** *Your hotel at 10am.*

❶ Atomic Testing Museum

Start your day at the **Atomic Testing Museum,** 755 E. Flamingo Rd. (less than 5 min. east of the Strip; ✆ **702/794-5161**), which charges $12 general admission, $9 for children ages 7 to 17, and free for children ages 6 and under. The museum will tell you everything imaginable about the atomic bomb and its development at the Nevada Test Site 50 miles northwest of Las Vegas. The museum's showstopper is a simulated bomb detonation as seen from a bunker.

Take Flamingo Road west, cross the Strip, then travel south (toward Los Angeles) on I-15. Turn onto 215 west and proceed to the Charleston Boulevard exit (about 22 miles). Turn right (east) on Charleston Boulevard to the:

❷ Red Rock Casino Resort Spa

This trend-setting casino opened in the spring of 2006. Park in the self-park garage. Take a short walk-through tour of this stunning property (p. 134), and enjoy lunch at the buffet, Mexican or barbecue restaurants, or the big food court.

After lunch, get back on Charleston Boulevard heading west. Cross over 215 and proceed to the:

❸ Red Rock Canyon National Conservation Area

At **Red Rock Canyon** (p. 267) start at the Visitor Center for an orientation on the remarkable geology, flora, and fauna of the Canyon. Pick up trail maps. (***Note:*** There is a $5-per-vehicle entrance fee.)

Take the one-way **Scenic Loop** (p. 271) stopping at the **Calico Tanks** (p. 271) trail head. Hike the Calico Tanks out-and-back trail (just under 3 miles round-trip). Most days you'll see very talented rock climbers perfecting their skills on the many rugged cliffs and boulders. Don't forget your water.

After the hike, complete driving the Scenic Loop. When the one-way loop dead-ends back at the two-lane road (NV 159), turn left to return to Las Vegas.

5

Getting to Know Las Vegas

Las Vegas means "the Meadows" in Spanish, and though it's hard to believe as you look at the vast expanses of asphalt and concrete, this entire area was once just another valley—albeit a large one—among the hundreds of valleys in this corner of the American Southwest. The largest city in Nevada, Las Vegas is located in the southernmost area of that wide flat plain.

The Anasazi first settled this area in a small central portion of the valley, surrounding a water hole. They were followed by Paiute Indians, pioneers, and eventually by ranchers, and then, in the 20th century, by gamblers and developers who built casinos, resorts, and housing.

One of the fastest growing cities in America, Las Vegas has concentrated the majority of tourist attractions in a centrally located area along Las Vegas Boulevard South, known as the Strip; this is the portion of the city you see in movies and on television, sparkling with bright and colorful lights. But there's more to Vegas than just the Strip, and while we do concentrate heavily in this book on those few glittering miles, we've also found a variety of attractions for families that will take you off that beaten, bedazzling path.

To the east of the Strip lies the Convention Center and a number of hotel chains focused on the business traveler; to the west are a few resort/hotels and several residential motels, plus stores, strip malls, and a family recreation center, as well as Las Vegas's Chinatown. Downtown, though it's been spruced up in recent years, is still oriented more to the hardcore gambler than families.

1 CITY LAYOUT

There are two main areas of Las Vegas: the **Strip** and **Downtown.** For the purposes of your family trip, this book focuses on the Strip and the areas around it, where the majority of attractions are located. Shuttles, city buses, and cabs can take tourists wherever they want to go outside this area, while visitors with cars should be able to quickly navigate their way to outlying sites.

Las Vegas Boulevard South (the Strip) is the starting point for addresses; any street crossing it will start with 1 East and 1 West (and go up from there) at its intersection with the Strip. Tropicana Boulevard is a major east-west route, as are Flamingo Road and Sahara Avenue.

Almost every new Strip hotel has an access road named after it, which should make finding the turnoff for your hotel easy.

Downtown has the Fremont Street Experience light and sound show, but that's the only attraction for families. There are no other amusements for children.

Confining yourself to the Strip is fine for the first-time visitor, but repeat customers (and you will be) should get farther out and explore.

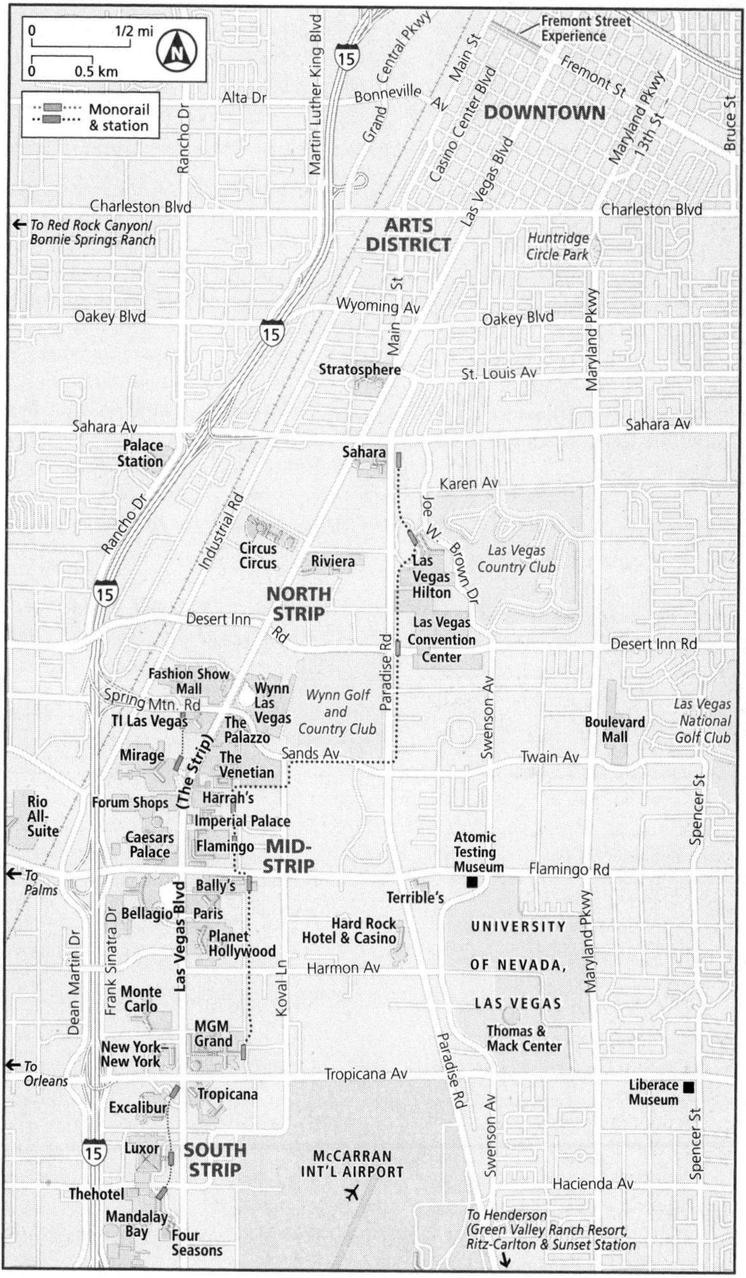
0
1/2 mi
0
0.5 km
N
Monorail & station
Fremont Street Experience
Fremont St
DOWNTOWN
Main St
Casino Center Blvd
Las Vegas Blvd
Maryland Pkwy
13th St
Bruce St
Grand Central Pkwy
Bonneville Av
Martin Luther King Blvd
15
Alta Dr
Rancho Dr
Charleston Blvd
Charleston Blvd
← To Red Rock Canyon/ Bonnie Springs Ranch
ARTS DISTRICT
Huntridge Circle Park
Wyoming Av
Main St
Oakey Blvd
Oakey Blvd
Maryland Pkwy
Stratosphere
St. Louis Av
Sahara Av
Sahara Av
Palace Station
Sahara
Karen Av
Rancho Dr
Industrial Rd
Joe W. Brown Dr
Circus Circus
Riviera
Las Vegas Hilton
Las Vegas Country Club
NORTH STRIP
Desert Inn Rd
Las Vegas Convention Center
Desert Inn Rd
Paradise Rd
Fashion Show Mall
Wynn Las Vegas
Wynn Golf and Country Club
Spring Mtn. Rd
TI Las Vegas
The Palazzo
(The Strip)
Swenson Av
Boulevard Mall
Las Vegas National Golf Club
Mirage
Sands Av
The Venetian
Twain Av
Rio All-Suite
Forum Shops
Harrah's
Imperial Palace
Spencer St
Caesars Palace
Flamingo
MID-STRIP
Atomic Testing Museum
Flamingo Rd
← To Palms
Bally's
Terrible's
Bellagio
Paris
Las Vegas Blvd
Hard Rock Hotel & Casino
UNIVERSITY OF NEVADA, LAS VEGAS
Planet Hollywood
Harmon Av
Dean Martin Dr
Frank Sinatra Dr
Koval Ln
Maryland Pkwy
Monte Carlo
MGM Grand
Thomas & Mack Center
New York–New York
← To Orleans
Tropicana Av
Paradise Rd
Tropicana
Liberace Museum
Excalibur
Swenson Av
Luxor
SOUTH STRIP
McCARRAN INT'L AIRPORT
Spencer St
Thehotel
Hacienda Av
Mandalay Bay
Four Seasons
To Henderson (Green Valley Ranch Resort, Ritz-Carlton & Sunset Station

Impressions

A few centuries from now archaeologists, studying the ruins of our civilization, will no doubt determine that Las Vegas was an important religious center, boasting dozens of massive temples to which pilgrims from afar brought bountiful offerings.

—Andres Martinez, *24/7: Living It Up and Doubling Down in the New Las Vegas*

THE STRIP

The Strip is probably the most famous 4-mile stretch of highway in the nation. Officially called Las Vegas Boulevard South, it contains most of the top hotels in town and offers almost all of the major showroom entertainment. First-time visitors will, and probably should, spend the bulk of their time on the Strip.

For the purposes of organizing this book, we've divided the Boulevard into three sections. The **South Strip** can be roughly defined as the portion of the Strip south of Harmon Avenue, including Planet Hollywood, MGM Grand, Mandalay Bay, Monte Carlo, New York–New York, Luxor, and several other megaresorts.

Center Strip is a long stretch of the street between Harmon Avenue and Spring Mountain Road, including Bellagio, Caesars, The Mirage, Treasure Island, Paris Las Vegas, Bally's, The Flamingo, Harrah's Las Vegas, The Venetian, and Palazzo, among other hotels and casinos.

North Strip stretches north from Spring Mountain Road all the way to the Stratosphere Tower and includes Wynn Las Vegas, The Riviera, Sahara, and Circus Circus, to name just a few of the accommodations and attractions.

EAST OF THE STRIP/CONVENTION CENTER

Paralleling the Strip to the east is Paradise Road, connected to the Strip by the Las Vegas Strip Monorail—which runs from Koval Lane to Sahara Avenue—as well as by road. The Las Vegas Convention Center is located on Paradise Road, as are the Hard Rock Hotel & Casino and the Las Vegas Hilton, among others.

Because Las Vegas is one of the nation's top convention cities (attracting more than 3.8 million conventioneers each year), the area around the Convention Center has really developed lately. The major hotel in this section is the Las Vegas Hilton, but you'll find many excellent smaller hotels and motels southward along Paradise Road. They offer close proximity to the Strip.

East of Paradise on Sahara Avenue, you'll find the Commercial Center, a large shopping center where many fine ethnic restaurants are located, along with an Asian market.

WEST OF THE STRIP

Hotels such as the Rio, Palace Station, Palms, Gold Coast, and the Orleans, along with timeshare developments and shops serving locals, are in this area, which includes Industrial Road/Dean Martin Drive and Decatur Boulevard. This is a far more suburban section of Las Vegas and, accordingly, the hotels and motels here can offer lower rates than those on the Strip. Running parallel to the Strip is Industrial Road, which turns into Dean Martin Drive at Twain Avenue and runs 9 miles south, providing a good north-south shortcut to avoid the often-clogged Strip. The fabulous International Marketplace (p. 222) is also located in this area.

Fun Facts **Bright Lights, Sin City**

More than 15,000 miles of neon tubing is used to light up the Strip and Downtown Vegas!

BETWEEN THE STRIP & DOWNTOWN

The area between the Strip and Downtown is a seedy stretch dotted with tacky wedding chapels, bail-bond operations, pawnshops, and cheap motels.

However, the area known as the **Gateway District** (roughly north and south of Charleston Blvd. to the west of Las Vegas Blvd. S.) is slowly but surely gaining a name for itself as an actual artists' colony. Studios, small cafes, and other signs of life are springing up, and we hope this movement lasts and grows.

DOWNTOWN

With the advent of the **Fremont Street Experience** (p. 172), Downtown has experienced a revitalization, though its hotels don't offer much in the way of anything for kids, so we don't recommend staying in this location with your family. Also, while there has been a strong effort to keep out unsavory elements, the area can still attract some unpleasant types. Nevertheless, the Glitter Gulch section of Fremont Street is clean, the crowds are low-key and friendly, and the light and music show—millions of light-emitting diodes (LEDs) attached to a 90-foot-tall, 4-block-long canopy that erupts to music throughout the evening—is as ostentatious as anything on the Strip. Las Vegas Boulevard runs all the way into Fremont Street Downtown, and beyond into North Las Vegas.

2 GETTING AROUND

For information on getting into town from the airport, see section 5, "Getting There," in chapter 3.

Once in town, it shouldn't be too hard to navigate your way up and down the Strip, where the hotels are noticeable landmarks. Luxor's pyramid is to the south and the Stratosphere, with its 1,149-foot-tall tower, anchors the Strip's north end.

That said, just because you know where you're going doesn't mean that it's easy to get there: Always allow plenty of time to travel to where you want to go, because sometimes just getting from your room to another part of your hotel can take 10 minutes or more, especially with children in tow. Outside your hotel, moving around is even more time-consuming: Resort properties are huge and what looks like it's just next door, across the street, or down the block is actually quite a distance. This, coupled with crowds wanting to see everything, can make walking along the Strip a slow process.

BY PUBLIC TRANSPORTATION

There are a number of free transportation services, courtesy of the casinos. A free elevated tram connects Mandalay Bay with Luxor and Excalibur; another connects Bellagio with Monte Carlo; still another links The Mirage and Treasure Island. Given how far apart even neighboring hotels can be, thanks to their size, and how they seem even farther apart on really hot days, these are blessed additions—and the more tourists who take them, the less traffic there might be on the Strip.

Tips Staying Off the Street

To make crossing the Strip safer and to help prevent traffic gridlock, pedestrian bridges and people movers have been built to help speed tourists on their way. Raised walkways, accessed from the street by escalators and elevators and from the mezzanine floors of many hotels, provide excellent photo opportunities. People movers, like those linking Excalibur and Luxor, glide tourists from hotel to hotel with a minimum amount of exertion, while monorails transport guests from property to property. It's possible to go from Mandalay Bay all the way to the Sahara without setting foot on the Strip sidewalk!

The $650-million **Las Vegas Strip Monorail** (**www.lvmonorail.com**), after numerous delays, finally began running in July 2004. Today, after considerable debugging, the monorail operates reliably. It runs between MGM Grand and the Sahara, with stops at Bally's-Paris, Flamingo-Caesars, Harrah's-Imperial Palace, Convention Center, Las Vegas Hilton, and Sahara. Covered walkways connect all the stations to the hotels and the Convention Center. Tickets cost $5 one-way, $12 for an all-day pass (the full 24 hr.), and $28 for a 3-day pass. This is an extremely convenient and comfortable way to travel along the Strip, though the North Strip casinos from The Riviera and Circus Circus are marginally served; it's a long walk from the monorail to the North Strip. Because the monorail stations are located 400 yards or more to the east of the Strip casinos they serve, expect a bit of a hike to access the stations (strollers might be in order for the smallest tykes or your little ones might be exhausted by the time you get to your destination). In fact, the monorail stations are located so far to the rear of the host casinos that it's faster to walk to your destination if it's less than a mile away.

The double-decker Deuce buses have served the Strip since October 2005. These are public buses operated by **Citizens Area Transit** (✆ **702/CAT-RIDE** [228-7433]), plying a route between the Downtown Transportation Center (at Casino Center Blvd. and Stewart Ave.) and a few miles beyond the southern end of the Strip. This is the least expensive "sightseeing tour" you'll ever take: The fare is $3 on the Strip Deuce bus, $1.25 for children 6 to 17 and seniors 62 and older, free for children 5 and under; you can also buy an all-day Deuce pass for $7 (through 2010). CAT buses also run commuter routes throughout the valley; fares are $1.75 off the Strip (going up to $2 in 2010), and $4 for an all-day pass (going up to $5 in 2010). CAT buses run 24 hours a day and are wheelchair accessible. Exact change is required, but dollar bills are accepted.

BY TAXI

Because cabs line up in front of all major hotels, they are an easy way to get around town. Cabs charge $3.30 at the meter drop and 30¢ for each additional 1/9 mile. A taxi from the airport to the Strip will run you $12 to $15, from the airport to Downtown $18 to $22, and between the Strip and Downtown about $10 to $12. You can often save money by sharing a cab with someone going to the same destination. (Up to five people can ride for the same fare.)

If you want to call a taxi, any of the following companies can provide one: **Desert Cab Company** (✆ **702/386-9102**), **Whittlesea Blue Cab** (✆ **702/384-6111**), and **Yellow/Checker Cab/Star Company** (✆ **702/873-2000**).

BY CAR

If you won't have your own car in Las Vegas, we recommend renting one. Your best bet for doing things together as a family is to get away from the Strip. Certainly there are family-friendly attractions on the Strip, but they're expensive and somewhat limited in number, especially if you're staying for more than a couple of days. Having a car will allow you to see Hoover Dam, Bonnie Springs, Mount Charleston, Red Rock Canyon, Lake Mead, and dozens of other memorable sights for less than you'd spend to ride two or three Strip roller coasters. You'll be able to sample some of the excellent local restaurants and economize on snacks and even meals by shopping at a supermarket. Many families stock a cooler in their hotel room with milk and orange juice so they can enjoy breakfast in their room. You can also rent a refrigerator at many of the major casino hotels for that purpose.

We should warn you that Las Vegas's growing population means a proportionate increase in the number of cars on its streets. Traffic is horrible and it's harder and harder to get around town with any certainty of swiftness. A rule of thumb is to avoid driving on the Strip whenever you can, and avoid driving at all during peak rush hours (8–9:30am and 4:30–6pm). That said, places with addresses some 60 blocks east or west from the Strip are actually a 10-minute drive away—provided there is no traffic.

A Word on Parking . . .

Free, but far from hassle-free, parking garages in Vegas range from the standard three- and four-story concrete boxes to dizzyingly huge, multilevel, multicolored, and multicoded labyrinths. That's why some are patrolled by men on bicycles; according to one guard with whom I've spoken, 80% of his job consists of helping people find the cars they parked and then lost. Here are some tips on making parking more of a pleasant experience:

- Only valet park if you have a 15- to 25-minute cushion when you leave: Valet parking may seem the quickest and easiest way to go, but in reality, it can be a huge hassle. Waits are particularly long if you try to retrieve your car after a show or even after the dinner hour in some of the plusher casinos. You'll be competing with the, oh, 150 to 300 people who also valet-parked that night, and they're just as eager as you are to get out.
- Write down the name, number, color, or code of your parking space: The reason I got to know that nice patrol-fellow so well is that I once lost my car for a good hour at the MGM Grand parking lot. For half an hour of that time, two patrol guys on bikes were searching for it with my license plate number. This is a long way of saying it's very easy to lose your car in these places, especially if it's a rental or if you've had a drink or two.
- Head to the casino parking if you're downtown: The public lots here are about the only ones in town that charge for parking. At the casinos, you may have to validate your ticket, but that's usually quite easily done (and won't even require a purchase on your part).

Tips **Quick Exits**

When visiting another hotel, tell the valet that you'll be only an hour, politely ask him "to keep it on the pad," then tip him a couple dollars as he takes your car. This usually ensures that you won't have to wait as long as a nontipper for you to get your vehicle back—a bonus with small children or in hot weather. Also, kindly tip the valet who returns your wheels. It's worth it!

Parking is usually a pleasure, because all casino hotels offer valet service (but not always; see below for parking tips). That means that for a mere $1 to $2 tip, you can pull up right to the door (though the valet usually fills up on busy nights). In those cases, you can use the gigantic, free, self-parking garages that all hotels have.

RENTING A CAR

National companies with outlets in Las Vegas include **Alamo** (✆ 877/227-8367; www.goalamo.com), **Avis** (✆ 800/230-4898; www.avis.com), **Budget** (✆ 800/527-0700; www.budgetrentacar.com), **Dollar** (✆ 800/800-3665; www.dollar.com), **Enterprise** (✆ 800/736-8227; www.enterprise.com), **Hertz** (✆ 800/654-3131; www.hertz.com), **Payless** (✆ 800/729-5377; www.paylesscarrental.com), and **Thrifty** (✆ 800/847-4389; www.thrifty.com).

Car-rental rates can vary even more than airline fares. The price you pay will depend on the size of the car, where and when you pick it up and drop it off, the length of the rental period, where and how far you drive it, whether you purchase insurance, and a host of other factors. A few key questions could save you hundreds of dollars:

- Are weekend rates lower than weekday rates? Ask whether the rate is the same for pickup Friday morning, for instance, as it is for Thursday night.
- Is a weekly rate cheaper than the daily rate? Even if you need the car for only 4 days, it may be cheaper to rent it for 7.
- Does the agency assess a drop-off charge if you don't return the car to the same location where you picked it up? Is it cheaper to pick up the car at the airport compared to a Downtown location?
- Are special promotional rates available? If you see an advertised price in your local newspaper, be sure to ask for that specific rate; otherwise, you may be charged the standard cost. Terms change constantly, and reservations agents are notorious for not mentioning available discounts unless you ask.
- Are discounts available for members of AARP, AAA, frequent-flyer programs, or trade unions? If you belong to any of these organizations, you may be entitled to discounts of up to 30%.
- How much tax will be added to the rental bill? Local tax? State use tax?
- What is the cost of adding an additional driver's name to the contract?
- How many free miles are included in the price? Free mileage is often negotiable, depending on the length of your rental.
- How much does the rental company charge to refill your gas tank if you return with the tank less than full? Though most rental companies claim these prices are competitive, fuel is almost always cheaper in town. Try to allow enough time to refuel the car yourself before returning it.

Some companies offer "refueling packages," in which you pay for an entire tank of gas upfront. The price is usually fairly competitive with local gas prices, but you don't get credit for any gas remaining in the tank. If a stop at a gas station on the way to the airport will make you miss your plane, by all means take advantage of the fuel purchase option. Otherwise, skip it.

Many packages are available that include airfare, accommodations, and a rental car with unlimited mileage. Compare these prices with the cost of booking airline tickets and renting a car separately to see if these offers are good deals. See section 10, "Packages for the Independent Traveler," in chapter 3 for more information on package deals.

Internet resources can also make comparison shopping easier. See section 12, "Planning Your Trip Online," in chapter 3, for tips on helpful websites.

Demystifying Renter's Insurance

Before you drive off in a rental car, be sure you're insured. Hasty assumptions about your personal auto insurance or a rental agency's additional coverage could end up costing you tens of thousands of dollars—even if you are involved in an accident that was clearly the fault of another driver.

If you already hold a **private auto insurance** policy, you're most likely covered in the United States for loss of or damage to a rental car and liability in case of injury to any other party involved in an accident. Be sure to find out whether you're covered in the area you're visiting, whether your policy extends to all persons who will be driving the rental car, how much liability is covered in case an outside party is injured in an accident, and whether the type of vehicle you're renting is included under your contract. (Rental trucks, sports utility vehicles, and luxury vehicles such as a Jaguar may not be covered.)

Most **major credit cards** provide some degree of coverage as well—provided they're used to pay for the rental. Terms vary widely, however, so be sure to call your credit card company directly before you rent.

If you're **uninsured,** your credit card may provide primary coverage as long as you decline the rental agency's insurance. This means that the credit card will cover damage or theft of a rental car for the full cost of the vehicle. If you already have insurance, your credit card may provide secondary coverage—which basically covers your deductible. *Credit cards will not cover liability,* or the cost of injury to an outside party and/or damage to an outside party's vehicle. If you do not hold an insurance policy, you may seriously want to consider purchasing additional liability insurance from your rental company. Be sure to check the terms, however: Some rental agencies cover liability only if the renter is not at fault; even then, the rental company's obligation varies from state to state. Bear in mind that each credit card company has its own peculiarities; call your own credit card company for details before relying on a card for coverage.

The basic insurance coverage offered by most car rental companies, known as the **Loss/Damage Waiver (LDW)** or **Collision Damage Waiver (CDW),** can cost more than $20 per day. It usually covers the full value of the vehicle with no deductible if an outside party causes an accident or other damage to the rental car. In all states but California, you will probably be covered in case of theft as well. (Las Vegas is the second-worst city in the nation for car theft, with an average of 52 cars stolen daily.) Liability coverage varies according to the company policy and state law, but the minimum is usually at least $15,000. If you are at fault in an accident, however, you will be covered for the full replacement value of the car but not for liability. In Nevada, you can buy additional liability coverage for such cases. Most rental companies will require a police report in

Tips Driving Safety

Because driving on the outskirts of Las Vegas—for example, coming from California or visiting Red Rock Canyon—involves passing through long stretches of uninhabited desert, you should take certain precautions: It's a good idea to check your tires, water, and oil before leaving; take at least 5 gallons of water in a clean container that can be used for either drinking or the radiator; pay attention to road signs that suggest when to turn off your car's air conditioner; and don't push your luck with gas—it may be 35 miles, or more, between stations. If your car overheats, do not remove the radiator cap until the engine has cooled. Once the temp has dropped, remove the cap slowly and add water to within an inch of the top of the radiator.

order to process any claims you file, but your private insurer will not be notified of the accident. Check your own policies and credit cards before you shell out money on this extra insurance, because you may be already covered.

Family-Friendly Accommodations

With more than 140,000 rooms for rent, including those in 18 of the nation's 21 largest hotels, Las Vegas should have more than enough room for you and your brood. But when a convention, holiday, fight, or other major event happens—and they do, almost weekly—all of a sudden, the rooms evaporate into the desert air, or at least skyrocket in price. However, with advance planning, you should be able to choose your vacation in a Vegas version of Paris, Venice, New York, ancient Rome, King Arthur's England, or simply a pleasant hotel with a gorgeous pool.

Hotel rooms in Vegas are low-priced compared to similar rooms in other vacation locations, but there are some drawbacks. Most hotels are casino-resorts, which means huge premises with long walks, through often-smoky casinos, to get between your room and anywhere else on the grounds. Minors cannot be unaccompanied at any time in casino areas, meaning that you'll have to walk with them whenever they want to go to the pool, the arcade, or the animal attractions.

Nongaming properties (yes, some places in Vegas actually do not have casinos) are located off the main drag, requiring a bit of planning and a car or cab in order for you and your kids to make it over to the Strip so that you can gape at all the wonderment it offers, such as volcanoes and talking statues. While these nongaming resident and apartment-style hotels, where each room comes with a fully equipped in-room kitchen, make it easy to cut meal costs by preparing food yourself, again, you will need a car to get to the market or convenience stores in order to take advantage of the pots, pans, and plates these hostelries provide.

Las Vegas's new identity as a resort location has yet to settle in completely. The pools at the self-proclaimed luxury resorts are often chilly, close early in the evening, and at most properties may partially shut down for half the year. Plus, some kids can quickly get bored with the whole pool experience, in which case, staying in a place with cool stuff to do, or at least an arcade and a lot of television stations to keep them occupied, is a good idea. Keep in mind that though these properties bill themselves as getaway locations with astounding shopping opportunities, there isn't a single bookstore in a hotel mall, so if your child likes to devour books on vacation, you should plan ahead and bring a supply or be prepared to make a special stop at the nearest bookshop (a Border's Express in the Fashion Show Mall). The same situation applies to CD stores, so it's a good idea to load up on music in advance.

The most important factors, after your family's needs and interests, naturally, are location and price, because at a certain point, most hotel rooms are surprisingly similar. Granted, some rooms are larger than others and some have nicer furnishings, but basically, your room is only a place to rest between sightseeing adventures.

Most of the time in Las Vegas, the difference between paying $69 for a room

Tips A Web Wonder

A little-known gem, **Travelaxe (www.travelaxe.com)**, offers a free, downloadable price-comparison program that will make your Las Vegas hotel search infinitely easier. The program searches the hotels and a host of discount travel websites for the best prices for your travel dates. Click on the price you like, and the program will send you straight to the website offering it. And, unlike most websites, Travelaxe prices include hotel tax, so you actually see the total price of the room.

and $250 for the same bed/bathroom/TV combo is the date you plan to stay, because Las Vegas has incredibly fluid room prices. Be aware that there is no standard for what is considered a child. Some hotels charge an extra-person fee for anyone over 7; others feel the cut-off age is 17; and some grinches will charge no matter how old or young the extra person. At certain properties, the extra-person fees are seasonal or changeable, based on "specials." Don't be afraid to ask.

One thing you'll notice is that while, in many cities, hotel chains have the corner on ultraluxurious or at least large substantial properties, in Las Vegas with its abundance of over-the-top supersize resorts, the usual standard-name hotels recede into the background. Sure, they're still nice (especially if you're on one of their frequent-visitor programs and get points for laying your head on the pillow), but they pale by comparison to the pyramids and palaces that are almost minicities unto themselves.

The one thing that is fixed about room prices is the tax; as of press time, you will pay an additional 9% tax in Clark County (where you'll find the major Strip hotels), and 10% in nearby Henderson for hotel room taxes.

You should know that price might not have anything to do with the quality of the hotel's clientele. Even the nicest hotels can have rowdy—well, let's be blunt, drunken—guests, especially if there's a holiday, convention, or big sporting event in town. And because the rooms are mass-produced—no matter how nice the hotel—you will hear plumbing noises and conversations (and sometimes more) from next door, along with the pitter-patter of feet in the room above you.

Many of the classic Las Vegas hotels have fallen to the wrecking ball and demolition experts, or have been renovated so they no longer resemble their old images. In their places are the new kids on the block—bigger, but not necessarily better.

Everyone thought entrepreneur Steve Wynn was nuts when he envisioned, then built, the huge Mirage, with its jungle foliage and erupting volcano. But the naysayers were mistaken; The Mirage was a success and the race to build successively more stupendous resorts was on. Excalibur, the MGM Grand, and Treasure Island began courting families, but the bottom-line executives quickly realized that Las Vegas would never be the next Orlando. Another nail in the family-friendly coffin was hammered home by Wynn who, in a firm antikid move, built Bellagio, which had a firm rule when it opened against children, not only in the casino, but property-wide. The MGM Grand, which also owns New York–New York, banished their kiddie-oriented ethos and, upon the taking over of Wynn's Mirage group (Bellagio, Treasure Island, and The Mirage), it revised the welcome with regard to families at those properties as well.

Meanwhile, Downtown, which had gotten progressively shabbier, underwent a major revitalization, thanks in great part to the Fremont Street Experience, a multimillion-dollar light show that draws crowds nightly to what is now a pedestrian promenade lined with kiosks and street entertainers. It's a nice place to visit, but we don't suggest you stay there with your family.

Steve Wynn's Wynn Las Vegas stands on the location of the old Desert Inn. It out-Bellagios Bellagio, with 2,700 rooms, a 15-story mountain, a 150-acre championship golf course, and two showroom extravaganzas.

The South Point, at the far south end of Las Vegas Boulevard, and the new 500-room Station casino, the Red Rock Resort on the far western side of town, are great choices for families wanting to take advantage of the area's outdoor recreational offerings.

Planet Hollywood has taken over the Aladdin. The Destination Group has taken over the Las Vegas Hilton. The Landry's restaurant chain has taken over the Golden Nugget. Harrah's Entertainment bought Caesars Entertainment, and MGM MIRAGE acquired Mandalay Resort Group. Nothing and no one stands still in this city of perpetual change.

The majority of visitors with families stay on the Strip, because that's where most of the attractions can be found. Downtown is not a suitable location for families—trust us on that one. Both to the east and west of the Strip you'll find decent to fine hotels, but you'll need transportation to get there and back. And while staying on the Strip provides you with heaps to do and see, keep in mind that the hotels are farther apart than they appear, especially while walking in 100°F (38°C) weather, or on a cold windy night, with children in tow.

The price guidelines that follow are rough, given the flexible nature of Vegas's room rates. But that doesn't mean you shouldn't call the hotels directly, or check the website deals, to see what kind of rates you can get.

We classified the recommended hotels below based on the average rack rate you can expect to be quoted on an average night, not when huge conventions are in town. Expect to pay a bit less than rack rates Sunday through Thursday, and a bit more on Friday and Saturday nights.

For more tips on accommodations, see p. 70.

Tips Check In

While checkout time is 11am in most hotels, your check-in time is usually 3pm. You can try to arrange an early check-in, but that isn't always an option. Conveniently, though, you can leave your baggage with the bellman, then go sightseeing, either in your hotel or nearby, until it's time to check in. Once in your room, call for your bags, and don't forget to tip when they come.

Las Vegas's Spas & Gyms

Hotel	Phone	Hours	Gym/Workout Room Fee	Min. Age	Spa Hours	Name	Notes
Planet Hollywood	702/785-5SPA	6am–7pm	$25	18	8am–8pm	Mandara Spa	$30 for nonhotel guests, multiple-day passes available; can use gym at 16+, but must have parent present if 16–17
Bally's	702/967-4366	6am–8pm	$22	18	8am–8pm	the Spa	
Bellagio	702/693-7111	6am–8pm	$25	18	6am–8pm	the Spa	Must be 16+ for workout room with parent; registered hotel guests only
Caesars Palace	702/731-7776	6am–8pm	$25	18	8am–6pm	Qua Spa	Nonhotel guests can use gym Mon–Thurs; $30; 17 and under admitted with guardian
Excalibur	702/597-7772	6am–9pm	$20	18	6am–9pm	Royal Treatment	$20 for nonhotel guests
Flamingo	702/733-3535	6am–8pm	$20	18	7am–8pm	the Spa	Nonhotel guests admitted
Four Seasons	702/632-5000	6am–9pm	free	18	6am–7pm	the Spa	Gym is free to hotel guests or those with spa service appt.; 16+ can use workout room with parent present
Green Valley Ranch	702/617-7777	6am–8pm	$35	18	8am–8pm	the Spa	Gym is free to hotel guests or those with spa service appt.
Hard Rock	702/693-5554	6am–8pm	$20	18	8am–8pm	the Spa	$25 if not staying at hotel
Harrah's	702/369-5189	8am–8pm	$20	18	9am–6pm	the Spa	3 days/$50; same fees for nonhotel guests; gym free with spa service; platinum players card can use gym for free
Las Vegas Hilton	702/732-5648	6am–8pm	$20	16	6am–8pm	the Spa	
Luxor	702/262-4000	8am–8pm	$25	18	6am–7pm	Nurture	

Mandalay Bay	702/632-7777	6am–8:30pm	$27	18	6am–8:30pm	Spa Mandalay	$30 if nonhotel guest
MGM Grand	702/891-1111	6am–8pm	$25	18	6am–8pm	the Spa	Gym for hotel guests only on weekends; $35 weekends
The Mirage	702/791-7472	5:30am–7:30pm	$25	18	9am–7pm	Spa Mirage	Hotel guests only
Monte Carlo	702/730-7777	6am–9pm	$22	18	8am–7pm	the Spa	$19 for gym and spa; $24 for nonhotel guests
New York–New York	702/740-6955	6:30am–8pm	$20	18	8am–6:30pm	the Spa	
Palms	702/942-7777	6am–8pm	$20	18	8am–7pm	the Spa	$25 for nonhotel guests
Paris Las Vegas	702/946-4366	Sun-Thurs 6am–7pm; Fri–Sat 6am–9pm	$25	18	7am–7pm	Spa by Mandara	$30 for nonhotel guests
Red Rock Resort	702/797-7878	5:30am–8pm	free	18	6am–8pm	the Spa	$50 for nonhotel guests
Rio	702/777-7777	6am–8pm	$22	18	8am–7pm	the Spa	Can use gym 3 consecutive days for $55
Treasure Island	702/894-7474	Sun–Thurs 6am–6pm; Fri–Sat, 6am–8pm	$22	18	7am–7pm	WET the Spa	Appt. available to nonhotel guests Mon–Thurs, subject to availability; can use gym 3 consecutive days for $55; spa treatments include use of workout room
Venetian	702/414-3610	5:30am–10pm	$35	18	8am–8pm	Canyon Ranch Spa	Gym and spa open to nonguests
Wynn Las Vegas	702/770-3900	6am–8pm	$25	16	6am–8pm	the Spa	Spa open to hotel guests only

All hours shown are 7 days a week unless otherwise noted.

Tips Beating the Heat

The hottest months in Las Vegas—July, August, and September—are the least popular months for travel to the desert—no doubt because the weather can get up to 118°F (48°C). However, because those are the most convenient months to travel with children, you can take advantage of the hotels' empty rooms and, with a few phone calls or mouse clicks, find the best possible deal.

1 CONDOMINIUMS & VACATION HOMES

Las Vegas is awash in new condominiums and timeshare developments, and the number of vacation homes available for short-term vacation rentals has grown exponentially. Vacation homes are freestanding; condos are essentially one- to three-bedroom accommodations in a larger building housing a number of similar units. Because condos tend to be part of large developments (frequently timeshares), amenities such as swimming pools, playgrounds, game arcades, and fitness centers often rival those found in the best hotels. Generally speaking, condo developments do not have restaurants, lounges, or spas. In a condo, if something goes wrong, someone is on hand to fix the problem. Vacation homes rented from property management companies, likewise, will have someone to come to the rescue should a problem arise, though there tend to be vastly varying degrees of responsiveness from company to company. If you rent directly from an owner, correcting problems is often more difficult, particularly when the owner doesn't live in the same area as the rental home.

In a vacation home, all the amenities are contained in the home (though planned developments may have community amenities available as well). Depending on the specific home, you might find a small swimming pool, hot tub, two-car garage, family room, game room, and even a home theater. Features found in both condos and vacation homes include a full kitchen, laundry room, TV, DVD/VCR, and frequently a stereo.

Timeshare condos are clones when it comes to furniture and decor, but single-owner condos and vacation homes are furnished and decorated in a style that reflects the taste of the owner. Vacation homes, usually one- to two-story houses located in a subdivision, very rarely afford an interesting view (some overlook lakes or natural areas); condos, especially the high-rise variety, sometimes offer exceptional vistas.

THE PRICE IS NICE

The best deals in lodging in the Las Vegas area are vacation homes and single-owner condos. Prices range from about $100 a night for one-bedroom condos and town homes to $300 to over $1,000 a night for three- to seven-bedroom vacation homes. Forgetting about taxes to keep things simple, let's compare renting a vacation home to staying at a moderate resort on the Strip. A family with two parents, two teens, and two grandparents would need three hotel rooms at the youngster-friendly Excalibur. At the lowest rate obtainable, that would run $119 per night per room, or $357 total for all three rooms. Rooms are each 354 square feet, so you'd have a total of 1,062 square feet. Each room has a private bathroom and a television.

Fun Facts Rapid Rate Changes

At larger hotels such as the MGM Grand, room rates can change hourly, based on demand. Special employees (called *rate clerks*) track the demand for rooms the way brokers watch the stock ticker and alter the room rates according to the number of bookings.

Renting for the same dates from Las Vegas Retreats, you can lodge in a 2,000-square-foot, four-bedroom, 2-bathroom, vacation home with a private pool a 10-minute drive from the Strip for $259, a savings of $98 per night from the Excalibur rate. With 4 bedrooms, both of the teens can have their own room. But that's not all; the home comes with the following features and amenities: private pool, 5 TVs (one in each bedroom and one big-screen TV in the family room), DVD player, CD player, fully equipped kitchen, 3-car garage, laundry room with full-size washer and dryer, fully furnished private covered patio, and gas grill. If you want to see how this home is furnished go to **www.lasvegasretreats.com/vacation-rentals/property/select-homes.html** and click on the home called Casa De Rosas. Click on that for rates, lots of photos, and other information.

By the way, one thing we like about Las Vegas Retreats is that this website has detailed information, including a dozen or more photos of each specific home. When you book, the home you've been looking at is the actual one you're reserving. Like rental car agencies, some vacation home companies don't assign you a specific home until the day you arrive. These companies provide photos of a "typical home" instead of making information available on each of the individual homes in their inventory. In this case you have to take the company's word that the typical home pictured is representative of all their properties, and that the home you'll be assigned will be just as nice.

HOW THE VACATION-HOME MARKET WORKS

In the greater Las Vegas/Henderson area, there are several thousand rental homes, including stand-alone homes, single-owner condos (that is, not timeshares), and town homes. In the same area there are about 140,000 hotel rooms. Almost all the rental homes are owned by individuals who occupy the home for at least a week or two each year. The rest of the year the owner makes the home available for rent. Some owners deal directly with renters, while others enlist the assistance of a property management company.

Logic may suggest that the lowest rate can be obtained by dealing directly with owners, thus eliminating all middlemen. Although this is sometimes true, more often property management companies offer the best rates. With their marketing expertise and larger customer base, property managers can produce a higher occupancy rate than can the owners themselves. In addition, the property management companies, or at least the larger ones, can achieve economies of scale not available to an owner in regard to maintenance, cleaning, linens, and the like. If an owner signs with a property management company before his home is furnished, he can similarly piggyback on the management company's buying power in acquiring furniture and appliances. The combination of the higher occupancy rates and economies of scale add up to a win-win situation for owners, management companies, and renters alike.

SHOPPING FOR A VACATION HOME

The only practical way to shop for a vacation home is on the Internet, which makes comparisons between different prospective homes and rental companies relatively easy. On the downside, there are so many owners, rental companies, and individual homes to choose from that you could research yourself into a stupor. There are three primary types of websites in the home rental game. A property-management-company site showcases the inventory of homes it manages and is set up for direct bookings, likewise with individual owner sites. Listing sites list homes available for rent by individual owners and sometimes by property management companies. Usually on a listing site you're referred to the owner's or property management company's website for reservations.

The best websites provide:

- numerous photos and in-depth descriptions of individual homes to make comparisons quick and easy;
- an overview map or text description that reflects how distant a specific home or development is from the Strip, the airport, and other Las Vegas destinations;
- the ability to book the specific rental home you chose on the site;
- a prominently displayed phone number for non-Internet bookings and questions.

The best sites also are easy to navigate, let you see what you're interested in without logging in or giving personal information, and list memberships in such organizations as the Better Business Bureau.

Using a search engine such as Google or Yahoo, type "Las Vegas vacation rental homes" in the search box. This will produce a listing of the major management companies in the market and also yield a couple of listing sites, such as **Vacation Rental By Owner** (**www.vrbo.com**), a national listing site that puts prospective renters in direct contact with owners. The site is straightforward and always lists a large number of rental properties in Las Vegas, North Las Vegas, and Henderson. Another listing service with a good website is **Vacation Rentals 411, www.vacationrentals411.com**.

MAKING CONTACT

Once you've found a vacation home you like online, check around the website for a Frequently Asked Questions (FAQ) page. This should provide answers to most of the questions on your mind. If there's not a FAQ page, here are some of the things you'll want to check out on the phone with the owner or rental company:

1. How close is the home to the Strip and other places I want to visit?
2. Is the home or condo I see on the Internet the one I get?
3. Is the home or condo part of a timeshare development?
4. Are there any specials or discounts available?
5. Is everything included in the rental price or are there additional charges (cleaning charges are common)? What about taxes?
6. How old is the home I'm interested in?
7. Has it been refurbished recently?
8. What is the view from the property?
9. Is the property near any noisy roads?
10. What is your smoking policy?
11. Are pets allowed? (This is as important to those who want to avoid pets as to those who want to bring their pet.)
12. Is the pool heated?
13. Is there a fenced backyard where children can play?

14. How many can be seated at the main dining table?
15. Is there a separate dedicated telephone at the property?
16. Is high-speed Internet access available?
17. Are linens and towels provided?
18. How far are the nearest supermarket and drugstore?
19. Are childcare or babysitting services available?
20. Are restaurants nearby?
21. What is required to make a reservation?
22. What is your change/cancellation policy?
23. What is the check-out time?
24. What will we be responsible for in the way of cleaning, and so on, when we check out?
25. How will we receive our confirmation and arrival instructions?
26. What are your office hours?
27. What are the directions to your office?
28. What do we do if we arrive after your office has closed?
29. Who do we contact if something breaks or goes wrong during our stay?
30. How long have you been in business?
31. Do you belong to the Better Business Bureau?

2 SOUTH STRIP ACCOMMODATIONS

Staying on the South Strip puts you right in the heart of the most extravagantly kid-friendly hotels, along with providing you with plenty of eye candy, courtesy of hotels such as Luxor, Excalibur, and New York–New York. Many family-oriented attractions can also be found here; additionally, this is where you'll find the largest range of rates in this section of Las Vegas.

VERY EXPENSIVE

The Four Seasons ★★★ If you crave pure unabashed luxury, the Las Vegas branch of this famously plush hotel is exactly where you belong. You'll be pampered like royalty in rooms decorated in quiet good taste with quality furnishings. Located on the top five floors of Mandalay Bay, with a separate driveway, entrance, and registration area, the nongaming Four Seasons' rates are higher for a basic room than any other hotel's in town. But included in those rates are amenities for which most hotels charge, making the calm peaceful Four Seasons a relative bargain among Las Vegas luxury resorts. Use of both the large health club (with weight training and cardio machines) and the hotel's private pool cabanas (at least $75 at most hotels) is free. Room amenities—including incredibly fluffy feather pillows, down comforters, and plush robes—are definitely a step up from the Vegas standard. Children get their own robes, and rooms are childproofed in advance. Use of strollers, highchairs, and playpens is complimentary, and all the hotel's restaurants, as well as room service, have children's menus. Best of all, children get a welcome package at check-in, which includes popcorn and soda for teens and toys and cookies for smaller kids. And if you'd like to bodysurf, guests have access to all the pools at Mandalay Bay (p. 109), but the Four Seasons also has its own pool.

3960 Las Vegas Blvd. S., Las Vegas, NV 89119. ✆ **877/632-5000** or 702/632-5000. Fax 702/632-5195. www.fourseasons.com. 424 units. $329–$600 double; from $400 suite. Extra person $30. Children 17 and

Tips Fighting the Crowds

Boxing matches draw huge crowds to Las Vegas. According to newspaper reports, the matches have also been known, from time to time, to attract unsavory organized-criminal groups who flock to Strip hotels. If there's a fight scheduled during your trip, you may want to book a hotel off the Strip and plan an activity for fight night that will keep you away from Las Vegas Boulevard.

under stay free in parent's room. Cribs/rollaways free. AE, DC, DISC, MC, V. Free self- and valet parking. Pets under 25 lb. only. **Amenities:** 2 restaurants (Continental, American); heated outdoor pool with free cabanas; health club (free to guests) and spa; concierge; car-rental desk; courtesy car; full 24-hr. business center with faxing, delivery, and secretarial service; 24-hr. room service; in-room massage; babysitting; overnight laundry service; overnight dry cleaning; nonsmoking rooms; executive-level rooms. *In room:* A/C, TV/VCR w/pay movies, dataport, minibar, fridge, coffeemaker, hair dryer, iron/ironing board, safe.

EXPENSIVE

MGM Grand Hotel/Casino ★★★ The MGM Grand was once the flagship of kid-friendly Vegas, but oh how times have changed. While we were researching this book, a PR rep went out of her way to let us know that the MGM Group did not wish to be known as family oriented. The amusement park, which used to be in the back—one of the true kid-friendly spots on the Strip—closed and was replaced by the new pool, convention center, and luxury high-rise condo towers. Even so, though it may talk the not-for-children talk, this hotel, more than any of the other MGM holdings—Treasure Island, The Mirage, and the adult-oriented Bellagio—(p. 116, 115, and 109, respectively) is a wonderful place for families to stay, with plenty for children to do and see.

For starters, there's the **Lion Habitat** (p. 172) and **CBS Television City,** where children ages 10 and older can play critic—attending screenings of new television programs (with a parent) and rating shows. The pool area, where not-for-free artists will braid hair into elaborate styles and apply temporary tattoos, sits on 6½ landscaped acres. Along with a Jacuzzi and standard pools, the MGM Grand also boasts the longest lazy river ride in Vegas; flotation devices are available for rent, along with cabanas. There's an arcade (p. 184), a food court with plenty of options, and restaurants such as **Wolfgang Puck Bar & Grill, Emeril's New Orleans Fish House** (Creole/Cajun), and **NOBHILL.** These, along with the buffet, **Stage Deli,** and the **Rainforest Cafe,** are reviewed in chapter 7. For nighttime entertainment, the hotel offers *KÀ,* the Cirque du Soleil extravaganza that will blow child and adult minds alike, the adults-only *La Femme,* a headliner showroom, and an events area for sporting matches and larger concerts. Add a convenient location and helpful staff and you have a complete city of entertainment for the wee and teen ones, and for those who pay for them.

The MGM Grand also boasts the luxurious **Grand Spa,** an Asian-themed retreat that offers massages, high-priced pedicures, facials, aromatherapy scrubs, and other treatments. The health club—$25 a day—has a full complement of equipment, ranging from weights to state-of-the-art computerized cardio machines.

However, all of this fun, fun, fun needs to be housed in a large, large, large area, and alas, the signage is hard to read, so getting around inside this monstrosity can become a Sisyphean task. We "lost" the elevators to our room several times, though the attentive

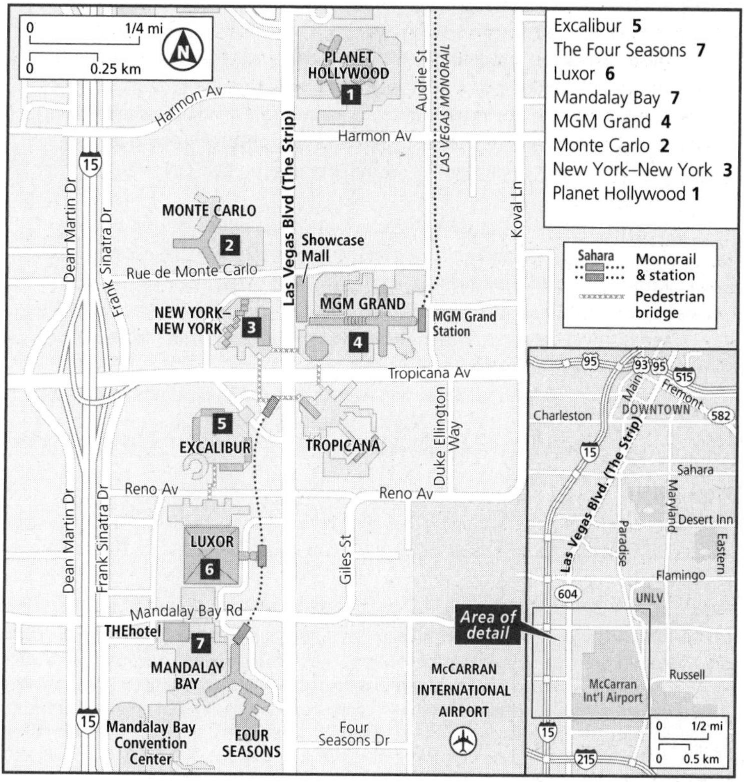

staff luckily recognized our befuddled expression and pointed us in the right direction. Also, getting from room to pool can take awhile, especially if the hotel is crowded, because, this being Vegas, the pathway circumnavigates the casino.

The rooms at the MGM Grand are done in a vaguely mid-'30s style, with light wood and neutral camel tones. Black-and-white photos of stars, lions, and celebrities decorate the walls, and there are plenty of lamps. The bathrooms are a good size; however, the bathtubs are small. Children should be reminded that the retractable clothesline is not a toy. The premier suites boast a far nicer array of toiletries than the standard rooms and bungalow suites, and unless you stay in the premier suites, you must request turndown service.

The MGM Grand also has a service to ease your travel experience; it's one of several hotels to offer airport reservations and check-in at Las Vegas's McCarran International Airport. This satellite desk, located in south baggage claim near the exit from the C and D gates, is open from 9am to 11pm. There you can also make reservations for shows at both the MGM Grand and New York–New York and, for an extra fee, shuttle and luggage transportation can be arranged to either hotel.

Fun Facts Cleaning Up

- The MGM Grand launders 12,000 bath towels, 18,000 washcloths, 11,000 sheets, and 15,000 pillowcases every day. Kids should be glad they don't have to make the beds here! MGM launders more than 29 million pounds of sheets annually for its guests in the largest privately owned laundry in Nevada: It takes an average of 22 miles of sheets each day to freshen the beds!
- Bellagio, one of MGM Grand's sister hotels, generates 44,000 pounds of dirty linen daily, including 10,000 king-size sheets, 10,000 pillowcases, 7,500 bath towels, 9,000 washcloths, and 4,000 bath rugs.
- In 1 month, Circus Circus sends 403,000 bath towels, 357,000 hand towels, and 800,000 sheets to its laundry service, Mission Industries, to be cleaned for the hotel's 3,770 rooms.
- A tablecloth lasts about 35 washes, sheets about 100 washings, and towels 60. Approximately 25% of MGM Grand's linen that has been deemed unserviceable is recycled; sheets become pillowcases, towels become cleaning rags, and so on.

—from the *Las Vegas Review-Journal*

3799 Las Vegas Blvd. S. (at Tropicana Ave.), Las Vegas, NV 89109. ✆ **800/929-1111** or 702/891-1111. Fax 702/891-1030. www.mgmgrand.com. 5,034 units. $69–$299 double; $189–$2,500 suite. Extra person $25. Children 12 and under stay free in parent's room. Cribs free; rollaways $25 per night. AE, DC, DISC, MC, V. Free self- and valet parking. **Amenities:** 15 restaurants (all major cuisines); casino; events arena; showroom; cabaret theater; wedding chapel; outdoor pool complex; health club and spa; Jacuzzi; sauna; concierge; tour desk; car-rental desk; business center; 24-hr. room service; in-room massage; laundry service; dry cleaning; nonsmoking rooms; executive-level rooms. *In room:* A/C, TV w/pay movies, dataport, hair dryer, iron/ironing board, safe.

Monte Carlo Resort & Casino ★★ At first look, this hotel with its marble lobby looks imposing and too formal for children, especially with the slightly suggestive statues out front. Additionally, depending on season and availability, there may be an extra charge for children staying in a parent's room. But despite those slight negatives, this is a kid-friendly place to stay, especially for older children and teens. The rooms, accessible without going through the casino, are spacious and decorated in traditional European style. And while there's no discount at the **Monte Carlo Buffet** (p. 166), and none of the hotel's restaurants offer children's menus, the restaurants—including **Dragon Noodle Co.** (p. 146) and the **Monte Carlo Brew Pub** (p. 150)—have a large selection that kids will find appealing. Standard options—pizza, burgers, hot dogs, ice cream—are available at the food court.

The main attraction for children, aside from master magician **Lance Burton** (p. 234) and an adequate arcade, is the huge pool area, which includes a kiddie pool, a lazy river, and a wave pool.

Parents will appreciate that the health club charges a very reasonable (for Vegas) $19 a day for use of the large and well-maintained facilities, including steam rooms and

Fun Facts **Plenty of Room at the Inn**

The MGM Grand is one of the world's largest hotels, with more than 5,000 rooms. It would take a person 13 years and 8 months to sleep in every one of them!

whirlpools. Those priming themselves for Wimbledon or who just want to practice their backhands can take advantage of the three tennis courts, lit for night use.

3770 Las Vegas Blvd. S. (btw. Flamingo Rd. and Tropicana Ave.), Las Vegas, NV 89109. ✆ **800/311-8999** or 702/730-7777. Fax 702/730-7250. www.monte-carlo.com. 3,014 units. Sun–Thurs $69–$179 double, $149–$279 suite; Fri–Sat $109–$279 double, $189–$469 suite. Extra person $25. Children 11 and under stay free in parent's room, depending on season. Cribs/rollaways free. AE, DC, DISC, MC, V. Free self- and valet parking. **Amenities:** 9 restaurants (all major cuisines); casino; showroom; wedding chapel; large wave pool with lazy river and separate kiddie pool; health club and spa; Jacuzzi; sauna; tour desk; business center; 24-hr. room service; in-room massage; babysitting; laundry service; dry cleaning; nonsmoking rooms; executive-level rooms. *In room:* A/C, TV w/pay movies, dataport, hair dryer, iron/ironing board.

New York–New York Hotel & Casino ★ New Yorkers will tell you that, for the most part, this hotel is nothing like their city, and some seem to almost resent this caricature of their hometown. But people from everywhere else love this place, especially since the terrorist attacks of September 11, 2001. Within days of that tragedy, a spontaneous tribute—T-shirts from hundreds of police and fire departments—covered the shrubbery around the miniature New York Harbor (complete with fireboats that shoot water) in front of the hotel. Since then, New York–New York has installed a permanent memorial to the lives lost, including two large flags that can be seen from the roller coaster as it whizzes by.

A complete refurbishing of the smallish guest rooms in a '40s-inspired decor was completed in 2004. All 64 different room layouts have attractive though dinky bathrooms that may disappoint parents, as will the fact that each extra person is $30, no matter what their age. But what the heck, it's your vacation, and kids love the New York–New York experience. Manhattan Express, the aforementioned roller coaster, zips around miniature Manhattan landmarks, and loads of junk food include pizza, candied apples, hot dogs, and ice cream. They'll also be able to see one-third replicas of Rockefeller Plaza, a subway station, and Central Park as you escort them about. The **Coney Island Emporium Arcade** (p. 178) is the best hotel arcade in town—large, clean, and well-lit, with both traditional boardwalk and video games, as well as really nice tiled bathrooms.

Although only the **ESPN Zone** restaurant offers a children's menu, **America** and **Chin Chin** (all reviewed in chapter 7) have kid-friendly and vegetarian food, as do **Gonzalez Y Gonzalez** and **Il Fornaio. Schrafft's** features great frozen custard that's especially popular with the kid set. Additionally, the spectacular Greenwich Village–themed **Village Eateries** food court offers up a better, though more expensive, grade of pizza, burgers, sandwiches, smoothies, and other counter treats than the usual fast food.

The major drawback—aside from the not-so-big health club and the surcharge for children—is that the bland pool is right next to the parking lot. ***Tip:*** Rooms next to the roller coaster tend to rumble.

3790 Las Vegas Blvd. S. (at Tropicana Ave.), Las Vegas, NV 89109. ✆ **800/NY-FOR-ME** (693-6763) or 702/740-6969. Fax 702/740-6700. www.nynyhotelcasino.com. 2,035 units. Sun–Thurs from $75 double; Fri–Sat from $159 double. Extra person $30. No discount for children. Cribs/rollaways free. AE, DC, DISC,

Tips So Your Trip Goes Swimmingly . . .

Part of the delight of the Vegas resort complexes is the gorgeous pools—what could be better for beating the summer heat? But there are pools and there are *pools,* so you'll need to keep several things in mind when searching for the right one.

During the winter, it's often too cold or windy to do much lounging, and even if the weather is amenable, the hotels often close part of their pool areas during winter and early spring. The pools are also not heated for the most part, but they largely don't need to be.

Most hotel pools are shallow, chest-high at best (the hotels want you gambling, not swimming). Diving is impossible—not that a single pool allows it anyway. Some resorts, such as The Mirage, The Venetian, and MGM Grand, offer adults-only pool areas, where you can find nightclub-style party-hearty action—and occasionally topless sunbathing—during the day (for a fee running $20–$40 per person).

And finally, during those hot days, be warned that sitting by pools next to heavily windowed buildings, such as The Mirage and Treasure Island, will allow you to experience the same thing a bug does under a magnifying glass with a sun ray directed on it. Regardless of the time of year, be sure to slather the sunscreen on yourself and your kids; there's a reason you see so many lobster-red people roaming the streets. Many pool areas don't offer much in the way of shade.

At any of the pools, you can rent cabanas (which often include TVs, special lounge chairs, and special poolside service), but these should be reserved as far in advance as possible, and with the exception of the Four Seasons and the Ritz, where they are complimentary, most cost a hefty fee. If you are staying at a chain hotel, you will most likely find an average pool, but if you want to spend some time at a better one, be aware that most of the casino-hotel pool attendants will ask to see your room key. If they are busy, you might be able to sneak in or at least blend in with a group.

MC, V. Free self- and valet parking. **Amenities:** 9 restaurants (all major cuisines); casino; showrooms; roller coaster; outdoor pool; small health club and spa; Jacuzzi; sauna; video arcade with carnival midway games; concierge; tour desk; 24-hr. room service; laundry service; dry cleaning; nonsmoking rooms; executive-level rooms. *In room:* A/C, TV w/pay movies, dataport, hair dryer, safe.

Planet Hollywood Resort & Casino ★ Planet Hollywood has its pluses for families: You could stay here for a week and never know that there's a casino on-site, which is a rarity in Las Vegas. Additionally, each room is no more than seven doors away from an elevator. And then there's the mall.

For years the former Aladdin drew its inspiration, of course, from the *Arabian Nights* tales, which in turn are based on the Islamic culture and folklore of North Africa and the eastern Mediterranean. The casino and hotel presented the theme in whimsical storybook fashion with some Las Vegas neon and glitter tossed in for good measure. All this—except maybe the neon and glitter—has been buried by the sands of time. Planet Hollywood now has a major "sleek and glamorous" look, completed in 2007. The hotel portion of the property is managed by Sheraton. In addition, Westgate, a 50-story luxury vacation-ownership and condominium tower directly connected to Planet Hollywood, is scheduled for completion in 2009, for a final Hollywood-style face-lift and total makeover.

Ringing the casino on the north, east, and south, the Miracle Mile Shops underwent a similar redesign, going from the streets of a mythical Arabian city to a sleeker, more urbanized, and contemporary look. The new mall was rechristened Miracle Mile Shops, in part as a nod to the 1½ miles of retail space.

Rooms are nice, serviceable, and forgettable, barely distinguishable from other hotel rooms in the same price range. However, the large bathrooms do stand out—the rooms' separate showers and bathtubs, as well as an enclosed toilet area, are features usually found at more expensive hotels.

The two pools are pleasant, and you'll find a vast selection of restaurants in the Miracle Mile Shops, including **Todai** sushi and seafood buffet (p. 143) and Trader Vic's, with its Strip-side outdoor patio. There are more than a dozen other offerings, in case you get tired of Planet Hollywood's excellent Spice Market Buffet.

3667 Las Vegas Blvd. S., Las Vegas, NV 89109. ✆ **866/919-7472** or 702/785-5555. Fax 702/785-5558. www.planethollywoodresort.com. 2,567 units. $99 and up double. Extra person $30. Children 11 and under stay free in parent's room, depending on season. Cribs/rollaways free. AE, DC, DISC, MC, V. Free self- and valet parking. **Amenities:** 13 restaurants (all major cuisines); 6 bars/lounges; casino; events arena; 2 outdoor pools; health club and spa; Jacuzzi; sauna; watersports equipment/rental; concierge; tour desk; car-rental desk; business center; 24-hr. room service; in-room massage; babysitting; laundry service; dry cleaning; nonsmoking rooms; executive-level rooms. *In room:* A/C, TV w/pay movies, dataport, high-speed Internet access (for a fee), hair dryer, iron/ironing board, safe.

MODERATE

Excalibur ★★ This medieval-themed hotel was built with families in mind—it's full of things for kids to see and do, and "the Realm" concept definitely produces some "whoas" from children. Excalibur's decor is based on the romantic ideals of the Middle Ages, filtered through fairy tale cartoons, sword-and-sorcery movies, and 1980s post-modern design. In other words, it's a Middle Ages mishmash that manages to capture the essence of life in a medieval village—loud, claustrophobic (low ceilings in the hallways and guest rooms), and crowded. Thankfully, the resemblance ends there; unlike a feudal village, Excalibur is neither plague-ridden nor stinky.

We must stress that this hotel—along with its sister up the Strip, Circus Circus—is still going strong by catering to families (offering lots for kids to do in a pretty cool environment) at a time when many over-the-top Vegas hotels are going out of their way to be kid unfriendly. Along with an IMAX movie theater, there is a well-stocked **arcade** full of the latest video games and the dinner show ***Tournament of Kings*** (p. 178 and 238, respectively). Located on the second floor is the Village Square, with meandering streets, souvenir shops, and the food court.

Kids and adults alike get excited over the **Krispy Kreme** factory (p. 156), also on the second floor. And though enthralled throngs watch in fascination as the fried dough chunks slide from racks into their sugar-glaze bath, alas, there are no free samples. The second floor also hosts the hotel's restaurants, including a food court, the **Round Table buffet** (p. 165), **Regale, Sir Galahad's,** and the **Steakhouse at Camelot,** a pricey hearty-eaters prime rib and steakhouse that is really more of an adult dining option. This floor also has the entryway to the people mover (really, a moving sidewalk) to **Luxor.** There's also a free tram to **Luxor** and **Mandalay Bay,** which is a lot of fun to ride.

Tips Sign Up to Save

Almost every hotel with a casino in Las Vegas has a players club or another similar type of frequent-gambling program. Sign up (free) to receive a plastic card with a magnetic strip, which you insert in the slot machines, or, if you are playing the tables, hand to your dealer. The card tracks your gambling action and habits and you rack up points by your length of play and the amount of money you feed into the machine. (At the tables, the pit boss notes your average bet and length of play.) What are the advantages? Well, simply by signing up, you can end up with a mailbox full of offers to stay in Vegas again at significantly discounted rates. If you plan on returning to Vegas within a year, it's a good use of your time to stand in the line at the promotions desk and join the club.

Rooms have noticeably low ceilings, and the windows have curved arches above them on the outside, blocking out a small portion of the view. On the lower floors, these factors can make for an exceptionably Rapunzel-like closed-in feeling. The rooms are decorated primarily in earth and woodsy tones, with Arts and Crafts–style bedspreads, faux-antique furniture, and heraldic art hung on the walls. Without dust ruffles on the beds, we got a nice view of the box springs. And there are no bathtubs, so keep this in mind if your little ones are bathers. Some guests who have stayed in Tower 2 have complained about noise from the roller coaster at New York–New York across the street, which runs from 10am through 11pm. Though we experienced no problems during our stay, you might want to take the coaster into consideration if you or your children are light sleepers. Note also that cellphones do not work well on the lower floors, which might make dial-happy teenagers unhappy.

If the rooms aren't exactly stellar, the staff is incredibly accommodating, moving us twice after we had been assigned problematic accommodations. Staff members are generally friendly and very kid tolerant, because families are the hotel's bread and butter.

3850 Las Vegas Blvd. S. (at Tropicana Ave.), Las Vegas, NV 89109. ✆ **800/937-7777** or 702/597-7777. Fax 702/597-7163. www.excalibur.com. 4,008 units. $69–$191 double. Extra person $20. Children 12 and under stay free in parent's room. Cribs/rollaways free. AE, DC, DISC, MC, V. Free self- and valet parking. **Amenities:** 5 restaurants (buffet, American, Italian, steak); casino; showrooms; wedding chapel; outdoor pool; video arcade; tour desk; car-rental desk; 24-hr. room service; laundry service; dry cleaning; nonsmoking rooms. *In room:* A/C, TV w/pay movies, dataport, hair dryer.

Luxor ★★★ For 15 years, Luxor's theme was all Egypt, all the time, and there was no skimping on the cornucopia of Cleopatrania contained within. But in 2007–08, Luxor invested $300 million to remodel most of the public areas, removing as much of the ancient Egyptian theme as it could. Exterior-wise, however, it's still that big bronze pyramid at the south end of the Strip. At night, balls of light roll down its sides and the top of the pyramid shoots out a giant 315,000-watt light beam—the world's brightest, according to the hotel's talking animatronic camels, located in the Giza Galleria of shops. Yes, that's right, talking camels! Kids love them, and so do adults for that matter, and it's rare to find the gabbing dromedaries without a cluster of tourists hanging on their every word and jostling to take their photos.

Nice Places to Visit (but You Wouldn't Want to Stay There)

Bellagio This is a beautiful hotel, designed for the rich and those who would prefer not to come in contact with children. The hotel states on the website, on the phone, and in person that persons under the age of 18 are not permitted on the premises—even with their guardians—unless they're guests of the hotel or have tickets or reservations for a show or restaurant. This harsh rule seems flexible: On our visits we saw slews of kids with adults moving through the lobby and Via Bellagio (p. 206). A casino security person told us that, for the most part, they practice don't-ask-don't-tell with regard to escorted and well-behaved children. Other folks have reported that they have seen families without room keys turned away at the hotel's revolving door. If you want to visit the conservatory or see Cirque du Soleil's *O* (p. 233), be prepared to answer staff's questions and possibly encounter hostile glares from guests who were promised a childfree zone.

3600 Las Vegas Blvd. S., at the corner of Flamingo Road (✆ **888/987-6667** or 702/693-7444; www.bellagio.com).

Imperial Palace If your child is 6 or older, your room will be an extra $19 per night, and depending on who's at the front desk, the crib and rollaway rentals can be either $15 or free, so even if you can get the lowest rate of $59, you're not saving much. Because there's little for kids to enjoy here, just drop in to see the Auto Collections (p. 186). During the summer there's a Hawaiian luau. But basically this hotel is for gamblers, not families.

3535 Las Vegas Blvd. S., between Sands Avenue and Flamingo Road (✆ **800/634-6441** or 702/731-3311; www.imperialpalace.com).

Mandalay Bay Despite the fabulous pool area with waves for bodysurfing and boogie boarding, this is not the place to stay with children. The hotel, with its beautiful Southeast Asian decor, cultivates a hip adults-only clientele, emphasized by its room policy: Any extra person, be they 7 months or 7 years old, costs an extra $35 a night. Add in the crib or rollaway rental ($20), and you might as well stay at the far kid-friendlier Caesars, Venetian, or Monte Carlo. Plus the food selection for children is virtually nil. However, the Shark Reef aquarium (p. 177), with its new Komodo dragon, is worth a visit.

3950 Las Vegas Blvd. S., at Hacienda Avenue (✆ **877/632-7800** or 702/632-7777; www.mandalaybay.com).

Rio All-Suite Hotel & Casino While the idea of an "all-suite hotel" may seem appealing, in the Rio's case this just means larger rooms with unusual-for-Vegas refrigerators. Rollaways are free, but each extra person runs $30 per night, no matter how old the child. Cribs are also free, but the hotel has a limited number available and there's no guarantee one will be available for you. Stay elsewhere and visit for the buffet (p. 168) or the free *Masquerade in the Sky* show (p. 173).

3700 W. Flamingo Rd., at I-15 (✆ **888/PLAYRIO** [752-9746] or 702/252-7777; www.harrahs.com).

The hotel's main entrance, on the casino level, is breathtaking. As you enter the lobby through the pyramid, you are greeted by a mix of Art Nouveau and Art Deco—beautiful and soothing, full of marble and dark wood, with hanging glass lamps and wall sconces. There's a less fancy, smaller lobby on the north side by the towers for tour group check-in only, but they didn't snarl at us when we used it accidentally.

The pyramid guest rooms open onto the huge open-air atrium, and the windows slant, which is sort of cool, but naturally, the higher you go, the more they slant, which could get a bit frustrating for the taller folks in your group. These rooms have shower-only bathrooms, making baths a nonoption. ("But Mom, doesn't using the pool count as a bath?") Very cool for kids are the 39-degree high-speed "inclinators"—that's what an elevator is when it works inside a pyramid. (Really, they are part conveyance, part thrill ride—check out that jolt when they come to a halt!) The larger tower rooms do indeed have bathtubs (some are of the wonderful whirlpool variety), though in family travel mode, you may not want one of the suite options, which have the tub in the bedroom under the window. All rooms lost the Egyptian motif in the recent redecoration, but oddly, there were no bedside lamps, which made the in-bed reading of Shakespeare's *Antony and Cleopatra* a bit difficult. But the mattresses were comfy and the room was quiet.

The hotel is great for kids with an interest in mummies—they're everywhere, from the gift shops to the **More** buffet (p. 165). There are also enough attractions to keep the kids amused: There's a fantastic **arcade,** plus an excellent motion simulator, *In Search of the Obelisk,* and **Bodies: The Exhibition.** Reliable family dining spots include **Pyramid Café** and **La Salsa** (p. 150). The pool area is really nice, with four dunking options, all of which accept kids. There are lifeguards on duty, but as with all hotels, a parent or other responsible adult must be present.

3900 Las Vegas Blvd. S. (btw. Reno and Hacienda aves.), Las Vegas, NV 81119. ✆ **800/288-1000** or 702/262-4000. Fax 702/262-4137. www.luxor.com. 4,400 units. Sun–Thurs $69–$249 double, Fri–Sat $99 and up double; $149 and up whirlpool suite; $249–$800 other suites. Extra person $25. Children 11 and under stay free in parent's room. Cribs $15; rollaways $25. AE, DC, DISC, MC, V. Free self- and valet parking. **Amenities:** 9 restaurants (all major cuisines); casino; showrooms; wedding chapel; 4 outdoor pools; health club and spa; 18,000-sq.-ft. video arcade with the latest Sega and more; tour desk; car-rental desk; courtesy car or limo; business center; shopping arcade; 24-hr. room service; dry cleaning; nonsmoking rooms; executive-level rooms. *In room:* A/C, TV w/pay movies, hair dryer, iron/ironing board.

3 CENTER STRIP ACCOMMODATIONS

Center Strip boasts 10 of the world's largest and most famous hotels, along with Las Vegas's most concentrated shopping opportunities, with three major malls and numerous retail promenades. Center Strip also features the finest pools in town (at The Flamingo, Mirage, and Caesars), white tigers, a sirens-vs.-pirates live extravaganza, a regularly erupting volcano, a larger-than-life dancing-waters show, and even an exact half-size replica of the Eiffel Tower. Despite the visual stimuli, however, Center Strip megaresorts are less family oriented than those along the South Strip.

VERY EXPENSIVE

Caesars Palace ★★★ Now this is Vegas—over-the-top, goofy, and kitschy. In the past few years, Caesars has actually toned down its theme a bit; some of its previous obvious vulgarity has been sacrificed on the altar of restraint, much to our disappointment. Still, do your children need mirrors over the bed? We thought not. You might, so if planning on

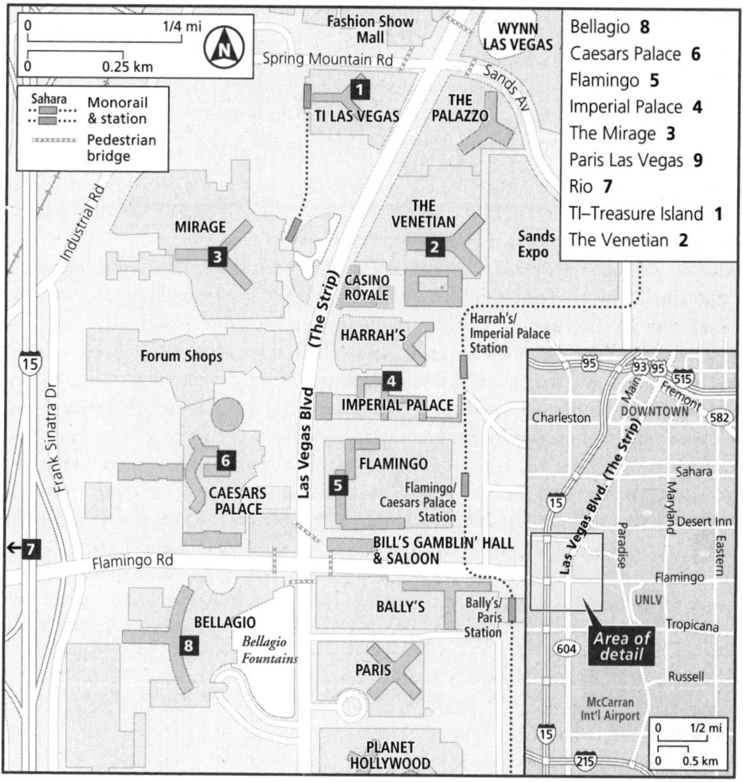

separate rooms from the kids, ask what they can do for you at the front desk. Gladiators greet you on arrival, cocktail waitresses wear togas, and everywhere are arches, statues, and columns. Chariots and temples line the entryways and it's all gloriously silly. But historical and educational, too. Really.

Like the Caesars' empire, this hotel is vast and sprawling, making navigation a bit difficult, especially because there's just so much to gape at. But once you get the hang of following the signage, you'll be moving as quickly as the bow to Nero's fiddle. Rooms, occupying five towers, tend toward classical themes—Greco-Roman statues and architectural details (and the aforementioned mirrored ceilings in some rooms). The newer rooms are less neo-Roman in their decor and are very nicely appointed with great views. All bathrooms have oversize tubs and marble floors. You should make sure that your room doesn't have a tub in the center of the room—that detail could make bathing a bit too much of a family experience for anyone's taste.

With 10 restaurants and a food court in the hotel, plus 11 more in the Forum Shops, you won't be at a loss to take care of your hungry brood. Along with the hotel's 24-hour coffee shop, Café Lago, wherein you'll find the small buffet, Caesars features Bradley

Fun Facts Darling, You Look Marble-Ous

The majority of the art in the Caesars Palace casino replicates masterpieces created centuries after the fall of Rome. Most of the marble statues there are replicas of classic Renaissance works, including Michelangelo's *David*. There is, however, one non-European style statue gracing the property—the golden statue of *Brahma*, the Hindu god of good fortune, which was donated by a Thai gambler.

Ogden, winner of the prestigious 2004 James Beard award for "Best New Restaurant." Additionally, **Spago** (perfect for your gourmets-to-be) can be found in the Forum Shops, along with **La Salsa** and the **Cheesecake Factory,** reviewed in chapter 7.

Located in the Garden of the Gods, the pool area features attractive granite mosaics, sea horses and griffins, and a **Snackus Maximus.** If you'd prefer not to rest on your laurels poolside, there are also tennis courts and a $25-a-day health club with a rock-climbing wall and state-of-the-art machines.

The Forum Shops features laser shows, animatronic statues, and high-end clothes and accessories, along with kiosks of children's gladiator costumes, toga sleep shirts, and assorted schlock. But then, without schlock, it wouldn't really be Vegas, would it?

3570 Las Vegas Blvd. S. (just north of Flamingo Rd.), Las Vegas, NV 89109. © **800/634-6661** or 702/731-7110. Fax 702/866-1700. www.caesarspalace.com. 3,348 units. From $99 standard double, $109–$300 "run of house deluxe" double; $549–$1,000 suite. Extra person $30. Children 17 and under stay free in parent's room. Cribs free; rollaways $20. AE, DC, DISC, MC, V. Free self- and valet parking. **Amenities:** 21 restaurants (all major cuisines); casino; wedding chapel; 4 outdoor pools; health club and spa; concierge; tour desk; car-rental desk; business center; shopping arcade; 24-hr. room service; laundry service; dry cleaning; nonsmoking rooms; executive-level rooms. *In room:* A/C, TV w/pay movies, dataport, hair dryer, iron/ironing board, safe.

Paris Las Vegas ★★ *Zut alors!* Not content with miniaturizing Rome, Egypt, and New York, Las Vegas turned its eyes to gay Paree, and before you could say *"vive la difference,"* there was a half-scale replica of the Eiffel Tower, a *petit* Louvre (sans artwork) and *demi*-Arc de Triomphe, fountains, and other landmarks higgledy-piggledy heaped about with no sense of the real city's geography. Nor of its language. Kindly point out to your children that "le car rental" is not real French. However, along with these pseudo-*français* touches—including the staff uttering *"bonjour"* and *"merci"* at every turn—there is real attention to detail and comfort here.

The lobby, designed to replicate chunks of Versailles, glistens under ornate crystal chandeliers. The Eiffel Towerette's legs rest on the casino floor; its spire, whence you can gaze on the Strip or dine at the *très* overpriced Eiffel Tower restaurant, shoots upward. It's always a lovely twilight in this fantasy Paris; streetlights gleam along the cobblestone paths that wind through the casino and Le Boulevard shopping area.

The theme fades slightly at the rooms, which are luxurious with thick carpets and drapes and plenty of marble, but only with the faintest hint of a French accent. The bathrooms are attractive, with larger-than-average tubs; but, frankly, the public *pissoirs* off the casino have more of the flavor (though, thankfully, not the scent) of Paris. Rooms that face west will give you a great view of Bellagio's fountains, though the water jets and music can be noisy.

In the real Paris, tourists can eat cheaply at local cafes and patisseries. Oh, that this were true here. Because Paris Las Vegas's perfectionist bakers feel that the Nevada water is not perfect for their art, H_2O is imported from the City of Lights for all the bread and pastries, which are baked on-site. You may not be able to taste the difference, but your wallet will feel it. **Le Village Buffet** and **Mon Ami Gabi** (p. 167 and 152, respectively) are not inexpensive, but they do offer decent to fine versions of French food. Several cafes also offer basic sandwiches and salads, plus a branch of the Paris sweet and pastry shop, **Lenôtre** (p. 157).

The second-floor 2-acre pool, nestled between the Eiffel and hotel towers and surrounded by trees and marble planters, is a lovely place to spend an afternoon soaking up the rays and the view.

3655 Las Vegas Blvd. S., Las Vegas, NV 89109. ✆ **888/BONJOUR** (266-5687) or 702/946-7000. Fax 702/946-4405. www.parislasvegas.com. 2,916 units. \$99–\$229 double; \$350 and up suites. Extra person \$30. Children 17 and under stay free in parent's room. Cribs free; rollaways \$10. AE, DC, DISC, MC. V. Free self- and valet parking. **Amenities:** 11 restaurants (French, American, Italian, more); casino; showrooms; 2 wedding chapels; outdoor pool; health club and spa; concierge; tour desk; business center; shopping arcade; 24-hr. room service; laundry service; dry cleaning; nonsmoking rooms; executive-level rooms. *In room:* A/C, TV w/pay movies, dataport, hair dryer, iron/ironing board, safe.

The Venetian ★★★ European glamour abounds at this ornate casino resort. Outside, you can frolic along the Bridge of Sighs and take photos of the Campanile and Doge's Palace. The beautiful lobby's recessed ceiling is covered with hand-painted copies of Venetian art, surrounded by elaborate gold-leaf frames, but if you spend too much time staring upward, you'll miss out on the marble floors, aged stone, and statues. And you'll probably get lost, too. We visited several times and always got turned around, lost, or generally disoriented.

The luxurious decor in the main parts of the hotel carries through to the large rooms. All are suites, decorated with richly patterned fabrics. The sitting room, with a foldout couch, is a few steps down from the sleeping area. There's even a half-canopy over the bed, adding to the European feel. The sumptuous marble bathrooms have two sinks, makeup areas, deep tubs, separate showers, and enclosed toilets. West-facing rooms will give you a view of the sirens-and-pirates show across the street at Treasure Island, but the sounds will also leak in; the fracas ends at midnight. Also, *under no circumstances* should you or your kids touch, jiggle, or fiddle with anything in the minibar—you will be charged for simply moving items about (trust us—there are computer sensors under each item). The hotel will, however, provide a fridge free of charge, along with devices for the hearing impaired. ***Note:*** The newer Venezia Tower rooms have their own check-in desk and are even more luxe than the regular ones (kids will find the plasma-screen TV in the bathroom quite cool).

Several good choices for kid-type food here include the **Grand Lux Café** (p. 157), which has over 150 choices of (oversize) plates from which to choose, along with a good food court featuring Nathan's hot dogs, Italian food, and sandwiches. There's also a casual Chinese restaurant, Noodle Asia.

Although the hotel is elaborately detailed, the five pools are disappointingly stark in comparison. Located on the fourth-floor roof, they offer a view, with minimal shade and plantings.

Parents looking to get away from it all should try the lavish **Canyon Ranch SpaClub,** the finest hotel spa in town. You'll find nutritionists, physical therapists, and acupuncturists on the staff, and vibrating massage chairs that you rest in during pedicures—what

Tips Surfing for Savings

Before you take your trip to Vegas, go online and sign up at the casino websites to be notified of promotional deals by e-mail. And, again, we strongly recommend that once you've arrived in Vegas, you should join the players clubs at every casino you visit. Before long, you'll be getting glossy postcards in your mailbox with deals to lure you back to Sin City.

more could you want? The $35-a-day fee is high, but it does include a full day's worth of classes ranging from regular aerobics to yoga, Pilates, rock climbing, and dance.

The **Grand Canal Shoppes** is a stupendous mall complete with nearly four-score stores, seven eateries, costumed performers, and gondola rides. ***Tip:*** This is one of only a few hotels on the Strip without a buffet. Plan your eating accordingly.

3355 Las Vegas Blvd. S., Las Vegas, NV 89109. ✆ **888/2-VENICE** (283-6423) or 702/414-1000. Fax 702/414-1100. www.venetian.com. 3,000 units. $179–$499 double. Extra person $35. Children 12 and under stay free in parent's room. Cribs free; no rollaways. AE, DC, DISC, MC, V. Free self- and valet parking. **Amenities:** 18 restaurants (all major cuisines; no buffet); casino; showroom; wedding chapel; 5 outdoor pools; health club and spa; video arcade; concierge; tour desk; car-rental desk; business center; shopping arcade; 24-hr. room service; laundry service; dry cleaning; nonsmoking rooms; executive-level rooms. *In room:* A/C, TV w/pay movies, fax, dataport, fridge, hair dryer, iron/ironing board, safe.

EXPENSIVE

The Flamingo ★★★ The best pool in town and a generous discount for kids at the buffet make this a swell choice for your family, especially if you can land a good room rate. The Flamingo rose to fame as the first Vegas hotel built with the mob's money (in 1946)—and eventually Bugsy Siegel's blood. The hotel has been renovated numerous times, and Bugsy's suite, with its secret panels and hidden doors, was torn out with no regard for history (welcome to Las Vegas).

The hotel's giant pink facade, with the glowing lotus, is one of the most famous landmarks in Vegas, but negotiating the driveway under it leading to the valet can be confusing. Inside, the hotel is nice, bright, and light, but a bit overwhelmed by the casino: The gaming area spreads throughout the property, winding about like a cash-hungry python.

The rooms have no set or consistent style, due to the many additions and renovations over the years. Room configurations vary depending on the era in which the tower was built, but most rooms tend to be slightly larger than the Vegas norm, decorated in either beach-toned pastels or deeper jewel colors (ask for a recently renovated room—most have been redone since 2003). The bathrooms are everything you'd expect in a standard hotel: nothing to complain about, nothing to rave about, either.

The pool area is truly a wonder—15 acres of trees and tropical foliage with river rides, water slides, a kiddie pool, whirlpools, and spray misters to keep you cool. Islands are the homes to birds like ducks, swans, spoonbills, and naturally, flamingos. There are also ponds with turtles and koi. Window seats in the buffet provide an up-close view of much of the wildlife.

The **buffet** (p. 167) is half-price for children, truly a bargain in Las Vegas. There are seven other dining choices, including the ubiquitous steakhouse. **Jimmy Buffett's Margaritaville** is a decent chain restaurant with burgers, seafood, and Caribbean fare, while **Hamada** is reviewed on p. 160.

3555 Las Vegas Blvd. S. (btw. Sands Ave. and Flamingo Rd.), Las Vegas, NV 89109. ✆ **800/732-2111** or 702/733-3111. Fax 702/733-3353. www.harrahs.com. 3,642 units. $69–$299 double. Extra person $30. Children 17 and under stay free in parent's room. Cribs/rollaways free. Inquire about packages and time-share suites. AE, DC, DISC, MC, V. Free self- and valet parking. **Amenities:** 7 restaurants (American, Italian, Chinese, buffet, more); casino; showrooms; outdoor pool; 4 night-lit tennis courts; health club and spa; small video arcade; tour desk; car-rental desk; business center; shopping arcade; 24-hr. room service; in-room massage; babysitting; laundry service; dry cleaning; nonsmoking rooms; executive-level rooms. *In room:* A/C, TV w/pay movies, dataport, hair dryer, iron/ironing board, safe.

The Mirage ★ Tigers and dolphins are the main reasons to stay here, but overall, there are many better locations for families. Not that we don't adore the verdant tropical foliage, the huge aquarium at the check-in desk, the lush pool area, and the vanilla-scented air that floats throughout the property, but kids just aren't a high priority at The Mirage, as demonstrated by their charging an extra $30 per person per room, regardless of age, though cribs and rollaways are free.

If you decide to stay here because you love the animals and the location, and price is no object, here's a hint: Ask for what you want. For example, you'll want to ask for a room on the seventh floor or higher so you'll have a view of something aside from a wall; you should also ask for a room close to the elevators, or you'll be exhausted before you get out of the hotel; and finally, if you want it, ask for a room with a view of the volcano. But if you don't get a volcano room, fret not, you can watch the four-times-an-hour lava flow free from the street.

The rooms are decorated in camel and beige with red-toned accent colors—sort of dull, but tasteful nevertheless, while bathrooms sport the "see-we-have-marble-even-though-we're-small" theme. If we have one complaint, it's that you can get better bang for your room buck elsewhere. The service here, however, is quite good and the staff pleasant enough.

The pool area is wonderfully landscaped, but you have to traipse through the casino to get to it from your room, which can be tiresome for smaller kids. The health club costs $25 per day, and for that you get saunas, juice bar, lockers, machines, and free weights. Expect to pay $35 and up, plus tip, for treatments such as manicures and pedicures.

3400 Las Vegas Blvd. S. (btw. Flamingo Rd. and Sands Ave.), Las Vegas, NV 89109. ✆ **800/374-9000** or 702/791-7111. Fax 702/791-7446. www.mirage.com. 2,763 units. Sun–Thurs $99–$229 double, Fri–Sat and holidays $129–$229 double; $250–$3,000 suite. Extra person $30. No discount for children. Cribs/rollaways free. AE, DC, DISC, MC, V. Free self- and valet parking. **Amenities:** 12 restaurants (American, French, Italian, Brazilian, buffet, more); casino; showrooms; beautiful outdoor pool; health club and spa; concierge; tour desk; car-rental desk; business center; shopping arcade; 24-hr. room service; laundry service; dry cleaning; nonsmoking rooms; executive-level rooms. *In room:* A/C, TV w/pay movies, dataport, hair dryer, iron/ironing boards.

Tips **Keep Them Out!**

At most hotels, children 11 and under are forbidden to use the whirlpool—heed the warnings and keep your kids out, as violations are likely to attract the ire of adults seeking some sanctuary in the pool area. Anyway, the high heat isn't healthy for your tots.

TI–Treasure Island ★ TI? What's up with the new name? Why, Vegas grew up, that's what. Though Treasure Island is a good choice for families who want to stay on the Center Strip, that doesn't mean it welcomes kids with open arms (at least not until they grow up and learn to drink and gamble). In fact, you might feel a bit pillaged when hit with the $30 per-extra-person charge, with no discount for children. But, like its next-door sister The Mirage, the cribs and rollaways are free. And Treasure Island is a lot more fun, at a little less cost, than The Mirage, while not quite as kitschy as Excalibur.

Originally conceived (or so the legend goes) as a family-oriented alternative to The Mirage, Treasure Island tried to shed its family-fun-zone vibe when it was acquired by MGM, but luckily, it kept the pirate theme intact. We especially like the seaside village that fronts the hotel along the lagoon where the free spectacle, *Sirens of TI,* is performed nightly. The updated sirens-and-pirates show, which replaced the original pirates-vs.–British Navy extravaganza, is a bit risqué, earning a PG-13 rating.

The guest rooms are pretty spacious—bigger than those at the next-door-neighbor Mirage—and are appropriately decorated in gold tones and a French Regency style. What they aren't is tacky. In fact, the rooms are surprisingly classy, with ultracomfortable beds and excellent lighting (a problem in many other Strip hotels). What there isn't is drawer space; there are only a measly two drawers, so be advised that you'll either be living out of your suitcase or the closet. The big marble bathrooms feature large soaking tubs and an abundance of counter space. ***Warning:*** The tub in our room didn't have handrails and the tub bottom was slippery—a bad combination for young kids. If you have older kids, try to get a Strip-side room facing the sirens show—which goes on every evening until midnight. If your kids, however, go to bed early, note that some of the goings-on can get a bit noisy.

The pool is small (just 3½ ft. deep), amoeba-shaped, and pretty bland by Vegas standards (the staff didn't even bother to check our room keys the last time we were there—a sure sign of mediocrity). There's a small kiddie pool, but most kids tend to congregate in the main pool (much to the consternation of many adults).

When it comes to food, you'll find a revamped **buffet** (p. 166), plus a deli, a coffee shop, **Ben & Jerry's Ice Cream Store,** and **Krispy Kreme Doughnuts.**

Shops are housed in a mock village, but aside from some cool skull-themed items, there's nothing outstanding—souvenirs, T-shirts, and some jewelry. Shrug. You're better off spending your window-shopping time across the street at The Venetian. The small dark arcade will, however, keep kids (who are old enough to wander) busy long enough so you can have a romantic drink and watch the sirens show together from a table on the patio at **Social House,** TI's upscale sushi restaurant, like a real date.

Moms and dads looking for more escape time can go to the full-service spa and health club with a complement of machines, plus sauna, steam, whirlpool, massage, on-site trainers, TVs and stereos with headsets, and anything else you might need (including Sebastian grooming products in the women's locker room). It's $22 per day to use the facilities. Note that many of the spa services are ridiculously and outrageously overpriced: They charge $50 for a pedicure!

The greatest—albeit pricey—treat for kids at Treasure Island: the Cirque du Soleil production *Mystère.* The $66- to $105-a-ticket cost is prohibitive for most families, and it's probably too sophisticated for young kids (think 10 and over), but it is a very memorable experience, and adults and older children and teens usually rave about it.

Tip: A free tram travels between Treasure Island and The Mirage almost round-the-clock.

3300 Las Vegas Blvd. S. (at Spring Mountain Rd.), Las Vegas, NV 89109. ✆ **800/288-7206** or 702/894-7111. Fax 702/894-7446. www.treasureisland.com. 2,900 units. From $89 double; from $149 suite. Extra person $30. No discount for children. Cribs/rollaways free. Special promotions on the Web. Inquire about packages. AE, DC, DISC, MC, V. Free self- and valet parking. **Amenities:** 8 restaurants (American, Japanese, steakhouse, seafood, sushi, buffet, more); casino; showrooms; outdoor pool; health club and spa; very well-equipped game and video arcade; tour desk; car-rental desk; business center; shopping arcade; 24-hr. room service; laundry service; dry cleaning; nonsmoking rooms; executive-level rooms. *In room:* A/C, TV w/pay movies, fax, dataport, hair dryer, iron/ironing board, safe.

4 NORTH STRIP ACCOMMODATIONS

The North Strip offers thrill rides at the Sahara and Stratosphere, a huge indoor amusement park, and big-top acts at Circus Circus, all of which can keep your children amused for hours, if not days.

MODERATE

Sahara Hotel and Casino At first glance, this venerable gem seems a real bargain, especially if you have a NASCAR fan in the family, because one of the main lures is the **NASCAR Cafe.** However, if you need a crib or rollaway bed, you'll pay for it, and any child over 12 also hikes up your rates. It should also be noted that the Sahara feels it's not as well equipped as other hotels for children and discourages you from bringing yours—and yet, they added a roller coaster. Go figure.

The hotel is old school, a holdout from the glory days of the Rat Pack. It's not as shiny as some of its southerly neighbors, especially when compared to the similarly themed Luxor, but there is a certain amount of charm to the Moroccan decor—colored tiles and filigree metalwork set with glowing red and blue gems are a nice touch, but the "midnight at the oasis" concept is left at the door to your room (and the bedspreads at the Sahara are notorious for their unattractiveness). Bathrooms are clean, serviceable, and just fine. Hopefully, if you've got a room here, it's just to sleep in, because that's pretty much what they're designed for—and under those not-our-taste-at-all bedspreads are some of the comfiest mattresses in town, which is an unexpected and welcome bonus.

The hotel features a buffet and the NASCAR Cafe (p. 158), along with Mexican food, a coffee shop, and the inevitable steakhouse, all of which provide sustenance.

The Olympic-size pool, located at the foot of the parking garage, is heated only during the summer months, a drawback and chilly disappointment for those visiting during the winter holidays. But even without a pool, kids will have things to do; there's an arcade in the hotel, plus the NASCAR attractions. The **Adventuredome** at Circus Circus (p. 180) is just minutes away. ***Tip:*** Get a bellman when checking in; it's a long trek from valet parking's domed driveway to the front desk.

2535 Las Vegas Blvd. S. (at E. Sahara Ave.), Las Vegas, NV 89109. ✆ **888/696-2121** or 702/737-2111. Fax 702/791-2027. www.saharavegas.com. 1,720 units. $39 and up double. Extra person $20. Children 11 and

Tips **Extra! Extra!**

Because most rooms are stocked for only two guests, you may want to request enough towels and toiletries for your entire family before you arrive.

under stay free in parent's room. Cribs/rollaways $15. AE, DC, DISC, MC, V. Free self- and valet parking. **Amenities:** 5 restaurants (American, buffet, Mexican, more); casino; showrooms; outdoor pool; Jacuzzi; tour desk; car-rental desk; business center; shopping arcade; limited room service; laundry service; dry cleaning; nonsmoking rooms; executive-level rooms. *In room:* A/C, TV w/pay movies, hair dryer, iron/ironing board.

Stratosphere ★ Yes, it's a bit far from the rest of the Strip, but the Stratosphere, the tallest building west of the Mississippi at 1,149 feet, has incredibly thrilling rides, amazing views, a fabulous pool, and reasonable rates.

The rooms are nice, with touches of cherrywood and the usual hotel amenities. Some suites offer window-side Jacuzzis, but this might not be the right way to go with your family. The bathrooms in the standard rooms are just fine; the ones in the suites are larger.

Along with dining at the high-priced, high-in-the-sky Top of the World on the 106th floor of the tower, you can stave off your hunger at **Naga** for Chinese or at the ubiquitous **buffet.** Bless **Fellini's Ristorante** for offering half-size, half-priced portions for both children and adults. **Roxy's** features singing waitresses in poodle skirts serving diner food. **Lucky's** coffee shop is open 24 hours and also has a retro feel. And then there's a food court with a Mickey D's, plus a steakhouse and a Mexican grill–oyster bar combo.

Indoor and outdoor observation decks offer the most stunning city views you will ever see, especially at night. The pool, located on the eighth floor overlooking the Strip, is big and beautiful, a perfect place to relax after a wild ride on **Insanity,** a ride of the midway Scrambler ilk, only 909 feet above the ground, or the **Big Shot** bungee-style ride that shoots you up the needle atop Strat's 1,149-foot tower, or **X Scream,** a ride that rolls you over the edge and back. All three thrill rides are reviewed on p. 182.

The hotel also offers three shows, but only one that some deem acceptable for kids, the impersonator show, ***American Superstars,*** reviewed on p. 229.

2000 Las Vegas Blvd. S. (btw. St. Louis St. and Baltimore Ave.), Las Vegas, NV 89104. ✆ **800/99-TOWER** (998-6937) or 702/380-7777. Fax 702/380-7732. www.stratospherehotel.com. 2,500 units. Sun–Thurs $39 and up double, Fri–Sat $79 and up double; $89 and up suite. Extra person $15. Children 12 and under stay free in parent's room. AE, DC, DISC, MC, V. Free self- and valet parking. **Amenities:** 6 restaurants (American, buffet, Italian, Asian, more); casino; showrooms; large new pool area with great views of the Strip; children's rides and games located at the base of the Tower; concierge; tour desk; car-rental desk; shopping arcade; business center; 24-hr. room service; laundry service; dry cleaning; nonsmoking rooms; executive-level rooms. *In room:* A/C, TV w/pay movies, dataport, hair dryer, iron/ironing board, safe.

Fun Facts **Officer Dex, the K-9 Cop**

In December 2001, Officer Dex, a then 2-year-old German shepherd, joined the security team at the Stratosphere, making him the only K-9 casino security officer in Las Vegas. Dex is trained in article and person search, obedience, scouting, and tracking. He and his handler, Officer Lieberman, are available to assist local and federal officers as well as security teams at other gaming properties, but what they really enjoy doing is interacting with guests. If you see Dex on duty, ask Officer Lieberman if it's all right to pet him or have your photo taken together.

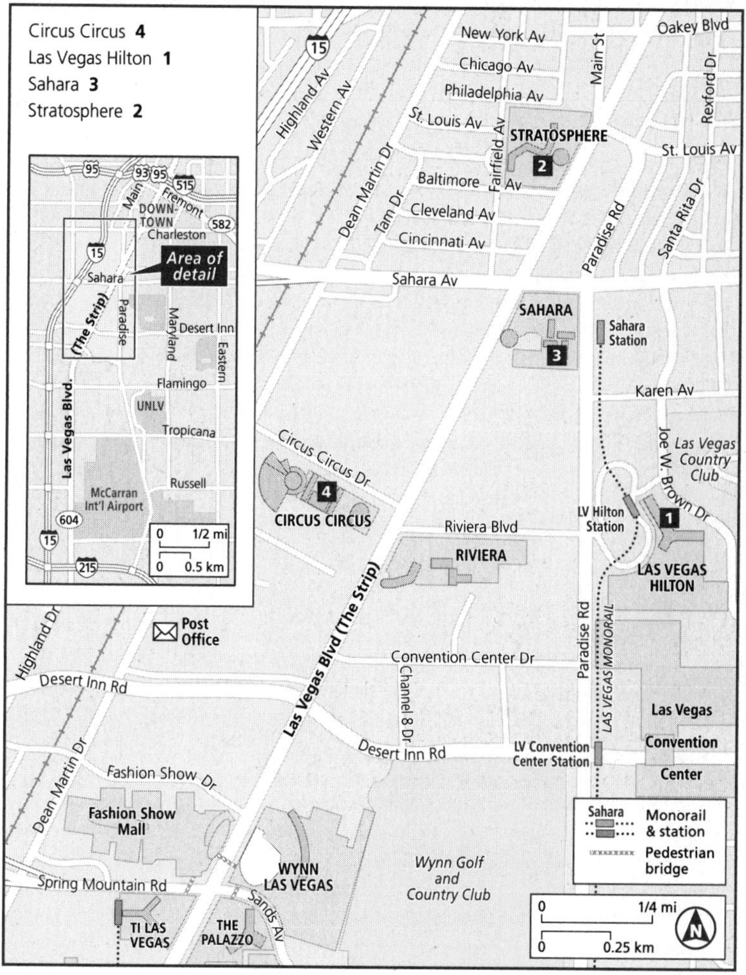

INEXPENSIVE

Circus Circus ★★ With free circus acts and a huge indoor amusement park, this place is an awesome spot for all but the most jaded and cynical of today's youth. Of course, the latter could be your kids, in which case you may want to just turn them loose at the **Adventuredome** (p. 180) and see if a spin on the Chaos roller coaster will knock some fun into them.

Fun Facts You Learn Something New . . .

You won't find record producer Sean "P. Diddy" Combs staying at Circus Circus; he allegedly suffers from coulrophobia, fear of clowns.

Circus Circus is unique among all of Vegas's casino hotels in that, according to placards placed throughout the property, children 13 and older can move freely about the property except in the casino, where they are forbidden. Those 12 and under must be accompanied by an older child. The curfew laws regarding arcades, however, still apply, and troublemakers can get themselves and their parents into all kinds of hot water.

Circus Circus was the first family-oriented casino in Las Vegas, and when it opened, the color scheme ran toward bilious and bright. One wag commented that the carpet was louder than the casino, and he wasn't far from the truth. Renovations have toned things down a bit, though the overall atmosphere of hectic fun remains. The midway level features dozens of carnival games, a large arcade (more than 300 video and pinball games), trick mirrors, and ongoing circus acts under the big top from 11am to midnight daily. The world's largest permanent circus (according to the *Guinness Book of World Records*), it features renowned trapeze artists, stunt cyclists, jugglers, magicians, acrobats, and high-wire daredevils. Spectators can view the action from much of the midway or get up close and comfy on benches in the performance arena. There's a "be-a-clown" booth where kids can be made up with washable clown makeup and red foam-rubber noses. They can grab a bite to eat in McDonald's (also on this level), and since the mezzanine overlooks the casino action, they can also look down and wave to Mom and Dad—or more to the point, Mom and Dad can look up and wave to the kids without having to stray too far from the blackjack table. (For better or worse, this is the only hotel that will let you leave your brood unattended in the main area of the property, making losing money at the casino not the only risk you may be taking here!) Circus clowns wander the midway creating balloon animals and cutting up in various ways.

Rooms here come in three varieties and price ranges. The cheapest and least attractive, the Manor rooms, are housed in low three-story buildings off of the main hotel. Guests park in front of their building. A gate to the property that can be opened only with your room key ensures your safety, but you'll get what you pay for in terms of quality. The Skyrise Tower includes two pools and a casino, and these rooms are decorated in deep jewel tones. The West Tower, which houses the central registration desk and the shopping arcade, is connected to the Adventuredome theme park. These rooms are decorated in the same color scheme as those in the Skyrise Tower. The Casino Tower, where the circus acts perform, has rooms with darker earth tones. The bathrooms in every section are basic, clean, and serviceable, and they all have tubs and showers, except for a few designed for those with physical disabilities. The thousands of rooms here occupy sufficient acreage to warrant a free Disney World–style aerial shuttle (another kid pleaser) and minibuses connecting its many components.

Adjacent to the hotel is **Circusland RV Park,** with 399 full-utility spaces and up to 50-amp hookups. It has its own 24-hour convenience store, swimming pools, saunas, whirlpools, kiddie playground, fenced pet runs, video-game arcade, and community room. The rate is $25 and up Sunday to Thursday, $35 and up Friday and Saturday.

The **Pink Pony** coffee shop and the **buffet** (p. 158 and 168, respectively) are popular with the kids, and the eponymous Steakhouse has proven a consistent favorite with locals for a number of years, though a lot of people we know don't think it's all that good. The **Pizzeria** offers children's specials.

2880 Las Vegas Blvd. S. (btw. Circus Circus Dr. and Convention Center Dr.), Las Vegas, NV 89109. ✆ **702/794-3986,** 800/634-3450, or 702/734-0410. Fax 702/734-5897. www.circuscircus.com. 3,763 units. Sun–Thurs $39 and up double; Fri–Sat $69 and up double. Extra person $12. Children 16 and under stay free in parent's room. Cribs/rollaways $12. AE, DC, DISC, MC, V. Free self- and valet parking. **Amenities:** 7 restaurants (American, buffet, Italian, Mexican, more); casino; wedding chapel; circus acts; 2 outdoor pools; midway-style carnival games; video arcade; tour desk; car-rental desk; shopping arcade; 24-hr. room service; laundry service; dry cleaning; nonsmoking rooms; executive-level rooms. *In room:* A/C, TV w/pay movies, hair dryer, safe.

5 ACCOMMODATIONS EAST OF THE STRIP

This area is close to both the Convention Center and the Strip, especially if you have a car. There are many chain hotels in this area in all price ranges, as well as some standout resorts like the Hard Rock and the Las Vegas Hilton. You will need a car, however, or have to use cabs to get to the Strip.

EXPENSIVE

Atrium Suites ★ Here's a way to have all the benefits of the Hard Rock Hotel & Casino without any of the issues that might arise when your just-turned-teenagers start hanging out with the cool college kids at the Hard Rock pool. Located next to the Hard Rock, but minus the swim-up blackjack tables and visible body modifications on the guests, the Atrium Suites is sedate, with a center atrium and waterfall. All rooms are suites, though some tend to be on the small size, and come equipped with a fridge, microwave, and coffeemaker, along with a wet bar. Small pets are permitted on the first floor. The fitness room is open 24 hours, so you can squeeze in a few minutes on the exercycle while the kids sleep in. The pool is plain, with a Jacuzzi.

4255 Paradise Rd. (north of Harmon Ave.), Las Vegas, NV 89109. ✆ **800/330-7728** or 702/369-4400. Fax 702/369-4330. www.atriumsuiteshotel.com. 201 units. $120–$200 double. Children 18 and under stay free in parent's room. Cribs free; rollaways $10. AE, DC, DISC, MC, V. Free self-parking. **Amenities:** Restaurant (American); outdoor pool; small exercise room with Nautilus, weights, and treadmills; Jacuzzi; sauna; concierge; free airport shuttle; business center; limited room service; dry cleaning; nonsmoking rooms; executive-level rooms. *In room:* A/C, TV w/pay movies, fridge, coffeemaker, hair dryer, iron/ironing board.

Tips **Know Your Room's Limits**

Most of the hotels oriented toward long-term stays and most all-suite hotels allow a maximum number of people to stay in a room, all for one fee, regardless of age. If you have five people in your party, no matter what their ages, you will have to get a room that sleeps six, rather than a room that sleeps four with a roll-away and an extra-person fee. Of course, desk staff and on-duty managers can be flexible at times, but it is best to assume that they will hold hard and fast to the guests-per-room maximum.

Carriage House ★★★ Finds This might seem an expensive place to stay when compared to some hotels on the Strip, but the rack rates are often deeply discounted, putting the Carriage House into the same category as many of the Strip hotels. The Carriage House is actually a timeshare, but at any given time, up to 50 units are available for rent, which translates into family-oriented vacation comfort. All suites have full kitchens, including cookware and dishes. Although the least expensive suites sleep only two, the larger units (deluxe and one- and two-bedroom suites) sleep four to eight, making this a great option for larger families. And they *are* roomy—one-bedroom condos range in size from 660 to 700 square feet; the two bedrooms are 1,200 square feet.

The rooms are decorated with a casual, summery feel in beiges, greens, and gold. Great care has been taken with the design of the furnishings—armchairs are built so that there's no strain on the body when standing up, especially good for seniors and those with back problems. The nice-size bathrooms are very clean; shower chairs are available for those who might need them.

There's a standard-size pool, whirlpool, and a basketball and paddle tennis court, with equipment available for free at the front desk. Pay-per-view movies and games are also available, as well as board games. Family bingo takes place on Thursday afternoons.

For those looking for a family atmosphere away from the smoky casinos yet close enough to easily see the sights, this is a perfect choice. ***Tip:*** If you can't find a parking place in the covered parking lot, park as close to the tennis court as possible to take advantage of the shade.

105 E. Harmon Ave. (at Koval Lane), Las Vegas, NV 89109. ✆ **800/221-2301** or 702/798-1020. Fax 702/798-1020, ext 112. www.carriagehouselasvegas.com. 201 units. Guest rooms and studio suites $129 (2 people maximum); suites $185–$300 (4–8 people maximum). Ask for discounted rates. Cribs, highchairs, and rollaways free. AE, DC, DISC, MC, V. Free self-parking. **Amenities:** Tennis court; concierge; tour desk; airport shuttle; laundry service; dry cleaning; nonsmoking rooms. *In room:* A/C, TV w/pay movies, dataport, full kitchen, hair dryer, iron/ironing board.

Courtyard by Marriott ★★ One of many Marriotts in Las Vegas, this upscale hotel is fresh and clean. Its location away from the Strip means more quality time together around the sparkling pool. Rooms are comfortable and bathrooms a nice size in this three-story, attractively landscaped building. Most rooms have king-size beds, and all have balconies or patios. It's bland compared to the snazzy Strip hotels that cost about the same or less, no doubt because this hotel is more for the business traveler rather than the vacationer.

3275 Paradise Rd. (btw. Convention Center Dr. and Desert Inn Rd.), Las Vegas, NV 89109. ✆ **800/321-2211** or 702/791-3600. Fax 702/796-7981. www.marriott.com/courtyard/travel.mi. 149 units. Sun–Thurs $159 and up double, Fri–Sat $189 and up double; $209 and up suite. No charge for extra person above double occupancy. Cribs/rollaways free. AE, DC, DISC, MC, V. Free parking at your room door. **Amenities:** Restaurant (American); outdoor pool; small exercise room; Jacuzzi; business center; limited room service; 24-hr. food market; laundry service; dry cleaning; nonsmoking rooms; executive-level rooms; coin-op laundry. *In room:* A/C, TV w/pay movies, dataport, coffeemaker, hair dryer, iron/ironing board.

Hard Rock Hotel & Casino ★★ If you worry that your children might be growing up too fast, you should steer clear of this hip hotel designed for MTV-viewing, Gen X–demographic, piña-colada-sucking vacationers who want to rock 'n' roll all night and party every day. But if the only way you'll have peace on vacation is to indulge your offspring, no doubt the Hard Rock will have your teens screaming that you are hip to be cool, while secretly wishing they'd brought fake IDs.

Keep in mind that if a calm vacation's all you ever wanted, you won't find it here. The casino, with its rock-star-themed versions of games (White Rabbit slot machines and Jimi Hendrix gambling chips, for instance), sits smack in the center of the main floor,

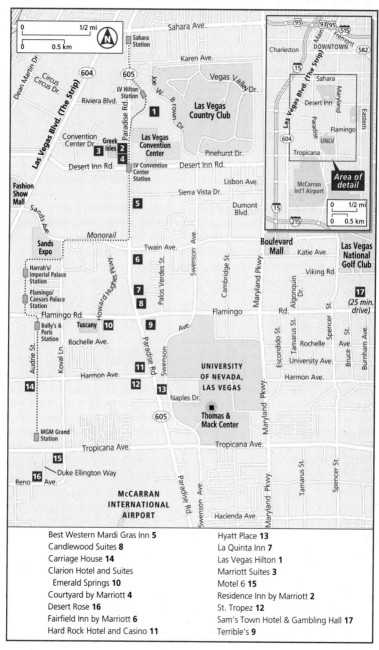

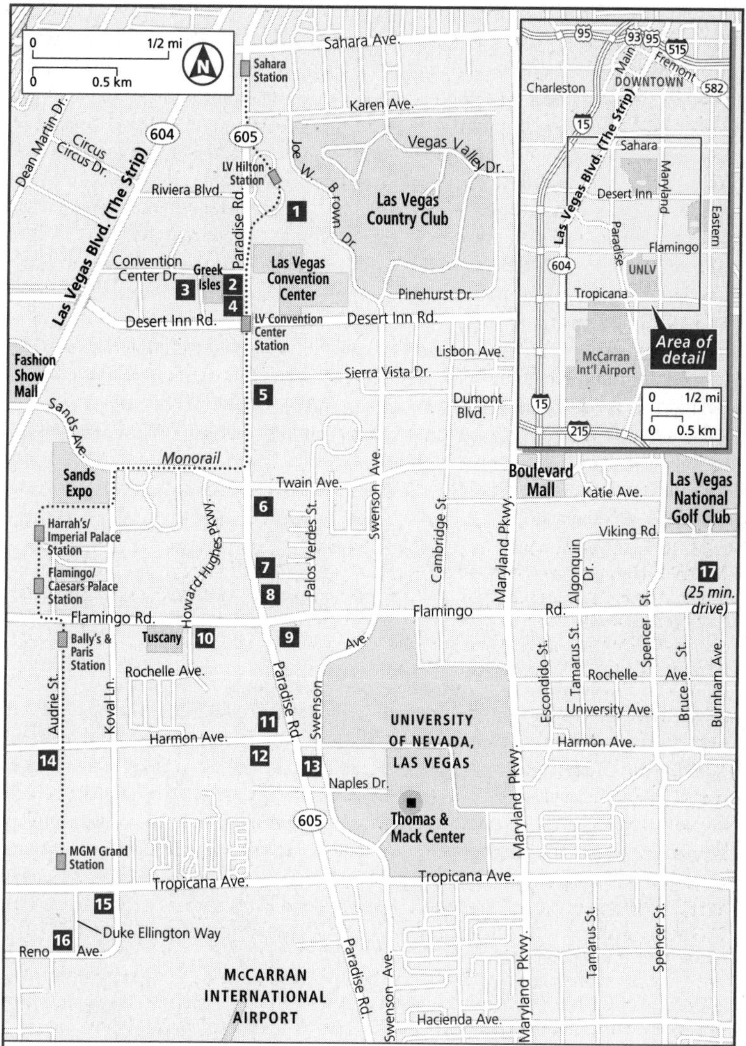

Best Western Mardi Gras Inn **5**
Candlewood Suites **8**
Carriage House **14**
Clarion Hotel and Suites Emerald Springs **10**
Courtyard by Marriott **4**
Desert Rose **16**
Fairfield Inn by Marriott **6**
Hard Rock Hotel and Casino **11**
Hyatt Place **13**
La Quinta Inn **7**
Las Vegas Hilton **1**
Marriott Suites **3**
Motel 6 **15**
Residence Inn by Marriott **2**
St. Tropez **12**
Sam's Town Hotel & Gambling Hall **17**
Terrible's **9**

and music blasts over the jingle-jangle of the slots. Everyone here—well, almost every-one—looks as if they stepped out of a casting call for *Blind Date* or the latest Vin Diesel action flick—think thousand-dollar tattoos and other surgical body modifications, tight T-shirts, skimpy skirts, and the chance to spot Ben Affleck, Lenny Kravitz, and Pamela Anderson (or reasonable facsimiles thereof) at the crap tables.

Enclosed in glass cases that ring the casino are costumes, instruments, and other rock memorabilia, including a floor-to-ceiling Beatles display and a collection of rock-star dolls and lunch boxes. Kurt Cobain, No Doubt, and the Rolling Stones are three of the many artists represented here. Over by the elevators, there's one large display of women who rock, which seems to marginalize the chicks—don't each of them deserve as much floor space as some of their male counterparts?

Check-in is easy: Just turn left as you walk in the front door. Rooms have that slacker-chic, Lost (Hipster Generation) in Space vibe popularized by movies such as *Drugstore Cowboy, Austin Powers,* and *Swingers.* The newer rooms are larger, with bigger bathrooms than the older rooms, and all have French doors (a unique touch in this city), and larger-than-the-Vegas-norm TV sets with specialty music channels. On a high note, the beds have feather pillows and the mattresses are surprisingly comfortable.

Restaurants include the **Hard Rock Cafe** (in another building), **Nobu, Mr. Lucky's 24/7,** and the smarmily named **Pink Taco** (reviewed on p. 162, 160, 163, and 163, respectively). The sundries shop has all manner of hipness—including Dirty Girl soap, Kama Sutra body oil, and pill cases shaped like prescription drug capsules. There's also a Hard Rock souvenir shop.

Girls—and guys—just wanna have fun by the pool, which features a swim-up (21-and-over) blackjack table and a sandy beach where lithe tan bodies splash in the cool shallow water. And we do mean cool—rock music is piped into the pool, so you've got the beat while doing the breaststroke. Daily, more than 1,600 piña coladas are served poolside, so the atmosphere can be a bit raucous, with more than a tinge of "let's hook up" hovering about.

If you're not a good sport or a suburban version of the Osbournes, you might hate the Hard Rock as a place to stay, especially when you factor its distance from the Strip (they have shuttles to take you there) and the prices. But you can always drop in for a visit.

4455 Paradise Rd. (at Harmon Ave.), Las Vegas, NV 89109. ✆ **800/473-ROCK** (473-7625) or 702/693-5000. Fax 702/693-5021. www.hardrockhotel.com. 657 units. Sun–Thurs $89 and up double, Fri–Sat $150 and up double; $250 and up suite. Extra person $35. Children 12 and under stay free in parent's room. Cribs $25 per night; rollaways free, available in suites only. AE, DC, MC, V. Free self- and valet parking. **Amenities:** 5 restaurants (American, Japanese, Mexican, more); casino; showroom; 2 outdoor pools with a lazy river ride and sandy beach bottom; small health club and spa; concierge; tour desk; 24-hr. room service; laundry service; dry cleaning; nonsmoking rooms; executive-level rooms. *In room:* A/C, TV w/pay movies, dataport, high-speed Internet access (for a fee), hair dryer, iron/ironing board.

Hyatt Place Las Vegas ★ (Value) Every Hyatt Place (formerly AmeriSuite) property is designed to look alike so that repeat guests will be able to find their way about with a minimum of thought or effort. So if you've seen one, you've seen them all. Not that that's a bad thing, just a bland one, especially in this town, where unique theatrical hotels are the norm. Catering to business travelers, high-school groups, and college sports teams, this corporate hotel offers large rooms in dark tones with microwaves, utensils, fridges, and foldout couches in all rooms. The TCB suites are larger, with a desk and workspace, but, alas, minus the Vegas-appropriate photos of Elvis wearing the lightning-bolt symbol engraved with the anagram for his slogan, "Takin' care of business." Such levity might distract from the regulation room styles, causing some poor AmeriSuite-conditioned traveler to lose his way to the vending machines.

Tips Always Ask

"Suite" can mean a number of things in Las Vegas, and frequently translates to "slightly larger room with a Jacuzzi tub, and maybe a fold-out couch." Less frequently, a suite will have either a partial kitchen with a minifridge and microwave or even a full kitchen. When unsure about what a hotel means by "suite," ask for specifics.

There's nary a slot machine on-site, but free shuttles can take you over to the centrally located Planet Hollywood Resort & Casino so you can experience the Strip in all its neon glory. We like that they provide *USA Today* gratis, which is more than can be said for the glitzier casino/hotels; their attitude seems to be that you can't gamble if you're reading the paper.

Occasional weekend and manager's specials (the law of supply and demand) can bring the rates significantly lower than the rack prices, and the large complimentary breakfast buffet helps offset the cost of the rooms. Every Wednesday, you can drop in on the manager's reception and gobble up the hot and cold hors d'oeuvres and soft drinks. Some kids may appreciate that Nintendo is available (for an hourly fee) and that the hotel is across the street from the Hard Rock Hotel. It's also close to the Strip. The pool is heated and basic. This isn't the most glamorous place to stay, but it definitely does the job.

4520 Paradise Rd., Las Vegas, NV 89109. ✆ **702/369-3366.** Fax 702/369-0009. www.amerisuites.com. 202 units. $89 and up double. Extra person $10. Children 17 and under stay free in parent's room. Cribs free; no rollaways. AE, DC, DISC, MC, V. Free self-parking. Small pets permitted on first floor. **Amenities:** Outdoor pool; fitness room; tour desk; free airport shuttle; business center; laundry service; dry cleaning; nonsmoking rooms; vending machines. *In room:* A/C, TV w/pay movies, high-speed Internet access (for a fee), hair dryer, iron/ironing board.

Marriott Suites ★ Extra-large comfortable rooms make this a good choice for families who don't want to experience the smoke and noise of the casino hotels, but still want to be close enough to visit the attractions. You will want to take a cab to the Strip in hot weather or if you have children who won't want to, or can't, make the long 3-block walk. The Convention Center is a block in the other direction. Rooms are attractively decorated, and French doors separate the sitting area from the bedroom. This is a fine choice if you want to stay off the Strip and don't mind paying high prices for the care and standards provided by a national chain.

325 Convention Center Dr., Las Vegas, NV 89109. ✆ **800/627-6667** or 702/650-2000. Fax 702/650-9466. www.marriott.com. 278 units. $189 and up suites (4 people maximum). Cribs free; no rollaways. AE, DC, DISC, MC, V. Free outdoor parking. **Amenities:** Restaurant (American); outdoor pool; small exercise room; Jacuzzi; concierge; tour desk; car-rental desk; business center; 24-hr. room service; laundry service; dry cleaning; nonsmoking rooms; executive-level rooms; coin-op laundry. *In room:* A/C, TV w/pay movies, dataport, minifridge, coffeemaker, hair dryer, iron/ironing board, safe.

Residence Inn by Marriott ★ Located on 7 acres of beautifully landscaped lawns, with tropical foliage and gardens, this link in the Marriott chain is a popular choice for business travelers and families. Most accommodations have working fireplaces—not that you'll need them in the summer, though during winter, it can actually get quite chilly in this desert town—along with their own patio or balcony. Studio suites, all with armchairs and queen-size beds, have adjoining sitting rooms with single-person fold-out sofas; these suites can sleep up to three, plus fit a crib. The deluxe penthouse suites add an upstairs bedroom with two queen-size beds, along with a bathroom, TV, and radio. These penthouses, which also have a dining room, sleep up to five, plus a crib. All accommodations have fully equipped kitchens, complete with dishwashers. Guests receive a complimentary basket of microwave popcorn and coffee.

3225 Paradise Rd. (btw. Desert Inn Rd. and Convention Center Dr.), Las Vegas, NV 89109. ✆ **800/331-3131** or 702/796-9300. www.marriott.com. 192 units. $139 and up studio (3 people maximum); $169 and up penthouse (6 people maximum). Rates include continental breakfast. Cribs free. AE, DC, DISC, MC, V. Free self-parking. Pet friendly. **Amenities:** Free buffets in lobby lounge; outdoor pool; guests have access to small exercise room next door at the Marriott Suites; Jacuzzi; dry cleaning; nonsmoking rooms; coin-op laundry. *In room:* A/C, TV w/pay movies, dataport, kitchenette, coffeemaker, hair dryer, iron/ironing board.

St. Tropez ★★ Finds Small, restful, and fairly secluded, this European style, all-suite hotel is worlds away from the glitter of the Strip, yet in reality, the Hard Rock Hotel & Casino is across the street and the Trop and MGM Grand are just a few long blocks to the west.

Rooms are large, almost Venetian in size, but without the Venetian prices. You have your choice of either a king-size or two double beds, with either a "private sleeping area" (the bed is to one side) or the "separate sleeping area," a suite that has the bed in a second room. Some suites come with an in-room whirlpool tub, and all have nice-size bathrooms. Rooms are tastefully decorated in subdued warm tones.

Lush landscaping surrounds the free-form pool and Jacuzzi, and there's a small fitness room. The grassy courtyard offers plenty of space for kids to run about, and you can often see them playing Frisbee and tag on the lawn. Free continental breakfast, with lots of doughnuts and pastries, is served daily. ***Tip:*** Off-season rooms can be half-price here.

455 E. Harmon Ave. (at Paradise Rd.), Las Vegas, NV 89109. ✆ **800/666-5400** or 702/369-5400. Fax 702/369-8901. www.sttropezlasvegas.com. 150 units. $99 and up double (5 people maximum). Children 11 and under stay free in parent's room. Cribs/rollaways free. AE, DC, DISC, MC, V. Free self-parking. **Amenities:** Outdoor pool; fitness room; tour desk; free airport shuttle. *In room:* A/C, TV w/pay movies, fridge, coffeemaker, hair dryer, iron/ironing board, safe.

MODERATE

Best Western Mardi Gras Inn Value Located a block from the Convention Center and a quick few blocks by car from the Strip, this well-run, clean, casino hotel is a reasonable choice for families, especially if parents want to do a little light gambling while the kids, who are old enough to be alone, play games or watch movies in the room. All accommodations are queen-bedded minisuites with sofa beds in the living room and eat-in minikitchens with wet bars, fridges, and coffeemakers. The grounds are nicely landscaped, and the inexpensive restaurant serves basic coffee-shop fare.

3500 Paradise Rd. (btw. Twain Ave. and Desert Inn Rd.), Las Vegas, NV 89109. ✆ **800/634-6501** or 702/731-2020. Fax 702/731-4005. www.mardigrasinn.com. 314 units. $69 and up double. Extra person $10. Children 17 and under stay free in parent's room. Rates include continental breakfast. Cribs free. AE, DC, DISC, MC, V. Free parking at your room door. **Amenities:** Restaurant; small casino; outdoor pool; Jacuzzi; tour desk; free airport shuttle; limited room service; nonsmoking rooms; coin-op laundry. *In room:* A/C, TV w/pay movies, dataport, kitchenette, fridge, coffeemaker, iron/ironing board.

Candlewood Suites ★ If you're planning on staying a week or longer in Las Vegas, this well-appointed hotel can be a real deal; stay for a month, and it's sinfully cheap. However, you'll want a car if you plan to do any sightseeing—it's relatively far from the action of the Strip, though the Hard Rock Hotel & Casino is close by. The bland rooms are decorated in grays and blues, the beds are reasonably comfortable, and the bathrooms are clean. Studios sleep two people maximum, a one-bedroom sleeps four or less, and every room has a fully equipped kitchen, along with TV, VCR, and CD player. You can also fax and copy for free at the front desk. ***Note:*** While this hotel is very expensive (for Vegas) if you stay for only 1 day, the longer you stay, the cheaper it becomes.

4034 Paradise Rd. (north of Harmon Ave.), Las Vegas, NV 89109. ✆ **800/315-2621** or 702/836-3660. Fax 702/836-3661. www.candlewoodsuites.com. 276 units. $99–$165 daily, weekly $69–$94 per day, monthly $59 per day studios (2 people maximum); $99–$189 daily, weekly $60–$104 per day, monthly $59 per day 1-bedroom (4 people maximum). Cribs free. AE, DC, DISC, MC, V. **Amenities:** Pool; weight room; Jacuzzi; tour desk; car-rental desk; business center; nonsmoking rooms; free laundry on each floor. *In room:* A/C, TV w/pay movies, VCR, dataport, full kitchens, hair dryer, iron/ironing board.

Clarion Hotel & Suites Emerald Springs ★ This is a friendly, low-key alternative to the Strip. Some parents may not like that a "gentlemen's club," that is, strip club, has opened up next door, though its signage is fairly well shielded from the hotel by tall plants. The hotel itself is pleasant, with a waterfall in the lobby, along with a sitting area that features a fireplace and TV. Typical of the inn's hospitality, there is a bowl of apples for the taking at the front desk, something we usually only see in more expensive hotels. Rooms are clean and nice, with bleached wood and a calming color scheme. Even the smallest accommodations (studios) offer small sofas, desks, and armchairs with hassocks. The pool is large, and there's a small exercise room.

325 E. Flamingo Rd. (btw. Koval Lane and Paradise Rd.), Las Vegas, NV 89109. ✆ **800/732-7889** or 702/732-9100. Fax 702/731-9784. www.choicehotels.com. 150 units. $99 and up studio; $129 and up whirlpool suite; $179 and up hospitality suite. Extra person $15. Children 18 and under stay free in parent's room. AE, DC, DISC, MC, V. Free self-parking. **Amenities:** Restaurant (coffee shop); outdoor pool; small exercise room; Jacuzzi; concierge; tour desk; car-rental desk; courtesy limo to airport or Strip; limited room service; nonsmoking rooms; executive-level rooms. *In room:* A/C, TV w/pay movies, pay-per-use Nintendo, dataport, kitchenette or wet bar, coffeemaker, hair dryer, iron/ironing board.

Desert Rose Resort ★★ (Finds) A good location, full kitchens, reasonable rates for this city, and it takes pets of any size—this place, formerly Hawthorn Suite, is a lifesaver for families. Just 1 block away from the intersection of Las Vegas Boulevard and Tropicana Avenue, this all-suite hotel is one of Las Vegas's best-kept secrets. The good-size suites are decorated in jewel tones, and all feature a fold-out couch in the living room. Bathrooms are clean and serviceable, and each room has a balcony, a unique feature in Las Vegas, where you're usually lucky if your hotel window slides open even 2 inches. There's a daily complimentary breakfast buffet with hot and cold dishes, plus an evening social hour with snacks. Families can splash in the large pool, play volleyball, or shoot hoops.

5051 Duke Ellington Way, Las Vegas, NV 89119. ✆ **800/527-1133** or 702/739-7000. Fax 702/739-9350. www.shellhospitality.com/hotels/desert_rose. 280 units. $89–$99 1-bedroom suite (4 people maximum); $119–$199 2-bedroom suite (6 people maximum). Rates include complimentary breakfast. Cribs free; no rollaways. AE, DC, DISC, MC, V. Free outdoor parking. Pets accepted. **Amenities:** Free afternoon snacks; bar; outdoor pool; small exercise room; Jacuzzi; concierge; business center; laundry service; dry cleaning; nonsmoking rooms; coin-op laundry. *In room:* A/C, TV w/pay movies, dataport, full kitchen, hair dryer, iron/ironing board.

Fairfield Inn by Marriott ★ Cheerful rooms and a comfortable lobby make this a pleasant place to stay. Units with king-size beds offer sofa beds, and up to five people are permitted in each room. The pool will keep you cool between sightseeing jaunts; and complimentary pastries, yogurt, fruit, and juices are served every morning in the lobby, while coffee, tea, and hot chocolate are provided all day. From this hotel, you can walk to several restaurants and the Strip is just minutes away.

3850 Paradise Rd. (btw. Twain Ave. and Flamingo Rd.), Las Vegas, NV 89109. ✆ **800/228-2800** or 702/791-0899. Fax 702/791-2705. www.fairfieldinn.com. 129 units. $99 and up (up to 5 people). Rates include continental breakfast. Cribs/rollaways free. AE, DC, DISC, MC, V. Free self-parking. **Amenities:** Outdoor pool; small exercise room; Jacuzzi; tour desk; airport shuttle; dry cleaning; nonsmoking rooms. *In room:* A/C, TV w/pay movies, dataport, hair dryer, iron/ironing board.

La Quinta Inn ★★ The California Mission exterior of this hotel makes it stand out along this section of Paradise Road, and once on the grounds, you'll feel an instant sense of relaxation. The staff is terrific—friendly and incredibly helpful. Families will appreciate the barbecue grills and picnic tables along with the attractive pools. The clean, pleasant rooms are spacious, and each has an oversize whirlpool tub in the bathroom. Executive rooms feature one queen-size bed, along with a minifridge, a wet bar, and a microwave, while the double queens are larger but have no kitchen facilities. Two-bedroom suites are perfect for families; they have full kitchens, a dining area, and a living room. Ground-floor accommodations have patios.

3970 Paradise Rd. (btw. Twain Ave. and Flamingo Rd.), Las Vegas, NV 89109. ✆ **800/NU-ROOMS** (687-6667) or 702/796-9000. Fax 702/796-3537. www.laquinta.com. 251 units. $99 and up standard double; $99 and up executive queen; $119 and up suite. Extra person $10. Children 17 and under stay free in parent's room. Rates include complimentary breakfast. Cribs free; rollaways $10. Inquire about seasonal discounts. AE, DC, DISC, MC, V. Free self- and valet parking. Pets welcome. **Amenities:** Restaurant; outdoor pool; fitness center; Jacuzzi; tour desk; car-rental desk; free Strip shuttle; nonsmoking rooms; coin-op laundry. *In room:* A/C, TV w/pay movies, dataport, coffeemaker, hair dryer, iron/ironing board.

Las Vegas Hilton ★ This classic Las Vegas hotel is where Elvis Presley performed during the last 8 years of his life. At the entrance, a giant bronze bust of the King commemorates the man whose name is synonymous with enormous excesses and Vegas style—and one of his sequined jumpsuits is enshrined near the entrance. Though it used to be a family-friendly hotel, the Hilton is now designed more for the business traveler. (The Convention Center is next door.) The large, well-maintained rooms were refurbished in 2006. There are small dressing areas off the bathroom in each room, another plus when several people are sharing a room.

Along with the buffet (p. 168), there's Mexican and Japanese food, as well as a food court with pizza, frozen yogurt, and sandwiches.

Active families will want to check out the 8-acre recreation deck on the third floor, with a swimming pool, six tennis courts lit for night play, Ping-Pong, and a putting green. Also on this level is a luxurious 17,000-square-foot state-of-the-art health club offering Nautilus equipment, Lifecycles, treadmills, rowing machines, three whirlpool spas, steam, sauna, massage, and tanning beds. There's a $20-per-day fee to use the facilities, but guests are totally pampered: All toiletries are provided; there are comfortable TV lounges; and complimentary bottled waters and juices are served in the canteen.

3000 Paradise Rd. (at Riviera Blvd.), Las Vegas, NV 89109. ✆ **888/732-7117** or 702/732-5111. Fax 702/262-5089. www.lvhilton.com. 3,174 units. $69 and up double. Extra person $35. Children 17 and under stay free in parent's room. Cribs free; rollaways $30 if you are not paying the extra person charge. AE, DC, DISC, MC, V. Free self- and valet parking. **Amenities:** 10 restaurants (American, Japanese, buffet, Mexican, more); casino; showrooms; outdoor pool; golf course adjacent; 6 tennis courts (4 night-lit); health club and spa; Jacuzzi; concierge; car-rental desk; business center; shopping arcade; 24-hr. room service; laundry service; dry cleaning; nonsmoking rooms; executive-level rooms. *In room:* A/C, TV w/pay movies, dataport, hair dryer, iron/ironing board.

Sam's Town Hotel & Gambling Hall ★★★ Off the beaten track, Sam's Town is a local favorite situated 5 miles from the Strip, which can be a hassle if you don't have a car. On the other hand, this casino hotel does provide shuttles to the Strip and has a variety of entertainment to keep kids and adults busy. Along with the pool, Sam's Town has a 56-lane bowling alley and an 18-screen, all-THX, all-stadium-seating multiplex, showing the latest releases. The main attraction here is the hotel's giant atrium, which combines real trees and fountains with animatronic animals. The splashing water *is* loud; nevertheless, we find it far more restful than the usual casino sounds of clanging slot machines. Wander about this seminatural environment before taking in the Sunset Stampede at Mystic Falls: Four times a day, at 2, 6, 8, and 10pm, the wolf atop the waterfall howls, and the show, with lights and sounds, begins. It lasts for 10 minutes, and younger kids will enjoy it, especially if you get there a few minutes early for a good spot close up.

The adequately sized rooms have a Western theme, and you can choose from mountain views (ask for a higher floor to take advantage of this) or a room with a view of the atrium, which the children will probably enjoy more.

There are nine dining choices here to keep you and yours sated, including the **Firelight Buffet** (p. 168), which features a different theme nightly.

Sam's Town also has two RV parks with more than 500 spaces, a good place to park your recreational rig close to plenty of casino action.

5111 Boulder Hwy. (at Flamingo Rd.), Las Vegas, NV 89122. ✆ **800/897-8696** or 702/456-7777. Fax 702/454-8014. www.samstownlv.com. 650 units. $50 and up double; $140 and up suite. Extra person $10. Children 15 and under stay free in parent's room. Cribs/rollaways free. AE, DC, DISC, MC, V. Free self- and valet parking. **Amenities:** 5 restaurants (American, Italian, buffet, more); huge casino; showrooms; movie theater; outdoor pool; bowling alley; video arcade; tour desk; car-rental desk; shuttle to Strip and Downtown; laundry service; nonsmoking rooms. *In room:* A/C, TV w/pay movies, dataport.

INEXPENSIVE

Motel 6 This reliable chain hotel accepts small pets, making it a good choice for families traveling with Fluffy or Fido. Its location, right next to the MGM Grand and only seconds away from the Strip, also makes it convenient for families who want access to the main drag without the hassle or expense. Finally, this is also a good call if other, nearby, big-name hotels are booked, because this is the largest Motel 6 property in the country, with a large lobby and bland but very clean rooms set inside two-story buildings. If you need a tub, be sure to ask for one; some rooms are shower only. Two pools will keep you busy and cool when you're not taking in the sights.

195 E. Tropicana Ave. (at Koval Lane), Las Vegas, NV 89109. ✆ **800/4-MOTEL-6** (466-8356) or 702/798-0728. Fax 702/798-5657. www.motel6.com. 608 units. Sun–Thurs from $39 single; Fri–Sat from $70 single. Extra person $6. Children 16 and under stay free in parent's room. AE, DC, DISC, MC, V. Free parking at your room door. Small pets accepted. **Amenities:** 2 outdoor pools; Jacuzzi; tour desk; nonsmoking rooms; coin-op laundry. *In room:* A/C, TV w/pay movies.

Terrible's ★ (Finds) One of the best reasons to stay here is so that for years to come, you'll have a family joke about how your hotel in Las Vegas was Terrible's. Are you laughing? Well, you should be—laughing all the way to the bank with the money you'll save by staying here. Seriously. This is a nice, cheap, clean, and "just-fine" hotel that gives the impression of being darn family friendly. The place gets its name from Ed "Terrible" Herbst; the Herbst family owns a chain of local gas stations and has spent tons of money to upgrade what was once a flea trap into a decent place to stay with large rooms, pleasant bathrooms, and a serviceable pool. It's a cheap cab ride or short drive to the Strip, there's a free shuttle to the airport, and the restaurants on the property are adequate.

4100 Paradise Rd. (at Flamingo Rd.), Las Vegas, NV 89109. ✆ **800/640-9777** or 702/733-7000. Fax 702/691-2484. www.terribleherbst.com/casinos/lasvegas. 400 units. Sun–Thurs $35 and up double; Fri–Sat $59 and up double. Extra person $10. Children 12 and under stay free in parent's room. Cribs/

rollaways $10. AE, DC, DISC, MC, V. Free self- and valet parking. **Amenities:** 2 restaurants (American, buffet); outdoor pool; exercise room; airport shuttle; 24-hr. room service; laundry service; nonsmoking rooms; convenience store. *In room:* A/C, TV w/pay movies, pay-per-use Nintendo, dataport, coffeemaker, hair dryer.

6 ACCOMMODATIONS WEST OF THE STRIP

There's not much to do in this area, which, fortunately, is a short cab or car ride to the Strip. However, the Orleans does provide plenty of entertainment for families.

EXPENSIVE

Desert Paradise ★★★ (Finds) A really nice timeshare that rents out units, Desert Paradise offers apartment living, and we mean living large, for families. Big one-bedroom apartments sleep four; the bigger two-bedroom apartments sleep six, and each unit has a small patio or balcony (with sliding doors), covered parking (a bonus in the summer), its own washer and dryer, along with a full-size kitchen and breakfast nook—truly roomy accommodations, all decorated in sand and beige. The overall impression is "wow, this is huge," except for the bathrooms, which are smallish in comparison to the rest of the place, though the dressing area/vanity mitigates that to some extent. The beds, including the fold-out couch in the living room, are comfy, and there is a TV both in the living and the sleeping quarters.

A barbecue area and picnic tables further enhance the family-resort atmosphere. The verdant lawns provide a great place for kids to frolic (there were plenty of well-behaved children with parents and grandparents on-site when we stayed), while in the main building, a large-screen TV lounge allows guests to gather for the news or sports events. There are frequent manager's receptions. The atmosphere is relaxing and family oriented, making this a great place for spending quality time, while its proximity to the Strip allows for sightseeing and exploring.

5165 S. Decatur Blvd., Las Vegas, NV 89118. ✆ **800/424-1943** or 702/579-3600. Fax 702/257-0363. www.desertparadiseresort.com. 152 units. $119–$219 1-bedroom (4 people maximum); $149–$299 2-bedroom (6 people maximum). Cribs/rollaways free. AE, DC, DISC, MC, V. Free self-parking. **Amenities:** Outdoor pool; fitness center and spa; concierge; nonsmoking rooms. *In room:* A/C, TV/VCR with full cable, full kitchen, hair dryer.

MODERATE

Budget Suites of America This hotel is conveniently located across from the wonders of the Orleans (see below), and if there's no place else to stay and you don't mind that all the rooms allow smoking, this could be an option for you and yours. The good-size rooms are all very, very clean, though they do reek of smoke. But not to be ultrafussy (okay, we are, but that's because we have your children to think about), they are all ultimately sort of depressing, with bright teal carpet and boring beige furniture. Not even the full-size stove and fridge or the groovy rock-formation outdoor decor could brighten our spirits about staying there, and, frankly, it's actually because these aren't really hotels or timeshares; they are, for the most part, places for people to live who can't or won't, for any number of reasons, get apartments. Granted, some families with kids do stay here, especially in the summer. But unless you've exhausted all other options, do you really want to stay in a place that has to state on its prerecorded reservation line that they do not accept collect or third-party phone calls?

Accommodations, Dining & Entertainment West of the Strip

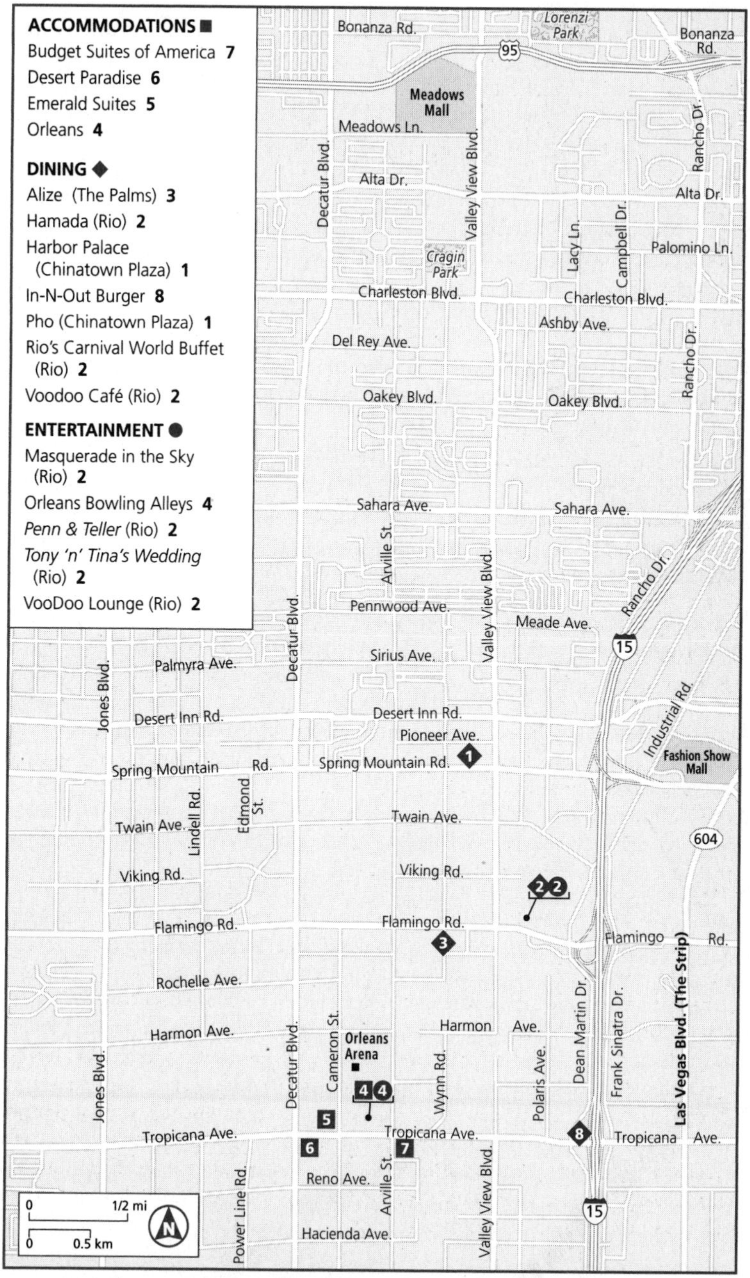

4205 W. Tropicana Ave. (at Wynn). ✆ **888/611-0414** or 702/889-1700. Fax 702/227-8099. www.budgetsuites.com. 1-bedroom (3 people maximum) $69 and up daily, $239 and up weekly; 2-bedroom (5 people maximum) $119 and up daily, $339 and up weekly. AE, DC, DISC, MC, V. Free parking at your room door. **Amenities:** Outdoor pool; Jacuzzi; coin-op laundry. *In room:* A/C, TV w/pay movies.

Emerald Suites If your hotel of choice is full, you can always check into this clean, all-suite hotel. But if you need a crib or a rollaway, you won't get them here for love or money. This hotel, like the nearby Budget Suites, has weekly and monthly rates, and this being Vegas, some people—and families—live here for long periods of time for all sorts of reasons. The Emerald Suites designates some rooms as nonsmoking, though management points out that it's difficult to enforce the rule, so you might end up with a nonsmoking room with a stale-smoke stench. That said, and all things being equal, if you are hard up for a place to stay, this hotel will do you just a bit better that the nearby Budget Suites; though, like its neighbor, the Emerald does not accept third-party or collect calls.

Bright colors and sort of Swedish modern carpets and fabrics set this apart from other similar suite hotels with their bland decor. Additionally, there's a fully equipped kitchen. The pool doesn't have much shade. Thankfully, the Orleans (see below), with its many family-oriented activities, is close by, and the Strip is 4 blocks away. But unless the Consumer Electronics Show or other huge convention is in town, you should be able to find hotels with more kid-friendly amenities in this price range.

4777 S. Cameron St., Las Vegas, NV 89103. ✆ **866/847-2002** or 702/365-5500. Fax 702/216-5547. www.emeraldsuites.com. 98 units. 1-bedroom suite (3 people maximum) $69 and up daily, $329 and up weekly; 2-bedroom suite (5 people maximum) $119 and up daily, $359 and up weekly. Children under 12 stay free. No cribs or rollaways. AE, DC, DISC, MC, V. Free self-parking. **Amenities:** Outdoor pool; Jacuzzi; nonsmoking rooms; coin-op laundry. *In room:* A/C, satellite TV w/pay movies, dataport, full kitchen, hair dryer, iron/ironing board.

Orleans ★★ Now here's something for everyone—bowling, movies, gambling, a showroom, an events arena, two pools, child care, restaurants, a food court, a shuttle to the Strip—all at a reasonable price, mainly because there are nearly 1,500 rooms, it's too far from the Strip to walk, and there's really nothing much else nearby. But then some may say, "With this wealth of distractions around us, why go elsewhere?" Kids will enjoy getting the free Mardi Gras beads handed out in the restaurants, and parents will enjoy the decent prices for room and board.

The hotel is decorated to resemble the New Orleans of MGM musicals and Disneyland, more faux than French Quarter. Nevertheless, check out the mannequins leaning over balconies, frozen in a perpetual celebration.

The L-shaped rooms feature brass headboards on the beds, plenty of floral prints, and lace curtains to create a New Orleans–1880s feel. The bathrooms are large, though a closet, rather than a rod for hanging one's clothes, would be nicer. Suites are larger, with dark wood, oval tubs in the bathrooms, and something families with several kids may or may not find pleasant—four TVs!

The two outdoor pools will do a fine job of keeping you cool; they are nowhere near as elaborate as those at the Strip resorts, but you aren't paying Strip prices.

With 70 lanes, the bowling center (p. 199) is more like a superhighway, but the size ensures that you can almost always get rolling without a wait. A megaplex theater screens a variety of new movie releases, at least one of which will usually fall within your approved ratings scale. If your kids are sports nuts, the 9,000-seat arena hosts a minor-league hockey team and other sporting events. Take advantage of the Kid's Tyme child-care center and enjoy up to 3 hours of childfree time in the casino, the showroom, or your own room. If you feel like dining on the premises, a dozen restaurants include a fairly authentic Cajun/Creole place and a buffet. Children may enjoy **Don Miguel's,** a basic but satisfying Mexican restaurant, where you can watch tortillas being made.

4500 W. Tropicana Ave. (west of the Strip and I-15), Las Vegas, NV 89103. ✆ **800/ORLEANS** (675-3267) or 702/365-7111. Fax 702/365-7500. www.orleanscasino.com. 1,886 units. $39–$160 standard double; $175–$225 1-bedroom suite. Extra person $15. Children 14 and under stay free in parent's room. AE, DC, DISC, MC, V. Free self- and valet parking. **Amenities:** 8 restaurants (American, French, Italian, Cajun/Creole, buffet, more); casino; events arena; showroom; 18 movie theaters; 2 outdoor pools; 70-lane bowling center; health club; Kid's Tyme children's center offering amusements and day care for kids 12 and under; video arcade; concierge; tour desk; car-rental desk; airport shuttle; 24-hr. room service; laundry service; dry cleaning; nonsmoking rooms; executive-level rooms. *In room:* A/C, TV w/pay movies, dataport, hair dryer, iron/ironing board.

7 ACCOMMODATIONS OUTSIDE OF LAS VEGAS

HENDERSON

Expensive

Green Valley Ranch ★★★ This is a resort in every sense of the word. Located in Henderson, about 25 minutes southeast of Las Vegas and closer if coming from the airport, this luxurious getaway combines Strip action (gambling, grown-up nightclub, and fine dining) with kid-friendly fun (movie theaters, arcade, and a beach pool—which has sand instead of concrete around the edges). The casino is located on one side of the property, so it can be completely avoided. Wood, stone, and plush drapes and carpets give this resort (part of the huge Station Casinos chain) a high-end feel that rivals Bellagio, without the attitude or prices.

Rooms have big closets, and the bathrooms have big bathtubs. The beds are supercomfy and the bathrobes are soft. There are great, though sometimes smoggy, views of the Las Vegas Valley from the pools (which are closed Nov–Apr). One pool is for all guests; the private pool is for those who rent cabanas, but even at the noncabana pool, you'll enjoy large chaise longues and wide beds (designed for poolside reclining and sprawling) in a sunscreen-soaked daze.

Dining options abound. Hank's is a plush, masculine chophouse and martini bar named after someone who neither ate meat nor drank alcohol. Other fine dining options include Terra Verde for Italian and the ultrahip Sushi + Sake that specializes in . . . well, take a guess. The Feast Around the World Buffet is one of Las Vegas's best, and for those who like their carbs served with butter and maple syrup there's an Original Pancake House. An informal Chinese bistro, an Irish pub, and a food court with Panda Express and Villa Pizza among others complete the culinary collage. The District at Green Valley Ranch, an open-air mall across the parking lot with 70 shops, has another dozen eateries, including a Cheesecake Factory and popular P.F. Chang's Chinese.

The Spa offers treatments such as massage therapies, facials, body wraps, exfoliation, and the like. At the salon, you can get manicures, pedicures, and the usual hairstyling.

One of the best things about Green Valley Ranch for families is its location, just 15 minutes southeast of the Strip. It's a perfect launching pad for outings to Lake Mead, Hoover Dam, and the Black Canyon of the Colorado, among others.

2300 Paseo Verde Dr. (at I-215), Henderson, NV 89012. ✆ **866/782-9487** or 702/617-7777. Fax 702/617-7778. www.greenvalleyranchresort.com. 574 units. Sun–Thurs $159 and up double; Fri–Sat $209 and up double. Extra person $12. Children 11 and under stay free in parent's room. Cribs/rollaways free. AE, DC, DISC, MC, V. Free self- and valet parking. **Amenities:** 8 restaurants (all major cuisines); nightclub; casino; outdoor pool; health club and spa; Jacuzzi; sauna; concierge; business center; 24-hr. room service; in-room massage; laundry service; dry cleaning; nonsmoking rooms; executive-level rooms. *In room:* A/C, TV w/pay movies, dataport, high-speed Internet access (for a fee), coffeemaker, hair dryer, iron/ironing board, safe.

Red Rock Casino Resort Spa ★★★ Located about 10 miles west of the Strip on Charleston Boulevard and isolated from any other property of similar stature, Red Rock attempts to make itself a destination worth the trip. It's an impressive place, with a low, curving, monolithic roofline meant to echo the desert landscape and slopes of the nearby Red Rock Canyon. Inside, the decor and layout represent the continuing Station Casino's mission to fuse the wow factor with the practical desires of its local fan base. Stone, wood, and glass predominate, more casually attractive and subtle than austere or intimidating; again, forms and colors are often meant to echo the surrounding geography. The overall impression is of an accessible, upscale, desert spa hotel, as opposed to the more glitzy palaces on the Strip.

For families Red Rock Resort is perfectly situated for such active endeavors as hiking, road biking, horseback riding, mountain biking, and rock climbing, and it offers an adventure program with guided outings for most of these activities.

Rooms and suites are extremely mod in appearance and modern in amenities, mixing chocolate browns and other earth tones with high-tech gadgetry and high-end appointments. Best of all, however, are the guest-room views. West-facing rooms look out onto Red Rock Canyon; east-facing rooms peer down the valley to the Las Vegas Strip.

Dining couldn't be better for families. In the full-service department there's Salt Lick BBQ, Cabo Mexican Restaurant, T-Bones Chophouse, and Terra Rossa for Italian cuisine. The Feast Buffet, one of Las Vegas's best, and a food court featuring Fatburger, Panda Express, Villa Pizza, Starbucks, Ben & Jerry's Ice Cream, Rubio's Fresh Mexican Grill, and Capriotti's Sandwich Shop round out the calorie-busting options.

Several of the restaurants open onto the pool area, which—while not staggeringly huge—is quite elegant. Tiers of outdoor lounges and patios look over smaller wading pools and rentable cabanas, plus the inevitable pool bar. As you proceed through the casino, the atmosphere gets a more and more "local" feeling to it; the entrance on the resort's far end is in fact specifically geared to locals, with close parking on the outside and an assortment of games set up right inside the door. This is also where you find the attached movie theater and KidsQuest children's complex, making it convenient to drop off the offspring en route to some adult time in the casino or a romantic dinner. The spa at Red Rock Resort can hold its own with any on the Strip, and in its variety of treatments and amenities offered, surpasses most.

11011 W. Charleston Blvd. (off I-215), Las Vegas, NV, 89135. ✆ **866/767-7773** or 702/797-7777. Fax 702/797-7745. www.redrocklasvegas.com. 414 units. Sun–Thurs $199 and up double; Fri–Sat $219 and up double. Extra person $35. Children 11 and under stay free in parent's room. Cribs/rollaways $15. AE, DC, DISC, MC, V. Free self- and valet parking. **Amenities:** 8 restaurants (all major cuisines); nightclub; casino; outdoor pool; health club and spa; Jacuzzi; sauna; concierge; business center; 24-hr. room service; laundry service; dry cleaning; nonsmoking floors; executive-level rooms. *In room:* A/C, plasma-screen TV, dataport, iPod sound system, high-speed Internet access (for a fee), coffeemaker, hair dryer, iron/ironing board, safe.

Inexpensive

Sunset Station ★ Located about 25 minutes from the Strip, in the bedroom community of Henderson, close to **Ethel M's Chocolate Factory and Cactus Gardens** (p. 191) and the **SportCenter** (121 E. Sunset Rd.; ✆ **702/317-7777;** www.sportcenteroflasvegas.com) family sport park, Sunset Station isn't really a major destination hotel, but it's good

Accommodations, Dining & Attractions in Henderson

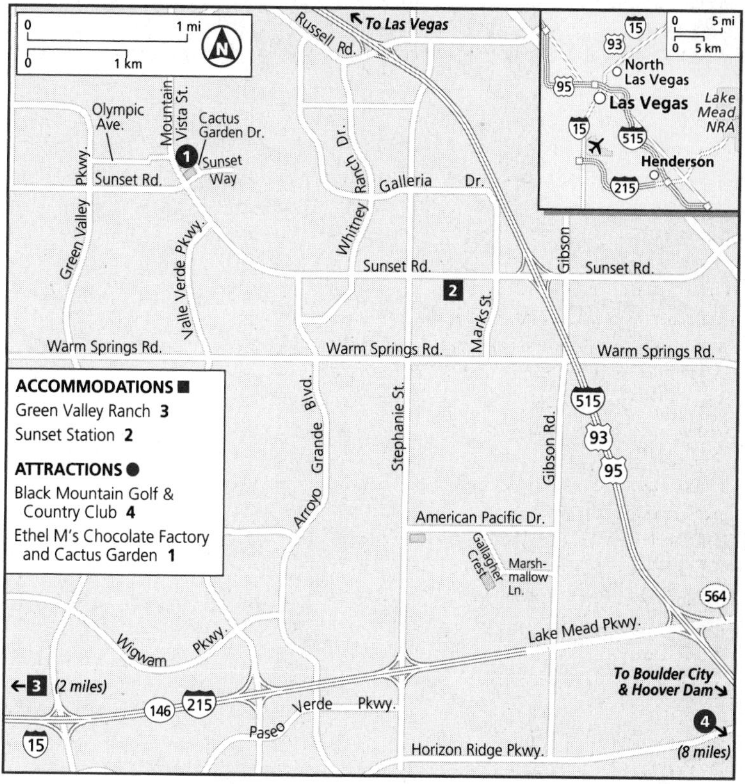

to know about in case your other options are booked. By Vegas standards, it's pricey for what you get (a basic hotel that charges $15 for cribs and rollaways and an additional $15 for an extra person), but it can be a good option if you place a high priority on accommodations that offer child care. Though it's far from the madding crowds of tourists, expect to find plenty of locals here for both the food and gambling; they definitely make use of the available child-care facilities. The entire hotel is done in a vaguely Mediterranean, south-of-Spain theme—soft ocher, warm earth tones—carried through to the standard-size rooms with basic, clean bathrooms, and to one of the eight restaurants: **Capri** serves Italian food. The outside pool does its job for daytime enjoyment; the fitness room, while nothing ultrafancy, is perfectly adequate; 13 movie screens and a decent arcade can keep you and your family entertained in the evening.

1301 W. Sunset Rd., Henderson, NV 89014. ✆ **888/786-7389** or 702/547-7777. Fax 702/547-7744. www.sunsetstation.com. 457 units. Sun–Thurs $59–$89; Fri–Sat $99–$169. Extra person $15. Cribs/rollaways $10. AE, DC, DISC, MC, V. Free self- and valet parking. **Amenities:** 8 restaurants (all major cuisines); food court; nightclub; casino; 13 movie theaters; outdoor pool; fitness room; concierge; free shuttle to Strip and airport; 24-hr. room service; child care (for a fee); laundry service; nonsmoking rooms. *In room:* A/C, TV w/pay movies, dataport, high-speed Internet access (for a fee), hair dryer, iron/ironing board.

7 Family-Friendly Dining

In the past decade, Las Vegas has experienced a restaurant boom, with celebrity chefs opening outposts in almost every hotel. Once purely a destination for gamblers, partiers, and wedding parties, the Strip is now the new mecca for adventurous palates weaned on, and educated by, the Food Channel. Food used to be cheap in Vegas, because the casinos (a) wanted you to spend most of your money gambling and (b) wanted you to feel like you'd gotten something—like a surf-and-turf special or an all-you-can-eat spread—for a bargain, so that your inevitable losses didn't seem so tragic. Then came food awareness—let's call it cuisine consciousness—and Vegas's entrepreneurs saw an opportunity to lure high rollers and their appetites, along with garden-variety gourmands, into the brand-new casino/resorts.

In came name chefs—Wolfgang, Emeril, Bradley Ogden, Joël Robuchon, Mario Battali, Bobby Flay—plus upscale, high-priced eateries such as **Lutèce, Picasso,** and **Alizé**—the list is mouthwateringly, and expensively, long.

At first glance, it seems that there are now fewer low- to mid-priced options and that it's easier to go broke at the dinner tables than at the gaming tables. Oh sure, you can eat three meals a day at food courts—**McDonald's, Nathan's,** and pizza are staples at most of the hotels, with **Krispy Kreme Doughnuts** a popular choice for breakfast and dessert—but at a certain point, you may want, or need, some variety. With a little forethought, the average visitor—especially ones with hungry mouths to feed—can find a cornucopia of reasonably priced eats. And that's where the Las Vegas gourmet boom has its advantages.

Buffets, once a stolid bastion of plain food, now offer international dishes and "stations" for Asian, Mexican, Italian, Middle Eastern, and other cuisines, along with large salad bars. Lunch menus, lower-priced gourmet cafes, and cantinas also provide a way for you and yours to sample celebrity chefs' cooking without squandering your children's college fund on the experience.

And while certain restaurants decline to seat families with children under 5 years old, most are more than happy to accommodate all ages, providing children's menus, highchairs, and booster seats. Some even go so far as to cook special off-menu dishes to order for your children. Upscale chain restaurants such as **P.F. Chang's China Bistro** and the **Cheesecake Factory** offer dependable choices and large portions, while the themed chains—**Planet Hollywood, Rainforest Cafe, ESPN Zone, NASCAR Cafe,** and similarly souvenir-slinging restaurants—provide varying levels of food in an entertaining environment. So grab a fork, tie on your napkin, and dive in. *Bon appétit!*

Note: In the listing descriptions after each review, following the website (or phone number if the restaurant doesn't have a website listed), we detail whether a restaurant has a children's menu and whether it's equipped with highchairs and booster seats. If any of these amenities is missing from the listing description, it means the restaurant doesn't offer that particular service.

1 TIPS FOR DINING IN LAS VEGAS

GETTING IN

The most logical time-tested advice is that if you want to celebrate your budding Iron Chef's birthday at **Nobu** or just want to eat at a specific place at a specific date and time, you should make reservations immediately after you make your hotel reservation, giving both your hotel and home phone number, and confirm your reservation once you arrive in town. Or you can have the concierge at your hotel call and make reservations for you. You should always make a reservation, no matter what, just to be safe, though we must say that during the down season (midsummer)—even with a chef's convention of more than 1,000 all staying at a hotel where we wanted to try out some of the restaurants—we still had no problem walking in and getting seated. Again, we don't recommend chancing it, but if you do show up without a reservation, here are our hints for getting a table:

- **Go early,** right at opening, for lunch and dinner. Prime time for lunch is between 12:30 and 2pm, but restaurants open for lunch at 11 or 11:30am. Your best bet for dinner is arriving between 5:30 and 6pm.
- **Dress nicely.** That means shirts with collars (polo or button-down) on men and boys, no shorts or jeans for men, and nice blouses or casual dresses for women and girls. Often, a lightweight sweater is advisable; it can sometimes get chilly in restaurants.
- **Take whatever seats are available.** Remember, you're walking in without a reservation and you have kids, so don't be surprised if you're seated a bit away from the center of the action; other tables may have been already reserved.

SAVING MONEY

You can spend upwards of $250 a day on food for a family of four without ever having a memorable meal. And that bites. But with a small amount of planning, there's no reason that you won't be able to sample some celebrity-chef fare without busting the bank, or at least keeping your food costs at a manageable level. One way is to get your rooms off the Strip at a place offering complimentary continental breakfasts, or at an apartment-style hotel where you can use the in-room kitchen facilities for some of your meals. Granted, staying away from the main section of the city requires some planning and usually a car, or you could end up spending what you were trying to save in food costs on cab fares to and from the Strip.

Keep in mind that on the Strip, food-court stands such as Nathan's offer breakfast specials of standards such as pancakes, eggs, and bacon. Buffets are best saved for a late breakfast or an early lunch; kids can stuff themselves, then perhaps rest in the room watching TV or playing games for a couple of hours during the hottest part of the day, emerging refreshed and still semi-full in time for more sightseeing and an early dinner. Dinner can be as simple as appetizers and dessert or as elaborate as you like. Most restaurants offer kids' menus for all meals, though the lunch and dinner selections of burgers, spaghetti and pizza, and chicken fingers may get repetitive for some children.

Some fine restaurants—**Emeril's, Delmonico Steakhouse,** and **Mon Ami Gabi,** for example—offer lunch menus, providing an alternative, dare we say cheaper, way to sample their cuisines. Others, such as **Border Grill, Chinois,** and **Spago,** have more casual spinoffs that serve signature dishes at far lower prices.

We wish that more hotels had minibars and fridges so we could take doggie bags back to our rooms, because the portions are huge at many restaurants, most notably the

Tips Dining Out in Peace

Bring pencils or pens and paper with you, so the kids have something to do while waiting for their food. This is also a great time for them to write postcards, so keep some handy. If you get caught without even a crayon and the waiter won't lend you a pen, have a few word games at your disposal—I Spy, for example, or have someone choose a category (movies, actors, food, and so on) and, in turn, each person must name something in the category. The catch is that the person with the next turn must name something that starts with the last letter of the previous answer. (Example: orange, eggplant, tomato, onion . . .)

We're sure your kids have lovely manners, but if you happen to be ferrying around a child who decides to make a ruckus at the table, try a trick that's worked for us. Promptly remove him or her from the premises for a supervised time-out. Don't yell, don't threaten, just quietly keep a beady eye on the tyke until he calms himself down. It's highly effective for the majority of kids and makes a lasting impression on siblings. After the third time-out on the pavement, we promise you that you won't have to do it again.

Bend the rules. If you don't usually let your children drink soda pop, perhaps as a treat when out for a meal (or behind your back—we're realists!), you can let them have some. And letting the kids order a Shirley Temple or Roy Rogers (7-Up or cola and grenadine with a cherry) always adds importance to a night out.

Think ahead before venturing out for dinner. If your little ones have had a long day seeing the sights, make time for them to nap before you go out to eat. (You won't mind the chance to put your feet up either.) You're on vacation, so don't dine early unless you plan to eat at a restaurant where reservations are hard to come by. There is no joy in returning to a hotel room to watch TV. With everyone relaxed and happy, mealtime can be a leisurely and enjoyable way to recap the adventures of day. Encourage each of the children to tell what they enjoyed best that day and discuss the family's plans for tomorrow.

Carnegie Deli, Cheesecake Factory, and its sister, **Grand Lux Café.** Sharing an order—if you can come to a consensus—is a great way to eat. You can, however, rent small fridges at most hotels for $10 and up per day. Consider appetizers as main courses—many, such as the quesadillas at **Border Cantina,** are large enough for two. Family-style dining is expected at Asian restaurants such as **Chin Chin** and **P.F. Chang's,** as well as **Lotus of Siam,** considered by some to be the best Thai restaurant in the United States. Order a couple of dishes and some rice, and you've got a complete meal for a reasonable price. Dim sum—small Chinese dishes of many varieties—is a filling and inexpensive breakfast/lunch option available at several Chinese restaurants.

And then there's that old standby, pizza—try the gourmet versions at **Wolfgang Puck Bar & Grill** or **California Pizza Kitchen,** go for a standard pie picked up from the nearest food court, or have **Metro Pizza** (p. 163) deliver to your room.

Tips: Stock Up on Staples

If you have a car, you can use it to stock up on staples that you'd pay inflated prices for on the Strip. Drive just a couple miles into the suburbs to a big supermarket and stock up on soft drinks, snacks, cereal, bananas, and other foodstuffs, so you don't have to pay the inflated prices in the resorts. It may be worth your while to bring along a cooler to keep things cold in your room. Flamingo and Tropicana avenues, east and west, are littered with Albertson's, Smith's, and Raley's, and Maryland Parkway is loaded with strip malls and discount stores.

ABOUT PRICE CATEGORIES

The restaurants in this chapter are arranged first by location, and then by the following price categories (based on the average cost of a dinner entree): **Very Expensive,** where most entrees cost more than $20; **Expensive,** where the majority of entrees are $15 to $20; **Moderate,** where the majority of entrees are $10 to $15; and **Inexpensive,** where entrees are under $10 (sometimes well under). We've also made sure to provide you with children's menu information, where applicable. In Very Expensive and Expensive restaurants, expect to spend no less than twice the price of the average entree for your entire meal with a tip; you can usually get by on a bit less in moderate and inexpensive restaurants. Dessert-restaurant pricing is based on the cost of one dessert. Buffets and Sunday brunches are gathered in a separate section at the end of this chapter.

2 RESTAURANTS BY CUISINE

American

America (South Strip, $$, p. 146)
Bradley Ogden ★★ (Center Strip, $$$$, p. 151)
Cheesecake Factory ★ (Center Strip, $$, p. 155)
ESPN Zone (South Strip, $$, p. 147)
Hard Rock Cafe (East of the Strip, $$, p. 162)
Harley-Davidson Cafe (South Strip, $$, p. 147)
In-N-Out Burger ★ (South Strip, $, p. 148)
Monte Carlo Brew Pub ★★★ (South Strip, $, p. 150)
NASCAR Cafe (North Strip, $$, p. 158)
NOBHILL ★★★ (South Strip, $$$$, p. 142)
Rainforest Cafe ★ (South Strip, $$$, p. 145)
Verandah ★ (South Strip, $$$$, p. 148)

Asian

Chinois ★★★ (Center Strip, $$, p. 156)
Dragon Noodle Co. ★ (South Strip, $$, p. 146)
Grand Wok and Sushi Bar ★ (South Strip, $$$, p. 144)

Buffets/Brunches

Buffet at TI ★ (Center Strip, $$, p. 166)
Circus Buffet (North Strip, $, p. 168)
Excalibur's Round Table Buffet (South Strip, $$, p. 165)

Key to Abbreviations: $$$$ = Very Expensive $$$ = Expensive $$ = Moderate $ = Inexpensive

Flamingo Paradise Garden Buffet ★ (Center Strip, $, p. 167)
Las Vegas Hilton Buffet ★ (East of the Strip, $, p. 168)
Luxor, More Buffet ★★ (South Strip, $$, p. 165)
MGM Grand Buffet (South Strip, $$$, p. 165)
The Mirage Cravings Buffet ★★ (Center Strip, $$$, p. 166)
Monte Carlo Buffet ★ (South Strip, $$, p. 166)
Paris's Le Village Buffet ★★★ (Center Strip, $$$, p. 167)
Planet Hollywood's Spice Market Buffet (South Strip, $$$, p. 167)
Rio's Carnival World Buffet ★ (West of the Strip, $$$, p. 168)
Sam's Town Firelight Buffet ★ (East of the Strip, $, p. 168)

California

California Pizza Kitchen (Center Strip, $$, p. 155)
Spago ★★★ (Center Strip, $$$$, p. 153)
Wolfgang Puck Bar & Grill ★★ (South Strip, $$$, p. 145)

Chinese

Chin Chin (South Strip, $$, p. 146)
Harbor Palace (West of the Strip, $, p. 151)
168 Shanghai ★ (West of the Strip, $, p. 151)
P.F. Chang's China Bistro (South Strip, $$, p. 147)

Deli

Canter's Deli ★ (Center Strip, $$, p. 155)
Player's Deli (South Strip, $, p. 151)

Desserts

Krispy Kreme (various locations, $, p. 156)
Lenôtre ★★★ (Center Strip, $, p. 157)
Voodoo Café (West of the Strip, $, p. 163)

Diner/Coffee Shop

Calypsos (South Strip, $, p. 148)
Mr. Lucky's 24/7 ★★ (East of the Strip, $, p. 163)
Pink Pony ★ (North Strip, $, p. 158)
Player's Deli (South Strip, $, p. 151)
Tiffany's Cafe at White Cross Drugs ★ (North Strip, $, p. 158)

French

Alizé ★★★ (West of the Strip, $$$$, p. 169)
Bouchon ★★★ (Center Strip, $$$$, p. 169)
Mon Ami Gabi ★★ (Center Strip, $$$$, p. 152)
Picasso ★★ (Center Strip, $$$$, p. 169)

International

Grand Lux Café ★ (Center Strip, $$, p. 157)

Italian

Metro Pizza ★ (East of the Strip, $, p. 163)

Japanese

Hamada ★ (various locations, $$, p. 160)
Mizuno's ★★ (South Strip, $$$$, p. 142)
Nobu ★★★ (East of the Strip, $$$$, p. 160)
Sushi Moto (West of the Strip, $, p. 151)
Todai ★ (South Strip, $$$$, p. 143)

Mexican

Border Grill ★★ (South Strip, $$$, p. 144)
Border Grill Cantina ★★ (South Strip, $$, p. 146)
El Sombrero ★ (Downtown, $, p. 164)
La Salsa (various locations, $, p. 150)
Pink Taco (East of the Strip, $, p. 163)

Romantic Dining
Alizé ★★★ (West of the Strip, $$$$, p. 169)
Bouchon ★★★ (Center Strip, $$$$, p. 169)
Hugo's Cellar ★★★ (Downtown, $$$$, p. 169)
Mon Ami Gabi ★★ (Center Strip, $$$$, p. 152)
Picasso ★★ (Center Strip, $$$$, p. 169)

Sandwiches
Capriotti's ★ (North Strip, $, p. 158)

Seafood
Second Street Grill ★ (Downtown, $$$$, p. 164)

Southern/Cajun/Creole
Delmonico Steakhouse ★★ (Center Strip, $$$$, p. 152)
Emeril's New Orleans Fish House ★★ (South Strip, $$$$, p. 141)
House of Blues ★ (South Strip, $$$, p. 144)

Thai
Lotus of Siam ★★★ (East of the Strip, $, p. 162)

Vietnamese
Pho (West of the Strip, $, p. 151)

3 SOUTH STRIP

VERY EXPENSIVE

Emeril's New Orleans Fish House ★★ SOUTHERN/CAJUN/CREOLE Many of the kids we know, ages 4 on up, think Emeril is the bam. One cooking-show-addicted mom of our acquaintance swears that her baby's first words were "pork fat," but she might just be exaggerating the teeniest bit. No matter, it proves the point: Emeril Lagasse is a bona fide superstar with a young following; he even has his own line of children's cookware and a cookbook for kids. If your child is as nuts about him as some of the ones we know, you'll definitely want to treat the little one—and yourself—to a meal here. To eat at one of his restaurants is to understand why he inspires such a passionate following. We sampled tasty double-cut pork chops with gnocchi and mushrooms, plus Cajun-spiced rib-eye steak with Emeril's trinity of spices, and his famous smashed potatoes, along with fish dishes. You may want to consider coming at lunch, rather than at the busier, and more expensive, dinner seating.

But if you eat at this restaurant (designed to look like a sidewalk cafe in New Orleans—replete with vines and Spanish moss) rather than at Emeril's Delmonico Steakhouse (p. 152) up the way at The Venetian, it should be because you really want to try what Emeril does with fish—such as the jumbo Gulf shrimp wrapped in bacon or the barbecued salmon on andouille sausage. Share some awesome appetizers—think crab cakes or sinfully good seared scallops. The gumbo, served at both lunch and dinner, is thick with seafood and is rich, redolent, and dark with spices, and there's a winning selection of salads at both lunch and dinner.

Try to save room for dessert—there's banana cream pie with banana crust and caramel sauce, and individual lemon-pudding cakes with just the perfect balance of sweet and tart—edible sunshine, seriously. Chocolate freaks should delve into the lethal double-chocolate flourless cake with Godiva milkshake and cherry compote. This is a perfect place for a fancy dessert with the kids no matter where you've eaten dinner.

In the MGM Grand, 3799 Las Vegas Blvd. S. ✆ **702/891-7374.** www.emerils.com. Highchairs, boosters. Reservations required. Main courses $12–$18 at lunch, $28–$45 at dinner (more for lobster). AE, DC, DISC, MC, V. Daily 11:30am–2:30pm and 5:30–10:30pm.

Mizuno's ★★ JAPANESE Mizuno's is the perfect place to take fussy eaters, budding gourmands, and vegetarians. The food is fresh and fun, and because this is Vegas, you get quite a show to go along with your meal. Guests are seated around a tabletop grill, called *teppan,* where your personal chef arrives with cleaver in hand to prepare your *teppanyaki* (stir-fried) meal. You can choose either the one-meat-item Samurai dinner or the two-item combo Shogun, with reduced price options for children under 12; vegetarians get sautéed veggies. All dinners come with miso soup and a small salad. Fried rice is made as you watch. There's sushi and *gyoza* (steamed-then-fried dumplings, aka pot stickers) for appetizers, but you'll want to save room for the light and tasty entrees. Want chicken with extra garlic? No problem. Like extra onions, or no onions with your steak? Your chef is happy to oblige as he rapidly chops, sautés, and stirs ingredients together. The strobe lights start as he tosses shakers and juggles knives, giving a real showbiz feel to the whole meal. It's satisfyingly flashy, and satisfyingly good as well. One dad told us that Mizuno's is the only place in all of Vegas where his two kids will actually eat their veggies and that they beg to come here. Now that's an endorsement!

In the Tropicana Resort & Casino, 3801 Las Vegas Blvd. S. ✆ **702/739-2713.** www.tropicanalv.com. Kids' menu, highchairs, boosters. Reservations recommended. Full Samurai dinners mostly $17–$25; Shogun combination dinners $26–$35; kids' menu $9.95. AE, DC, DISC, MC, V. Daily 5–10:45pm.

NOBHILL ★★★ **Finds** AMERICAN This is a pricey, adult-looking restaurant, but, surprisingly, it's rather kid friendly, and good to boot. "We're a neighborhood restaurant," explained one of the staff members. "And we don't like to leave out any of the family." Indeed, we were delighted to see a family with a 5-year-old and a 7-year-old happily eating away in the modern yet comfortable room. When we inquired, our server told us that parents regularly bring their children here and that most kids order the chicken tetrazzini (cream sauce, chicken, noodles, and black truffles!) and the appetizer sampler, which features duck confit rolls, marinated beef empanadas, and grilled swordfish satay.

Executive chef Sven Mede will also specially make pasta or other entrees for children who might not want to try seasonal dishes such as pork loin with polenta cake or lamb served with goat-cheese tortellini. And the wee ones can always happily dig away at the whipped potato sampler, featuring five types of spuds emulsified with tasty things such as cheese and bacon, garlic, and mushrooms.

This is a serious restaurant, make no mistake, but it's nice that the entire staff realizes children of fine diners will most likely grow up to be as enthralled by food as their parents—and the parents we spied on were encouraging this by sharing bites of their poached squab, seared foie gras, and fried soft-shell crab with their well-behaved offspring. Children aren't the only ones catered to at NOBHILL; upon placing our order, we were asked if we had any allergies or if we had reservations for a show, in order to allow the chef to adjust to our needs.

The theme of the chef/proprietor Michael Mina's restaurant is San Francisco, with its wealth of seafood and agricultural abundance, emphasizing organic vegetables and fruits and the free-range poultry and meats of Northern California. Appetizers included a charcuterie plate, Tomales Bay shellfish platter, and a crab Louis salad. The desserts are splendid as well—cable car crème brûlée, lemon-strawberry pie, and a selection of homemade ice creams. Ask in advance for the special glass-enclosed booths, which look like old-style private train cars, for a truly intimate family dining experience.

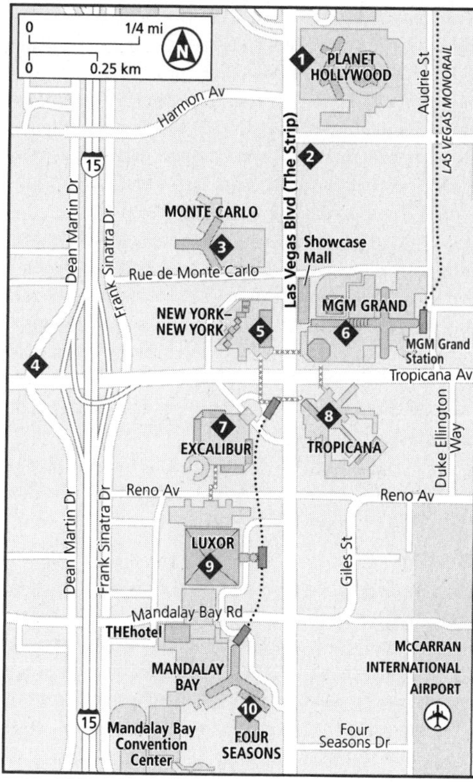

RESTAURANTS
America (New York-New York) **5**
Border Cantina (Mandalay Bay) **10**
Border Grill (Mandalay Bay) **10**
Calypsos (Tropicana) **8**
Chin Chin (New York-New York) **5**
Dragon Noodle Co. (Monte Carlo) **3**
Emeril's New Orleans Fish House (MGM Grand) **6**
ESPN Zone (New York-New York) **5**
Grand Wok and Sushi Bar (MGM Grand) **6**
Hamada (MGM Grand) **6**
Harley Davidson Café **2**
House of Blues (Mandalay Bay) **10**
In-N-Out Burger **4**
La Salsa (Planet Hollywood) **1**
La Salsa (Luxor) **9**
Mizuno's (Tropicana) **8**
Monte Carlo Brewpub (Monte Carlo) **3**
NobHill (MGM Grand) **6**
P.F. Chang's China Bistro (Planet Hollywood) **1**
Players Deli (Tropicana) **8**
Rainforest Café (MGM Grand) **6**
Todai (Planet Hollywood) **1**
Verandah (The Four Seasons) **10**
Wolfgang Puck Bar & Grill (MGM Grand) **6**

BUFFETS
Excalibur's Round Table Buffet **7**
Luxor's More Buffet **9**
MGM Grand Buffet **6**
Monte Carlo Buffet Bar & Grill **3**

In the MGM Grand, 3799 Las Vegas Blvd. S. ✆ **702/891-7337.** Highchairs, boosters. Reservations recommended. Main courses $29–$50. AE, DC, MC, V. Daily 5:30–10:30pm, last seating at 10pm.

Todai ★ JAPANESE Instead of basing the children's menu on age, Todai, a Japanese sushi/seafood buffet chain, takes a different tack—the charge for your children depends on their height. At any one time, Todai offers over 40 different types of sushi and rolls along with a variety of hot dishes, including teriyaki, tempura, dumplings, chicken wings, fried rice, and vegetables. Salads range from the basic potato with mayo to the hot pickled cabbage, kimchi. An endless array of desserts includes a couple very odd ones—green tea cheesecake and piña colada tofu—along with cookies, flourless chocolate cake, and puddings. We like it here, but sushi purists complain that the rice for the sushi is extruded and formed by machine. Nevertheless, this is the best bet for families who want an unlimited Asian food feast. And if it happens to be one of your birthdays, your meal is on the house.

In Miracle Mile Mall at Planet Hollywood, 3663 Las Vegas Blvd. S. ✆ **702/892-0021.** Highchairs, boosters. Reservations accepted for large parties. Children 5 ft. and under half price. Lunch Mon–Thurs $15, Fri–Sun $17; dinner Mon–Thurs $26, Fri–Sun $28. AE, DC, DISC, MC, V. Lunch Mon–Sat 11:30am–2:30pm, Sun 11:30am–3pm; dinner Sun–Thurs 5:30–9pm, Fri–Sun 5:30–9:30pm.

EXPENSIVE

Border Grill ★★ MEXICAN The "Two Hot Tamales" television program is no longer aired, but long before there were hundreds of cable channels, Mary Sue Milliken and Susan Fenniger carved out an empire making fresh, light, Mexican food with a *nuevo* twist. The Vegas outpost of their most famous restaurant is every bit as yummy as the ones in Santa Monica and Pasadena, and there's even a lower-priced cantina that serves a truncated and less expensive menu (p. 146). The location, at Mandalay Bay, the southernmost point of the Strip, puts it a bit out of the way, but for devotees or the curious, it's worth a special trip. The prices and the hours at both locations also make this a sound choice for families staying next door at the Four Seasons or who've come to view Shark Reef.

We loved the enchiladas, made with citrus-marinated chicken and a poblano chili sauce, and our test child went wild over the chicken *chilaquiles,* a casserole made with corn tortillas, cheese, and different salsas. The tacos were a successful choice, as were all the appetizers, though $8 was a steep tariff for guac and chips. Sharing a plate of assorted tamales and a salad is enough food for two any-size people, but our portion-control issues may be different than yours. Ordering off the children's menu gives kids the option of tacos, tamales, grilled turkey, or fish. Desserts for kids include cookies and ice cream, but we preferred the flan and the Mexican chocolate pie.

In Mandalay Bay, 3950 Las Vegas Blvd. S. © **702/632-7403.** www.mandalaybay.com. Kids' menu, highchairs, boosters. Reservations recommended. Main courses $8–$35. AE, DC, DISC, MC, V. Sun–Thurs 11am–10:30pm; Fri–Sat 11am–11pm.

Grand Wok and Sushi Bar ★ ASIAN This is one of the only places you'll find Thai food on the entire Strip, and you'll pay dearly for it by comparison to the Thai joints along Sahara Boulevard. No matter, the pad Thai is light and sweet, perfectly seasoned, served with garnishes of shredded cabbage, carrots, and chopped peanuts. The simmered albacore with garlic sauce is tasty, with just the right amount of spice. Portions—especially the soups—are large enough to share, so you'll be able to sample several items from the extensive Pan-Asian menu. Along with Thai food, there are traditional Chinese dishes, Vietnamese rice noodle soup (*pho,* pronounced "fuhr"), Indonesian dishes, and sushi. Kids get a kick out of the minced shrimp "lollipops" on sugar-cane sticks. Adults may want to try one of the fine sakes with their meal. This restaurant is very popular with the MGM Grand's Asian clientele, which is always a good sign.

In the MGM Grand, 3799 Las Vegas Blvd. S. © **702/891-7777.** www.mgmgrand.com. Highchairs, boosters. Reservations not accepted. Main courses $8.95–$30; sushi $4.50–$14. AE, DC, DISC, MC, V. Restaurant Mon–Thurs 11am–10pm, sushi bar 5–10pm; both open Fri–Sat 11am–midnight, Sun 11am–10pm.

House of Blues ★ SOUTHERN/CAJUN/CREOLE The blues and folk music meet Disneyland with a New Age overlay here. Decorated with folk art, outsider art, and found art, this huge funky shack serves up a (loud) all-ages gospel brunch buffet with eggs, fried chicken, bourbon-glazed ham, salads, and way too much other stuff in the main showroom every Sunday. The restaurant, separate from the nightclub so that all ages can dine here, provides regular meals. We like the burgers the best of everything on the regular menu, and we'd love it if the Sunday brunch fried chicken migrated over to the main menu. Along with ribs and gumbo, they serve jambalaya, grilled tuna, steak, and salads. It's above adequate for a chain, with some interesting selections (voodoo shrimp with Dixie beer reduction), but sometimes it seems like they're trying too hard (those andouille sausage po' boys again). The children's menu, which is fine for light or super fussy eaters, features a grilled-cheese sandwich, pasta, or chef salad. Blah. Kids

Tips **If Your Kids Are Really Picky . . .**

Many Las Vegas restaurants will fax you their menus, so you and your kids can agree, in advance, where you'd like to have special, or just regular, meals.

might be happier with the main-menu burger or the rib "fingers" from the appetizer menu. Desserts are nothing special. For lunch, spend your money at one of Emeril's places instead: You'll get better, more original food for your money.

In Mandalay Bay, 3950 Las Vegas Blvd. S. ✆ **702/632-7600.** www.hob.com. Kids' menu, highchairs, boosters. Main courses $14–$30; kids' menu $6.95–$7.95. AE, DC, DISC, MC, V. Breakfast daily 7:30–11am; full meals Mon–Thurs 11am–midnight, Sat–Sun 11am–1am. Gospel brunch in the showroom Sun (2 seatings) 10am and 1pm.

Rainforest Cafe ★ AMERICAN Part of a chain, this ecologically themed restaurant is entirely smoke-free—a rarity in Vegas. Animatronic animals (including a misplaced dinosaur) blink, roar, and twitch their ears and tails as a rainstorm passes overhead. There's a huge saltwater aquarium and a waterfall, and at breakfast, magicians from Houdini's Magic Store wander around performing sleight-of-hand and close-up magic. And yes, there's a souvenir shop with T-shirts, safari clothes, stuffed animals, and coffee mugs. We scored a very cool leopard-spotted onesie jumper from a rack next to a winking gorilla. But back to the food—which is really pretty good; for once, the owners seem to have paid just as much attention to it as to the decor.

In keeping with the tropical theme, the food has exotic names cloaking its mostly kid-friendly ingredients, but the dishes are all described in detail, so you and your family can decide more easily. Some items, such as the Rasta Pasta with walnuts, broccoli, and red peppers may be a little too way-out for some kids, but there are pizza, Buffalo wings, fried chicken, and pot roast, along with ribs, and large salads for the finicky. The 12-and-under set can choose from the kids' menu, which comes with a soda, milk, or juice. The most awesome kids' meal was Jurassic Chicken Tidbits—dinosaur-shaped deep-fried nuggets—but the Rainforest Rascal burger plate was also a good choice. Vegetarian adults and kids will find something for them on both menus, and the desserts are huge.

In the MGM Grand, 3799 Las Vegas Blvd. S. ✆ **800/929-1111** or 702/891-8580. www.mgmgrand.com. Kids' menu, highchairs, boosters. Reservations accepted. Main courses $13–$30; kids' menu $6.99–$7.99. AE, DC, DISC, MC, V. Sun–Thurs 8am–midnight; Fri–Sat 8am–1am.

Wolfgang Puck Bar & Grill ★★ CALIFORNIA This branch of the celebrity-chef's populist chain is bright and lively, featuring the famous multicolored mosaics designed by Puck's artistically ambitious wife Barbara Lazaroff and his even more famous huge wood-burning pizza ovens. This is an affordable choice for parents who want to have a gourmet-lite experience with their kids without breaking the bank, especially during happy hour, when appetizers are available at reduced prices. Well, okay, maybe your kids aren't into pesto pizza or goat cheese, but the ravioli is good and the salads are large and fresh, making it a welcome change from food court, coffee shop, or buffet fare. Puck's signature Chinese chicken salad is full of crunchy fried wontons and cabbage, and the basic Caesar salad is large enough for two. Another good option for sharing is the truffled potato chips with bleu cheese.

In the MGM Grand, 3799 Las Vegas Blvd. S. ✆ **800/929-1111** or 702/891-3000. www.mgmgrand.com. Highchairs, boosters. Reservations recommended. Main courses $12–$32. AE, DC, MC, V. Sun–Thurs 11:30am–10:30pm; Fri–Sat 11:30am–11:30pm.

MODERATE

America AMERICAN Take a gastronomic tour of the USA at this brightly colored restaurant. Your kids can practice their geography and cultural history while ordering Buffalo wings—they're from upstate New York, not the prairies—and Cobb salad, which comes from Hollywood. The menu features American food, with a dish's point of origination spelled out next to each item. Some of these are a bit random, such as the fried mozzarella sticks from Santa Monica and the Seattle lobster chopsticks. And our neighbors down Mexico way might be a bit surprised to find out that America, the restaurant, has annexed Tijuana, the city, for America, the country, via the Caesar salad. On the main wall, a 90×20-foot map of the United States (complete with mountains, rivers, and forests) provides distraction and/or nonchalant educational opportunities. The food is good, especially for such an ambitious concept.

In New York–New York, 3790 Las Vegas Blvd. S. ✆ **800/693-6763** or 702/740-6451. www.nynyhotelcasino.com. Highchairs, boosters. Main courses $8–$23. AE, DC, DISC, MC, V. Daily 24 hr.

Border Grill ★★ MEXICAN No kids' menu, but you don't really need it; you can share dishes, sampling the quesadillas, tacos, and empanadas also found at the main Border Grill restaurant. We liked the chicken mole quesadilla, but alas, the complex dark sauce was not a child pleaser. Our test child much preferred the *carne asada* (steak), the grilled fish tacos, and, naturally, the *taquitos*—corn tortillas rolled around shredded beef, deep fried, and served with guacamole and salsa. No desserts that we could find, but adults may appreciate the margaritas and fine tequilas on hand.

In Mandalay Bay, 3950 Las Vegas Blvd. S. ✆ **702/632-7403.** www.mandalaybay.com. Highchairs, boosters. Reservations not accepted. Main courses $9–$14. AE, DC, DISC, MC, V. Daily 11:30am–10pm.

Chin Chin CHINESE *Chin chin* means "to your health" in Chinese, and this chain, which got its start on chic Sunset Plaza in West Hollywood, uses no added MSG in the preparation of its fresh light food. Along with noodles, which symbolize longevity to the Chinese, Chin Chin serves salads, wokked meats and veggies, plus dim sum (various small dishes of Chinese food), a filling meal any time of day. At breakfast, a traditional eggs, waffles, and bacon buffet shares space with dim sum, noodles, and *congee,* a rice porridge, which can be ordered off the menu. The light and airy room features an open kitchen, so kids can watch their food being prepared.

In New York–New York, 3790 Las Vegas Blvd. S. ✆ **800/693-6763** or 702/740-6300. www.nynyhotelcasino.com. Highchairs, boosters. Main courses $9–$16. AE, DC, DISC, MC, V. Mon–Fri 7:30am–11pm; Sat–Sun 8am–11pm.

Dragon Noodle Co. ★ ASIAN Sushi and Chinese food come together in this campily decorated restaurant (think lots of red paint, dragons, and hanging fringed lamps). Food is cooked in an open kitchen, something kids love to watch, especially when the wok flares up. Everything can be prepared for take out, though unless you're staying in the Monte Carlo, it could be cold by the time you get back to your place. And forget about carrying sushi around in 100°F (38°C) weather. We really like the Chinese food here—the chow fun with beef and chop suey are solid choices, as are the kid-pleasing lemon chicken (battered and fried with a lemon sauce), the orange chicken (battered and fried with a chili-orange sauce), and the honey chicken (more battered and fried chicken morsels, this time with a honey glaze). If you'd like to throw in a vegetable or two (please do), there's spinach with soy and garlic and Chinese broccoli with oyster sauce, along with a selection of tofu dishes that even most nonvegetarians will like. Fried rice, egg rolls, wontons, and soups are traditional hunger busters that won't do the same to your budget. The barbecued pork appetizer is tasty and the fried chicken and noodle salad are light and refreshing. Menu items can be modified and ingredients adjusted to your desires.

In the Monte Carlo Resort & Casino, 3770 Las Vegas Blvd. S. (btw. Flamingo Rd. and Tropicana Ave.). ✆ **702/730-7965.** www.monte-carlo.com. Highchairs, boosters. Reservations recommended. Main courses $10–$22; sushi $5 and up. AE, DC, DISC, MC, V. Sun–Thurs 11am–11pm; Fri–Sat 11am–midnight; sushi bar daily 5pm–close.

ESPN Zone AMERICAN Sports enthusiasts will thrill to this themed chain, where some sporting event is always airing on the TVs and memorabilia line the walls. The food is all-American armchair-quarterback fare—think burgers, grilled steaks, fried chicken fingers, and the ever-popular cheese fries, though they have tried to hit a home run with the health conscious by including grilled fish, pasta, and a subpar apple, blue cheese, and walnut salad, with the inexplicable addition of roasted red peppers. Kids under 10 have their own menu, which includes a drink with their order of chicken tenders, PB&J, hot dog, grilled cheese, pasta, or miniburgers. The same miniburgers, called sliders, are on the appetizer menu in a "cluster of six," while nachos, called Zone Queso Chips, have bacon on them for an extra-cholesterol kick (as do the aforementioned cheese fries). Desserts are big enough for two or three adults. When the kids are done eating, send them upstairs to play video games so you can share a peaceful moment together watching bass fishing. This is Vegas—be prepared for the sports souvenir shop right outside the door.

In New York–New York, 3790 Las Vegas Blvd. S. ✆ **702/933-3776.** www.espnzone.com. Kids' menu, highchairs, boosters. Main courses $12–$26; kids' menu at lunch and dinner $6.99. AE, DC, DISC, MC, V. Mon–Sat 11am–midnight; Sun 11am–11pm.

Harley-Davidson Cafe AMERICAN Harley-Davidson motorcycles were once the hog of choice for one-percenters—the outcasts of society, the rebels, the grungy, leather-clad badasses you wouldn't want your kids to grow up and be. But now, doctors, lawyers, and other "upstanding" citizens—many of whom spend upwards of $18,000 for their hog—head on down the highway, riding America's number-one motorcycle for fun. Let your kids take an up-close gander at the motorcycle memorabilia as they sink into black simulated leather booths and chow down on sloppy Joes, Roadhouse Chicken Wings, and, of course, the Harley Hog sandwich. There are also salads as well as vegetarian fare on the menu, no doubt because the demographics and image of bikers has changed so much during the past 2 decades. But not to give short shrift to Harley-Davidson's rowdy history, there is a menu of over 20 hard liquor drinks available in souvenir glasses.

3725 Las Vegas Blvd. S. (btw. Harmon and Tropicana aves.). ✆ **702/740-4555.** Highchairs, boosters. Reservations accepted. Main courses under $10–$20. AE, DC, DISC, MC, V. Daily 11am–midnight.

P.F. Chang's China Bistro CHINESE With menu items developed in conjunction with acclaimed chef Barbara Tropp (San Francisco's China Moon Café and author of *China Moon Cookbook* and *Modern Art of Chinese Cooking*), P.F. Chang's China Bistro serves a decent selection of favorite Chinese dishes. Although you won't find exotic items such as shark fin or birds nest on the menu, you will get sizable portions of traditional Chinese restaurant items: Mongolian beef, orange-peel chicken, and sweet-and-sour pork, along with egg rolls, Peking duck, noodle dishes (we liked the Singapore street

Moments **Tea for Two**

High tea—with its dainty finger sandwiches, scones thickly slathered with clotted cream, and tiny frosted cakes, not to mention a choice of different teas, served with either milk or lemon—is a lovely and relaxing way to spend an afternoon with your children, especially if they are Anglophiles or prone to throwing tea parties with their dolls and pets. The **Verandah** ★ at the child-loving Four Seasons serves high tea Monday through Thursday from 3 to 4pm (Fri–Sun it's for private parties only), replete with the requisite cucumber and cress sandwiches, scones, and pastries. You might want to pack ladylike hats and gloves and plan to make this a dress-up playtime by inviting any historical personages or invisible princesses and fantasy friends from your child's imagination. And if high tea's not your cup of tea, the Verandah offers children's menus for breakfast, lunch, and a dinner buffet. (In the Four Seasons, 3960 Las Vegas Blvd. S.; ✆ **877/632-5000;** www.fourseasons.com; afternoon tea $30 per person; AE, DC, DISC, MC, V.)

noodles with shrimp and curry, but kids might find its yellow color and spiciness a bit off-putting), cashew chicken, and the signature lettuce wraps. It's all good, even the nontraditional desserts—Great Wall of Chocolate Cake and the deep-fried banana rolls with coconut ice cream. The room itself (with replicas of Xian statues—life-size terracotta warriors found in an emperor's gravesite) is lovely.

In the Planet Hollywood, 3667 Las Vegas Blvd. S. (at Harmon Ave.). ✆ **702/836-0955.** Highchairs, boosters. Reservations accepted. Main courses $8–$18 (many under $10), some less at lunch. AE, DC, DISC, MC, V. Sun–Thurs noon–midnight; Fri–Sat noon–1am.

INEXPENSIVE

Calypsos DINER/COFFEE SHOP Building your own burger is one of the prime attractions at this cheery coffee shop, which also features salads, including a dessert camouflaging itself among the leafy-green offerings: strawberries heaped atop pound cake, served with frozen yogurt. For the health-conscious, there's a pineapple boat filled with cottage cheese, honeydew, cantaloupe, and other fruits, but we prefer the classic coffee shop fare such as the burger with barbecue sauce, grilled onions, bacon, and pineapple, followed by a fudge sundae. Your kids will, too.

In the Tropicana, 3801 Las Vegas Blvd. S. ✆ **702/739-2222.** Highchairs. Reservations not accepted. Main courses $7–$20. AE, MC, V. Daily 24 hr.

In-N-Out Burger ★ **Value** AMERICAN This Southern California classic roadside, family-owned, drive-through burger chain has always made a point of serving fresh, high-quality, fast food. Potatoes for the fries are hand cut at each location; the meat is always fresh, not frozen; shakes are made with real ice cream; and all burgers can be customized for your desires. None of the special variations are listed on the menu, but they have gained mythic stature among those in the know. Try the Animal Style—grilled onions, extra sauce, and pickles—or the protein, which comes wrapped in lettuce with no bun; or the grilled cheese, which has no burger, just cheese, lettuce, and tomatoes. A Flying

Value Cheap Eats

Gone are Vegas's days of **super-cheap buffets,** but a few holdouts offer meals for a bit less than the Strip average (though most really cheap dining establishments are in ickyish, smoky, old hotels). Also note that these places cut no discount for children; even kindergartners will pay full price. Nevertheless, if you feel that you *must* experience this vestige of Old Las Vegas, try one of the following.

At its two locations, **Arizona Charlie's** buffet, 740 Decatur Blvd. (✆ **702/258-5200**) and 4575 Boulder Hwy. (✆ **702/951-9000;** www.arizonacharlies.com), offers basic food at cheap prices—breakfast for $5.29 ($6.99 at the Decatur location), lunch for $6.99/7.99, and dinner for $8.75/$9.99. Children 2 and under eat free. The **Gold Coast** buffet, 4000 W. Flamingo Rd. (✆ **702/367-7111**), provides seven serving stations. Breakfast is $6.95, lunch $8.45, dinner and Sunday brunch $12.95, Sunday steak night will set you back $12.95, and Thursday seafood night is $17.95. Children 2 and under eat free. **Main Street Station,** 200 Main St. (✆ **702/387-1896;** www.mainstreetcasino.com), is 2 blocks from the Fremont Street Experience and offers a buffet with a variety of cuisines. Breakfast is $6.99, lunch $7.99, and dinner $10.99. The Tuesday night T-bone special is $13.29, and Sunday brunch runs $10.99. Children 2 and under eat free. **The Orleans,** 4500 W. Tropicana Ave. (✆ **702/365-7111;** www.orleanscasino.com), also delivers low-price buffets of cuisines of the world. Breakfast is $6.95, lunch $8.95, and dinner $13.95. Children 2 and under eat free.

Hot dog lovers should check out the **Gold Coast Casino,** 3959 Las Vegas Blvd. S. (✆ **702/367-7111;** www.goldcoast.com), where a dog from the cart near the sports bar is $1.25. **Slots A Fun Casino,** 2890 Las Vegas Blvd. S. (✆ **702/734-0410**), has a much-lauded hot dog, which made it into a PBS special on the best hot dogs in all of the United States (though some people we know don't think they're anything particularly special!). These casinos allow children, accompanied by their parents, to go to the snack bars.

Beef eaters can find a complete filet-cut sirloin steak dinner for $6.95, served day and night at **Ellis Island** (✆ **702/733-8901;** www.ellisislandcasino.com). And an $8.95 steak and shrimp dinner can be had 24/7 at the Hard Rock's **Mr. Lucky's 24/7** coffee shop (✆ **702/693-5000;** www.hardrockhotel.com).

You can also save big at hotel food courts (with McDonald's, Nathan's, and more adventurous fare), which offer inexpensive alternatives to buffet or restaurant breakfasts. MGM Grand, Monte Carlo, and The Venetian have particularly good food courts with lots of interesting choices. You can save big bucks at breakfast, and the kids will be happy with familiar choices. On the other hand, buffets can be good value at lunch or dinner for kids under 10 because of the desserts—they're part of the buffet and you can eat as much as your stomach (or parent!) allows. Note also that children under 10 are charged half price at many Strip hotel buffets.

Dutchman has two slices of cheese and two patties with nothing else; if you just want mustard and ketchup with your meat and cheese, ask for the Old Fashioned. If you like your fries crisp, ask for well-done and they'll fry them twice. Along with their "secret items," the chain has a couple other peculiarities: Numbers of certain Bible chapters and verses (Revelation 3:20, John 3:16, Proverbs 3:15, and Nahum 1:7) are printed on the underside of soda cups, malt cups, and burger wrappers, which may be disturbing to some; and no phone numbers are listed for individual locations—they can only be reached through the 800 number. In addition to the Strip-side In-N-Out, you can find this quirky drive-through on the road to Nellis Air Force Base (51 N. Nellis Blvd.), west of the North Strip (2900 W. Sahara Blvd.), and on the east end of town (4705 S. Maryland Pkwy.).

4888 Dean Martin Dr. (at Tropicana Rd.). ✆ **800/786-1000.** www.inandout.com. Highchairs, boosters. Reservations not accepted. Main courses $1.45–$5.50. Cash only, no credit cards; ATM on-site. All branches Sun–Thurs 8am–1am; Fri–Sat 8am–1:30am.

La Salsa (Value) MEXICAN This pioneering chain of Mexican fast food/casual dining restaurants created the concept of the salsa bar, where different types of fresh salsas can be self-served onto your freshly made tacos and burritos. La Salsa was also the first fast-food Mexican chain to grill chicken and beef for tacos and is credited with popularizing soft tacos, *carne asada* (grilled steak), and black beans, all of which were quite an innovation when the chain launched more than 20 years ago. Its Vegas locations mean that vegans can eat vegetable, rice, and lard-free bean burritos or tacos and that no one has to worry about the food being too spicy, because you can choose your salsas, all of which are rated by heat. An order of tacos comes two to a plate, burritos are large, and the chips are good and fresh. All food can be custom-ordered—we overheard one slinky teen asking for a rice, tomato, and lettuce taco. Whatever! Along with this branch and several noncasino locations, you can find this popular taco stand at the Planet Hollywood Miracle Mile Shops (3663 Las Vegas Blvd. S.; ✆ **702/892-0645**), Caesars Palace (3570 Las Vegas Blvd. S.; ✆ **702/735-8226**), The Riviera (2901 Las Vegas Blvd. S.; ✆ **702/734-5110**), and Neonopolis Downtown (450 Fremont St.; ✆ **702/384-1720**).

In Luxor, 3900 Las Vegas Blvd. S. ✆ **702/739-1776.** www.luxor.com. Reservations not accepted. Main courses $5–$11. AE, DC, DISC, MC, V. All branches open daily 11:30am–10pm.

Monte Carlo Brew Pub ★★★ (Value) AMERICAN Huge, loud, and fun, this restaurant is no longer a brewpub, but it still serves pizzas, burgers, and salads, along with a long list of beers. TVs are tuned to different stations, so guests can watch (forget about hearing) sports, news, and other programs. Exposed bricks, copper tubing, and brew vats add to the casual and lively decor. Kids are welcome until 9pm, when live music begins. We really liked the barbecued chicken pizza, house salad, juicy cheddar burger, and the jalapeño poppers that literally popped with flavor. Pass on the Buffalo wings, which came soaked in a thin, unpleasant, vinegary pepper sauce. The nachos are large enough for a family of four, plus Spot the dog. Did we mention chicken fingers? Yum! There's ice cream, cheesecake, and a huge chocolate brownie smothered in ice cream and fudge sauce for dessert. This informal, reasonably priced hotel-dining barn is a great change of pace from buffets and coffee shops with enough choices on the menu for everyone. We loved it, and so did the other families scattered about.

In the Monte Carlo Resort & Casino, 3770 Las Vegas Blvd. S. (btw. Flamingo Rd. and Tropicana Ave.). ✆ **702/730-7777.** www.montecarlo.com. Highchairs, boosters. Reservations not accepted. Main courses $8–$17. AE, DC, DISC, MC, V. Thurs and Sun–Mon 11am–11pm; Fri–Sat 11am–midnight.

Las Vegas's Chinatown

Las Vegas's Chinatown (4255 Spring Rd.; www.lvchinatown.com) is a 5-minute drive from Treasure Island, but almost a world away, despite its strip-mall atmosphere. Along with stores carrying a variety of exotic goods, there are over half-a-dozen family-friendly restaurants serving food from the Far East. **Pho** (✆ **702/227-8618**), a Vietnamese soup shop named for the soup itself, serves a big hot pot with raw beef (it cooks instantly in the hot broth), bean sprouts, leaves, and lime, along with a regular menu of Vietnamese dishes like spring rolls wrapped in a delicate rice paper and stuffed with shrimp, noodles, and herbs. **Sushi Moto** (✆ **702/871-1532**) offers sushi as well as basic Japanese foods.

Both **168 Shanghai** ★ (✆ **702/889-8700**) and **Harbor Palace** (✆ **702/253-1688**) serve dim sum from the traditional metal carts that are pushed through the restaurant, stopping at each table. Your waitress will lift up each dish, showing you the contents, which can range from the not-for-the-squeamish (chicken feet) to the most sedate and succulent items such as *shu mai*—thin-skinned dumplings filled with shrimp—or fluffy *cha su bao,* the Chinese barbecued-pork sandwich. Each diner is given a small dish of mustard and hot sauce for dipping; the addition of soy sauce is at your discretion. The dim sum dishes for vegetarians are meager (Chinese broccoli, no oyster sauce, please), but the regular menu offers some options.

Player's Deli DELI/DINER/COFFEE SHOP Sample sandwiches named for Las Vegas and gambling terms include the Baccarat, Ace-High, One-Armed Bandit, King of Clubs, and more. Also served are bagels and lox, eggs, pizza, wings, and matzo ball soup. You'll find this fun snack spot near the sports bar.

In the Tropicana Resort & Casino, 3801 Las Vegas Blvd. S. ✆ **702/739-2222.** www.tropicanalv.com. Highchairs. Reservations not accepted. Main courses $8–$13. AE, MC, V. Daily 9am–9pm.

4 CENTER STRIP

VERY EXPENSIVE

Bradley Ogden ★★ **Moments** AMERICAN Noted chef and owner Bradley Ogden has dubbed his cooking "Farm Fresh American cuisine," buying exclusively from American producers and farmers. In 2004, Bradley Ogden became the first Las Vegas restaurant to be named the nation's Best New Restaurant by the James Beard Foundation. Cooking with Ogden is his son Bryan, graduate of the Culinary Institute of America. A softly lit bastion of understated elegance, Bradley Ogden is a special-occasions sort of restaurant, but is relaxing and unpretentious all the same. Menus change daily, though such signatures as the foie gras, Kobe-style New York strip steak, the seasonal oysters, the blue cheese soufflé appetizer (not to be missed), and the selection of artisan American cheeses are always in place. Other recommendations include any of the seafood dishes. Selection varies with the season, but is always exciting. Seared dayboat scallop in spring onions

Tips Call in Advance

When making reservations, reserve the highchairs and booster seats you'll need, making it easier for the staff to accommodate you; some restaurants have limited numbers.

soup with pea tendrils, Wisconsin pheasant with sweet potato spaetzle, oak-grilled lamb rack with fava bean and cumin, and clay-pot Guinea hen with Kara Kara orange sauce are typical of the variety. Desserts are both delicious and whimsical—Carnival Jubilee with a snow cone, mini–funnel cake, ice cream sandwich, sweet hot pretzel with a trio of fondue sauces, cotton candy, rhubarb upside-down cake with vanilla crème fraîche ice cream, and the intriguing chocolate childhood tasting. Allow enough time to dine (at least 2 hr.) if you plan to see the Celine show. A four-course, prix-fixe pre-theater menu is available. Lunch and bar menus also change daily. ***Tip:*** The leisurely pace of dining makes Bradley Ogden a bad choice for kids (or anyone else) that can't sit still for a couple of hours.

In Caesars Palace, 3570 Las Vegas Blvd. S. ✆ **702/731-7731.** www.harrahs.com. Highchairs, boosters. Reservations accepted. Main courses $29–$48 (changes daily with menu). AE, DC DISC, MC, V. Daily 5pm–close. Bar & Lounge day menu 2:30–5pm; night menu 5–11pm.

Delmonico Steakhouse ★★ SOUTHERN/CAJUN/CREOLE You may want to save dinner here for the adults and bring your Emeril-adoring offspring for lunch, because the food at Delmonico is very adult, as are the prices. Lunchtime features a juicy burger with bacon, Swiss cheese, caramelized onions, and Creole fries. The spicy, tomato-glazed chicken sandwich with A.O.K. sauce is the most upscale barbecue food ever. For good measure, throw in some truffle Parmesan potato chips or smashed potatoes, and your child won't mind forgoing dinner. Appetizers—including the barbecue shrimp in tangy sauce with a rosemary biscuit and the steak tartare—are served at both lunch and dinner, as are soups and salads. A true Emerilphile should go for the gumbo, and the kid-pleasing French onion soup comes with an English muffin smothered in Swiss cheese. Desserts, especially the flourless chocolate–peanut butter cake with peanut butter mousse, fudge sauce, and toasted peanuts, are rich, flavorful, luxurious, and satisfying.

In The Venetian, 3355 Las Vegas Blvd. S. ✆ **702/414-3737.** www.emerils.com. Highchairs, boosters. Reservations strongly recommended for dinner. Lunch $14–$39; dinner $28–$48. AE, DC, DISC, MC, V. Sun–Thurs 11:30am–2pm and 5–10pm; Fri–Sat 5–10:30pm.

Mon Ami Gabi ★★ Moments FRENCH Tile floors and dark wood booths enhance the feeling of dining in a Parisian bistro circa 1909, and the menu is traditional French grill food, such as steaks, soups, salads, and, of course, *pommes frites,* served in an elegant and charming atmosphere. Come early and make sure to ask for patio seating, where you are slightly elevated above the Strip and can watch the passersby. Although there is no children's menu, young ones will find a variety of soups, salads, crepes, quiches, omelets, and sandwiches at lunch; at dinner, more adult food comes into play, though soups and sides can certainly fill young ones' tummies. At both, guests are presented with a baguette of freshly baked bread upon being seated, and our waiter steadily brought us more as needed.

The portions are massive, even by Vegas standards, so once again, sharing is a wise option. We especially liked the pepper steak and the mussels with leek cream, along with

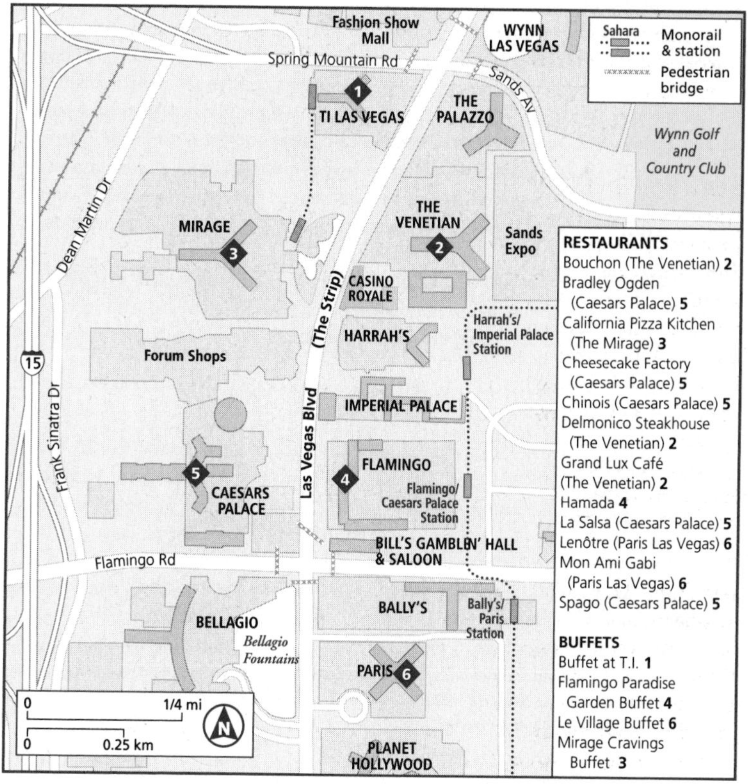

the endive and the frisee salads. Desserts, naturally, are big enough for four. Even though the menu has less for children at dinner, nighttime on the Strip patio offers a wonderful view of the water ballet across the street at the Bellagio. Every 15 minutes, the fountains dance and cascade in time to classical and pop music as you savor your fine meal, making this a romantic spot for couples, but without the formality of other adult restaurants.

In Paris Las Vegas, 3655 Las Vegas Blvd. S. ✆ **702/944-4224.** www.monamigabi.com. Highchairs, boosters. Reservations recommended, though you cannot specifically reserve a table on the patio. Lunch $10–$32; dinner $19–$40. AE, DC, DISC, MC, V. Lunch Mon–Fri 11:30am–4pm, Sat–Sun 11am–4pm; dinner Sun–Thurs 4–11pm, Fri–Sat 4pm–midnight.

Spago ★★★ CALIFORNIA Spago for kids? Sure, why not treat them, if you think they'd enjoy beets layered with goat cheese, crispy Asian duck, or any other of Wolfgang Puck's signature dishes? If you're not ready to commit to the more expensive indoor restaurants (reservations, please), grab a seat at the less formal "outdoor" cafe overlooking the Forum Shops and order up the Jewish pizza. (Yes, that's its creator's designation.) You'll have to ask for it by name, because this dish—crème fraîche and salmon on a thin, wood-fired, pizza crust—is not on the menu. Puck's signature Chinese chicken salad can be found here (as well as at Wolfgang Puck Bar & Grill at the MGM Grand and, of

Sweets for the Sweet

Traditional gelato is a low-fat low-sugar version of ice cream, made without eggs and whipped to a dense rich texture. Gelato Las Vegas–style takes the health kick a bit further; it's made without any milk products at all, so that lactose-intolerant individuals and vegans can enjoy a creamy, smooth, frozen dessert. The base of this miracle dessert is vegetable oils and cellulose, a plant fiber: Think tofu, in a good way; in a very good way—whipped, sweetened, and fabulously flavored. Some flavors are also made sugar free, using Splenda, maltose, or aspartame—ask your server.

Give it a try at the Bellagio at **Cafe Gelato** (3600 Las Vegas Blvd. S.; ✆ **702/693-7111**), where they scoop up gelatos of many varieties, along with serving pastries and smoothies. They are open from 7am to 11pm, daily.

course, Chinois, also at Caesars), but its omnipresence in Vegas doesn't detract from its wonderfulness—soy mustard dressing, crisp wontons, and lettuces tossed with roasted chicken. For the less adventurous, there's meatloaf, pasta, and fish, all treated with herbs and seasonings in a way that will make you rethink food. The desserts, including homemade sorbets and the brownie sundae, are luxurious. If you think that the prices are more than you'd like to spend on the kids, consider getting a sitter or ordering a pay-per-view movie for them and treating yourselves to this gourmet experience.

In the Forum Shops at Caesars Palace, 3570 Las Vegas Blvd. S. ✆ **702/369-6300.** Highchairs, boosters. Reservations recommended for the dining room; not accepted at the cafe. Dining room main courses $31–$50; cafe main courses $12–$28. AE, DC, DISC, MC, V. Dining room nightly 5:30–10pm. Cafe Sun–Thurs 11am–11pm, Fri–Sat 11am–midnight.

EXPENSIVE

Empress Court CHINESE Often mentioned as the best Chinese/pan-Asian restaurant in Las Vegas, it's certainly one of the most expensive. Empress Court is reminiscent of the finest restaurants in Hong Kong, somewhat hidden in a dedicated corner of the second floor. The main dining room features Chinese art and artifacts and plush sofas; there are also three private dining rooms, and outdoor terraces overlook Caesars' Garden of the Gods swimming pools and gardens. Here you'll find traditional Chinese delicacies, such as bird's nest, abalone, and shark's fin, along with a variety of fresh seafood, especially lobster, squab, fantail shrimp, and crispy whole fish, as represented by the large fish tank that greets you when you exit the elevator. A few exotic dishes include melon soup with pork, curry chicken, and lacquered Peking duck. But there's also the usual cashew chicken, Mongolian beef, and lo mein, albeit costing three times more than what you're accustomed to paying; the Vegetarian Feast accommodates nonmeat eaters with varied tofu dishes. The kids will especially love the mango crème brûlée and chocolate-filled fried banana for dessert.

In Caesars Palace, 3570 Las Vegas Blvd. S. ✆ **702/731-7731.** Highchairs, boosters. Reservations recommended. Main courses $18-$39. AE, DC, DISC, MC, V. Wed-Sun 5-11pm.

MODERATE

California Pizza Kitchen CALIFORNIA Bright, light, and loud, this chain caused a sensation when it opened over 20 years ago—finally, gourmet food mainstreamed out of chic celebrity chefs' open kitchens and into the malls, eventually landing in the freezer section of your local supermarket. Here is a plethora of pizza—Thai pizza, pear and Gorgonzola cheese pizza, barbecued chicken pizza, pizza with odd sauces, tandoori chicken, stinky cheese, peanuts, potatoes, and just to keep the traditionalists at bay, pepperoni. All are good, depending on where your taste lies. The basic five-cheese is always going to make someone happy; you can order cheeseless if that's your choice, and should you prefer salads to slices, they have those too. We like the Thai Crunch salad with chicken, wontons, and cabbage in peanut dressing. It's a chain, so it's reliable. It's full of families (there's even a special kids' section on the chain's website at **www.cpk.com/menu/cpkids_menu.aspx**), so yours is welcome. The California pizzas and pastas are large enough to share between two adults, as are the Neapolitan pizzas with thin crusts and more traditional toppings; salads come in (large) half and (even larger) full portions. The kids' menu features kid-size pasta, salads, and a variety of pizzas, including the barbecue chicken pizza; all kids' meals come with a drink.

In The Mirage, 3400 Las Vegas Blvd. S. ✆ **702/791-7111.** Additional locations in the Fashion Show Mall, 3200 Las Vegas Blvd. S. ✆ 702/893-1370, and Town Square, 6659 Las Vegas Blvd. S. ✆ 702/896-5154. www.cpk.com. Kids' menu, highchairs, boosters. Main courses $7–$18; kids' menu $4.99. AE, DC, DISC, MC, V. Sun–Thurs 11am–midnight; Fri–Sat 11am–2am.

Canter's Deli ★ (Finds) DELI Canter's Deli at TI is a transplant from Los Angeles that dates back to 1931 and has branched once in its 78-year-history: to Treasure Island, adjacent to the sports book, in 2004. And now that the Stage Deli in the Forum Shops has closed and gone home to New York, this is the best deli on the Strip. The half-pound 5-inch-high pastrami, corned beef, and pastrami-corned beef condo sandwiches are the mainstays; Canter's in L.A. serves 5,000 pounds of pastrami per month. Of course, the matzo ball soup is another favorite; some southern Californians claim it cures not only colds, but the flu, not to mention hunger pangs. The barley-bean soup is "famous," as are the knishes, blintzes, chopped liver, and "slightly hot" pickles. Also try the New York cheesecake and chocolate-chip racetrack cake.

In Treasure Island, 3300 Las Vegas Blvd. S. ✆ **702/894-6390.** www.lasvegas.cantersdeli.com. Highchairs, boosters. Reservations accepted for large parties only. Main courses $12–$19.95; sandwiches $10–$18. AE, DC, DISC, MC, V. Daily 11am–midnight.

Cheesecake Factory ★ AMERICAN Be prepared, the portions are huge here—even the lunch-size portions of pasta and salads are too much for most adults, and if you have guilt issues about leaving food on your plate, you may want to eat elsewhere. Their slogan is NO ONE GOES HOME HUNGRY FROM HERE, and they're right. Most people go home overstuffed. With more than 200 items on the menu (well, that includes desserts, too), everyone should find something pleasing in this faux-bistro-styled restaurant. The food is dependable, especially if you stick to the more basic items, though maybe you think avocado-stuffed, deep-fried egg rolls are a good idea. We preferred the standard burger, the Santa Fe salad, and the tacos to the more highfalutin attempts (miso-glazed salmon, for instance). The room is loud, loud, loud, so kids aren't frowned upon in the least, though you won't find an actual children's menu. There are also dozens of flavors of cheesecake for dessert; being purists, we opted for the basic plain and loved it.

The Kult of Krispy Kreme

Part of Krispy Kreme's original attraction was its elusiveness. For decades, these doughnuts were legendary across the United States for their sweet coating and crisp, golden crust that gave away into the fluffy, but not too yeasty, interior. Visitors to the South, the only region in the United States where Krispy Kremes were sold, were urged by friends and family to bring back a box, usually of the Original Glazed doughnuts, as a delicious souvenir.

But by 1996, Krispy Kreme had migrated to New York City, in 1999 it arrived in California, and today there's at least one Krispy Kreme shop in almost every state. So elusiveness may no longer be the magnet, but you'll still see lines of people waiting for their dozen hot and fresh treats no matter which branch you head to.

Why? Aside from the great taste, another part of Krispy Kreme's attraction is the immediacy of a sinfully indulgent (and fresh!) experience. Each store that makes the doughnuts cooks two runs a day, one in the morning and one in the late afternoon. You really, really want to be there then to grab a hot, fresh Original Glazed right off the rack and feel it melt in your mouth. Luckily, Las Vegas, a city known for allowing—nay, encouraging—decadent behavior, has plenty of Krispy Kreme outlets to satisfy your cravings: The **Venetian,** 3377 Las Vegas Blvd. S. (✆ **702/414-3408**) in the food court, open 24 hours; **Circus Circus,** 2880 Las Vegas Blvd. S. (✆ **702/733-9944**); and **Fitzgeralds,** 301 Fremont St. (✆ **702/366-0150**).

True Krispy Kreme connoisseurs head for the **Excalibur,** 3850 Las Vegas Blvd. S. (✆ **702/736-5235**), where the shop is open 24 hours a day, and doughnuts are made from 6 to 11am and again from 6 to 10pm. The real thrill about the Excalibur's Krispy Kreme, located on the second floor of the hotel, is that you can stand slack-jawed in anticipation in front of a glass wall, watching the raw doughnuts flip into the hot grease, then flip back out cooked and golden onto the tray where they're drenched with a warm, damp, sugary coating before arriving in the cases for your buying and eating pleasure.

In the Forum Shops at Caesars Palace, 3570 Las Vegas Blvd. S. ✆ **702/792-6888.** www.cheesecakefactory.net or www.harrahs.com. Highchairs, boosters. Reservations accepted. Main courses $10–$24. AE, DC, DISC, MC, V. Mon–Thurs 11:10am–11:30pm; Fri 11:10am–12:30am; Sat 10:10am–12:30am; Sun 10:10am–11:30pm.

Chinois ★★★ Value ASIAN Once he conquered Italian food and created gourmet pizza, Wolfgang Puck, like Caesar, did not rest on his laurels; he forayed into the realm of Chinese cooking, blended it with French, and Chinois was born. This outpost of Puck's famous Santa Monica eatery is divided into a pricey downstairs restaurant and a more playful, less expensive cafe upstairs, which is where we suggest you and your family eat. We like the steamed salmon with citrus soy sauce, the duck with pineapple sauce served with ginger and scallion pancakes, and the wok-fried catfish in ginger and ponzu sauce, all served family style for sharing. The vegetable fried rice is light and fluffy, probably the best we've ever had, and the garlic tofu is deeply satisfying. The yummy sushi selection is very extensive.

In the Forum Shops at Caesars Palace, 3500 Las Vegas Blvd. S. ✆ **702/737-9700.** www.wolfgangpuck.com. Highchairs, boosters. Reservations recommended. Main courses $13–$38. AE, MC, V. Sun–Thurs 11am–10pm; Fri–Sat 11am–11pm.

Grand Lux Café ★ INTERNATIONAL The Cheesecake Factory's not-so-little sister joins the international set, with an equally large menu of gargantuan dishes served 24 hours a day, every day. Art Nouveau styling gives the Grand Lux the feel of a Viennese cafe (ca. 1900), but the choices scream, "Welcome to the 21st century!" Asian nachos—fried wonton skins topped with peanut sauce, chicken, wasabi, and cheese—stand out as an egregious example of a food consultant run amok, as do the coconut–macadamia nut–crusted chicken skewers and the Santa Fe roll—sort of a Southwestern egg roll meets deep-fried burrito concept. Ugh. There's also a caramel-coated fried chicken claiming Thai flavors (garlic and ginger), which just screams insulin and cholesterol overload. However, the Vietnamese summer roll, which is one of the few relatively greaseless appetizers, is good, as are the salads, many of which are carried over from the Cheesecake Factory. We liked that the waiter and the kitchen were able to handle a complex variation of Madeira chicken for our fussy eater who wanted no cheese, no mushrooms, no asparagus, and no sauce, and got exactly what he ordered—a plain chicken breast with plain mashed potatoes. Vegetarians will find a decent selection, plus sides (mashed sweet potatoes—yum). Desserts are big enough for three adults; we appreciated the fresh baked chocolate chip cookies, a whole dozen of them; they were simple and are probably the best item on the menu. There's a kid-size breakfast available, and if you ask your server, she or he may be able to work with you on a lunch or dinnertime meal customized for your kid.

In The Venetian, 3355 Las Vegas Blvd. S. ✆ **888/2-VENICE** (283-6423) or 702/414-3888. www.venetian.com. Highchairs. Reservations accepted. Main courses $9–$26 (most under $15). AE, DC, DISC, MC, V. Daily 24 hr.

INEXPENSIVE

Lenôtre ★★★ Finds DESSERTS Ooh la la. Desserts made the Parisian way—delicious and decadent. Please thank Paris Las Vegas for bringing you this branch of the famous French cafe/shop (run by world-renowned pastry chef Gaston Lenôtre, now in his late 80s), which also makes smooth, rich, chocolate candies and breakfast pastries. Try their most popular dessert: chocolate mousse surrounding pistachio cream filling dubbed the Millennium—though they might want to rethink that name. If you feel that fruit might be a more salubrious sweet, the Charlotte features strawberries, along with vanilla custard supported by a ladyfinger crust. There's also Tarte Tatin (a caramelized apple tart) and other seasonal fruit tarts, plus heaps of chocolatey goodness. You can start your

Tips Chillin' Out

If your hotel does not provide a fridge in your room, inquire about renting one. The cost runs about $10 to $15 a day for a small icebox. Because cold bottled water costs $2 at hotel convenience stores, you could easily save the rental charge by buying water, juice, and sodas outside the hotel and chilling them in your room. Plus, you'll have a place to stash leftovers for a quick breakfast—cold chow mein, anyone?

morning at Lenôtre in a more sensible fashion, with a cheese croissant, baguette, or apple turnover; the fresh desserts get loaded into the cases around 9:30am.

In Paris Las Vegas, 3655 Las Vegas Blvd. S. ✆ **702/946-7000.** www.harrahs.com. Reservations not accepted. Pastries $3–$7. AE, DC, DISC, MC, V. Daily 6:30am–11pm.

5 NORTH STRIP

MODERATE

NASCAR Cafe AMERICAN Concept over content here—this is all-American food, with a slight Southern twist; after all, NASCAR got its start in the South, back in the days of moonshining, when bootleggers would build super-charged stock cars to outrun the revenuers. The food here is not bad, just not great, but the atmosphere makes up for it—race memorabilia festoon the walls and NASCAR races play on video screens. Race fans will love to look at all the photos, autographed items, and car parts while downing burgers and ribs—check out Carzilla, the largest NASCAR ever built, which serves as the bar downstairs. If you don't know Dale, Jr., from Michael Schumacher, or the Daytona 500 from the Monaco Grand Prix, you're better off elsewhere.

In the Sahara, 2535 Las Vegas Blvd. S. ✆ **702/734-7223.** www.nascarcafelasvegas.com. Highchairs, boosters. Reservations not accepted. Main courses $9–$21. AE, DC, DISC, MC, V. Mon–Thurs 11am–10pm; Fri-Sat 10am–midnight; Sun 9am–10pm.

INEXPENSIVE

Capriotti's ★ **Value** SANDWICHES A favorite with locals, Capriotti's certainly builds the best and most eclectic selection of sandwiches close to the Strip, and at the best prices. Along with traditional Italian subs, cheesesteaks, and hot-sausage sandwiches, you'll find veggie burgers, hot dogs, and even a tofu turkey sub. Try the much-loved Bobbie (real turkey, cranberry sauce, and dressing) or any of the other of Cap's specials. Keep in mind that these sandwiches are very large; the so-called small is 9 inches long, while the large tops out at almost 20 inches. If you're planning a side trip or picnic, this is where you should pick up your victuals. ***Note:*** A couple dozen branches of this shop are scattered around town, though this one is our favorite; check the website for other locations.

322 W. Sahara Ave. ✆ **702/474-0229.** www.capriottis.com. Reservations not accepted. Sandwiches $8–$15. AE, DC, DISC, MC, V. Mon–Fri 10am–5pm; Sat 11am–5pm.

Pink Pony ★ DINER/COFFEE SHOP Kid-friendly is the operative theme at this coffee shop, where your children will get crayons and a circus place mat to color. The striped walls and circus paintings will delight, as will the prices. The food is fine for kids and for those who have grown tired of standing in lines and want a simple meal.

In Circus Circus, 2880 Las Vegas Blvd. S. ✆ **877/224-7287** or 702/734-0410. www.circuscircus.com. Kids' menu, highchairs, boosters. Main courses $7–$16; kids' menu $4–$7. AE, DC, DISC, MC, V. Daily 24 hr.

Tiffany's Cafe at White Cross Drugs ★ DINER/COFFEE SHOP Just a close walk from the Stratosphere, this is a real, old-fashioned, coffee shop/diner that's been in business for over 60 years. Open 24 hours, it's located inside a pharmacy, so picturesque

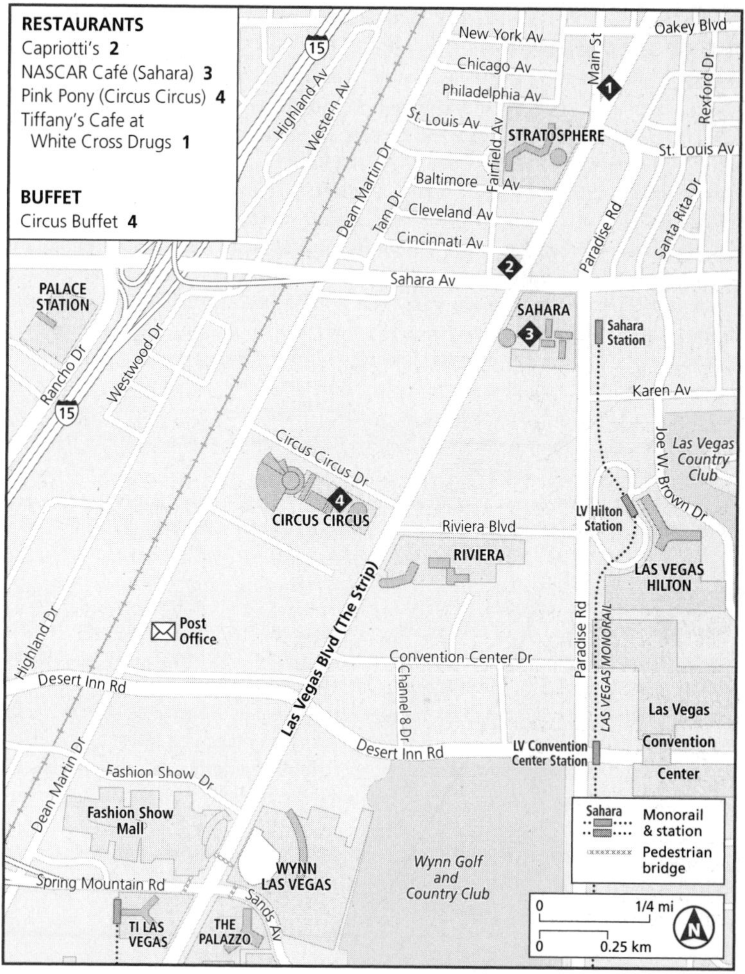

it isn't. Take your kids here, pull up to the fountain, and order thick creamy shakes (the best in Vegas), 1/3-pound burgers, slices of pie, or meatloaf, so they can see what all the other retro diners are merely *trying* to be. The food is not only good, it's a bargain. ***Note:*** The neighborhood here remains stubbornly rough in appearance, and that can be a turnoff. Keep alert if you come here at night.

In White Cross Drugs, 1700 Las Vegas Blvd. S. ✆ **702/383-0196.** 1 highchair. Reservations not accepted. Main courses $4–$9. No credit cards. Daily 24 hr.

6 EAST OF THE STRIP

VERY EXPENSIVE

Nobu ★★★ JAPANESE If you want to experience a modern gourmet Japanese restaurant, this is the place, but if dragon rolls and volcanoes are more your sushi speed, go elsewhere. Nobuyuki Matsuhisa is the reigning king of modern Japanese cooking, whose acclaimed restaurants—Nobu, Ubon (Nobu backward), and Matsuhisa—serve both the raw and the cooked in a delicate fusion of Japanese, Peruvian, and French cuisine. The Nobus in New York, Malibu, Miami, and London are very, very good restaurants, and, luckily, the landlocked Las Vegas version lives up to its heritage. Leave behind your expectations of standard Japanese cuisine when you enter this beautiful room, with its black-rock sculpture and bamboo walls. This is sushi supreme (the fish is flown in daily from Tokyo), and you'll want to taste the yellowtail with jalapeño, the tuna tataki with ponzo sauce, and Kobe beef carpaccio, along with the changing *omakase* (chef's choice) dinners, which can feature items like seared Kobe with foie gras or seared salmon in a delicate sauce. Well-behaved children are welcome (there is chicken teriyaki on the menu for the fussy eater), but you may want to get a sitter, allowing you to savor this restaurant as a romantic, gourmet getaway.

In the Hard Rock Hotel & Casino, 4475 Paradise Rd. ✆ **702/693-5090.** www.hardrockhotel.com. Highchairs. Reservations suggested. Main courses $22–$55; sushi $5 and up per order. AE, DC, DISC, MC, V. Daily 6–11pm.

MODERATE

Hamada ★ JAPANESE This reliable restaurant has been rated as the Top Japanese Restaurant in Nevada by Zagat's and the readers of the *Las Vegas Review-Journal.* Hamada serves good, dependable, Japanese food. There's nothing earthshaking about the food, served in bamboo-decorated rooms festooned with hanging banners, but there's a certain confidence in knowing you'll get the same food every time. The sushi is fresh, basic, standard stuff with a few now-traditional rolls (think California roll, dragon roll, and their siblings) thrown in. Tempura, teriyaki, and sukiyaki, along with noodle dishes, form different combos.

Lunch specials served in *bento* boxes—lacquered wooden platters with separate areas for each item, not unlike upscale TV-dinner plates—include teriyaki, tempura, sushi,

Fun Facts **Did You Know?**

Celebrity watchers know that Nobuyuki Matsuhisa counts many stars as guests at his restaurants, some of whom are occasionally spotted dining at Nobu in Las Vegas, and that actor Robert De Niro is an investor. Fans of the Iron Chef cooking show will also recognize the name Nobu: New York's Nobu restaurant is where Japanese Iron Chef Masaharu Morimoto worked as executive chef—when not performing as the Iron Chef in Kitchen Stadium—until he opened his own eponymous restaurant, Morimoto, in Philadelphia in 2002. At Nobu, he carried on and advanced founder Matsuhisa's vision, creating some of the signature dishes for the Nobu restaurants worldwide.

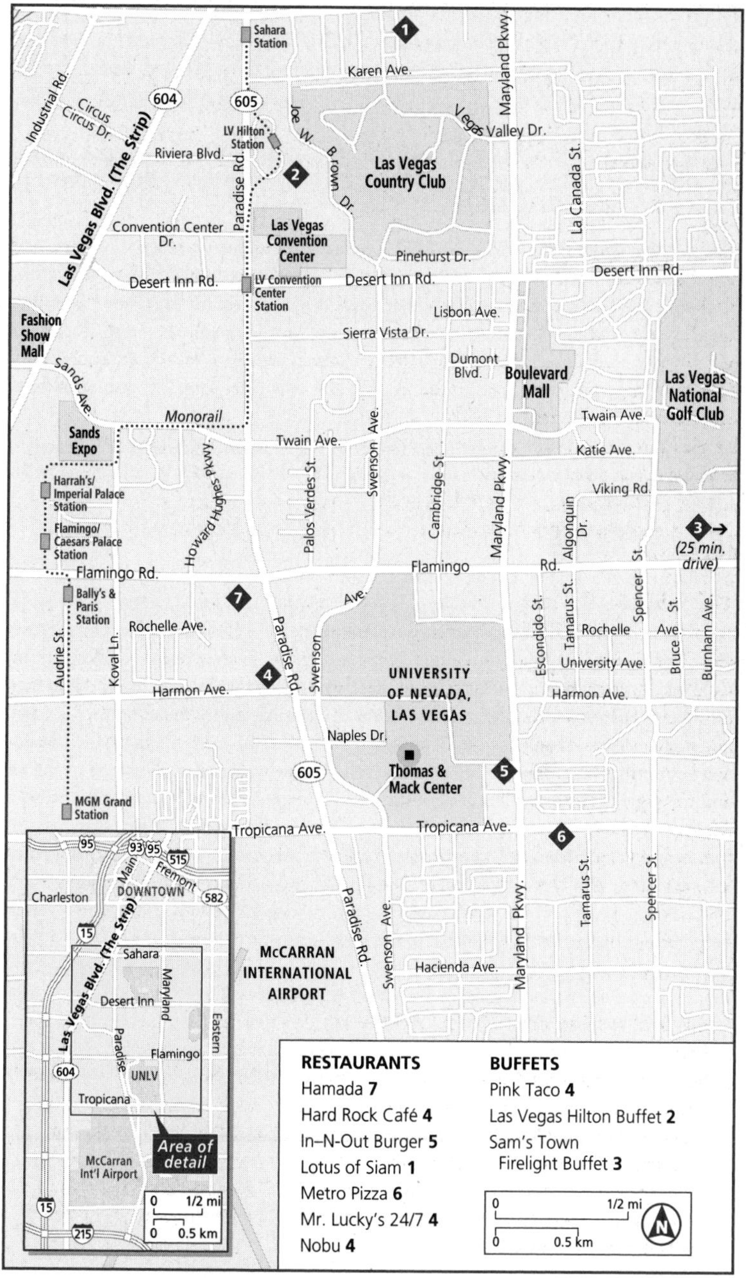
Sahara Station
Karen Ave.
Maryland Pkwy.
604
605
Industrial Rd.
Circus Circus Dr.
Las Vegas Blvd. (The Strip)
LV Hilton Station
Vegas Valley Dr.
Joe W. Brown Dr.
Riviera Blvd.
Paradise Rd.
Las Vegas Country Club
La Canada St.
Convention Center Dr.
Las Vegas Convention Center
Pinehurst Dr.
Desert Inn Rd.
LV Convention Center Station
Lisbon Ave.
Sierra Vista Dr.
Fashion Show Mall
Sands Ave.
Dumont Blvd.
Boulevard Mall
Las Vegas National Golf Club
Monorail
Twain Ave.
Sands Expo
Katie Ave.
Harrah's/ Imperial Palace Station
Howard Hughes Pkwy.
Palos Verdes St.
Swenson Ave.
Cambridge St.
Viking Rd.
Algonquin Dr.
Flamingo/ Caesars Palace Station
(25 min. drive)
Flamingo Rd.
Bally's & Paris Station
Rochelle Ave.
Audrie St.
Koval Ln.
Escondido St.
Tamarus St.
Spencer St.
Bruce St.
Burnham Ave.
University Ave.
Harmon Ave.
UNIVERSITY OF NEVADA, LAS VEGAS
Naples Dr.
Thomas & Mack Center
MGM Grand Station
Tropicana Ave.
McCARRAN INTERNATIONAL AIRPORT
Hacienda Ave.
95
93
515
Main
Fremont
Charleston
DOWNTOWN
582
15
Sahara
Maryland
Desert Inn
Eastern
Paradise
Flamingo
UNLV
Tropicana
Area of detail
McCarran Int'l Airport
215
0 1/2 mi
0 0.5 km
N
RESTAURANTS
Hamada 7
Hard Rock Café 4
In–N-Out Burger 5
Lotus of Siam 1
Metro Pizza 6
Mr. Lucky's 24/7 4
Nobu 4
BUFFETS
Pink Taco 4
Las Vegas Hilton Buffet 2
Sam's Town Firelight Buffet 3

and, inexplicably, potato salad, along with rice, miso soup, and salad. They're definitely a bargain, but only the original Hamada (365 E. Flamingo Rd.; ✆ **702/733-3005**) is open for lunch. The Hamada at The Flamingo (3555 Las Vegas Blvd. S.; ✆ **702/733-3455**) and the Rio (3700 W. Flamingo Rd.; ✆ **702/777-7923**) also feature a *teppan* grill for searing and stir-frying food before your eyes. Both locations are open from 5 to 11pm daily. All locations serve *udon* soup—huge bowls of fat noodles with tempura shrimp and vegetables floating in a clear broth.

Original location, 365 E. Flamingo Rd. ✆ **702/733-7305.** www.hamadaofjapan.com. Highchairs, boosters. Main courses $16–$32; sushi $4–$10. AE, DC, DISC, MC, V. Lunch daily 11am–3pm; dinner daily 5–12:30pm, till 11pm at Rio and Flamingo.

Hard Rock Cafe AMERICAN Give this place the dubious respect it deserves; the Hard Rock was the progenitor of the theme restaurant as we know it today. Full of rock souvenirs like scarves, jackets, guitars, hats, and platinum records from bona fide superstars as well as those who made the grade if only for a moment, the Hard Rock serves decent burgers, good salads, and huge desserts, along with loud music and a party atmosphere. If your kids love rock music, they'll love this place. You, on the other hand, may not.

Near the Hard Rock Hotel & Casino, 4475 Paradise Rd. ✆ **702/733-8400.** www.hardrock.com/locations/cafes. Kids' menu, highchairs, boosters. Main courses $8–$18; kids' menu $6.95. AE, DC, DISC, MC, V. Sun–Thurs 11am–11pm; Fri–Sat 11am–midnight.

INEXPENSIVE

Lotus of Siam ★★★ (Value) THAI There's virtually nowhere on the Strip to get Thai food, so a visit to Lotus of Siam is worth the cab fare for a *prik king* (a seasoned curry with green beans) fix. When *Gourmet* magazine's Jonathan Gold declared this small Thai restaurant (in a giant shopping center loaded with other Asian eateries) the best Thai restaurant in America, some locals were stunned, while others crowed rapturously that they'd known it all along. Luckily, Lotus of Siam has pretty much ignored the hype and hoopla—with the exception of reprinting reviews and posting them on their walls—and instead has stayed focused on its cooking. The lunch buffet at $9 is one of the best around, with more than a dozen dishes, including fried spring rolls and garlicky chicken wings, two soups, salad, vegetarian specialties (we loved the glass noodles with tofu and mushrooms), pad Thai, and several curries (which were warm and flavorful with spices, but not hot at all). Desserts included sliced fruits and delicious deep-fried banana rolls. If you'd like to order off the menu, you can adjust the spiciness to your comfort level, but be prepared, the higher range of hotness is truly, tearfully painful.

953 E. Sahara Ave., #A-5. ✆ **702/735-3033.** www.saipinchutima.com. Highchairs, boosters. Reservations strongly suggested for dinner. Lunch buffet $9; other dishes $9–$18. AE, MC, V. Mon–Fri 11:30am–2:30pm; Sun.-Thurs 5:30–9:30pm, Fri-Sat 5:30-10pm.

Commercial Center

The appropriately named Commercial Center at 953 E. Sahara Ave., just west of Maryland Parkway, features numerous authentic Korean and Thai restaurants, along with the plainly, but perfectly, named Asian Market, which is full of unique delicacies like *poki-poki*—thin cookies rolled around a sweet filling, then dipped in frosting.

Metro Pizza ★ ITALIAN Consistently voted Best Pizza by the citizens of Las Vegas in polls from the *Las Vegas Review-Journal,* Citysearch.com, and Zagat's, Metro features a variety of pizzas—"regular" with crisp crusts; stuffed, which sandwiches layers of cheese and toppings between two crusts and tops with sauce; specialty pizzas like barbecued chicken and a sauceless white pizza; and East Side pizzas, which have slices, rather than a blanket, of cheese—along with calzones, baked ziti, and their highly addictive garlic Romano or spicy Atomic french fries. Meat eaters can dig into the Stockyard pizza, while vegetarians will appreciate the Casa Verde pizza, with veggies, and the Wrigley Field stuffed pizza with broccoli, green peppers, and mushrooms. Vegans will groove the cheeseless La Costa, topped with mushrooms, tomatoes, and broccoli. They also feature dine-in specials and desserts from Ferrara's of Little Italy. But best of all—they deliver to hotels!

1395 E. Tropicana Ave. ✆ **702/736-1955.** www.metropizza.com. Highchairs, boosters. No reservations. Main courses and pizzas $9–$23. AE, DISC, MC, V. Mon–Thurs 11am–10pm; Fri–Sat 11am–11pm; Sun noon–10pm.

Mr. Lucky's 24/7 ★★ DINER/COFFEE SHOP This is, in our opinion, the best hotel coffee shop for families in Las Vegas, if only because pop-cultured kids will like the groovy blue-and-orange menus, the blaring rock music, and overhead TVs playing videos. Feel like a Vegas insider by asking for the secret, off-the-menu, steak and shrimp special, offered at $8.95. The burgers are good, and breakfasts are filling. We liked the pancakes and the omelets, as well as the smoothies. Salads are huge. Afterward, stroll around the hotel and take in the collections of rock memorabilia.

In the Hard Rock, 4455 Paradise Rd. ✆ **800/473-ROCK** (473-7625) or 702/693-5592. www.hardrockhotel.com. Kids' menu, highchairs, boosters. Reservations not accepted. Main courses $8–$16; kids' menu $6–$7. AE, DC, DISC, MC, V. Daily 24 hr.

Pink Taco MEXICAN The loud rock music might make you want to turn away, but then you'd miss out on good Mexican food (tamales, quesadillas, tacos, and the like) served in a large room nicely decorated with folk art. Take a hint from us: Come early and sit on the patio, where you'll be far away from the margarita-maddened crowd. If you want to take advantage of half-priced appetizers to fill your family, happy hour runs Monday through Friday from 4 to 7pm. Along with the price-break on starters, they also offer two-for-one beers and house margaritas, and half-off appetizers, meaning the bar area and main room can get raucous. Again we stress: Retreat to the patio.

In the Hard Rock, 4455 Paradise Rd. ✆ **702/693-5525.** www.hardrockhotel.com. Highchairs, boosters. Reservations not accepted. Main courses $8–$15. AE, DC, DISC, MC, V. Sun–Thurs 11am–10pm; Fri–Sat 11am–midnight. Bar open until 3am Fri–Sat.

7 WEST OF THE STRIP

INEXPENSIVE

Voodoo Café (Moments) DESSERTS Perfect for older kids, the Voodoo Café offers a spectacular view from the 50th floor of the Rio, coupled with a selection of tempting desserts in a setting straight out of *I Walked with a Zombie* or *The Serpent and the Rainbow.* The voodoo vibes are emphasized with elaborate *veves* (symbols) painted on the walls of the purple, black, and red room. The *veves* are accurately executed and designed to invoke or celebrate the different gods—known as *loas*—of success, happiness, love, luck, and wealth (all appropriate for a casino).

Avoid the entrees, which are large, spicy, and not the best Cajun food in Vegas. Instead, grown-ups should relax while enjoying an exotic drink such as the Headshrinker or Witch Doctor, while 'tweens and teens take in the spooky atmosphere, astounding view, and virgin cocktails with ghost-shaped stirrers. The bananas Foster are flambéed at the table—very flashy and fun, though you may want to make sure your server has flamed off all the alcohol before the kids sample it. The plate of chocolate desserts features flourless chocolate cake, homemade chocolate ice cream, crème brûlée, and a mini milkshake; ask that they make the milkshake without alcohol if the kids are having it. At night, the upstairs level becomes a bar/nightclub, strictly off-limits for those under 21, and there is a dress code (no sneakers, flip-flops, torn jeans, or T-shirts) for the restaurant and nightclub.

In the Rio, 3700 W. Flamingo Rd. ✆ **702/777-7923.** www.harrahs.com. Highchairs, boosters. Reservations recommended. Desserts $6–$9. AE, DC, MC, V. Daily 5–11pm. Lounge 5pm–3am.

8 DOWNTOWN

Note: Restaurants in this section can be found on the "Downtown Attractions & Dining" map on p. 181.

VERY EXPENSIVE

Second Street Grill ★ *Finds* SEAFOOD Though the Grill is tucked away in an obscure corner of Downtown's obscure Fremont Hotel, it's one of the great seafood restaurants in Las Vegas. What's more, though it's been around for more than 15 years, it's one of Vegas's greatest unknown restaurants; if you're stuck for a nice place to eat, you can almost always get in here on short notice. The seafood served at the Second Street Grill is flown in fresh from around the Pacific Rim and that region's influence is felt throughout the menu. The blackened ahi and mahimahi might not be to kids' tastes, but the filet mignon smothered with Maui onion rings will be. There are also pork chops, pasta, and a bargain special. Appetizers include shrimp and duck tacos, crab cakes, and chicken wrapped in lettuce. For dessert, try some mango sorbet or the Hawaiian pineapple boat (floating with tropical fruit); kids will love the macadamia nut cheesecake and the chocolate explosion.

In the Fremont Hotel & Casino, 200 E. Fremont St. ✆ **800/634-6182** or 702/385-3232. www.fremontcasino.com. Boosters. Entrees $20–$30. AE, DC, MC, V. Sun–Mon and Thurs 6–10pm; Fri–Sat 6–11pm.

INEXPENSIVE

El Sombrero ★ MEXICAN At first glance, this squat adobe building, with bars across tiny windows and a heavy security door, looks like a Juárez jailhouse. But the neon sign gives it away: This is El Sombrero, the first Mexican cantina and the oldest restaurant in Las Vegas (opened in 1950). What's more, only two chefs have overseen things here in its entire 59-year history; the current one, Jose Aragon, has run the kitchen since 1976 and the menu has barely changed since then. Huevos are available for lunch and dinner; they're served ranchero style (covered with salsa) and with chorizo. The house special is a burrito enchilada-style (floating in red or green sauce), otherwise known as "smothered." Other entrees include *carne asada* (steak), *chile verde* and *colorado* (pork with green or red sauce), and *camarones* (shrimp). If you need to get away from it all and pretend you're anywhere but Vegas, this is the place to do it.

807 S. Main St. ✆ **702/382-9234.** Reservations not accepted. Highchairs, boosters. Entrees $8–$14. MC, V. Mon–Sat 11am–9pm.

9 BUFFETS

Most buffets are great deals for families. You get a vast amount of food for the money, the majority offer discounts for children, and you need to tip only about a dollar per person, rather than 15% of the bill. In addition, you can have food on the table in a matter of a minute or two, handy especially for very young and hungry kids. Selections are varied, so you can almost always find something for everyone, and drinks and desserts are included in the price. Lunch buffets are the most cost-effective; there's little difference in quantity from dinner, but the price is always lower. Consider having your largest meal midday (as recommended by most nutritionists), followed by a lighter less pricey supper. Las Vegas buffets used to be homogeneous, without much to recommend one over another, but today the differences, both in quality and price, are more discernible.

SOUTH STRIP

For a map of the buffets below, see the "South Strip Dining" map on p. 143.

Expensive

MGM Grand Buffet At breakfast, omelet and lox stations provide variety to this otherwise average buffet. If you ask nicely, the staff will get you plain yogurt instead of the sweeter berry flavors on display. Lunch and dinners have the usual carving stations, veggies, and salad bar. The children's prices and the selection make it a good choice for family lunches or dinners. Also available: low-fat, sugar-free desserts. At all meals, you get a full pot of coffee on your table. There's also a champagne brunch on weekends.

3799 Las Vegas Blvd. S. ✆ **702/891-7777.** www.mgmgrand.com. Highchairs, boosters. Breakfast $14.50; lunch $17.50; dinner $25.99 except Fri–Sat $27.99; Sat–Sun brunch $25.99; children 3 and under eat free; children 4–12 breakfast $9.50, lunch $10.99, dinner $14.99, Sat-Sun brunch $11.99. AE, DC, DISC, MC, V. Daily 7am–10pm.

Moderate

Excalibur's Round Table Buffet One of the nicest features of this bustling buffet is that the menus for the day's meals are posted overhead before you get to the entrance so that you can decide whether you really want to eat here. The large room resembles a hospital cafeteria enlivened by heraldic flags draped about. The food is adequate and heavy on the starch.

3850 Las Vegas Blvd. S. ✆ **702/597-7777.** www.excaliburlasvegas.com. Highchairs, boosters. Breakfast $11.99; lunch $13.99; dinner $16.99; children 3 and under eat free; $2 off for children 4–12. AE, DC, DISC, MC, V. Daily 7am–11pm.

Luxor's More Buffet ★★ Luxor remodeled the Indiana Jones fun out of this buffet, but the food remains fresh and tasty, including plenty of salads (the tabbouleh and hummus were especially yummy), plus delectable Korean-style short ribs. The Chinese and

Tips **Beware Buffet Lines**

At the more popular buffets, beware of humongous, ridiculous buffet lines, especially on weekends or in high season. Basic strategy is to arrive early for breakfast and early or late for lunch or dinner. If you arrive at prime time, resign yourself to a long wait.

pasta stations doled up some fine, ethnic options with several choices (important for kids); and the Mexican was surprisingly good, with an actual kick of spice to it (important for some adults). There wasn't enough chocolate for us on the dessert bar, but the mini crème brûlées were nice, and there are sugar-free desserts as well. This is a popular buffet, so lines can get ferociously long. ***Tip:*** The menu is posted at the entrance, so you can decide whether you want to eat here before you make the trudge down the ramp.

3900 Las Vegas Blvd. S. ✆ **800/288-1000** or 702/262-4000. www.luxor.com. Highchairs, boosters. Breakfast $12.99; lunch $14.99; dinner $19.99; Sat-Sun brunch $18.99; children under 4 eat free; discount prices for children 4–11, breakfast $9.99; lunch $10.99; dinner $13.99; brunch $11.99. AE, DC, DISC, MC, V. Daily 7am–10pm.

Monte Carlo Buffet ★ A "courtyard" under a painted sky, the Monte Carlo's buffet room has a Moroccan market theme with murals of Arab scenes, Moorish archways, Oriental carpets, and walls hung with photographs of, and artifacts from, Morocco. Dinner includes a rotisserie (for chicken and pork loin or London broil), a Mongolian grill, a pasta bar, a taco/fajita bar, a baked potato bar, numerous salads, and more than a dozen desserts, plus frozen yogurt and ice-cream machines. Lunches are similar. At breakfast, the expected fare is supplemented by an omelet station, and choices include crepes, blintzes, and corned beef hash. Fresh-baked New York–style bagels are a plus, and there's a champagne brunch on weekends.

3770 Las Vegas Blvd. S. ✆ **702/730-7777.** www.monte-carlo.com. Highchairs, boosters. Breakfast $11.95; lunch $13.95; dinner $18.95; Sun brunch $18.95; children 2 and under eat free; $9 for children 3–12. AE, DC, DISC, MC, V. Daily 7am–10pm; Sun brunch 7am–3pm.

CENTER STRIP

For a map of the buffets below, see the "Center Strip Dining" map on p. 153.

Expensive

Buffet at TI ★ The pirate decor has been deep-sixed to Davy Jones's locker in favor of a contemporary (generic) look, but the food has been similarly upgraded from passable to recommendable. The serving area is sparkling clean and well-organized; though it's small by center Strip standards, the traffic flow is orderly and efficient. The sushi station greets you as you walk in, then the Middle Eastern (try the dolma) and Asian (Korean short ribs). The Tennessee- and North Carolina–style barbecue leads you into the American cuisine, with corn pudding, collard greens, and pulled pork. Made-to-order salads, custom pasta (choose your noodles and sauces), pizza, and antipasto round out the offerings. Don't miss the desserts in the back of the room, especially the pies, cakes, and hard-packed ice cream.

3300 Las Vegas Blvd. S. ✆ **702/894-7111.** www.treasureisland.com. Highchairs, boosters. Breakfast $13; lunch $16; dinner Mon–Thurs $21; Fri–Sun $26; Sat–Sun brunch $20; children 3 and under eat free; children 5–10 half-price. AE, DC, DISC, MC, V. Daily 7am–10:30pm.

The Mirage Cravings Buffet ★★ Completely remodeled and retooled in 2005, the Mirage Cravings provides the best value among the Center Strip "gourmet buffets," such as Le Village at Paris and the ultraexpensive (and more-for-adults) Bellagio Buffet. The room has a high-tech feel with its stainless steel, brass, and a couple of dozen video monitors out front playing sensual video loops of food. Open and airy, the traffic flow is well designed, so you can usually get in and out of the serving stations without much waiting. Dim sum is served at every meal, along with abundant seafood, bagels and lox at breakfast, good sushi, wood-fired pizzas, on-site smoked meats, and gelato for dessert.

3400 Las Vegas Blvd. S. ✆ **800/791-7111.** www.mirage.com. Highchairs, boosters. Breakfast $13.95; lunch $17.95; dinner $22.95; champagne brunch $22.95; all meals free for children 4 and under; age 5–10 breakfast $9.95, lunch $12.95, dinner $16.95, brunch $16.95. AE, DC, DISC, MC, V. Mon–Fri 7am–10pm; Sat–Sun 8am–10pm.

Paris's Le Village Buffet ★★★ This is the only buffet in Las Vegas that successfully carries out its host hotel's theme in its entirety. As well as incorporating the hotel's decor into the buffet area, Le Village Buffet has based the entire spread, from salad to sugary finale, around the hotel's *parlez-vous* premise. All of France is represented at Le Village Buffet, in a two-thirds replica of a French village that is charming in that Vegas-y fake way, but is the nicest buffet dining room in the entire city. If you want to sample all the cuisine of France without a vacation to five or so regions of that country, this is the place to do it. Though this is the second-most expensive buffet in town, for the variety and the well-executed concept, it's worth it.

Each buffet station reflects the specialties of a specific French region. In Brittany, you have crepes made to order, while Normandy features seafood and quiche. Burgundy, known for its farming and hunting, serves up the carving station with chateaubriand sauce and cherry sauce Escoffier. Hearty Alsace serves stews, while the Mediterranean region of Provence features made-to-order pastas. Be sure to sample a crepe from Le Village's one-of-a-kind cooked-to-order crepe station. Desserts include tarts, pastries, and bananas Foster.

3665 Las Vegas Blvd. S. ✆ **702/946-7000.** www.harrahs.com. Highchairs, boosters. Breakfast $14.99; lunch $17.99; dinner $24.99; champagne brunch $24.99; children 3 and under eat free; $3 off for children 4–10, $5 off breakfast. AE, DC, DISC, MC, V. Mon–Fri breakfast 7–11am, lunch 11am–3:30pm, dinner 3:30–10pm; Sat–Sun brunch 11am–3:30pm, dinner 3:30–10pm.

Planet Hollywood's Spice Market Buffet ★ Take the escalator down to the "basement" level of the PH casino to this "superbuffet" with everything from cracked king crab legs to litchi nuts; the other seafood selections included mussels, rock shrimp, crab-stuffed sole, catfish, seafood Newberg, salmon, and crab salad. Individual serving islands were dishing up Italian, including lobster risotto and eggplant Parmesan; action Chinese in flaming woks; Mexican; and American, with sweet-potato fritters and barbecued ribs. Are your kids adventurous? Have them try a few items from Las Vegas's biggest Middle Eastern island: baba ganouj, tabbouleh, tzatziki, falafel, tahini, tandoori chicken, marinated lamb, saffron basmati rice, and Moroccan veggies. Reward their expanding culinary tastes with chocolate-covered strawberries, strawberry shortcake, brownies, or soft-serve ice cream.

3667 Las Vegas Blvd. S. ✆ **702/785-5555.** www.planethollywoodresort.com. Highchairs, boosters. Breakfast $14.99; lunch $17.99; dinner $25.99; Sat–Sun brunch $21.99; all meals free for children 4 and under; children 5–12 breakfast $8.50; lunch $10.50; dinner $15.50; Sat–Sun brunch $12.50. AE, DC, DISC, MC, V. Daily 7am–10pm.

Moderate

Flamingo Paradise Garden Buffet ★ Value This is one of the nicest buffet rooms in Las Vegas, especially if you can be seated by the large windows overlooking the fish ponds and waterfalls. Watch the swans and ducks swim languidly by as you eat selections chosen from the soup/salad/pasta bar, stir-fry station, or from the international food stations offered at lunch and dinner (their offerings change monthly). Desserts include sugar-free options, along with cookies, cakes, and really good brownies. Breakfast includes fresh-baked breads and the ubiquitous omelet station. The moderate prices for families, plus the view, make this a great place to eat.

3555 Las Vegas Blvd. S. ✆ **702/733-3111.** www.harrahs.com. Highchairs, boosters. Breakfast $14.99; lunch $16.99; dinner $21.99; Sat–Sun champagne brunch $19.99; children 2 and under eat free; discount price for children 3–12. AE, DC, DISC, MC, V. Daily 7am–10pm.

NORTH STRIP

For a map of the buffets below, see the "North Strip Dining" map on p. 159.

Inexpensive

Circus Buffet There are over 50 choices at this, the Strip's cheapest buffet, so kids can have a blast sampling everything from the steam tables. For the most part, adults rate it in a word: cheap. Low price, low quality. It's been remodeled a few times over the years, but the food seems never to change. Think of it as fuel for your next adventure, rather than as a dining experience.

2880 Las Vegas Blvd. S. ✆ **877/224-7287** or 702/734-0410. www.circuscircus.com. Highchairs, boosters. Breakfast $10.49; lunch $12.49; dinner $13.94; children 5 and under eat free; AE, DC, DISC, MC, V. Daily 7am–2pm; 4:30-10pm.

EAST OF THE STRIP

For a map of the buffets below, see the "Dining East of the Strip" map on p. 161.

Inexpensive

Las Vegas Hilton Buffet ★ Gone is the old sports theme, replaced with a sort of a generic outdoorsy look, but luckily, the kitchen still serves good food. Prime rib is served at lunch and dinner; the salad bar is fresh; and the desserts tasty and not overwhelmingly sugary. At dinner, there's the addition of an all-you-can-eat crab and shrimp station, while on Fridays there are additional seafood selections.

3000 Paradise Rd. ✆ **888/732-7117** or 702/732-5111. www.lvhilton.com. Highchairs, boosters. Breakfast $10.99; lunch $12.99; dinner $15.99; children 3 and under eat free; $1-$2 off for children 4–12. DC, DISC, MC, V. Daily 7am–9pm.

Sam's Town Firelight Buffet ★ The huge wall of flames here is really impressive, and the room is open to the atrium with its Sunset Stampede light show, making this a nice room, especially for kids. Along with the usual food choices, there's a Mexican and Chinese food station, and it's fun to get your ice cream scooped at the dessert station. Prices are higher on Wednesday for steak, Thursday for Pacific Rim cuisine, Friday for the seafood buffet, and Saturday for prime rib.

5111 Boulder Hwy. ✆ **702/456-7777.** www.samstownlv.com. Highchairs, boosters. Breakfast $5.99; lunch $7.99; dinner Sun–Tues $10.99; dinner Wed, Sat $13.99; dinner Thurs $11.99; dinner Fri $17.99; Sat–Sun champagne brunch $10.49; all meals free for children 3 and under; children 4-10 breakfast $4.99; lunch $3.99; dinner $6.99-$13.99; brunch $4.99. AE, DC, DISC, MC, V. Mon–Fri 7am–3pm; Sat–Sun 8am–3pm; daily 4–9pm.

WEST OF THE STRIP

Expensive

Rio's Carnival World Buffet ★ (Overrated) Gorge yourself with food from around the world, if you (and more important, your kids) can stand to wait in line. Locals have long voted this one of the best buffets in town, but unless you're coming for the *Masquerade in the Sky* (p. 173), it's not really worth going out of your way; the food isn't good enough to pay off for the long lines. If you do want to try beating the crowd, plan on a late lunch at 2 or 3pm or an early dinner starting about 4 or 5pm. Remodeled and reopened in summer 2004, stations now include Chinese, Italian, Mexican, seafood,

American, sushi, baked potato, barbecue, pizza, *teppanyaki,* and a unique Oriental noodle-soup bar with *pho,* hot and sour *tom yum* soup, and more. Low-fat and sugar-free desserts are included along with the full-strength cakes, pies, and puddings.

In the Rio, 3700 W. Flamingo Rd. ✆ **888/752-9746** or 702/252-7777. www.harrahs.com. Highchairs, boosters. Breakfast $14.99; lunch $16.99; dinner $23.99; champagne brunch $23.99; Village Seafood $34.99 adults, $22.99 children; children 3 and under eat free; $4 off for children 4–8. AE, DC, MC, V. Daily 7am–10pm.

10 JUST THE TWO OF US: ROMANTIC DINING

Where to go when it's just the two of you? Try any of the romantic restaurants below, all of which happen to be French.

While we think the patio of **Mon Ami Gabi** (p. 152) is the most casual and affordable romantic dining spot in Las Vegas, other passionate couples who've snagged a sitter for the night may wish to indulge themselves at the incredibly romantic **Picasso** ★★, in Bellagio, 3600 Las Vegas Blvd. S. (✆ **702/693-7111;** www.bellagio.com). Tables overlook the Bellagio fountains and are themselves surrounded by $30 million dollars worth of Picasso artwork. Chef Julian Serrano's prix-fixe dinners and tasting menus hold their own in this elegant environment, where attentive servers pamper you without intruding.

Bouchon ★★★, in The Venetian (3355 Las Vegas Blvd. S., ✆ **702/414-6200;** www.bouchonbistro.com), offers up an elegant and intimate French bistro setting (there's also lovely outside patio dining available in good weather)—and genius Thomas Keller, arguably the best chef in the United States. The classic menu changes daily, but expect such delicacies as pâté, Snow Creek oysters, and caviar.

For a romantic stroll down memory lane to old Las Vegas, have dinner at **Hugo's Cellar** ★★★, in Four Queens (202 E. Fremont St.; ✆ **702/385-4011**), in the lower level of the '60s downtown casino. Every lady (and man too, if he likes) gets a rose on entering the dim, wood and brick, Rat Pack–like room with big booths. Salads are prepared tableside from a cart with a flourish; all meals come with chocolate-dipped fruit as a finish. Our waiter described himself as "the new kid": He'd only worked at Hugo's for 17 years.

Alizé ★★★, in the Palms Resort & Casino (4321 W. Flamingo Rd.; ✆ **702/951-7000**), opened by the former chef at Napa, and freshly launched at the Palms, has received ecstatic reviews as the best restaurant in Las Vegas, which is saying a lot. The view, coupled with the superlative food (think Chilean sea bass with caramelized citrus fruit, Muscovy duck with cherry reduction, a palate-cleansing sorbet course, and voluptuous chocolate desserts), creates the most fabulously romantic dining experience in the whole city.

Reservations are a must for any of the above-mentioned restaurants.

For information on babysitters and child-care services, see section 14 of chapter 3, "Planning a Family Trip to Las Vegas," beginning on p. 73.

8 What Kids Like to See & Do in Las Vegas

The overwhelming number of attractions and distractions for tourists in the touristy parts of Las Vegas serve to enhance the city's reputation as an escape from reality and an oasis of nonstop fun. Despite Las Vegas's emphasis on grown-up pleasures, there is a surprising amount of child-friendly activities, many free or low cost, and some even educational, to be found in what wags call Sin City.

Cruising the Strip hotels is a great pastime, especially during the heat of the day. You and your kids can stroll through an ersatz Venice while a simulated storm rolls overhead or experience the same-style deluge in a mall that replicates the Grand Canyon. Where else but in Las Vegas can you explore ancient Rome and Venice, then frolic down the Champs Elysée and through Greenwich Village, followed by a trip to the South Seas? If the around-the-world-in-80-hours experience gets to be too much, there are also parks and playgrounds awaiting you and your picnic basket. And let's not forget Las Vegas's museums—ranging from the silly and serious to the enlightening and the ludicrous—as well as the factory tours where you can see how candy and cars are made.

First-time visitors, or those with limited time, will definitely want to spend most of their stay exploring the Strip, perhaps concentrating on one section a day, if possible. (We've divided the itineraries by sections of the Strip.) One of the kindest things casino planners did was to provide free amusements. And while we doubt they had altruistic aims, it's a bonus for families, particularly those on a budget, or otherwise. We'd recommend that any itinerary you come up with should include an animal attraction, several of which are free, and a free show such as the statues at Caesars or *Masquerade in the Sky* at the Rio.

Older kids should take a roller coaster ride; coasters can be found at several hotels, giving kids and their families an adrenaline-pumping charge. The **Adventuredome,** one of the world's largest indoor amusement parks, offers a couple of thrill rides, as well as more sedate rides for younger kids. With rides, games, attractions, and a miniature tour of the world, both ancient and modern, the Strip can keep a visitor occupied for a week, but with judicious planning and use of people movers, trams, the monorail, and taxis, the highlights of these few miles of many marvels can be seen in a day, if you want to rush from one end of the Strip to the other.

Getting around the Strip is simple, but the crowds can be overwhelming. Cabs are useful for getting places in relatively good time (except on weekend nights), and they are always air-conditioned. Consider them for trips from one end of the Strip to another, or if the little ones and you are exhausted. The monorail is also good for longer Strip trips, though it can be a hike from the west side of the Strip. Rental cars can be handy, especially because valet parking is free, as are the parking garages; just drive to one hotel, see the nearby sites, and leave for the next stop.

A day away from the Strip is a must. A drive out to Red Rock Canyon, Hoover Dam, or Old Nevada/Bonnie Springs Ranch offers a stunning contrast to the neon-soaked cityscape. Getting to these locations is simple with a car, but tours can easily be arranged through your hotel. ***A reminder:*** Be prepared—Las Vegas is a huge, huge place. Just getting from your room to the sidewalk can take 20 minutes, easily tiring out even the hardiest of underage adventurers. With younger children, your best bet is to pick an area of the Strip (South, Center, or North) and stay within in it for the day. Not that that's a tall order; there's plenty to do and see at every hotel, and the flashing lights and ringing bells hypnotize youngsters as well as adults.

Of course, during the hot summer months, your hotel's pool and air-conditioned arcade may be the main attractions for the kids!

1 ATTRACTIONS FOR KIDS

Luckily, most of Las Vegas's attractions appeal to all ages, and most accept children of every age group. Many are free (see "Free Attractions," above), and some can almost be construed as educational. But no matter what, they are all fun.

Big-Top Acts & Midway at Circus Circus ★★ **All ages,** though older kids may want to go play the arcade games. Parents who can trust their teenagers will appreciate the philosophy of this family-oriented hotel: Kids 13 and over can explore the arcade and midway, watch the big-top acts without adults, and are allowed to supervise younger children, as long as they all stay off the casino floor. This allows the adults to escape for a brief time. But you should spend some time with your children, watching the acrobats, jugglers, and clowns in the world's largest indoor circus; the performers are all good and you could easily use up 2 hours just watching the shows and another strolling the midway; your video gamers will be kept amused for at least that long. The games, not unlike the adult versions on the casino floor below, will suck up plenty of quarters as your kids try to win tickets redeemable for gewgaws and gimcracks. There's also a face-painting booth, where little ones can get made up like clowns, and a McDonald's for the peckish. The entire arcade and big-top area are nonsmoking zones, though, at times, the drift of cigarette smoke from the casino below can sort of defeat the concept. Older kids may get bored because the acts aren't that daring—no juggling of chainsaws—but they'll enjoy watching for a bit until the pull of the arcade becomes too insistent.

Tip: The stairs up to the arcade and circus viewing area can be difficult for toddlers to manage on their own (we saw one little girl trying futilely to catch up with her mom), so you may want to hold on to them while going up or down.

In Circus Circus, 2880 Las Vegas Blvd. S. ✆ **800/634-3450** or 702/734-0410. Free admission. Daily 11am–midnight.

Fountain Shows at the Forum Shops **Ages 4 & up.** Every hour on the hour, two sets of fountains at the Forum Shops come alive for 10 minutes with lasers, fog, and moving, talking statues. In the original wing, the Bacchus fountain's statues bring Greek myths to life, while in the second wing, the Battle for Atlantis pits two bratty god children—one fire, one water—against each other in a battle for their father's kingdom, Atlantis. ***Warning:*** The loud noises and explosions of the shows may be too much for

Value Free Attractions

It's easy to spend a small fortune on vacation, especially in this tourist town where almost everything—from slot machines to shopping malls—seems geared to separating you from your Benjamins as quickly as possible. But don't despair, you can find plenty of fun on—or near—the Strip for free.

Bellagio Fountains Set to a wide variety of music ranging from opera to pop songs and classical to Broadway, the fountains at Bellagio erupt up to 240 feet in the air and dance every half-hour Mondays through Fridays from 3 to 8pm, Saturdays and Sundays from noon to 8pm, and every 15 minutes nightly from 8pm to midnight (3600 Las Vegas Blvd. S.; ✆ **888/987-6667** or 702/693-7444; www.bellagio.com).

Circus Circus Clowns, acrobats, and jugglers perform every half-hour from 11am to midnight (2880 Las Vegas Blvd. S.; ✆ **877/634-3450** or 702/734-0410; www.circuscircus.com).

Everything Coca-Cola and **M&Ms World** Located in the Showcase Mall, these are quick, self-guided tours of the American icons' histories. You can also experience a desert rainstorm every 45 minutes at the Showcase Mall souvenir shop (3785 Las Vegas Blvd. S.; ✆ **702/736-7611**).

Fremont Street Experience Downtown spiffed up its image by installing a canopy with 12.5 million light-emitting diodes and a sound system and turning Fremont Street into a pedestrian walkway. Four times nightly, the neon goes off and the LEDs display broad-quality and spectacular light shows. (Fremont St., btw. Main St. and Las Vegas Blvd.; www.vegasexperience.com).

The Grand Canal Shoppes Vaguely historical (performers in Renaissance costumes and replicas of the Bridge of Sighs and St. Mark's Square, complete with real, bossy pigeons and living statues), this mall masquerades as Venice in its heyday. It's relaxing to sit under the blue faux sky and watch the singing gondoliers steer their fares along the waterway (3355 Las Vegas Blvd. S.; ✆ **888/283-6423** or 702/414-4500; www.venetian.com).

Lion Habitat The MGM Grand displays big beautiful cats sure to provoke plenty of oohs and aahs. The lions are on duty daily from 11am to 10pm (3799 Las Vegas Blvd. S.; ✆ **800/929-1111** or 702/891-1111; www.mgmgrand.com).

younger kids. The Forum Shops are a pleasant way to pass an afternoon browsing, especially if you have little ones; strollers are provided gratis.

In Caesars Palace, 3570 Las Vegas Blvd. S. ✆ **800/634-6661** or 702/731-7110. www.harrahs.com. Free admission. Daily every hour.

Fremont Street Experience ★ **All ages.** Up until the mid-'90s, Fremont Street, aka Glitter Gulch, was a grubby and gritty old Downtown area. But then the street was closed, and a huge canopy light show was developed by a private corporation and funded by 10 Downtown hotels. Today, Fremont Street, a pedestrian walkway that takes about 20 minutes to stroll and people-watch, boasts a grid-work of 12.5 million LEDs, strobes,

Masquerade in the Sky Seven times a day, from 3 to 9:30pm, Mardi Gras–styled floats move along tracks suspended from the ceiling at the Rio All-Suite Hotel & Casino, while costumed participants toss beads from the floats and lip-sync to the songs, followed by a stage-show extravaganza on the casino floor, complete with a giant peacock and sequin-covered dancers. Best place to watch is from the second-floor balcony (3700 W. Flamingo Rd.; ✆ **800/PLAYRIO** [742-9746] or 702/252-7777; www.harrahs.com).

Mirage Volcano The volcano in front of The Mirage erupts every hour on the hour daily from dusk to 11pm (3400 Las Vegas Blvd. S.; ✆ **800/374-9000** or 702/791-7111; www.mirage.com).

Paris Las Vegas You may not be able to see Paris in the springtime, but Paris Las Vegas is available anytime, complete with cobblestone streets and twinkling streetlamps (3655 Las Vegas Blvd. S.; ✆ **888/BONJOUR** [266-5687] or 702/946-7000; www.parislv.com).

Sirens of TI This is the retooled pirate battle that raged outside Buccaneer Bay in front of Treasure Island for 10 years. The new show, performed at 7, 8:30, 10, and 11:30pm, is somewhat sexier, with "sirens" luring the pirates off their ship and into Sirens Cove for what can only be some X-rated activity. There are some fireworks and explosions that all kids will enjoy, but it might be tough to explain to the younger ones just what's going on. Also, the new show is nearly 20 minutes longer than the defunct 8-minute pirate battle—a long time to stand squashed in a crowd with a 40-pound kid on your shoulders—the only way the short ones can see a thing (3300 Las Vegas Blvd. S.; ✆ **800/288-7206** or 702/894-7111; www.treasureisland.com).

Sports Hall of Fame Sports fans will love this huge collection of athletic items displayed throughout the ground floor of the Las Vegas Club Hotel and Casino Downtown. It's available for viewing round-the-clock. The collection includes signed bats used in the World Series, autographed photos, T-shirts, and much more (18 Fremont St.; ✆ **800/634-6532** or 702/385-1664; www.vegasclubcasino.net).

robotically controlled mirrors, and a 540,000-watt sound system. Five times a night, a 6-minute spectacle of light and sound floods the promenade. Music from the 218 speakers plays throughout the evening, enhancing your stroll through the cafes and shops. Look for the old neon signs from casinos of the past, which the Neon Museum has restored and displayed.

Fremont St. (btw. Main St. and Las Vegas Blvd.), Downtown. www.vegasexperience.com. Free admission. Shows nightly.

GameWorks **Ages 6 & up.** This chain arcade is youth-action central with video games designed by Steven Spielberg and his DreamWorks team. Kids will love the Jurassic Park

If I Could Talk to the Animals

Animal lovers will have a field day in Las Vegas, where a large variety of animals, including rare big cats, piranhas, penguins, flamingos, hammerhead sharks, and more are part of the attractions. Regional fauna are also well represented at local museums and zoos.

See Scaly & Furry for Free! The big cats at the Lion Habitat at the MGM Grand, 3799 Las Vegas Blvd. S. (✆ **800/929-1111** or 702/891-1111; www.mgmgrand.com), sleep and frolic as you stroll through a clear tub. Look up—one might even be walking over your head. At The Flamingo, 3555 Las Vegas Blvd. S. (✆ **800/732-2111** or 702/733-3111; www.harrahs.com), hundreds of birds, including the hotel's namesake, wander about on their own islands surrounding the pool area. All of these attractions are free.

Play with the Dolphins & Observe the Big Cats At The Mirage, 3400 Las Vegas Blvd. S. (✆ **800/374-9000** or 702/791-7111; www.mirage.com), dolphins swim and frolic in a huge pool, bouncing balls back to their trainer and to children who squeal with delight. The animals in the Secret Garden change regularly, but can include black panthers, white tigers, snow leopards, and even an elephant. Admission is $15 for those 13 and over, $10 for kids ages 4 to 12, and free for those 3 and under.

Shark Reef Along with watching sharks, moray eels, and piranhas go about their fishy business, and a Komodo dragon go about its "living-dinosaur" business, visitors to the Shark Reef at Mandalay Bay, 3950 Las Vegas Blvd. S. (✆ **877/632-7800** or 702/632-7777; www.mandalaybay.com), can participate in educational programs offered weekdays that include a 1-hour guided tour. Admission is $17 for adults, $11 for children 5 to 12, free for those 4 and under. Open daily 10am to 11pm.

Meet the Locals Check out the region's reptiles and other critters at the **Southern Nevada Zoological-Botanical Park,** 1775 N. Rancho Dr. (✆ **702/647-4685**), a quaint old-fashioned zoo. Here you will find Midas and Maniac Girl, a pair of lions born in 1998, along with a family of rare Barbary apes and swamp wallabies, as well as sidewinders, coyotes, and cougars. Admission is $8 for those 13 and over, admission for children 2 to 12 is $6, and free for children under 2. It's open daily 9am to 5pm. Admission is free at the **Marjorie Barrick Museum,** at the University of Nevada, Las Vegas, 4505 Maryland Pkwy. (✆ **702/895-3381**), which has a collection of live, local reptiles. The Wild Nevada Room at the funky **Las Vegas Museum of Natural History,** 900 Las Vegas Blvd. N. (✆ **702/384-3466**), displays a tableaux of different desert environments, complete with sights, sounds, and smells. It also has dioramas of taxidermied animals from around the world, a tank of live sharks, and animatronic dinosaurs. Admission is $8 for adults, $7 for students, and $4 for children 3 to 11; those under 3 get in for free. It's open daily 9am-4pm.

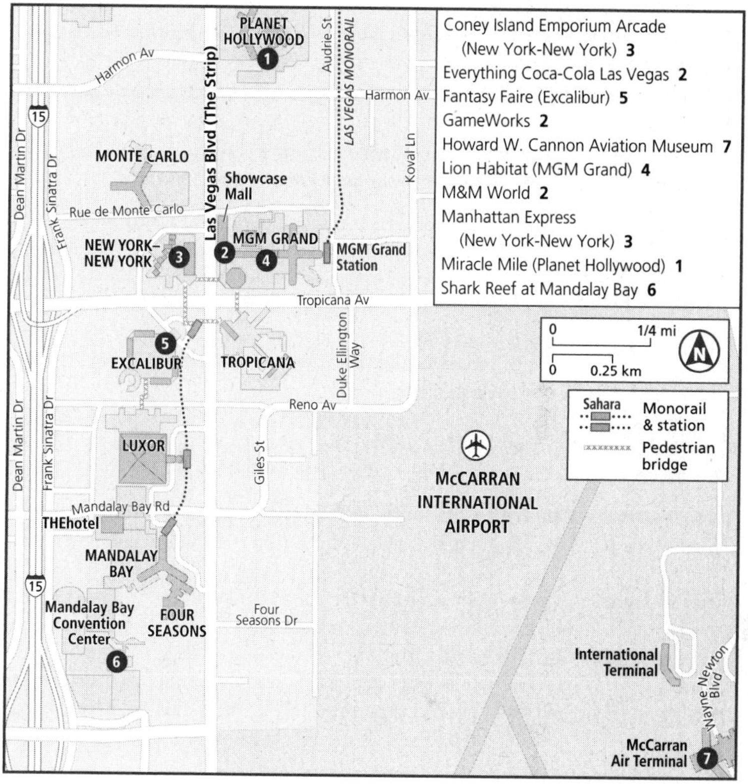

game, virtual racing, a virtual reality batting cage, and other distracting, and somewhat pricey, video games. Cash is not accepted for play; you'll have to buy a game card. With the standard version, $15 gets you $15 in game play, $20 gets you $25, or $25 gets you $35. Alternatively, you can purchase a block of time ($20 for 1 hr., $25 for 2 hr., $30 for 3 hr., all day for $35 or, if you get there at opening or closing, you can buy 2 hr. for $20). Your payment goes on a debit card that is then inserted into the various machines to activate them. Games average $1 to $2 each. For a separate fee, there's also a rock-climbing wall in the center of the arcade, where climbers are cheered on by their friends and bystanders. When the climb is completed, the successful climber gets a T-shirt. Adults who wish to have a cocktail and snacks can do so at the Arena Bar & Grill, while kids will find burgers, pizza, and other child-friendly food at either Jax Grill or the GW Grill.

Adults should supervise younger children, but those 10 and older should be able to handle the complex games, most of which are geared for junior high schoolers and older. This is a very popular spot with both locals and visitors. We were unhappy about the litter on the floor and the deplorable state of the women's bathroom on one evening visit, but found the place more pleasant in the day. You're probably better off playing earlier rather than the later night hours, when it gets very crowded.

Tips Insider Info

A good place to view the Sky Parade light show is from the balcony at Fitzgeralds Casino/Hotel.

In the Showcase Mall, 3785 Las Vegas Blvd. S. ✆ **702/432-GAME** (432-4263). www.gameworks.com. AE, DC, DISC, MC, V. Sun–Thurs 10am–midnight; Fri–Sat 10am–1am. Hours may vary.

Gondola Ride **All ages.** This slow cruise through the Grand Canal Shoppes is no thrill ride, but it is an experience. If you're lucky, you'll be serenaded by your own gondolier, but if you are a party of just two, you may end up sharing the four-seater boats with another couple. Small children will be more excited than teens to pass under bridges and to be looked at by groups of people dining, shopping, and, occasionally, just staring. The long lines, especially on weekends, however, can be overwhelming, especially because the ride lasts just a few minutes.

In The Venetian, 3355 Las Vegas Blvd. S. ✆ **888/2-VENICE** (283-6423) or 702/733-5000. www.venetian.com. Admission: Indoor $15 adults, $8 children 2–12; outdoor $16 adults, $8.50 children 2–12, free for children under 2. AE, DC, DISC, MC, V. Sun–Thurs 10am–11pm; Fri–Sat 10am–midnight.

Lied Discovery Children's Museum ★★★ Finds **Ages 3 months–10 years.** Designed specifically for children, this hands-on museum makes learning fun with interactive exhibits that let kids touch, poke, and prod to their hearts' content. Parents with babies and toddlers will especially appreciate the Baby Oasis, with special toys to encourage little brains and bodies, and the Parents' Resource Room. Children 5 and under can play in the Desert Discovery area, playing with soft boulders, pulleys, and shovels as they "build" a desert. Older kids can bang on steel drums, see what it's like to play basketball from a wheelchair, and stand inside a giant soap bubble. All of this can keep you busy for at least 2 hours. Creativity Workshops, free with admission, allow kids to drop in and make cool stuff. These are offered all day.

833 Las Vegas Blvd. N. (half-block south of Washington, across the street from Cashman Field). ✆ **702/382-3445.** www.ldcm.org. Admission $8 adults; $7 seniors, military, and children 1–17. AE, DC, DISC, MC, V. Tues–Fri 9am–4pm; Sat. 10am–5pm; Sun noon–5pm.

Madame Tussaud's Wax Museum ★ **All ages.** Oh, don't your children yearn to throw their arms around Brad Pitt or go up for a rebound against Shaquille O'Neal? Well, Madame Tussaud's allows just this kind of horseplay. In fact, they encourage it by selling you overpriced cameras and film at the entrance. Don't be a sucker—stock up in advance at a local convenience store or pharmacy. Trust us; you'll want snapshots of your child with at least one of the waxy statues that pack the place. Hopefully, your children will recognize some of the older mannequins, so you won't feel like a geezer trying to explain Frank Sinatra and Tony Bennett, or even Elvis.

Alas, for the gruesomely inclined children, there's no Chamber of Horrors like the one in London's Tussaud's (it's historical, really!), but there are some pretty horrifyingly realistic figures, especially the Reverend Schuller statue, which was so lifelike it scared the be-je—the be-jones—out of us, and the minuscule Prince (the Artist Who Preferred to Be Known as a Symbol). Princess Di is there, along with Joan Rivers, Madonna, Elvis, George W. Bush, Barack Obama, and sports figures such as Michael Jordan. A guest book at the end of the self-guided tour (which takes anywhere from 15–45 min.) allows you

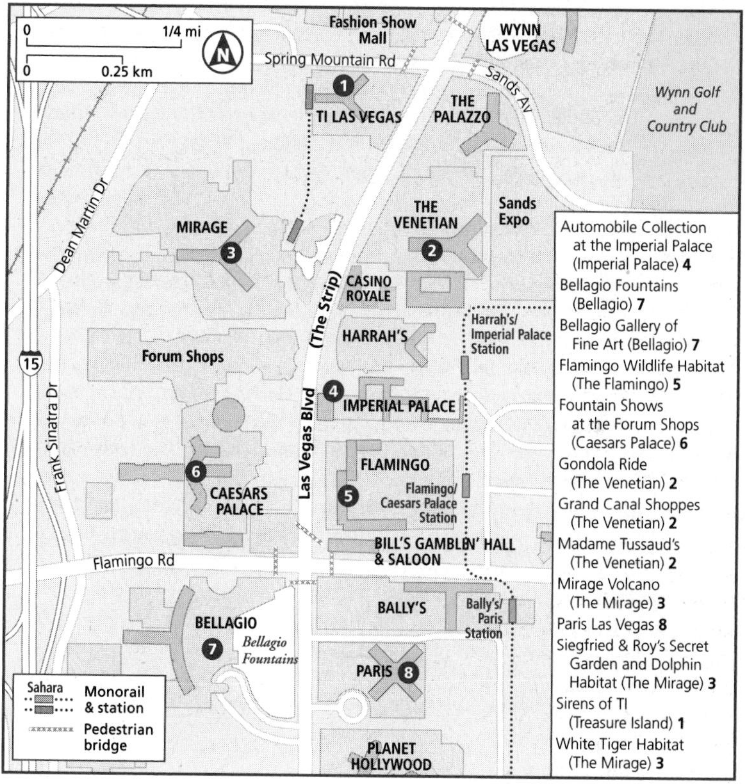

to vote for the next star to be preserved in paraffin. Just so you don't feel like you have gone totally pop-culture crazy, there's also an educational display, which explains the history of the museum's founder Madame Tussaud (a feminist role model if ever there was one) and how the dummies, I mean celebrity figures, are made.

In The Venetian, 3377 Las Vegas Blvd. S. ✆ **702/862-7800.** www.mtvegas.com. Admission $25 adults, $18 seniors and students, $15 children 3–12. AE, DC, DISC, MC, V. Daily 10am–11pm.

Shark Reef at Mandalay Bay ★★ All ages. It's entirely appropriate that a Las Vegas casino celebrates sharks and other man-eaters, dontcha think? Ironic, cynical adult observations aside, this is a perennial fave with kids because there's nothing cooler than seeing plenty of flesh-eating, living, swimming death machines up close. Along with sharks, there are moray eels, stingrays, and a school of piranhas, which luckily have a naturalist-type guide standing next to the open tank to keep out curious fingers. Feeding time is usually around 2pm, but there are no guarantees, so don't plan your visit in the hopes of (or desire to avoid) seeing the South American killers swarm on hapless goldfish. In 2008, the Reef received a 7-foot-long 87-pound Komodo dragon, about as close to a prehistoric creature as can be seen on this post-historic planet. The free audio devices provide plenty of prerecorded information, and the guides throughout the attraction are

Arcades Abound

A handful of hotels on the Strip have video arcades, and a few have put extra thought into their execution of a room that holds so much importance to both kids and adults. By far the nicest, cleanest, and most varied is the **Coney Island Emporium Arcade** in **New York–New York,** 3790 Las Vegas Blvd. S. (✆ **702/736-4100;** www.nynyhotelcasino), open 8:30am to 1am Sunday through Thursday, and 8:30am to 2am Fridays and Saturdays. Along with video games, there are numerous boardwalk-style games, all housed in a bright, light room with hardwood floors. Another plus: You board the Manhattan Express roller coaster from a corner in this arcade. **Fantasy Faire,** 3850 Las Vegas Blvd. S. (✆ **702/597-7700;** www.excalibur.com), is open Sunday through Thursday from 10am to 11pm, and Friday and Saturday from 10am to 1am. You can try out motion rides there and experience 70mm Dolby, with seats that move in synch with the onscreen action. **Games of the Gods** at Luxor, 3900 Las Vegas Blvd. S. (✆ **702/262-4000;** www.luxor.com)—located on the mezzanine attractions level—is packed with games and full of children and teens busily dropping quarters into race rides and other video-themed amusements daily from 11am to 10:30pm. One special feature is a virtual roller coaster, which you get to design and then virtually ride. **Circus Circus,** 2880 Las Vegas Blvd. S. (✆ **702/734-0410;** www.circuscircus.com), open daily from 9am to midnight, is surrounded by a big-top show with midway games and a separate room for video and pinball, featuring over 200 machines, along with a McDonald's. At the midway, children under 13 must be accompanied by someone older than 13, but those over 13 can play on their own. For more on Las Vegas's arcades (names, hours, phone numbers, comments), see the arcade chart above.

very helpful, answering questions about all of the finny beasts. We have only two complaints and those are minor: The "sunken temple" is a mite confusing, especially because some of the fish—most notably the famous piranhas—have nothing to do with the Asian artwork surrounding them; and some people, especially those with mobility issues, may find it a bit of a trek from the rest of the resort/casino. ***Tip:*** Don't go right after having your hair done; it's very humid inside.

In Mandalay Bay, 3950 Las Vegas Blvd. S. ✆ **877/632-7800** or 702/632-7777. Admission $17 adults, $11 children 5–12, free for children 4 and under. AE, DC, DISC, MC, V. Daily 10am–11pm.

Siegfried & Roy's Secret Garden and Dolphin Habitat ★★★ Value All ages. These two attractions in one are among the best bargains in Las Vegas, because once you pay, you can stay as long as you like wandering between the cages of large, exotic cats in the Secret Garden and watching the dolphins play, and because it's a relatively cheap attraction. Besides, what kids don't love animals?

Siegfried and Roy's famous white tigers became rather infamous when one of them either did what tigers all do, eventually, and attacked his beloved owner/trainer, or—depending on whether you buy this story—helped said beloved owner/trainer when the latter was having a medical emergency. Either way this story is played, it explains why the

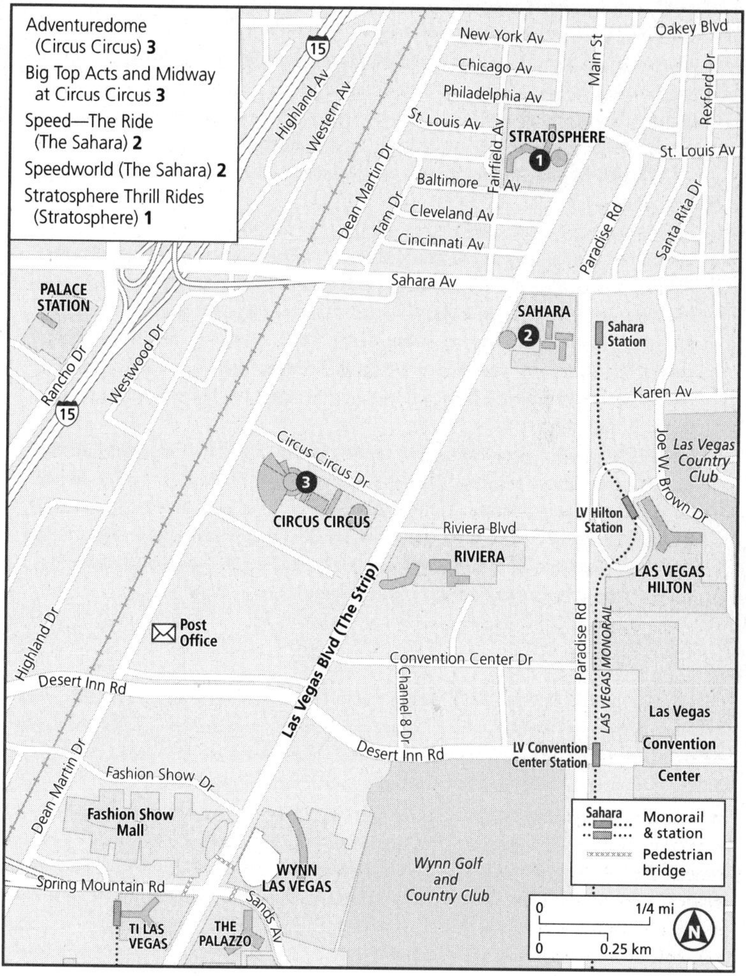

Secret Garden habitat is still up; no matter what, the tiger is not to blame (this may provide a good opportunity to discuss with your kids the dangers inherent in interacting with wild animals). In addition to the white tigers, you'll find dozens of the dynamic duo's animals exhibited amid lush landscaping. Because the animals—including black panthers, white lions, a snow leopard, and an elephant—are rotated between the Garden and the duo's home/game preserve, the inhabitants can vary from visit to visit. An audio wand allows you to learn more about the huge felines as they sleep, play, and wrestle just a few feet away from you. The close-up atmosphere gives perspective on the actual size and ferocity of these endangered species.

Tips Photo Ops

In a town full of nothing but Artificial Wonders of the World, camera shutters will be kept busy clicking. For those looking for Christmas card possibilities, gather your brood around the famous vintage **"Welcome to Las Vegas"** sign on the outskirts of town (or call up Jesse Garon, an Elvis impersonator, at ✆ **702/588-8188**—and see if you can pay him to pose in his pink Caddie along with you).

From there, you can choose among posing with the replica of Michelangelo's David, the talking animatronic statues at **The Forum Shops at Caesars Palace,** or the nontalking lions at the **MGM Grand Lion Habitat** (glass safely between you and Kitty, of course—you'll need a polarizing filter on your camera to capture them properly). More kitty critters can be found at The Mirage behind bars at **Siegfried & Roy's Secret Garden.** Ask nicely, and maybe a trainer at the **Dolphin Habitat** will get a finny friend to leap behind you at just the right moment.

If beasties aren't your thing, you can stand with a gladiator back at **Caesars** or with one of the roaming Italian Renaissance–dressed figures (Casanova, perhaps) at **The Venetian.** Confuse the folks at home and pose by the **Statue of Liberty** outside New York–New York (while the tugboats shoot water into the air), or really confuse them with shots of you amid the gorgeously arranged seasonal flora in **The Conservatory** at Bellagio.

In the Dolphin Habitat, you'll watch the dolphins leap, cackle, and bounce balls to their handlers (or to the lucky kids in the audience who get to toss the balls back to the sea mammals). These dolphins are not "trained" like those at certain parks; instead, they act out of their own desire to play and have fun. All the dolphins in this exhibit have been born in captivity; none have been taken from the ocean, and they seem to be quite happy here, breeding regularly and behaving in what their handlers feel is a natural manner. The large dolphin pool, which holds 2.5 million gallons of seawater, is designed so you can watch the dolphins interact with their human guardians, and then walk below ground to observe them playing in the depths.

In The Mirage, 3400 Las Vegas Blvd. S. ✆ **800/374-9000** or 702/791-7111. www.mirage.com. Admission $15, children 4–12 $10; free for children under 4. AE, DC, DISC, MC, V. Weekdays 11am–5:30pm; weekends and major holidays 10am–5:30pm; last admission 5pm. Hours subject to change and vary by season.

2 THRILL RIDES

Adventuredome ★★ **All ages.** Enclosed in this big pink dome are 5 acres of fun, including the world's largest indoor roller coaster, a flume ride, an inverter ride, and Chaos, a spinning amusement that whisks riders randomly though three dimensions. There are also some soothing kiddie rides to comfort preschoolers after seeing the menacing, life-size, animatronic dinosaurs that populate Adventuredome. Toddlers can ride with their parents on four rides, including a Ferris wheel, along with watching clown acts

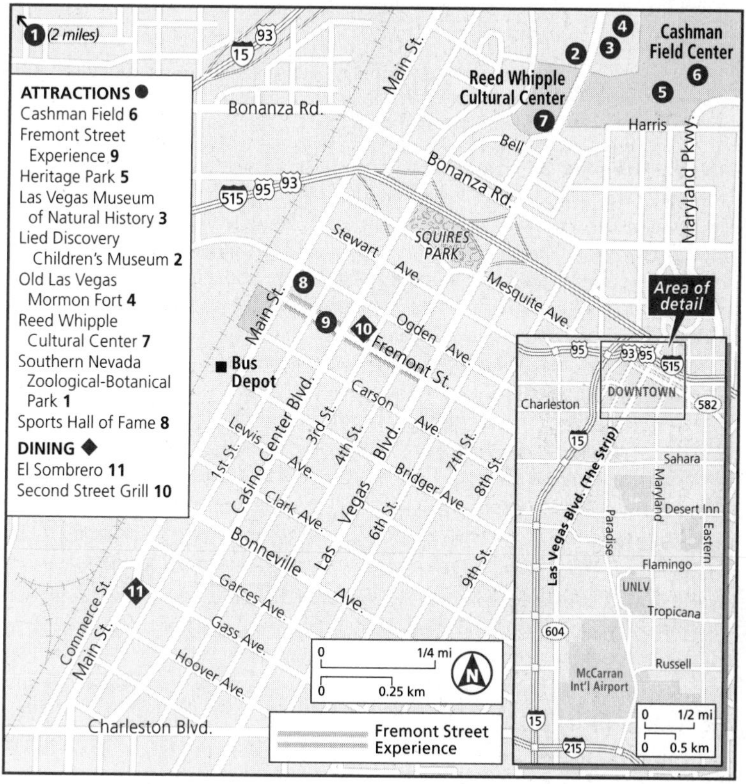

and puppet shows. Some rides are designed for children 33 to 54 inches tall; others restrict riders to those over 42 or 48 inches. The Rim Runner roller coaster is a real heart stopper and the flume ride gets you very wet if you ride in the front. One virtual-reality game/ride involves yelling, clapping, and stomping your feet while wearing VR goggles and responding to your "host," who can actually see you and direct your actions, while it feels as though you're moving through 3-D rooms of a castle, trying to escape, and winning as many points as possible. Almost as much fun is watching the folks play the game, as they kick and flail in their seats, shouting and laughing. There's also the inevitable arcade for video-game junkies. Expect to spend at least 3 hours here.

2880 Las Vegas Blvd. S. (behind Circus Circus). ✆ **702/794-3939.** www.adventuredome.com. Free admission; pay per ride $4–$7; daily pass $25 adults, $15 children 33–47 in.; children under 33 in. ride some attractions free with parents. AE, DC, DISC, MC, V. Park hours vary seasonally but usually Mon–Thurs 10am–6pm; Fri–Sat 10am–midnight; Sun 10am–8pm.

Manhattan Express ★★ Blaze through the boroughs of New York, whip by the Statue of Liberty, and take the world's first "heartline" twist and dive roll, which allows the rider to feel negative g's by simulating a barrel roll in a jet fighter. With drops of 144 feet, speeds up to 67 mph, and one long rush along the Coney Island–style coaster at

New York–New York, this is considered one of the best attractions in the city. The height restrictions may upset smaller kids who'll want to sit in the cool yellow taxicabs and race above the Strip and through the casino. Take them to the midway and let them play video games instead.

3790 Las Vegas Blvd. S. ✆ **800/NY-FOR-ME** (693-6763) or 702/740-6969. www.nynyhotelcasino.com. $12 per ride; $25 all-day pass. AE, DC, DISC, MC, V. Mon–Thurs 11am–6pm; Fri–Sat 10am–midnight. Must be 33 in. or taller to ride the smaller rides, 48 in. bigger rides.

Speed—The Ride ★ This is a monster roller coaster that uses electromagnetic "slingshot" technology to propel you from 0 to 70 mph in 4 seconds flat. You've never felt such acceleration (unless you're an astronaut). You roar out of the NASCAR area inside the Sahara and make an immediate sharp right turn to travel parallel to the Strip, zip through a misty tunnel, and go around a 360-degree loop. From there, you accelerate again from 35 to 70 mph to climb up a 224-foot-tall needle, straight up, before dropping down and replaying the entire course in reverse. The whole thing takes 90 seconds at most, but it'll then require another 60 minutes for you to regain any steadiness on your feet. Note that Speed "closed for the season" in late 2008 and hasn't reopened at press time; it's possible that it won't reopen, so be sure to call before you go.

Sahara Hotel & Casino, 2535 Las Vegas Blvd. S. ✆ **888/696-2121** or 702/737-2111. www.saharavegas.com. Single ride $10; all-day ride pass $20. AE, DC, DISC, MC, V. Sun–Thurs 10am–11pm; Fri–Sat 11am–1am.

Speedworld ★ Riders on the Cyber Speedway must be 48 inches or taller to hop into these 7/8 replica NASCAR racers, which rock 'n' roll as they speed down a video version of the Las Vegas Speedway or the Strip itself. Drivers can adjust the tire pressure, aerodynamic wing angles, horsepower, braking response, transmission torque, and suspension before the race starts. The separate 3-D motion simulator with goggles will take you on a jostling race experience as you zoom along at what feels like 200 mph. At press time this attraction was closed; be sure to check with the hotel if you plan on visiting.

Sahara Hotel & Casino, 2535 Las Vegas Blvd. S. ✆ **888/696-2121** or 702/737-2111. www.saharavegas.com. Single ride $10; all-day ride pass $22. AE, DC, DISC, MC, V. Thurs–Mon 2–10pm.

Stratosphere Thrill Rides ★★ **Ages 9 & up.** Calling these heart-stoppers "thrill rides" is a bit of an understatement; two of them are downright frightening, providing an adrenaline rush unlike anything we've ever experienced. **Insanity** is Disney's Mad Tea Party–type ride, where the seats are suspended from above rather than attached from below, and spin madly over the side of the tower 920 feet above the ground. As you stand in line for the **Big Shot,** keep in mind that soon you will be strapped onto a tiny seat at the top of the tallest building west of the Mississippi, and thrust approximately 16 stories straight up the needle. You pause at the top for a split second, and then are dropped like a rock (your stomach stays at the top). Both rides are great, fun, and will provide quality bonding time with your kids if you ride them together. A third thrill ride, **X Scream,** is a giant teeter-totter-style device that propels you in an open car off the side of the 100-story tower and lets you dangle there weightlessly before returning you to relative safety. It's tame and not in the same category as the first two; give it a pass. Children under 48 inches not allowed on any of the rides.

Atop the Stratosphere, 2000 Las Vegas Blvd. S. ✆ **800/99-TOWER** (998-6937) or 702/380-7777. Admission for the Tower $10; individual ride tickets $8; $3 off for children, seniors, and hotel guests; combo package (Tower and rides) $24 (if you dine in the buffet room or Top of the World, there's no charge to go up to the Tower). AE, DC, DISC, MC, V. Sun–Thurs 10am–1am; Fri–Sat 10am–2am. Hours vary seasonally. Minimum height requirement for rides is 48 in.

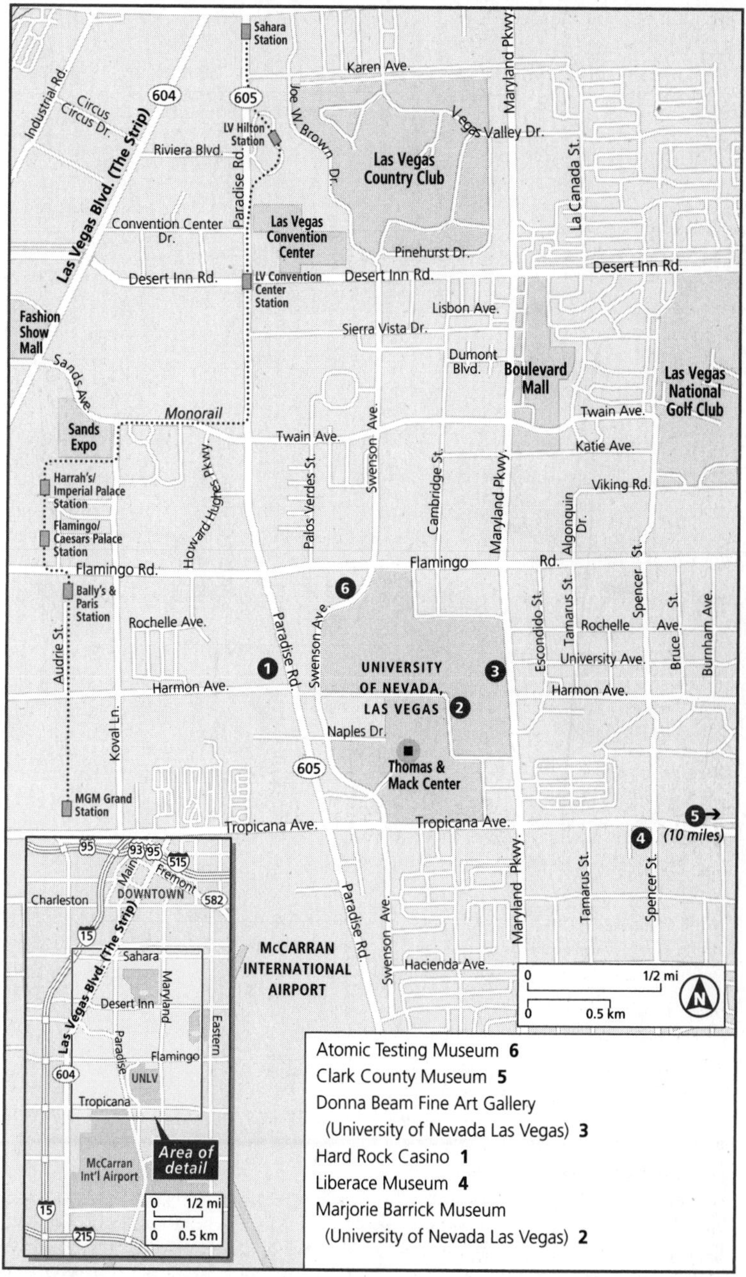

Atomic Testing Museum **6**

Clark County Museum **5**

Donna Beam Fine Art Gallery (University of Nevada Las Vegas) **3**

Hard Rock Casino **1**

Liberace Museum **4**

Marjorie Barrick Museum (University of Nevada Las Vegas) **2**

Las Vegas's Arcades

Hotel	Phone	Name	Hours	Notes/Special Features
Bally's	702/739-4111	The Arcade Room	Sun–Thurs 9am–11pm; Fri–Sat 9am–midnight	Normal arcade
*Circus Circus	702/734-0410	no name, just an area on the Midway	Daily 9am–midnight	200+ games, plus the Midway and a McDonald's; children 12 and under must be accompanied by a child 13+ or an adult; children 13 and over can play on their own
*Excalibur	702/597-7700	Fantasy Faire	Sun–Thurs 10am–11pm; Fri–Sat 10am–2am	Current arcade games and carnival games of skill and chance; Magic Motion Rides (70mm film, five-channel Dolby stereo sound, specially designed seats that move in sync with the on-screen action)
The Flamingo	702/733-3111	The Arcade	24 hr.	"Very small area," according to the hotel
*GameWorks	702/432-4263	GameWorks	Sun–Thurs 10am–midnight; Fri–Sat 10am–2am	47,000 sq. ft.; 250+ games; world's tallest free-standing rock-climbing structure (75 ft.)
Green Valley Ranch Resort	702/617-7777	The Arcade	Daily 10am–10pm	"Just a normal video arcade"
Las Vegas Hilton	702/732-5111	Sports Zone	Sun–Thurs 10am–10pm; Fri 10am–midnight; Sat 8am–midnight	Video and virtual reality games
*Luxor	702/262-4000	Games of the Gods	Daily 11am–11pm	Video, pinball, and interactive and simulator games/rides; includes a roller coaster simulator where you ride on a coaster you design yourself
MGM Grand	702/891-7777	no name, just an area	Mon–Thurs 10am–10pm; Fri–Sun 10am–midnight	Skill, redemption, video and virtual reality games; also games geared for the 12-and-under set

The Mirage	702/791-7111	The Arcade	Sun–Thurs 9am–10pm; Fri–Sat 9am–midnight	Video games only; small area near pool
Monte Carlo	702/730-7777	Backstreet Arcade	Sun–Thurs 9am–10pm; Fri–Sat 9am–midnight	60 video and redemption games
*New York–New York	702/736-4100	Coney Island Emporium	Daily 24 hrs.	32,000 sq. ft., midway games, laser tag, 8-person Daytona racing simulator, 200+ coin-op games; starting point for the Manhattan Express roller coaster; unaccompanied minors 17 and under not allowed Sun–Thurs after 10pm, Fri–Sat and school holidays after midnight; and from Memorial Day to Labor Day, after midnight
Palms	702/942-7777	no name, just an area	Sun–Thurs 8am–10pm; Fri–Sat 8am–midnight	Video games only
Rio	702/777-7777	Fun & Games Arcade	Daily 11am–11pm	Video, virtual reality, and redemption games
*Sahara	702/734-7223	Pit Pass Arcade	Daily 10am–11pm	120 interactive games, redemption and standard video games; part of the NASCAR Cafe; also available: Cyber Speedway racing simulators and Speed—The Ride roller coaster
*Stratosphere	702/380-7777	The Arcade	Daily 10am–11pm	Video games, some mechanical redemption games, and virtual soccer
Treasure Island	702/894-7111	no name, just an area	Sun–Thurs 10am–10pm; Fri–Sat 9am–midnight	Video games and a few games for children; considerably downsized from previous incarnation

**Notable arcades noted by asterisk; all minors must be accompanied by parents/adult 21 or over unless noted; no video arcades: Planet Hollywood, Bellagio, Four Seasons, Hard Rock, Harrah's, Mandalay Bay, Paris, The Venetian.*

3 ART GALLERIES & HISTORY MUSEUMS

When Steve Wynn opened Bellagio he stocked it with art—real art: Millions of dollars worth of Impressionist masterpieces, plus Picassos, Matisses, and Warhols. Like everything Wynn did, the concept was a success. Riding on the concept that Vegas visitors wanted cultcha along with all-you-can-eat-shrimp buffets, the Guggenheim came to The Venetian, followed by the separate Guggenheim and Hermitage collaboration in the same hotel. When the MGM Group bought The Mirage and ousted Steve Wynn, he took most of his artwork with him, to be displayed in Wynn Las Vegas.

Along with the art galleries and museums in these relative newcomers to the Vegas cultural scene, there are museums celebrating the city, its history, and its denizens, including Elvis, Liberace, and the Mormons. One of the world's largest collections of automobiles is at the Imperial Palace, while the Liberace Museum boasts the world's largest rhinestone. See below for more information.

Atomic Testing Museum ★★★ **Ages 8 & up.** If you are looking for some brain stimulation to escape the midway atmosphere of the casinos, try the Atomic Testing Museum, created in association with the Smithsonian Institution. The museum presents the story of the development of nuclear weapons. In particular, the Nevada Test Site located just north of Las Vegas is featured. This museum is instructive and cerebral and offers much to look at (and much to read for a full encounter). The strength of the experience is greatly enhanced by the overall design, which re-creates settings with fine attention to materials. For example, the entrance to the 8,000 square feet of exhibit space is a replica of the stainless steel facade of the Wackenhut guard station located at the Nevada Test Site. A good balance of videos and interactive stations here can engage anyone with a curiosity about the subject matter. Exhibit spaces configured like a bunker convey a sense of mystery and danger. This scheme sounds oppressive, but it deftly communicates the power and secrecy of the nuclear program. In one of two small theaters, the brief, overpowering experience of witnessing a nuclear test explosion is alone worth the price of admission. ***Tip:*** The Atomic Testing Museum requires more mental energy than gawking at faux volcanoes and sphinxes, so visit when you're well rested.

755 E. Flamingo Rd. ✆ 702/794-5151. www.atomictestingmuseum.org. $10 adults; $7 seniors, military, and students with ID; free for children 6 and under. Mon–Sat 9am–5pm; Sun 1–5pm.

Auto Collections at the Imperial Palace ★★ **All ages.** Antique, vintage, rare, and notable—or notorious—cars make up this huge, beautifully displayed collection of automobiles. The collection is so large that the exhibits are changed regularly, but expect to see several Duesenbergs (the museum has the world's largest collection, valued at over $50 million), JFK's 1962 "bubbletop" Lincoln Continental, and Cadillacs belonging to FDR and Herbert Hoover. Other cars of the stars and celebrities of bygone days include Al Capone's and Marilyn Monroe's Cadillacs, and Howard Hughes's 1954 Chrysler, which was installed with a special air-purification system that cost more than the car itself. Over 200 vehicles are on display, including one of only 51 revolutionary Tucker automobiles ever manufactured.

In the Imperial Palace Hotel, 3535 Las Vegas Blvd. S. ✆ **800/634-6441** or 702/794-3174. www.autocollections.com. Admission $6.95 adults, $3 seniors and children 11 and under, free for children under 4 and AAA members. Check website and ever-present hawkers in front of Imperial Palace for free admission coupon. AE, DC, DISC, MC, V. Daily 9:30am–9:30pm.

Bass Pro Shops Outdoor World ★★ Ages 4 & up. What child doesn't like cute, fuzzy, stuffed animals? Well, you won't find them here. What you will find, however, is a stuffed (as in taxidermy) specimen of just about every critter and fish on the face of the earth, all placed decoratively among tents, sleeping bags, canoes, archery supplies, Wellington boots, and safari hats. Far from trite moose heads or your eternally contented, glassy-eyed museum specimen, these beasts have been stuffed to look ready for action. There's a bear busy attacking an RV, combative elk with locked antlers, deer fending off mountain lions, and whales cruising serenely under the bass boats. Never was there a store better designed to divert the children while dad shops.

Adjoining the Silverton Hotel and Casino, 3333 Blue Diamond Rd. ✆ **702/730-5200.** Free admission. Mon–Sat 9am–10pm; Sun 10am–7pm.

Bellagio Gallery of Fine Art ★ Ages 10 & up. First, the drawback: According to Bellagio, children under 18 are not permitted in the hotel unless their families are registered guests, or tickets have been purchased in advance for a gallery or show, or if reservations are already made at a restaurant. Now, when we were there, we saw many a youngster traipsing about with an adult in tow, and somehow it just didn't seem like all those families were staying there or had tickets for the Cirque de Soleil show *O.* The security person we spoke to said there's an unofficial "don't-ask" policy as long as kids stay well behaved, but on the other hand, we were told—both on the phone and in person—that children under 18 were *verboten.*

Now for the good part: This is an important gallery, even though its originator, Steve Wynn, is no longer associated with Bellagio. Past exhibits have included Impressionists; the mobiles of Alexander Calder; the art of Fabergé, jeweler to the Imperial Court of Russia, which featured many of his intricately designed and bejeweled eggs; Andy Warhol celebrity portraits; Ansel Adams photographs; and a large exhibit of Monets.

The museum gift shop next door is stocked full of great gift and crafts items, most of which are designed for children, which is odd, given the hotel's seeming antipathy toward them. And then there's that ticket price. Do let us point out that the Louvre and London's National Gallery collections—both of which are, needless to say, quite a bit larger and both of which, one can safely say, do have some notable works—cost a whole lot less as a family excursion.

In Bellagio, 3600 Las Vegas Blvd. S. ✆ **877/957-9777** or 702/693-7871. www.bellagio.com. Admission $15 adults; $12 students with ID, Nevada residents, and seniors 65 and older. Reservations suggested, but walk-ins taken every 15 min. AE, DC, DISC, MC, V. Daily 9am–10pm.

Clark County Museum ★★★ (Finds) Ages 5 & up. One of the high points of this unique museum is Heritage Street, where historic homes from important periods of Clark County history have been restored to re-create the lifestyles of their times. There's also a mining exhibit, a ghost town, and a pueblo, making this an educational yet fun place to spend an afternoon walking about. Strollers can be easily accommodated, which is good, because young children may tire of walking around and looking at old buildings.

1830 S. Boulder Hwy., E. Las Vegas. ✆ **702/455-7955.** www.co.clark.nv.us/parks/clark_county_museum.htm. Admission $1.50 adults; $1 seniors, military, and children 3–15. AE, DC, DISC, MC, V. Daily 9am–4:30pm.

Donna Beam Fine Art Gallery ★ (Finds) Ages 10 & up. Located on the campus of the University of Nevada, Las Vegas, this gallery displays traveling exhibitions, as well as works by UNLV's students and faculty. It also serves as a training ground for students

Hey, Sport!

Sports are a major part of the American psyche and Las Vegas plays right into it. Here are some activities and attractions your young sports fans will like:

Eat at ESPN Zone You'll be surrounded by sports-themed items and souvenirs while you munch sports-fan food (New York–New York, 3790 Las Vegas Blvd. S.; ✆ **702/933-3776;** www.espnzone.com). See p. 147.

Visit the Sports Hall of Fame This is the world's largest personal collection of athletic memorabilia, including Muhammad Ali's boxing gloves, baseball cards, and bats from the World Series (Las Vegas Club Hotel and Casino, 18 Fremont St.; ✆ **702/385-1664;** www.vegasclubcasino.net). See p. 173.

Watch a Local Team Play Whether it's baseball, basketball, or hockey, college or pro, Las Vegas has plenty of sports year-round. See p. 241 for a complete listing of teams and their contact numbers.

Visit the Las Vegas Mini Gran Prix If your kids like racing, they'll love taking these go-karts for a spin. For those with driver's licenses, real Gran Prix cars are available. (1401 N. Rainbow Blvd.; ✆ **702/259-7000;** www.lvmgp.com). See p. 194.

Play Sport-Themed Arcade Games at GameWorks State-of-the-art video games allow players to kick soccer balls, swing bats, and perform other sporty feats in the comfort of their local arcade (in the Showcase Mall, 3785 Las Vegas Blvd. S.; ✆ **702/432-GAME** [432-4263]). See p. 173.

Browse at Field of Dreams This chain boutique offers a variety of autographed sports items, including photos, jerseys, cards, and balls (Rio, 3700 W. Flamingo Rd.; ✆ **702/221-9144;** or at Caesars Palace, 3500 Las Vegas Blvd. S.; ✆ **702/792-8233**). See p. 224.

studying gallery management. Exhibits change 7 to 15 times a year. Children who are fascinated by art will definitely enjoy this; the other 99% of kids will find it dull.

University of Nevada, Las Vegas, Alta Ham Fine Arts Building, 4505 Maryland Pkwy. ✆ **702/895-3893.** finearts.unlv.edu/facilities/donna-beam_gallery. Free admission. Mon–Fri 9am–5pm; Sat 10am–2pm.

Howard W. Cannon Aviation Museum ★ Finds **All ages.** Open 24 hours a day, this free museum at McCarran Airport is located on level 2, above baggage claim, and details the history of aviation in Nevada from the first flight to the introduction of the commercial jet. Plane fans will love it and plain folks will learn a little something. Plus, it's a better, more family-oriented way to kill time at the airport than pulling slots.

5757 Wayne Newton Blvd. ✆ **702/455-7968.** Free admission. Daily 24 hr.

Las Vegas Museum of Natural History ★ **All ages.** "Cool, totally cool," lauded one preteen, entranced by the shark tank with its undulating, sharp-toothed denizens. The slightly old and dusty taxidermy displays of bears, wolves, and the like also got high marks, as did the motion detector–activated dinosaurs, which roar and move when you enter the room. (Some smaller kids startle because of this, so you may want to explain the situation first.) This is a fun museum in the old-school diorama style and is definitely worth checking out, especially because it is located next to the Mormon Fort (p. 190) and close to the Lied Discovery Children's Museum (p. 176). The African Gallery details the fossils of primitive man found on the continent; one high point is the replica skulls enclosed in light boxes that illuminate when you press a button. Nifty. Make sure you visit the desert environment, complete with sights, sounds, and smells of the living desert. The sharks are fed Monday, Wednesday, and Friday at 2pm—if that's the sort of thing you'd enjoy watching as a family.

900 Las Vegas Blvd. N. ✆ **702/384-3466.** www.lvnhm.org. Admission $7 adults; $6 seniors, students with ID, and military; $3 children 3–11; free for children 2 and under. AE, DC, DISC, MC, V. Daily 9am–4pm.

Liberace Museum ★★ **All ages.** "He was Grandma's Elton John." That's the easiest way to explain Liberace to your children, and we can't think of a kid who won't be excited over some part of the monumental (even by Vegas standards) excesses displayed here. The first half of the museum is dedicated to Liberace's life, his cars, and his pianos. His story is indeed a distillation of the American dream—son of immigrants, Lee (nee Walter) Liberace vowed to become "the most famous pianist in the world." And boy howdy, did he succeed! His first entry in the *Guinness Book of World Records* was as the world's fastest pianist; he also set records in his time as the most highly paid. Even today, his name lives on as a symbol of kitsch and flamboyance.

The men in your family will no doubt be awestruck by the late pianist's collection of automobiles, including a rhinestone-encrusted limousine; a replica of a London taxicab; and a red, white, and blue Rolls-Royce used in the 1976 Bicentennial celebration. Check out the pink Volks Royce, a customized version of a VW bug with a Rolls-Royce grille. The piano collection features a rhinestone-covered piano and many rare antique models, but this will probably bore most kids; even we were a little ho-hum over this part. A video program and photographic chronology of Liberace's life, his cars, and pianos are housed in the front part of the museum.

The real wows, however, are heard in the second museum building—the one that has the musical score to "Beer Barrel Polka" laid out in mosaic. That's where Lee's clothes and jewels, including the world's largest rhinestone—do we sense a theme here?—are displayed. And what a Barbie doll fantasy closet—multicolored, high-collared, insanely spectacular, sequined, spangled, and rhinestoned within an inch of their seams clothes! Among the splendor and sparkle, there's a monkey-fur jacket, a green Chinese-style number, and a striking black and red outfit that will make any Gothy teen perk up. A small display of Las Vegas historical artifacts, a cafe, and a gift shop round out the visit.

Fun Facts Muy Macho

Lest anyone call Liberace a sissy for wearing ermine and pearls, point out that his furs alone could weigh up to 200 pounds, and he would stride out on stage wearing a huge fur cape and fling it open, revealing a heavy and elaborately sparkling ensemble. After accepting his applause, the fur would be driven off stage by a "show-fur" in the custom Volks Royce, and then Lee would begin to play the piano in his bejeweled garb, his fingers encumbered by the massive rings now on display at the museum. Now that's a macho man!

1775 E. Tropicana Ave. (at Spencer St.). ✆ **702/798-5595.** www.liberace.com. Admission $13 adults, $8.50 seniors 65 and over and students 6 "through college," free for children 10 and under. AE, DC, DISC, MC, V. Tues–Sat 10am–5pm; Sun noon–4pm.

Marjorie Barrick Museum **All ages.** Previously known as the Marjorie Barrick Natural History Museum at UNLV, the name has been shortened and altered, which makes it more easily distinguished from the Las Vegas Museum of Natural History. Located on the UNLV campus, this free museum offers examples of Mexican folk art, Native American pottery, traveling art exhibits (changed every 8 weeks), and other worthwhile, somewhat dry, displays based around the collections and interests of the museum's patroness, Marjorie Barrick. For kids, the real thrill is getting close to the glass cages of the live snakes (who, if you are lucky—or unlucky, depending on your view—will be dining on mice when you drop by), lizards, and tortoises on display. Remind younger kids to please not tap the glass.

On the UNLV campus, 4505 S. Maryland Pkwy. ✆ **702/895-3381.** http://hrcweb.nevada.edu/Museum. Free admission. Mon–Fri 8am–4:45pm; Sat noon–4pm.

Old Las Vegas Mormon Fort **All ages.** It's hard to believe that from this tiny structure sprang the glittering giant that is Las Vegas today, but in 1855, Mormons moving westward stopped here because of the freshwater springs, and stayed, in what was then an oasis, to build a fort, with a post office and other buildings that became a way station for travelers. Within 2 years, the hot weather and a dispute between two church leaders caused a schism, and the Mormons sold their land to a rancher. Eventually, the area was deeded to the San Pedro, Los Angeles, and Salt Lake Railroad. In 1905, trains came to Vegas, and the town was finally born around the remnants of this adobe fort. This is a good place to stop and take a look on the way to or from the Lied Discovery Children's Museum (p. 176) or the Museum of Natural History (p. 188). It is outdoors, so make sure you have hats and sunblock.

500 E. Washington Ave. ✆ **702/486-3511.** http://parks.nv.gov. Admission $3 adults, $2 children 6–12, free for children 5 and under. No credit cards. Mon–Sat 8am–4:30pm.

4 FACTORIES & FOOD

IN LAS VEGAS

Everything Coca-Cola Las Vegas Overrated **All ages.** The giant Coke-bottle-shaped window indicates you're in the right place to purchase everything Coca-Cola. Or, at least almost everything. From key chains to T-shirts, postcards, and replicas of vintage glasses and trays, this monofocused monolith is here to sell Coke. Upstairs you can taste samples of Coke from around the world, plus buy items with the Coke logo in different languages.

In the Showcase Mall, 3785 Las Vegas Blvd. S. ✆ **702/270-5952.** Free admission. Daily 10am–11pm.

M&Ms World ★ **All ages.** Along with being a store full of all things M&Ms (including the candy-coated chocolate, pajamas, and lunch boxes), this multistoried building also serves as a 3-D movie theater. The half-hour movie, *I Lost My M in Las Vegas,* stars (plain) Red M and (peanut) Yellow M, and all ages will enjoy it. Expect to be badgered into buying lavender or pastel pink M&Ms; you can mix and match colors by weight.

Or, if you like, try a box of the Mars Company's upscale chocolate, Ethel M's, also conveniently available in the gift shop.

In the Showcase Mall, 3785 Las Vegas Blvd. S. ✆ **702/736-7611.** Free admission. Sun–Thurs 9am–11pm; Fri–Sat 9am–midnight. Movie screens continuously every 30 min. Sun–Thurs 10am–6pm, Fri–Sat 10am–8pm.

National Vitamin Company Factory **All ages.** Advertised in all the local tourist attraction magazines, this quick, self-guided tour takes you through a vitamin and cosmetic company, giving you a behind-the-scenes look at how the stuff is made and packaged. There are also educational displays, and, afterward, you get free samples. This being Vegas, there's also a gift shop where you can buy hair-care products, herbs, and vitamins. The smoothie bar is considered by locals to make one of the best such drinks in the West. This place is especially good for the budding scientist or cosmetic collector.

7440 S. Industrial Rd. ✆ **702/269-9600.** www.nationalvitamin.com. Free admission. Tours during business hours Mon 7am–3pm; Tues–Sat 7am–4pm.

IN NEARBY HENDERSON

There are two factories about 6 miles from the Strip in the town of Henderson that offer free tours, and if that's your kind of thing, well, you won't be entirely alone on your visit; they are a favorite with tour groups. If you do put these factories on your to-do list, it's best to see them on a weekday, when they're fully operative.

To get to Henderson, drive south on Las Vegas Boulevard South to Sunset Road. Then, continue straight on Sunset Way, rather than following Sunset Road to the right. Turn left onto Cactus Garden Drive. You will soon see Ethel M's Chocolates, a good place to begin. Ron Lee's World of Clowns is approximately 3 miles away from Ethel M's. To get there, turn right off Cactus Garden Drive onto Sunset Way, and then left onto Sunset Road. Follow Sunset Road south to Stephanie. Turn right on Stephanie and left on Warm Springs Road. Drive past the light at Marks to Carousel Parkway, a long driveway on your right.

Ethel M's Chocolate Factory and Cactus Garden **All ages.** This is a self-guided tour, with audio and visual explanations of the processes involved in creating sweet treats. The mixtures bubble and boil before you, separated from hungry faces by a thick glass wall. The candy bits travel down conveyer belts where they are covered in chocolate and gently jiggled before being boxed by hand, an absolutely hypnotizing process. Kids should also like watching the employees behind the glass and trying to figure out what they are saying. After you finish this brief portion of the tour, you get to watch a kindly factory worker demonstrate up close how the chocolate-enrobing machines work. (*Enrobing* is the candy-making word for "covering.") After, you'll get a piece of freshly enrobed candy. Then comes the really fun part—a trip to the chocolate shop for a free sample, plus plenty of sweet goodies to buy, including ice cream. We were happy to note that the shop sells both sugar-free candy and ice cream. There's also a picture of the actual Ethel M, Ethel Mars, the mom of the founder of Mars Candy, making this a nice addition to your trip to M&Ms World (p. 190).

The factory is surrounded by a **2½-acre cactus and wetlands garden,** which features 350 species of rare and exotic cacti from the arid areas of South and Central America, with signs provided for self-guided tours. The showpiece of the cactus garden is the water-reclamation plant. Built on ecological principles, only natural means—algae, fish, and plants—are used to clean all the water used at the candy factory. The cleaned water is then used to irrigate the cactus garden and the wetlands area. Any extra water goes to

Fun Facts Trivia: Viva Las Vegas

1. Gambling was legalized in Nevada in
   - a. 1931
   - b. 1918
   - c. 1877
   - d. 1849
2. Fremont Street was the site of Las Vegas's first
   - a. elevator
   - b. paved street
   - c. streetlight
   - d. all of the above
3. Though Las Vegas is known for its casinos, it also has numerous churches, synagogues, and other places of worship. Approximately how many?
   - a. 1,200
   - b. 500
   - c. 140
   - d. 70
4. The Spanish words "las vegas" mean
   - a. "the winners"
   - b. "the meadows"
   - c. "the sands"
   - d. "the losers"
5. Las Vegas is famous for its neon. How many miles of neon tubing are along the Strip and in Downtown?
   - a. 15,000 miles
   - b. 400 miles
   - c. 1,500 miles
   - d. 4 miles

local water companies for nonpotable uses. This section is a really neat way to show how Mother Nature can be used to undo some of mankind's messes. Plus, the fish are fun to watch.

Tip: If you get there at opening, not a lot of candy is being made; the factory gets busier as the day goes on, but by 2:30pm, production has slowed back down. The early bird does catch the worm, or chocolate in this case; we were given multiple samples because nobody else was there, or maybe they just thought we looked hungry. You may not, however, want to have your darlings eating multiple helpings of toffee and truffles at 9am. Bottom line—if you want to see full production, aim for arrival between 10am and 1pm, but if you'd like an extra helping of chocolate, go at opening.

2 Cactus Garden Dr. (just off Mountain Vista and Sunset Way in the Green Valley Business Park), Henderson. ✆ **888/627-0990.** www.ethelm.com. Free admission. Daily 8:30am–7pm. Closed Dec 25.

6. There are how many hotel swimming pools in the Las Vegas area?
   a. 17
   b. 27
   c. 35
   d. 50+

ANSWERS

1: **a** Gambling was legalized in 1931. In 1909, the state passed a no-gambling law, which forbade even flipping a coin for the cost of a drink; no one in Las Vegas, however, really paid much attention to the law.

2: **d** Fremont Street was also the location of the city's first hotel, Hotel Nevada, opened in 1905.

3: **b** Over 40 faiths are served at 500-plus places of worship.

4: **b** Rafael Rivera bestowed the name in 1829, after founding the site located in a grassy valley.

5: **a** 15,000 miles of neon tubing makes nighttime Las Vegas one of the most recognizable cityscapes in the world.

6: **d** There are over 50 hotel pools; unfortunately, many close (or aren't heated) in the winter. The ones that are heated and do stay open include Bellagio, Caesars, Circus Circus, Excalibur, Flamingo, Golden Nugget, Green Valley Ranch, Las Vegas Hilton, Luxor, MGM Grand, Mirage, Monte Carlo, Paris, Plaza, and Tropicana.

5 KID-FRIENDLY TOURS

If you'd rather relax and leave the driving to someone else or if you'd like to try something more daring in sightseeing, almost every hotel in Las Vegas has a sightseeing desk where clerks can arrange any kind of tour you'd like to anywhere you want to go, whether you want to travel by helicopter, limo, horse, Humvee, foot, or bus.

GRAND CANYON TOURS The Grand Canyon is hundreds of miles away from Las Vegas, so if you happen to pass it on your way in or out of town, it's—to put it mildly—worth a stop. If experiencing the natural wonder is an important part of your trip, and you want to make the huge detour, there are dozens of sightseeing tours departing from

For Your Little Race Car Enthusiast

Race car fans are a very specific subset of sports fans, and Las Vegas has everything race car–themed you could want to get your kid revved up—from food to actual drivable scale models of NASCAR vehicles, virtual car races, an amazing auto museum, a tour of a race car factory, and more. Listed below are some of the best race car–related activities in town.

Eat at the NASCAR Cafe Theme aplenty here, with autographed team jackets, actual cars, and a genuine love of NASCAR. ***Tip:*** Eat *after* the rides (Sahara Hotel, 2535 Las Vegas Blvd. S.; ✆ **888/696-2121** or 702/737-2111; www.saharavegas.com)!

Watch the Races at the Las Vegas Motor Speedway Weekly events here include stock car races, motocross, and hot rod races, but this is also a major stop on the NASCAR circuit. Some of the top races in the country are held here from March through December, with tickets at this 250,000-seat racecourse at times exceeding $100. But January and February, you can see races for under $10. There are tours available when races aren't on. The action takes place at 7000 Las Vegas Blvd. N.; (✆ **800/644-4444;** www.lvms.com).

Tour the Shelby American Sports Car Museum and Assembly Area Located next to the Las Vegas Motor Speedway, this free museum displays a dozen classic Shelby American cars (the Shelby Cobra is considered by enthusiasts to be the finest American sports car ever built—designer Carroll Shelby also worked for Ford and created the Mustang Cobra for that company); the working auto assembly plant shows cars in every stage of production. The museum is located at 6755 Speedway Blvd. (✆ **702/942-7325;** www.shelbyamerican.com).

Visit the Liberace Museum While the ladies ooh and aah over the world's largest rhinestone, check out the customized cars that Liberace collected (1775 E. Tropicana Ave.; ✆ **702/798-5595;** www.liberace.com).

Explore the Auto Collections at the Imperial Palace This constantly changing display features Duesenbergs, vintage commercial vehicles, cars owned by presidents, and, most impressively, a Tucker, one of the 51 manufactured before the company went out of business (Imperial Palace Hotel, 3535 Las Vegas Blvd. S.; ✆ **702/794-3174;** www.autocollections.com).

Race on a Track **Las Vegas Mini Gran Prix,** 91401 N. Rainbow Blvd. (✆ **702/259-7000;** www.lvmgp.com), has go-karts and mini Gran Prix racers.

the city daily. The major operator of Grand Canyon tours, **Scenic Airlines** (✆ **800/634-6801** or 702/638-3300; www.scenic.com), runs full-day and overnight tours with hiking, along with their deluxe, full-day guided air-ground tours starting at $279 per person ($249 for children 2–11); the price includes a bus excursion through the national park, a flight over the canyon, and lunch. All their tours include flightseeing.

Scenic Airlines also offers tours to other points of interest and national parks, including Bryce Canyon and Monument Valley. Ask for details when you call.

UNIQUE DESERT TOURS If you would like a personalized tour of Las Vegas, one that takes you off the beaten path, call **Creative Adventures, Ltd.** ★★★ (✆ **702/893-2051**). Founder and tour guide Char Cruze really knows the city and its outlying areas. Whether you would like to take one of her structured tours, or work with her to devise one suited to your family's interests and tastes, Char can deliver. A fourth-generation Las Vegan whose family has been here since 1855, and who can tell you firsthand about the opening of The Flamingo, Char has extensively studied southern Nevada's geology and desert wildlife, its regional history, and its Native American cultures. And the thrilling stories she tells are all factual as well as fun.

From haunted mines to mobsters, Char takes you there literally and figuratively as you visit sacred Paiute land, ghost towns, ancient petroglyphs, and many historical landmarks in the city. Along with her storytelling skills, Char brings along visual aids, such as a board of labeled rocks to help illustrate her lecture on local geography. Prompt, knowledgeable, and thoughtful, Char provides tours unlike any other in Las Vegas and is well worth the expense. If you don't have a vehicle with you, Char can rent transport according to the size of your group. She is also knowledgeable about handling clients with disabilities.

Depending on your itinerary, the cost is $10 per hour per person; transportation is extra. Obviously, if you use your own car, you'll save the cost of the rental vehicle. This is an economical tour option, as well as a unique way of seeing the area. It's a good idea to make arrangements with her prior to leaving home to ensure she's available.

9

Las Vegas for the Active Family

Both tourist and local families take advantage of the variety of indoor and outdoor sports and activities in greater Las Vegas. Family fun centers and sports parks provide a variety of rides and activities, while parks—city, county, and state—offer recreational activities ranging from swings to horseshoes. You'll also find educational aspects to several parks, because they're often home to museums, historical sites, and ecological preserves.

Expect to drive or taxi to most of the in-city locations. Recreational sports such as rock climbing, cycling, horseback riding, and hiking happen in areas well outside the city—Bonnie Springs, Lake Mead, Mount Charleston, Red Rock Canyon, and Valley of Fire—and are covered in chapter 12, "Side Trips from Las Vegas."

1 PLACES TO RUN & WALK

Sometimes it seems as though the only walking anyone does in Las Vegas is to and from his or her room and up and down the Strip, but the city does have beautiful botanical gardens and public parks. Keep in mind, however, that most parks are not located close to the expensive real estate on the Strip.

NATURE WALKS & BOTANICAL GARDENS

Springs Preserve ★★ **All ages.** Las Vegas's newest cultural attraction is the Springs Preserve, a $250-million park and environmental study area that opened in spring 2008 and preserves Big Springs, the original Mojave Desert oasis that supported indigenous people for thousands of years, inspired the Spanish name Las Vegas (the Meadows), and attracted settlers to the big valley that surrounded it. Developed and managed by the Southern Nevada Water Authority, this attraction encompasses 180 acres, with 2½ miles of hiking trails surrounded by wetlands, 176,000 square feet of museum space, an 1,800-seat outdoor amphitheater, and a desert botanical garden with 30,000 plants. A guest services building contains a gift shop and cafe. Under construction is a 79,000-square-foot building that will house the new Nevada State Museum, opening in 2009.

333 S. Valley View Blvd. ✆ **702/822-7700.** www.springspreserve.org. Admission adults $19, students $13, children 5–17 $11. Daily 10am–10pm during summer; 10am–6pm rest of the year; trails close at dusk.

UNLV Xeric Garden ★ **All ages.** The beautifully landscaped desert garden, in front of the Marjorie Barrick Museum on the university's campus, is at its most colorful from February through May, when the flowers bloom. But year-round, the strange and wonderful plants in this xeriscape make for a scenic walk through a surreal landscape. Free brochures about the plants are available in the museum's gift shop. Throughout the

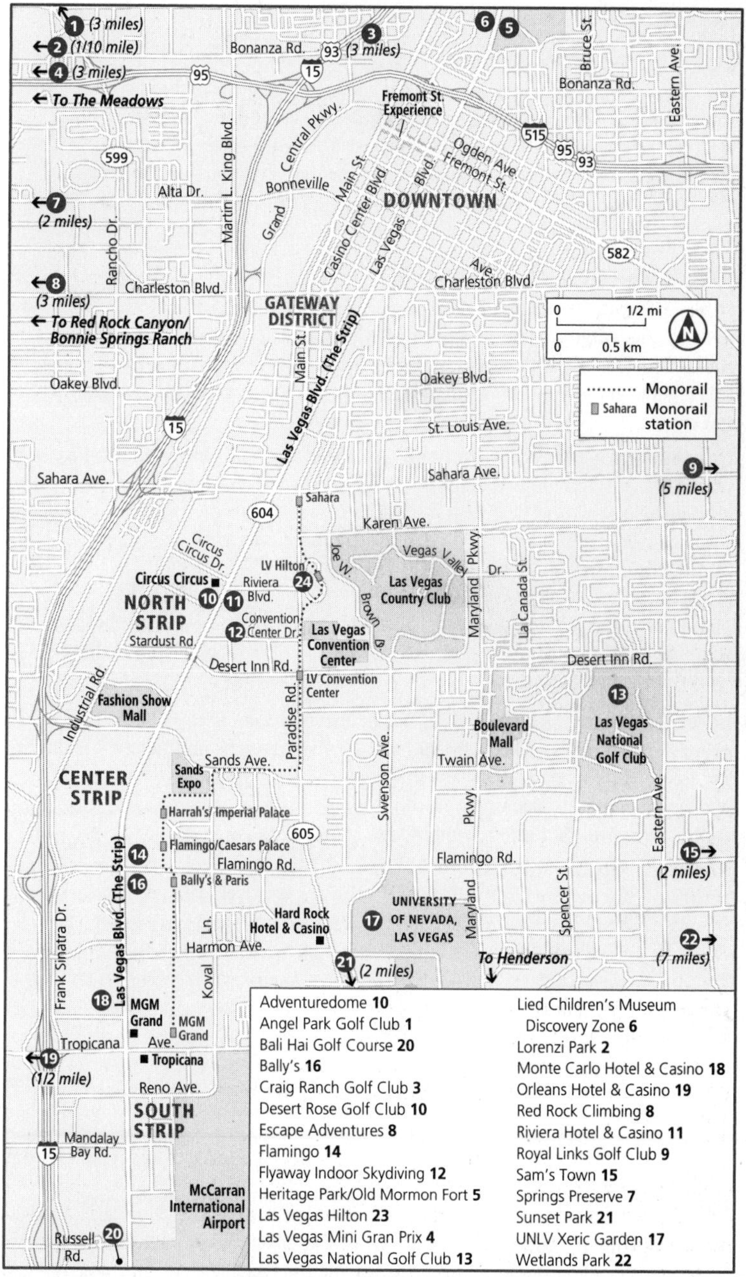
1 (3 miles)
2 (1/10 mile)
4 (3 miles)
To The Meadows
3 (3 miles)
Bonanza Rd.
Fremont St. Experience
Bruce St.
Eastern Ave.
Ogden Ave.
Fremont St.
Central Pkwy.
Martin L. King Blvd.
Alta Dr.
Bonneville
Main St.
Casino Center Blvd.
Las Vegas Blvd.
Grand
DOWNTOWN
7 (2 miles)
Rancho Dr.
Charleston Blvd.
8 (3 miles)
To Red Rock Canyon/ Bonnie Springs Ranch
GATEWAY DISTRICT
Las Vegas Blvd. (The Strip)
Oakey Blvd.
St. Louis Ave.
Sahara Ave.
9 (5 miles)
0 1/2 mi
0 0.5 km
Monorail
Sahara Monorail station
Sahara
Karen Ave.
Circus Circus Dr.
LV Hilton
Joe W. Brown Dr.
Vegas Valley Dr.
Maryland Pkwy.
La Canada St.
Circus Circus
Riviera Blvd.
Las Vegas Country Club
NORTH STRIP
Convention Center Dr.
Las Vegas Convention Center
Stardust Rd.
Desert Inn Rd.
LV Convention Center
Industrial Rd.
Fashion Show Mall
Paradise Rd.
Boulevard Mall
Las Vegas National Golf Club
Sands Ave.
Twain Ave.
Sands Expo
CENTER STRIP
Swenson Ave.
Harrah's/Imperial Palace
Flamingo/Caesars Palace
Flamingo Rd.
15 (2 miles)
Bally's & Paris
Spencer St.
UNIVERSITY OF NEVADA, LAS VEGAS
Hard Rock Hotel & Casino
Koval Ln.
Harmon Ave.
Frank Sinatra Dr.
21 (2 miles)
To Henderson
22 (7 miles)
MGM Grand
Tropicana Ave.
Tropicana
19 (1/2 mile)
Reno Ave.
SOUTH STRIP
Mandalay Bay Rd.
McCarran International Airport
Russell Rd.
Adventuredome 10
Angel Park Golf Club 1
Bali Hai Golf Course 20
Bally's 16
Craig Ranch Golf Club 3
Desert Rose Golf Club 10
Escape Adventures 8
Flamingo 14
Flyaway Indoor Skydiving 12
Heritage Park/Old Mormon Fort 5
Las Vegas Hilton 23
Las Vegas Mini Gran Prix 4
Las Vegas National Golf Club 13
Lied Children's Museum Discovery Zone 6
Lorenzi Park 2
Monte Carlo Hotel & Casino 18
Orleans Hotel & Casino 19
Red Rock Climbing 8
Riviera Hotel & Casino 11
Royal Links Golf Club 9
Sam's Town 15
Springs Preserve 7
Sunset Park 21
UNLV Xeric Garden 17
Wetlands Park 22

 campus are trees and other plants with labels. By the concert hall, a stand of weeping willows provides shade for a picnic or rest.

4505 Maryland Pkwy. ✆ **702/895-1421.** Free admission. Daily dawn–dusk.

Wetlands Nature Preserve ★ All ages. Five miles of trails—including walking trails, dirt trails, a concrete ADA trail, and crossover trails—weave through this 130-acre nature preserve where wildlife roams, and indigenous and migratory birds flock. Rare fossilized footprints of a dinosaur are displayed at the visitor center. Picnicking is allowed; plan to spend at least 2 hours strolling along the trails and watching the birds.

7050 Tropicana Blvd. E. ✆ **702/455-7522.** www.co.clark.nv.us/parks. Free admission. Daily dawn–dusk. Visitor center daily 9am–3pm.

PARKS & PLAYGROUNDS

Clark County has over 50 parks and playgrounds, and the City of Las Vegas administers to an additional 50. A complete listing can be found at **www.accessclarkcounty.com/parks**. State parks can be found online at **http://parks.nv.gov**. The following are the largest parks in the city, with a variety of activity areas, and are the sites of many festivals and events.

Heritage Park/Old Mormon Fort All ages. The Old Mormon Fort, part of the Old Las Vegas Mormon State Historic Park, adjacent to the city's Heritage Park, draws tourists, historians, and field trips, but locals come here for the Heritage's playgrounds and picnic grounds. There's also a desert demonstration garden, also known as a xeriscape, which displays different drought-resistant plants. Tour the fort, and then have a picnic lunch.

500 E. Washington Ave. ✆ **702/486-3511.** www.parks.nv.gov. Free admission to Heritage Park. Admission to Old Mormon Fort $3 adults, $2 children 6–12, free for children 5 and under. Park daily 7am–9pm. Fort daily 8am–4:30pm.

Lorenzi Park ★ All ages. With picnic and barbecue areas along with slides and swings, sports fields, tennis courts, and a wheelchair fitness course, this park is a favorite for local families. The artificial lake is stocked with fish for catching or feeding, and waterfowl will beg for the crumbs you scatter. This is the site of the annual Sammy Davis, Jr., Festival, which honors the performer and civil rights pioneer. There is a unique garden for the blind, with scented and textured plants, that the sighted will also enjoy. The Nevada State Museum (✆ **702/486-5205**) is also located on the park grounds, allowing you to fit a picnic and play time in with a trip to the museum, which is stuffed full of taxidermied animals and a variety of other features, such as a replica of Bugsy Siegel's hotel suite and Paiute Indian artifacts. Note that the museum will move to the Springs Preserve in 2009.

> **Tips License Required**
>
> For fishing licenses, required for those 13 and older, and for more fishing information, contact the Department of Wildlife at ✆ **702/486-5127.**

3333 W. Washington Ave. ✆ **702/229-6297.** Free admission. Hours vary by area and season.

Sunset Park ★ All ages. This huge park (and lake!) features something for almost everyone, with multiuse fields and areas dedicated to specific sports including disc-golf, horseshoes, and radio-controlled boating. Residents of Las Vegas make good use of the ball fields, a swimming pool, tennis courts, and the walking/jogging track. The lake is available on a year-round basis for fishing. The State of Nevada Department of Fish and Wildlife stocks the lake with trout in the cooler winter months and catfish in the summer months; a fishing license, with a trout stamp, is required for anyone 13 and older. The Renaissance Festival–Age of Chivalry event is held here annually.

2601 E. Sunset Rd. ✆ **702/455-8200.** www.accessclarkcounty.com/depts/parks/locations/pages/Sunset_Park_Lake.aspx. Free admission. Hours vary by area and season.

2 FAMILY FUN CENTERS & INDOOR PLAYGROUNDS

Las Vegas Mini Gran Prix **Ages 4 & up.** The main attraction at this 7-acre family fun center with a roller coaster, slide, arcade, and snack bar is the opportunity to race on four different minitracks. Height requirements vary from ride to ride, but children must be at least 36 inches for any of the attractions. Children 42 inches to 54 inches can drive themselves on the Kiddie Karts (two rides per ticket), while taller kids can speed around on go-karts. There's also a mini Gran Prix course for those 16 and older. On the roller coaster, adults ride free with a paying child (who gets two rides per ticket); for the mini Gran Prix cars, children ride for free with a paying adult. Yes, it's a bit confusing, but you will have fun.

1401 N. Rainbow Blvd. ✆ **702/259-7000.** www.lvmgp.com. Rides $6.50 each, $30 for 5. Sun–Thurs 10am–10pm; Fri–Sat 10am–11pm.

3 SPORTS

BICYCLING The **Las Vegas Valley Bicycle Club** (www.vegasbikeclub.org/page_rides.html) hosts rides throughout the week. Check the website for the itineraries, which can be anywhere from 13 to 45 miles. The length of the rides may make them impractical for some kids; however, they are welcome with their guardians. Helmets are required, and you will need a bike; all manner of bike equipment can be rented from **Escape Adventures,** 8221 W. Charleston Blvd. (✆ **702/596-2953;** www.escapeadventures.com), starting at $40 first day; $35 for half-day or an additional day. If biking around the city doesn't strike your fancy, Escape Adventures also provides guided bike and hiking tours of the desert areas outside of Las Vegas.

BOWLING Bowling is astoundingly popular in Las Vegas. The 56-lane alleys at **Sam's Town & Gambling Hall,** 5111 Boulder Hwy. (✆ **702/456-7777;** www.samstownlv.com), are open 24 hours, while the 70-lane **Orleans,** 4500 W. Tropicana Ave. (✆ **702/365-7111;** www.orleanscasino.com), is open 24 hours on weekdays. Bowling costs at each facility vary depending on day and time, but expect to pay about $3 a game per person, plus $2.25 for shoe rental; midnight bowling for $1 per game per person is offered from Monday through Thursday, midnight to 8am.

GOLF Desert golfing strikes something atavistic in even the highest-scoring duffer, and Las Vegas, with more than 60 courses—more than 30 of which are public, resort, or semiprivate—is a world-class location for teeing off. Players who have designed courses

Not for the Faint of Heart

If the thrill rides weren't exciting enough for your teenagers, they might want to try sky diving. Check out **Flyaway Indoor Skydiving,** 200 Convention Center Dr. (✆ **877/545-8093** or 702/731-4768; www.flyawayindoorskydiving.com), where you don a special flight suit and receive a 20-minute training session in weightless movement before a jet engine under the floor blasts on, keeping you hovering above the ground for another 15 minutes in its exhaust (no fumes, just air). There are no age requirements, but you must be between 40 and 230 pounds. Look for coupons in tourist magazines for discounts on the $32 ticket price. Open daily 10am to 6pm.

include greats Arnold Palmer, Jack Nicklaus, and Chi Chi Rodriguez. If you have any doubt about golf's impact on Las Vegas, consider this: The University of Nevada, Las Vegas offers a bachelor's degree in recreation with a PGA-approved emphasis on professional golf management. Greens fees can range from as low as $40 upward into the hundreds of dollars for a round of golf, depending on the course, season, and time of day you choose to play. You should also factor in renting a cart, because you won't want to carry your bags in the heat. Golf is a great family activity; all ages can play (little ones should have their own clubs) on the Vegas courses, and many courses offer reduced rates for junior golfing in the afternoon. (Juniors must walk.)

Serious golfers should contact **American Golf** (✆ **800/468-7918;** www.americangolf.com), a nationwide reservations service that's based in Arizona. They can help you arrange golf packages and book hard-to-get tee times in Las Vegas.

Local favorite **Angel Park Golf Club,** 100 S. Rampart Blvd. (✆ **888/629-3929** or 702/254-4653; www.angelpark.com), is a 36-hole par-70/71 public course. Arnold Palmer originally designed the Mountain and Palm courses; several years later, the Palm course was redesigned by Bob Cupp. The Palm Course, with gently rolling fairways, offers golfers of all abilities a challenging yet forgiving layout. The Mountain Course has rolling natural terrain and gorgeous panoramic views. In addition to these two challenging 18-hole courses, Angel Park offers a night-lit Cloud 9 Course (12 holes for daylight play, 9 at night), where each hole is patterned after a famous par-3. You can reserve tee times up to 60 days in advance with a credit card guarantee. Greens fees run between $75 and $135, with discounted twilight rates available. Juniors, those golfers under 17, can call the club daily and find out when "they are letting the juniors out." This arcane phrase means that once the course clears out from duffers finishing up their rounds (usually about 3 hr. before dark), the youngsters can come on for a quick 18 holes. However, all juniors, who pay the incredibly low rate of $35, must be accompanied by an adult; they should ask for the "junior card holder rate." **Bali Hai Golf Club,** 5160 Las Vegas Blvd. S. (✆ **888/427-6678;** www.balihaigolfclub.com), is one of the area's newest and most exclusive golf addresses. This multimillion-dollar course, built in 2000, is located on the Strip just south of Mandalay Bay. Done in a wild South Seas theme, the par-72 course has over 7 acres of water features, including an island green, palm trees, and tropical foliage everywhere you look. All golf carts are equipped with global positioning satellite (GPS) tracking systems. And celebrity chef Wolfgang Puck opened his newest Vegas eatery here. All this glamour will cost you; greens fees run from $150 to $325, and even at those prices, tee times are often booked 6 months in advance. Unfortunately, they do not offer junior rates, but, as with all courses, all ages are allowed to golf here.

Two new greens have recently been added to **Black Mountain Golf & Country Club** in nearby Henderson at 500 Greenway Rd. (✆ **702/565-7933;** www.golfblackmountain.com), a 27-hole, par-72 semiprivate course. Unpredictable winds can make your game a challenge on this course, which has greens fees ranging from $40 to $120. Expect to see wildlife here, including roadrunners. Juniors can walk the course from noon on for $15.

Greens fees are a bargain at **Craig Ranch Golf Club,** 628 W. Craig Rd., between Losee Road and Martin Luther King Jr. Boulevard (✆ **702/642-9700**), a flat, 18-hole, par-70 public course with many trees and bunkers, where both narrow and open fairways feature Bermuda turf. You can reserve tee times 7 days in advance, and expect to pay $19 walking, $30 with cart. Juniors can walk on after noon for a $5 fee, or ride for $16. Another public course accepting tee time reservations 7 days in advance is the 18-hole, par-71 **Desert Rose Golf Club,** 5483 Clubhouse Dr., 3 blocks west of Nellis Boulevard, off Sahara Avenue (✆ **702/431-4653**). Built in 1964 and designed by Dick Wilson and Joe Lee, the course's narrow fairways feature Bermuda turf. The greens fees can range from $49 to $59, cart included.

The 1996 Las Vegas Invitational, won by Tiger Woods, was held at the **Las Vegas National Golf Club,** 1911 Desert Inn Rd., between Maryland Parkway and Eastern Avenue (✆ **702/734-1796**), an 18-hole, par-72 public course. The steep greens fees from $129 to $159 include cart rental. The classic layout of this course includes over half a dozen water hazards. Discounted tee times are often available. Reservations are taken up to 60 days in advance for a $5 to $7 fee. There is no junior rate.

Legendary Scottish golf holes, including St. Andrews Road Hole and the Postage Stamp at the Royal Troon, are among the famous fairways on the British Open tour that are faithfully re-created at the **Royal Links Golf Club,** 5995 East Vegas Valley, east of Boulder Highway, between Flamingo and Sahara (✆ **702/450-8000**), making for a unique game and an interesting history lesson. The 19th hole is designed to resemble a medieval castle, complete with an English pub inside. You can expect to pay $125 to $250 for the greens fee; there is no junior rate here.

ROCK CLIMBING If you want to try your hand at this strenuous desert sport, which works out both the mind and body, see p. 270 for more information on outdoor rock climbing in the Las Vegas area. However, you should consider practicing at an indoor climbing facility before scrambling up the walls of Red Rock Canyon. **Nevada Climbing Center,** 3065 E. Patrick Lane (✆ **702/898-8192**), offers a 35-foot challenge; both **GameWorks** (p. 173) and **Adventuredome** (p. 180) have smaller versions in amusement zone environments. True indoor climbing enthusiasts will want to head to **Red Rock Climbing Center,** 8201 Charleston Blvd. (✆ **702/254-5604**), where textured terrain mimics caves, roofs, buttresses, and other rock formations. The floor is padded and shoes and a harness can be rented. First-timers will pay $35, which includes a lesson and rental of the harness and shoes. More experienced climbers can pay $15 for a day pass, with an $8 shoe and harness fee. A day pass for kids (11 and under) is $10. Acrophobes may want to buy a boulder pass for $12, which will keep them climbing at a lower height.

TENNIS Tennis buffs should choose one of the many hotels in town that has tennis courts, because locals keep the public courts in the parks busy. You should reserve a hotel court when you make your room reservations. Some hotels beyond those in this section do have tennis courts, but because they're not particularly child friendly, we didn't list them in the accommodations chapter or here.

Bally's (✆ **702/739-4111;** www.harrahs.com) has eight night-lit hard courts and a pro shop. Fees per hour are $10, $15 for nonguests. Hours vary seasonally. Reservations are required at The **Flamingo** (✆ **702/733-3444;** www.harrahs.com), which has four outdoor hard courts, all lit for night play. Open to the public daily from 7am to 7pm (closes 6pm Sat–Sun), rates are $20 per hour for nonguests, $12 for guests. Lessons are available, and there's also a pro shop. The **Las Vegas Hilton** (✆ **702/732-5111;** www.lvhilton.com) has four night-lit courts and two day-only courts; fees are $10 for hotel guests and $15 for nonguests, per day. The **Riviera Hotel & Casino** (✆ **702/734-5110**) has only two courts, both available for night play; for nonguests the charge is $10 an hour, and hotel guests play free.

In addition to hotels, the **University of Nevada, Las Vegas (UNLV),** Harmon Avenue just east of Swenson Street (✆ **702/895-3009;** www.unlv.edu), has a dozen courts (all lit for night play) that are open weekdays from 6am to 9:45pm, weekends 8am to 9pm. Rates are $5 per person per day. You should call before going to find out whether a court is available.

4 CLASSES & WORKSHOPS

Throughout the year, there are numerous free and low-cost activities for children and families available through **Clark County Parks and Community Services** ✆ **702/455-8200;** www.accessclarkcounty.com/parks). They offer a changing calendar of classes, workshops, and activities for children of all ages—as well as for adults and seniors—at locations throughout the greater Las Vegas area. Recent offerings included laser tag, fossil hunting, and horseback riding. Workshops for teens emphasize academic and leadership skills. Teens and 'tweens can attend seasonal dances and parties, while younger kids can participate in classes such as Alphabet Art, music, dance, and gymnastics. E-mail or call for a brochure, published four times a year, outlining what's available.

For the Special-Needs Child

The **Adaptive Recreation Center** (✆ **702/229-4905;** www.lasvegasnevada.gov/information/5168.htm) is a service of the city of Las Vegas and is the only Adaptive Recreation Program in the state. As of this writing, the center is open only to residents of Nevada. Designed for those with special needs, the recreation program offers after-school activities for ages 7 to 21, while ages 14 to 21 can participate in the Dynamic Teen Recreation program. There are also additional individual and team sports activities offered. For additional information, write to ARP, 749 Veterans Memorial Dr., Las Vegas, NV 89101.

Lorenzi Park, 3333 W. Washington Ave., where the Adaptive Recreation Program bases most of its activities, features a wheelchair fitness course and a garden for the blind, both of which are open to the public.

Lied Discovery Children's Museum ★★★ Ages 10 & under. This innovative museum (p. 176) provides a number of ongoing art, arts and crafts, science, and cultural workshops. Some cost $3 above admission, but most are free. Check the website's Calendar of Events for a 3-month schedule.

833 Las Vegas Blvd. N. (a half-block south of Washington, across the street from Cashman Field). ✆ **702/382-3445.** www.ldcm.org. Admission $8 adults, $7 seniors and children 1–17. AE, DC, DISC, MC, V. Tues–Fri 9am–4pm; Sat 10am–5pm; Sun noon–5pm.

10

Shopping for the Whole Family

Shopping in Las Vegas falls into two categories—tourist and local. Tourists tend to stick to the hotel shopping malls and retail areas to sate their spending urges, while locals flock primarily to the malls, which—as in any urban center—are vast. You'll find many of the same large chain shops (such as bebe, Banana Republic, and Gap) in both styles of shopping venues, but local malls also host numerous department stores ranging from Sears to Neiman Marcus in addition to branches of national retail shops.

Fashion Show Mall, the only hotel-less shopping mall located on the Strip, underwent a massive renovation, which added more stores, including New York's venerable Bloomingdale's and a Nordstrom. The expansion makes Fashion Show Las Vegas's largest mall, at 2 million square feet, even eclipsing the Boulevard Mall, another Vegas supershopping structure, which boasts 1.2 million square feet of shopping space.

Outlet shopping has become a big business in Las Vegas; there are regularly scheduled tours to both the Primm outlets and the closer Las Vegas Outlet Center, where consumers can find deep discounts on clothing, accessories, and household goods. A second related venue, Las Vegas Premium Outlets, is located near Downtown with 120 outlet shops. Las Vegas is also a popular spot for collectors who search for finds along Charleston Boulevard, starting in the middle of the 1600 block of East Charleston Boulevard, where little stores in old houses dating from the 1930s line the street.

The majority of stores throughout Las Vegas accept American Express, Discover, MasterCard, and Visa, in addition to debit cards with a Visa or MasterCard logo, and traveler's checks. Some stores also accept traditional ATM cards requiring a PIN.

Most traditional stores in Las Vegas open at 10am and close at 7pm. Malls, whose openings and closings vary by location, have expanded hours on weekends and holidays; mall stores generally follow the hours of the mall itself. The physical spaces of hotel arcades are always open to tempt wee-hour window-shoppers, but their actual hours vary from shop to shop,

Top Toys for Kids

In Vegas, logos are everywhere, and most souvenirs are nothing more than overpriced junk with a logo stamped on it. But you will find some cool stuff for kids, if they don't find it first. Here are our favorite Vegas children's toys:

- Excalibur's **Princess Hats:** These cone-shaped hats come in fuchsia, royal blue, and gold and silver, and from the cone hangs a neat veil ($9). Our 7-year-old wore hers all day long.
- The Mirage's **Stuffed White Tigers:** They come in a number of sizes; the $22 version is absolutely irresistible and is of good quality.
- Of course, you can't go wrong with two of the cheapest gifts in the hotel gift stores: **used casino dice** ($1–$2) and **playing cards** (75¢–$1.50).

hotel to hotel, with some shops keeping traditional hours and others open round-the-clock.

The sales tax in Las Vegas is 7.75%.

1 THE SHOPPING SCENE

SHOPPING DISTRICTS

For the most part, Las Vegas's main shopping districts are the malls and hotel shopping promenades (see below), with the notable exception of Maryland Parkway, a long swath that runs parallel to the Strip to the east. There, in addition to the huge Boulevard Mall, you'll find drugstores, a Toys "R" Us, and vintage shops, hipster clothing emporia, and tattoo parlors.

Malls

Boulevard Mall Anchored by Sears, JCPenney, Macy's, Dillard's, and Marshalls, the Boulevard's 150-plus stores are geared to the average consumer. The wide variety of shops—offering moderately priced shoes and clothing for the entire family, books and gifts, jewelry, and home furnishings, plus more than a dozen fast-food eateries—means you can find just about anything you need here. The shops and restaurants are arranged in arcade fashion on a single floor occupying 1.2 million square feet. The mall is open Monday through Saturday from 10am to 9pm, and Sunday from 11am to 6pm. 3528 S. Maryland Pkwy. (btw. Twain Ave. and Desert Inn Rd.). ✆ **702/732-8949.** www.blvdmall.com.

Fashion Show Mall Presently comprising more than 250 shops, restaurants, and services, this luxurious and centrally located mall is anchored by Neiman Marcus, Saks Fifth Avenue, Macy's, Dillard's, Bloomingdale's, and Nordstrom. Thanks to a $300-million expansion completed in the fall of 2003, Fashion Show now sports a wild, high-tech Strip entrance. The centerpiece of the expansion is the Cloud, the largest stainless-steel screen in existence: 479 feet long, 160 feet wide, up to 21 feet thick, and 182 feet tall. The 900-ton structure is actually a video screen, running ads from stores inside the mall, complete with a concert-quality sound system. Valet parking is available, and you can even arrange to have your car hand-washed while you shop. The mall is open Monday through Friday from 10am to 9pm, Saturday from 10am to 8pm, and Sunday from 11am until 6pm. 3200 Las Vegas Blvd. S. (at the corner of Spring Mountain Rd.). ✆ **702/369-0704.** www.thefashionshow.com.

The Meadows Fountains and trees enhance the Meadows' ultramodern, high-ceilinged interior, comprising 144 shops, services, and eateries, anchored by four department stores: Macy's, Dillard's, Sears, and JCPenney. In addition, there is a full array of apparel for the entire family (including maternity wear, petites, and large sizes), 15 shoe stores, an extensive food court, and shops purveying toys, books, CDs and tapes, luggage, gifts, jewelry, home furnishings, and accessories. Thankfully, there are a few comfortable conversation/seating areas for resting your feet between purchases. The Meadows is open Monday through Saturday from 10am to 9pm, and Sunday from 10am to 6pm. 4300 Meadows Lane (at the intersection of Valley View and U.S. 95). ✆ **702/878-3331.** www.themeadowsmall.com.

Factory Outlets

Las Vegas has two big factory outlet centers, one just a few miles past the southern end of the Strip (see below) and the other just off I-15 near Charleston Boulevard on the way to Downtown.

Dedicated bargain hunters may want to make the roughly 40-minute drive along I-15 (there's also a $10 shuttle from New York–New York) to the Fashion Outlet at Primm (✆ **888/424-6898;** www.fashionoutletlasvegas.com), right on the border of California and Nevada. On your left will be a large factory outlet with some designer names prominent enough to make that drive well worthwhile—Kenneth Cole, Donna Karan, even Williams-Sonoma, among several others (p. 276).

Las Vegas Outlet Center You'll save up to 75% off retail prices here, where 130 air-conditioned outlets vie for your cash and credit cards. This bargain shopper's heaven features kids' clothes at Oshkosh B'Gosh, along with offerings from Danskin, Billabong, Liz Claiborne, Perry Ellis, Calvin Klein, Levi's, Nike, Dress Barn, Leggs/Hanes/Bali, Converse, Dickies, Reebok, Jockey, Van Heusen, and Tommy Hilfiger. Housewares and home goods include Bose (electronics), Royal Doulton, Waterford (crystal), and Black & Decker (tools). Children will enjoy the carousel; there is also a food court. Open Monday through Saturday from 10am to 9pm and Sunday from 10am to 8pm. 7400 Las Vegas Blvd. S. (at Warm Springs Rd.). ✆ **702/896-5599.** www.premiumoutlets.com.

Las Vegas Premium Outlets The sister mall to the Las Vegas Outlet Center, this one is more accessible but potentially uncomfortable in the deep of winter and height of summer: It's not enclosed, so you walk from store to store exposed to the elements. You'll save between 20% and 65% at 120 stores, including Armani Exchange, Coach, Dolce & Gabbana, and Polo Ralph Lauren at the high end, and Bass, Levi's, Rave, and Eddie Bauer in the midrange. The food court has both indoor and outdoor munching. Open Monday to Saturday 10am to 9pm, Sunday 10am to 8pm. 875 S. Grand Central Pkwy. (near Charleston). ✆ **702/474-7500.** www.premiumoutlets.com.

Hotel Shopping Promenades

Just about every Las Vegas hotel offers some shopping opportunities. The following have the most extensive areas. The physical spaces of these shopping centers are always open, but individual stores keep unpredictable hours. All hotels have convenience stores, which should be able to provide you with film, batteries, and disposable cameras.

Note: The Forum Shops at Caesars, the Grand Canal Shoppes at The Venetian, and the Miracle Mile Shops at Planet Hollywood—as much sightseeing attractions as shopping opportunities—are in the must-see category.

BALLY'S You can always dispatch the kids to the video arcade while you shop in the Avenue Shoppes, which include several gift shops, art galleries, and a pool-wear shop. The offerings are meager by comparison to other hotel arcades, but the recent addition of a walkway to neighbor Paris Las Vegas has added more stores and restaurants.

BELLAGIO Via Bellagio, in Las Vegas's most notoriously kid-unfriendly hotel, features the most glamorous and expensive collection of stores in any hotel. Armani, Chanel, Prada, Hermès, and Gucci are among the clothiers featured here. Fred Leighton, with its impressive selection of vintage and modern gems, and American standard-bearer Tiffany provide additional sparkle. Children of guests should be accompanied by parents prepared to whip out the platinum card. Otherwise, spend your time shopping someplace fun.

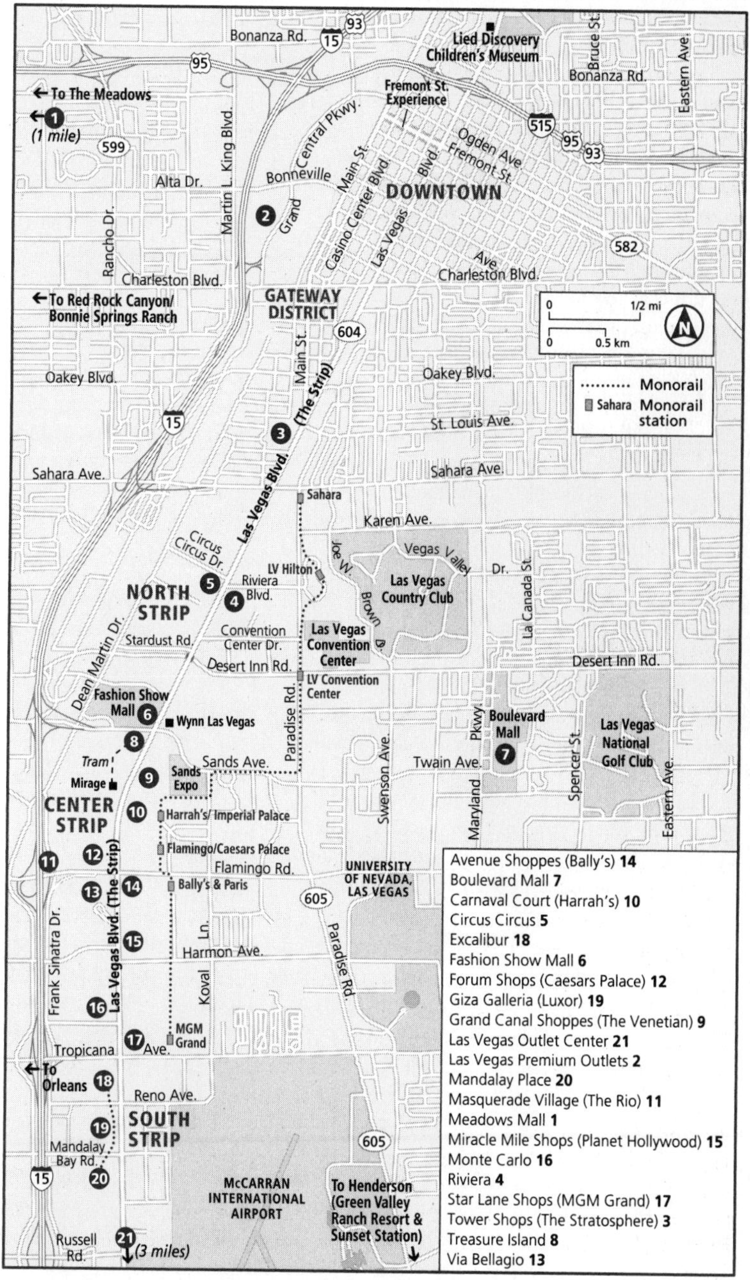
Bonanza Rd.
Lied Discovery Children's Museum
Bonanza Rd.
Bruce St.
Eastern Ave.
To The Meadows
1
(1 mile)
Fremont St. Experience
Central Pkwy.
Martin L. King Blvd.
Ogden Ave
Fremont St.
Alta Dr.
Bonneville
Main St.
Casino Center Blvd.
Las Vegas Blvd.
DOWNTOWN
2
Grand
Rancho Dr.
Charleston Blvd.
Charleston Blvd.
Ave
To Red Rock Canyon/ Bonnie Springs Ranch
GATEWAY DISTRICT
0 1/2 mi
0 0.5 km
N
Main St.
Oakey Blvd.
Oakey Blvd.
Monorail
Sahara Monorail station
3
Las Vegas Blvd. (The Strip)
St. Louis Ave.
Sahara Ave.
Sahara Ave.
Sahara
Karen Ave.
Circus Circus Dr.
Joe W. Brown Dr.
Vegas Valley Dr.
LV Hilton
Riviera Blvd.
5
4
Las Vegas Country Club
NORTH STRIP
La Canada St.
Dean Martin Dr.
Stardust Rd.
Convention Center Dr.
Las Vegas Convention Center
Desert Inn Rd.
Desert Inn Rd.
LV Convention Center
Fashion Show Mall 6
Wynn Las Vegas
Paradise Rd.
Pkwy
Boulevard Mall
Las Vegas National Golf Club
8
Tram
Sands Ave.
Swenson Ave.
Twain Ave.
7
Mirage
9
Sands Expo
Maryland
Spencer St.
Eastern Ave.
CENTER STRIP
10
Harrah's/ Imperial Palace
Flamingo/Caesars Palace
11
12
Flamingo Rd.
UNIVERSITY OF NEVADA, LAS VEGAS
13
14
Bally's & Paris
Las Vegas Blvd. (The Strip)
Frank Sinatra Dr.
15
Harmon Ave.
Koval Ln.
Paradise Rd.
16
17
Ave.
MGM Grand
Tropicana
To Orleans
18
Reno Ave.
19
SOUTH STRIP
Mandalay Bay Rd.
20
McCARRAN INTERNATIONAL AIRPORT
To Henderson (Green Valley Ranch Resort & Sunset Station)
Russell Rd.
21
(3 miles)
Avenue Shoppes (Bally's) 14
Boulevard Mall 7
Carnaval Court (Harrah's) 10
Circus Circus 5
Excalibur 18
Fashion Show Mall 6
Forum Shops (Caesars Palace) 12
Giza Galleria (Luxor) 19
Grand Canal Shoppes (The Venetian) 9
Las Vegas Outlet Center 21
Las Vegas Premium Outlets 2
Mandalay Place 20
Masquerade Village (The Rio) 11
Meadows Mall 1
Miracle Mile Shops (Planet Hollywood) 15
Monte Carlo 16
Riviera 4
Star Lane Shops (MGM Grand) 17
Tower Shops (The Stratosphere) 3
Treasure Island 8
Via Bellagio 13

CAESARS PALACE Even if you don't like to shop, Caesars Palace's shopping areas are a must-see. The Appian Way, an impressive selection of shops, is highlighted by an 18-foot-high Carrara-marble replica of Michelangelo's *David.* But the real draw is the fabulous **Forum Shops ★**. Independently operated, this 250,000-square-foot Rodeo-Drive-meets-the-Roman-Empire affair overwhelms visitors who enter through a 48-foot triumphal arch entryway. Beneath the painted Mediterranean sky that changes as the day progresses from rosy-tinted dawn to twinkling evening stars, you'll find acres of marble, lofty Corinthian columns with gold capitals, and a welcoming goddess of fortune under a central dome. The architecture and sculpture here span a period from 300 B.C. to A.D. 1700, framing 70 prestigious emporia including Louis Vuitton, Christian Dior, Armani Exchange, bebe, Gucci, Ann Taylor, and Gianni Versace, along with many other clothing, shoe, and jewelry stores. Every hour on the hour, the Festival Fountain show commences, when seemingly immovable "marble" animatronic statues of Bacchus (a bit tipsy), a lyre-playing Apollo, Pluto, and Venus come to life for a 7-minute revel with dancing waters and high-tech laser effects.

Hey, Big Spenders!

This is the perfect vacation. My husband likes to gamble; we like to shop. And trust me, my daughters and I can do more damage in an hour at a Vegas mall than he can in an hour on the tables!

—Laura, mother of 13- and 16-year-old girls

In 1998, the Forum Shops added an extension. The centerpiece is a giant Roman Hall, featuring a 50,000-gallon circular aquarium and another fountain that also comes to life with a show of fire (don't stand too close—it gets really hot), dancing waters, and animatronic figures as the mythical continent of Atlantis rises and falls every hour.

In this shopping area, you'll find a number of stores for adults, including a DKNY, Emporio Armani, Niketown, Fendi, and Guess. Kids' Castle stocks clothes for the wee ones. Also in the shops are Wolfgang Puck's Chinois (p. 156) and the Cheesecake Factory (p. 155).

The latest expansion debuted in 2004: Another 175,000 square feet of space between the existing building and the Strip, featuring a three-story open courtyard.

The shops at Caesars are open Sunday to Thursday from 10am to 11pm and Friday and Saturday from 10am to midnight. Strollers and wheelchairs are available, free of charge.

CIRCUS CIRCUS Between the casino and Adventuredome (p. 180), about 15 shops offer a wide selection of gifts and sundries, logo items, toys and games, jewelry, liquor, resort apparel for the entire family, T-shirts, homemade fudge/candy/soft ice cream, and, appropriately, clown dolls and puppets. The newer shopping arcade, adjacent to the Adventuredome, is themed as a European village with cobblestone walkways and fake woods, decorated with replicas of vintage circus posters.

EXCALIBUR Kids will enjoy shopping for plastic swords, the perfect accessory for horned Viking hats and princess crowns also available in the shops of the Realm. Dragon's Lair features items ranging from pewter swords and shields to full suits of armor. Merlin's Mystic Shop carries crystals, luck charms, and gargoyles. Other shops carry more conventional wares: gifts, candy, jewelry, women's clothing, and Excalibur logo items. At Fantasy Faire, you can have your photo taken in Renaissance attire. And, most important, they have a branch of Krispy Kreme Doughnuts!

HARRAH'S Harrah's has an outdoor shopping center called Carnaval Court with a bandstand and a bar. It's small and crowded, especially when a band is playing and the margaritas are flowing. The highlight is a Ghirardelli Chocolate store, a branch of the famous San Francisco–based chocolate company.

LUXOR The Giza Galleria is a 20,000-square-foot shopping arcade with eight full shops, including the kids' shop Tiny Tuts, a tie and sock shop, plus a metaphysical gimcracks shop, a place to purchase logo items (your name in hieroglyphics on mugs and T-shirts), and more. Adjacent to the Giza Galleria is the Cairo Bazaar with plenty of Egyptian-themed statuary, jewelry, and knickknacks.

MANDALAY BAY Mandalay Place is a small boutique mall in an expansion of Mandalay Bay on a sky bridge between Mandalay Bay and Luxor. Its 100,000 square feet house 40 or so shops, including 55 Degrees, a wine shop; Nike Golf; Oilily, an interesting children's store from Holland; Chocolate Swan; and the Burger Bar, which serves a $60 Kobe beef and foie gras hamburger.

MGM GRAND You can still find the semibanished figures from the hotel's original *Wizard of Oz* diorama along Star Lane Shops, more than a dozen upscale emporia, which line the corridors en route from the parking garage. Studio Walk is another shopping area, adjacent to the main casino, which features some upscale boutiques, souvenir shops, and several restaurants.

MONTE CARLO RESORT & CASINO An arcade of retail shops here includes several upscale clothing, timepiece, eyewear, and gift boutiques plus a Lance Burton magic paraphernalia shop, and Bijoux Terner $10 Boutique, where all items are $10 or less.

PLANET HOLLYWOOD The stores in the Miracle Mile Shops—over a street scene reminiscent of Rodeo Drive—are an assortment of the usual-suspect mid- and high-end name brands, including Sur La Table, a cookware and kitchen supply boutique—no doubt for those who have just hit the jackpot and would rather buy expensive enamel pots and ceramic knives instead of expensive jewelry. Desert Brats has clothes for kids, which are far more charming than the store's name.

THE RIO The 60,000-square-foot, two-story Masquerade Village is done up as a European village. It features a wide variety of shops, including Hippy Chic for tie-dyed clothing and retro stuff and the N'awlins store, which includes "authentic" voodoo items, Mardi Gras masks, and so forth.

THE RIVIERA The Riviera has a fairly extensive shopping arcade comprising art galleries, jewelers, a creative photographer, and shops specializing in women's shoes and handbags, clothing for the entire family, furs, gifts, logo items, toys, phones and electronic gadgets, and chocolates.

THE STRATOSPHERE The internationally themed second-floor Tower Shops promenade, housing more than 50 stores, is entered via an escalator from the casino. Some shops are in "Paris," along the Rue Lafayette and Avenue de l'Opéra (there are replicas of the Eiffel Tower and Arc de Triomphe in this section), while others occupy Hong Kong and New York City streetscapes. It's fine for shopping if you are staying there, but pales by comparison to Caesars, The Venetian, Paris Las Vegas, and Planet Hollywood.

TREASURE ISLAND The Treasure Island Store, a basic hotel gift/sundry shop, also offers a good amount of pirate-themed merchandise, including some cool skull stuff, which kids may like. Fans of Cirque du Soleil will find their logo items at the Crow's

Nest, en route to the Mirage monorail, and also in a shop near the ticket office. TI also has a pedestrian bridge to the Fashion Show, adding 200 more shops to the mix.

THE VENETIAN ★ Directly accessible from the outside, so you can avoid the casino and other hotel distractions, the Grand Canal Shoppes are a direct challenge to Caesars' shopping eminence. You'll find the usual high- and medium-end brand names: Mikimoto, Movado, Rockport, Davidoff, Marshall Russo, Lior, Caché, Kenneth Cole, Ann Taylor, BCBG, bebe, Banana Republic, a Blue Man Group shop, and more, plus Venetian glass and papermakers under a painted, cloud-studded blue sky. As you stroll through Renaissance-era Venice, gondoliers float by and sing. If you pay them (p. 176), you can take the lazy ride down and back, serenaded by your gondolier, who has perfected his Italian accent to ensure your illusion remains in place. Along the way, actors pose as living statues. The stroll (or float) ends at a miniature (though not by all that much) version of St. Mark's Square, the central landmark of Venice. Here, you'll find opera singers, strolling musicians, glass blowers, and other bustling marketplace activity. The Venetian's "Phase Two" hotel addition, the Venezia Tower, opened in late 2003 and adjoins the Canal Shoppes at the far end of St. Mark's Square.

WYNN LAS VEGAS The Wynn Esplanade at Wynn Las Vegas is a *trés chic et trés* dear lineup of upscale shops and boutiques including Brioni, Oscar de la Renta, Graff, Jean Paul Gaultier, and Manolo Blahnik. The only stop your kids will enjoy is the Penske-Wynn Ferrari Maserati dealership, but you must pay admission to walk through the door and the salesmen break out in hives if a child gets within 20 feet of a car. A Ferrari merchandise store, however, lurks next door with model toy Ferraris that go for about what you paid for your car at home.

2 SHOPPING A–Z

We've tried to keep you as close to the Strip as possible with these shops, but for some items, you may need to venture further afield. For stores with multiple locations, we've listed those nearest the Strip.

ANTIQUES & COLLECTIBLES

Academy Fine Books and Antiques These shops, arranged in a square, are nothing much to look at, but inside, if you have the patience, you'll find some treasures; kids who have an interest in cool old stuff will enjoy looking at, well, cool old stuff. Individual store hours vary, but most are closed on Sunday and Monday. 2014–2034 Charleston (at Eastern Ave.). ✆ **702/471-6500.**

Antiques at the Market This is another group of antiques shops lurking in mini-mall formation. The market consists of a number of individuals operating stalls under one roof, each with his or her own specialty, though, at times, some stalls look more like gussied-up garage sales. If your family enjoys rummaging around for treasures, oddities, or just something unique, you might get lucky here. Open Monday through Saturday from 10am until 6pm, Sunday from noon until 5pm. 6663 S. Eastern Ave. (btw. Sunset and Warm Springs roads). ✆ **702/307-3960.**

Red Rooster Antique Mall Individual stalls fill this mall, which sometimes offers real finds for collectors of all ages. Individual store hours vary. 307 W. Charleston Blvd. (at I-15). ✆ **702/382-5253.**

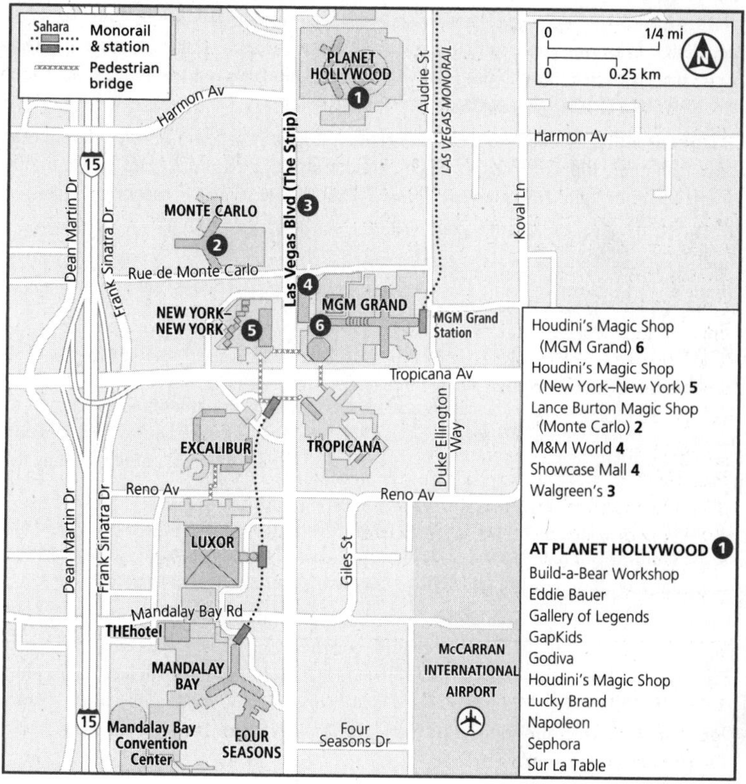

ARTS & CRAFTS

Jo-Ann Whether its beading, sewing, decoupage, or any other number of arts and crafts, Jo-Ann has the supplies you'll need, plus a helpful staff to guide you. Open Monday through Saturday from 9am to 9pm and Sunday 10am until 7pm. 4628 W. Sahara Ave. ✆ **702/878-9549.** www.joann.com.

BABY & PRESCHOOLER CLOTHES & ITEMS

Along Came a Spider This store features name-brand children's clothing, such as Diesel and Juicy. You can find some toys and accessories here as well. Open Monday through Friday from 10am until 9pm, Saturday from 10am to 8pm, and Sunday from 11am until 6pm. Fashion Show Mall, 3200 Las Vegas Blvd. S. ✆ **702/735-2728.**

Babies "R" Us The name says it all. Clothes, toys, strollers, car seats, furniture, disposable diapers, cribs—everything you'll need for babies and toddlers at this branch of the nationwide chain. Open Monday through Saturday from 9:30am until 9:30pm, and Sunday from 11am to 7pm. 2150 N. Rainbow Blvd. ✆ **702/647-8514.** www.babiesrus.com.

BOOKS

Albion Books Value Six thousand square feet of used books, including first editions, vintage children's books, pop and sci-fi, pulp fiction, and bestsellers, both hard and paperback. You're welcome to take a seat and browse through your finds before purchasing. Open Monday through Saturday 10am-6pm, Sunday noon to 6pm. 2466 E. Desert Inn Rd. ✆ **800/485-1864.** www.abebooks.com/home/albionbco.

Barnes & Noble Books on every subject for all ages, plus bestsellers are offered at this branch of the nationwide chain. Open Monday through Saturday, 9am to 10pm, and Sunday 9am to 9pm. 3860 Maryland Pkwy. ✆ **702/734-2900.** www.barnesandnoble.com.

B. Dalton This nationwide chain sells a wide selection of books on all subjects. It stocks bestsellers and has a large children's section. Open Monday through Friday from 10am to 9pm, Saturday from 10am to 8pm, and Sunday from 11am to 6pm. 3680 S. Maryland Pkwy. ✆ **702/735-0008.**

Bell Book & Candle Finds This musty, dusty shop, a Las Vegas landmark, stocks books on witchcraft, along with herbs, expensive aromatherapy oils, and candles. Kids who are into this sort of stuff will appreciate the spooky vibes; atheists, skeptics, and the religiously strict will not. We found the free "lucky beans" improved our wins at the slots; maybe they help with math tests, too! Open daily 11am to 7pm. 1725 E. Charleston Blvd. ✆ **702/386-2950.** www.lasvegasbbc.com.

Borders Along with a huge selection of books and magazines for all ages, this branch of the nationwide chain also has a decent cafe. Open Monday through Saturday 9am to 11pm, Sunday 9am to 9pm. 2323 S. Decatur Blvd. ✆ **702/258-0999.** www.borders.com.

Borders Express Waldenbooks, located in the Fashion Show Mall, is the only bookstore on the Strip. This national chain—bought out by and replaced with Borders Express—has books for all ages; you'll find a large selection of all subjects here, plus a children's section as well as bestsellers. Open Monday through Saturday from 10am to 9pm, and Sunday from noon until 6pm. The Fashion Show Mall, 3200 Las Vegas Blvd. S. ✆ **702/733-1049.** www.borders.com.

Dead Poet Books Finds The owners of this used bookstore wanted to name the store after the man from whose estate they bought their start-up stock, but they never did get his name, so they just called him the "dead poet." The unknown gentleman's good taste in books lives on at this store, a book lover's haven, with a large selection for children and young adults. This place is a good, low-cost way to start a young book-lover's library. Open daily from 10am to 6pm. 937 S. Rainbow Blvd. ✆ **702/227-4070.**

Learning Is Fun Teachers and parents will find books, toys, learning games, and supplies—including posters, bulletin boards, paints, and paper—to help expand their children's minds and skills. It's a perfect place to load up before a long road trip. Open Monday through Friday from 10am to 7pm, Saturday from 10am until 6pm, and Sunday from noon until 5pm. 204 S. Decatur Blvd. ✆ **702/258-5437.**

Psychic Eye More a metaphysical minimall than a bookshop, you'll find crystals, T-shirts, candles, and tabletop fountains along with actual reading material here, making this a good stop for children into glittery gewgaws, crystals, and Indian-print fabrics, as well as the more mystical in books. All three branches keep the same hours; Monday through Saturday 10am to 9pm, Sunday 11am to 6pm. 4500 E. Sunset Rd. ✆ **702/451-5777.** 6848 W. Charleston Blvd. ✆ **702/255-4477.** 2755 S. Nellis Blvd. ✆ **702/432-4666.** www.pebooks.com.

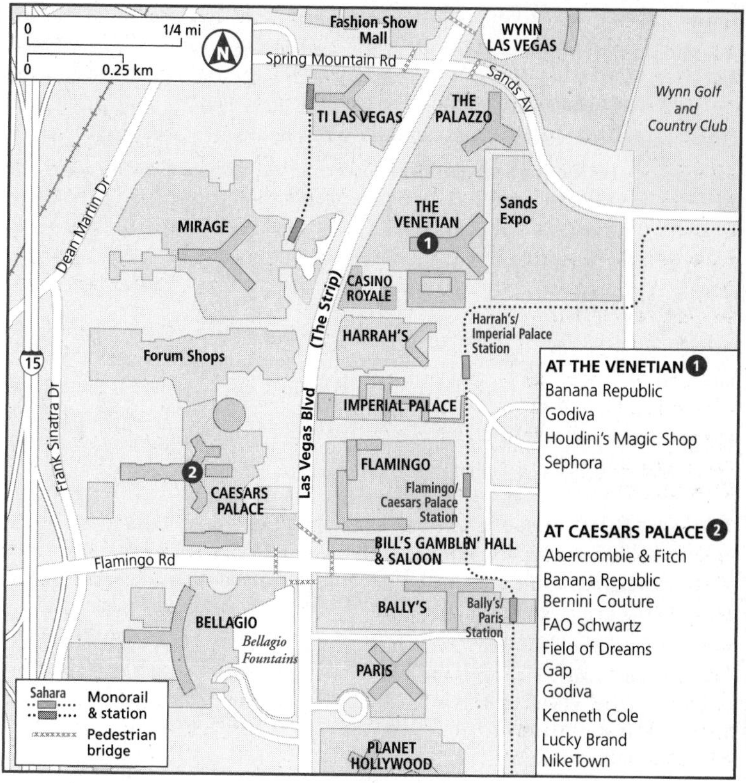

CANDY, CHOCOLATE & SWEETS

Godiva Sinful, rich, decadent chocolates in gleaming gold boxes, the perfect pick-me-up after a hard day shopping. All casino locations are open Sunday through Thursday from 10am to 11pm, Friday and Saturday from 10am until midnight. In Caesars Palace, 3570 Las Vegas Blvd. S. ✆ **702/734-8855.** Miracle Mile Shops, 3667 Las Vegas Blvd. S. ✆ **702/731-6798.** The Venetian, 3377 Las Vegas Blvd. S. ✆ **702/732-1577.** The Fashion Show Mall, 3200 Las Vegas Blvd. S. ✆ **702/369-5832.** www.godiva.com.

M&Ms World The sheer volume of chocolate overwhelms here; along with candy (Mars products, all shades of M&Ms, and the upscale boxed Ethel M. brand), you can purchase M&M-themed pajamas, T-shirts, mugs, and other souvenirs. You can also see a 3-D movie starring the M&Ms. Open Sunday through Thursday from 9am to 11pm, Friday and Saturday from 9am to midnight. In the Showcase Mall, 3785 Las Vegas Blvd. S. ✆ **702/736-7611.**

COMICS

Alternate Reality Comics This is the place in Vegas for all your comic book needs. They have a nearly comprehensive selection, with a heavy emphasis on the underground comics. But don't worry—the superheroes are here, too. Open Sunday through Tuesday from noon until 6pm and Wednesday through Saturday from 11am to 7pm. 4800 S. Maryland Pkwy. ✆ **702/736-3673.**

Cosmic Comics Superheroes share shelf space with the antiheroes of underground and alternative comics providing local kids—and grown-ups—an escape from the omnipresent desert environment into fantasy. Open daily from 11am to 7pm. 3330 E. Tropicana Ave. ✆ **702/451-6611.** http://jbrocius.home.mindspring.com.

Silver Cactus Comics About 10 minutes from the Strip, this well-stocked shop features rare collectible comics, current issues, and hard-to-find action figures. (Never, never call them dolls!) Open Monday through Saturday from 11am until 8pm, Sunday 11am to 6pm. 480 N. Nellis Blvd. ✆ **702/438-4408.** www.silvercactuscomics.com.

COOKWARE

Sur la Table If you or your honey wins big and you've been craving a duck press, a lemon peeler, or a complete set of matching stainless steel pots and pans, this is the place. Aprons, potholders, seasonal cookie cutters, coffee mugs, plus kid-oriented gear and baking kits can also be found here. Open Sunday through Thursday from 10am to 11pm, Friday and Saturday from 10am until midnight. Aladdin/Planet Hollywood, Miracle Mile Shops, 3663 Las Vegas Blvd. S. ✆ **702/732-2706.** www.surlatable.com.

COSMETICS

Sephora This branch of the famous chain has any color of nail polish you can imagine, every color of lipstick you could desire, and much more. Teen and 'tween girls will go nuts here. Indulge them with the store's own brand, which comes in small trial sizes, or load up on the cutting-edge colors from the likes of Urban Decay and Benefit. Fans of Chanel products should try Bourjois, a French company that is astoundingly similar in quality, yet far less expensive. For the younger, pre-makeup set, there are cool hair clips, headbands, and ponytail holders. The spa and body care kits—perfect for slumber parties or as birthday gifts—can keep girls (and women) of all ages busy in their hotel room. Both stores are open Sunday through Thursday from 10am until 11pm, and Friday and Saturday from 10am until midnight. Miracle Mile Shops, 3663 Las Vegas Blvd. S. ✆ **702/737-0550.** The Venetian, 3377 Las Vegas Blvd. S. ✆ **702/735-3896.** www.sephora.com.

COSTUMES

Halloween Mart Finds A favorite with local Goths, it's Halloween 365 days of the year at this warehouse full of costumes and masks for all ages, plus props and all your haunted house needs. Other holidays don't get the short shroud, uh, shrift, here, either. They also stock Christmas lights, Santa suits, Easter bunny outfits, and more. Open Monday through Friday from 9am to 6pm, Saturday from 10am to 4pm. 6230 S. Decatur Blvd. ✆ **702/740-4224.**

Party City Every day is a party at Party City, which features costumes at Halloween, plus all the things you'll need for a baby shower, birthday party, or even a Tiki-themed party. Open Monday through Friday from 9am until 9pm, Saturday from 8:30am until 9pm, and Sunday from 10am until 6pm. 4020 Maryland Pkwy. ✆ **702/893-4600.**

Serge's Showgirl Wigs Both this shop and the less pricey Serge's Wig Outlet, across the way, offer an astounding array of hirsute replicas, ranging from the elaborate to the subtle. This is where showgirls get their glossy locks. Serge's can also make custom wigs and toupees and carries hair-care products. Children are welcome at both stores, though

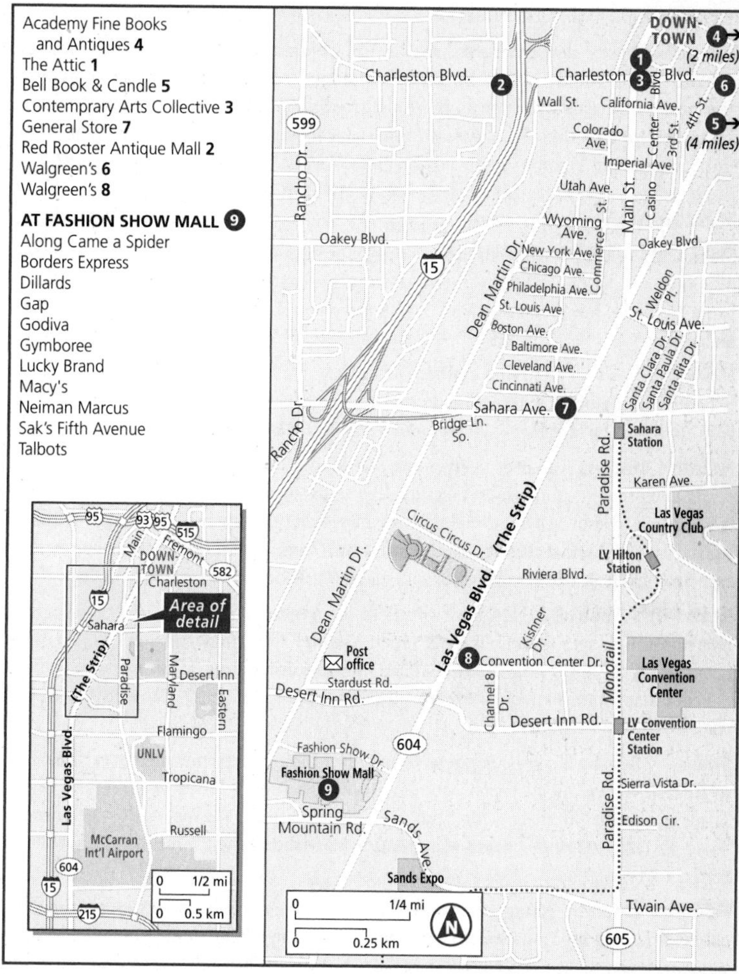

they may enjoy seeing (and trying out) the more colorful, goofier wigs at the outlet rather than the towering showgirl versions. Open Monday through Saturday, from 10am until 6pm. 953 E. Sahara Ave. ✆ **702/732-1015.** www.showgirlwigs.com.

DEPARTMENT STORES

Dillard's You'll find apparel for the entire family plus shoes, accessories, and more at this stolid retailer. All locations are open Monday through Saturday from 10am to 9pm and Sunday from noon until 6pm. Fashion Show Mall, 3200 Las Vegas Blvd. S. ✆ **702/733-2008.** The Meadows, 4200 Meadows Lane. ✆ **702/870-2039.** Boulevard Mall, 3700 S. Maryland Pkwy. ✆ **702/734-2111.** www.dillards.com.

Kmart This retailer (which can get pretty crowded on weekends) offers inexpensive clothing for the whole family, along with household items and small appliances. Open daily 8am until 10pm. 2975 E Sahara Ave. ✆ **702/457-1037.** www.kmart.com.

Macy's Quality clothes for teens, adults, and children, along with china, sheets, towels, and other household goods from this New York–based retailer. The latest fashions, top designers, and classic styles can all be found here. All locations are open Monday through Thursday from 10am to 9pm, Friday from 10am to 10pm, Saturday from 10am to 9pm, and Sunday from 11am to 7pm. Fashion Show Mall, 3200 Las Vegas Blvd. S. ✆ **702/731-5111.** The Meadows, 4100 Meadows Lane. ✆ **702/258-2100.** The Boulevard, 3634 S. Maryland Pkwy. ✆ **702/791-2100.** www.macys.com.

Marshalls Adult and children's clothing, plus housewares, are sold at this nationwide discount store. Open Monday through Saturday from 9:30am to 9:30pm and Sunday from 11am to 7pm. Boulevard Mall, 3740 S. Maryland Pkwy. ✆ **702/737-1117.** www.marshalls online.com.

Mervyn's All ages will find clothes and housewares at reasonable prices at this nationwide discount store. Open Monday through Saturday from 9am to 10pm and Sunday 9am to 9pm. The Meadows, 4700 Meadows Lane. ✆ **702/870-9000.**

Neiman Marcus Expect to find one-of-a-kind pieces of jewelry to accessorize your designer clothes at this high-end retailer. Expect to swoon over the shoes. Teens who love to shop will be especially enthralled by the high fashions. Open Monday through Friday from 10am to 8pm, Saturday from 10am until 7pm, and Sunday from noon to 6pm. Fashion Show Mall, 3200 Las Vegas Blvd. S. ✆ **702/731-3636.** www.neimanmarcus.com.

Saks Fifth Avenue New York comes to Las Vegas; you'll find a large and high-end selection for all ages and tastes here. Open Monday through Wednesday from 10am to 8pm, Thursday and Friday from 10am to 9pm, Saturday from 10am to 7pm, and Sunday noon to 6pm. Fashion Show Mall, 3200 Las Vegas Blvd. S. ✆ **702/733-8300.** www.saks.com.

Sears They stock everything here, from power tools to perfume, dresses to drills, boots to lingerie—bless them! Open Monday through Saturday 10am to 9pm, and Sunday 10am to 7pm (to 6pm Sun for Boulevard Mall location). The Meadows, 4000 Meadows Lane. ✆ **702/259-4200.** Boulevard Mall, 3450 S. Maryland Pkwy. ✆ **702/894-4200.** www.sears.com.

Target Loved by young and old alike, this discount retailer stocks everything, from cool clothes and hip housewares (including goods designed by Phillipe Starck) to cans of bug spray and boxes of detergent. Open Monday through Saturday from 8am until 10pm and Sunday 8am to 9pm. 4001 S. Maryland Pkwy. ✆ **702/732-2218.** www.target.com.

T. J. Maxx This is where clothes and housewares go for discounting; you'll find some buys here for everyone. Open 9:30am to 9:30pm Monday through Saturday, Sunday 11am to 6pm. 4000 S. Maryland Pkwy. ✆ **702/733-7730.** www.tjmaxx.com.

Walmart If you need it, they probably have it—and at low prices. Open daily, 24 hours. 3075 E. Tropicana Ave. ✆ **702/451-8900.** www.walmart.com.

DRUGSTORES

Sav-On Over-the-counter medications, cosmetics, baby needs, and more, along with a pharmacy. Store open daily from 7am to 10pm. Pharmacy open Monday through Friday from 8am to 9pm, Saturday 9am to 5pm, and Sunday from 10am to 5pm. 1360 E. Flamingo Rd. ✆ **702/731-5373.** www.savon.com.

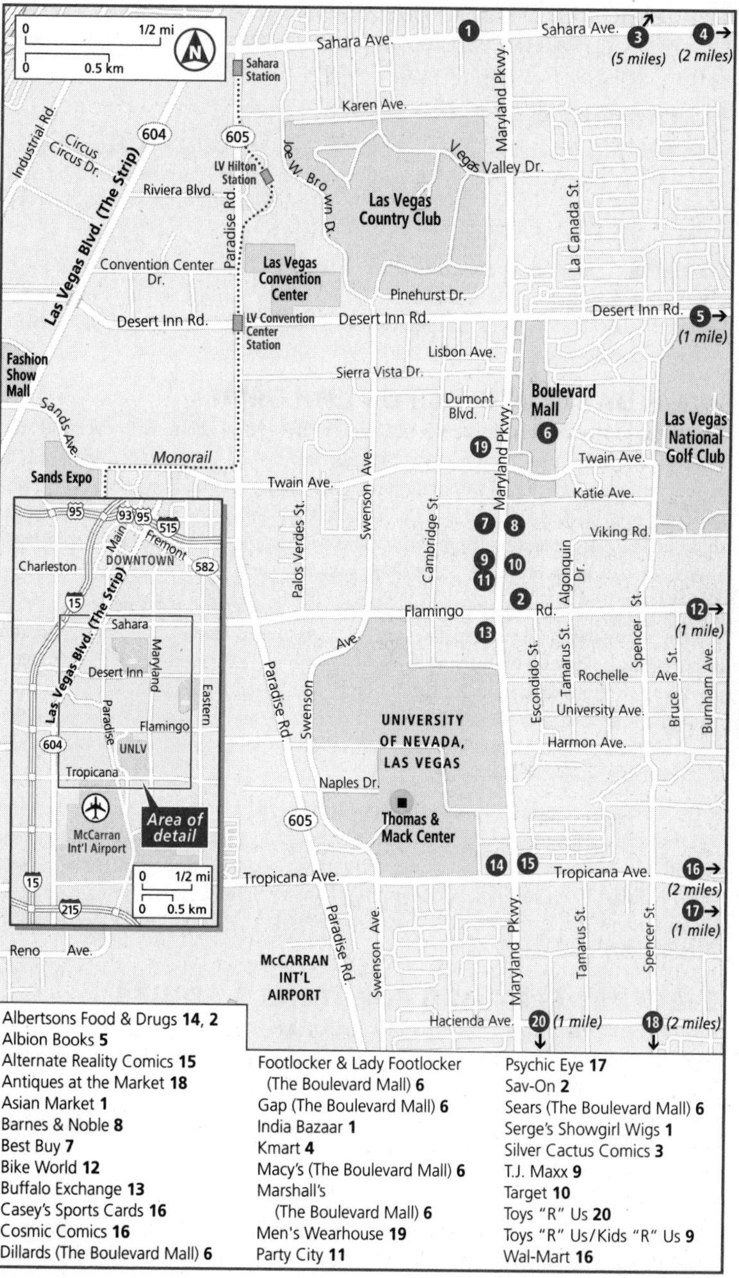

Albertsons Food & Drugs **14**, **2**
Albion Books **5**
Alternate Reality Comics **15**
Antiques at the Market **18**
Asian Market **1**
Barnes & Noble **8**
Best Buy **7**
Bike World **12**
Buffalo Exchange **13**
Casey's Sports Cards **16**
Cosmic Comics **16**
Dillards (The Boulevard Mall) **6**
Footlocker & Lady Footlocker (The Boulevard Mall) **6**
Gap (The Boulevard Mall) **6**
India Bazaar **1**
Kmart **4**
Macy's (The Boulevard Mall) **6**
Marshall's (The Boulevard Mall) **6**
Men's Wearhouse **19**
Party City **11**
Psychic Eye **17**
Sav-On **2**
Sears (The Boulevard Mall) **6**
Serge's Showgirl Wigs **1**
Silver Cactus Comics **3**
T.J. Maxx **9**
Target **10**
Toys "R" Us **20**
Toys "R" Us/Kids "R" Us **9**
Wal-Mart **16**

Walgreens Convenient locations open 24 hours, with pharmacies open round-the-clock, and pharmacists on staff throughout the day and night. Well stocked for baby needs, cosmetics, over-the-counter medications, and much more. We love it. 3025 Las Vegas Blvd. S. ✆ **702/836-0818.** 3765 Las Vegas Blvd. S. ✆ **702/739-9638.** 1101 Las Vegas Blvd. S. ✆ **702/471-6840.** 4905 W. Tropicana Ave. ✆ **702/889-0911.** www.walgreens.com.

ELECTRONICS

Best Buy If you can plug it in, they have it, along with cellphones, cameras, games, CDs, DVDs, and more. Open Monday through Thursday 10am to 9pm, Friday and Saturday from 10am to 10pm, and Sunday from 10am until 7pm. 3820 S. Maryland Pkwy. ✆ **702/732-8283.** www.bestbuy.com.

CompUSA Home and personal electronics, including rows of televisions, videos and DVD players, cellphones, and cameras. Open Monday through Friday from 10am to 9pm, Saturday 10am to 7pm, and Sunday 10am to 6pm. 3535 W. Sahara Ave. ✆ **702/252-0149.** www.compusa.com.

EVERYDAY CLOTHING FOR CHILDREN

GapKids Cute and classic are the key notes of this global chain, with over 500 stores worldwide. Jeans, shirts, dresses, skirts, and accessories—all your kid-clothing needs can be met easily here. Designed with both form and function in mind, the clothes here won't fall apart even if they fall out of style. The staff is helpful and patient. Open Sunday through Thursday 10am to 10pm, Friday and Saturday 10am to midnight. Miracle Mile Shops, 3663 Las Vegas Blvd. S. ✆ **702/862-4042.** www.gap.com.

Gymboree This chain store stocks sturdy play clothes for toddlers to age 7. The stretchy solids and patterned separates are designed to mix, match, coordinate, and, most importantly, hold up. The Fashion Show Mall location is open Monday through Saturday 10am to 9pm, and Sunday 11am to 6pm. The Meadows location is open Monday through Friday 10am to 9pm, Saturday 10am to 8pm, and Sunday 11am to 6pm. Fashion Show Mall, 3200 Las Vegas Blvd. S. ✆ **702/369-8909.** The Meadows, 4300 Meadows Lane. ✆ **702/880-4228.** www.gymboree.com.

Kids "R" Us Located in the same building as Toys "R" Us (p. 225), next to the Meadows mall, this vast nationwide chain store sells shoes and clothes, both casual and formal, for toddlers on up to age 12-ish, along with some cribs and a small selection of car seats. Open Sunday 10am to 7pm, Monday from 9am to 9pm, Tuesday through Thursday 10am to 9pm, Friday 10am to 10pm, Saturday 9am to 10pm. 4550 Meadows Lane. ✆ **702/877-9070.** www.kidsrus.com.

EVERYDAY CLOTHING FOR TEENS & ADULTS

Abercrombie & Fitch This national retailer has caught a lot of flack for its racy catalogs and its unpleasant, inappropriate thong underwear for 7-year-olds. That aside, A&F stocks Ts, jeans, skirts, and shirts that are comfy and low-key, many of which are emblazoned with their logo. Both locations open Sunday through Thursday 10am to 11pm, Friday and Saturday from 10am until midnight. Caesars Palace, 3500 Las Vegas Blvd. S. ✆ **702/731-0712.** www.abercrombie.com.

Banana Republic Banana Republic's clothes feature classic lines, but with a fashionable edge for both men and women, including slacks, sweaters, shirts, and skirts in the latest shades and fabrics. Sizes favor the lean; girls and women over size 12 may be disappointed to find few items that work for them, aside from scarves and hats. Open Sunday

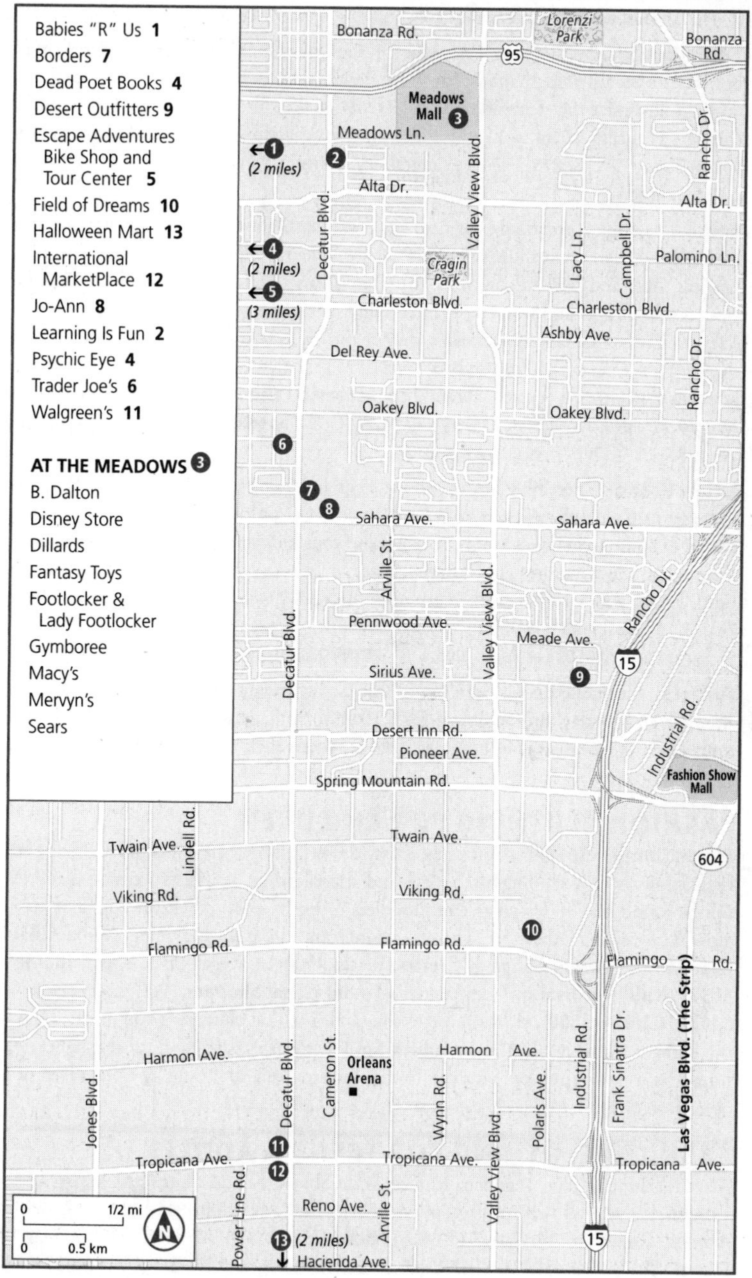
Babies "R" Us 1
Borders 7
Dead Poet Books 4
Desert Outfitters 9
Escape Adventures Bike Shop and Tour Center 5
Field of Dreams 10
Halloween Mart 13
International MarketPlace 12
Jo-Ann 8
Learning Is Fun 2
Psychic Eye 4
Trader Joe's 6
Walgreen's 11
AT THE MEADOWS 3
B. Dalton
Disney Store
Dillards
Fantasy Toys
Footlocker & Lady Footlocker
Gymboree
Macy's
Mervyn's
Sears
Bonanza Rd.
Lorenzi Park
95
Meadows Mall
Meadows Ln.
(2 miles)
(2 miles)
(3 miles)
Alta Dr.
Decatur Blvd.
Valley View Blvd.
Rancho Dr.
Cragin Park
Lacy Ln.
Campbell Dr.
Palomino Ln.
Charleston Blvd.
Ashby Ave.
Del Rey Ave.
Oakey Blvd.
Sahara Ave.
Arville St.
Pennwood Ave.
Meade Ave.
Sirius Ave.
15
Desert Inn Rd.
Pioneer Ave.
Industrial Rd.
Fashion Show Mall
Spring Mountain Rd.
Twain Ave.
Lindell Rd.
604
Viking Rd.
Flamingo Rd.
Harmon Ave.
Orleans Arena
Cameron St.
Wynn Rd.
Polaris Ave.
Frank Sinatra Dr.
Las Vegas Blvd. (The Strip)
Jones Blvd.
Tropicana Ave.
Power Line Rd.
Reno Ave.
Hacienda Ave.
0 1/2 mi
0 0.5 km
N

through Thursday 10am to 11pm, Friday and Saturday from 10am until midnight. Caesars Palace, 3500 Las Vegas Blvd. S. ✆ **702/650-5623.** The Venetian, 3377 Las Vegas Blvd. S. ✆ **702/733-1566.** www.bananarepublic.com.

Eddie Bauer By shopping here, you can look outdoorsy and never leave the house, but the clothes are more than just for show; designed for outdoors men and women, they do hold up under the elements. The colors are low-key, the styles classic. Open Sunday through Thursday 10am to 11pm, Friday and Saturday from 10am until midnight. Premium Outlets Shops, 875 S. Grand Central Pkwy. (near Charleston). ✆ **702/387-5557.** www.eddiebauer.com.

Gap The original standard-bearer for egalitarian fashion is allegedly moving away from their brief dalliance with low-rise pants cut for scrawny, hipless waifs paired with belly-bearing tops, and back (thankfully) to its bread and butter—some of which includes clothes that fit girls and women over size 8 and men's fashions for a variety of shapes and sizes. As always, the Gap stocks jeans, khakis, and Ts, as well as basics in the latest fashion shades, plus accessories. For hours of each of Vegas's five Gap branches, check the mall hours in which they're located. Forum Shops at Caesars Palace, 3500 Las Vegas Blvd. S. ✆ **702/737-1550.** Boulevard Mall, 3580 S. Maryland Pkwy. ✆ **702/734-6620.** Fashion Show Mall, 3200 Las Vegas Blvd. S. ✆ **702/796-0010.** www.gap.com.

Lucky Brand Incredibly hip, expensive jeans and T-shirts let your teens tell the world that you care enough to spend your hard-earned cash on their trends. The lining inside the fly of some styles reads LUCKY YOU. Maybe your kids should wait until they're 18 for these. Open Sunday through Thursday 10am to 11pm (9pm at the Fashion Show location), Friday and Saturday from 10am until midnight. Miracle Mile Shops, 3663 Las Vegas Blvd. S. ✆ **702/733-6613.** Fashion Show Mall, 3200 Las Vegas Blvd. S. ✆ **702/369-4116.** Forum Shops at Caesars, 3500 Las Vegas Blvd. S. ✆ **702/369-2536.** www.luckybrandjeans.com.

Talbots Restrained good taste in an East Coast preppy style is the hallmark of this store. Open Monday through Friday from 10am to 9pm, Saturday 10am to 8pm, Sunday from 11am to 6pm. Fashion Show Mall, 3200 Las Vegas Blvd. S. ✆ **702/893-1706.** www.talbots.com.

FASHION CLOTHING FOR CHILDREN

Along Came a Spider Suits, ties, dressy dresses, along with miniature versions of the latest adult styles, including camouflage and animal prints, as well as accessories and toys can be found here. Sizes range from toddlers to up to sizes 7 to 12 in boys and 16 for girls. We love the clothes here. The same store reappears as the charmingly dubbed **Kids' Castle** in the **Forum Shops** at Caesars Palace, 3500 Las Vegas Blvd. S. (✆ **702/369-5437**). **Kids' Karnival** in The Venetian's **Grand Canal Shoppes,** 3377 Las Vegas Blvd. S. (✆ **702/414-3800**), stocks more of the same cool kid clothes. If you prefer to go to the Fashion Show Mall, **Along Came a Spider** is open there Monday through Friday from 10am until 8pm, on Saturday from 11am to 8pm, and Sunday from 11am until 6pm. Fashion Show Mall, 3200 Las Vegas Blvd. S. ✆ **702/735-2728.**

FASHION CLOTHING FOR TEENS & ADULTS

A prowl through The Venetian, Miracle Mile Shops, Forum Shops at Caesars, or the Fashion Show Mall will turn up any number of chic boutiques and chains, including **Armani Exchange** (✆ 702/733-1666), **bebe** (✆ 702/735-8885 or 702/892-0406), **Diesel** (✆ 702/791-5927), **DKNY** (✆ 702/650-9670), and **BCBG** (✆ 702/737-0681 or 702/735-2947), all of which can put you and your teens in the latest au courant styles for a pretty penny, and whose hours mirror those of the mall in which they are located.

GIFTS & SOUVENIRS

Hotel logo shops and sundry stores offer a variety of Vegas-themed items that strive for good taste—and often come up just a little short, but, alas, not enough to make them appallingly fabulous. If you wish to move beyond your hotel, we offer the following suggestions.

Contemporary Arts Collective This is a gift shop full of pink flamingos and Vegas-specific items. There should be something here for every camp fancy; take pleasure in the fact your children may not yet recognize the ironic aspect to these iconic souvenirs. The galleries also stock paintings and other art by local artists. Open Tuesday through Saturday 11am until 5pm, but call before your make the trip, because hours can vary. 231 W. Charleston Blvd. ✆ **702/382-3886.**

Showcase Mall Native Americana (think kachina dolls, feathered dream catchers, and pottery) to all-American bad taste (dice clocks, again), this mall has it all. Every Vegas souvenir you could imagine—and some you'd prefer not to imagine—are here for your buying pleasure. But it's not only a mall; it's an "experience," in that very special Las Vegas way. Not to be outdone by Caesars, Aladdin/Planet Hollywood, and The Venetian, the Showcase has installed a Grand Canyon simulacrum where every 45 minutes the clouds roll in and a thunderstorm erupts, only to be gradually replaced with a gentle sunrise and the sounds of chirping birds. There's also a rope bridge you can walk over. Open 8am until 1am daily. 3785 Las Vegas Blvd. S. ✆ **702/597-3122.**

Souvenir Savvy

My favorite souvenir is my T-shirt from MGM Grand with the picture of the lion and the words, "Here human, human, human."

—Victoria, 12

GROCERY STORES & MARKETS

Albertsons Food and Drugs This grocery store can meet all your food needs. It also has sundries, over-the-counter medications, pet food, disposable diapers, and more. Both stores are open daily 24 hours. 1300 E. Flamingo Rd. ✆ **702/733-2947.** 2300 E. Tropicana Ave. ✆ **702/739-8461.** www.albertsons.com.

Trader Joe's Finds This store sells gourmet food—fresh, frozen, and canned—at budget prices. Trader Joe's carries its own line of comestibles, including sodas and juices, plus international treats, a large range of desserts, and candies, along with unique products from small manufacturers. Trader Joe's emphasizes making and keeping food as wholesome and natural as possible; the dairy products are hormone-free, and preservatives are nonexistent or kept at a minimum. The refrigerated selection of sandwiches and salads is great for picnics. Open daily 8am to 10pm. 2101 S. Decatur Blvd. ✆ **702/367-0227.** www.traderjoes.com.

INTERNATIONAL GROCERIES

Asian Market Japanese food items dominate in this good-sized market full of *poki-poki* (rolled cookies dipped in chocolate and filled with creamy goop), colorful jelly candies, and ice cream, plus rice, noodles, frozen fish, sauces, and other exotic items. Open daily from 9am to 9pm. Commercial Center, 953 E. Sahara Blvd. ✆ **702/734-7653.**

International Marketplace (Finds) The International Marketplace is the biggest, most fabulous food store in all of Las Vegas (we think). A world, literally, of food is for sale here. Items from England (burdock root soda, teas, chocolates, beans, cookies, and so on) share shelf space with Indonesian and Dutch delicacies. There is an astounding array of Indian curry mixes, Armenian foods, teas and coffees from around the globe, Middle Eastern breads and spices and their uniquely flavored, shockingly green drink, tarragon soda. The refrigerated food section stocks items as diverse as goose uterus (don't ask), steak, chicken, and cuttlefish. You'll also find Hawaiian hot dogs, Mexican sausages, and Filipino ice cream (including purple yam, cheese and corn, and durian flavors) in the freezer; and Japanese vegetable chips, plus strange, brightly glowing candies, Asian sauces and soups, dried fungus, juices, sodas, and more on the shelves lining this warehouse-size market. Kids will be wowed by the colorful selection of snacks in their neon packaging. Give them a budget of $5 and they'll go wild buying things to share—and maybe learn a little bit about different cultures while they're at it. The International Marketplace also stocks woks, specialty stoves, and ovens. If you plan to load up on exotic items, or to spend more than $20, it's probably worth paying for a $10 membership card, which gives you discounts. Open Monday through Saturday from 8am to 6pm. 5000 S. Decatur Blvd. ✆ **702/889-2888.**

MAGIC & GAGS

Houdini's Magic Shop The staff at these magic emporia are more than happy to demonstrate their wares. Expect to have coins and cards pulled from behind ears and to see plenty of ring and scarf tricks. Buying a trick here and having to learn it and then perform it seamlessly will impress upon children that practice does make perfect. For slackers, there's a huge selection of gags including foaming sugar, soap that turns your hands black, and that perennial favorite, the whoopee cushion. The Houdini Museum is located next door to The Venetian's shop. Shop hours mirror those of their respective malls. New York–New York, 3790 Las Vegas Blvd. S. ✆ **702/740-6418.** Miracle Mile Shops, 3663 Las Vegas Blvd. S. ✆ **702/314-4674.** The Venetian, 3377 Las Vegas Blvd. S. ✆ **702/796-0301.** MGM Grand, 3799 Las Vegas Blvd. S. ✆ **702/736-2883.** www.houdini.com.

Lance Burton Magic Shop Located close to magician Lance Burton's theater in the Monte Carlo Resort & Casino, this magic shop has plenty of tricks up its sleeve, along with Lance Burton–related items. A staff member can demonstrate the sleight of hand. And we're happy to say that there's nary a whoopee cushion or squirting flower in sight. Open daily 9am until midnight. In the Monte Carlo Resort & Casino, 3770 Las Vegas Blvd. S. ✆ **702/730-7518.**

MENSWEAR

Bernini Couture High fashions and basics for the preening male. Think chinchilla baseball jackets, leather pants, and other Liberace-esque items. Open daily from 10am to midnight. Caesars Palace, 3500 Las Vegas Blvd. S. ✆ **702/893-1786.**

Men's Wearhouse Low prices, good service, and a quick turnaround on alterations make this national chain a favorite with fashion-conscious men old enough to care about such things. This store doesn't carry jeans or T-shirts, but it does have a large selection of suits, ties, and casual wear in name brands and quality fabrics. Open Monday through Friday from 10am to 9pm, Saturday from 9:30am to 6pm, and Sunday from 11am to 6pm. 1159 E. Twain Ave. ✆ **702/892-9035.** www.menswearhouse.com.

Napoleon Despite the name's connotations, this shop does not handle clothes purely for men under 5 feet 7 inches tall. In actuality, Napoleon carries a fine selection of menswear for all shapes and sizes in good fabrics, cuts, and colors. Open Sunday through Thursday from 10am to 11pm, Friday and Saturday from 10am until midnight. Miracle Mile Shops, 3663 Las Vegas Blvd. S. ✆ **702/733-6005.** www.napoleonfashions.com.

MUSIC

Sam Goody With Tower Records and Virgin Megastore gone, Sam Goody is the last large media box store in southern Nevada. It has a comprehensive selection of CDs, DVDs, and video games, along with books and media-storage devices. 3680 S. Maryland Pkwy. ✆ **702/734-1424.** www.samgoody.com.

SHOES

Department stores in the major shopping malls (p. 205) carry a wide selection of children's shoes. The following are specialty shops, some of which are sized more for teens than children.

Footlocker & Lady Footlocker All manner of athletic shoes are sold here, which your child may prefer as fashion statements instead of for the purpose for which they were designed. The Meadows location is open Monday through Friday from 10am to 9pm, Saturday from 10am to 9pm, and Sunday from 10am to 6pm. You can visit the Maryland Parkway location from 10am to 9pm Monday through Friday, Saturday from 9:30am to 6pm, and Sunday from 11am to 5pm. The Meadows, 4300 Meadows Lane. ✆ **702/878-8226.** 3500 S. Maryland Pkwy. ✆ **702/731-3639.** www.footlocker.com.

Jimmy Choo Popularized by the gals in *Sex and the City,* these pricey shoes, most with high heels, are only for girls whose feet have finished growing. And even then, at $300 and up, does she really need them? We were secretly relieved when the lusted-for pair didn't fit, and thanked our wide-footed genes. Open Sunday through Thursday from 10am to 11pm, Friday and Saturday from 10am until midnight. Caesars Palace, 3500 Las Vegas Blvd. S. ✆ **702/691-2097.** www.jimmychoo.com.

Kenneth Cole These stores carry hip men's and women's shoes, along with other products such as jackets, purses, and belts. While you won't find any kids' shoes here, your bigger 'tweens and most teens can be fitted in a variety of shoes in the latest styles. Open Sunday through Thursday 10am to 11pm, Friday and Saturday from 10am to midnight. Caesars Palace, 3500 Las Vegas Blvd. S. ✆ **702/794-2653.** The Venetian, 3377 Las Vegas Blvd. S. ✆ **702/836-1916.** www.kennethcole.com.

New Balance This athletic shoe store carries its own brand, in various styles, for infants, children, and adults, in widths ranging from AA to EEEE. Along with athletic shoes, including cross trainers and running shoes, New Balance carries an adult line called Dunhams, which are basic, casual shoes. What you don't see in stock can be ordered and shipped. This location is open Monday through Saturday from 10am to 9pm, Sunday from 11am to 6pm. The District at Green Valley, 2260 Village Walk Dr. ✆ **702/678-6262.** www.newbalance.com.

SPORTING GOODS & SPORTSWEAR

Bike World Bikes for everyone—from the 2-year-old to the 80-year-old—along with bike gear, clothes, helmets, and accessories are for sale at this professional and friendly shop. Open Monday through Friday from 10am to 6pm, Saturday from 10am until 5pm, and Sunday 10am to 5pm. 2320 E. Flamingo Rd. ✆ **702/735-7551.**

Desert Outfitters Stop here for almost all your desert hiking, backpacking, and camping needs, including hats, tents, canteens, and the like (but you'll have to find the shoes elsewhere). If you feel like prospecting for gold, this is the place to load up on maps, tools, and local lore. Open Monday through Friday 10am until 5pm, Saturday 10am to 4pm. 3340 Sirius Ave. ✆ **702/362-7177.**

Escape Adventure Bike Shop and Tour Center Whether you want to buy a high-end racing bike a la Lance Armstrong or are just looking for a new set of spokes for your Schwinn, the Cyclery has it. The shop also does repairs and rents bikes, and is the headquarters for Escape Adventure tours. Open Monday through Friday from 10am until 6pm, Saturday 9am to 6pm, and Sunday from 10am until 4pm. 8221 W. Charleston Blvd. ✆ **702/596-2953.** www.escapeadventures.com.

Niketown Sports clothes and shoes by Nike for men, women, and children, including the latest in superquick dry fabrics. Every Wednesday at 6pm, the Nike running club meets here to stretch out and warm up for 3- and 6-mile runs, followed by snacks. Open Sunday through Thursday from 10am to 11pm, Friday and Saturday from 10am until midnight. Caesars Palace, 3500 Las Vegas Blvd. S. ✆ **702/650-8888.** http://niketown.nike.com.

SPORTS MEMORABILIA

Casey's Sports Cards With hundreds of thousands of sports cards in stock, this store deals to both the serious collector and the hobbyist. It's handled some of the world's hardest-to-find cards. Open Monday through Friday noon to 5pm, Saturday from 11am to 3pm, Sunday 1 to 3pm. 3421 E. Tropicana Ave. ✆ **702/458-6394.**

Field of Dreams Framed and mounted sports memorabilia, including autographs, photos, balls, gloves, and players' cards, all with certificates of authenticity, are sold here. They have Michael Jordan; they can get you Babe Ruth. Excellent for browsing and for boning up on sports history. The shop in the Rio is open daily from 10am to midnight. The Caesars store hours are also daily 10am until midnight. Rio, 3700 W. Flamingo Rd. ✆ **702/221-9144.** Caesars Palace, 3500 Las Vegas Blvd. S. ✆ **702/792-8233.** www.fieldofdreams.com.

Gallery of Legends Even more sports memorabilia—signed, sealed, and delivered with certificates of authenticity in a 1,200-square-foot store. When do these superstars have time to play? Don't their hands get tired from all that signing? Overwhelming. Sunday through Thursday 10am to 11pm, Friday and Saturday from 10am until midnight. Miracle Mile Shops, 3663 Las Vegas Blvd. S. ✆ **702/471-8300.** www.galleryoflegends.net.

TOYS & GAMES

Build-a-Bear Workshop This is just too cute. You select an empty fur husk that will become your bear's body (they also have tigers, horses, and other cute critter skins), which is then stuffed with fluff before you give it a (plastic) heart and a name. Then you pay. Your bear is registered, and then you can buy heaps of clothes and accessories for him/her/it. It's oddly compelling for adults (people have proposed via the bears), and kids love it, too. Sunday through Thursday 10am to 11pm, Friday and Saturday from 10am until midnight. Miracle Mile Shops, 3663 Las Vegas Blvd. S. ✆ **702/836-0899.** www.buildabear.com.

Disney Store This chain store carries all things Disney, but with an emphasis on the more modern creations, including *Little Mermaid, Beauty and the Beast,* and whatever else the studio has recently released or rereleased. You will find some of the classics—Mickey, Minnie, Pluto, and Goofy—but they are overwhelmed by the Incredibles and their ilk, making this more for pop-encultured kids than their nostalgic parents. Open Monday through Saturday 10am to 9pm, Sunday 10am to 6pm. The Meadows, 4300 Meadows Lane. ✆ **702/258-2692.** www.disneystore.com.

Fantasy Toys At this store, you can indulge your child's desire to be a child. The "fantasy" here means your little one's imagination, rather than weirdly costumed action figures from a grisly blockbuster sci-fi movie. You'll find mind-stimulating gifts for all age groups from newborns to 'tweens, including mobiles, Lincoln Logs, Tinkertoys, and even motor scooters. Open daily 7am to 10pm. The Meadows, 4300 Meadows Lane. ✆ **702/258-7448.**

FAO Schwarz From outside, the giant Trojan horse nods his head to welcome you into the ultimate toy store for kids and adults. If you can tear yourself and your children away from the store's own line of stuffed animals—some of the softest, most plush, lovable animals ever—you'll find three levels to explore. Along with a room dedicated solely to all things Barbie, there is a special area for Gene—a glamorous 1940s movie star doll—and her friends, a *Star Wars* boutique, G.I. Joes, electronic games, plus thousands of offerings from Steiff, Fisher-Price, and other well-known manufacturers. A special section is dedicated to costumes, and another area holds trains and erector sets. You can walk around inside the Trojan horse, which is set up like a treehouse, and if your children are really, really good, you can arrange for them to have a birthday party or sleepover at the store. This is one of our favorite places to spend hours and money. ***Note:*** Though many FAO Schwarz branches closed across the country when the company declared bankruptcy, this branch has remained open through thick and thin. Open Sunday through Thursday 10am to 11pm, Friday and Saturday 10am to midnight. Caesars Palace, 3500 Las Vegas Blvd. S. ✆ **702/796-6500.** www.fao.com.

Toys "R" Us Toys, toys, toys: battery operated, wind-up, push, pull, and stationary. It's huge, it can be loud (especially on weekends and around the holidays, when it can, at times, resemble a personal definition of hell), and though it's not as posh as FAO Schwarz, they do have sales and specials, and children will be busy for hours looking at all the stuff they'll want you to buy them. It's a good place for preplanning your holiday and birthday gift buying, so bring paper and pencil. Batteries are thoughtfully sold here for the toys that need them. Kids "R" Us, a clothing and kid supply store (p. 218), is on the same property. Both locations are open Sunday 10am to 7pm, Monday from 9am to 9pm, Tuesday through Thursday 10am to 9pm, Friday 10am to 10pm, and Saturday 9am to 10pm. 4000 S. Maryland Pkwy. ✆ **702/732-3733.** 4550 Meadows Lane. ✆ **702/877-9070.** www.toysrus.com.

VINTAGE & USED SHOPS

The Attic The former star of a Visa commercial, the Attic shares a large space with Cafe Neon, a coffeehouse that also serves Greek-influenced cafe food (so you can take a break during your shopping). The store offers plenty of vintage clothing choices on many racks. Expect that all your child's dress-up desires will be met or surpassed here. Open Monday through Thursday from 10am until 5pm, Friday from 10am until 6pm, and Saturday from 11am until 6pm. 1018 S. Main St. ✆ **702/388-4088.** www.theatticlasvegas.com.

Buffalo Exchange Though this is actually a branch of a chain of stores spread out across the western United States, you shouldn't let the chain part keep you away; this store has plenty of cool stuff and good prices. Staffed by plenty of incredibly hip alt-culture kids, it is stuffed with dresses, shirts, pants, and so forth, both vintage and slightly worn, as well as remainder and discontinued fashions. We've seen Prada, Donna Karan, and other designers come through in addition to 1960s golf sweaters, retro cocktail dresses, and the like. But like any vintage shop, the contents are hit-or-miss, though the large stock ensures the chance of finding something. The store is open Monday through Saturday from 10am to 8pm and Sunday from 11am until 7pm. 4110 S. Maryland Pkwy. (at Flamingo). ✆ **702/791-3960.** www.buffaloexchange.com.

11

Entertainment for the Whole Family

During its first few decades as Sin City, Las Vegas had a great formula for stage entertainment, delivering one or more of the following: pretty girls dancing in skimpy sparkling outfits, a comedian, or a big-name star (though in later years, it became formerly big-name stars) headlining. Then, the show ran and the guests were in and out of the showroom and back to the gambling tables in less than 2 hours.

During the building boom of the '90s and the advent of the megacasino, many of the huge new hotels sought to lure guests through larger-than-life fanciful themes and a confusing array of outdoor spectacles ranging from pirate battles to fire-belching volcanoes to dancing fountains. Coming at the same time as the short-lived campaign to represent Las Vegas as a family destination, the themes and street extravaganzas were misinterpreted as proof that the major hotels were getting behind the family-friendly press releases. Alas, the over-the-top themes and colossal outdoor productions were about market share pure and simple, about getting more adults into the casino. Though the come-ons were in fact pretty juvenile, establishing a family clientele was the last thing the casinos intended.

The one-upmanship along the Strip was also manifest in the showrooms. Modest headliner and production shows gave way to eye-popping presentations with huge casts, staged in custom theaters seating audiences numbering in the thousands.

You can still see showgirls in their daring outfits (or without them, for that matter), but now they have full-blown productions behind them involving fire, ice, and light shows. These days, headliners are signed to 2-year contracts, Broadway shows come through town and land at hotel resorts, and some top-flight performances such as the Cirque du Soleil productions and Blue Man Group, draw visitors to Vegas just to see their shows.

There's no longer any doubt that one of Las Vegas's biggest draws is its entertainment. Really! It has internationally known headline acts, local favorites, showgirls, comics, impersonators—both the female drag version and the faux-celebrity types—animals, and magicians appearing at hotels throughout the city. Add to all those stage shows the sporting events; rock concerts; Broadway shows; local, community-supported orchestras, dance, and theater (all of which can make a pleasant change from the onslaught of sequins and disappearing doves that are the staple of many resort shows); and much much more, and you can begin to understand the allure of all of Vegas's entertainment possibilities.

Of course, the options are more numerous for adults, but don't fret—Vegas also has entertainment that's quite suitable for the whole family, most notably magicians using animals, ranging from the afternoon delight of Mac King to the over-the-top effects of Cirque du Soleil's *KÀ*. And parents who don't object to their kids watching Christina Aguilera and Britney Spears videos may not mind taking their kids to the early showing of *Jubilee!*, though, for some kids, seeing seminude women dancing in real life while seated next to their parents might be disconcerting or uncomfortable; you may feel the same degree of discomfort, too.

For families, an evening out at a big-ticket production show can run into the hundreds of dollars. However, lower-priced options provide a decent entertainment value, though you will not be seeing the same level of showmanship and production as you would at, say, Bette Midler. Will your kids enjoy the lower-priced shows? Most likely, especially your younger ones. Will you? Sure, especially if your children are having fun.

Sporting events in Las Vegas range from university football, basketball, and volleyball games to major boxing and golf matches, national rodeo finals, and local minor league hockey and baseball games.

The local performing arts scene also provides families with opportunities to see ballet, symphony orchestras, and plays. The Rainbow Company Children's Theatre and the Nevada Ballet perform regularly, and the Las Vegas Philharmonic works hard to prove that there's more to Vegas than the jingle of slot machines and the purr of Elvis impersonators.

Las Vegas, with both its production shows and local performing arts groups, offers opportunities for families to share time together, whether they're seeing a tiger disappear or watching a ballet troupe interpret Pink Floyd. Whatever you choose, know that spending an afternoon or evening at a show with your family (whatever that show may be) will almost definitely provide many lasting memories for you and your family.

1 WHAT'S PLAYING WHERE

Most acts in Las Vegas sign a contract their first time in the city. If all goes well, they'll renew and extend their contract. If things go really well, they'll last forever or may move to a different, bigger location. Some shows eventually close for any number of reasons, including lack of interest from the general public. Las Vegas is showbiz Darwinism at its most refined, though what passes as the fittest is sometimes baffling, though always amusing. The following section will describe each of the major production shows appropriate for families currently playing in Las Vegas, arranged alphabetically by the title of the production. But first, here's a handy list arranged by hotel:

- **Bellagio:** Cirque du Soleil's *O* (unique circus-meets-performance-art theatrical experience; ages 5 and up)
- **Excalibur:** *Tournament of Kings* (medieval-themed revue; all ages)
- **Harrah's:** *Legends in Concert* (musical impersonators; ages 5 and up)
- **Las Vegas Hilton:** *Laugh Out Loud with the Scintas* (music and variety, impressions; ages 5 and up)
- **MGM Grand:** *KÀ* (Cirque du Soleil's epic adventure featuring martial arts; ages 10 and up)
- **The Mirage:** *LOVE* (Cirque du Soleil production based on the music of the Beatles; ages 10 and up)
- **Monte Carlo:** *Lance Burton: Master Magician* (magic show and revue; ages 5 and up)
- **Planet Hollywood:** *Tony n' Tina's Wedding* (lighthearted comedy; ages 10 and up)
- **Plaza:** *Viva Las Vegas* (Las Vegas–style revue; ages 7 and up)
- **Rio:** *Penn & Teller* (sarcastic, abrasive magic show; ages 5 and up)
- **Stratosphere:** *American Superstars* (an impression-filled production show; ages 7 and up)
- **Treasure Island:** Cirque du Soleil's *Mystère* (unique circus performance; ages 10 and up)
- **Tropicana:** *Jubilee!* (Las Vegas–style revue; 7:30pm show only for families, ages 8 and up; all other shows feature topless numbers, ages 16 and up)

Buying Show Tickets

Las Vegas shows, once a great bargain, are now expensive. Before plunking down your cash, check the freebie visitor magazines for discount coupons. Also check the half-price ticket outlet, **Tix4Tonight,** with four locations—Hawaiian Marketplace (near the MGM Grand), a booth just South of The Riviera, Fashion Show Mall, and Four Queens Downtown—all open from 11am to 8pm (if you're driving, avoid the super-congested Hawaiian Marketplace location). This discounter sells tickets for same-day shows for half price, plus a $3 service fee. Open 2 to 9pm, it's first-come, first-served. Generally speaking, you won't find tickets available for top-tier productions such as the Cirque du Soleil shows, Blue Man Group, Danny Gans, and Bette, because, among other reasons, they sell out every night. Many, if not most, of the other shows turn up at Tix4Tonight, some routinely, some periodically. Tix4Tonight additionally offers coupons on its website, www.tix4tonight.com, that are good for discounts on the service fee.

If you're nervous about waiting until the last minute to purchase your tickets, most tickets are now available from **Ticketmaster** at ✆ **702/474-4000** or online at **www.ticketmaster.com**. Expect to pay full price, however.

- **The Venetian:** *Blue Man Group* (hilarious multimedia production featuring percussion on instruments crafted from PVC pipe; ages 5 and up)
- **Wynn Las Vegas:** *Le Rêve* (aquatic epic with diving, acrobatics, and synchronized swimming; ages 10 and up)

2 MAJOR PRODUCTION SHOWS

Note: Although every effort has been made to keep up with the volatile Las Vegas show scene, keep in mind that the following reviews may not be indicative of the actual show you'll see, but the basic concept and idea will most probably be the same. What's more, shows can close without warning, even ones that have been running just shy of forever, so it's a good idea to always call the venue ahead of time to check whether it's open and what the show really is. And while you have them on the phone, find out if ticket prices include tax or drinks, just so you know which potential hidden costs you might be slammed with when you show up.

American Superstars **Ages 5 & up.** Impersonator shows allow the audience to experience almost seeing their favorite stars in real life, but without having to pay a fortune and traipse all over to do so. (And, in the case of someone like Elvis, it would be pretty darn impossible, anyway, to catch the King in concert.) Here, Madonna, Prince, Christina Aguilera, and Michael Jackson (not maybe the best idea given Jacko's unfortunate publicity) are all re-created, live, in their most iconic phase (no lip-syncing allowed!), in all their pop glory—sparkling costumes, beards, sunglasses, whatever it takes to make sure you know who's being impersonated. The show is opened by a good Elvis, followed by a Prince who shakes his bon-bon quite credibly. Madonna is from the lingerie era of her career, and the version of modern poptress Aguilera is spot-on. Country fans will appreciate the fine voice of Tim McGraw. The Michael Jackson impersonator is good, but we found ourselves asking why and cringing a bit when watching that one. If your kids are fans of one or more of these performers in real life, or are just pop music fans, they're more than likely to enjoy this show, and you will, too, as the skills of the impersonators will no doubt impress you, at least a bit! (While this show focuses more on pop music, the *Legends in Concert* show—see below—is geared more toward such musicians as the Blues Brothers, Jackie Wilson, and Whitney Houston. However, both shows deliver solid entertainment, so it's more about what your kids would prefer when choosing a show instead of which is better.) Shows are Sunday through Tuesday at 7pm, Wednesday, Friday, and Saturday at 6:30 and 8:30pm. In the Stratosphere, 2000 Las Vegas Blvd. S. ✆ **800/99-TOWER** (998-6937) or 702/380-7711. www.stratospherehotel.com. Tickets $43 adults, $32 children 5–12 (including tax and gratuity).

The Wisdom of Youth

Las Vegas is better than Disneyworld, a hundred times! There's so much cool stuff! Wednesday Dad and Susan got married, last night we saw Blue Man Group, and tomorrow we're going to O. I love it here, all of us do!

—Kasey, age 9, in Las Vegas with her three siblings, her two stepsiblings, her dad, stepmom, and her stepgrandparents

Blue Man Group **Ages 5 & up.** Kids will love this, period. Three men painted all blue ("I want to be one for Halloween," we overheard one tyke proclaiming afterward) do outrageous things with breakfast cereal, Jell-O, Twinkies, marshmallows, and more. The blue men—sort of innocent aliens/curious children/gentle beings from another place and time—make percussive music by playing PVC pipes and generally spread merriment and mischief using everyday objects during the 1¼-hour show (which some have said seemed longer). We found it to be a thought-provoking, uplifting, light-hearted experience, and the kids around us were spellbound. As an adult, you might find yourself squirming at times, especially if high-concept performance art is not your bag (until the uplifting, hysterical finale), but you and your children will surely discuss the show at length afterward. Be warned—the front rows get wrapped in waterproof plastic for a reason. Shows are Sunday through Thursday at 7:30pm, and Saturday at 7:30pm and 10:30pm. In The Venetian, 3355 Las Vegas Blvd. S. ✆ **800/BLUE-MAN** (258-3626) or ✆ 702/414-7469. www.blueman.com. Tickets $77, $99, $126 (including tax).

Cirque du Soleil's KÀ **Ages 5 & up.** A departure for Cirque du Soleil in many ways, *KÀ*, at the MGM Grand, is unique in that it is the first Cirque production that attempts to tell a linear story. That story follows twins who have been separated and must each make a journey to meet their destiny. That journey is the focus of the show, and the twins travel through beaches, mountains, forests, and blizzards; face warriors and whimsical sea and forest creatures; and witness remarkable feats of strength and agility. All these, of course, completely overshadow the storytelling and relegate the story to something you're vaguely conscious of from time to time, but nothing more. If there is a single star of *KÀ*, it is the gantry stage. From the pit emerges a large deck, supported by a boom, that is manipulated with computer precision to spin, tilt, raise, and lower throughout the show, all with surprising fluidity and speed. Not to knock the performers, who are as lithe and powerful as any cast of humans has a right to be, but the stage is an incredible industrial

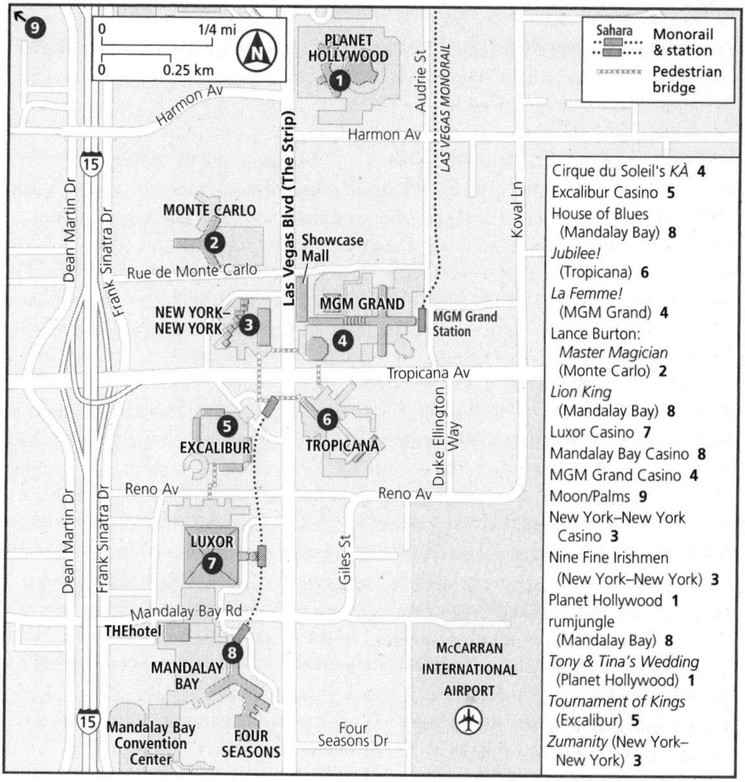

achievement. In one of the most breathtaking scenes, the stage tilts fully vertical as warriors loose arrows toward it and their intended victims scramble to find purchase. The arrows appear to stick in the stage, giving the "attacked" performers the handholds they need to dance and spin and flip their way up the vertical wall. As the performers ascend the wall, the "arrows" (which are actually 80 retractable pegs built into the stage) retract and the stage appears to shrug off the performers like so much detritus—an effect that is both unforgettable and disturbing. *KÀ* may not be quite what you expect of a Cirque performance. Although *KÀ* does display some of the whimsy of *Mystère* and *O,* the overall impression of *KÀ* is shock, awe, and menacing power. If you are in a show-going mood, you can easily see both *KÀ* and *Mystère* in a single vacation without feeling over-Cirqued. In fact, we recommend it. *KÀ* is a fearsome production, and an elegant foil for the playful *Mystère.* Though children as young as 5 years old are welcome, they'll have the sneeples scared out of them before the show even begins. The theater itself creates a menacing atmosphere with the look of an enchanted Asian foundry from space, complete with 30-foot bursts of flame. Bottom line, leave the kids with a sitter unless they are at least 8 years old. Finally, your wascally boys will love it; *KÀ* will definitely be the high point of their vacation and possibly the high point of all their days on earth. Children 17 and under must be accompanied by an adult. Usual showtimes 7 and 9:30p.m. Dark Sunday and Monday. In the MGM Grand, 3799 Las Vegas Blvd. S. ✆ **800/929-1111.** www.mgmgrand.com/ka. Tickets $69, $99, $125, $150 (no tax or fees included).

Cirque du Soleil's *LOVE* **Ages 5 & up.** *LOVE,* like most Cirque du Soleil shows, is nothing if not an overwhelming spectacle. But this latest Cirque extravaganza is a definite departure from what might be loosely called the norm. First, it's heavily multimedia, combining extensive video effects projected onto a variety of screens with dancers, acrobats, and aerialists in outlandish costumes and bizarre props, all driven by the most powerful soundtrack ever, perhaps, produced. And because music, especially familiar music, is the force behind the visuals and theatrics, *LOVE* is grounded in a reality that the audience shares, which renders this show unified and accessible in a way that *Mystère* approximates, but that *O* and even *KÀ,* with its loose plot line, can never be. That's not to imply, however, that *LOVE* doesn't have its extreme flights of fancy. The teaming of Cirque and the Beatles is, simply put, a marriage made in psychedelic heaven. Only Cirque could so effectively choreograph, costume, and showcase the characters, images, themes, humor, whimsicality, and all-around 1960s optimism, exuberance, and magic that the Beatles continue, 40 years later, to embody. One thing's for sure: The acoustics are outstanding. More than 6,000 speakers surround you, with one installed in the backrest of every seat in the house. The soundtrack consists of full songs, medleys, snippets of tunes down to a bar or two that disappear as soon as you recognize them, along with Beatles banter and fragments from recording sessions, plus suitably surreal transitions holding it all together. For the finale, umbrellas spread confetti all over the room to "Hey Jude" and predictably, the show ends on "Sgt. Pepper's Lonely Hearts Club Band": We hope you have enjoyed the show and we're sorry but it's time to go. The audience is sorry, too. *LOVE* is a sure winner for kids—it's fast-paced, zany, and wild. If your children's exposure (or yours, for that matter) to Beatles music is limited, not to worry, they'll be die-hard fans before the curtain falls.

LOVE plays in the space where Siegfried and Roy used to perform, but the new theater underwent a mere $120 million worth of renovations. There's not a bad seat in the 2,000-seat theater-in-the-round, but the top $150 ticket might be too close. Since all the action occurs on the elevated stages and above, the eye-level $99 and $125 seats are better. Usual showtimes are Thursday through Monday, 7 and 10pm. Dark Tuesday and Wednesday. In the Mirage, 3400 Las Vegas Blvd. S. ✆ **702/792-7777** or 800/963-9634. www.mirage.com or www.cirquedusoleil.com. Tickets $69 (upper level), $99 (upper-mid), $125 (mid-level), $150 (floor level) plus tax.

Cirque Du Soleil's *Mystère* **Ages 8 & up.** Part circus, part surrealist stage show, Cirque du Soleil's performances have defied description since the Canadian troupe first began performing its strange blend of dance, acrobatics, and mime over 20 years ago. When *Mystère* opened a decade ago in Vegas, there was nothing like it on the Strip, and even today, with its four siblings and the performance group the Blue Man Group at The Venetian (see above), *Mystère* is still a standout: Acrobats and gymnasts twirl, contort, and float through the air to the strains of haunting music; performers drop from giant bungee cords and scale vertical poles; and stilt-walkers prowl the stage in this show, considered by many to be the best production in Las Vegas. Children and adults alike will be awestruck by the feats of the 72 performers who bend and twist, defying physics and gravity. Plus there's a clown and a giant snail. Though all ages are admitted, this show is more suited for older children and teens; it can be a little scary at times, with some erotic overtones. The best view is from the center rows. Shows are Wednesday through

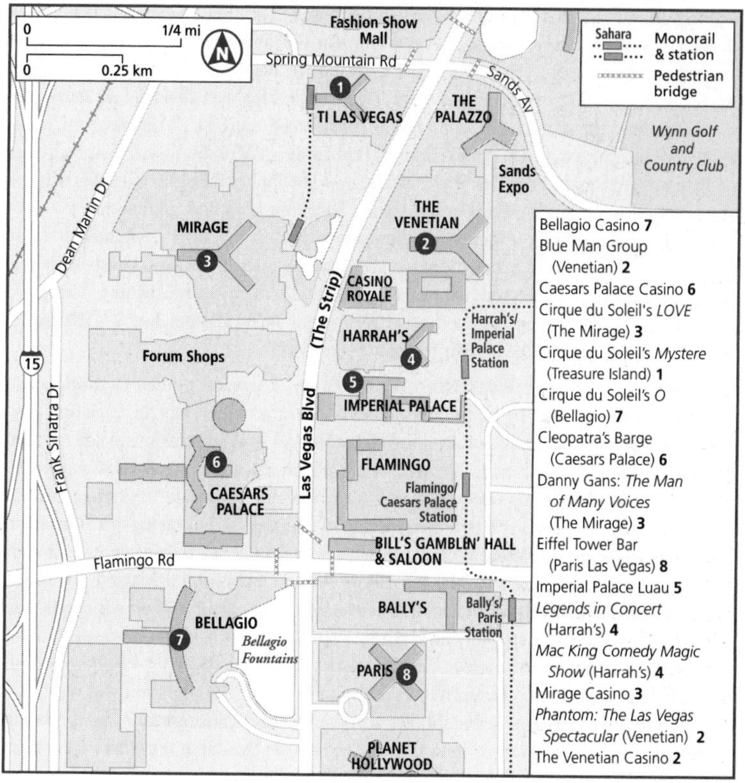

Saturday at 7 and 9:30pm. In Treasure Island, 3300 Las Vegas Blvd. S. ✆ **800/288-7206** or 702/392-1999. www.treasureisland.com. Tickets $60–$95 (plus tax and surcharge).

Cirque Du Soleil's *O* **Ages 8 & up.** This astounding show features a 1.5 million-gallon pool of water into which performers dive, out of which they rise, and above which they fly, making *O* (a homophone of the French word *eau,* meaning water, and of the gasps you'll hear from the audience) a cross between a Busby Berkeley musical and a surrealist montage. There is a plot (our hero loses his red scarf and experiences many strange adventures trying to retrieve it), but it's secondary to the action on stage, which includes carousel horses descending from the ceiling, synchronized diving, a water ballet, and a fountain that erupts during the hour-and-a-half show. This is truly phenomenal entertainment for all ages, which, like most Cirque shows, defies description; you must see it and experience the dreamlike world into which the performers draw you. You'll get the best view from the center seats somewhat up from the floor. Children under 18 must be accompanied by an adult. Shows are Wednesday through Sunday at 7:30 and 10:30pm. In the Bellagio, 3600 Las Vegas Blvd. S. ✆ **888/488-7111** or 702/693-7722. www.bellagiolasvegas.com/pages/ent_main.asp. Tickets $99–$150 (including tax and surcharge).

Danny Gans: The Man of Many Voices **Ages 8 & up.** Affable, talented Gans may be the man of many voices, but, unfortunately, unless your children are retro-buffs, they will not recognize many of the impressions he does so well. They may, however, laugh at some of the jokes. Gans can impersonate over 400 celebrities, and on any given night, he'll perform about 80 or so of them, depending on the crowd. Teens may recognize Bruce Springsteen, but be baffled by the Spencer Tracy/Katherine Hepburn dialogue spouting from Gans's talented throat. The "Twelve Days of Christmas," sung in 12 different voices, will make kids laugh even if they don't recognize Paul Lynde or Woody Allen. His speech at the end about his inspiration to perform may inspire some, but make older kids roll their eyes. If your child is an aspiring actor or has a good background in vintage film and television, this might be a good call. Otherwise, you may be better off spending an evening at a show he or she can relate to. The showroom has good seating throughout, and you're really there to hear (not see) him, anyway. Shows are Tuesday, Wednesday, Friday, and Saturday at 7:30pm. In the Mirage at Encore, the Danny Gans Theatre, 3400 Las Vegas Blvd. S. ✆ **800/963-9634** or 702/792-7777. Tickets $95–$120 (with tax and surcharge)

Lance Burton: Master Magician **Ages 5 & up.** There are numerous magic acts in Vegas of varying degrees of charm and opulence, most of which rely on huge bombastic effects and plenty of animals, while ignoring the fine art of legerdemain—sleight of hand, close-up magic. If you want to see an evening magic show that won't leave you feeling like your pocket has been picked, this is the act to see. Burton, a true Southern gentleman via Lexington, Kentucky, offers low-key delivery and dry humor, along with producing dozens of ducks out of nowhere and turning a dove into confetti. His work with coins, candles, and other objects won him his title as World Champion of Magic from Federation International Society de Magic, but he can make cars come and go with equal ease. The show is housed in a specially built theater, reminiscent of a Victorian music hall, but with modern touches; the comfy seats come with cup holders, an especially thoughtful touch for families. There really isn't a bad seat in the room, though you will want to be as close to the action as possible. Shows are Tuesday and Saturday at 7 and 10pm and Wednesday through Friday at 7pm. In the Lance Burton Theater at the Monte Carlo Resort & Casino, 3770 Las Vegas Blvd. S. ✆ **877/386-8224** or 702/730-7160. www.lanceburton.com. Tickets $60–$70 (plus tax and surcharge).

Aloha, Las Vegas!

For those who want to take a brief detour to the South Pacific during their explorations of Paris, Egypt, Rome, and other exotic locales in Vegas, the **Imperial Palace,** 3535 Las Vegas Blvd. S. (✆ **800/634-6441** or 702/731-3311; www.imperialpalace.com), provides an evening of island-themed entertainment and (naturally, this being Vegas) an all-you-can-eat island buffet with unlimited mai tais and piña coladas, and nonalcoholic fruit punch. Exotic drumming, hula dancing, torch lighting, conch blowing, and the wearing of flower leis are all part of evening fun here, Tuesdays and Thursdays, from April through October.

This is a sort of goofy fun evening (adults will welcome the free tropical drink to get them in the mood), but the dancing is amazing, and the drumming invigorating. A meal and show runs $40 for adults and $22 for children ages 2 to 12. Free for children under 2.

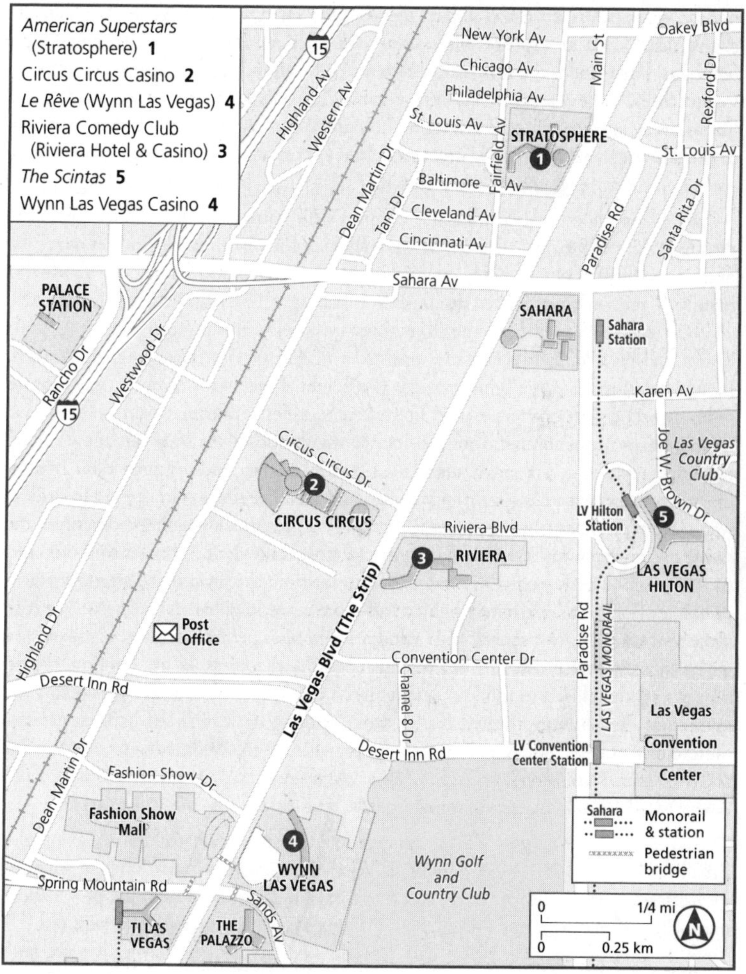

Legends in Concert **Ages 5 & up.** For more than 2 decades, this show has been pleasing crowds of all ages with impersonations of classic stars (Elvis, the Supremes, and more) to the more time-specific (Prince). Instead of lip-syncing, these impersonators—um, re-creations—actually sing and speak (and when called for, play instruments) just like the stars they're dressed up to be. Overall, they succeed on all counts. Acts are accompanied by a live band, and dancers of both genders do their darnedest in gauzy, skimpy outfits, dancing to different artists' greatest hits. The acts change seasonally (expect a more country flair during December's rodeo finals), but Elvis is always in the house here. Other re-creations have included the Blues Brothers, Madonna, Prince, Jackie Wilson, and Whitney Houston—a sort of middle-of-the-road demographic spread that will appeal to everyone from grandparents on down through the generations. This 90-minute show has no age minimums, but kids over 5 will enjoy it the most. Both this show and *American Superstars,* reviewed above, deliver solid entertainment. However, there is a slight oldies edge at *Legends,* while *Superstars* goes more for the contemporary pop emphasis. That aside, the only real difference is location: *Legends'* home at Harrah's is Center Strip, while *American Superstars* is located on the North Strip at the Stratosphere. Shows are Monday through Saturday at 7:30 and 10pm. At Harrah's, 3475 Las Vegas Blvd. S. © **800/392-9002.** www.harrahslasvegas.com. Ticket prices and times not yet announced.

Le Rêve **Ages 5 & up.** *Le Rêve* is a wet concoction of someone else's dreams. The protagonist is a nocturnal voyager in a red dress who ventures forth from her own bed of dreams. Like Cirque du Soleil's *O, Le Rêve* (French for "the dream") features water, lots of it, in the form of plunge pools, fountains, sprays, torrents, and squirts. The production requires a specially constructed amphitheater seating 2,100 where no seat is more than 42 feet from the action (and the front rows are given water-protective clothing and a discounted price of $99 versus the maximum of $150). Performed in the round, the show's cast of more than 70 internationally assembled gymnasts, acrobats, synchronized swimmers, and dancers execute their impressive routines within an expansive, mysterious tank of water. Mechanical lifts hoist various configurations of the stage out of a seemingly bottomless reservoir. The set is augmented by fire, smoke, and dripping skin. At times the performers perch atop a rising column, and at other times they appear to walk on water. Sometimes they are hoisted straight up into the dome's opening. Sometimes they swing on trapezes, their exquisitely strong and athletically defined bodies shimmering in the show lights, or they dangle in suspended contortions as if in a Michelangelo rendition of hell. For kids, *O* is definitely lighter and more accessible than *Le Rêve. Le Rêve* is the more sensual of the two shows, and includes one topless performer whose acrobatic feats are so amazing that it takes a while to register that she's topless. In our opinion, the first 15 rows are too close and too low to take in the whole of this expansive production that makes use of the entire theater. If you drive, parking in Wynn's self-parking garage is more convenient than using valet parking. Showtimes are Wednesday to Sunday, 7:30 and 10:30pm. Dark Monday and Tuesday. In Wynn Las Vegas, 3131 Las Vegas Blvd. S. © **702/770-9966** or 888/320-7110. www.wynnlasvegas/le_reve. Tickets $94–$150 (plus tax).

The Lion King **All ages.** This adaptation of a Disney animated movie, a longtime Broadway kid's favorite, has now come to Vegas. Tony-award-winning director Julie Taymor discarded glitzy special effects and made stage music instead with puppets, dancers, masks, billowing clouds, and imagination, drawing strongly on African folk traditions. This show is genuinely moving, even—dare I say it?—better than the movie. Reserve far in advance for this show—it's worth planning your trip around. At the Mandalay Bay Theatre, 3950 Las Vegas Blvd. S. © **702/632-4766.** www.mandalaybay.com/entertainment/LionKing.aspx. Tickets $53–$168 (plus tax).

Mac King Comedy Magic Show **All ages.** Goofy, beguiling, funny, sweet, and, at $25 a ticket, possibly the best show deal in Vegas—Mac King is the perfect show for children and adults. His costuming is straight off *Green Acres* (plaid suit, bowl haircut), his humor is broad, his tricks impeccable, and he seems so charmingly astounded when they work (when they don't he shrugs it off with, "That would have been cool, though," while working the "failed" trick into part of a larger scheme). At least one child will be called up on stage to help with a trick, and a pair of grown-ups will be drawn into a complex card trick involving the magician's cloak of invisibility. Whether turning himself into a white tiger (sort of) or playing with flying food, King makes every trick fresh, as though this is the first time he's tried it; and that sort of attitude is infectious. The hour-long show is brilliant, and a must-see. Shows are Tuesday through Saturday at 1 and 3pm. At Harrah's Las Vegas, 3475 Las Vegas Blvd. S. ✆ **800/838-9383** or 702/369-5000. www.harrahs.com. Tickets $25 (plus tax and gratuity).

Penn & Teller **Ages 12 & up.** This is the show for cynical, bored teens, for know-it-alls, wiseacres, and, well, for anyone over 12. The Bad Boys of Magic, Penn and Teller (Penn speaks, Teller suffers) brought their bullets and wood chippers with them to this one. Penn and Teller deconstruct magic, explaining its history, laying out its scams. Using cards, knives, and bullets, they'll perform an illusion; do the stunt again, pulling the scales from the audience's eyes by explaining how the trick works; and then—when the audience thinks they have it all figured out—perform another, similar trick without explanation, leaving the audience gaping. This is a clever, smart show: It's irreverent, sarcastic, and, at times, disturbing (the bunny/wood chipper trick, plus other cool but gory effects, makes this a show for older kids, despite the hotel being willing to admit any paying customer ages 5 and up). But you will leave the theater after an hour and a half thinking about the nature of reality, illusion, and deception and wanting to see the show again, just to see if you can catch the sleight of hand, the distraction, the wire, the false bottom, and maybe, maybe figure out how these two masters do it. Their loyal fans follow the duo on their website, **www.pennandteller.com**. All seats are good for this show, though, as in most cases with magic acts, closer is better. Shows are Saturday through Wednesday at 9pm. In the Rio Hotel & Casino, 3700 Las Vegas Blvd. S. ✆ **888/746-7784** or 702/777-7776. www.playrio.com. Tickets $75 or $85 (plus tax and gratuity).

Phantom—The Las Vegas Spectacular **Ages 8 & up.** Shortened to a mere 95 minutes, the longest-running show in Broadway history has finally descended upon Las Vegas, but with a face-lift. But *Phantom* fans need not be alarmed. Andrew Lloyd Webber and Hal Prince have personally revamped the show; all of Webber's songs will be sung and the story line remains the same. The Venetian built a custom theater to house the show, and enhanced illusions, expanded set designs, and more spectacular effects differentiate the Las Vegas version from its Broadway cousin. *Phantom—The Las Vegas Spectacular* is based on the novel *Le Fantôme de l'Opéra* by Gaston Leroux. In it, the Paris Opera House is haunted not by a ghost, but by a masked man residing in the catacombs of the Opera House. While spreading havoc and terror over all associated with the Opera House, the Phantom falls madly in love with the soprano singer Christine and vows to transform her into a star. The fusion of all aspects of the musical, from the costumes to

Tips Our Favorites

Our vote for **best show?** It's a tossup between *KÀ* at MGM Grand, *O* at Bellagio, and *Mystère* at Treasure Island, all by Cirque du Soleil. Any must be seen to be believed—and even then you may not believe it, but you won't be forgetting the experience anytime soon. The **smartest show in town** is Penn & Teller at the Rio. The only reason we don't call it the **best magic show** is so that we can acknowledge the delightful Lance Burton at Monte Carlo. **Best we-aren't-sure-what-the-heck-to-call-it** is *Blue Man Group* at The Venetian. **Best for the whole family** is *The Lion King* at Mandalay Bay.

the haunting lyrics by Webber, will tug at your imagination and your emotions. If you drive, give yourself lots of extra time to park and make it to the showroom. The Venetian showrooms are toward the rear of the property around the corner from the V Bar nightspot. Showtimes are 7pm Monday through Saturday; 9:30pm Monday and Saturday. Dark Tuesday. In The Venetian, 3355 Las Vegas Blvd. S. ✆ **702/414-9000.** www.venetian.com or www.phantomlasvegas.com. Tickets $69–$158 (plus tax and surcharge).

Tony n' Tina's Wedding **Ages 10 & up.** Tony and Tina are getting married, and you, plus the entire audience, are invited to participate in this unique interactive theatrical experience. Because the audience is indistinguishable from the cast, expect plenty of surprises and some unpredictable behavior from "guests" of the Nunzio and Vitale families during the ceremony and reception, where you'll feast at the wedding buffet (pretty darn good Italian food), eat cake, and dance during the 2½-hour production. Older children and teens will enjoy following the plot twists and the spontaneous interaction with the actors. This wacky, zany, and fun show is unlike any other in Vegas, and has been an off-Broadway classic since it debuted in the mid-1980s. Shows take place nightly at 7pm. At Planet Hollywood, 3667 Las Vegas Blvd. S. ✆ **702/949-6450.** www.tonylovestina.com. Tickets $86 and $137.

Tournament of Kings **All ages.** Galloping horses! Swordplay! Pounding the table! Singing! Shouting! Good vs. evil! Eating with your hands! *Tournament of Kings* is the big all-ages show at Excalibur. It's pretty darn fun for kids, and although a bit long for grown-ups, it definitely delivers plenty of live action.

As you enter the large arena surrounding a dirt floor, you'll take your assigned seat in sections named after countries and decorated with medieval flags and ye olde signage. Not to give away too much of the ending, but unless you like rooting for the loser, or want to be on the side of Ultimate Evil, avoid the Dragon section like the plague by asking in advance to sit elsewhere. If you want to back a winner, go for, say, France, Norway, or Ireland. If you prefer the "if you're not cheating, you're not playing" dictum, you might request Russia at the ticket booth.

The story involves Britain's King Arthur inviting the various kings of Europe over for a little jousting, sword play, and the like. Aside from the king of Russia taking a few cheap shots, it's good, clean fun until the evil wizard Mordred crashes the party and attempts to destroy civilization. Arthur rallies the kings along with his son Christopher (who knew?) to battle Mordred. Never mind that Arthur didn't have a son named Christopher, as loudly pointed out by one child who had obviously read his *Knights of the Roundtable* near us on our last visit! Instead, get into the spirit and loudly cheer your champion! Beat your fists on the table! Tear apart your roasted game hen with your bare hands and wave its legs in the air! See why kids like it so much?

While the hour and a half of pageantry and spectacle is going on in front of you, you're getting fed a meal, because, after all, this is a dinner theater. The food is adequate, but barely so—pitchers of cola and salty cream of tomato soup with rolls, followed by a rather nicely cooked game hen, some dry potato wedges, and a vegetable. (We got broccoli.) Dessert is a bland apple turnover. The very best part—no utensils because this is the 12th century, and cutlery did not become popular for another 200 years or so.

Warning: The show features chemical fog, pyrotechnics, and dirt, as well as horses, so those with allergies or asthma should definitely take this into consideration before going. Also, this show might not be the best thing for younger children who could be upset by live fights (including a bloodless simulated throat slitting), creepy masks, or by flames, explosions, and swirling spotlights. On the other hand, your young child may thrive on

The Men Who Could Be (the) King

Las Vegas has cornered the market in fakery (note all the architecture that replicates other places and times), and much of its current low-cost entertainment is based on the art of illusions—and we don't mean just the magic acts. In addition to the female impersonator shows (not suitable for kids) and the full-production celebrity impersonators, there can be up to half a dozen Elvises in Las Vegas working the lounges at any one time. The best performer is usually the one who appears in *Legends in Concert* at Harrah's.

that sort of thing. . . . Shows are Wednesday through Monday at 6 and 8:30pm. Dark Tuesday. In Excalibur, 3850 Las Vegas Blvd. S. ✆ **800/937-7777** or 702/597-7600. Tickets $62 (includes tax and dinner).

3 HEADLINER SHOWROOMS

Vegas entertainment made its name with its showrooms, though its glory days are somewhat behind it, gone with the Rat Pack themselves. For a long time, Vegas headliners were something of a joke; only those on the downhill side of fame were thought to play there, and children weren't welcome in them anyway. But with all the new performance spaces offered by the new hotels, and the high admission prices, Vegas suddenly has credence again, especially in, of all things, the rock scene. Both the Hard Rock Hotel & Casino's the Joint and the House of Blues are attracting the most current and popular acts who find it hip, rather than humiliating, to play Sin City, and some of those acts actually make it a point of catering to their fans by insisting that their shows allow all ages inside. However, the classic Vegas showroom itself does seem headed the way of the dinosaurs; many of the hotels have shuttered theirs. As for the remainder, one is pretty much like any other, with the exception of the Hard Rock and House of Blues (hence their detailed descriptions below), and, in any case, audiences go based on the performer rather than the space itself. Check with your hotel or look in those free magazines in your room to see who is in town when you are and whether the show is appropriate (and/or will be enjoyable) for your children.

Hard Rock Hotel & Casino's The Joint Formerly just about the only game in town in terms of good rock bookings, the Joint, with a 1,400-seat capacity, now faces some stiff competition from the House of Blues. For example, when Alanis Morissette came to town, she played the Hard Rock, but her opening act, Garbage, played the House of Blues. On the other hand, it was here that the Rolling Stones chose to do a show during their arena tour—this was the smallest venue the band had played in years, and, as you can imagine, it was one hot ticket. When the Hard Rock Hotel & Casino opened in 1995, the Eagles were the first act to appear. Since then, the facility has presented Ziggy Marley, Marilyn Manson, Tori Amos, the Black Crowes, Beck, Tears for Fears, the Red Hot Chili Peppers, and Counting Crows, to name a few kid faves, along with Stephen Stills and Bob Dylan, who may be more appealing to adults.

The venue is not a preferred one, however; it's worth going only if a favorite performer is playing or if it's an opportunity to see a big artist play a smaller-than-usual room, or if there's an all-ages show, and you want to show your kid a good time. Though there's sometimes table seating, it's usually festival style, making personal space at a premium during a crowded show, and though the floor is slightly raked, this still makes for poor sightlines, especially for smaller kids. ("We get them as young as six," said the helpful lady at the box office when asked about age limits.) The balconies upstairs, if you can get to them, aren't much better, because once the bodies are packed in about two deep, the stage is completely obscured. Unless you want to brave the crush at the very front (sure, you should—it's a rock show!), we suggest standing at the rail toward the back, which not only elevates you slightly above the crowd (improving those sightlines), but also protects one side of your body from the crowd. ***Note:*** Children must be accompanied by an adult here.

Showroom Policies: Smoking permitted for some shows; seating is either preassigned or general, depending on the performer. **Price:** $55 to $140, depending on the performer (tax and drinks extra). **Showtimes:** 7 or 8:30pm (nights of performance vary, as do age requirements). **Reservations:** You can reserve up to 30 days in advance. In the Hard Rock Hotel & Casino, 4455 Paradise Rd. ✆ **800/473-7625** or 702/693-5000. www.hardrockhotel.com.

House of Blues The House of Blues at Mandalay Bay goes head-to-head with the Joint at the Hard Rock Hotel & Casino. Probably the most comfortable and user-friendly place to see a rock show in Vegas, especially for children and teens, the House of Blues is a good, intimate room with a cozy floor surrounded by a bar area, and an upstairs balcony area that has actual theater seating. (The balcony might actually be a better place to see a show because the sightlines are unobscured, unlike down below, where posts and such can obstruct the view.) The Disney-bayou decor—with corrugated tin and weathered wood, plus walls covered in outsider/primitive/folk art from various Southern artists—can be a bit twee and overly nouveau-riche folksy, but kids do love to stare at all the stuff. The House of Blues has rock and blues shows just about every night, and, as mentioned, nationally recognized acts are flocking to the place: Billy Idol, X, Garbage, the B-52s, the Pretenders, the Wallflowers, Reverend Horton Heat, Etta James, Al Green, the Go-Gos, the Neville Brothers, and even the spoken word by Henry Rollins are just some of the acts who have performed here since the club opened.

Headliner Stadiums

Two arenas are worth a special mention because they often feature major entertainers and are open to all ages. **Sam Boyd Stadium,** the outdoor stadium for the University of Nevada, Las Vegas (UNLV) at 7000 E. Russell Rd., has been host to such major acts as Paul McCartney, U2, the Eagles, and Metallica. The **Thomas & Mack Center,** the university's indoor arena, located on the campus at 4505 Maryland Pkwy., has a more comprehensive concert schedule, which, in the past, has included Phish, Van Halen, Celine Dion, and Michael Bolton as well as shows such as Disney on Ice and the Ringling Brothers and Barnum & Bailey Circus. To reach either of the above, call ✆ **702/895-3900** or visit **www.thomasandmack.com**.

Ticketmaster (✆ **702/474-4000**) handles ticketing for concerts at these arenas, though tickets to some events can be purchased through the university (✆ **702/739-3267;** www.unlvtickets.com).

Showroom Policies: Smoking permitted; seating is either preassigned or general, depending on the performer (some shows are all general admission, with everyone standing on the floor). **Price:** $15 to $125, depending on the performer. **Showtimes:** Vary, but usually 8pm. Age requirements vary by acts. **Reservations:** You can buy tickets as soon as shows are announced; lead time varies with each artist. In Mandalay Bay, 3950 Las Vegas Blvd. S. ✆ **877/632-7800** or 702/632-7600. www.hob.com/venues/clubvenues/lasvegas.

4 COMEDY CLUBS

Although Las Vegas is the proving ground for many comics and a place where visitors can catch both top-name and rising stars, unfortunately, most clubs are 21 and over. Below is the exception.

Riviera Comedy Club **Ages 12 & up.** Featuring a rotating lineup of comedians, and designed to resemble a classic basement comedy club (rows of tables, a semicircular stage with a spotlight and microphone), this is the only all-ages comedy spot in Las Vegas. Children 12 and older are welcome, though expect that they will hear some raunchy language and some off-color jokes, staples of comics and many PG-13 movies during the $1^1/_2$-hourlong show; the 10:30pm show is even more "blue." Along with comics, hypnotists and ventriloquists occasionally share the bill. Dinner and show combos are also available. Performances are nightly at 8:30 and 10:30pm. In The Riviera, 2901 Las Vegas Blvd. S. ✆ **800/634-6753** or 702/794-9433. www.rivierahotel.com/entertainment_comedyclub.asp. Tickets $38; dinner/show combos $50 and $60.

5 SPECTATOR SPORTS

Las Vegas isn't especially well known for its sports teams. The only consistent spectator sports are those featuring teams from the University of Nevada, Las Vegas; the rest of the city's sports teams, such as they are, resemble a bad soap opera, in which the characters get amnesia, disappear for years, or change their names and reappear as their twin. Sin City's minor league baseball team, the Stars, changed their name to the 51s and became a farm team for the Los Angeles Dodgers. The city's hockey team, the Thunder, took a powder break, and was replaced by the Wranglers.

A major venue for car racing, **Las Vegas Motor Speedway** draws major race events to Las Vegas, as well as providing a venue for demolition derbies, dirt biking, and go-kart races.

Because the city has several top-notch sporting arenas, there are important annual events that take place in Las Vegas, details for which can be found in the listings of major conventions (p. 33) and the "Las Vegas Calendar of Kid-Friendly Events" (p. 34). In addition to those listings, the **PGA Tours Las Vegas Senior Classic** is held each April in nearby Summerlin, and the **Las Vegas Invitational** takes place in Las Vegas each October. The **National Finals Rodeo** is held in UNLV's Thomas & Mack Center each December and the **Professional Bull Riders Tour** takes place in late October to early November. From time to time, you'll also find NBA exhibition games, professional ice-skating competitions, or gymnastics exhibitions.

Finally, Las Vegas is well known as a major location for championship **boxing matches.** These are held in several Strip hotels, most often at Caesars or the MGM Grand, but sometimes, also, at The Mirage and Mandalay Bay. Tickets are hard to come by for these matches and are quite expensive. We suggest that if your children truly wish to watch a boxing match, you spring for the pay-per-view, rather than the insanity of the stadium during a match.

Tickets for sporting events at hotels are available either through **Ticketmaster** (✆ **702/893-3000**) or through the hotels themselves. (Why pay the service charges if you don't have to?)

PROFESSIONAL TEAMS

The 51s ★★ Las Vegas's local minor league team used to be known as the Stars, but after becoming the Los Angeles Dodgers' farm team, they took on this moniker, a tribute to alleged UFO spotting site, Area 51, located 90 minutes from Las Vegas. Their logo is an alien, and their fans truly love them. Home games are played seasonally at Cashman Field, which is also the site of preseason Major League exhibition games. Cashman Field, 850 Las Vegas Blvd. N. ✆ **702/474-4000.** http://lasvegas.51s.milb.com. General admission $7, reserved seating $9, plaza level $10, field level $12.

MAJOR SPORTS VENUES

Outside of Hotels

Las Vegas Motor Speedway ★★ The first new superspeedway to be built in the Southwest in over 2 decades, this venue seats 107,000. Included in the $100-million state-of-the-art motor-sports entertainment complex are a 1½-mile super-speedway, a 2½-mile FIA-approved road course, paved and dirt short-track ovals, and a 4,000-foot drag strip. Also on the property are facilities for go-kart and Motocross racing, along with specialty racing opportunities such as Legends Car and Sand Drag. The new speedway is accessible via shuttle buses to and from the Imperial Palace hotel, though some of the other major hotels have their own shuttles to the Speedway. Free tours are offered. 7000 Las Vegas Blvd. N., directly across from Nellis Air Force base (take I-15 N. to Speedway exit 54). ✆ **702/644-4443** for ticket information. www.lvms.com. Tickets $20–$262 (higher prices for weekend passes to major events).

Baby Bikers

Motocross, known colloquially as dirt biking, attracts many families, both as spectators and as participants. A women's league recently formed, and kids as young as 4 years old are racing on small bikes with 50cc (cubic centimeters; the engine size) engines called "teeny 50s." These peewee dirt bike competitions are held at Las Vegas Motor Speedway. Check out **www.dirtbikekids.com** for more information.

University of Nevada, Las Vegas ★★ The university hosts three major sports venues: the Thomas & Mack Center, Cox Pavilion, and Sam Boyd Stadium. The Thomas & Mack Center, located on the campus at 4505 Maryland Pkwy., hosts the UNLV Running Rebels basketball team, as well as being the site of the rodeo finals, bull-riding championships, and concerts. The 3,000-seat Cox Pavilion, also on the campus, at 4505 Maryland Pkwy., is home to the UNLV volleyball teams and UNLV's Lady Rebels basketball team, as well as being the site of other indoor events. Sam Boyd Stadium, at 7000 East Russell Rd., is the site of UNLV Rebels' football games, as well as being a concert venue for bands like U2, the Eagles, and Metallica. Tickets for events at the Sam Boyd

Las Vegas's Sports Venues, Stadiums & Local Performing Arts Venues

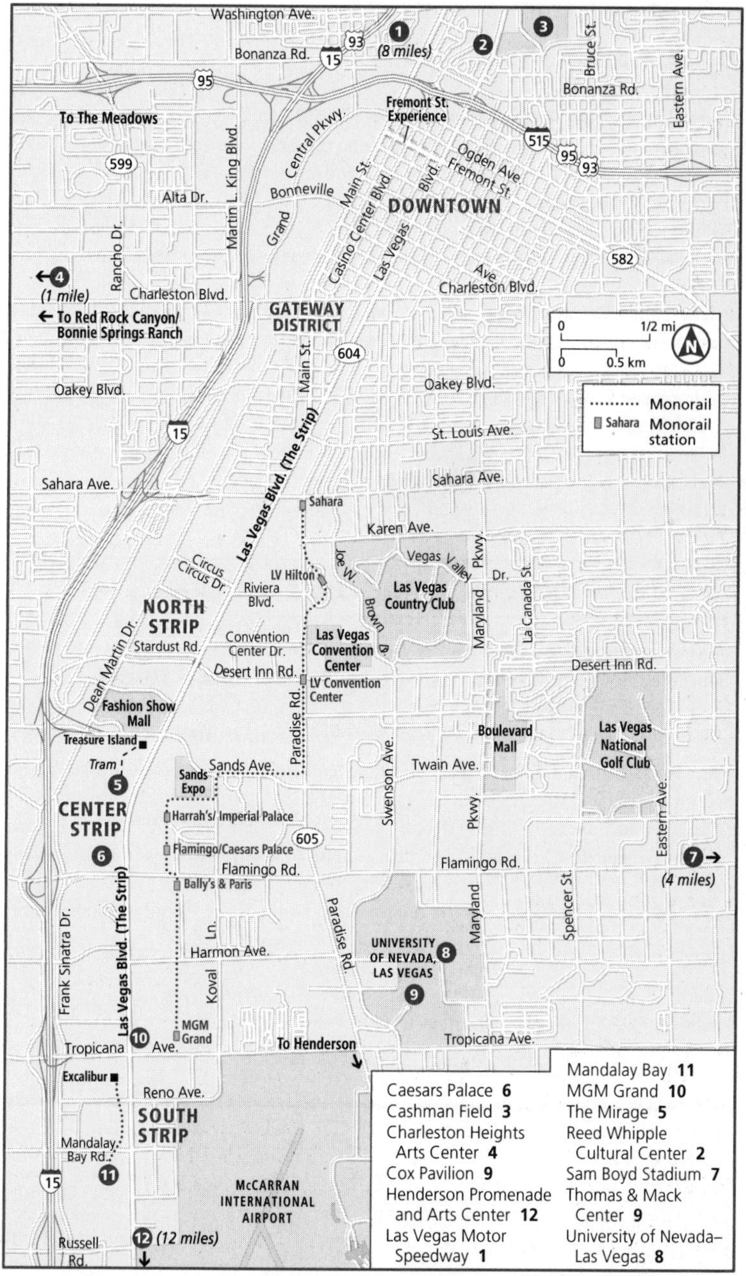

Stadium, Cox Pavilion, and the Thomas & Mack Center can be purchased through the campus's ticketing agency. 4505 Maryland Pkwy. and 7000 E. Russell Rd. ✆ **702/739-3267** for ticket information. www.unlvtickets.com for event listings at all UNLV venues. Tickets $10 and up depending on event.

MAJOR SPORTS VENUES

In Hotels

Caesars Palace (✆ **800/634-6698** or 702/731-7110) has a long tradition of sporting events, from Evel Knievel's attempted motorcycle jump over its fountains in 1967 to Grand Prix auto races. Mary Lou Retton has tumbled in gymnastic events at Caesars, and Olympians Brian Boitano and Katarina Witt have taken to the ice, as has Wayne Gretzky. Additionally, well over 100 world-championship boxing contests (not the best place for children—under any circumstance) have taken place at Caesars Palace since the hotel opened.

The **MGM Grand's Garden Events Arena** (✆ **800/929-1111** or 702/891-7777) is a major venue for professional boxing matches, rodeos, tennis, ice-skating shows, World Figure Skating Championships, and more.

Mandalay Bay (✆ **877/632-7400**) has been hosting a number of boxing matches in its 12,000-seat Events Center, and The **Mirage** (✆ **800/627-6667** or 702/791-7111) also features occasional championship boxing matches. You may wish to avoid these hotels during boxing matches, as that type of sporting event can draw raucous, and according to *Los Angeles Times* reports, decidedly unsavory types to the area.

6 LOCAL PERFORMING ARTS

The local performing arts scene in Las Vegas provides cultural events of all types, whether your tastes lean toward light musicals, classical music, or ballet. We've chosen the most family-friendly ones for you—the ones where a child asking questions about plot points or wanting to go to the restroom won't be frowned upon (usually).

Las Vegas Youth Orchestras **All ages.** Sponsored in part by the Clark County School District and the City of Las Vegas, the Las Vegas Youth Orchestras consist of four divisions based on age and experience; the annual concert for all the orchestras takes place in December, with other concerts, including a performance by the Youth Philharmonic with the UNLV Philharmonic, taking place throughout the year. The coaching staff, conductors, and other services are provided by the Clark County School District; the City of Las Vegas provides a rehearsal hall and storage at Reed Whipple Center, sponsors one concert a year, and has commissioned music written specially for the LVYO. Reed Whipple Cultural Center, 821 Las Vegas Blvd. N. ✆ **702/229-6211.** www.lvyo.org. Tickets $6 adults; $3 students, seniors, and visitors with disabilities.

Nevada Ballet Theatre **Ages 5 & up.** This much-beloved ballet company is the beneficiary of funds raised at the annual All-You-Can-Eat Ice Cream Festival held in September in nearby Summerlin, where the theater stages a special performance. The company, whose season runs from December though May, offers performances geared toward the entire family, usually held at stages on the UNLV campus. Along with the much-adored *Nutcracker* (staged at the Judy Bayley Theatre at UNLV), their 2005–06 season included the classic *A Midsummer Night's Dream.* At University of Nevada, Las Vegas, 4505 Maryland Pkwy. ✆ **702/243-2623.** www.nevadaballet.com. Tickets $35–$49, $75.

Look & Listen

Families interested in a one-stop cultural experience should check out the **Charleston Heights Arts Center,** 800 S. Brush St. (✆ **702/229-6383**), a city-run facility that showcases both visual and performing arts, with events coordinated by the cultural affairs division of the city's Department of Parks and Leisure. Along with gallery space for national and regional artists, its concert halls feature anything from the Eastern European folk sounds of klezmer to jazz to classical music, and such musicals as the Rainbow Theatre's *Snoopy!* have been staged in the 375-seat theater.

Rainbow Company Youth Theatre **Ages 4 & up, depending on play.** This award-winning theater company, supported by the City of Las Vegas, is housed at the Reed Whipple Cultural Center, and performs there and at other locations, including the Charleston Heights Arts Center (see "Look & Listen," below). Annually, the company stages five shows, which have included the musicals *Meet Me in St. Louis* and *The Little Mermaid,* and the drama *The Effect of Gamma Rays on Man in the Moon Marigolds.* Thanks to city support and funding, ticket prices are kept low, making this an affordable community resource. At the Reed Whipple Cultural Center, 821 Las Vegas Blvd. N. ✆ **702/229-6211.** www.rainbowcompany.info. Tickets $7 adults, $5 seniors and children 13–18, $3 children 12 and under. Combo show tickets for all 5 shows $12–$28; for 3 shows, $7–$18.

7 WHAT TO DO IF YOU'VE GOTTEN A BABYSITTER

It's Vegas! Do we really need to tell you what to do if you've made suitable arrangements for your munchkins? You can't walk two steps in this town without finding something that will entertain you. Nevertheless, we've given you some options below.

For information on babysitters and child-care services, see section 14 "Babysitters & Child-Care Centers," of chapter 3, beginning on p. 73.

BARS

Eiffel Tower From this chic and elegant room, in the restaurant on the 11th floor of the Eiffel Tower, you can look down on everyone (in Vegas)—just like a real Parisian! (Just kidding, Francophiles.) But really, this is a date-impressing bar, and, because there's no cover or minimum, it's a cost-effective alternative to the overly inflated food prices at the restaurant. Drop by for a drink, but try to look sophisticated. Then you can cop an attitude and dismiss everything as gauche—or droit, depending on which way you are seated. Open daily until 1am. In Paris Las Vegas, 3655 Las Vegas Blvd. S. ✆ **702/948-6937.**

Fontana Bar So you've been avoiding Bellagio, either because you've got too many kids or too little cash. Well, here's a way to do Bellagio without kids or cash. The Fontana Bar could be the least expensive night out in the most expensive hotel on Earth. You'll find some of the best lounge entertainment in Vegas here, with comfortable seating and great acoustics; an outdoor patio overlooks the Lake Bellagio fountain show; and you get it all for the price of one drink. The frou-frou cocktails and hard liquor aren't cheap, but beers are $6 to $7 and juice and soft drinks are even less. The entertainment starts at 5pm and runs till 1am Sunday to Thursday, 2am Friday to Saturday. The earlier the go, the more you'll have the place to yourself. Open daily 11am to 11pm. In Bellagio, 3600 Las Vegas Blvd. S. ✆ **888/488-7111** or 702/693-7722. www.bellagiolasvegas.com. 1-drink minimum.

Nine Fine Irishmen One of the most upbeat, high-energy, and friendly bars you'll find anywhere, Nine Fine Irishmen is the go-to place for live Celtic music, good Irish food (this is NOT an oxymoron), cold draft Guinness, and small-batch Irish whiskeys. Best of all, if you don't look quite as fresh as you did before your child-rearing years, you won't be surrounded by the buff, beautiful, see-and-be-seen crowd. Built in Ireland and shipped to America, the two-story pub is wood paneled throughout, with bars on both levels. A bandstand on the lower level is home to talented Celtic singers, dancers, and bands. The bandstand is visible from the stairway and the upper level. No hidden agendas here, Nine Fine Irishmen is just for fun. Open daily 11am to 11pm. In New York–New York, 3790 Las Vegas Blvd. S. ✆ **702/740-6463.** www.nynylasvegas.com or www.ninefineirishmen.com. Occasional cover charge.

VooDoo Lounge In an amazing Vegas sleight of hand, this bar is supposedly located on the 51st floor of the Rio, but, in reality, is on the 41st. (The number 4 is considered unlucky in Chinese culture—it's a homophone for "death"—and is thus avoided by casino hotels eager to draw Asian gamblers.) Numerical trickery aside, the view from the lounge's balcony is astounding—the entire Strip is laid out glistening with neon. The lounge's tropical drinks—with names such as Shrunken Head, High Priestess, and What the Witch Doctor Ordered—are potent and pricey, and are made by handsome bartenders who flip and toss the bottles with considerable showmanship and flair; they are almost as much fun to watch as the sparkling lights of the Strip. The decor carries out the voodoo theme with mysterious symbols and beaded flags covering the walls. The dress code basically translates as no jeans or T-shirts. From 9pm on, there are live bands. Open daily 5pm to 2:30am. In the Rio All-Suite Hotel & Casino, 3700 W. Flamingo Blvd. ✆ **702/252-7777.** Cover $20 after 8pm.

CASINOS

What? You didn't come to Las Vegas for the Liberace Museum? We are shocked. *Shocked.*

Yes, there are gambling opportunities in Vegas. We've noticed this. You will, too. The tip-off will be the slot machines in the airport as soon as you step off the plane. And the slot machines in the convenience stores as soon as you drive across the state line. Let's not kid ourselves, gambling is what Vegas is about. The bright lights, the shows, the showgirls, the buffets—it's all there just to lure you in and make you open your wallet. (The free drinks certainly help ease the latter as well.)

You can disappoint them casinos if you want, but what would be the point? *This is Las Vegas.* You don't have to be a high roller. You would not believe how much fun you can have at a nickel slot machine. You won't get rich, but neither will most of those guys playing the $5 slots.

Of course, that's not going to stop anyone from trying. Almost everyone plays in Vegas with the hopes of winning The Big One. That only a few ever do win doesn't stop them from trying again and again and again. That's how the casinos make their money, by the way.

But we're not going to give you a lecture here. Enjoy the time you have in the casinos while you can—because they are strict about not letting anyone underage into their hallowed halls, so, if this is the only time you have away from your kids while you're in Las Vegas, this may be your only opportunity to take part in the gambling hoopla that Las Vegas is so famous for.

Casino choice is a personal thing. Some like to find their lucky place and stick with it, while others love to take advantage of the nearly endless choices that Vegas offers. Everyone should casino-hop at least once to marvel (or get dizzy) at the decor/spectacle and the sheer excess of it all. But beyond decoration, there isn't too much difference. You've got your slot machines, your gaming tables, and your big chandeliers.

Don't be a snob, and don't be overly dazzled by the fancy casinos. Sometimes you can have a better time at one of the older places Downtown, where stakes are lower, pretensions are nonexistent, and the clientele is often friendlier. Frankly, real gamblers—and by that we don't necessarily mean high rollers, but those who play to win regardless of the amount of said win—head straight for Downtown for these precise reasons, caring not a whit about glitz and glamour. Even if you don't take your gambling as seriously as that, you may well want to follow their example. After all, it's getting harder and harder to find cheap tables (where you can play a hand of blackjack, for example, for less than $10) on the Strip—so take your hard-earned money to where you can lose it more slowly; or, lose it all in one fantabulous hand of a very glamorous poker game; whatever floats your boat.

SOUTH STRIP

Excalibur As you might expect, the Excalibur casino is replete with suits of armor, stained-glass panels, knights, dragons, and velvet and satin heraldic banners, with gaming action taking place beneath vast iron-and-gold chandeliers fit for a medieval castle fortress. This all makes it fine for kitsch-seekers, but anyone who hates crowds or is sensitive to noise will hate it. The overall effect is less like a castle and more like a dungeon. (We really only recommend it if you're staying there anyway, and even then, we advise you to look beyond this one.) Excalibur's 100,000-plus square feet of gaming facilities also include a race and sports book, a keno lounge, a poker room, blackjack, minibaccarat, Caribbean stud, craps, roulette, pai gow poker, Big Six, and slot/video-poker machines. 3850 Las Vegas Blvd. S. ✆ **877/750-5464** or 702/597-7777. www.excalibur.com.

Luxor More accessible than ever thanks to the air-conditioned people mover from Excalibur and the monorail from Mandalay Bay, Luxor has been completely remodeled and, in our opinion, improved immeasurably. Gone is the space-wasting central area that used to contain the bathrooms, cashiers, and casino offices. This additional space gives the casino a much more airy feel, which produces a low claustrophobia level—in parts, you can see all the way up the inside of the pyramid. The Players Club, the MGM MIRAGE slot club also valid at sister properties such as Mandalay Bay, Excalibur, New York–New York, MGM Grand, Monte Carlo, Bellagio, The Mirage, and Treasure Island, offers rewards of cash, merchandise, meals, and special services to slot and table players. Sports action unfolds on 17 large-screen TVs and 128 personalized monitors in Luxor's race and sports book. Additional gaming facilities include blackjack, craps, roulette, poker, baccarat, pai gow, Big Six, and slot/video-poker machines. 3900 Las Vegas Blvd. S. ✆ **800/288-1000** or 702/262-4000. www.luxor.com.

Mandalay Bay You'll find "elegant" gaming in a prefab, deliberate, and expansive way, with a very high ceiling that produces a very low claustrophobia factor. It's definitely the place to go if you're looking for less hectic, less gimmick-filled play. The layout makes it look airy, and it's marginally less confusing and certainly less overwhelming than many other casinos. Because it is at the far south end of the Strip, there are fewer walk-in players, but the presence of the House of Blues and the popularity of the **rumjungle nightclub** (p. 251) can mean a late-night influx of customers. There's a big, ultracomfortable sports book (what casinos call the room where you bet on sports), complete with armchairs that could well encourage a relaxed gambler to fall asleep, including a live daily sports-radio show. Other gaming available includes poker, blackjack, craps, roulette, baccarat, minibaccarat, Let-It-Ride, Caribbean stud, pai gow poker, Big Six, and slot/video-poker machines. Players should sign up for the Players Club, the MGM MIRAGE player-reward system, to get the comps that come with pitting your bankroll against the casino's. 3950 Las Vegas Blvd. S. ✆ **877/632-7000** or 702/632-7000. www.mandalaybay.com.

MGM Grand Las Vegas's largest casino at 171,500 square feet—we've been to countries that were smaller!—is divided into four themed areas, in a futile attempt to make it seem smaller. The original *Wizard of Oz* decorations have been removed, but spend an hour in here and you may feel like Dorothy after she was whisked away by the twister. You will get lost at least once. The sports casino houses a big poker room and a state-of-the-art race and sports book. And the French Riviera–themed Monte Carlo casino has a luxurious marble-columned and gold-draped private high-end gaming area. Carousels of progressive slots unique to the MGM Grand include the very popular Majestic Lions high-frequency $1 slot machines that pay out more than $1 million daily, and the Lion's Share $1 slots, which are capable of jackpots exceeding $1 million each at any time. Additional gaming facilities include a keno lounge, blackjack, craps, roulette, baccarat, minibaccarat, pai gow, pai gow poker, Caribbean stud, Let It Ride, Casino War, Big Six, and slot/video-poker machines. 3799 Las Vegas Blvd. S. ✆ **800/929-1111** or 702/891-7777. www.mgmgrand.com.

New York–New York Another theme-run-wild place: tuxes on the backs of gaming chairs, change carts that look like yellow cabs, and so forth, all set in a miniature New York City. Crammed into the casino are such landmarks as Greenwich Village, Wall Street, Little Italy, and Times Square. The most obvious resemblance to the real New York, however, is the casino's virtually gridlocked pedestrian traffic. Simply put, avoid this place if you're a little claustrophobic. Even if you can handle jostling crowds, you're still in for a major case of sensory overload. Serious gamblers understandably may sniff at it all and prefer to take their business to a less congested venue, especially if they don't regard gambling as a contact sport. Everyone else should drop in and gawk for a couple of minutes. There's blackjack, craps, roulette, baccarat, minibaccarat, Caribbean Stud, Let It Ride, Casino War, Big Six, and slot/video-poker machines. New York–New York participates in the MGM MIRAGE Players Club, also valid at sister properties such as the MGM Grand and The Mirage. 3790 Las Vegas Blvd. S. ✆ **888/693-6763** or 702/740-6969. www.nynyhotelcasino.com.

Orleans This is not a particularly special gambling space, though it does have a low claustrophobia level, but, if you're staying here and don't want to venture out of the hotel, it'll do. Another plus is that they sometimes play Cajun and zydeco music over the sound system, so you can two-step while you gamble, which can make losing somewhat less painful. It has all the needed tables—blackjack, craps, and so forth—plus plenty of slots, including the popular Wheel of Fortune machine, which works like those other roulette-wheel slots, but in this case, actually plays the theme song from the TV show. It will even applaud for you if you win. Because Orleans is popular with locals, there are lots of video-poker options. And because it's not on the Strip, you'll find cheaper table minimums. 4500 W. Tropicana Ave. ✆ **800/675-3267** or 702/365-7111. www.orleanscasino.com.

CENTER STRIP

Bellagio The slot machines here are mostly encased in marble and fine woods. How's that for upping the ante on classy? In all fairness, Bellagio comes the closest to re-creating the feel of gambling in Monte Carlo (the country, not the next-door casino), but its relentless good taste means that this is one pretty forgettable casino. After all, we are suckers for a wacky theme that screams "Vegas," and European class just doesn't cut it. Sure, there are good touches—we always like a high ceiling to reduce the claustrophobia index, and the place is laid out in an easy-to-navigate grid with ultrawide aisles, so walking through doesn't seem like such a crowded collision-course maze. Anyway, the cozy sports book has individual TVs and entirely denlike leather chairs—quite comfortable. And stop off for a peek into Bobby's Room, which hosts the biggest poker games in town. 3600 Las Vegas Blvd. S. ✆ **888/987-6667** or 702/693-7111. www.bellagio.com.

Caesars Palace Caesars' casino is simultaneously the ultimate in gambling luxury and the ultimate in Vegas kitsch. Cocktail waitresses in togas parade about as you gamble under the watchful gaze of faux-marble Roman statues. The very high ceiling in certain areas of the casino makes for a very low claustrophobia level. Although we love it, the casino has become somewhat confusing and unmanageable because of its size and meandering layout, like Caesars itself.

A notable facility is the state-of-the-art **Race and Sports Book,** with huge electronic display boards and giant video screens. (Caesars pioneered computer-generated wagering data that can be communicated in less than half a second and has sophisticated satellite equipment that can pick up the broadcast of virtually any sporting event in the world.) The domed VIP slot arena of the Forum Casino (minimum bet is $5, but you can wager up to $1,500 on a single pull!) is a plush, crystal-chandeliered precinct with seating in roomy, adjustable chairs. Gamblers can accumulate bonus points toward cash back, gifts, gratis show tickets, meals, and rooms by joining the Total Rewards players club that is also valid at sister properties like Bally's, Paris Las Vegas, Harrah's, and The Flamingo. Club membership also lets you in on grand-prize drawings, tournaments, and parties.

The most upscale of the Caesars' gaming rooms is the intimate, European-style casino adjoining the **808** restaurant. Total facilities in all three casinos contain craps tables, blackjack, roulette, baccarat, minibaccarat, Let It Ride, Caribbean Stud, pai gow poker, two Big Six wheels, slot/video-poker machines, and a keno lounge. 3570 Las Vegas Blvd. S. ✆ **800/634-6661** or 702/731-7110. www.harrahs.com.

The Mirage Gamble in a Polynesian village in one of the prettiest casinos in town. It has a meandering layout, and the low ceiling makes for a medium claustrophobia level, but neither of these aspects is overwhelming. This remains one of our favorite places to gamble. Facilities include a plush European-style high-limit lounge for high rollers at baccarat, blackjack, and video poker; an elegant minibuffet serves meals to gamblers there. Slot and table players can join the MGM MIRAGE Players Club, also valid at sister hotels such as Treasure Island and MGM Grand, and work toward points for cash rebates, special room rates, complimentary meals and/or show tickets, and other benefits. The elaborate race and sports book offers theater stereo sound and a movie-theater-size screen. Other gaming facilities here: 75 blackjack tables, craps, roulette, baccarat, minibaccarat, pai gow, pai gow poker, Big Six, Casino War, and slot/video-poker machines.

It's one of the most pleasant, and popular, casinos in town, so it's very crowded more often than not. 3400 Las Vegas Blvd. S. ✆ **800/627-6667** or 702/791-7111. www.mirage.com.

The Venetian "Tasteful" is the watchword in these days of classy Vegas gaming, and consequently, with the exception of more hand-painted Venetian art re-creations on parts of the ceiling, The Venetian's casino is interchangeable with those found at Mandalay Bay, the Monte Carlo, and to a certain extent, Bellagio. All that gleaming marble, columns, and such is very nice, but after a while, also a bit ho-hum. Besides, this is Vegas, and we want our tacky theme elements, by gosh. The lack thereof, combined with poor signage, may be why this casino is so hard to get around—every part looks exactly the same. It's not claustrophobic, but it can be confusing. Plus, there is no giant slot machine. On the other hand, you can access the casino directly from the St. Mark's Square re-creation out front. Facilities include a relatively small but comfortable sports book, poker, blackjack, craps, roulette, pai gow poker, baccarat, and slot/video-poker machines. 3355 Las Vegas Blvd. S. ✆ **888/2-VENICE** (283-6423) or 702/414-1000. www.venetian.com.

Wynn Las Vegas At 110,000 square feet, the Wynn casino is among the larger in town. Situated in the middle of the ground floor, two things strike you immediately. First, most of the main pedestrian walkways run around the perimeter of the casino rather than through it, and second, the high ceilings canopy the slots instead of the table games. Speaking of which, the Wynn casino offers an amazing variety of games. In addition to the usual suspects (blackjack, craps, roulette, and so on), 3-card poker, Let It Ride, pai gow poker, Caribbean Stud, and Crazy 4 Poker are also dealt. Video poker and slots are low return in denominations of less than a dollar and there's really nothing worth playing unless a progressive runs up. If you're willing to bet $1 or higher, there are plenty of full-pay video poker machines. Hotel room key cards double as slot cards. For nonguests regular slot cards are available. The best blackjack tables deal double deck with the dealer hitting soft 17s, and double after split. Minimum bets for table games are high, usually $10. Wynn Las Vegas, 3131 Las Vegas Blvd. S. ✆ **800/320-WYNN** (320-9966) or 888/320-7173. www.wynnlasvegas.com.

NORTH STRIP

Circus Circus This vast property has three full-size casinos that, combined, comprise one of the largest gaming operations in Nevada (more than 100,000 sq. ft.). More importantly, it has an entire circus midway set up throughout, so you are literally gambling with trapeze stunts going on over your head. The other great gimmick is the slot machine carousel—yep, it turns while you spin the reels. The MGM MIRAGE Players Club offers slot/video-poker and table players the opportunity to earn points redeemable for cash, discounted rooms and meals, and other benefits at any of the sister properties. The Circus Bucks progressive slot machines here build from a jackpot base of $500,000, which players can win on a $2 pull. Gaming facilities include a 10,000-square-foot race and sports book with 30 video monitors ranging from 13 to 52 inches, poker tables, blackjack, craps, roulette, a Big Six wheel, Let It Ride, pai gow poker, dice, Caribbean Stud, and slot/video-poker machines. Unfortunately, the casino is crowded and noisy, and there are lots of children passing through (making it more crowded and noisy). That, plus some low ceilings (not in the Big Top, obviously), makes for a very high claustrophobia rating, though the new commedia dell'arte clown motif (as opposed to the old garish circus motif) has upgraded the decor. 2880 Las Vegas Blvd. S. ✆ **877/224-7287** or 702/734-0410. www.circuscircus.com.

EAST OF THE STRIP

Hard Rock Hotel & Casino This is where Gen X goes to gamble. The Hard Rock has certainly taken casino decor to a whole new level. The attention to detail and the resulting playfulness is admirable, if not incredible. Gaming tables have piano keyboards at one end; some slots have Fender guitar fretboards as arms; gaming chips have band names and/or pictures on them; slot machines are similarly rock-themed (check out the Jimi Hendrix machine!); and so it goes. The whole thing is set in the middle of a circular room, around the outskirts of which are various rock memorabilia in glass cases. Rock blares over the sound system, allowing boomers to boogie while they gamble. A Back Stage Pass allows patrons to rack up discounts on meals, lodging, and gift-shop items while playing slots and table games. The race and sports book here provides comfortable seating in leather-upholstered reclining armchairs. Gaming facilities (with selected non-smoking tables) include blackjack, roulette, craps, Caribbean Stud, Let It Ride, pai gow poker, and slot/video-poker machines. All this is genuinely amazing, but the noise level is above even that of a normal casino. 4455 Paradise Rd. ✆ **800/473-ROCK** (473-7625) or 702/693-5000. www.hardrockhotel.com.

DANCE CLUBS

Cleopatra's Barge This is a small, unique lounge set in part on a floating barge—you can feel it rocking. The bandstand, a small dance floor, and a few (usually reserved) tables are here, while others are seated around the boat on "land." It's a gimmick, but one that makes this far more fun than other, more pedestrian, hotel bars. Plenty of dark makes for romance, but blaring volume levels mean you will have to scream those sweet nothings. Check out the bare-breasted figurehead on the ship's prow who juts out over the hallway going past the entrance. She could put someone's eye out. Open nightly from 8:30pm until 3am. In Caesars Palace, 3570 Las Vegas Blvd. S. ✆ **702/731-7110.** No cover.

Moon (Finds) Moon is aptly named. Located at the top of the Palms's Fantasy Tower, you're halfway into orbit when you walk in, and closer yet when you ascend the steel-and-glass spiral staircase that leads to the VIP balcony and patio. This place will definitely put you in a lunar frame of mind, with its color-changing glass floor tiles, laser beams flitting hither and yon, and space-age metallic waitress and dancer outfits. The large rectangular dance floor is surrounded by large VIP booths. The roof—35 feet above the dance floor—retracts, allowing the mingling of stars inside and out; when it's closed, the ceiling serves as a giant screen that projects images from the cameras focused on the action. But no matter where you go or what you do, you'll always get your money's worth from the view of the sprawling Las Vegas Valley out the floor-to-ceiling windows or outside on the patio behind the main bar. Open Tuesday and Thursday to Sunday 10pm till "late." In the Palms Resort & Casino, 4321 W. Flamingo Rd., ✆ **702/942-7777.** Cover Fri–Sat $50; Sun, Tues, Thurs $25.

rumjungle Now, normally our delicate sensibilities wince at such overkill, and we tend to write off such efforts as just trying a bit too hard. But surprisingly, rumjungle really delivers the great fun it promises. The fire-wall entrance gives way to a wall of water; the two-story bar is full of the largest collection of rum varieties anywhere, each bottle illuminated with a laser beam of light; go-go girls dance and prance between bottles of wine, to dueling congas; and the food all comes skewered on swords. It's all a bit much, but it works, it really does. rumjungle is one of the hottest clubs in Vegas, with lines of partyers out the door every night, ready to dance to live world-beat music. Get there early (before 10pm) to avoid lines/guest lists/the cover charge, and consider having dinner (served until 9pm); it's costly, but it's a multicourse, all-you-can-eat feast of flame-pit-cooked Brazilian food. For the amount of food and the waiving of the cover charge, the $40 dinner is a good deal. Then dance it all off all night long. The club is open 'til 2am Tuesday to Thursday, until 4am Friday, Saturday, and Monday nights. In Mandalay Bay, 3950 Las Vegas Blvd. S. ✆ **702/632-7408.** Cover $10–$20.

MAJOR PRODUCTION SHOWS

Crazy Horse Paris *Crazy Horse Paris* is part of Vegas's new, classy, adult entertainment resurrection. Allegedly the same show that has been running for years in a famous racy French nightclub, this show is just a bunch of pretty girls taking their clothes off. Except that the girls are smashingly gorgeous, with the kind of bodies just not found on real live human beings, and they take their clothes off in curious and, yes, artistic ways, gyrating on *pointe* shoes while holding on to ropes or hoops, falling over sofas while lip-syncing to French torch songs—in short, it's what striptease ought to be, and by gosh, if strip clubs were this well staged we'd go to them all the time. But $60 a ticket is a great deal to pay for arty nudie fun, especially when the routines, no matter how clever or how naked (the girls get down to a postage-stamp-size triangle covering the naughtiest of their bits, so they aren't "nude," but talk about a technicality), start to seem alike after a while. Shows are Wednesday through Monday at 8 and 10:30pm. In the MGM Grand, 3799 Las Vegas Blvd. S. ✆ **877/880-0880** or 702/891-7902. Tickets $55–$65 (includes tax and gratuity).

Jubilee! A classic Vegas spectacular, crammed with singing, dancing, magic, acrobats, elaborate costumes and sets, and, of course, bare breasts. It's a basic revue, with production numbers featuring homogenized versions of standards (Gershwin, Cole Porter, some Fred Astaire numbers) sometimes sung live, sometimes lip-synced, and always accompanied by lavishly costumed and frequently topless showgirls. Humorous set pieces about Samson and Delilah and the sinking of the *Titanic* (!) show off some pretty awesome sets. (They were doing the *Titanic* long before a certain movie, and recent attendees claimed the ship-sinking effect on stage here was better than the one in the movie.) The finale features aerodynamically impossible feathered and bejeweled costumes and headpieces designed by Bob Mackie. So what if the dancers are occasionally out of step, and the action sometimes veers into the dubious (a Vegas-style revue about a disaster that took more than 1,000 lives?) or even the inexplicable (a finale praising beautiful and bare-breasted girls suddenly stops for three lines of "Somewhere Over the Rainbow"?). Shows are Saturday through Thursday at 7:30 and 10:30pm. In Bally's Las Vegas, 3645 Las Vegas Blvd. S. ✆ **800/237-7469** or 702/967-4111. Tickets $61–$101 (including tax and gratuity).

Zumanity *Zumanity* is the first Cirque du Soleil production to chart a decidedly adult course. Celebrating love, both physical and emotional, in all of its myriad forms, *Zumanity* is the buzz of the Las Vegas show scene. If you're comfortable with sexuality, including your own, *Zumanity* will wash over you like a torrid desert wind. If not, you're in for an hour and a half of varying degrees of revulsion and a lot of squirming in your seat. *Zumanity* is zany, raucous, and decidedly outrageous. It is lovable in its humor and insightful in its understanding of sex. The visually hypnotic production seamlessly blends its challenging theme with Cirque du Soleil's signature music, color, acrobatics, and dance. *Zumanity* is sometimes very tender but at other moments quite hard-edged. Urging us to look at how we define human beauty and making a plea for the acceptance of differences, *Zumanity* delivers a powerful message. As the production unfolds, you witness an artful sequence of sexual vignettes celebrating heterosexual sex, gay sex, masturbation, sex between obese lovers, sex with midgets, group sex, sado-masochistic sex, and sex between the very old. As the name "Zumanity" implies, sex, and the varied emotions we bring to it, is a defining element of our humanity. Sex is happy, sex is sad, sex is of the moment, sex is transcendent, sex is funny, sex is bewildering. And as *Zumanity* so ably demonstrates, sex is a window into our essential being. Shows are Tuesday, Wednesday, and Friday through Sunday at 7:30 and 10:30pm. In the New York–New York Hotel & Casino, 3790 Las Vegas Blvd. S. ✆ 702/740-6815. www.zumanity.com. Tickets $75–$155 (including tax and gratuity).

12

Side Trips from Las Vegas

From the strange desert formations of Red Rock and Valley of Fire to the pine trees and cool breezes of Mount Charleston, the area surrounding Las Vegas is rich with natural beauty. Whether you decide to take a guided tour or drive yourself, you'll discover that there is more to Las Vegas than just casinos and roller coasters (though those, too, can be found outside the city limits).

The city of Las Vegas is modern and overdeveloped, layered with concrete and minimalls. In stark contrast, the outlying deserts and mountains are raw, wild, and untamed. If you visit Las Vegas with your kids, you owe it to yourself, and to them, to see the natural wonders that lie less than an hour away from the artificial miracles of the Strip. Go ahead! Breathe some fresh air, frolic in the forest, or take a trip back in time. You'll be glad you did.

To interest the kids, let them know that, as different as Vegas the city is from its surrounding areas, they are deeply interconnected. For instance, the miles of lights, exploding volcanoes, and dancing fountains all over the city would not be able to exist were it not for Hoover Dam.

The excursions in this chapter, with the exception of the Grand Canyon trip, will take you anywhere from 20 to 60 miles outside of town for memorable family-travel experiences. In these surrounding areas, there are plenty of opportunities for outdoors recreation in truly astounding environments. (But, if you're really partial to gambling, riding thrill rides, and shopping, and haven't gotten your fill yet in Vegas, you can find those same opportunities outside of the city, in Primm.)

1 HOOVER DAM & LAKE MEAD

30 miles SE of Las Vegas

You must take your kids to see the Hoover Dam (www.usbr.gov/lc/hooverdam). It is an engineering and architectural marvel, one of the wonders of the modern world, and, without it, Las Vegas, nay, the Southwest as we know it today, would not exist. Plus, most kids think that all that rushing water is cool. If your children appear antsy or bored at the visitor center, you may want to skip the actual tour of the dam, but, trust us, you should try to wheedle, connive, or bribe them into taking it: They'll learn something and see some amazing sights, including an up-close-and-personal view of the dam.

Be sure to wear comfortable shoes, because the tour involves quite a bit of walking—something that, unfortunately, your child may be too young to complete on their own. Those kids aged 6 years and up will enjoy it the most; any younger, and you'll probably be in for a struggle. For the most comfortable tour, try to arrive early in the morning, when the dam first opens; you'll not only beat the desert heat, but also the crowds, because 2,000 to 3,000 people visit the dam daily.

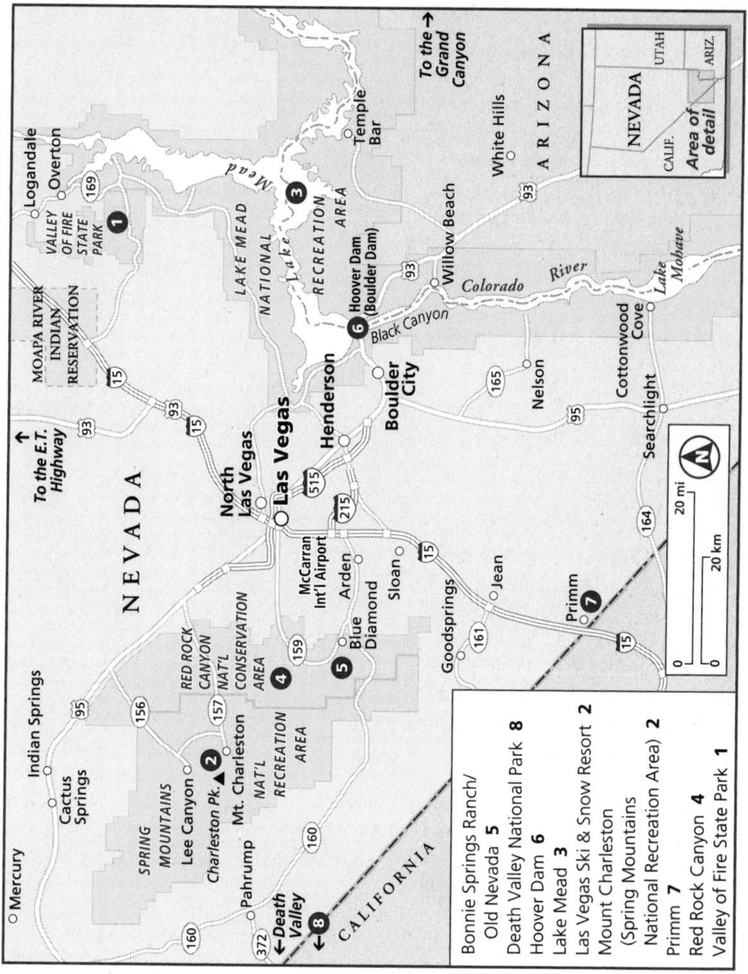

After touring the dam, you can have lunch in Boulder City, and, if you are up for a long drive, perhaps go back to Vegas the long way through **Valley of Fire State Park** (© **702/397-2088;** www.parks.nv.gov/vf.htm), a landscape of wind and water-hewn formations of red sandstone, about 6 miles from Lake Mead. ***Note:*** Fill up your gas tank and buy drinking water before you start! Or, you can spend the rest of the day at Lake Mead—hiking, boating, or scuba diving in season. At Lake Mead, there's also the option of an old-fashioned sternwheeler tour. Alternatively, some families prefer to combine Hoover Dam with a trip to **Bonnie Springs Ranch** (© **702/875-4191;** www.bonniesprings.com). For more on the ranch, see section 4, "Bonnie Springs Ranch/Old Nevada," later in this chapter.

GETTING THERE

Drive east on either Flamingo or Tropicana to U.S. 515 S., which automatically becomes I-93 and takes you right to the dam. This is a beautiful and dramatic drive; as you go through Boulder City, you come over a rise and Lake Mead is suddenly spread before you. (Be aware that at this point, the road narrows to two lanes and traffic can slow considerably, meaning that on busy tourist days, the drive can take an hour or more, another good reason to get an early start.) Go past the Lake Mead turnoff, and, as you near the dam, you will see a five-story parking structure to your left jutting out from the canyon wall. Parking there costs $7, cash only. (Free parking is also on the Arizona side of the dam, which is easily accessible.)

SUV or passenger van tours to and from Las Vegas are available through **Action Tours.** A 4-hour tour of the Hoover Dam includes a brief stop at Lake Mead for pictures and costs $65. Call ✆ **702/566-7400** or visit **www.actiontours.com** for details.

HOOVER DAM ★★

Without Hoover Dam, there would be no glittering lights and chiming slot machines in Las Vegas; its fountains would not dance nor would its swimming pools exist. In fact, the growth of the entire Southwest, not just Las Vegas, can be tied directly to the electricity generated by the dam, and the controlled water use it provides.

Before the dam was built, the Colorado River had run unchecked for millions of years, its turbulent waters carving out the Grand Canyon. When settlers came en masse and agriculture began as an industry, the river's natural behavior (drying up most of the year, and then flooding when fed by the melting snow in the Rocky Mountains) caused severe hardships. Crops, lives, and property were consistently lost, progress was stalled, and so the powers that be, in this case Congress, stepped in.

In 1928, Congress—strongly urged by the seven states through which the Colorado runs during its 1,400-mile journey to the Gulf of California—authorized the construction of a dam intending that "A mighty river, now a source of destruction, is to be curbed and put to work in the interest of society." Construction began in 1931 and was completed in 1936, 2 years ahead of schedule and $15 million under budget. During those 5 years, more than 5,200 laborers worked 24 hours a day, and the project generated significant advances in engineering, machinery production, and construction. The completed dam served its purpose, stopping the annual floods and conserving water for agricultural, industrial, and domestic use. Equally important, Hoover Dam, now one of the world's major electrical generating plants, provides low-cost, pollution-free, hydroelectric power to neighboring communities. The cost of building the dam, $165 million, has been repaid many times over by the sale of its electricity to a number of California cities and the states of Nevada and Arizona.

A massive curved wall, 660 feet at its base, tapering to 45 feet across at the top where the road crosses it, the Hoover Dam towers 726½ feet above the bedrock, acting as a plug between the canyon walls. The dam holds back up to 9.2 trillion gallons of water in Lake Mead, the reservoir created by its construction. Four concrete intake towers on the dam's lakeside drop the water down about 600 feet to drive turbines and create power, after which the water spills out into the river, continuing south to the Gulf of California.

The dam has become a major sightseeing attraction along with Lake Mead, a huge local recreation site and the nation's largest artificial reservoir.

On your way to Hoover Dam, 7 miles to the west on U.S. 93, you'll pass through Boulder City, which was built to house the dam's managerial and construction workers.

Fun Facts Did You Know . . .

- Five million 8-cubic-yard buckets of cement were used to create the Hoover Dam—enough concrete to pave a two-lane highway between Miami and Los Angeles?
- The minimum wage paid on the dam construction project was $4 a day? Comparatively, those wages of 50¢ an hour weren't bad, because most of the workers' Depression-era peers were making an average of 5¢ per hour!
- Ninety-six men died while building, excavating, blasting, and scaling mountains during dam construction, and on-the-job injuries totaled about 1,500 a month? However, though 96 workers were killed during the construction, contrary to popular myth, none were accidentally buried as the concrete was poured. (It was poured at a rate of only 8 in. at a time.)
- In summer, the canyon rocks are so hot you can literally fry an egg on them?
- Lake Mead contains enough water to cover the entire state of Pennsylvania to a 1-foot depth?
- The dam was originally called Boulder Dam because of its Boulder Canyon site, then renamed Hoover Dam in 1930 to honor Herbert Hoover's years of work making the project a reality? Unofficially, it was renamed Boulder Dam by FDR, who did not wish to honor Hoover; it finally regained the name Hoover Dam under Truman, who, in 1947, asked the 80th Congress to find out just what the "dam" name really was.
- It took 6½ years to fill the lake created by the Hoover Dam?
- Hoover Dam is 726½ feet high and weighs over 6,600,000 tons?

Boulder City's higher elevation offered lower temperatures than the area surrounding the dam, making it a more appealing location for a community. Within a single year, the city emerged from the wasteland, with a population of 6,000. By 1934, Boulder City was Nevada's third-largest town.

TOURING THE DAM

Things have changed at Hoover Dam since the September 11, 2001, terrorist attacks, and, for those with children, the tour itself has become much more manageable—you are left to discover the dam and its history on your own. Fans of the old tour may be disappointed by this truncated version, but newcomers won't miss a thing. Whereas before you were on a structured group tour, with a guide moving you at a steady pace, now the visit is self-guided, and you can linger or move on as the mood strikes you. The exchange for this is the ability to see what you want to see, and what your kids can handle, without being tied into a structured tour. If the children get bored watching one of the two movies at the Visitor Center, you can traipse right along and take the elevator to the fifth-floor observation deck, without having to wait. Want to watch the water roar for 20 minutes? Go ahead, look as long as you like. If the kids are getting cranky or you're getting tired, you're free to cut the visit short and head on out for a snack.

Your tour begins at the Visitor Center, where your admission to the center, the exhibit hall across the street, and your self-guided sightseeing of the dam are covered in one admission price ($11 for adults, $9 for ages 4–16 and seniors, free for children 4 and under).

The three-story **Hoover Dam Visitor Center,** built in 1995, features a rooftop overlook with an unobstructed view of Lake Mead, the dam, the power plant, the Colorado River, and the Black Canyon. This is one of the tour's many fabulous photo opportunities. The ground-floor Reception Lobby is the ticketing station as well as the place where exhibits, memorabilia, and photographs are displayed and where the two informational videos are screened continuously. By watching these, you'll learn more about the importance of water, the events leading up to the construction of Hoover Dam, and the many benefits it confers. The Plaza Level includes interactive displays on the environment, habitation, and development of the Southwest; the people who built the dam; and related topics. The third-floor Overlook Center provides an astounding view of Lake Mead, the dam, the power plant, the mighty Colorado River, and Black Canyon. Along with the awe-inspiring vista, sculpted bronze panels (far less interesting to children) demonstrate how Lake Mead and Hoover Dam benefit Arizona, Nevada, and California.

While you are at the dam, make sure to take in all the exterior details, including the floors inlaid with the wheel of the zodiac, a compass, and the American eagle as well as the sculptural tributes to those who died building the dam, including the dam's mascot, a black dog who was killed when a truck inadvertently ran him over some years after the dam's completion. On the grounds of the dam, you may also be able to spot wildlife, including ravens, cormorants, an occasional bighorn sheep, and the lively antelope ground squirrels. When you return to your car, note the cactus garden at the top of the escalators, which was installed by the movie company who made the Chevy Chase movie *National Lampoon's Vegas Vacation* to make the location look more "desertlike." Hollywood being what it is, the plants they chose for their desert atmosphere are not native to this region, but they do look nice, especially when they bloom in the spring. ***Tip:*** It is highly recommended that persons with defibrillators do not take the tour. Additionally, some areas may be difficult to navigate with strollers and wheelchairs. For more information on the dam, surf over to its website at **www.usbr.gov/lc/hooverdam**.

The self-guided tour around the dam begins with an elevator ride to the fifth-floor observation deck. You'll get to walk along the top of the dam, watch the water roil, and learn about this stupendous monument from the displays and the guides. Six guides, each with his or her own spiel, are strategically placed and are able to answer any questions you or your kids might have. The self-guided tour can take up to 2½ hours or as little as 30 minutes, depending on your family's level of interest.

Tips Travel Time

The least-crowded times to visit are during the first 2 hours of each day. Also, keep in mind that the busiest season is in the summer from Memorial Day until Labor Day. Spring break is also a busy time at the dam. The slowest months are January and February. When visiting, make sure to bring bottled water and wear a hat and sunscreen, as you will be outside for part of your explorations.

LAKE MEAD NATIONAL RECREATION AREA ★★

The 1.5-million-acre Lake Mead National Recreation Area was created in 1936 around Lake Mead, a man-made reservoir lake resulting from the construction of Hoover Dam. Later, Lake Mohave, to the south, was formed with the construction of Davis Dam. The entire area is administered by the National Park Service, except for the dam itself, which is administered by the Bureau of Reclamation. Before the two lakes—comprising over 290 square miles—emerged, this desert region was brutally hot, dry, rugged, and unfit for human habitation. Today, it attracts about 9 million visitors annually, making it one of the nation's most popular playgrounds. At a maximum elevation of 1,221$^1/_2$ feet (lower today after years of drought in the Southwest), Lake Mead itself extends up to 110 miles upstream toward the Grand Canyon. Backed by spectacular cliff and canyon scenery, its 550-mile shoreline forms a perfect setting for a wide variety of watersports and desert hiking.

Run by the National Park Service, the **Alan Bible Lake Mead Visitor Center,** 4 miles northeast of Boulder City on U.S. 93 at Nev. 166 (✆ **702/293-8990**), provides information on all area activities and services, and contacts for renting accommodations, boats, and fishing equipment. There you can pick up trail maps and brochures, view informative films, and find out about scenic drives, accommodations, ranger-guided hikes, naturalist programs and lectures, bird-watching, canoeing, camping, lakeside RV parks, and picnic facilities. The center is open daily from 8:30am to 4:30pm. The center also sells books and videotapes about the area.

Seven Crown Resorts provides the accommodations, boat rentals, and fishing equipment for Lake Mead. You can make reservations with them either by calling ✆ **800/752-9669** or visiting www.sevencrown.com.

You can also find information on the Lake Mead National Recreation Area on the Web at **www.nps.gov/lame**.

In 2000, the park service began to charge **entry fees** for the first time; $5 per vehicle (this covers all passengers in the vehicle) gets you entry that is valid for 5 days, or $3 per individual for 5 days.

LAKE MEAD & VICINITY'S OUTDOOR ACTIVITIES

This is a lovely area for scenic drives amid the dramatic desert scenery. One popular route follows the Lakeshore and North Shore Scenic Drives along the edge of Lake Mead. From these roads, panoramic views of the blue lake are set against a backdrop of the browns, blacks, reds, and grays of the desert mountains. North Shore Scenic Drive also leads through areas of brilliant red boulders and rock formations, and you'll find a picnic area along the way.

BOATING & FISHING Under the auspices of Seven Crown Resorts (✆ **800/752-9669** or 702/293-3484; www.sevencrown.com), WaveRunners, fishing boats, patio boats, and personal watercrafts can be rented at **Lake Mead Resort and Marina.** This store also carries groceries, clothing, marine supplies, sporting goods, water-skiing gear, fishing equipment, and bait and tackle. You can get a fishing license here ($69 a year or $18 for 1 day; $9 for children 12–15; children 11 and under may fish without a license). The knowledgeable staff can direct you to good fishing spots. Largemouth bass, striped bass, channel catfish, crappie, and bluegill are found in Lake Mead; rainbow trout, largemouth bass, and striped bass in Lake Mohave. You can also arrange here to rent a fully equipped houseboat at **Echo Bay,** 40 miles northeast.

Other convenient Lake Mead marinas offering similar rentals and equipment are **Las Vegas Bay** (✆ **702/565-9111**), which is even closer to Las Vegas, and **Callville Bay** (✆ **702/565-8958**), which is the least crowded of the five on the Nevada shore.

CAMPING Available on a first-come, first-served basis, all of the campsites along Lake Mead's shoreline are equipped with running water, picnic tables, and grills. They are administered by the **National Park Service** (✆ **702/293-8990;** www.nps.gov/lame), with a $10 per night charge at each campsite.

CANOEING The **Alan Bible Lake Mead Visitor Center** (see "Lake Mead National Recreation Area," above) can provide a list of outfitters who rent canoes for trips on the Colorado River. There's one catch, however: A canoeing permit ($13 per person) is required in advance for certain areas near the dam and is available from the **Bureau of Reclamation**'s concessionaires, Boulder City Outfitters, located at 1631 Industrial Rd. in Boulder City. This fee includes a $3 national parks service fee. Call the company at ✆ **928/767-4747** or visit the bureau website **www.usbr.gov/lc/hooverdam/paddlecraft/canoenew.html** for information.

HIKING The best season for hiking is November to March, as it's really too hot the rest of the year. The **Alan Bible Lake Mead Visitor Center** (see above) offers detailed trail maps. Three trails, ranging in length from .75 to 6 miles, originate at the Visitor Center. The 6-mile trail goes past remains of the railroad built for the dam project. Be sure to take all necessary desert-hiking precautions (see the "Take a Hike: Desert Hiking Advice" box on p. 266). From November to March, the park offers a number of free, ranger-guided hikes; check its website at **www.nps.gov/lame** for information about upcoming hikes. You must call the visitor center to make reservations for these guided hikes (✆ **702/293-8990**).

LAKE CRUISES A delightful way to enjoy Lake Mead is on a cruise aboard **Lake Mead Cruises'** ***Desert Princess*** ★ (✆ **702/293-6180;** www.lakemeadcruises.com), a Mississippi-style paddle-wheeler. Cruises depart year-round from a terminal near **Lake Mead Lodge** (see below). Enjoy the relaxing, scenic trip from an open promenade deck or from one of two fully enclosed, climate-controlled decks. The trip takes you through Black Canyon and past colorful rock formations known as the Arizona Paint Pots en route to Hoover Dam. Your best family bets would be the brunch ($37 adults, $18 children 11 and under) or the narrated midday cruises ($22 adults, $10 children), each of which is 1½ hours long. The cocktail/dinner cruises ($46 adults, $25 children) last 2 hours, and can include a spectacular view of Hoover Dam lit up for the night, depending on the time of year. The three sunset dinner/dance cruises with live music ($58 adults) are not recommended for kids. Meals (basic, decent food that's hardly gourmet, but you're there for the view) are served in a pleasant, windowed, air-conditioned dining room. Call ✆ **702/293-6180** for departure times. Reservations are strongly recommended.

RAFTING Through **Black Canyon/Willow Beach River Adventures** (the Bureau of Reclamation's concessionaires), located in the Hacienda Hotel and Casino, Nev. 93, Boulder City (✆ **800/455-3490;** www.blackcanyonadventures.com), you can take a motorized raft trip down the Colorado River. Your raft, complete with guide, is boarded below Hoover Dam, and you then slowly go downstream to Willow Beach, Arizona, where a bus will return you to your point of origination. During your 3½- to 4-hour ride on the water, your guide will discuss the history of Hoover Dam, the history and geography of the area, the Native American tribes, and the local flora and fauna. As this is a flat-water trip, you won't get wet. Sunblock and hats are advised no matter what the

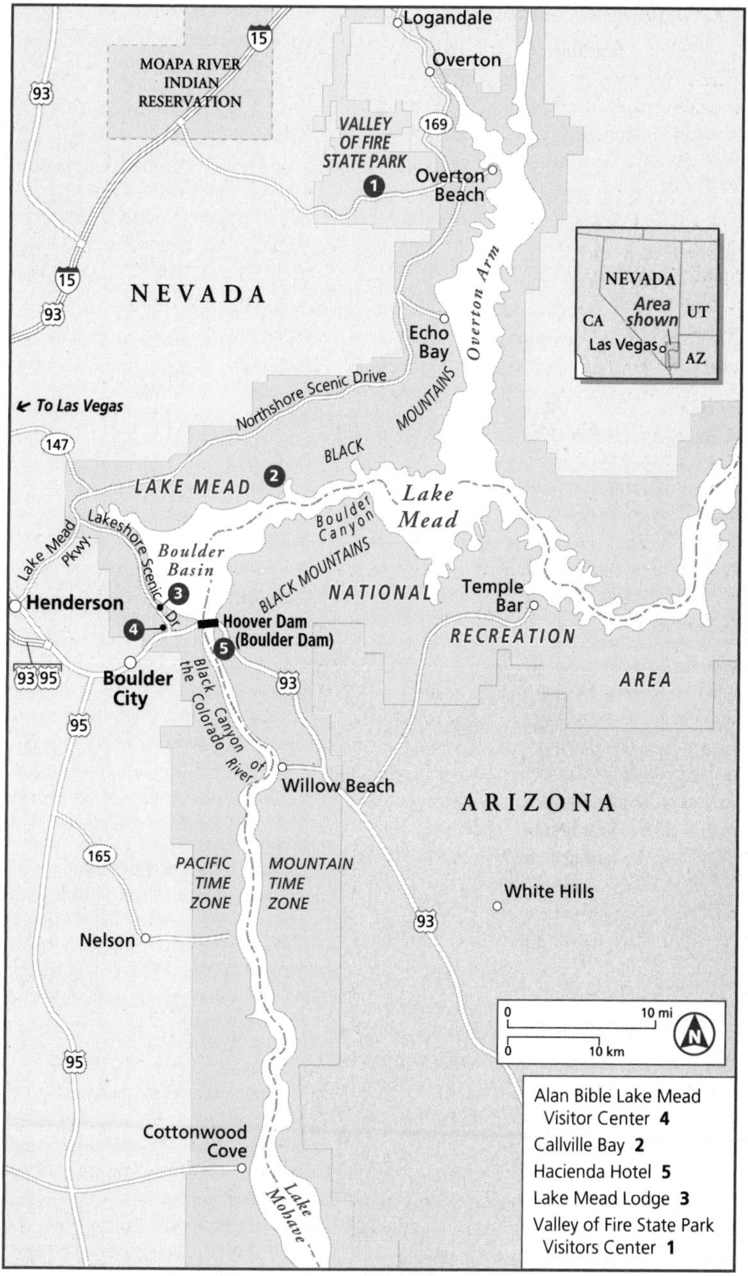
Logandale
15
MOAPA RIVER INDIAN RESERVATION
Overton
93
VALLEY OF FIRE STATE PARK
169
Overton Beach
1
15
NEVADA
93
Overton Arm
Echo Bay
NEVADA
CA
Area shown
UT
Las Vegas
AZ
Northshore Scenic Drive
To Las Vegas
BLACK MOUNTAINS
147
LAKE MEAD
2
Lake Mead
Boulder Canyon
Lake Mead Pkwy.
Lakeshore Scenic Dr.
Boulder Basin
BLACK MOUNTAINS
Henderson
3
NATIONAL
Temple Bar
4
Hoover Dam (Boulder Dam)
5
RECREATION
93 95
Boulder City
Black Canyon of the Colorado River
93
AREA
95
Willow Beach
ARIZONA
165
PACIFIC TIME ZONE
MOUNTAIN TIME ZONE
White Hills
93
Nelson
0
10 mi
0
10 km
N
95
Cottonwood Cove
Lake Mohave
Alan Bible Lake Mead Visitor Center 4
Callville Bay 2
Hacienda Hotel 5
Lake Mead Lodge 3
Valley of Fire State Park Visitors Center 1

season. The cost is $83 for adults, $51 for 5- to 12-year-olds, free for those 5 and under. Hotel pickups can be arranged for an additional cost of $44 per person. These rafting tours are offered year-round, weather permitting.

The best time to run the river is in the fall through December. The spring is prettiest with new green foliage seen on the beaches and in the side canyons. The spring, along with January and February, however, tends to be the windiest time of year. Headwinds can whip up 3-foot waves and make forward progress grueling. If winds of more than 15 mph are forecast, go another day. Summers are hot, and the canyons tend to hold the heat. The 53°F (12°C) water, however, provides some natural cooling.

SCUBA DIVING There's good visibility for scuba diving in Lake Mead October to April, lessened in summer months when algae flourishes. A list of good dive locations, authorized instructors, and nearby dive shops is available at the **Alan Bible Lake Mead Visitor Center** (see above). There's also an underwater, designated diving area near Lake Mead Marina.

WHERE TO STAY & DINE AROUND LAKE MEAD

In addition to the hotels listed below, there are a number of little hotels in Boulder City.

Hacienda Hotel and Casino Located on Hwy. 93, 3½ miles south of Boulder City, the Hacienda is a standard gaming hotel, complete with nice rooms, a casino, and a two-screen movie theater showing first-run flicks, which is almost a necessity, because the in-room TVs do not have cable. Double rooms have two queen-size beds, suites, a king-size bed with a couch or loveseat (neither folds out). This hotel, with a buffet and food court, is a safe bet for families looking to stay close to the lake. There's also a steakhouse if you feel like having a sit-down meal after a day of boating and sightseeing. The hotel can also arrange helicopter tours over Hoover Dam and Lake Mead, ranging from $29 to $99 (✆ **702/294-2200**).

Nev. 93, Boulder City, NV 89005. ✆ **800/245-6380** or 702/293-5000. www.haciendaonline.com. 325 units. Sun–Thurs $49 and up double, $85 suite; Fri–Sat $79 double, $105 suite. Extra person $3. Children 4 and under stay free in parent's room. Cribs $3, rollaways $5. AE, DC, DISC, MC, V. Pets accepted for $20 per animal. **Amenities:** 3 restaurants (cafe, buffet, and steakhouse); food court; movie theater; outdoor pool. *In room:* A/C, TV (no cable).

Lake Mead Lodge (Value) This rustic and comfortable bungalow-style lodge is an easy drive from Hoover Dam. It's beautifully situated right on the lake, and surrounded on three sides by desert. The rooms are pleasant, with wood-paneled ceilings and walls of white-painted brick or rough-hewn pine, and all offer full private bathrooms. There is a suite with three rooms and a small kitchen, which might be good for families staying a few days. (There are plans to add a second suite.) The pool is rudimentary, but you might want to relax with a good book in one of the gazebos on the property. About a half-mile down the road is the marina, where you can while away a few hours over cocktails on a lakeside patio. The marina is the area's headquarters for boating, fishing, and watersports; it also houses a large shop (for details, see the "Boating & Fishing" section, above).

There's a nautically themed restaurant (✆ **702/293-3484**) at the marina, its rough-hewn pine interior embellished with various seafaring iconography. It's open 7am to 9pm daily. (It closes an hour later during the summer.) The restaurant serves hearty breakfasts; sandwiches, salads, and burgers at lunch; and steak-and-seafood dinners. And Boulder Beach, also an easy walk from the lodge, has waterfront picnic tables and barbecue grills.

322 Lakeshore Rd., Boulder City, NV 89005. ✆ **800/752-9669** or 702/293-2074. 42 units. Early Mar to late Nov $90 and up double; the rest of the year $75 and up double. Children 4 and under stay free in parent's room, $6 per night per person 5 and over. Rollaways $6. DISC, MC, V. Pets accepted for $10 per animal. **Amenities:** Outdoor pool; picnic area with barbecue pit. *In room:* A/C, TV w/basic cable.

BOULDER CITY

Consider poking around Boulder City on your way back to Vegas. Founded in 1936, Boulder City was the first planned community in the United States. The company town for those building Hoover Dam, it was created by the wives who came with their husbands and turned a temporary site into a real community, since aided by the recreational attractions and attendant businesses of Lake Mead. It doesn't look like much as you first approach it, but once you are in the heart, you'll discover that it's quite charming. The town has some antiques and curio shops, and a number of family-style restaurants as well as burger and Mexican joints; the most fun for kids is the **Happy Days Diner,** a retro coffee shop with a soda fountain, red-vinyl booths, and decent '50s comfort food, at 512 Nevada Hwy. (✆ **702/293-4637**); it's right downtown.

2 VALLEY OF FIRE STATE PARK ★★

60 miles NE of Las Vegas

In contrast to the modern developments in Las Vegas, much of the Mojave Desert around the city resembles a Martian landscape—a seemingly lifeless tundra where misshaped rock formations erupt from the vivid red earth. Shaped by time, climate, and subterranean upheaval, these majestic canyons, cliffs, and ridges provide a striking contrast to the man-made monuments of Sin City.

The 36,000-acre **Valley of Fire State Park** (✆ **702/397-2088;** www.parks.nv.gov/vf.htm) typifies the mountainous red Mojave Desert. Deriving its name from the crimson sandstone formations created 150 million years ago by a great shifting of sand, the park continues to be shaped by the geologic processes of wind and water erosion. Mysterious, loaded with petroglyphs, and totally inhospitable, this was a sacred place for Native Americans, where only the men came as a test of their manhood; it is still a natural wonder that must be seen to be appreciated. The otherworldly rock formations, fiery outcroppings blazing under the relentless sun, are surreal, beautiful, and strange beyond comprehension. There is nothing green in the area and no plant life as far as the eye can see. No wonder this park has been used as a location for various sci-fi movies: It is unlike any other place on earth; studios, even with all the modern technology available to them, cannot reproduce Nature's handiwork in this case.

Although it's hard to imagine while you're driving through the park in the sweltering Nevada heat, for billions of years, these rocks were under hundreds of feet of ocean, which began to rise some 200 million years ago. The ocean's waters became shallower and shallower over time, until the sea made a complete retreat, leaving a muddy terrain traversed by ever-diminishing streams. Eventually, a great sandy desert covered much of the southwestern part of the American continent until about 140 million years ago. Over these eons, winds, massive fault action, and water erosion sculpted fantastic formations of sand and limestone. Oxidation of iron in the sands and mud and the effect of groundwater leaching the oxidized iron—in other words, rust on a huge scale—turned the rocks the many hues of red, pink, russet, lavender, and white that can be seen today. Logs of ancient forests washed down from faraway highlands and became petrified fossils, which can be seen along two interpretive trails.

The centuries between 2000 B.C. and 300 B.C., when human beings occupied the region, were much wetter and cooler than now. Although these early residents didn't live in the Valley of Fire itself, the men of the tribes traveled here to hunt bighorn sheep for a source of food, clothing, blankets, and hut coverings, using a notched stick called an *atlatl* that is depicted in the park's petroglyphs, while the women and children caught rabbits, tortoises, and other small game.

In the Valley of Fire's next historical phase, from 300 B.C. to A.D. 700, the climate became warmer and drier. Bows and arrows replaced the atlatl, and the hunters and gatherers discovered farming. Corn, squash, and beans were cultivated by the Anasazi people, whose communities began replacing small nomadic family groups. These ancient people wove watertight baskets, mats, hunting nets, and clothing. Around A.D. 300, they learned how to make sun-dried ceramic pottery. Over time, other tribes, notably the Paiutes, migrated to the area, and by A.D. 1150, they had become the dominant group. Unlike the Anasazi, the Paiutes were still nomadic and used the Valley of Fire region seasonally. The Paiutes were the inhabitants found by white settlers when they entered the area in the early to mid-1800s. The pioneers diverted river and spring waters to irrigate their farmlands, destroying the nature-based Paiute way of life. Now about 300 descendants of those Paiute tribespeople still live on the Moapa Indian Reservation (about 20 miles northwest) that was established along the Muddy River in 1872.

Dedicated in 1935, Valley of Fire is Nevada's oldest and largest state park. Since that time, the park's notable rock formations have been named for the shapes they vaguely resemble—a duck, an elephant, seven sisters, domes, beehives, and so on. You can have fun with your family by looking for these and renaming formations to suit your visions. Look for Mouse's Tank, named for a fugitive Paiute called Mouse who hid there in the late 1890s. It is a natural basin that collects rainwater (hence the "tank" appellation). You can hike to see Native American **petroglyphs** etched into the rock walls and boulders—some dating from as early as 3,000 years ago. These can be observed on self-guided trails. Petroglyphs at Atlatl Rock and Petroglyph Canyon are both easily accessible. It is unlawful to remove rocks, plants, or animals from the park; there is a $250 fine per object if you're caught. Make sure to tell your children about this law, so you don't encounter any problems. And, naturally, carving your initials on the rocks is also illegal. In summer, when temperatures are usually over 100°F (38°C), you may have to settle for driving through the park in an air-conditioned car.

Your first stop on your visit through this bizarre landscape should be the **Visitor Center** on Nev. 169, 6 miles west of North Shore Scenic Drive (✆ **702/397-2088;** www.parks.nv.gov/vf.htm). It's open daily 8:30am to 4:30pm and is worth a quick stop for information and a bit of history before entering the park. Exhibits on the premises explain the origin and geologic history of the park's colorful sandstone formations, describe the ancient peoples who carved their rock art on canyon walls, and identify the plants and wildlife you're likely to see. Postcards, books, slides, and film are on sale here, and you can also pick up hiking maps and brochures or have your park-related questions answered by rangers.

GETTING THERE

From Las Vegas, take I-15 N. to exit 75 (Valley of Fire turnoff). However, the more scenic route is to take I-15 N., then travel Lake Mead Boulevard (exit 45) east to North

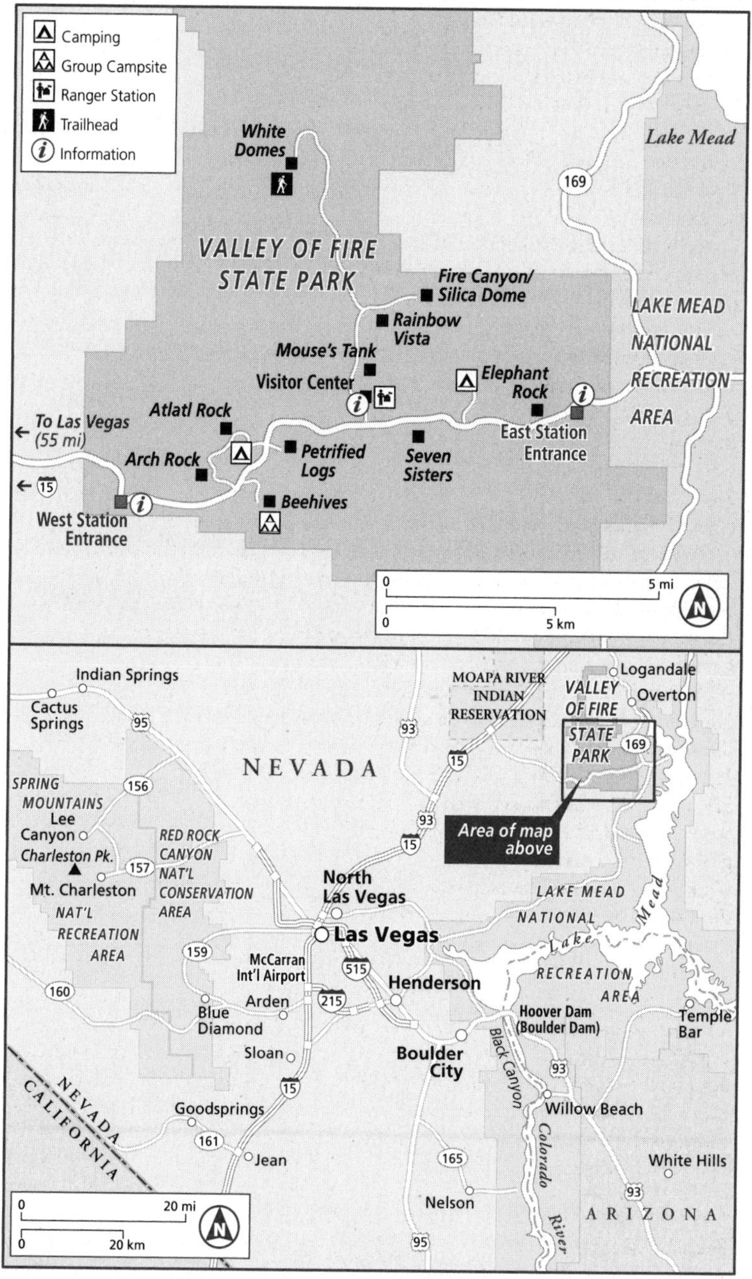
Camping
Group Campsite
Ranger Station
Trailhead
Information
White Domes
VALLEY OF FIRE STATE PARK
Fire Canyon/ Silica Dome
Rainbow Vista
Mouse's Tank
Visitor Center
Elephant Rock
Atlatl Rock
To Las Vegas (55 mi)
Arch Rock
Petrified Logs
Seven Sisters
East Station Entrance
15
West Station Entrance
Beehives
Lake Mead
169
LAKE MEAD NATIONAL RECREATION AREA
0
5 mi
0
5 km
N
Indian Springs
Cactus Springs
95
MOAPA RIVER INDIAN RESERVATION
VALLEY OF FIRE STATE PARK
Logandale
Overton
93
169
NEVADA
15
SPRING MOUNTAINS
156
Lee Canyon
93
Area of map above
Charleston Pk.
RED ROCK CANYON NAT'L CONSERVATION AREA
15
157
Mt. Charleston
NAT'L RECREATION AREA
North Las Vegas
LAKE MEAD NATIONAL RECREATION AREA
Las Vegas
159
McCarran Int'l Airport
515
Lake Mead
160
Arden
215
Henderson
Blue Diamond
Hoover Dam (Boulder Dam)
Temple Bar
Sloan
Boulder City
Black Canyon
93
15
NEVADA
CALIFORNIA
Goodsprings
Willow Beach
161
Jean
Colorado River
165
White Hills
93
Nelson
ARIZONA
0
20 mi
0
20 km
N
95

Tips Take a Hike: Desert Hiking Advice

Except in summer, when temperatures can reach 120°F (49°C) in the shade, the Las Vegas area is great for hiking. The best hiking season is November to March.

Hiking in the desert is exceptionally rewarding, but it can be dangerous. Here are some safety tips:

1. Don't hike alone.
2. Carry plenty of water and drink it often. Don't assume spring waters are safe to drink. A gallon of water per person per day is recommended for hikers.
3. Be alert for signs of heat exhaustion (headache; nausea; dizziness; fatigue; and cool, damp, pale, or red skin).
4. Gauge your fitness accurately. Desert hiking may involve rough or steep terrain. Don't take on more than you can handle.
5. Check weather forecasts before starting out. Thunderstorms can turn into raging flash floods, which are extremely hazardous to hikers.
6. Dress properly. Wear sturdy walking shoes for rock scrambling, long pants (to protect yourself from rocks and cacti), a hat, sunscreen, and sunglasses.
7. Carry a small first-aid kit.
8. Be careful when climbing on sandstone, which can be surprisingly soft and crumbly.
9. Don't feed or play with animals, such as the wild burros in Red Rock Canyon. (It's actually illegal to approach them.)
10. Be alert for snakes and insects. Though they're rarely encountered, you'll want to look into a crevice before putting your hand into it.
11. Visit park or other information offices before you start out and acquaint yourself with rules and regulations and any possible hazards. It's also a good idea to tell the staff where you're going, when you'll return, how many are in your party, and so on. Some park offices offer hiker registration programs.
12. Follow the hiker's rule of thumb: Take only photographs and leave only footprints.

Shore Scenic Road (Nev. 167), and proceed north to the Valley of Fire exit. The first route takes about an hour, the second, about 1½ hours.

There is a $6 per vehicle admission charge to the park, regardless of how many people you cram inside.

Plan on spending a minimum of an hour in the park, though you can spend a great deal more time. It can get very hot in there (nothing relieves the sun beating down on all that red and reflecting off it) and there is no water, so be certain to bring a liter, maybe two, per person. In the summer, consider a gallon per person. Without a guide, you must stay on paved roads, but don't worry if they end; you can always turn around and come back to the main road again. You can see a great deal from the car, but there are also hiking trails.

Char Cruze of **Creative Adventures, Ltd.** (p. 195) also offers a fantastic tour, which can be tailored to your family's interests (✆ **702/893-2051**).

The Valley of Fire can also be visited in conjunction with Lake Mead. From **Lake Mead Lodge,** take Nev. 166 (Lakeshore Scenic Dr.) heading north, make a right turn on Nev. 167 (North Shore Scenic Dr.), turn left on Nev. 169 (Moapa Valley Blvd.) west—a spectacularly scenic drive—and follow the signs. Valley of Fire is about 70 miles, approximately an hour, from Hoover Dam itself.

WHAT TO SEE & DO

No food concessions or gas stations are in the park; however, you can obtain meals or gas on Nev. 167 or in nearby **Overton** (15 miles northwest on Nev. 169). A fertile valley town replete with trees, agricultural crops, horses, and herds of cattle, Overton is quite a change in scenery from the Valley of Fire's looming ruddy formations. On your way in or out of the quaint burg, treat your family to a meal or snack at **Inside Scoop ★**, 395 S. Moapa Valley Blvd. (✆ **702/397-2055**), open Tuesday through Thursday 10am to 8pm, Friday and Saturday 10am to 9pm, and Sunday 11am to 8pm. This sweet, old-fashioned, ice-cream parlor is run by extremely friendly people who offer a proper menu of fresh food and classic sandwiches, including a vegetarian option. Consider coming by here on your way into the park and picking up box lunches (perfect for picnicking in the park), and then coming by afterward for a much-needed ice cream.

You might also want to stop at the **Lost City Museum ★**, 721 S. Moapa Valley Blvd. (✆ **702/397-2193**), on the southern edge of town. This little museum, surrounded by reconstructed wattle-and-daub pueblos, displays artifacts dating back 12,000 years from the ancient Anasazi village that was discovered in the region in 1924. This village had reached one of the highest levels of Native American culture in the United States. Clay jars, dried corn and beans, arrowheads, seashell necklaces, and willow baskets of the ancient Pueblo culture that inhabited this region between A.D. 300 and 1150 are thoughtfully and informatively exhibited. You'll also find exhibits about Mormon farmers who settled the valley in the 1860s. In addition, there's a large collection of local rocks—petrified wood, fern fossils, iron pyrites, green copper, and red iron oxide. Kids seem especially fascinated by the purple glass bottles—manganese blown bottles turned purple by the ultraviolet rays of the sun. Admission is $3 for adults, $2 for seniors 65 and older, and free for children 17 and under. The museum is open daily 8:30am to 4:30pm. Closed Thanksgiving, December 25, and January 1.

Hiking trails, shaded picnic sites, and **two campgrounds** are in the park. Most sites are equipped with tables, grills, water, and restrooms. A $14 per vehicle per night camping fee is charged for use of the campground; if you're not camping, it costs $6 per vehicle to enter the park.

3 RED ROCK CANYON ★★★

19 miles W of Las Vegas

If you need a break from Las Vegas and its overstimulating hustle and glow, soothe your senses and spend some family time at Red Rock Canyon, less than 20 miles away from the neonopolis's glittering Strip. A visit to this magnificent, unspoiled vista is a refreshing break from the hubbub and neon of Vegas. And what makes the canyon even more appealing is that you and yours can spend a good part of the day out here, taking in the unique natural wonders, and still make it back to your hotel in time for the Bellagio fountain show or the *Blue Man Group*. You can drive the panoramic 13-mile **Scenic**

Drive (open daily 6am–dusk) or explore the park in more depth on foot, making it perfect for both athletes and armchair types. You'll find many interesting sights and trail heads along the drive itself, allowing you to get out and stretch your legs or just take in the views. The wider **National Conservation Area** offers hiking trails and internationally acclaimed rock-climbing opportunities (especially notable is the 7,068-ft. Mount Wilson, the highest sandstone peak among the bluffs). Picnic areas can be found along the drive and in nearby **Spring Mountain Ranch State Park,** 5 miles south, which also offers plays in an outdoor theater during the summer. Because Bonnie Springs Ranch (see the next section) is just a few miles away, it makes a great base for exploring Red Rock Canyon.

GETTING THERE

Just drive west on Charleston Boulevard, which becomes Nev. 159. Virtually as soon as you leave the city, the red rocks begin to loom around you. The Visitor Center will appear on your right.

Finally, the adventurous, in-shape family can go **by bike.** Not very far out of town (at Rainbow Blvd.), Charleston Boulevard is flanked by a bike path that continues for about 11 miles to the Visitor Center/Scenic Drive. The path is hilly but not difficult if you're in reasonable shape. However, exploring Red Rock Canyon by bike should be attempted only by exceptionally fit and experienced bikers. Bike equipment can be rented from **Escape Adventures/Las Vegas Cyclery,** 8221 W. Charleston Blvd. (✆ **702/596-2953;** www.escapeadventures.com), starting at $40 per day. They also offer guided tours (p. 281).

Just off Nev. 159, you'll see the **Red Rock Canyon Visitor Center** (✆ **702/515-5350;** www.redrockcanyon.blm.gov), which marks the actual entrance to the park. There, you can pick up information on trails and view history exhibits on the canyon. The center is open daily from 8:30am to 4:30pm. Red Rock Canyon can also be combined with a visit to Bonnie Springs Ranch.

ABOUT RED ROCK CANYON

Some 600 million years ago, the forces of nature began forming Red Rock Canyon. During most of its history, Red Rock Canyon was below a warm shallow sea. Then, about 225 million years ago, massive fault action and volcanic eruptions caused this seabed to begin rising. As the waters receded, sea creatures died and the calcium in their bodies combined with sea minerals to form limestone cliffs studded with ancient fossils. Some 45 million years later, the region was buried beneath thousands of feet of windblown sand. The landscape was as arid as the Sahara. As time progressed, iron oxide and calcium carbonate infiltrated the sand, consolidating it into cross-bedded rock.

> **Tips** **Wild Weather**
>
> Although it can get very hot in Red Rock during the summer, it can also get very cold there during the winter. A recent trip in March to Red Rock and Bonnie Springs found the latter closed—due to snow!

Winds and water shaped the sandstone monoliths into arches, natural bridges, and massive sculptures, and painted them a stunning palette with gray-white limestone, pink and crimson oxidized minerals, dolomite, black mineral deposits, and orange and green lichen stains.

As shallow streams began carving the Red Rock landscape, logs washed down from ancient highland forests and gradually fossilized, their molecules replaced by quartz and

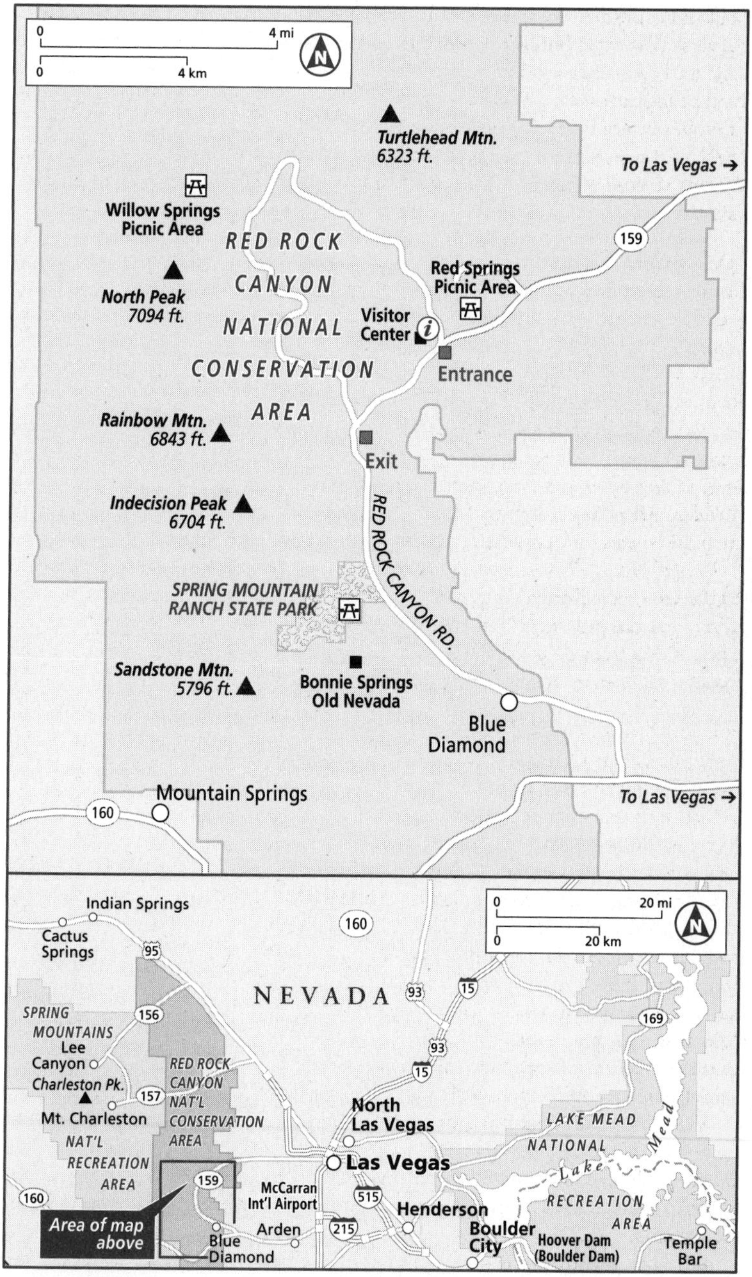
0
4 mi
0
4 km
N
Turtlehead Mtn.
6323 ft.
To Las Vegas →
Willow Springs
Picnic Area
RED ROCK
CANYON
NATIONAL
CONSERVATION
AREA
159
Red Springs
Picnic Area
North Peak
7094 ft.
Visitor
Center
i
Entrance
Rainbow Mtn.
6843 ft.
Exit
Indecision Peak
6704 ft.
RED ROCK CANYON RD.
SPRING MOUNTAIN
RANCH STATE PARK
Sandstone Mtn.
5796 ft.
Bonnie Springs
Old Nevada
Blue
Diamond
Mountain Springs
160
To Las Vegas →
Indian Springs
Cactus
Springs
95
160
0
20 mi
0
20 km
N
NEVADA
93
15
SPRING
MOUNTAINS
156
Lee
Canyon
169
93
RED ROCK
CANYON
NAT'L
CONSERVATION
AREA
15
Charleston Pk.
157
Mt. Charleston
NAT'L
RECREATION
AREA
North
Las Vegas
LAKE MEAD
NATIONAL
Lake Mead
Las Vegas
159
McCarran
Int'l Airport
160
515
RECREATION
AREA
Henderson
Area of map
above
Arden
215
Boulder
City
Hoover Dam
(Boulder Dam)
Temple
Bar
Blue
Diamond

other minerals, becoming petrified wood. These stone logs, which the Paiute Indians believed were weapons of the wolf god, Shinarav, can be viewed in the **Chinle Formation** at the base of the Red Rock Cliffs. About 100 million years ago, massive fault action began dramatically shifting the rock landscape here, forming spectacular limestone and sandstone cliffs and rugged canyons punctuated by waterfalls, shallow streams, and serene oasis pools. Even now, spring-fed areas of lush foliage contrast the harsh rocks and steep cliffs jutting 2,000 feet above the valley floors.

The seismic activity is exemplified by the **Keystone Thrust Fault,** dating back about 65 million years, where two of the earth's crustal plates collided, forcing older limestone and dolomite plates from the ancient seas over younger red and white sandstones.

Red Rock's valley is home to more than 45 species of mammals, including bighorn sheep, about 100 species of birds, 30 kinds of reptiles and amphibians, and an abundance of plant life. Ascending the slopes from the valley, you'll see cactus and creosote bushes, aromatic purple sage, yellow-flowering blackbrush, yucca and Joshua trees, and, at higher elevations, clusters of forest-green pinyon, juniper, and ponderosa pines. In spring, this desert blooms with extraordinary wildflowers.

Archaeological studies of Red Rock have turned up pottery fragments, stone tools, pictographs (rock drawings), and petroglyphs (rock etchings), along with other ancient artifacts. They show that humans have been in this region since about 3000 B.C. (some experts say as early as 10,000 B.C.). You can still see remains of early inhabitants on hiking expeditions in the park. (It's the same, sad Anasazi to Paiutes to white settlers progression related in the Valley of the Fire section above.)

In the latter part of the 19th century, Red Rock was a mining site and later a sandstone quarry that provided materials for many buildings in Los Angeles, San Francisco, and early Las Vegas. By the end of World War II, however, as Las Vegas developed, many people became aware of the importance of preserving the canyon. In 1967, the Secretary of the Interior designated 62,000 acres as Red Rock Canyon Recreation Lands under the auspices of the Bureau of Land Management, and later legislation banned all development except hiking trails and limited recreational facilities. In 1990, Red Rock Canyon became a National Conservation Area, further elevating its protected status; its current acreage is 197,000.

WHAT TO SEE & DO

Begin with a stop at the **Visitor Center** (**© 702/515-5350;** www.redrockcanyon.blm.gov); not only is there a $5 per vehicle fee to pay, but you can pick up a variety of helpful literature: history, guides, hiking trail maps, and lists of local flora and fauna. There, you can also view exhibits that tell the history of the canyon and depict its plant and animal life. The center also has a fascinating video about Nevada's thousands of wild horses and burros, protected by an act of Congress since 1971. Furthermore, you can obtain permits for hiking and backpacking there. Call ahead to find out about ranger-guided tours as well as informative guided hikes offered by groups such as the Sierra Club and the Audubon Society. Also ask about the free *Junior Ranger Discovery Book* filled with fun, family activities. Other books and videotapes are on sale here, including a guidebook identifying more than 100 top-rated climbing sites.

The Visitor Center also offers astronomy programs, for those interested in stargazing; details can be found on the website or by calling the center. A campsite, located 2 miles past the visitor center, has barbecue grills (bring your own fuel), picnic tables, trash pickup, and pit toilets. A campground host is on-site if you need any help. Campsites are on a first-come, first served basis, and cost $10 per night. Pets are permitted, but must be on a leash at all times.

The easiest thing to do with your family is to **drive the 13-mile scenic loop ★★**. It's a one-way loop and once you start, you are committed to driving the whole thing, which can take as little as 40 minutes or as long as you like, depending on whether you stop and get out to admire your surroundings. Anywhere along the way, you can stop the car to gaze at any number of fabulous views and sights, have a picnic, or take a walk or hike. Point out to your kids how dramatically the milky-white limestone alternates with the iron-rich red rocks and show them the evergreen forest, a strange sight in the desert, through the limestone canyons.

For the most part, **hiking** is best left to in-shape adults and athletic young adults, who can read maps and enjoy clambering and climbing. However, if you're up to it, we can't stress enough that the way to really see the canyon is by hiking, because the trails are the best way to explore the park. Most of the trails are designated "easy," but that is fairly subjective. One trail is designed especially for children, the **Lost Creek Children's Discovery Trail,** which is .7 mile and suitable for all ages. The hike to the Calico Tanks may be the best hike at Red Rock Canyon. Though short (under 3 miles round-trip), this hike is moderately strenuous and should not be undertaken by children under age 8. The trail winds up a narrow, rocky canyon, terminating at the Calico Tanks, a natural water repository situated high on a ridge overlooking the Las Vegas Valley. Children love the adventure and easy boulder hopping. Adults and kids alike are wowed by the views from the top.

A trail appropriate for children 8 years and up is the **Moenkopi Trail.** Originating at the Visitor Center and traversing undulating open terrain in a broad desert valley, the short loop trail takes a little more than an hour to walk.

All of the canyon's hikes involve a certain amount of effort, because you have to scramble over rocks on even the shorter hikes. Younger children, the out of shape, and the clumsy may wish to stand by the side and just take in the scenery. Be sure to wear good shoes—the rocks can be slippery—and take a map with you. You probably won't get lost forever without one (usually other hikers are around to help you out—eventually!), but you can get lost, which could be very upsetting for all concerned. It is often tough to find a landmark, and once deep into the rocks, everything looks the same, even with the map. Consequently, give yourself extra time for each hike (at least an additional hour except for Lost Creek and Moenkopi trails), regardless of its billed length, to allow for the lack of paths, getting disoriented, and simply slowing down and admiring the scenery. Many tourists make the mistake of heading off without proper footwear or water, a sure recipe for disaster. Get this straight: Good shoes and adequate drinking water are not optional, nor is sunscreen. Regarding water, on trails of 3 miles or less, a liter should get you by. On longer trails, 2 liters is a minimum. Adjust the quantities upward in the hotter months, but never downward regardless of season. You can check out the hikes in advance at **www.redrockcanyon.blm.gov/activities/hiking.asp**.

As you hike, keep your eyes peeled for lizards, the occasional desert tortoise, herds of bighorn sheep, birds, and other critters. There are also minicaves to explore and rocks to climb. On trails along Calico Hills and the escarpment, look for "Indian marbles," a local name for small, rounded sandstone rocks that have eroded off larger sandstone formations. Look, but don't touch: *You should not take these or any other rocks with you as souvenirs; it is illegal.* Petroglyphs are also tucked away in various locales, but don't be tempted to add your own: The park is a National Conservation Area controlled by the federal government. The fines—which vary by offense—are steep for desecrating the monuments, taking plants and rocks, and for harassing (trying to touch, chasing, and so on) the animals in the park.

Biking is another option for seeing the park; riding a bicycle would be a tremendous way to travel the loop. There are also terrific off-road mountain biking trails, with levels from amateur to expert. If you don't want to go on your own, **Escape Adventures** (**© 702/596-2953;** www.escapeadventures.com) offers a half-day, 18-mile bike ride through Red Rock.

After you tour the canyon, drive over to Bonnie Springs Ranch (see below) for lunch or dinner.

4 BONNIE SPRINGS RANCH/OLD NEVADA ★★

About 24 miles W of Las Vegas, 5 miles from Red Rock Canyon

Bonnie Springs Ranch/Old Nevada is a kind of Wild West theme park with a zoo, ghost town, accommodations, and a restaurant. Admission to the zoo and Old Nevada is covered in one low fee. If you're traveling with kids, a day or overnight trip to Bonnie Springs/Old Nevada is recommended, but it is surprisingly appealing for adults, too. It could even be a romantic getaway, offering horseback riding, gorgeous mountain vistas, proximity to Red Rock Canyon, and temperatures 5° to 10° cooler than on the Strip.

For additional information, contact **Bonnie Springs Ranch/Old Nevada** at **© 702/875-4191** or **www.bonniesprings.com**.

If you're **driving,** a trip to Bonnie Springs Ranch can be combined easily with a day trip to Red Rock Canyon; it is about 5 miles farther on. But you can also stay overnight at the Bonnie Springs Hotel to make this destination more than just a day trip.

GETTING THERE

From anywhere on Las Vegas Boulevard South (the Strip), drive north to Charleston Boulevard, make a left onto Charleston Boulevard, and take it west for 25 miles (6 miles past the Red Rock Visitor Center). Bonnie Springs/Old Nevada is on the right side. A wooden arch with an OLD NEVADA sign marks the entrance.

For those without transportation, there's a shuttle service, **Star Land Tours/Bonnie Springs Shuttle** (**© 702/493-0416**), which will pick you up at your Vegas hotel and take you out to Bonnie Springs for $45 round-trip per person. The shuttle fee includes admission to Old Nevada and the zoo.

WHAT TO SEE & DO AT BONNIE SPRINGS RANCH

For kids, the **zoo** (its admission is covered in the entrance fee to Old Nevada) is the big draw at Bonnie Springs Ranch, located right next door to Old Nevada, on the same property, at 1 Gunfighter Lane, with the same hours, daily 10am to 6pm from May through September, and 10am to 5pm October through April. In addition to the petting zoo with potbellied pigs, llamas, goats, and sheep, wire enclosures hold all manner of creatures, including wolves and bobcats. Parents and some children may find this a bit prehistoric in comparison to the zoos located in large urban centers. However, the creatures are healthy and well cared for, and the ranch provides a home for wild horses, many of whom would starve to death if not rounded up and placed here.

The zoo includes an aviary, housing peacocks, Polish chickens, peachface and black-mask lovebirds, finches, parakeets, ravens, ducks, pheasants, and geese. Keep your eyes peeled for the peacocks roaming free; with luck, they will spread their tails for a photo op. With greater luck, some of the angelic, rare white peacocks will do the same. It may be worth dropping by just in the hopes of spotting one in full fan-tailed glory.

Riding stables offer guided trail rides into the mountain area on a continuous basis throughout the day (9am–3:15pm fall–spring, until 5:45pm in summer). Children must be at least 6 years old to participate. Cost is $50 per person for the hourlong guided ride through the surrounding hills. For more information, call © **702/875-4191.**

WHAT TO SEE & DO IN OLD NEVADA

Old Nevada ★★ (© **702/875-4191**) is a re-creation of an 1880s frontier town, built on the site of a very old ranch. Though a bit hokey, it's got a certain charm, and children up to age 12 (before teenage cynicism kicks in) will certainly get a kick out of the authentic-looking Western town (and you just might, as well!). Rustic buildings are entirely made of weathered wood, and the town lies right in front of beautiful mountains with layered red rock. Hollywood could not have done any better.

The block-long town, with its well-replicated places of business (a blacksmith shop, a working mill), a saloon, and a museum that has a potpourri of items from the Old West and Old Las Vegas (antique gaming tables and slot machines, typewriters, and a great display of old shoes including lace-up boots) also has (of course) an old-fashioned general store, which functions as a gift shop. Additionally, there's a wax museum, which pales beside the free **stage melodramas** that take place three times a day in the (all ages allowed) saloon. These melodramas (staged at 11:30am, 2 and 4:30pm in the summer; 11:30am, 1:30 and 3:30pm in the winter; dark Monday and Tuesday) are entirely tongue-in-cheek—the actors are goofy and know it, and the plot is hokey and fully intended to be that way. Somehow, however, all of these factors just heighten the fun you have while watching them. Kids will like the interactivity of the audience who, in response to cue cards held up by the players, boo and hiss the mustache-twirling villain, sob in sympathy with the distressed heroine, and laugh, cheer, and applaud as the cards instruct. It's hugely silly and hugely fun, provided you all play along. Kids love it, though younger ones might be scared by the occasional gunshot.

Immediately following each melodrama, a free **Western drama** is presented outside the saloon on the street, involving a bank robbery, a shootout, and the trial of the bad guy. A judge, prosecuting attorney, and defense attorney are chosen from the audience, the remainder of whom act as the jury. The action always culminates in a hanging, which some younger kids might find disturbing. None of this is a particularly polished act, but the dialogue is quite funny and the whole thing is performed with enthusiasm and affection.

Throughout the area, during the hours of operation, "cowboys" (costumed actors) continually interact with visiting kids, who, on the weekends, are given badges so that they can join a "posse" hunting for bad guys (also costumed actors). There are also ongoing, somewhat clumsy **stunt shootouts** on the street in this wild frontier town, staged by said actors, and some rather unsavory characters (more actors) occasionally languishing in the town jail, at least until their lunch break!

The town (in all of its block-long pseudo–ghost town glory) also has replicas of a turn-of-the-20th-century church and stamp mill; the latter, having original 1902 machinery, was used for crushing rocks to separate gold and silver from the earth. In the **Old Nevada Photograph Shoppe,** on the main street, you can dress up in period costumes and have a tintype picture taken with a 120-year-old camera. You can also tour the remains of the **old Comstock Lode silver mine,** behind the saloon, though there isn't much to see there. And if you must, you can shop for a variety of "Western" souvenirs (though, to us, this is when the real tourist trap part of Old Nevada kicks in).

There is plenty of parking in Old Nevada; weekends and holidays, a free shuttle train that your youngest kids will love takes visitors from the parking lot to the entrance. Admission to Old Nevada is charged by vehicle—$20 per car for up to 6 people in the car. The park is open daily from 10:30am to 5pm November to April, until 6pm the rest of the year, and admission also includes entrance into Bonnie Springs Ranch, with its zoo.

WHERE TO STAY & DINE

Bonnie Springs Motel ★ This is really a hoot; a funky, friendly, little place in the middle of nowhere—though nowhere is really a gorgeous setting. The motel is in two double-story buildings and offers regular rooms, "Western" rooms, "specialty theme" rooms, and kitchen suites.

Unfortunately, the specialty rooms (decorated in theatrical Chinese, Native American, Gay '90s, and Spanish themes) are off-limits to kids, but children are allowed in the Calico West rooms and kitchen suites, which have sleeper sofas in the living room. The Western-motif Calico West rooms sleep four and are quite large, though long and narrow. All of these Calico West rooms have private balconies or patios, and mountain views. The family suites, which are also Western themed and sleep six, come with fully equipped kitchens, bedrooms, living rooms (with convertible sofas), and dressing areas; these are also equipped with two phones and two TVs and are available for long-term rentals. DVDs and players are also available for rental, and a tiny train takes you around the grounds and on a short tour of the desert. The motel also offers a special breakfast horseback ride package for guests, at a cost of $35. Guests of the motel receive free admission into Old Nevada.

1 Gunfighter Lane, Old Nevada, NV 89004. ✆ **702/875-4400.** Fax 702/875-4424. www.bonniesprings.com. 50 units. Sun–Thurs $85–$95 double, Fri–Sat $100–$110 double (4 people maximum); Sun–Thurs $150 fantasy suite, Fri–Sat $165 fantasy suite (4 people maximum); Sun–Thurs $125 family suite, Fri–Sat $140 family suite (6 people maximum). Extra person $5. $100 deposit required on family suites; $10 key and phone deposit for all rooms. Cribs/rollaways free, unless they are for an extra person, in which case the $5 extra person fee applies. AE, MC, V. **Amenities:** Outdoor pool. *In room:* A/C, TV w/pay movies, DVDs available to rent, coffeemakers.

Bonnie Springs Ranch Restaurant This perfect family place has a lot of character, with a heavily rustic decor (complete with stone floors, log beams, raw wooden chairs made from tree branches, lanterns, a roaring fire in winter, and plenty of dead animals adorning the walls). It's a bit touristy, but small-town touristy. The food is basic—steak, ribs, chicken, burgers, and potato skins; pancakes and eggs for breakfast; most of it is greasy but good, with a children's menu featuring chicken fingers, steak, and other kid pleasers. For parents who want a break, a cozy bar is attached to the restaurant; its walls are covered with thousands of dollar bills with messages on them—what would be a classic neighborhood bar, if it were actually in a neighborhood!

In Bonnie Springs Ranch, 1 Gunfighter Lane. ✆ **702/875-4300.** www.bonniesprings.com/restaurant.html. Highchairs, boosters. Main courses $15–$25; kids' menu $5–$10. AE, MC, V. Daily, 9am–9pm.

5 SPRING MOUNTAINS NATIONAL RECREATION AREA

25 miles NW of Las Vegas

Part of the 316,000-acre **Spring Mountains National Recreation Area** (known locally as Mount Charleston), this mountainous area offers stunning natural beauty year-round. Under an hour from Las Vegas, Mount Charleston makes a quick, easy, and lovely getaway from the Strip. There are five separate eco-zones within the park, based on elevation. During the summer, it can be 30°F (–1°C) cooler here than on the Strip, and the green forests with pine trees beckon hikers. **Robber Roost,** 3 miles north of Nev. 157, on Nev. 158, is an 850-yard hiking loop (just under .5 mile), which weaves past caves, where, allegedly, real bandits hid out from lawmen. This is the easiest and shortest trail in the park, suitable for children 8 and over, with moderate athletic ability. Hiking trails, descriptions, and directions to each of the trails can be found at **www.fs.fed.us/r4/htnf/districts/smnra.shtml.**

From roughly Thanksgiving through Easter, depending on weather conditions, you can ski and snowboard at the **Las Vegas Ski and Snowboard Resort** (© **702/645-2754;** www.skilasvegas.com), located within the recreation area. The only snow sport facility in the Mount Charleston area, it rents equipment and clothing and also provides snowboarding and skiing lessons. A snack bar is on-site. The following information is for the 2008–09 ski season and may change during subsequent years. Call or e-mail the **Las Vegas Ski and Snowboard Resort** (ridenski@lvssr.com) to check for rate changes and get the most up-to-date information: Group rates for skiing or snowboarding lessons—based on groups of three or more—for 2 hours of instruction are $35 per person providing their own equipment and lift ticket, $90 including tickets and equipment. Children must be over 8 years old for these lessons. All-day instruction, lasting 5 hours, for one or two people is $500. Private instruction is also available hourly for $125 per hour. There is also a special children's program for kids ages 4 to 12 from 9:30am to 3:30pm. The $125 fee includes equipment and lunch. The half-day children's program is $90 and goes from 9:30am to noon, and does not include lunch.

The all-day pass for adults is $50 and $30 for children 12 and under. Those 60 and over can ski or snowboard all day for $30.

Complete ski equipment rental (skis, poles, and boots) is $35 no matter whether they are rented for a full day or for the 3-hour afternoon session. Skis alone are $25 and poles are $5. Snowboards, either in a complete package (including boots) or with the board alone, can be rented for $35. The fee is the same whether rented for the full day or for the shorter afternoon session. Snow clothes can be rented as well; bib and jacket together are $30 for the full day. Rented separately they are $20 each for a full day.

GETTING THERE

Mount Charleston is easily accessible from the Strip. Take Las Vegas Boulevard north to Spring Mountain Road. Turn west on Spring Mountain and merge onto I-15 N. Take I-15 N. to U.S. 95 N. and follow that to Nev. 157 (Kyle Canyon). Turn left on 157, and the signs will announce your arrival in the recreation area.

WHERE TO STAY

Mount Charleston Hotel This rustic-style hotel (think log walls and fireplaces in the public areas) becomes a bustling ski resort during the winter months. During the summer, it provides an excellent, though slightly expensive, location for families who want to hike in the Mount Charleston area. Rooms are attractive, offering a comfortable place to rest up, and most have stunning views of the surrounding area. Suites sleep four with the pullout couch. The website lists room rate specials. The restaurant, featuring what staff calls "middle of the road, tasty" food (they're right), serves reasonably priced breakfasts, lunches, and dinners, and provides a children's menu as well.

2 Kyle Canyon Rd. (Nev. 157), Mount Charleston, NV 89124. ✆ **800/794-3456** or 702/872-5500. www.mtcharlestonhotel.com. 63 units. $99–$129 double; $119–$149 suite. Extra person $5. Children 11 and under stay free in parent's room. No cribs or rollaways. AE, DC, DISC, MC, V. **Amenities:** Restaurant (American); coffee shop; bar; whirlpool; Jacuzzi; sauna; arcade. *In room:* A/C, TV w/pay movies, coffeemaker.

Mount Charleston Lodge Located at the very top of Nev. 157, and designed primarily as a honeymoon and vacation getaway for couples, Mount Charleston Lodge provides rustic log cabins that sleep two to four people. Two cabins have full kitchens; all have whirlpool tubs and fireplaces. Designed mainly for skiers, the Lodge's rates go up approximately $15 during December and on all major holidays. On weekends, during September and October, the Lodge restaurant adds German food to its extensive menu (ostrich, elk, and buffalo burgers in addition to beef, plus pizza, desserts, and breakfast) and throws a big Oktoberfest celebration.

1200 Old Park Rd., Mount Charleston, NV 89124. ✆ **800/955-1314** or 702/872-5408. www.mtcharlestonlodge.com. 23 units. $145–$256. Extra person $10. No cribs or rollaways. AE, DISC, MC, V. **Amenities:** 24-hr. restaurant (American). *In room:* A/C, TV w/pay movies (in some cabins), kitchenette, coffeemaker, Jacuzzi, fireplace.

6 PRIMM

35 miles S of Las Vegas

Best known for its outlet shopping (p. 206), Primm is located half an hour south of Las Vegas, on I-15, right before the border with California. (It was formerly named Stateline.) There are three hotels, including a golf resort, in Primm, but, really, you're better off staying in Las Vegas.

Primm, in its entirety, can be found on the Web at **www.primmvalleyresorts.com**.

Crime buffs will enjoy looking at Bonnie and Clyde's death car, Clyde's death shirt, and Al Capone's car at **Primm Valley Resort & Casino** (31900 Las Vegas Blvd. S.; ✆ **800/386-7867** or 702/386-7867), within walking distance from Buffalo Bill's.

However, the main reasons to come here with your family, aside from making sure that the heavily discounted clothes fit them, are the thrill rides at **Buffalo Bill's Resort and Casino** (31900 Las Blvd. S.; ✆ **800/386-7867** or 702/382-1212; www.primmvalleyresorts.com). There's the **Desperado,** a steep, exciting roller coaster that zips through the casino, dropping 225 feet and reaching speeds of 85 mph. And the **Adventure Canyon** log flume ride will definitely leave you sopping wet. If that's not enough for thrill lovers, there's the **Turbo Drop,** which will plunge you 170 feet in milliseconds. **MaxFlight Cyber Coaster** allows you, through the miracle of virtual reality and motion simulators, to design your own roller coaster ride, and then take it, and the **Vault,** another 3-D ride, offers you a series of interactive adventures.

To ride these, you must be over 48 inches, with the exception of the flume ride, which allows smaller children to ride with an adult. For those 36 to 48 inches, there's also a **Frog**

Hopper, which raises riders 20 feet up in the air and gently brings them down; the ride is four cycles long.

Rides range from $3 to $8; the best buy, if you plan to stay awhile, is a wristband. For $33, you can ride everything all day long, plus see a feature movie in the casino's theater (generally screening G and PG family-oriented flicks) and get a small soda and popcorn. Alternatively, a $24 wristband is good for 3 hours, which might be plenty of time to get your child's ya-yas out. For $15, those under 48 inches can get a Little Wranglers wristband that's good for all-day Frog Hoppers, plus a movie, soda, and popcorn. For more information, call the recorded ride hot line at ✆ **702/679-7433.**

7 THE GRAND CANYON: GRAND CANYON WEST

121 miles SE of Las Vegas

The Grand Canyon—the name is at once both entirely apt and entirely inadequate. How can words sum up the grandeur of 2 billion years of the earth's history sliced open by the power of a single river? Once an impassable and forbidding barrier to explorers and settlers, the Grand Canyon is today a magnet that each year attracts millions of visitors from all over the world. The pastel layers of rock weaving through the rugged ramparts of the canyon, the interplay of shadows and light, the wind in the pines, and the croaking of ravens on the rim—these are the sights and sounds that never fail to transfix the hordes of visitors who gaze awestruck into the canyon's seemingly infinite depths.

With more than four million people each year visiting the South Rim of the Grand Canyon, and traffic congestion and parking problems becoming the most memorable aspects of most people's trips, you might want to consider an alternative to the South Rim. For most travelers, this means driving around to the North Rim; however, it's open only from mid-May to late October and itself is not immune to parking problems and traffic congestion. Plus, it's pretty far away from Las Vegas.

So, if you want to go to the canyon on your own (not taking a tour), we recommend Grand Canyon West as your best option if you're going to the canyon as a "side trip" from Las Vegas. Visiting Grand Canyon West, on the Hualapai Indian Reservation, is favored by people short on time, or who want to go to the new Skywalk attraction, or who want to fly down into the canyon (something that isn't permitted within Grand Canyon National Park). Note that the drive to and from Grand Canyon West involves spending some 28 miles on gravel, so expect lots of dust and some rough stretches. Also remember that Grand Canyon West is particularly popular with tour buses from Las Vegas (because it's about the closest spot to Las Vegas that actually provides a glimpse of the Colorado River and Grand Canyon National Park), and the constant helicopter traffic here precludes any sort of tranquil canyon experience. That said, you're still at the Grand Canyon, which is pretty, well, awesome, no matter what.

The **Skywalk** attraction opened in 2007 to great fanfare: It's a 500-ton U-shaped steel-and-glass walkway that juts 70 feet over the edge of the Canyon, which drops along sheer cliff faces for 4,000 feet to the Colorado River below. The walkway has a see-through glass bottom and sides; five layers of tempered floor glass are nearly 4 inches thick and weigh 90 tons. Massive anchors made from 84 rods of high-strength steel, embedded nearly 46 feet into the bedrock, hold the structure over the canyon. Skywalk is designed to withstand 100-mph winds coming from all directions and an 8.0 magnitude earthquake 50 miles away, and can hold 72 millions pounds. In short, it's not going to drop nearly a mile to the canyon floor while you're standing on it. Good thing, too, since you pay $30 for the opportunity. Visitors wear special booties to keep from scratching the glass or slipping on it.

For information on Grand Canyon West, contact **Hualapai Reservations,** P.O. Box 538, Peach Springs, AZ 86434-0538 (© **888/255-9550** or 928/769-2230; www.destinationgrandcanyon.com/indexe.html).

GUIDED TOURS

Generally, tourists visiting Las Vegas don't drive the hundreds of miles to Arizona to see the Grand Canyon National Park from the North or South rims. Instead, they take one of dozens of sightseeing tours departing from the city daily, which will bring you there. One major operator, **Scenic Airlines** (© **800/634-6801** or 702/638-3300; www.scenic.com), runs deluxe, 8-hour, guided air-ground tours for $244 per person ($224 for children 2–11); the price for the tour, which begins with a narrated flight over the canyon, includes a bus excursion through the national park as well as lunch. In addition to the full-day tours, the company offers overnight tours with hiking and flightseeing. Scenic also offers flight tours to other points of interest and national parks, including an 11-hour trip combining the Grand Canyon and Bryce Canyon in Utah (270 miles from Las Vegas), and a flight tour of Monument Valley, which is located on Navajo land straddling the border between Arizona and Utah (approx. 450 miles from Las Vegas, and a 12-hr. tour with Scenic). Ask for details when you call.

GETTING THERE

Be aware that at least 14 miles of the route heading to Grand Canyon West from Las Vegas features dirt roads, making a trip there almost impossible if it has rained recently. From Vegas, take Nev. 93, south, approximately 30 miles past Hoover Dam to Pearce Ferry Road (signed for Dolan Springs and Meadowview). Turn left onto Dolan Springs/Meadowview and continue for 28 miles on this road, and then turn right onto gravel Diamond Bar Road, which is signed for Grand Canyon West. Another 14 miles down this road brings you to the Hualapai Indian Reservation, and onto the paved road, which demarcates the reservation. A little farther along, you'll come to the Grand Canyon West Terminal (there's actually an airstrip here), where visitor permits and bus-tour tickets are sold.

DISCOVERING THE CANYON

Located on the Hualapai Indian Reservation on the south side of the Colorado River, **Grand Canyon West** (© **702/565-8761;** www.grandcanyonwest.com) overlooks the rarely visited west end of Grand Canyon National Park. Although the view is not as spectacular as at either the South Rim or the North Rim, Grand Canyon West is noteworthy for one thing: It is one of the only places where you can legally fly down into the canyon. This is possible because the helicopters operate on land that is part of the Hualapai Indian Reservation. At this point, the south side of the Colorado lies within the reservation, while the north side of the river is within Grand Canyon National Park. Helicopter tours are operated by **Papillon Helicopters** (© **800/528-2418** or 928/638-2419; www.papillon.com), which charges $120 to $204 per person for flight tours to the bottom of the canyon; some tours also include pontoon boat cruises and meals—call for further information.

There are also guided **bus tours** along the rim of the canyon. These include time to do a bit of exploring at a canyon overlook. Tours stop at Eagle Point, where rock formations resemble various animals and people, and at Guano Point, where bat guano was

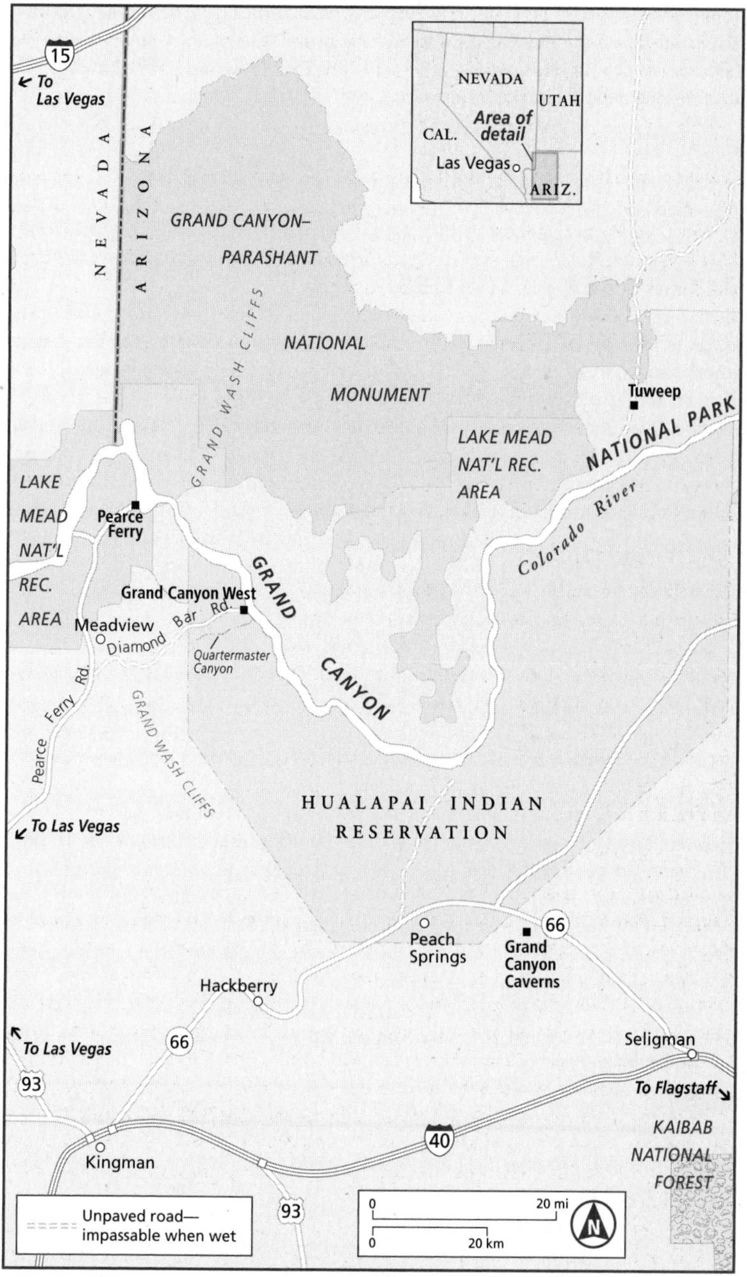
15
To Las Vegas
NEVADA
ARIZONA
GRAND CANYON–PARASHANT NATIONAL MONUMENT
GRAND WASH CLIFFS
NEVADA
UTAH
Area of detail
CAL.
Las Vegas
ARIZ.
Tuweep
NATIONAL PARK
LAKE MEAD NAT'L REC. AREA
LAKE MEAD NAT'L REC. AREA
Pearce Ferry
Colorado River
GRAND CANYON
Grand Canyon West
Meadview
Diamond Bar Rd.
Quartermaster Canyon
Pearce Ferry Rd.
GRAND WASH CLIFFS
To Las Vegas
HUALAPAI INDIAN RESERVATION
Peach Springs
66
Grand Canyon Caverns
Hackberry
66
To Las Vegas
93
Seligman
To Flagstaff
KAIBAB NATIONAL FOREST
40
Kingman
93
Unpaved road—impassable when wet
0
20 mi
0
20 km
N

once mined commercially. The tours to the South and West rims, which operate daily throughout the year, cost $115. Reservations are required at least 24 hours in advance.

If you'd just like to take in the view from this end of the canyon, head to **Quartermaster Point,** after first purchasing your sightseeing permit ($15) at the Grand Canyon West terminal. At Quartermaster Point, you'll find a trail that leads down a few hundred yards to a viewpoint overlooking the Colorado River.

Although we can only recommend a trip out to Grand Canyon West as a side trip from Las Vegas or for travelers who absolutely must fly down into the canyon, the drive out here is almost as scenic as the destination itself. Along Diamond Bar Road, the dirt road that leads to the Hualapai reservation, you'll be driving below the Grand Wash Cliffs, and for much of the way, the route traverses a dense forest of Joshua trees.

OTHER AREA ACTIVITIES

If you long to raft the Grand Canyon but have only a couple of free days in your schedule to realize your dream, then you have only a couple of options. Here at the west end of the canyon, it's possible to do a 1-day rafting trip that begins on the Hualapai Indian Reservation. These trips are operated by **Hualapai River Runners,** P.O. Box 538, Peach Springs, AZ 86434 (✆ **928/769-2219;** www.destinationgrandcanyon.com/runners.html), a tribal rafting company, and run between mid-March and late October. Expect a mix of white water and flat water (all of it very cold). Although perhaps not as exciting as longer trips in the main section of the canyon, you'll still plow through some pretty big waves (kids must be 8 or older to ride). Be ready to get wet! These trips stop at a couple of side canyons where you can get out and do some exploring. The trip lasts 10 hours and costs $328 per person, which includes transportation, equipment, vests, and a meal, plus a helicopter ride out of the canyon at the end of the trip. Groups of eight or more can also arrange a 2-day tour, if they wish.

Also in this area, you can visit **Grand Canyon Caverns** (✆ **928/422-3223;** www.gccaverns.com), just outside Peach Springs. The caverns, which are accessed via a 210-foot elevator ride, are open from Memorial Day to October 15, daily from 8am to 6pm, and other months, daily from 10am to 4pm. Admission is $15 for adults, $10 for children 4 to 12.

WHERE TO STAY & DINE NEAR THE GRAND CANYON

Grand Canyon Caverns Inn As the name implies, this motel is built on the site of the Grand Canyon Caverns, which are open to the public (see above). The curio store, general store, and restaurant/bar are located on the same property, a mile up the road, while the pool and laundry are adjacent to the rooms. There's a real sense of Americana here, a classic motel just off historic Route 66. Book early; for most of the year, the motel is used by the Elderhostel travel group and thus stays very busy.

P.O. Box 180, Peach Springs, AZ 86434. ✆ **928/422-3223.** www.gccaverns.com/inn.html. 48 units. $85–$95. Rollaways $5. AE, DISC, MC, V. Pets accepted with $50 deposit. **Amenities:** Restaurant (American); lounge; outdoor pool; coin-op laundry. *In room:* A/C, TV.

Hualapai Lodge ★ (Finds Located in the Hualapai community of Peach Springs, this lodge is by far the most luxurious accommodations anywhere in the region. (Though that's not saying much!) Guest rooms are spacious and modern, with a few bits of regional decor for character. Most people staying here are in the area to visit Grand Canyon West, to go rafting with Hualapai River Runners, or to hike in to Havasu Canyon. The dining room is just about the only place in town to get a meal.

900 Rte. 66, P.O. Box 538, Peach Springs, AZ 86434. ✆ **888/255-9550** or 928/769-2230. Fax 928/769-2372. www.destinationgrandcanyon.com/lodge.html. 60 units. $89–$99. Children 11 and under stay free

in parent's room. Extra person $10. Cribs/rollaways $10. AE, DC, DISC, MC, V. **Amenities:** Restaurant (American); concierge; tour desk; coin-op laundry. *In room:* A/C, TV, dataport.

8 OUTDOOR ACTIVITIES & TOUR COMPANIES

CYCLING

Escape Adventures (✆ **702/596-2953** or 800/596-2953; www.escapeadventures.com) rents bikes and biking equipment, starting at $35 per day, as well as providing guided and self-guided tours of Red Rock Canyon and Mount Charleston, which begin at $89 for a half-day self-guided tour and include the bike rental. These tours range from 7 to 23 miles and span experience and age levels, depending on your children's abilities. One that is definitely suited to children is a summer tour that's 18 miles and all downhill from the top of Mount Charleston (a shuttle takes you up the mountain).

HIKING

Desert hiking trails in the region include marked trails in both Red Rock Canyon and Valley of Fire. Keep in mind that in the summer, temperatures can soar to 120°F (49°C); the best time for exploring the beauty of the desert is November through March. If you'd prefer a guided hiking adventure in Red Rock, an experienced guide from **Grand Canyon Tours** (✆ **800/222-6966** or 702/655-6060; www.grandcanyontourcompany.com) will pick you up at your hotel and drive you into Red Rock for lunch and a 5- to 6-hour up-close walking tour of the formations for $119 per person (no discount for children). **Escape Adventures** (✆ **702/596-2953;** www.escapeadventures.com) offers a half-day guided hike through Red Rock for $89 per person. Guided tours are offered on a limited basis through the Red Rock Canyon visitor center, but reservations must be made in advance. A website specifically devoted to hiking in the Las Vegas area, www.hikinglasvegas.com, provides an overview of local hiking sights. Also see the "Take a Hike: Desert Hiking Advice" box, on p. 266, for more information on hiking in the desert.

HORSEBACK RIDING

Cowboy Trail Rides (✆ **702/387-2457;** www.cowboytrailrides.com) offers a variety of rides and trails in Red Rock Canyon and on Mount Charleston (at the 12-mile marker), ranging in price from $45 to $139. The high end is for a Red Rock Canyon sunset trail ride; it's about 2 hours, with the canyon providing a glorious backdrop for the end of the day. Riders then return to camp for a barbecue dinner (including a 16-oz. T-bone steak), joined by the cowboys for singalongs and marshmallow roasting. They also offer hour-and-a-half rides at $70. Riding stables at **Bonnie Springs Ranch** (✆ **702/875-4191;** see section earlier in this chapter) offer guided trail rides daily through the area close to Red Rock. Rates are $35 per person per hour. Wear tennis shoes, riding boots, or hiking boots and jeans for riding.

SKIING & SNOWBOARDING

From roughly Thanksgiving through Easter, depending on weather conditions, you can ski and snowboard at the **Las Vegas Ski and Snowboard Resort** (✆ **702/645-2754;** www.skilasvegas.com). It rents equipment and clothing and provides lessons. Adult all-day passes are $50; children 12 and under $30; afternoon passes good from 1 to 4pm are $5 less. For more information see p. 275.

Appendix: Fast Facts, Toll-Free Numbers & Websites

1 FAST FACTS: LAS VEGAS

AMERICAN EXPRESS There are about a dozen offices in town, but the closest one to the Strip is located inside the Fashion Show Mall at 3200 Las Vegas Blvd. S. (✆ **702/739-8474**), which is open daily from 8am to 6pm.

AUTOMOBILE ORGANIZATIONS Auto clubs will supply maps, suggested routes, guidebooks, accident and bail-bond insurance, and emergency road service. The **American Automobile Association (AAA)** is the major auto club in the United States. If you're traveling from outside the U.S. and belong to an auto club in your home country, inquire about AAA reciprocity before you leave. You may be able to join AAA even if you're not a member of a reciprocal club; to inquire, contact AAA (✆ **800/521-8124;** www.aaa.com).

BABYSITTERS See section 14, "Babysitters & Child-Care Centers," in chapter 3.

BANKS Banks are generally open from 9 or 10am to 5 and sometimes 6pm, and many have Saturday hours. ATMs are plentiful all around town. Also see "Cash & Credit" below.

BUSINESS HOURS International travelers, note that American offices are usually open weekdays from 9am to 5pm. Banks are open weekdays from 9am to 5pm or later, and sometimes on Saturday morning, although there's 24-hour access to the automated teller machines (ATMs) at most banks and other outlets. In Las Vegas, money is also available round-the-clock at casino cages—and every casino has at least one ATM. Shops, especially those in shopping complexes, tend to stay open late: until about 9pm weekdays and until 6pm weekends (including Sun).

CAR RENTALS See "Renting a Car" under section 2, "Getting Around," in chapter 5.

CASH & CREDIT It's extremely easy to obtain cash in Las Vegas. Most casino cashiers will cash personal checks and can exchange foreign currency, and just about every casino has a machine that will provide cash on a wide variety of credit cards.

CONVENTIONS Las Vegas is one of America's top convention destinations. Much of the action takes place at the **Las Vegas Convention Center,** 3150 Paradise Rd., Las Vegas, NV 89109 (✆ **702/892-0711**), which is the largest single-level convention center in the world. Its 3.2 million square feet include 144 meeting rooms. This immense facility is augmented by the **Cashman Field Center,** 850 Las Vegas Blvd. N., Las Vegas, NV 89101 (✆ **702/386-7100**). Under the same auspices, Cashman provides another 98,100 square feet of convention space. Additionally, there are massive convention facilities at many of the big hotels, including The Venetian, MGM Grand, Mandalay Bay, Las Vegas Hilton, and others.

CURRENCY EXCHANGE See "Money & Costs" in chapter 3.

DENTISTS & DOCTORS Hotels usually have lists of dentists and doctors should you need one. In addition, doctors and dentists are listed in the Centel Yellow Pages. Also see "Hospitals" below.

For physician referrals, call the **Desert Springs Hospital** (✆ **702/733-8800**). Hours are Monday to Friday 8am to 5pm.

DRINKING LAWS The legal age for purchase and consumption of alcoholic beverages is 21; proof of age is required and often requested at bars, nightclubs, and restaurants. Do not carry open containers of alcohol in your car or any public area that isn't zoned for alcohol consumption. The police can fine you on the spot. And nothing will ruin your trip faster than getting arrested for DUI ("driving under the influence"), so don't even think about driving if you've been drinking. Beer, wine, and liquor are all sold in all kinds of stores, pretty much round-the-clock; trust us, you won't have a hard time finding a drink in this town. It's even legal to have an open container (walking) on the Strip.

DRUGSTORES & PHARMACIES There's a 24-hour **Walgreens** (which also has a 1-hr. photo) at 3765 Las Vegas Blvd. S. (✆ **702/739-9638**), almost directly across from the Monte Carlo. **Sav-On** is a large 24-hour drugstore and pharmacy close to the Strip at 1360 E. Flamingo Rd., at Maryland Parkway (✆ **702/731-5373** for the pharmacy, 702/737-0595 for general merchandise). **White Cross Drugs,** 1700 Las Vegas Blvd. S. (✆ **702/382-1733**), open daily 8am to 9pm, will make pharmacy deliveries to your hotel during the day.

DRY CLEANERS Most hotels provide dry cleaning services with a 24-hour or less turnaround, but charge an arm and a leg. Local laundromats and dry cleaners, however, charge local prices.

ELECTRICITY For international visitors: Like Canada, the United States uses 110–120 volts AC (60 cycles), compared to 220–240 volts AC (50 cycles) in most of Europe, Australia, and New Zealand. If your small appliances use 220–240 volts, you'll need a 110-volt transformer and a plug adapter with two flat parallel pins to operate them here. Downward converters that change 220–240 volts to 110–120 volts are difficult to find in the United States, so bring one with you.

EMBASSIES & CONSULATES All embassies are located in the nation's capital, Washington, D.C. Some consulates are located in major U.S. cities, and most nations have a mission to the United Nations in New York City. If your country isn't listed below, call for directory information in Washington, D.C. (✆ **202/555-1212**) or log on to **www.embassy.org/embassies**.

The embassy of **Australia** is at 1601 Massachusetts Ave. NW, Washington, DC 20036 (✆ **202/797-3000;** www.austemb.org). There are consulates in New York, Honolulu, Houston, Los Angeles, and San Francisco.

The embassy of **Canada** is at 501 Pennsylvania Ave. NW, Washington, DC 20001 (✆ **202/682-1740;** www.canadianembassy.org). Other Canadian consulates are in Atlanta, Boston, Buffalo (New York), Chicago, Dallas, Denver, Detroit, Los Angeles, Miami, Minneapolis, New York, San Francisco, and Seattle.

The embassy of **Ireland** is at 2234 Massachusetts Ave. NW, Washington, DC 20008 (✆ **202/462-3939;** www.irelandemb.org). Irish consulates are in Boston, Chicago, New York, and San Francisco.

The embassy of **Japan** is at 2520 Massachusetts Ave. NW, Washington, DC 20008 (✆ **202/238-6700;** www.embjapan.org). Japanese consulates are located in Atlanta, Kansas City, San Francisco, and Washington, D.C.

The embassy of **New Zealand** is at 37 Observatory Circle NW, Washington, DC 20008 (✆ **202/328-4800;** www.nzemb.org). New Zealand consulates are in Los Angeles, Salt Lake City, San Francisco, and Seattle.

The embassy of the **United Kingdom** is at 3100 Massachusetts Ave. NW, Washington, DC 20008 (✆ **202/588-7800;** www.britainusa.com). British consulates are in Chicago, Los Angeles, and New York.

EMERGENCIES Dial ✆ **911** to contact the police or fire departments or to call an ambulance. This is a free call.

If you are an international visitor and encounter serious problems, contact **Traveler's Aid International** (✆ **202/546-1127;** www.travelersaid.org) to help direct you to a local branch. This nationwide, nonprofit, social-service organization geared to helping travelers in difficult straits offers services that might include reuniting families separated while traveling, providing food and/or shelter to people stranded without cash, or even emotional counseling. If you're in trouble, seek them out. In Las Vegas there is an office on 1640 E. Flamingo Rd. (✆ **702/369-4357**), which is open daily from 8am to 5pm. Similar services are provided by **Help of Southern Nevada,** 953 E. Sahara Ave., Ste. 208, in the Commercial Center on the northeast corner (✆ **702/369-4357;** www.helpsonv.org). Hours are Monday to Friday from 8am to 4pm.

GAMBLING LAWS You must be 21 to gamble in the United States; proof of age is required, so it's always a good idea to bring ID, especially if you look young.

HIGHWAY CONDITIONS For recorded information, call ✆ **877/687-6237.** You can also tune your radio to 970 AM for traffic news or 1610 AM for highway reports.

HOLIDAYS Banks, government offices, post offices, and many stores, restaurants, and museums are closed on the following legal national holidays: January 1 (New Year's Day), the third Monday in January (Martin Luther King, Jr., Day), the third Monday in February (Presidents' Day/Washington's Birthday), the last Monday in May (Memorial Day), July 4 (Independence Day), the first Monday in September (Labor Day), the second Monday in October (Columbus Day), November 11 (Veterans Day/Armistice Day), the fourth Thursday in November (Thanksgiving Day), and December 25 (Christmas). State offices, banks, and schools are closed on the last Friday of October in observance of Nevada Day.

HOSPITALS Emergency services are available 24 hours a day at **University Medical Center,** 1800 W. Charleston Blvd., at Shadow Lane (✆ **702/383-2000**); the emergency room entrance is on the corner of Hastings and Rose streets. **Sunrise Hospital and Medical Center,** 3186 Maryland Pkwy., between Desert Inn Road and Sahara Avenue (✆ **702/731-8000**), also has a 24-hour emergency room.

A branch of the **Fremont Medical Center** is located close to the Strip. The Wynn Road center, 4880 S. Wynn Rd., at Tropicana Avenue (✆ **702/871-5005**), is a 24-hour facility.

HOT LINES Emergency hot lines include the Rape Crisis Center (✆ **702/366-1640**), Suicide Prevention (✆ **702/731-2990**), and Poison Emergencies (✆ **800/446-6179**).

INSURANCE Check your existing insurance policies and credit card coverage before you buy travel insurance. You may already be covered for lost luggage, canceled tickets, or medical expenses. The cost of travel insurance varies widely, depending on the cost and length of your trip, your age, your health, and the type of trip you're taking.

Trip-Cancellation Insurance Trip-cancellation insurance helps you get your money back if you have to back out of a trip, if you have to go home early, or if your travel supplier goes bankrupt. Allowed reasons for cancellation can range from sickness to natural disasters to the State Department declaring your destination unsafe for travel. (Insurers usually won't cover vague fears, though, as many travelers discovered who tried to cancel their trips in Oct 2001 because they were wary of flying.) In this unstable world, trip-cancellation insurance is a good buy if you're getting tickets well in advance—who knows what the state of the world, or of your airline, will be in 9 months? Insurance policy details vary, so read the fine print—and especially make sure that your airline or cruise line is on the list of carriers covered in case of bankruptcy. For information, contact one of the following insurers: **Access America** (✆ 800/729-6021; www.accessamerica.com); **Travel Guard International** (✆ 800/826-4919; www.travelguard.com); **Travel Insured International** (✆ 800/243-3174; www.travelinsured.com); and **Travelex Insurance Services** (✆ 888/457-4602; www.travelex-insurance.com).

Medical Insurance Most health insurance policies cover you if you get sick away from home—but check, particularly if you're insured by an HMO. If you require additional medical insurance, try **MEDEX International** (✆ **800/351-1649;** www.medexassist.com) or **Travel Assistance International** (✆ **800/821-2828;** www.travelassistance.com; for general information on services, call the company's Worldwide Assistance Services, Inc. at ✆ **800/777-8710**).

Health Insurance for International Visitors Health insurance is highly recommended if you're traveling to Vegas from outside the United States. Unlike many European countries, the United States does not usually offer free or low-cost medical care to its citizens or visitors. Doctors and hospitals are expensive, and in most cases will require advance payment or proof of coverage before they render their services. Policies can cover everything from the loss or theft of your baggage and trip cancellation to the guarantee of bail in case you're arrested. Good policies will also cover the costs of an accident, repatriation, or death. Packages such as **Europ Assistance's Worldwide Healthcare Plan** are sold by European automobile clubs and travel agencies at attractive rates. **Worldwide Assistance Services, Inc.** (✆ **800/777-8710;** www.worldwideassistance.com) is the agent for Europ Assistance in the United States.

Though lack of health insurance may prevent you from being admitted to a hospital in nonemergencies, don't worry about being left on a street corner to die: The American way is to fix you now and bill the living daylights out of you later.

Insurance for British Travelers Most big travel agents offer their own insurance and will probably try to sell you their package when you book a holiday. Think before you sign. **Britain's Consumers' Association** recommends that you insist on seeing the policy and reading the fine print before buying travel insurance. The **Association of British Insurers** (✆ **087/0366-9366;** www.abi.org.uk) gives advice by phone and publishes *Holiday Insurance,* a free guide to policy provisions and prices. You might also shop around for better deals; try **Columbus Direct** (✆ **020/7375-0011;** www.columbusdirect.net).

Insurance for Canadian Travelers Canadians should check with their provincial health plan offices or call **Health Canada** (✆ **613/957-2991;** www.hc-sc.gc.ca) to find out the extent of their coverage and what documentation and receipts they must take home in case they are treated in the United States.

Lost Luggage Insurance On domestic flights, checked baggage is covered up to $2,500 per ticketed passenger. If you plan to check items more valuable than the standard liability, see whether your valuables are covered by your homeowner's policy, get baggage insurance as part of your comprehensive travel-insurance package, or buy Travel Guard's "BagTrak" product. Don't buy insurance at the airport, because it's usually overpriced. Be sure to take any valuables or irreplaceable items with you in your carry-on luggage, because many valuables (including books, money, and electronics) aren't covered by airline policies.

If your luggage is lost, immediately file a lost-luggage claim at the airport, detailing the luggage contents. For most airlines, you must report delayed, damaged, or lost baggage within 4 hours of arrival. The airlines are required to deliver luggage, once found, directly to your house or destination free of charge.

Car-Rental Insurance If you hold a private auto insurance policy, you are probably covered throughout the U.S. for loss or damage to the car and for liability in case a passenger is injured. The credit card you used to rent the car also may provide some coverage.

Car-rental insurance may not cover liability if you caused the accident. Check your own auto insurance policy, the rental company policy, and your credit card coverage for the extent of coverage: Is your destination covered? Are other drivers covered? How much liability is covered if a passenger is injured? If you rely on your credit card for coverage, you may want to bring a second credit card with you, because damages may be charged to your card and you may find yourself stranded with no money.

Car-rental insurance costs about $24 a day.

NEWSPAPERS & PERIODICALS There are two Las Vegas dailies: the *Las Vegas Review-Journal* and the *Las Vegas Sun.* The *Review-Journal*'s Friday edition has a helpful "Weekend" section with a comprehensive guide to shows and buffets. Additionally, there are two free, weekly, alternative papers, *City Life,* and *Las Vegas Weekly,* with club listings and many unbiased restaurant and bar reviews. And at every hotel desk you'll find a dozen or so free local magazines, such as *Vegas Visitor, What's On!, Showbiz Weekly,* and *Where to Go in Las Vegas,* which are chock-full of helpful information—even though almost all of it comes from paid advertising.

PARKING Valet parking is one of the great pleasures of Las Vegas, and it's well worth the dollar tip (given when the car is returned) to save walking a city block from the far reaches of a hotel parking lot, particularly when the temperature is over 100°F (38°C). Another summer plus: The valet will turn on your air-conditioning so that you don't have to get into an "oven on wheels."

PASSPORTS **For Residents of Australia:** You can pick up an application from your local post office or any branch of Passports Australia, but you must schedule an interview at the passport office to present your application materials. Call the **Australian Passport Information Service** at ✆ **131-232,** or visit the government website at www.passports.gov.au.

For Residents of Canada: Passport applications are available at travel agencies throughout Canada or from the central **Passport Office,** Department of Foreign Affairs and International Trade, Ottawa, ON K1A 0G3 (✆ **800/567-6868;** www.ppt.gc.ca). ***Note:*** Canadian children who travel must have their own passports. However, if you hold a valid Canadian passport issued before December 11, 2001, that bears the name of your child, the passport remains valid for you and your child until it expires.

For Residents of Ireland: You can apply for a 10-year passport at the **Passport Office,** Setanta Centre, Molesworth Street, Dublin 2 (✆ **01/671-1633;** www.irlgov.ie/iveagh). Those 17 and under and over 65 must apply for a 3-year passport. You can also apply at 1A South Mall, Cork (✆ **021/272-525**), or at most main post offices.

For Residents of New Zealand: You can pick up a passport application at any New Zealand Passports Office or download it from their website. Contact the **Passports Office** at ✆ **0800/225-050** in New Zealand or 04/474-8100, or log on to www.passports.govt.nz.

For Residents of the United Kingdom: To pick up an application for a standard 10-year passport (5-year passport for children 15 and under), visit your nearest passport office, major post office, or travel agency. You could also contact the **United Kingdom Passport Service** at ✆ **0870/521-0410** or search its website at www.ukpa.gov.uk.

POLICE For nonemergencies, call ✆ **702/828-3111.** For emergencies, call ✆ **911,** which is a free call.

POST OFFICE One convenient post office is at 3100 Dean Martin Dr., between Sahara Avenue and Spring Mountain Road (✆ **702/735-8519**). It's open Monday to Friday from 8:30am to 5pm. You can also mail letters and packages at your hotel, and there's a full-service U.S. Post Office in the Forum Shops in Caesars Palace. The **main post office** is at 1001 E. Sunset Rd. (✆ **702/361-9472**). It's open Monday to Friday from 8am to 9pm and Saturday from 8am to 4pm.

If you need to receive mail in Vegas but won't have a fixed place of residence for whatever reason, mail can also be sent to you, in your name, c/o General Delivery at the main post office of the city or region where you expect to be. (Call ✆ **800/275-8777** for information on the nearest post office.) The addressee must pick up mail in person and must produce proof of identity (driver's license or passport). Most post offices will hold your mail for up to 1 month.

SAFETY In Las Vegas, vast amounts of money are always on display, and criminals find many easy marks. Don't be one of them. At gaming tables and slot machines, men should keep wallets well concealed and out of the reach of pickpockets, and women should keep handbags in plain sight (on laps). If you win a big jackpot, ask the pit boss or slot attendant to cut you a check rather than give you cash—the cash may look nice, but flashing it can attract the wrong kind of attention. Outside casinos, popular spots for pickpockets and thieves are restaurants and outdoor shows, such as the volcano at The Mirage or the Treasure Island pirate battle, and on crowded public buses. Stay alert. Unless your hotel room has an in-room safe, check your valuables in a safe-deposit box at the front desk.

SHOW TICKETS See chapter 11, "Entertainment for the Whole Family," for details on obtaining show tickets.

TAXES Clark County hotel-room tax is 9%; in Henderson, it's 10%. The sales tax in Las Vegas is 7.75%.

TELEPHONE, TELEGRAPH, TELEX & FAX The telephone system in the United States is run by private corporations, so rates, especially for long-distance service and operator-assisted calls, can vary widely. Generally, hotel surcharges on long-distance and local calls are astronomical, so you're usually better off using a **public pay telephone,** which you'll find clearly marked in most public buildings and private establishments as well as on the street. Convenience grocery stores and gas stations always have them. Many convenience groceries and packaging services sell **prepaid calling cards** in denominations up to $50; these can be the least expensive way to call home. Many public phones at airports now accept American Express, MasterCard, and Visa credit cards. **Local calls** made from public pay phones in most locales cost either 25¢ or 50¢. Pay phones do not accept pennies, and few will take anything larger than a quarter.

You may want to look into leasing a cellphone for the duration of your trip.

Most long-distance and international calls can be dialed directly from any phone. **For calls within the United States and to Canada,** dial 1 followed by the area code and the seven-digit number. **For other international calls,** dial 011 followed by the country code, city code, and the telephone number of the person you are calling.

Calls to area codes **800, 888, 877,** and **866** are toll-free. However, calls to numbers in area codes **700** and **900** (chat lines, bulletin boards, "dating" services, and so on) can be very expensive—usually a charge of 95¢ to $3 or more per minute, and they sometimes have minimum charges that can run as high as $15 or more.

For **reverse-charge or collect calls,** and for person-to-person calls, dial 0 (zero) followed by the area code and number you want; an operator will then come on the line, and you should specify that you are calling collect, or person-to-person, or both. If your operator-assisted call is international, ask for the overseas operator.

For **local directory assistance** ("information"), dial ✆ 411; for long-distance information, dial 1, then the appropriate area code and 555-1212.

Telegraph and telex services are provided primarily by Western Union. You can bring your telegram into the nearest Western Union office (there are hundreds across the country) or dictate it over the phone (✆ **800/325-6000**). You can also telegraph money, or have it telegraphed to you, very quickly over the Western Union system, but this service can cost as much as 15% to 20% of the amount sent. You can find a Western Union office at 1350 E. Flamingo Rd. (✆ **702/732-0024**).

Most Las Vegas hotels have **fax machines** available for guest use (be sure to ask about the charge to use it, as charges tend to be very expensive), and many hotel rooms are even wired for guests' fax machines. A less-expensive way to send and receive faxes is to do it at stores such as FedEx Office, a national chain offering computer and copying services. There is a FedEx Office near UNLV at 4440 S. Maryland Pkwy. (✆ **702/735-4402**), and another branch is located Downtown at 830 4th St. (✆ **702/383-7022**).

There are two kinds of telephone directories in the United States. The **White Pages** list private households and business subscribers in alphabetical order. The inside front cover lists emergency numbers for police, fire, ambulance, the Coast Guard, poison-control center, crime-victims hot line, and so on. The first few pages will tell you how to make long-distance and international calls, complete with country codes and area codes. Government numbers are usually printed on blue paper within the White Pages. Printed on yellow paper, the **Yellow Pages** list all local services, businesses, industries, and houses of worship according to activity with an index at the front or back. (Drugstores/pharmacies and restaurants are also listed by geographic location.) The Yellow Pages also include city plans or detailed area maps, postal zip codes, and public transportation routes.

TIME ZONE Las Vegas is in the Pacific Standard Time zone, 3 hours earlier than the East Coast and 2 hours earlier than the Midwest. Nevada, like most of the rest of the United States (but not all of it), observes **daylight saving time** from 2am on the second Sunday in March through 2am on the first Sunday in November. Daylight saving time moves the clock 1 hour ahead of standard time. This results in long lovely summer evenings, when the sun sets as late as 8:30 or 9pm. For exact local time, call ✆ **702/248-4800.**

TIPPING Here are some rules of thumb:

In hotels, tip **bellmen** at least $1 per bag ($2–$3 per bag if you have a lot of luggage) and tip the **chamber staff** $2 to $4 per day (more if you've left a disaster area for him or her to clean up, or if you're traveling with kids or pets). Tip the **doorman** or **concierge** only if he or she has provided you with some specific service (for example, calling a cab for you or obtaining difficult-to-get theater tickets). Tip the **valet-parking attendant** $2 or $3 every time you get your car.

In restaurants, bars, and nightclubs, tip **service staff** 15% to 20% of the check, tip **bartenders** $1 to $2 per drink, and tip **checkroom attendants** $1 per garment. Tip the **doorman** only if he has provided you with some specific service (such as calling a cab for you). Tipping is not expected in cafeterias and fast-food restaurants.

Tip **cabdrivers** $2 to $5 for short hauls or 15% of the fare for longer rides.

As for other service personnel, tip **skycaps** at airports at least $1 per bag ($2–$3 per bag if you have a lot of luggage) and tip **hairdressers** and **barbers** 15% to 20%.

Tipping ushers at movies and theaters, and gas-station attendants, is not expected.

Casino dealers usually get a few dollars if you've had a big win.

TOILETS Large hotels, all of the casino hotels, and fast-food restaurants are probably the best bet for good, clean facilities.

VETERINARIAN If Fido or Fluffy gets sick while traveling, go to the **West Flamingo Animal Hospital,** 5445 Flamingo Rd., near Decatur Boulevard (✆ **702/876-2111**). Open 24 hours, they take Discover, MasterCard, and Visa, and they have an ATM.

VISAS For information about U.S. Visas go to **http://travel.state.gov** and click on "Visas." Or go to one of the following websites:

Australian citizens can obtain up-to-date visa information from the **U.S. Embassy Canberra,** Moonah Place, Yarralumla, ACT 2600 (✆ **02/6214-5600**), or by checking the U.S. Diplomatic Mission's website at **http://usembassy-australia.state.gov/consular**.

British subjects can obtain up-to-date visa information by calling the **U.S. Embassy Visa Information Line** (✆ **0891/200-290**) or by visiting the "Visas to the U.S." section of the American Embassy London's website at **www.usembassy.org.uk**.

Irish citizens can obtain up-to-date visa information through the **Embassy of the United States Dublin,** 42 Elgin Rd., Dublin 4, Ireland (✆ **353/1-668-8777**), or by checking the "Consular Services" section of the website at **http://dublin.usembassy.gov**.

Citizens of **New Zealand** can obtain up-to-date visa information by contacting the **U.S. Embassy New Zealand,** 29 Fitzherbert Terrace, Thorndon, Wellington (✆ **644/472-2068**), or get the information directly from the "For New Zealanders" section of the website at **http://usembassy.org.nz**.

WEATHER See "The Weather" under section 3 in "When to Go," chapter 3. For local weather information, call ✆ **702/248-4800.** The radio station 970 AM also gives regular weather reports for Vegas.

WEDDINGS Las Vegas is one of the easiest places in the world to tie the knot. There's no blood test or waiting period, the ceremony and license are inexpensive, chapels are open round-the-clock, and your honeymoon destination is right at hand. More than 140,000 marriages are performed here each year. Get a license Downtown at the **Clark County Marriage License Bureau,** 201 Clark Ave. (✆ **702/455-3156**), which is open Monday to

Thursday 8am to midnight, and from 8am Friday through midnight on Sunday. On legal holidays, it's open 24 hours. The cost of a marriage license is $55; the cost of the ceremony varies depending on where you go to have it done.

2 TOLL-FREE NUMBERS & WEBSITES

MAJOR U.S. AIRLINES

(*flies internationally as well)

Alaska Airlines/Horizon Air
✆ 800/252-7522
www.alaskaair.com

American Airlines*
✆ 800/433-7300 (in U.S. or Canada)
✆ 020/7365-0777 (in U.K.)
www.aa.com

ATA Airlines
✆ 800/435-9282
www.ata.com

Cape Air
✆ 800/352-0714
www.flycapeair.com

Continental Airlines*
✆ 800/523-3273 (in U.S. or Canada)
✆ 084/5607-6760 (in U.K.)
www.continental.com

Delta Air Lines*
✆ 800/221-1212 (in U.S. or Canada)
✆ 084/5600-0950 (in U.K.)
www.delta.com

Frontier Airlines
✆ 800/432-1359
www.frontierairlines.com

Hawaiian Airlines*
✆ 800/367-5320 (in U.S. and Canada)
www.hawaiianair.com

JetBlue Airways
✆ 800/538-2583 (in U.S.)
✆ 080/1365-2525 (in U.K. or Canada)
www.jetblue.com

Midwest Airlines
✆ 800/452-2022
www.midwestairlines.com

Nantucket Airlines
✆ 800/635-8787
www.nantucketairlines.com

North American Airlines*
✆ 800/371-6297
www.flynaa.com

Northwest Airlines
✆ 800/225-2525 (in U.S.)
✆ 870/0507-4074 (in U.K.)
www.nwa.com

Pan Am Clipper Connection
✆ 800/359-7262
www.flypanam.com

PenAir
✆ 800/448-4226 (in U.S.)
www.penair.com

United Airlines*
✆ 800/864-8331 (in U.S. and Canada)
✆ 084/5844-4777 in U.K.
www.united.com

U.S. Airways*
✆ 800/428-4322 (in U.S. and Canada)
✆ 084/5600-3300 (in U.K.)
www.usairways.com

Virgin America*
✆ 877/359-8474
www.virginamerica.com

Aeroméxico
✆ 800/237-6639 (in U.S.)
✆ 020/7801-6234 (in U.K., information only)
www.aeromexico.com

Air France
✆ 800/237-2747 (in U.S.)
✆ 800/375-8723 (U.S. and Canada)
✆ 087/0142-4343 (in U.K.)
www.airfrance.com

Air India
✆ 212/407-1371 (in U.S.)
✆ 91 22 2279 6666 (in India)
✆ 020/8745-1000 (in U.K.)
www.airindia.com

Air Jamaica
✆ 800/523-5585 (in U.S. or Canada)
✆ 208/570-7999 (in Jamaica)
www.airjamaica.com

Air New Zealand
✆ 800/262-1234 (in U.S.)
✆ 800/663-5494 (in Canada)
✆ 0800/028-4149 (in U.K.)
www.airnewzealand.com

Air Tahiti Nui
✆ 877/824-4846 (in U.S. and Canada)
www.airtahitinui-usa.com

Alitalia
✆ 800/223-5730 (in U.S.)
✆ 800/361-8336 (in Canada)
✆ 087/0608-6003 (in U.K.)
www.alitalia.com

American Airlines
✆ 800/433-7300 (in U.S. and Canada)
✆ 020/7365-0777 (in U.K.)
www.aa.com

Aviacsa (Mexico and southern U.S.)
www.aviacsa.com.mx

Bahamasair
✆ 800/222-4262 (in U.S.)
✆ 242/300-8359 (in Family Islands)
✆ 242/377-5505 (in Nassau)
www.bahamasair.com

British Airways
✆ 800/247-9297 (in U.S. and Canada)
✆ 087/0850-9850 (in U.K.)
www.british-airways.com

Caribbean Airlines (formerly BWIA)
✆ 800/920-4225 (in U.S. and Canada)
✆ 084/5362 4225 (in U.K.)
www.caribbean-airlines.com

China Airlines
✆ 800/227-5118 (in U.S.)
✆ 022/715-1212 (in Taiwan)
www.china-airlines.com

Continental Airlines
✆ 800/523-3273 (in U.S. or Canada)
✆ 084/5607-6760 (in U.K.)
www.continental.com

Cubana
✆ 888/667-1222 (in Canada)
✆ 020/7538-5933 (in U.K.)
www.cubana.cu

Delta Air Lines
✆ 800/221-1212 (in U.S. or Canada)
✆ 084/5600-0950 (in U.K.)
www.delta.com

EgyptAir
✆ 212/581-5600 (in U.S.)
✆ 020/7734-2343 (in U.K.)
✆ 09/007-0000 (in Egypt)
www.egyptair.com

El Al Airlines
✆ 972/3977-1111 (outside Israel)
✆ *2250 (from any phone in Israel)
www.el.co.il

Emirates Airlines
✆ 800/777-3999 (in U.S.)
✆ 087/0243-2222 (in U.K.)
www.emirates.com

Finnair
✆ 800/950-5000 (in U.S. and Canada)
✆ 087/0241-4411 (in U.K.)
www.finnair.com

Hawaiian Airlines
✆ 800/367-5320 (in U.S. and Canada)
www.hawaiianair.com

Iberia Airlines
✆ 800/722-4642 (in U.S. and Canada)
✆ 087/0609-0500 (in U.K.)
www.iberia.com

Icelandair
✆ 800/223-5500 ext 2 prompt 1 (in U.S. and Canada)
✆ 084/5758-1111 (in U.K.)
www.icelandair.com
www.icelandair.co.uk (in U.K.)

Israir Airlines
✆ 877/477-2471 (in U.S. and Canada)
✆ 700/505-777 (in Israel)
www.israirairlines.com

Japan Airlines
✆ 012/025-5931 (international)
www.jal.co.jp

Korean Air
✆ 800/438-5000 (in U.S. and Canada)
✆ 0800/413-000 (in U.K.)
www.koreanair.com

Lan Airlines
✆ 866/435-9526 (in U.S.)
✆ 305/670-9999 (in other countries)
www.lanchile.com

Lufthansa
✆ 800/399-5838 (in U.S.)
✆ 800/563-5954 (in Canada)
✆ 087/0837-7747 (in U.K.)
www.lufthansa.com

North American Airlines
✆ 800/359-6222
www.flynaa.com

Olympic Airlines
✆ 800/223-1226 (in U.S.)
✆ 514/878-9691 (in Canada)
✆ 087/0606-0460 (in U.K.)
www.olympicairlines.com

Philippine Airlines
✆ 800/I-Fly-Pal (800/435-9725; in U.S. and Canada)
✆ 632/855-8888 (in Philippines)
www.philippineairlines.com

Quantas Airways
✆ 800/227-4500 (in U.S.)
✆ 084/5774-7767 (in U.K. or Canada)
✆ 13 13 13 (in Australia)
www.quantas.com

South African Airways
✆ 271/1978-5313 (outside South Africa)
✆ 086/1 FLYSAA (086/135-9122; in South Africa)
www.flysaa.com

Swiss Air
✆ 877/359-7947 (in U.S. and Canada)
✆ 084/5601-0956 (in U.K.)
www.swiss.com

TACA
✆ 800/535-8780 (in U.S.)
✆ 800/722-TACA (8222; in Canada)
✆ 087/0241-0340 (in U.K.)
✆ 503/2267-8222 (in El Salvador)

Thai Airways International
✆ 212/949-8424 (in U.S.)
✆ 020/7491-7953 (in U.K.)
www.thaiair.com

Turkish Airlines
✆ 90 212 444 0 849 (international)
www.thy.com

United Airlines
✆ 800/864-8331 (in U.S. and Canada)
✆ 084/5844-4777 (in U.K.)
www.united.com

U.S. Airways
✆ 800/428-4322 (in U.S. and Canada)
✆ 084/5600-3300 (in U.K.)
www.usairways.com

Virgin Atlantic Airways
✆ 800/821-5438 (in U.S. and Canada)
✆ 087/0574-7747 (in U.K.)
www.virgin-atlantic.com

BUDGET AIRLINES

Aegean Airlines
✆ 210/626-1000 (in U.S., Canada, and U.K.)
www.aegeanair.com

Aer Lingus
✆ 800/474-7424 (in U.S. and Canada)
✆ 087/0876-5000 (in U.K.)
www.aerlingus.com

Aero California
✆ 800/237-6225 (in U.S. and Mexico)
www.aerocalifornia.com.mx

Air Berlin
✆ 018/0573-7800 (in Germany)
✆ 087/1500-0737 (in U.K.)
✆ 180/573-7800 (international)
www.airberlin.com

AirTran Airways
✆ 800/247-8726
www.airtran.com

Avolar
✆ 888/3-AVOLAR (888/326-8527; in U.S.)
✆ 800/21-AVOLAR (800/326-8527; in Mexico)
✆ 086/6370-4065 (in U.K.)
www.avolar.com.mx

BMI Baby
✆ 087/1224-0224 (in U.K.)
✆ 870/126-6726 (in U.S.)
www.bmibaby.com

Click Mexicana
✆ 800/112-5425 (in Mexico)
✆ 800/11-CLICK (800/112-5425; international)
www.clickmx.com

easyJet
✆ 870/600-0000 (in U.S.)
✆ 090/5560-7777 (in U.K.)
www.easyjet.com

Budget Carrier Aircraft Age & Fleet Size
(Source: www.airfleets.net)

For more airline information including aircraft age, fleet size, accident statistics, photos, and more, please see **www.airfleets.net.**

Airline	Aircraft Age (in years)	Fleet Size
Aegean Airlines	10.9	134
Aer Lingus	5.1	38
Air Berlin	7.3	92
AirTran Airways	4.2	134
Avolar	19.5	7
Click Mexicana	15.9	16
easyJet	2.5	123
Frontier Airlines	3.3	60
go!	6.3	5
Interjet	6.3	8
JetBlue Airways	3.1	128
Ryanair	2.9	137
Southwest Airlines	9.8	497
Spirit Airlines	3.9	42
Volaris	1.8	12
WestJet	3.1	65

Frontier Airlines
✆ 800/432-1359
www.frontierairlines.com

go! (Hawaii)
✆ 888/435-9462
www.iflygo.com

Interjet
✆ 800/101-2345 (in U.S.)
www.interjet.com.mx

JetBlue Airways
✆ 800/538-2583 (in U.S.)
✆ 801/365-2525 (in U.K. and Canada)
www.jetblue.com

Jetstar (Australia)
✆ 866/397-8170 (in U.S.)
www.jetstar.com

Ryanair
✆ 1 353 1 249 7700 (in U.S.)
✆ 081/830-3030 (in Ireland)
✆ 087/1246-0000 (in U.K.)
www.ryanair.com

Skybus
✆ no phone
www.skybus.com

Southwest Airlines
✆ 800/435-9792 (in U.S., U.K., and Canada)
www.southwest.com

Spirit Airlines
✆ 800/772-7117
www.spiritair.com

Virgin America
✆ 877/359-8474 (in U.S.)
www.virginamerica.com

Volaris
✆ 866/988-3527 (in U.S.)
✆ 800/7-VOLARIS (800/786-5274; in Mexico)
www.volaris.com.mx

WestJet
✆ 800/538-5696 (in U.S. and Canada)
www.westjet.com

CAR-RENTAL AGENCIES

Advantage
✆ 800/777-5500 (in U.S.)
✆ 021/0344-4712 (outside U.S.)
www.advantagerentacar.com

Alamo
✆ 800/GO-ALAMO (800/462-5266)
www.alamo.com

Auto Europe
✆ 888/223-5555 (in U.S. and Canada)
✆ 800/2235-5555 (in U.K.)
www.autoeurope.com

Avis
✆ 800/331-1212 (in U.S. and Canada)
✆ 084/4581-8181 (in U.K.)
www.avis.com

Budget
✆ 800/527-0700 (in U.S.)
✆ 087/0156-5656 (in U.K.)
✆ 800/268-8900 (in Canada)
www.budget.com

Dollar
✆ 800/800-4000 (in U.S.)
✆ 800/848-8268 (in Canada)
✆ 080/8234-7524 (in U.K.)
www.dollar.com

Enterprise
✆ 800/261-7331 (in U.S.)
✆ 514/355-4028 (in Canada)
✆ 012/9360-9090 (in U.K.)
www.enterprise.com

Hertz
✆ 800/645-3131
✆ 800/654-3001 (for international reservations)
www.hertz.com

Kemwel
✆ 877/820-0668
www.kemwel.com

National
✆ 800/CAR-RENT (800/227-7368)
www.nationalcar.com

Payless
✆ 800/PAYLESS (800/729-5377)
www.paylesscarrental.com

Rent-A-Wreck
✆ 800/535-1391
www.rentawreck.com

Thrifty
✆ 800/367-2277
✆ 918/669-2168 (international)
www.thrifty.com

MAJOR HOTEL & MOTEL CHAINS

Best Western International
✆ 800/780-7234 (in U.S. and Canada)
✆ 0800/393-130 (in U.K.)
www.bestwestern.com

Clarion Hotels
✆ 800/CLARION (800/252-7466) or 877/424-6423 (in U.S. and Canada)
✆ 0800/444-444 (in U.K.)
www.choicehotels.com

Comfort Inns
✆ 800/228-5150
✆ 0800/444-444 (in U.K.)
www.comfortinnchoicehotels.com

Courtyard by Marriott
✆ 888/236-2427 (in U.S.)
✆ 0800/221-222 (in U.K.)
www.marriott.com/courtyard

Crowne Plaza Hotels
✆ 888/303-1746
www.ichotelsgroup.com/crowneplaza

Days Inn
✆ 800/329-7466 (in U.S.)
✆ 0800/280-400 (in U.K.)
www.daysinn.com

Doubletree Hotels
✆ 800/222-TREE (800/222-8733; in U.S. and Canada)
✆ 087/0590-9090 (in U.K.)
www.doubletree.com

Econo Lodges
✆ 800/55-ECONO (800/552-3666)
www.choicehotels.com

Embassy Suites
✆ 800/EMBASSY (800/362-2779)
www.embassysuites.hilton.com

Fairfield Inn by Marriott
✆ 800/228-2800 (in U.S. and Canada)
✆ 0800/221-222 (in U.K.)
www.marriott.com/fairfieldinn

Four Seasons
✆ 800/819-5053 (in U.S. and Canada)
✆ 0800/6488-6488 (in U.K.)
www.fourseasons.com

Hampton Inn
✆ 800/HAMPTON (800/426-4766)
www.hamptoninn.hilton.com

Hilton Hotels
✆ 800/HILTONS (800/445-8667; in U.S. and Canada)
✆ 087/0590-9090 (in U.K.)
www.hilton.com

Holiday Inn
✆ 800/315-2621 (in U.S. and Canada)
✆ 0800/405-060 (in U.K.)
www.holidayinn.com

Howard Johnson
✆ 800/446-4656 (in U.S. and Canada)
www.hojo.com

Hyatt
✆ 888/591-1234 (in U.S. and Canada)
✆ 084/5888-1234 (in U.K.)
www.hyatt.com

InterContinental Hotels & Resorts
✆ 800/424-6835 (in U.S. and Canada)
✆ 0800/1800-1800 (in U.K.)
www.ichotelsgroup.com

La Quinta Inns & Suites
✆ 800/642-4271 (in U.S. and Canada)
www.lq.com

Loews Hotels
✆ 800/23-LOEWS (800/235-6397)
www.loewshotels.com

Marriott
✆ 877/236-2427 (in U.S. and Canada)
✆ 0800/221-222 (in U.K.)
www.marriott.com

Motel 6
✆ 800/4MOTEL6 (800/466-8356)
www.motel6.com

Omni Hotels
✆ 888/444-OMNI (888/444-6664)
www.omnihotels.com

Quality
✆ 877/424-6423 (in U.S. and Canada)
✆ 0800/444-444 (in U.K.)
www.qualityinn.choicehotels.com

Radisson Hotels & Resorts
✆ 888/201-1718 (in U.S. and Canada)
✆ 0800/374-411 (in U.K.)
www.radisson.com

Ramada Worldwide
✆ 888/2-RAMADA (888/272-6232; in U.S. and Canada)
✆ 080/8100-0783 (in U.K.)
www.ramada.com

Red Carpet Inns
✆ 800/251-1962
www.bookroomsnow.com

Red Lion Hotels
✆ 800/RED-LION (800/733-5466)
www.redlion.rdln.com

Red Roof Inns
✆ 866/686-4335 (in U.S. and Canada)
✆ 614/601-4075 (international)
www.redroof.com

Renaissance
✆ 888/236-2427
www.renaissance.com

Residence Inn by Marriott
✆ 800/331-3131
✆ 800/221-222 (in U.K.)
www.marriott.com/residenceinn

Rodeway Inns
✆ 877/424-6423
www.rodewayinn.com

Sheraton Hotels & Resorts
✆ 800/325-3535 (in U.S.)
✆ 800/543-4300 (in Canada)
✆ 0800/3253-5353 (in U.K.)
www.starwoodhotels.com/sheraton

Super 8 Motels
✆ 800/800-8000
www.super8.com

Travelodge
✆ 800/578-7878
www.travelodge.com

Vagabond Inns
✆ 800/522-1555
www.vagabondinn.com

Westin Hotels & Resorts
✆ 800/937-8461 (in U.S. and Canada)
✆ 0800/3259-5959 (in U.K.)
www.starwoodhotels.com/westin

Wyndham Hotels & Resorts
✆ 877/999-3223 (in U.S. and Canada)
✆ 050/6638-4899 (in U.K.)
www.wyndham.com

INDEX

Please see also Accommodations and Restaurant indexes, below.

General Index

AAA (American Automobile Association), 282
AARP, 56
Abercrombie & Fitch, 218
Above and Beyond Tours, 55
Academy Fine Books and Antiques, 210
Access America, 285
Accessible Journeys, 54
Accommodations, 93–135. ***See also*** **Accommodations Index**
best, 7–10
Bonnie Springs Ranch/Old Nevada, 274
Center Strip, 110–117
check-in time, 95
condominiums and vacation homes, 98–101
East of the Strip, 121–130
fridges in, 157
Grand Canyon West, 280–281
Henderson, 133–135
Lake Mead, 262–263
North Strip, 117–121
pet-friendly, 57
pools, 106
rates, 95–97, 99
reservations, 72
South Strip, 101–110
surfing for, 67
surfing for savings, 114
tipping, 289
tips on, 70–73
West of the Strip, 130–133
Adaptive Recreation Center, 202
Adventuredome, 180–181
Adventuring with Children, 63
Aer Lingus, 39
Age of Chivalry Renaissance Festival, 36
AIDSinfo, 30
Air Canada, 39, 40
Airfares, 42–43
surfing for, 66–67
Air New Zealand, 39–40
Air Tickets Direct, 43
Air travel, 39–46, 59–66
"almost" first-class experience in coach, 44–45
bankrupt airlines, 42
books on, 63, 64
canceled flights, 44
children traveling solo, 61–62
food tips, 64–66
for international visitors, 39–40
jet lag, 45
with live animals, 57–58
safety instructions, 63
seats for kids, 59–61
security measures, 40–41
Alamo car rentals, 90
Alan Bible Lake Mead Visitor Center (near Boulder City), 259, 260
Alaska Airlines, 39
food, 66
Albertsons Food and Drugs, 221
Albion Books, 212
Allegiant Air, 39
Alliance for Retired Americans, 56
Aloha, Las Vegas!, 234
Along Came a Spider, 211, 220
Alternate Reality Comics, 213–214
American Airlines, 39
food, 66
American Airlines Vacations, 58
American Automobile Association (AAA), 282
American Express, 282
emergency number, 49
traveler's checks, 48
American Foundation for the Blind, 55
American Golf, 200
***American Superstars,* 229–230**
Angel Park Golf Club, 200
Animal lovers, sights and attractions for, 174
Antiques and collectibles, 210
Antiques at the Market, 210
APEX (Advance Purchase Excursion), 40
Arcades, 178, 188
Armani Exchange, 220
Around the Clock Child Care, 73
Art galleries, 186–188
Arts and crafts, 211
Great Las Vegas Craft Festival, 34, 36
Asian Market, 221
ATMs (automated teller machines), 47
Atomic Testing Museum, 186
The Attic, 225
Attractions, 170–195
for animal lovers, 174
arcades, 178
art galleries and history museums, 186–190
free, 172–173
for kids, 171–180
photo ops, 180
sports-related, 188
thrill rides, 180–185
Australia
customs regulations, 32
embassy and consulates, 283
passports, 286
visas, 289
Auto Collections at the Imperial Palace, 186
Auto insurance, 91–92
Aviation Museum, Howard W. Cannon, 188
Avis car rentals, 90

Babies "R" Us, 211
Babysitters, 73, 282
Bali Hai Golf Club, 200–201
Ballet, 244
Bally's Las Vegas
entertainment, 252
shopping, 206
tennis, 202
Banana Republic, 218, 220
Banks, 282
Barnes & Noble, 212
Bars, 245–246
Baseball, 242
Bass Pro Shops Outdoor World, 187
BCBG, 220–221
B. Dalton, 212
Bebe, 220
Bellagio, 104, 109
casino, 249
entertainment, 228, 245–247, 249
fountains at, 172
Gallery of Fine Art, 187
shopping, 206
Bellagio Fountains, 172
Bellagio Gallery of Fine Art, 187
Bell Book & Candle, 212
Bell Trans, 40
Bernini Couture, 222
Best Buy, 218
Bicycling, 199, 281
Red Rock Canyon, 268, 272
BiddingForTravel, 67, 68
Big Shot (Stratosphere), 182
Big-Top Acts & Midway at Circus Circus, 171
Bike World, 223
Black Canyon/Willow Beach River Adventures, 260, 262
Black Mountain Golf & Country Club, 201
***Blue Man Group*, 230**
BluWay, 55
Boat cruises, Lake Mead, 260
Boating, Lake Mead, 259–260
Bonnie Springs Ranch, 255
riding stables at, 281
Bonnie Springs Ranch/Old Nevada, 272–274
Books, recommended, 26–27
Bookstores, 212
Borders, 212
Borders Express, 212
Boulder City, 263
Boulder Station, 74
Boulevard Mall, 205
Bowling, 199
Boxing matches, 102, 242
***Brain Quest for the Car: 1,100 Questions and Answers All About America* (Gold), 64**
British Airways, 39
Bucket shops (consolidators), 43
Budget car rentals, 90
Buffalo Bill's Resort and Casino (Primm), 276
Buffalo Exchange, 225–226
Buffets, 136, 149, 165–169
Build-a-Bear Workshop, 224
Business hours, 282
Bus travel, 46–47

Caesars Palace
casino, 249
entertainment and nightlife, 251
The Forum Shops, 180
Fountain Shows at the Forum Shops, 171–172
shopping, 208, 213, 218, 220, 222–225
sporting events, 244
staying at, 110–112
Cafe Gelato, 154
Calendar of events, 34–36
Callville Bay, 260
Cameras, digital, 41, 70
Camping, Lake Mead, 260
Canada
customs regulations, 31
embassy and consulates, 283
health insurance, 285
passports, 286
Canoeing, Lake Mead, 260
Car-rental insurance, 286
Car rentals, 90
insurance, 91–92
surfing for, 68
Carry-on luggage, 63
Car travel, 46, 89
to the airport, 40
driving safety, 92
Casey's Sports Cards, 224
Cashman Field Center, 282–283
Casinos, 246–251
Center Strip, 249–250
East of the Strip, 251
North Strip, 250
South Strip, 247–249
Cellphones, 38
Center Strip, 86
accommodations, 110–117
casinos, 249–250
restaurants, 151–158, 166–168
Chamber of Commerce, Las Vegas, 24, 28
Charleston Heights Arts Center, 245
Charter flights, 43
Child-care centers, 73–75
Chinatown, restaurants, 151
Chinese New Year, 34
Chinle Formation (Red Rock Canyon), 270
Cinco de Mayo Festival, 34
CineVegas International Film Festival, 35
Circus Circus, 172
arcade, 178
Big-Top Acts & Midway at, 171
casino, 250
free entertainment, 172
shopping, 208
staying at, 119–121
Circusland RV Park, 120
Cirque du Soleil's *KA*, 230–232
Cirque du Soleil's *LOVE*, 232
Cirque du Soleil's *Mystère*, 232–233
Cirque du Soleil's *O*, 233
Cirque du Soleil's *Zumanity*, 252
Citizens Area Transit, 88
***CityLife*, 29**
Citysearch, 29
Clark County Museum, 187
Clark County Parks and Recreation Department, 34
Clark County Rodeo and Fair, 34
Classical music, 244
Cleopatra's Barge, 251
Climate, 32–33
Clothing, 218–221
baby and preschooler, 211
everyday, 218, 220
fashion clothing, 220–221
menswear, 222–223
vintage and used, 225–226
Colds, kids with, 60
Comedy clubs, 241
Comics, 213–214
Commercial Center, restaurants, 162
CompUSA, 218

Comstock Lode silver mine, 273–274
Condominiums and vacation homes, 98
Coney Island Emporium Arcade, 178
Consolidators (bucket shops), 43
Contemporary Arts Collective, 221
Continental Airlines, 39
food, 66
Continental Airlines Vacations, 58
Convention dates, 33
Conventions, 282–283
Cookware, 214
Cosmetics, 214
Cosmic Comics, 214
Costumes, 214–215
Cowboy Trail Rides, 281
Crafts, 211
Great Las Vegas Craft Festival, 34, 36
Craig Ranch Golf Club, 201
Crazy Horse Paris, 252
Creative Adventures, 195, 266
Credit cards, 49
auto insurance, 91
***Cult Vegas* (Weatherford), 24–25**
Curfew, 52
Customs regulations, 30–32

Dance clubs, 251–252
***Danny Gans: The Man of Many Voices*, 234**
Daylight saving time, 288–289
Dead Poet Books, 212
Deep vein thrombosis, 44
Delta Airlines, 39
food, 66
Delta Vacations, 58
Department stores, 215–216
Desert Cab Company, 88
Desert Outfitters, 224
Desert Rose Golf Club, 201
Desert Springs Hospital, 283
Desert tours, 195
Diesel, 220
Digital cameras, 41, 70
Dillard's, 215
Dining, 136–169. *See also* Restaurants Index
best, 10–13
buffets, 136, 149, 165–169
Center Strip, 151–158, 166–168
cheap, 149
Chinatown, 151
Commercial Center, 162
by cuisine, 139–141
Downtown, 164
East of the Strip, 160–163, 168
food courts, 149
high tea, 148
menus for the blind, 54
North Strip, 158–159, 168
price categories, 139
reservations, 137
romantic dining, 169
saving money on, 137–138
South Strip, 141–151, 165–166
tipping, 289
tips on, 137–139
West of the Strip, 163–164, 168–169
Dirt biking (motocross), 242
Disabilities, travelers with, 53–55
Disney Store, 224–225
DKNY, 220
Doctors and dentists, 283
Dollar car rentals, 90
Dolphin Habitat, 180
Donna Beam Fine Art Gallery, 187–188
Downtown, 84
brief description of, 87
restaurants, 164
Drinking laws, 283
Driving safety, 92
Drugstores and pharmacies, 216, 218, 283
Dry cleaners, 283

Ear pressure, relieving, 45
East of the Strip/Convention Center
accommodations, 121–130
brief description of, 86
South Strip, 86
casino, 251
restaurants, 160–163, 168
The Strip, 77, 80
Echo Bay, 259
Economy-class syndrome, 44
Eddie Bauer, 220
Eiffel Tower, 245
Elderhostel, 56
Electricity, 283
Electronics, 218
El Rancho Vegas, 17–18
Elwell, Brenda, 55
Embassies and consulates, 283–284
Emergencies, 284
***Emerging Horizons*, 55**
Enterprise car rentals, 90
Entertainment and nightlife, 227–253
for adults, 245–253. *See also* Casinos
bars, 245–246
buying show tickets, 229
casinos, 246–251
comedy clubs, 241
dance clubs, 251–252
favorite shows, 237
headliner showrooms, 239–241
headliner stadiums, 240
list arranged by hotel, 228
local performing arts, 244–245
major production shows, 229–239, 252–253
Entry requirements, 29–30
Equifax, 49
Escape Adventure Bike Shop and Tour Center, 224
Escape Adventures, 199, 272, 281
Escape Adventures/Las Vegas Cyclery, 268
Ethel M's Chocolate Factory and Cactus Garden (Henderson), 191
***Everybody Smokes in Hell* (Ridley), 27**
Everything Coca-Cola Las Vegas, 172, 190
Excalibur
casino, 247
entertainment, 228, 238–239
Fantasy Faire, 178
Krispy Kreme shop, 156
shopping, 204, 208
staying at, 107–108
Experian, 49

Factory outlets, 206
Family Travel Files, 57
Family Travel Network, 57
***Family Travel Times* (newsletter), 63**
Fantasy Faire, 178
Fantasy Toys, 225
FAO Schwarz, 225

Fashion Show Mall, 205, 211–213, 215, 216, 218, 220
Fax machines, 288
***Fear and Loathing in Las Vegas* (Thompson), 27**
Festivals and special events, 34–36
Field of Dreams, 188, 224
The 51s, 242
Films, 25–26
CineVegas International Film Festival, 35
Friday Family Film Fest, 35
Fishing, 198
Lake Mead, 259
The Flamingo
birds, 174
staying at, 114–115
tennis, 202
Flyaway Indoor Skydiving, 200
FlyCheap, 43
Flying Wheels Travel, 54
Fontana Bar, 245–246
Food
air travel and, 64–66
stocking up on staples, 139
Food courts, 149
Food stores and markets, 221–222
Footlocker & Lady Footlocker, 223
Foreign visitors
air travel, 39–40
further travel for, 46–47
health insurance for, 285
safety for, 51
The Forum Shops, 180, 208, 220
Fountain Shows at the Forum Shops, 171–172
The Four Seasons, 101
Free attractions and entertainment, 172–173
Fremont Medical Center, 284
Fremont Street Experience, 172–173
Frequent-flier clubs, 43
Frequent-gambling programs, 108
Friday Family Film Fest, 35
Frommers.com, 68
Frommer's favorite family experiences, 4–7
Frontier Airlines, 39

Gallery of Legends, 224
Gambling laws, 284
Games of the Gods, 178
GameWorks, 173, 175–176, 188
Gans, Danny, 234
Gap, 220
GapKids, 218
Garden Events Arena (MGM Grand), 244
Gateway District (between the Strip and Downtown), 87
The Gay and Lesbian Community Center of Southern Nevada, 55
Gay Men's Health Crisis, 30
Gays and lesbians, Pride Festival, 34–35
***Gay Travel A to Z* (Ferrari), 56**
Gelato, 154
Gifts and souvenirs, 221
Giovanni's Room, 56
***Gladstones Games to Go: Verbal Volleys, Coin Contests, Dot Duel, and Other Games for Boredom-Free Days*, 64**
Godiva, 213
Golden Access Passport, 54
Golden Age Passport, 56
Golf, 199–201
Gondola Ride (The Venetian), 176
Google, 67
Grand Canal Shoppes, 114, 172, 220
The Grand Canyon (Grand Canyon West), 277–281
Grand Canyon Caverns, 280
Grand Canyon Tours, 193–194, 281
Grandma Dottie's Babysitting, 73
Great Las Vegas Craft Festival, 34, 36
Greyhound/Trailways, 47
***Grift Sense* (Swain), 27**
Grocery stores and markets, 221
Gymboree, 218

Halloween Mart, 214
Hard Rock Hotel & Casino
casino, 251
The Joint, 239–240
staying at, 122, 124
Harrah's Las Vegas
entertainment, 228, 236–237
shopping, 209
Hawaiian Airlines, 39
Headliner showrooms, 239–241
Health concerns, 50–51
Health insurance, 50, 285
Helicopter tours, Grand Canyon West, 278
Help of Southern Nevada, 284
Henderson
accommodations, 133–135
attractions, 191–192
Heritage Park/Old Mormon Fort, 198
Hertz car rentals, 90
Highway conditions, 284
Highways, 46
Hiking
advice on, 266
guided, 281
Lake Mead, 260
Red Rock Canyon, 271
Spring Mountains, 275
Valley of Fire State Park, 267
History of Las Vegas, 14–24
founding of Las Vegas, 16–17
1950s, 18–20
1960s, 20–21
1970s, 21–22
1980s, 22–23
1990s, 23–24
HIV-positive visitors, 30
Holidays, 284
Hoover Dam, 17, 254–258
Hoover Dam Visitor Center, 258
Horseback riding, 281
Bonnie Springs Ranch, 273
Hospitals, 284
Hotel Reservations Network, 72
Hotels, 93–135. *See also* Accommodations Index
best, 7–10
Bonnie Springs Ranch/Old Nevada, 274
Center Strip, 110–117
check-in time, 95
condominiums and vacation homes, 98–101
East of the Strip, 121–130
fridges in, 157
Grand Canyon West, 280–281
Henderson, 133–135

Lake Mead, 262–263
North Strip, 117–121
pet-friendly, 57
pools, 106
rates, 95–97, 99
reservations, 72
South Strip, 101–110
surfing for, 67
surfing for savings, 114
tipping, 289
tips on, 70–73
West of the Strip, 130–133
Hotels.com, 72
Hot lines, 284
Hotmail, 70
Hotwire, 67
Houdini's Magic Shop, 222
House of Blues, 240–241
Howard W. Cannon Aviation Museum, 188
Hualapai River Runners, 280
Humana Medical Center, 51

Imperial Palace Hotel, 109
Auto Collections at, 186, 194
entertainment, 234
Infants, 65
shopping, 211
Insanity (Stratosphere), 182
Insurance, 284–286
car-rental, 91–92
International Ameripass, 47
International Gay & Lesbian Travel Association (IGLTA), 55
International Mariachi Festival, 35
International Marketplace, 222
International visitors
air travel, 39–40
further travel for, 46–47
health insurance for, 285
safety for, 51
Internet access, 69–70
InTouch USA, 38
Ireland
embassy and consulates, 283
passports, 287
visas, 289
Itineraries, suggested, 76–83
for ages 7 to 9, 78–79
for ages 10 to 13, 79
the East Strip, 77, 80
for kids 7 and under, 76–77
for kids over 13, 79
natural and educational attractions, 82–83
for toddlers to age 6, 78
the West Strip, 80–82
***Ivory Coast,* The, (Fleming), 27**

Japan Airlines, 39
Japanese embassy and consulates, 284
Jazz in the Park, 35
JetBlue, 39, 40
Jet lag, 45
Jimmy Choo, 223
Jo-Ann, 211
Jubilee!, 252

***KA,* Cirque du Soleil's, 230–232**
Kenneth Cole, 223
Keystone Thrust Fault (Red Rock Canyon), 270
Kids' Castle, 220
Kids' Karnival, 220
KidsQuest, 74
Kids "R" Us, 218
Kmart, 216
Krispy Kreme, 156

Lake Mead Cruises, 260
Lake Mead National Recreation Area, 259–263
Lake Mead Resort and Marina, 259
***Lance Burton: Master Magician,* 234**
Lance Burton Magic Shop, 222
***Las Vegas: An Unconventional History* (Ferrari and Ives), 27**
Las Vegas Advisor (website), 28
Las Vegas Bay, 260
Las Vegas Chamber of Commerce, 24, 28
Las Vegas Convention and Visitors Authority (LVCVA), 2, 24, 28
Las Vegas Convention Center, 282
Las Vegas Hilton
entertainment, 228
tennis, 202
Las Vegas Invitational, 241
Las Vegas Kids (website), 28
Las Vegas Mini Gran Prix, 188, 194, 199
Las Vegas Motor Speedway, 194, 241, 242
Las Vegas Museum of Natural History, 174, 188–189
Las Vegas National Golf Club, 201
Las Vegas Outlet Center, 206
Las Vegas Premium Outlets, 206
***Las Vegas Review-Journal,* 29**
Las Vegas's Chinatown, 151
Las Vegas Ski and Snowboard Resort, 275, 281
Las Vegas Strip Monorail, 88
Las Vegas Valley Bicycle Club, 199
Las Vegas Youth Orchestras, 244
Layout of Las Vegas, 84–87
Learning Is Fun, 212
***Legends in Concert,* 235–236**
***Le Rêve,* 236**
Liberace Museum, 189–190, 194
Liberty Travel, 58
Lied Discovery Children's Museum, 176, 203
Lion Habitat, 172, 174, 180
***Lion King, The,* 236**
Lorenzi Park, 198
Lost children, 53
Lost City Museum, 267
Lost Creek Children's Discovery Trail, 271
Lost luggage insurance, 286
Lost or stolen wallet, 49–50
***LOVE,* Cirque du Soleil's, 232**
Lucky Brand, 220
Luxor
casino, 247
Games of the Gods, 178
shopping, 209
staying at, 108, 110

***Mac King Comedy Magic Show,* 236–237**
Macy's, 216
Madame Tussaud's Wax Museum, 176–177
Magic and gags, 222
Mail2web, 70
Malls, 205
Mandalay Bay, 109
casino, 247–248
entertainment, 240–241

Mandalay Bay *(cont.)*
International Mariachi Festival, 35
rumjungle, 251–252
Shark Reef at, 174, 177–178
shopping, 209
sporting events, 244
M&Ms World, 172, 190–191, 213
Manhattan Express, 181–182
The Man Who Invented Las Vegas (Wilkerson), 27
Marjorie Barrick, 174
Marjorie Barrick Museum, 190
Marshalls, 216
Martin Luther King, Jr., Parade, 34
***Masquerade in the Sky,* 173**
MasterCard
emergency number, 49
traveler's checks, 48
McCarran International Airport, getting into town from, 40
The Meadows, 205, 215, 216, 218, 223, 225
MEDEX International, 285
MedicAlert Identification Tag, 50
Medical insurance, 50, 285
Medical requirements for entry, 30
Melatonin, 45
Men's Wearhouse, 222
Mervyn's, 216
MGM Grand Hotel/Casino
casino, 248
entertainment, 228, 230–232, 244, 252
Lion Habitat, 172, 174, 180
shopping, 209
sporting events, 244
staying at, 102–104
Midwest Airlines, 39
Miracle Mile Shops, 213, 214, 218, 220, 222–224
The Mirage
casino, 249–250
Dolphin Habitat, 180
entertainment, 228, 232, 234, 244
shopping, 204
Siegfried & Roy's Secret Garden, 178–180
staying at, 115
Mirage Volcano, 173
Moenkopi Trail, 271
Moment's Notice, 43
Money and costs, 47–50
Monorail, Las Vegas Strip, 88
Monte Carlo Resort & Casino
entertainment, 228, 234
shopping, 209, 222
staying at, 104–105
Moon, 251
Mormons, 16
Old Las Vegas Mormon Fort, 190
Old Mormon Fort, 198
MossRehab Hospital, 54
Motocross (dirt biking), 242
Mount Charleston (Spring Mountains National Recreation Area), 275–276
Mousesavers.com, 28, 68
Movies, 25–26
CineVegas International Film Festival, 35
Friday Family Film Fest, 35
***Mystère,* Cirque Du Soleil's, 232–233**

Napoleon, 223
Narcotics, 30
National Finals Rodeo, 36, 241
National Vitamin Company Factory, 191
Natural History, Las Vegas Museum of, 174, 188–189
Neiman Marcus, 216
Nevada Ballet Theatre, 244
Nevada Climbing Center, 201
Nevada Commission on Tourism, 28
access information, 54
Nevada Shakespeare in the Park, 35–36
New Balance, 223
Newspapers and magazines, 286
New Year's Eve, 36
New York–New York Hotel & Casino
casino, 248
Coney Island Emporium Arcade, 178
entertainment, 246
Manhattan Express, 181–182
shopping, 222, 248, 253
Statue of Liberty, 180
staying at, 105–106
New Zealand
customs regulations, 32
embassy and consulates, 284
passports, 287
visas, 289
NFR Cowboy Christmas Gift Show, 36
Nightlife and entertainment, 227–253
for adults, 245–253. *See also* Casinos
bars, 245–246
buying show tickets, 229
casinos, 246–251
comedy clubs, 241
dance clubs, 251–252
favorite shows, 237
headliner showrooms, 239–241
headliner stadiums, 240
list arranged by hotel, 228
local performing arts, 244–245
major production shows, 229–239, 252–253
Niketown, 224
Nine Fine Irishmen, 246
North Strip, 86
accommodations, 117–121
casino, 250
restaurants, 158–159, 168
Northwest Airlines, 39
food, 66
Now, Voyager, 55

***O,* Cirque Du Soleil's, 233**
***Odysseus,* 56**
Oktoberfest, 35
Old Las Vegas Mormon Fort, 190
Old Mormon Fort, 198
Old Nevada, 272, 273–274
Old Nevada Photograph Shoppe, 273
Openlist, 29
Orleans Hotel & Casino
bowling, 199
casino, 248–249
child-care center, 75
staying at, 132–133
***Out and About,* 56**
Overton, 267

Package tours, 58–59
Packing tips, 37–38
Palms Resort & Casino, 74
dance club, 251

Parents Without Partners, 55
Paris Las Vegas, 173
entertainment, 245, 249
staying at, 112–113
Parking, 89–90
Parks and playgrounds, 198–199
Party City, 214
Passports, 286–287
Payless car rentals, 90
***Penn & Teller*, 237**
Petroglyphs
Red Rock Canyon, 271–272
Valley of Fire State Park, 264
Pets, traveling with, 57
PGA Tours Las Vegas Senior Classic, 241
***Phantom–The Las Vegas Spectacular*, 237–238**
Pickpockets, 52
Planet Hollywood Resort & Casino
entertainment, 228, 238
shopping, 209, 214, 221
staying at, 106–107
Planning a family trip, 28–75
accommodations, 67, 70–73
babysitters and child-care centers, 73–75
customs regulations, 30–32
entry requirements, 29–30
health concerns, 50–51
Internet access, 69–70
money and costs, 47–50
online, 66–69
packing tips, 37–38
red alert checklist, 31
safety concerns, 51–53
specialized travel resources, 53–58
traveling to Las Vegas, 39–46
visitor information, 28–29
when to go, 32–33
Players clubs, 108
Poison control center, 51
Police, 287
Pools, 106
Post office, 287
Prescription medications, 50
Presley, Elvis, 19–21, 25
impersonator shows, 239
Priceline, 67
Pride Festival, 34–35
Primm, 276–277
Princess Hats (Excalibur), 204
Professional Bull Riders Tour, 241
Psychic Eye, 212

Qantas, 39
Quartermaster Point, 280
Quikbook, 72
Quiz, 192–193
***QVegas*, 55–56**

Race and Sports Book, 249
Race car-related activities, 194
Rafting
Grand Canyon West, 280
Lake Mead, 260, 262
Rainbow Company Youth Theatre, 245
The Rat Pack, 19, 20
Red Rock Canyon, 267–272
Red Rock Canyon Visitor Center, 268
Red Rock Casino Resort Spa, 74
Red Rock Climbing Center, 201
Red Rooster Antique Mall, 210
Reservations
hotel, 72
restaurant, 137
Restaurants, 136–169. *See also* Restaurants Index
best, 10–13
buffets, 136, 149, 165–169
Center Strip, 151–158, 166–168
cheap, 149
Chinatown, 151
Commercial Center, 162
by cuisine, 139–141
Downtown, 164
East of the Strip, 160–163, 168
food courts, 149
high tea, 148
menus for the blind, 54
North Strip, 158–159, 168
price categories, 139
reservations, 137
romantic dining, 169
saving money on, 137–138
South Strip, 141–151, 165–166
tipping, 289
tips on, 137–139
West of the Strip, 163–164, 168–169
Rio All-Suite Hotel & Casino, 109
entertainment, 228, 237
Masquerade in the Sky, 173
shopping, 209
Riviera Comedy Club, 241
Riviera Hotel & Casino
entertainment, 241
shopping, 209
tennis, 202
Robber Roost, 275
Rock climbing, 201
Rodeos
Clark County Rodeo and Fair, 34
National Finals Rodeo, 36
Royal Links Golf Club, 201
rumjungle, 251–252

Safety concerns, 51–53, 287
Sahara Hotel & Casino
Speed-The Ride, 182
Speedworld, 182
Saks Fifth Avenue, 216
Sam Boyd Stadium, 240
Sam Goody, 223
Sam's Town & Gambling Hall, 199
San Gennaro Feast, 35
Santa Fe Station, 74
SATH (Society for Accessible Travel & Hospitality), 55
Sav-On, 216
Scenic Airlines, 194, 278
Scuba diving, Lake Mead, 262
Sears, 216
Seasons, 32–33
Security measures, air travel, 40–41
Senior travel, 56–57
Sephora, 214
Serge's Showgirl Wigs, 214–215
Seven Crown Resorts, 259
Shark Reef at Mandalay Bay, 174, 177–178
Shelby American Sports Car Museum and Assembly Area, 194
Shoes, 223

Shopping, 204–226
antiques and collectibles, 210
baby and preschooler clothes and items, 211
bookstores, 212
candy, chocolate and sweets, 213
clothing, 218–221
baby and preschooler, 211
everyday, 218, 220
fashion clothing, 220–221
menswear, 222–223
vintage and used, 225–226
comics, 213–214
cookware, 214
cosmetics, 214
costumes, 214–215
crafts, 211
department stores, 215–216
districts, 205–210
drugstores, 216, 218
electronics, 218
gifts and souvenirs, 221
grocery stores and markets, 221
magic and gags, 222
music, 223
shoes, 223
sporting goods and sportswear, 223–224
sports memorabilia, 224
tips, 68–69
toys and games, 204, 224–225
vintage and used shops, 225–226
Showcase Mall
attractions, 172, 176, 188, 190, 191
shopping, 213, 221
SideStep, 66
Side trips from Las Vegas, 254–281
Siegel, Bugsy, 17
Siegfried and Roy, 21, 22, 178
Siegfried & Roy's Secret Garden, 178–180
Sights and attractions, 170–195
for animal lovers, 174
arcades, 178
art galleries and history museums, 186–190
free, 172–173
for kids, 171–180
photo ops, 180
sports-related, 188
thrill rides, 180–185
Silver Cactus Comics, 214
Sinatra, Frank, 20, 23
Single parents, 55
Singleparenttravel.net, 55
***Sirens of TI*, 173**
Site59.com, 67
Skiing, Las Vegas Ski and Snowboard Resort, 275, 281
Skydiving, 200
Skywalk (the Grand Canyon), 277–278
Sleeping, air travel and, 45, 63
Smarter Travel, 67
Snacks, for air travel, 65
Snowboarding, Las Vegas Ski and Snowboard Resort, 281
Society for Accessible Travel & Hospitality (SATH), 55
South Coast Hotel & Casino, babysitting service, 75
The Southern Nevada Center for Independent Living Program, 54
Southern Nevada Zoological-Botanical Park, 174
South Strip
accommodations, 101–110
casinos, 247–249
restaurants, 141–151, 165–166
Southwest Airlines, 39
vacation deals, 58
***Spartacus International Gay Guide*, 56**
Special events and festivals, 34–36
Special-needs children, 202–203
Spectator sports, 241–244
Speed-The Ride, 182
Speedworld, 182
Spirit Airlines, 39
Sporting goods and sportswear, 223–224
Sports and activities, 196–203
classes and workshops, 202–203
parks and playgrounds, 198–199
running and walking, 196–199
Sports Hall of Fame, 173, 188
Sports memorabilia, 224
Spring Mountains National Recreation Area (Mount Charleston), 275–276
Springs Preserve, 196
Star Land Tours/Bonnie Springs Shuttle, 272
Statue of Liberty, 180
Stratosphere
entertainment, 228, 229–230, 236
shopping, 209
staying at, 118
Stratosphere Thrill Rides, 182
The Strip, 84, 86. *See also* Center Strip; East of the Strip/Convention Center; Mid-Strip; North Strip; South Strip; West of the Strip
staying off the street, 88
Sunrise Hospital and Medical Center, 284
Sunset Park, 198–199
Sunset Station, 74
Sur la Table, 214
Syringe-administered medications, 30

Talbots, 220
Target, 216
Taxes, 287
Taxis, 88
tipping, 289
Telegraph and telex services, 288
Telephones, 287–288
Television shows, 25–26
Temperatures, average, 32
Tennis, 201–202
Texas Station Gambling Hall & Hotel, 74
Theater, 245
Nevada Shakespeare in the Park, 35–36
Thomas & Mack Center, 240
Thrifty car rentals, 90
Thrill rides, 180–185
Buffalo Bill's Resort and Casino (Primm), 276–277
Ticketmaster, 229, 240
Time zones, 288–289
Tipping, 289
TI-Treasure Island, 116–117
entertainment, 228
shopping, 209–210
Sirens of TI, 173

Tix4Tonight, 229
T. J. Maxx, 216
Toilets, 289
Tony n' Tina's Wedding, 238
Tourist information, 28–29
Tournament of Kings, 238–239
Tours, 193–195
 the Grand Canyon, 278, 280
 Hoover Dam, 257–258
 package, 58–59
Toys and games, 204, 224–225
 for air travel, 64
Toys "R" Us, 225
Trader Joe's, 221
Train travel, 46
Transportation, 87–92
 from the airport, 40
Transportation Security Administration (TSA), 41–42
TransUnion, 49
Travel Assistance International, 285
Travelaxe, 28, 67, 94
Travelers Advantage, 43
Traveler's Aid International, 284
Traveler's checks, 47–48
Travelex Insurance Services, 285
Travel Guard International, 285
TravelHub, 43
Traveling to Las Vegas, 39–46
Travel insurance, 42
Travel Insured International, 285
Travel with Your Kids, 57
Tree & Menorah Lighting Ceremonies, 36
Trip-cancellation insurance, 285
Tropicana, entertainment, 228

United Airlines, 39
 food, 66
United Kingdom
 customs regulations, 32
 embassy and consulates, 284
 health insurance, 285
 passports, 287
 visas, 289
United States Tour Operators Association, 58
United Vacations, 58
University Medical Center, 284
University of Nevada, Las Vegas (UNLV)
 sports venues, 242, 244
 tennis courts, 202
UNLV Xeric Garden, 196, 198
US Airways, 39
 food, 66
US Airways Vacations, 58

Vacation Fun Mad Libs: World's Greatest Party Game (Price), 64
Vacation homes, 98
Vacation Together, 58
Valley of Fire State Park, 255, 263–267
Vegas.com, 29
Vegas4Visitors, 29
Vegetarians and vegans, 65
The Venetian, 180
 casino, 250
 entertainment, 229, 230, 232, 237, 238, 250
 Gondola Ride, 176
 Grand Canal Shoppes, 114, 172, 220
 Madame Tussaud's Wax Museum, 176–177
 shopping, 210, 213, 214, 220–223
 staying at, 113
Veterinarian, 289
Videotape, air travel and, 41
Virgin Atlantic Airways, 39
Visa (credit card)
 emergency number, 49
 traveler's checks, 48
Visas, 29–30, 289
Visitor information, 28–29
Visitor's Guide, Las Vegas Chamber of Commerce, 24
Visit USA, 46
VooDoo Lounge, 246

Walgreens, 218
Walmart, 216
We Are Family, 55
Weather, 32–33, 289
Websites, 28–29
 for family travel, 57
 traveler's toolbox, 69
Weddings, 289–290
"Welcome to Las Vegas" sign, 180
Western Union, 49
West of the Strip, 86
 accommodations, 130–133
 restaurants, 163–164, 168–169
 suggested itinerary, 80–82
Wetlands Nature Preserve, 198
Whale Hunt in the Desert: The Secret Las Vegas of Superhost Steve Cyr (Castleman), 26–27
Wheelchair accessibility, 53–55
Whittlesea Blue Cab, 88
Wynn Las Vegas
 casino, 250
 entertainment, 229, 236
 shopping, 210

X Scream (Stratosphere), 182

Yahoo! Mail, 70
Yellow/ Checker Cab/ Star Company, 88
Young, Brigham, 16

Zoos
 Bonnie Springs Ranch, 272–273
 Southern Nevada Zoological-Botanical Park, 174
Zumanity, 252–253

Accommodations

Atrium Suites, 121
Best Western Mardi Gras Inn, 126
Bonnie Springs Motel, 274
Budget Suites of America, 130, 132
Caesars Palace, 110–112
Candlewood Suites, 126–127
Carriage House, 122
Circus Circus, 119–121
Clarion Hotel & Suites Emerald Springs, 127
Courtyard by Marriott, 122
Desert Paradise, 130
Desert Rose Resort, 127
Emerald Suites, 132

Excalibur, 107–108
Fairfield Inn by Marriott, 127–128
The Flamingo, 114–115
The Four Seasons, 101
Grand Canyon Caverns Inn, 280
Green Valley Ranch, 133–134
Hacienda Hotel and Casino (Boulder City), 262
Hard Rock Hotel & Casino, 122, 124
Hualapai Lodge (Grand Canyon West), 280
Hyatt Place Las Vegas, 124–125
Lake Mead Lodge (Boulder City), 262–263
La Quinta Inn, 128
Las Vegas Hilton, 128
Luxor, 108, 110
Marriott Suites, 125
MGM Grand Hotel/Casino, 102
The Mirage, 115
Monte Carlo Resort & Casino, 104–105
Motel 6, 129
Mount Charleston Hotel, 275–276
Mount Charleston Lodge, 276
New York-New York Hotel & Casino, 105–106
Orleans, 132–133
Paris Las Vegas, 112–113
Planet Hollywood Resort & Casino, 106–107
Red Rock Casino Resort Spa, 134
Residence Inn by Marriott, 125–126
Sahara Hotel and Casino, 117–118
St. Tropez, 126
Sam's Town Hotel & Gambling Hall, 128–129
Stratosphere, 118
Sunset Station, 134–135
Terrible's, 129–130
TI–Treasure Island, 116–117
The Venetian, 113–114

Restaurants

Alizé, 169
America, 146
Arizona Charlie's, 149
Bonnie Springs Ranch Restaurant, 274
Border Grill, 144, 146
Bouchon, 169
Bradley Ogden, 151–152
Buffet at TI, 166
California Pizza Kitchen, 155
Calypsos, 148
Canter's Deli, 155
Capriotti's, 158
Cheesecake Factory, 155
Chin Chin, 146
Chinois, 156–157
Circus Buffet, 168
Delmonico Steakhouse (Castleman), 152
Dragon Noodle Co., 146–147
Ellis Island, 149
El Sombrero, 164
Emeril's New Orleans Fish House, 141–142
Empress Court, 154
ESPN Zone, 147
Excalibur's Round Table Buffet, 165
Flamingo Paradise Garden Buffet, 167–168
Gold Coast, 149
Gold Coast Casino, 149
Grand Lux Café, 157
Grand Wok and Sushi Bar, 144
Hamada, 160, 162
Happy Days Diner (Boulder City), 263
Harbor Palace, 151
Hard Rock Cafe, 162
Harley-Davidson Cafe, 147
House of Blues, 144–145
Hugo's Cellar, 169
In-N-Out Burger, 148, 150
Inside Scoop (Overton), 267
La Salsa, 150
Las Vegas Hilton Buffet, 168
Lenôtre, 157–158
Lotus of Siam, 162
Luxor's More Buffet, 165–166
Main Street Station, 149
Metro Pizza, 163
MGM Grand Buffet, 165
The Mirage Cravings Buffet, 166–167
Mizuno's, 142
Mon Ami Gabi, 169
Mon Ami Gabi (Castleman), 152–153
Monte Carlo Brew Pub, 150
Monte Carlo Buffet, 166
Mr. Lucky's 24/7, 149, 163
NASCAR Cafe, 158, 194
NOBHILL, 142–143
Nobu, 160
168 Shanghai, 151
The Orleans, 149
Paris's Le Village Buffet, 167
P.F. Chang's China Bistro, 147–148
Pho, 151
Picasso, 169
Pink Pony, 158
Pink Taco, 163
Planet Hollywood's Spice Market Buffet, 167
Players Deli, 151
Rainforest Cafe, 145
Rio's Carnival World Buffet, 168
Sam's Town Firelight Buffet, 168
Second Street Grill, 164
Slots A Fun Casino, 149
Spago, 153–154
Sushi Moto, 151
Tiffany's Cafe at White Cross Drugs, 158–159
Todai, 143
Verandah, 148
Voodoo Café, 163–164
Wolfgang Puck Bar & Grill, 145–146

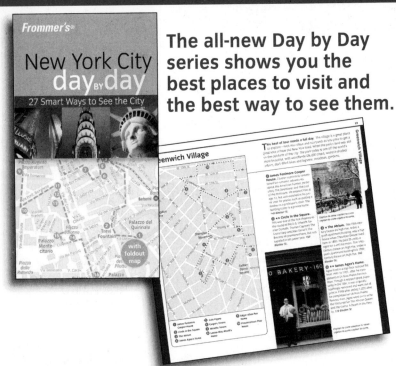

Frommer's® Complete Travel Guides

Alaska
Amalfi Coast
American Southwest
Amsterdam
Argentina
Arizona
Atlanta
Australia
Austria
Bahamas
Barcelona
Beijing
Belgium, Holland & Luxembourg
Belize
Bermuda
Boston
Brazil
British Columbia & the Canadian Rockies
Brussels & Bruges
Budapest & the Best of Hungary
Buenos Aires
Calgary
California
Canada
Cancún, Cozumel & the Yucatán
Cape Cod, Nantucket & Martha's Vineyard
Caribbean
Caribbean Ports of Call
Carolinas & Georgia
Chicago
Chile & Easter Island
China
Colorado
Costa Rica
Croatia
Cuba
Denmark
Denver, Boulder & Colorado Springs
Eastern Europe
Ecuador & the Galapagos Islands
Edinburgh & Glasgow
England
Europe
Europe by Rail
Florence, Tuscany & Umbria
Florida
France
Germany
Greece
Greek Islands
Guatemala
Hawaii
Hong Kong
Honolulu, Waikiki & Oahu
India
Ireland
Israel
Italy
Jamaica
Japan
Kauai
Las Vegas
London
Los Angeles
Los Cabos & Baja
Madrid
Maine Coast
Maryland & Delaware
Maui
Mexico
Montana & Wyoming
Montréal & Québec City
Morocco
Moscow & St. Petersburg
Munich & the Bavarian Alps
Nashville & Memphis
New England
Newfoundland & Labrador
New Mexico
New Orleans
New York City
New York State
New Zealand
Northern Italy
Norway
Nova Scotia, New Brunswick & Prince Edward Island
Oregon
Paris
Peru
Philadelphia & the Amish Country
Portugal
Prague & the Best of the Czech Republic
Provence & the Riviera
Puerto Rico
Rome
San Antonio & Austin
San Diego
San Francisco
Santa Fe, Taos & Albuquerque
Scandinavia
Scotland
Seattle
Seville, Granada & the Best of Andalusia
Shanghai
Sicily
Singapore & Malaysia
South Africa
South America
South Florida
South Korea
South Pacific
Southeast Asia
Spain
Sweden
Switzerland
Tahiti & French Polynesia
Texas
Thailand
Tokyo
Toronto
Turkey
USA
Utah
Vancouver & Victoria
Vermont, New Hampshire & Maine
Vienna & the Danube Valley
Vietnam
Virgin Islands
Virginia
Walt Disney World® & Orlando
Washington, D.C.
Washington State

Frommer's® Day by Day Guides

Amsterdam
Barcelona
Beijing
Boston
Cancun & the Yucatan
Chicago
Florence & Tuscany
Hong Kong
Honolulu & Oahu
London
Maui
Montréal
Napa & Sonoma
New York City
Paris
Provence & the Riviera
Rome
San Francisco
Venice
Washington D.C.

Pauline Frommer's Guides: See More. Spend Less.

Alaska
Hawaii
Italy
Las Vegas
London
New York City
Paris
Walt Disney World®
Washington D.C.

FROMMER'S® PORTABLE GUIDES

Acapulco, Ixtapa & Zihuatanejo
Amsterdam
Aruba, Bonaire & Curacao
Australia's Great Barrier Reef
Bahamas
Big Island of Hawaii
Boston
California Wine Country
Cancún
Cayman Islands
Charleston
Chicago
Dominican Republic
Florence
Las Vegas
Las Vegas for Non-Gamblers
London
Maui
Nantucket & Martha's Vineyard
New Orleans
New York City
Paris
Portland
Puerto Rico
Puerto Vallarta, Manzanillo & Guadalajara
Rio de Janeiro
San Diego
San Francisco
Savannah
St. Martin, Sint Maarten, Anguila & St. Bart's
Turks & Caicos
Vancouver
Venice
Virgin Islands
Washington, D.C.
Whistler

FROMMER'S® CRUISE GUIDES

Alaska Cruises & Ports of Call
Cruises & Ports of Call
European Cruises & Ports of Call

FROMMER'S® NATIONAL PARK GUIDES

Algonquin Provincial Park
Banff & Jasper
Grand Canyon
National Parks of the American West
Rocky Mountain
Yellowstone & Grand Teton
Yosemite and Sequoia & Kings Canyon
Zion & Bryce Canyon

FROMMER'S® WITH KIDS GUIDES

Chicago
Hawaii
Las Vegas
London
National Parks
New York City
San Francisco
Toronto
Walt Disney World® & Orlando
Washington, D.C.

FROMMER'S® PHRASEFINDER DICTIONARY GUIDES

Chinese
French
German
Italian
Japanese
Spanish

SUZY GERSHMAN'S BORN TO SHOP GUIDES

France
Hong Kong, Shanghai & Beijing
Italy
London
New York
Paris
San Francisco
Where to Buy the Best of Everything

FROMMER'S® BEST-LOVED DRIVING TOURS

Britain
California
France
Germany
Ireland
Italy
New England
Northern Italy
Scotland
Spain
Tuscany & Umbria

THE UNOFFICIAL GUIDES®

Adventure Travel in Alaska
Beyond Disney
California with Kids
Central Italy
Chicago
Cruises
Disneyland®
England
Hawaii
Ireland
Las Vegas
London
Maui
Mexico's Best Beach Resorts
Mini Mickey
New Orleans
New York City
Paris
San Francisco
South Florida including Miami & the Keys
Walt Disney World®
Walt Disney World® for Grown-ups
Walt Disney World® with Kids
Washington, D.C.

SPECIAL-INTEREST TITLES

Athens Past & Present
Best Places to Raise Your Family
Cities Ranked & Rated
500 Places to Take Your Kids Before They Grow Up
Frommer's Best Day Trips from London
Frommer's Best RV & Tent Campgrounds in the U.S.A.
Frommer's Exploring America by RV
Frommer's NYC Free & Dirt Cheap
Frommer's Road Atlas Europe
Frommer's Road Atlas Ireland
Retirement Places Rated